IV

seventh edition

Psychology of Adolescence

KARL C. GARRISON
Professor Emeritus, University of Georgia

KARL C. GARRISON, JR.
Columbus College

Prentice-Hall, Inc., Englewood Cliffs, New Jersey

Library of Congress Cataloging in Publication Data

GARRISON, KARL CLAUDIUS, 1900–
 Psychology of adolescence.

 Bibliography: p.
 Includes indexes.
 1. Adolescent psychology. I. Garrison, Karl C.,
joint author. II. Title. [DNLM: 1. Adolescent
psychology. WS462 G242p]
BF724.G33 1975   155.5   74-20724
ISBN 0-13-734996-3

PRINTED IN THE UNITED STATES OF AMERICA

10 9 8 7 6 5 4 3 2 1

Prentice-Hall International, Inc., London
Prentice-Hall of Australia, Pty. Ltd., Sydney
Prentice-Hall of Canada, Ltd., Toronto
Prentice-Hall of India Private Limited, New Delhi
Prentice-Hall of Japan, Inc., Tokyo

contents

part two

Adolescent Development and Change

part three

Cultural and Social Influences

part four

Contemporary Issues and Problems

part five

The Future is Now

preface

This seventh edition is a complete reworking of the previous edition. It combines the efforts of the original author with those of a younger student of sociology who has worked closely with ·the original author throughout his life. These students of adolescence bring together the material presented in the first six editions with the thinking of a contemporary student of adolescence. This should provide a balanced point of view which is needed in a study of present-day adolescents.

The impact of education, technology, and the cultural revolution of the past two or more decades has made it imperative that we give special consideration to the diversity of cultures found among adolescents, existing subcultures, changed life styles, and varied youth movements. The new authorship has brought forth new points of view and a better understanding of the present generation of adolescents.

The materials have been selected to introduce the reader to basic experimental studies dealing with adolescents and thus lay the foundation for a critical appreciation of additional studies and new developments taking place at the present time. Never before has society witnessed such rapid and far-reaching changes as those that are now taking place throughout the world. Thus, never before have the apparent generation gap and many intergenerational conflicts been more clearly shown. The writers have drawn on their own experiences when this seemed most appropriate. They have further attempted to present theoretical backgrounds for many of the problems that are discussed. This should help in unifying the materials presented and in making them more relevant to contemporary adolescents.

The present approach to understanding the adolescent takes the total personality into consideration; it views the adolescent as a bio-cultural product. Biologically the adolescent period has been extended downward in age due to earlier maturation of boys and girls; from a cultural and social point of view it has been extended upward into the college years. We have attempted to view the adolescent largely from a sociopsychological point of view and evaluate his development and personality in terms of the entire matrix of forces that he has encountered. Since each individual is unique, both in terms of his biological makeup and his experiences, it is most difficult to present specific principles applicable to all individuals. We have attempted to recognize both individual differences between groups of adolescents, and have drawn upon sources from many areas of study.

We have drawn heavily from recent scientific studies, from current source materials, and from our own experiences and observations, and have tried to give credit to the major sources of our information. However, it is difficult to give adequate credit to all sources to which we are indebted. To you who have furnished special help, suggestions, and encouragement we express our thanks. To the college students we have encountered and from whom we have received help or suggestions we are indebted.

K. C. G.

K. C. G., JR.

part one

Society, Adolescence, and Marginality

In our study of adolescence we are especially concerned with one period, although it is not necessarily detached from other periods of development. We further regard development as the area of psychology that is concerned with behavioral changes and relationships, progressive changes, and the interactions between a physiologically changing individual and environmental circumstances and events. Such changes involve the genetic endowment of the individual, historical events and interactions since the time of conception, and present circumstances and conditions.

In the first of the three chapters that comprise part one, we attempt to give a clear meaning to the adolescent period and present the basic theories underlying adolescence. In the second chapter we present the period of adolescence as one of uncertainty and transition from childhood to adulthood. The last chapter of part one deals with generational continuity. The generation gap between youth and adults in contemporary American society reflects a real and serious conflict of attitudes, interests, and values. Adolescents are described as marginal—they are no longer children but are not yet accepted as adults. Under these conditions adolescent subcultures have developed throughout the industrial countries of the world.

1

adolescence: meaning and historical perspective

The attention focused on adolescence since the 1950s is without parallel in history. Because of this attention, many people tend to look upon adolescence as a period separate from other periods of life. It is important to recognize (1) that adolescence is a stage in the continuous growth process, and (2) no single description characterizes all adolescents even in a common general culture.

This period of life is momentous; it is fraught with changes, difficulties, and special problems. When one looks back upon his teen years he is frequently puzzled at his reactions to many situations. Thus, adults sometimes fail to understand the behavior of adolescents, even though they were once adolescents. Throughout this text the writers attempt to provide insight into the nature, origin, and significance of the behavior during this stage of life.

THE MEANING OF ADOLESCENCE

In many cases the disagreements about the meaning of adolescence stem from different assumptions about its characteristics and scope.

Also, theoretical differences result from the diverse educational backgrounds of the investigators and their methods of studying human development. A student of developmental psychology is likely to construct a theory of adolescence based upon findings from his method of studying development and will ignore results obtained from other methods. Since the different theories are not all-inclusive but depend upon systematic (and biased) findings, there is a need to integrate different theoretical positions.

Definition and Relationship

Adolescence has been a growing concern to Western society for the past century. This concern may be seen in the descriptive label given to this period of life as a "storm and stress" period. For a long time this period was described as a transitory one the individual inevitably passes through in his growth from childhood to adulthood, or maturity. Biologically adolescence has been extended downward, as evidenced by the median age of puberty in girls. This earlier physiological development, combined with an increased period of schooling demanded by our complex industrial and technological society, has increased the length of this period of life so as to give it an independent status to accompany other life periods. Some students of human development have referred to childhood, adolescenthood, and adulthood (Konopka, 1966: 5). Thus, we may think of the divisions of life as early childhood, childhood, preadolescence, adolescence, postadolescence, early adulthood, middle adulthood, and late adulthood.

ADOLESCENCE AS A PHYSIOLOGICAL PHENOMENON. The word "adolescence" is derived from the Latin verb *adolescere,* meaning "to grow up," to grow into maturity. The most important physiological changes that signify the beginning of adolescence involve the sex glands. The hormones from the sex glands bring the reproductive organs to maturity, and the individual becomes potentially capable of reproduction. This is emphasized by Flaherty (1969) in his definition of adolescence. He states:

> Basically, adolescence is a period of time between puberty and maturity; it is marked by the appearance of secondary sexual characteristics. The age range may vary from twelve to twenty years, although the variation is peculiar to the individual. The change in adolescence encompasses gonadal maturity and a replacement of emotional security in the home for emotional security in wider society (181–82).

ADOLESCENCE AS A SOCIAL PHENOMENON. The beginning of adolescence is primarily physiological in nature; physiological maturity occurs through biological developmental processes. It is frequently assumed that emotional and social maturity occur concomitantly with biological maturity, through interacting with social forces. While this assumption is open to serious question, the effects of physiological changes seem to be greatly modified by social expectations and social institutions. Sociological correlates appear in the nature of sexual adjustments in different cultures and in various social situations.

There is a tendency for the adolescent to be more mature physically than socially in some societies. Western countries, in particular, have developed a complex culture that requires a long period of training for the individual to master and fully participate in as an adult. Educational plans, work laws and opportunities, and age of marriage are factors that have an important bearing on the end of adolescence and the beginning of adulthood. For example, the lengthened period of education has increased childhood dependency and consequently prolonged adolescence. This change is discussed more fully in Chapter 10.

Societies differ as to how freely they permit young people to accumulate knowledge and experience, especially that which might be contrary to the attitudes, beliefs, and values of the adults. Adults select the cultural content that is given to children and adolescents and protect them from contrary experiences. This may be observed in religious, political, and social teachings in particular, and tends to postpone social maturity to some time beyond physiological maturity.

Economic and social evolution has progressed to the point where power no longer depends on physical prowess. For example, even an army, which depends markedly upon physical skill, strength, and endurance is controlled by generals and colonels. Adolescents and post adolescents are required to defer to older persons whose biological capacities are less. Thus, we can see the application of the statement so well illustrated during the Vietnam War: "The elders make war; youth fight the battles." There is a pronounced lag between physiological maturity and full social development. As a society grows in complexity the lag becomes greater, and adolescence, as socially defined, extends further into physical adulthood.

ADOLESCENCE AS A CULTURAL PHENOMENON. Adolescence as a cultural phenomenon is described by Eisenstadt as follows:

> The transition from childhood and adolescence to adulthood, the development of personal identity, psychological autonomy and self-regulation, the attempt to link personal temporal transition to general cultural images and to cosmic rhythms, and to link psychological maturity to the emulation of definite role models—these constitute the basic elements of any archetypal image of youth. However, the ways in which these various elements become crystallized in concrete figurations differ greatly from society to society and within sectors of the same society (1968: 53).

Concerning the stages of adolescence Flaherty states:

> This is a time which may be divided into three phases: preadolescence, early adolescence, and late adolescence. The preadolescent is content with his body proportions and is usually self-assured, energetic, enthusiastic, and content with himself. Early adolescence corresponds to puberty. This

period is marked by the acquisition of secondary sexual characteristics and ability to produce. The late adolescent has a more serious concept of life and is interested in courtship, marriage and vocational opportunities along with social and political problems (191).

ADOLESCENCE AS AN IN-BETWEEN PERIOD. The adolescent period has been described as an in-between period. The transition from childhood to adulthood is not sudden. During this transition period the individual displays many childlike characteristics, even though he is striving to be grown-up in nature. Observations of, and experiences with, individuals during the teen period reveal that there is a fairly distinct time during which the individual cannot be treated as a child, and actually resents such treatment. Yet this same individual is by no means fully mature, and cannot be classed as an adult. During this transition from childhood to adulthood, therefore, the subject is referred to as an adolescent.

The term teen-ager is widely used in the United States when referring to adolescents and postadolescents. Teen-agers usually dislike being called teen-agers because the word has been associated with adult criticisms of them. Actually, this feeling is not confined to the United States. Until the term became synonymous with juvenile delinquency, the Germans called their teen-agers *Halbstarke,* or "half-strong ones." No one ever called them teen-agers in the United States until the 1930s, when the word sneaked into the language from sources unknown. Roughly at this same time systematic sociology, itself coming of age, recognized the teen-ager in the United States as a major group to be analyzed and studied (*Newsweek,* 1966: 57).

The in-between nature of adolescence is more marked in highly industrialized societies than in rural or agricultural societies. Adolescents are prevented from realizing the goal of ego identification through adult-oriented institutions and processes. This frequently makes them a minority group within a larger group, and we find many minority groups of adolescents with their own peculiar culture. These are described in Chapter 9. Each minority group of adolescents has its own peculiar problems; therefore any discussion of adolescent problems must take into consideration the particular people or population being studied. Also, age differences are important in making generalizations from studies of adolescents. Important changes take place during the growing teen years; the adolescent seventeen-year-old girl is quite different in many ways from what she was at age twelve or thirteen. These differences frequently account for variations in findings from studies of adolescents.

Extended Adolescence

From the Webster Groves study (Johnstone and Rosenberg, 1968) came evidence that adolescents from high socioeconomic backgrounds antici-pate periods of extended adolescence. This evidence is based on case studies of 686 sixteen-year-olds in Webster Groves, Missouri, during October 1965. Data were collected from questionnaires administered in public and parochial schools and by interviewing and observing the same students.

By analyzing the data gathered it was possible to divide the adolescents into three groups depending on the father's profession or job and the amount of their parents' education. The three groups consisted of (1) the "highs," or those who had a father in one of the professional or managerial fields and with at least one parent holding a college degree; (2) the "intermediates," or those who had parents in either one of these categories but not in both; and (3) the "lows," who had parents that did not meet either of the categories.

One of the primary questions under study was how the groups differed in their "anticipation of adulthood." These were listed in three categories: marriage, career readiness, and car ownership. In all areas students from lower-class backgrounds had a "greater sense of urgency" to get married earlier, to begin a career immediately after completion of schooling, and to get a car if they did not already have one before graduation from high school. Girls and boys from economically advantaged backgrounds showed their orientation toward longer periods of adolescence by their willingness to delay marriage until they were well into their twenties. In addition they were less urgent about establishing themselves economically, and although their career goals were considerably higher than the lows, they were content to postpone them. These students were also less likely than the lows to own, or have the intention of owning, a car before leaving high school, which implies a reconciliation of extended adolescence with its dependency.

From this and other aspects of the Webster Groves study it appears that most adolescents from the upper class accept their adolescent dependency and anticipate extending their carefree days, knowing at the same time they are secure in their social positions. This may be observed among many school dropouts. This has also been an important factor in bringing forth an extended subculture that is frequently at variance with the admonitions of the conventional home and established institutions such as the church.

Middle-class adolescents with low academic aptitude face difficult problems in the extended school years. Many of them become dropouts from school or become troubled adolescents. Special attention is given in later chapters to these and other adolescents who fail to meet the expectations of their family and others with whom they have been identified. Lower-class youth are considerably more encouraged to establish their independence by seeking marriage, securing a job, and buying a car with a small down-payment. These are symbols of adulthood and are a means of expressing one's independence.

HISTORICAL PERSPECTIVE

Centuries before the birth of psychology as a science there were philosophical, educational, theological, and psychological theories of human development that led to an understanding (or in many cases misunderstanding) of human development in general and adolescence in particular. And, although G. Stanley Hall is usually considered by psychologists in the United States to be the father of adolescent psychology, such scholars as Plato, Aristotle, Francke, Froebel, Comenius, Rousseau, John Locke, Herbart, and Pestalozzi were concerned with theories of human development.

The Contributions of G. Stanley Hall

G. Stanley Hall was among the first students of human development to use scientific methods in studying adolescents and to advance a psychology of adolescence (1916). He expanded Darwin's concept of biological evolution into a psychological theory of *recapitulation*. He pointed out that the experiential history of the human species had become part of the genetic structure of each individual. According to the law of recapitulation the individual organism during its development goes through the same stages that occurred during the evolution of mankind. That is, the individual relives the development of the human race from its early animal-like primitive existence to the more civilized ways of modern man.

A corollary to Hall's theory of recapitulation is his concept of human development through stages of growth. Hall proposed a four-division pattern consisting of infancy, childhood, youth, and adolescence. The period of infancy comprised the first four years, which was followed by the period of childhood—the years from four to eight. Youth consisted of the years eight to twelve, which includes part of the period we usually refer to as preadolescence. Adolescence is the period from puberty until full physical maturity is reached, which according to Hall is comparatively late—between the twenty-second and twenty-fifth years. These years correspond to what we now term adolescence and postadolescence, or youth. Hall described adolescence as a period of *Sturm und Drang*, "storm and stress."

In relation to the recapitulation theory, adolescence corresponds to the period when the human race was in a turbulent, transitional stage. The turbulent stage of adolescence, according to Hall, is revealed in the emotional life of the adolescent, which oscillates between opposites. Gaiety, exuberance, ecstasy, and laughter may be followed by depression, despair, gloom, and melancholy. In late adolescence the individual recapitulates the stage of the beginning of modern civilization. This is the end of the developmental process; during this period the individual reaches maturity.

Studying Adolescents

The methods of studying adolescents reflect philosophical and scientific trends in other areas of learning. G. Stanley Hall made use of diaries for gathering data about the nature, interests, and activities of adolescents, since the adolescent period is characterized by a pronounced interest in diaries. Adolescent diaries frequently reveal a great deal about the aspirations and problems of their authors that cannot be obtained from other sources. Such autobiographical material is, however, subject to a certain amount of error, such errors arising primarily from the sampling of those who keep diaries and from the selection of materials to be included in a diary.

Studies of adolescents in primitive cultures by Margaret Mead and other anthropologists have furnished us with useful data about the nature of adolescence and the influence of cultural forces on adolescent development and behavior. The experimental method was introduced in early psychological studies in an attempt to make psychology an exact science. Although this method has been generally regarded as the most accurate one, there are many problems related to adolescents for which it is not suitable.

Buhler (1969) describes three main approaches that might be used in studying human life as a whole. The first of these is primarily *statistical* and usually involves cross-sectional data. In this approach, certain behaviors, functions, or productions of groups of people are studied with respect to age distributions and perhaps with respect to social and educational correlations. Concerning this approach Buhler states: "In this type of study, the individual is seen only as the member of a group and only in a fraction of his life. The material gained from this kind of study does not give us a picture of an individual's life as a whole; it is unrelated to humanistic concepts" (738).

Opposite to the statistical approach is the *biographical* approach, in which the investigator attempts to see one individual in the total context of his development. The emphasis in this approach lies on the characterization of the individual personality and his life style, partly in psychoanalytic terms and partly in terms of Murray's *need* concepts.[1] "The third approach is *developmental*. Developmental steps are used here as the main theoretical frame of reference. The problem with this approach is the criterion for subdivisions into phases. In view of life's continuity, phases represent an artifact. The justification of dividing life into phases is derived from the other fact that, in spite of life's continuity, certain *changes of direction* and certain *new categories of behavioral experiences* can be stated that come to pass with certain time limits" (738).

The developmental method described by Buhler is closely related to the *longitudinal* method, which makes use of repeated measurements of the same individuals over relatively long periods. This method has been used extensively in studying adolescent growth curves for height and weight, blood pressure and pulse rate, change of interests and attitudes, and social-sexual development. Each of these techniques has its place in

---

1 Lewin (1935) stressed the influence of needs on life space. Categories of needs are presented and discussed in Chapter 2.

research on adolescents, but at the same time, each has its limitations. It is not the province of this discussion to present a complete description of the different methods and their limitations. Rather, the reader should simply know that many methods are available for studying adolescents.

DEVELOPMENTAL TASKS OF
THE ADOLESCENT

In a given society there are certain roles expected of individuals at different stages of life. The processes of growing to fulfill such roles have been termed "developmental tasks" (Havighurst, 1948: 86). There are two major forces that interact to create these tasks: the expectations of society, or the "cultural patterns" in which the individual grows and learns, and the changes that take place in the individual organism as a result of growth and maturation. The cultural expectations vary within a particular society from home to home and with different communities. There are, however, certain developmental tasks encountered by the great majority of American children and adolescents. The major developmental tasks of late childhood, early adolescence, and late adolescence are presented in Table 1-1.

In studying the materials of Table 1-1 the reader should keep in mind that these tasks may be grouped in different ways and that their achievement is gradual and continuous in nature. Some appear during the early adolescent years, whereas others appear during late adolescence or postadolescence. Much of the material of forthcoming chapters will deal with problems related to the achievement of these tasks.

ACHIEVING AN APPROPRIATE DEPENDENCE-INDEPENDENCE PATTERN. It is during the adolescent years that boys and girls establish close relationships with others and develop increased independence from parents. To retain affection for the parents without continued dependence upon them is the desired goal. Teen-agers desperately want to break away from close parental control, yet they feel a strong need for parental guidance. They want freedom in making plans, choosing friends, buying clothes, and spending money, but at the same time, they need the security of a close and happy home relationship.

Although much friction frequently exists in the family during the time adolescents are attempting to develop independence, only 10 percent of the youth between ages fifteen and twenty-one interviewed in a Louis Harris poll (1971) indicated that they thought their parents had been too strict; the great majority (81 percent) felt their upbringing had been about right. The resolution of conflict is made difficult when parents are very strict and authoritative and allow little freedom to their children.

ACHIEVING AN APPROPRIATE AFFECTIONAL PATTERN. An individual must feel accepted and loved during his early childhood in order to feel

TABLE 1-1 Important Developmental Tasks of Late Childhood, Early Adolescence, and Late Adolescence of American Children and Adolescents

TASK	LATE CHILDHOOD	EARLY ADOLESCENCE	LATE ADOLESCENCE
Achieving an appropriate dependence-independence pattern	Growth in self-identification. Accepting physical characteristics, aptitudes, and abilities	Establishing independence from adults in self identification and emotional independence	Establishing self as an independent person. Making own decisions on matters concerning self
Achieving an appropriate affectional pattern	Forming friendships and peers on sharing basis	Accepting self as a person worthy of affection	Building a strong affectional bond with another person
Achieving a sense of belonging	Establishing peer loyalty and identification	Accepting and adjusting to special groups with whom identified	Accepting an adult role in different groups
Acquiring an appropriate sex role	Identifying with peers of the same sex	Learning role in heterosexual situations	Becoming attached to a member of the opposite sex. Preparing to accept future sex role
Developing intellectual skills and concepts	Developing concepts and skills essential for everyday living	Developing intellectual, language, and motor skills essential for individual and group participation	Developing intellectual, language, and motor skills and understanding for assuming civic responsibility
Developing conscience, morality, and a set of values	Acquiring moral concepts and elementary values	Acquiring moral concepts and values as guides to behavior	Acquiring standards and ethical concepts. Acquiring a philosophy of life

11

secure in his social relations during late childhood and adolescence, to attain emotional stability during marriage, and to enable him to more satisfactorily meet frustrations and difficulties throughout life. Although the adolescent finds much gratification in achievement, he finds even more in the affectional relations within his home and among his peers. Close affectional patterns established with a relatively small number of persons provide the necessary feeling of being wanted.

ACHIEVING A SENSE OF BELONGING. Learning to interact with others of a group is an important developmental task of early childhood. The child must not only interact, but he must also feel that he belongs, is liked by, and accepted as a part of a group. Although at first the child usually learns to interact with groups of his own sex, he must later learn to live with others of both sexes. The task of learning to get along with age-mates of both sexes continues throughout the high school years and into college years or employment. It is closely related to the task of learning the appropriate sex role and is important in relation to successful social relations during later years.

ACQUIRING AN APPROPRIATE SEX ROLE. In our culture the child tends to identify himself with his own sex at an early age, largely on the basis of dress and play activities, particularly the toys with which he plays. During late childhood there is a tendency to identify with peers of the same sex, although actual antagonism toward members of the opposite sex appears only where cultural patterns tend to promote such behavior.

At pubescence the difference between the sexes becomes greater. Each sex develops characteristics distinctly masculine or feminine, characteristics peculiar to and necessary for the part sex plays in the process of life. Sometimes girls find it difficult to determine just what society expects of them, especially since the role of women in our society is in a state of transition. Unlike their Pilgrim sisters, they can choose between following a career and raising a family.

The task of learning the appropriate sex role involves the acceptance and learning of socially approved adult male and female roles. Generally, most boys and girls find it easy to accept their respective sex roles, although accurate and honest information about sex is badly needed by all adolescents. One major problem faced by teen-agers is the directing of the sex drive into culturally desirable channels. Here, sex education and guidance should be most helpful.

DEVELOPING INTELLECTUAL SKILLS AND CONCEPTS. The growing adolescent must acquire sufficient intellectual skills and concepts to enable him to function effectively and harmoniously in the social order. The increasing complexity of our social order has brought with it additional educational demands. Thus, educational attainments are essential both for effective living and for making a living. The adolescent must not only acquire certain intellectual skills and concepts, but he must also acquire a better understanding of himself as a growing person and come to accept his possibilities and limitations.

ATTAINING ECONOMIC INDEPENDENCE. Another task important for adolescent boys, and increasingly more so for girls, is that of attaining economic independence. In our society a person's occupation is of prime importance; most parents encourage their children to remain in school and to prepare for some vocation that will provide financial security and a favorable social status. Usually, the adolescent is free to select an occupation within the limits imposed by his inherited characteristics and by his financial ability to prepare for such an occupation.

Thus, the choice of and preparation for a vocation is a developmental task which becomes increasingly important as the individual matures and nears the end of his schooling. Studies show that occupational planning and preparation are chief concerns of a majority of adolescents. However, there is necessarily a period of delay between the desire for adult status and its fulfillment, so that the paralyzing force of anxiety often appears.

DEVELOPING CONSCIENCE, MORALITY, AND A SET OF VALUES. The infant must lean entirely on external standards of right and wrong. The goal, however, is for internal discipline gradually to replace external controls. Young adolescents may not be consciously struggling with the problem of developing a "philosophy of life," but they are concerned with ethical and moral problems and are constantly trying to fit into their lives the moral and ethical values passed on to them throughout earlier years from their parents and others. As they grow up, they must acquire a better understanding of the meaning of life and the role of religion in daily living.

Unless the adolescent develops some standard or system of values, he will be without a stable guide to help him in making the decisions he will be required to make later. The kinds of choices he makes are extremely important in relation to his future adjustments and happiness, and much of what he does as an adult and a citizen in a democratic society will be the result of the philosophy of life developed during his adolescent years.

SUMMARY

Adolescence has been a growing concern of industrial societies. Questions have been raised about the existence of adolescence, as we view it today, prior to the Industrial Revolution. It has been recognized as a biological phenomenon for many centuries; as a social phenomenon, it seems to be of more recent origin. Perhaps much of the disagreement over the definition of adolescence arises from the different assumptions of what characterizes adolescence. The terms teen-ager, youngster, and youth are used to symbolize the adolescent, largely for want of a particular term to designate the period from puberty to complete maturity.

Adolescence may be regarded from a physiological or biological viewpoint or from a cultural and social. The beginning of adolescence is usually regarded as physiological—the beginning of full sexual development with the first menstruation on the part of the girl. The period of adolescence has been extended even beyond the teen years, especially in families of high socioeconomic status.

Although much of the concern about adolescents seems to have developed out of our industrial-technological environment, many early scholars have dealt with theories of human development. However, the contributions of G. Stanley Hall stand out most prominently.

Comparison of adolescents in different cultures shows that problems vary somewhat with culture. There will also be some variation in the nature and intensity of problems. However, it should be noted that puberty, which ushers in the period of adolescence, is a biological phenomenon; its relationship to development into manhood will vary with cultures.

The developmental tasks of adolescence were outlined from Havighurst. The major tasks of this period are: (1) achieving an appropriate dependence-independence pattern; (2) achieving an appropriate affectional pattern; (3) achieving a sense of belonging; (4) acquiring an appropriate sex role; (5) developing intellectual skills and concepts; (6) attaining economic independence; and (7) developing conscience, morality, and a set of values.

REFERENCES

BELLER, E. KUNO. "Theories of Adolescent Development." In *Understanding Adolescent Development*, J. F. Adams, ed. Boston: Allyn and Bacon, Inc., 1968.

BENEDICT, RUTH. *Patterns of Culture*. New York: New American Library, 1950.

BUHLER, CHARLOTTE. "Humanistic Psychology as an Educational Program." *American Psychologist* (1969), 24:736–42.

EISENSTADT, S. N. "Archetypal Patterns of Youth." In *Adolescence: Contemporary Studies*, Alvin E. Winder and David L. Angus, eds. New York: American Book Co., 1968.

FLAHERTY, LAURENCE A. "Adolescence Between Home and Society." In *Children, Psychology, and the Schools*, Bryant Feather and Walter S. Olson, eds. Glenville, Ill.: Scott, Foresman and Co., 1969.

HALL, G. STANLEY. *Adolescence*. 2 vols. New York: Appleton, 1916.

HARRIS, LOUIS. "The Younger Generation, It Turns Out, Is Not Breathing Fire." *Life* magazine (January 8, 1971), 1:22–27, 30.

HAVIGHURST, ROBERT J. *Developmental Tasks and Education*. Chicago: University of Chicago Press, 1948.

JOHNSTONE, JOHN W. and LARRY ROSENBERG. "The Webster Groves Study."

Understanding Adolescence: Current Developments in Adolescent Psychology. Boston: Allyn and Bacon, Inc., 1968. Pp. 324–28.

KONOPKA, GISELA. "Group Work with Adolescents." *Mental Health in Virginia* (Summer 1966), pp. 5–7.

LEWIN, K. *A Dynamic Theory of Personality.* New York: McGraw-Hill, 1935.

MANNHEIM, KARL. "The Problem of Generations." In *Essays on the Sociology of Knowledge,* Paul Kecskemeti, ed. London: Routledge and Kegan Paul, 1953.

MEAD, MARGARET. "Adolescence in Primitive and Modern Society." In *Readings in Social Psychology,* G. E. Swanson, T. M. Newcomb, and E. L. Hartley, eds. New York: Henry Holt, 1952.

———. *Growing Up in New Guinea.* New York: New American Library, 1953.

MUUSS, ROLF E. *Das Problem der Schulreife und Versucheiner Losung.* Unpublished Thesis. Teachers College, Flensburg Murwik, 1951.

———. *Theories of Adolescence.* 2nd ed. New York: Random House, Inc., 1968.

Newsweek (March 21, 1966), p. 57. "The Teenagers."

SEBALD, HANS. *Adolescence: A Sociological Analysis.* New York: Appleton-Century-Crofts, 1968.

RECOMMENDED READINGS[2]

AUSUBEL, D. P. *Theory and Problems of Adolescent Development.* New York: Grune and Stratton, 1954.
The author categorizes the theories of adolescent development and presents problems of adolescents as they grow and develop in an industrialized society.

BELLER, E. KUNO. "Theories of Adolescent Development." In *Understanding Adolescent Development,* James F. Adams, ed. Boston: Allyn and Bacon, Inc., 1968.
Theories of adolescent development are presented and organized in the following categories: biological, psychological, psychosocial, sociological, psychoanalytic, and anthropological.

BERNARD, HAROLD. *Adolescent Development.* Scranton, Pa.: Intext Educational Publishers, 1971. Chapter 1.
In this chapter the author presents the following perspectives of adolescence: physiological, cultural, individual, demographic, and the statistical versus the spectacular.

DEMOS, J. and V. DEMOS. "Adolescence in Historical Perspective." *Journal of Marriage and the Family* (1969), 31:630–38.
The authors review the literature on adolescence from the time of G. Stanley Hall (1900) to the present. The writers point out that the concept of adolescence is related to changes in American life, especially in family structure in the cities.

HORROCKS, JOHN E. "Theories and Points of View on Adolescence." *The Psy-*

---

2 Consult the Appendix for a selection of recent references dealing with the adolescent period.

chology of Adolescence. 3rd ed. Boston: Houghton Mifflin Company, 1969. Chapter 2.

A review of the stages of adolescent development is presented, along with a description of the following theories of adolescent development: Gesell's growth patterning process, Freud's developmental theory, departures from the Freudian position, developmental tasks, Erikson's psychological tasks, Lewin's field theory, and the S-R behavior theory.

MUUS, ROLF E. *Theories of Adolescence.* 2nd ed. New York: Random House, Inc., 1968.

The philosophical and historical roots of theories of adolescence are presented, followed by a rather complete description of the following theories: psychoanalytic, geiteswissenschaftliche, cultural anthropology, social psychology, Gesell's sequence of development, central European stage, and Jean Piaget's cognitive theory. The summary should be helpful to the reader.

2

adolescence: uncertainty and transition

In a rapidly changing society many problems emerge for which there are no ready-made answers. Parents are uncertain of what and how to teach their children. Children are troubled about what choices to make, what models to emulate, and what to think and believe. In industrially developed countries television, prolonged education, and other educational media have provided children and adolescents with increased opportunities to acquire more knowledge and understanding to guide them in their thinking and problem-solving than past generations were able to acquire in a lifetime; yet the complexity of our society has presented adolescents with problems of growing up that were largely unknown to past generations. Thus, transition growth from childhood to adulthood becomes more difficult and complex with each decade. This has produced a generation of youth similar to immigrants who are struggling as they grapple with the unfamiliar conditions of life in a new era (Mead, 1970: 72).

THE ADOLESCENT
AS A BIOCULTURAL PRODUCT

Although every generation of adolescents goes through similar biological changes, each faces problems that are different from those of previous generations. In addition these problems vary from culture to culture and within a single culture. This may be observed in the United States where many adolescents are to a large degree "outside" the mainstream of adolescent culture. These may be thought of as the forgotten or neglected teenagers. Thus, adolescents in the United States cannot be thought of in a strictly monolithic manner. We have various groups of adolescents, each group with different cultural norms.

Much has been said about the problems of adolescents. In fact, the adolescent age has been described by some as the problem age. The question arises: Are the problems of adolescent boys and girls a result of the nature of adolescents or of the culture in which they live and grow? All societies and all cultures recognize the changing status of the child as he approaches adulthood, but they do so in different ways. A study of the problems and adjustments of adolescents in cultures very different from our own may help in answering this question.

Puberty in Different Cultures

An outstanding difference between our culture and other cultures is that at puberty in some cultures there are ceremonies that usher boys and girls into manhood or womanhood, whereas in our culture there exists an in-between period during which a person is considered neither a child nor an adult (Mead, 1939). The lengthy period between childhood and adulthood is one of the prime characteristics of adolescence in American society.

In our culture, adolescence is a period when new heterosexual relationships are formed. Although there is no strict taboo about boys and girls playing together at an early age, they tend to separate into different games and activities. A different relationship may be noted as they mature physically and sexually.

In Samoa, boys and girls are strictly separated from age nine or ten until after puberty. The opposite sexes may not touch each other, sit together, eat together, address each other familiarly, or in any way really associate with each other. At puberty, the taboos between the sexes are lessened. After two or three years, these separate groups of boys and girls tend to disappear and sexual relations usually begin. Premarital sexual relations are accepted by the Samoan society except in the case of the Taupo, who is the princess of the village and must remain a virgin until she marries (Mead, 1939).

In the Arapesh society a boy's father selects a bride for his son, then takes her into his home and "grows her" for his son. The girl grows up with her future husband and treats him and his brothers as she would her own brothers. There is no taboo on the association of boys and girls. However, during the preadolescent period sexual relations are forbidden. The boy's parents act as chaperones, protecting the girl. They may relax their strictness on her after the first menstruation period ceremony has been performed. The couple drifts from a brother-sister relationship into marriage.

In Pondoland there is no strict separation of the sexes at any time, although boys and girls are separated by the fact that men and women eat apart and do many other things separately. Marriages are officially arranged by the parents, but only after the boy and girl have agreed to the match. Subordination of individual desires to those of the group is emphasized. Parents feel very responsible for their children, and children have little choice in what they will do, since they all get married and live in a hut in the boy's father's domain.

PUBERTY CEREMONIES. Several authors, among whom G. Stanley Hall is prominent, have given us full and vivid descriptions of puberty ceremonies among the more "primitive" tribes. In connection with these ceremonies Ruth Benedict (1934) early stated:

> In order to understand puberty institutions, we do not most need analyses of the necessary nature of *rites de passage;* we need rather to know what is identified in different cultures with the beginning of adulthood and their methods of admitting to the new status. Not biological puberty, but what adulthood means in that culture conditions and puberty ceremony (24).

In other words, the physiological facts of adolescence are socially interpreted. Furthermore, the interpretation of puberty in the male's life cycle differs from that in the female's. In most primitive cultures the adult prerogatives of men are greater than those of women, and consequently it is more common for societies to take special note of this period in the lives of boys than in the lives of girls. However, the puberty rites for boys and girls may be celebrated in the same tribe in identical ways. This may be noted in the rites for adolescents in the interior of British Columbia, where the purpose is to provide training for manhood and womanhood and work. In Africa and Australia, more attention is directed toward the boy. Among such cultures the most elaborate and important ceremonials are those which transfer the youth to the society of men and thus to the tribal life. Sometimes physical ordeals inflicted by adult members of the group are involved. The boy must accept the ordeal stoically to prove his courage and manhood. The ceremony brings the adolescent boy to man's estate and to full participation in the activities of the men of the tribe.

Puberty rites for girls are designed primarily to promote marriage. Among tribes of Central Africa, the girl is segregated, sometimes for several years, fed sweets and fatty foods, and allowed no physical activity. During her stay at the fatting-house she is taught her future duties, and at the end of this period she is ready for marriage. No special treatment is accorded the bridegroom. When a Takuma maiden reaches the age of twelve or thirteen, long pubertal ceremonies are held for her introduction into womanhood (Schultz, 1959). After three months of isolation the Takuma maidens are brought out on the third day of the festival. They must submit to much torture during this stage of their development. However, they yield unprotestingly, believing they cannot attain womanhood without the suffering. Afterwards, they may marry.

Certain practices saturated with particular moral and religious connotations are handed down through tribal ceremonies. Among the Yahgan of South America, a prominent part of their ceremony consists of group singing and dancing, usually late at night. The songs are communications to an evil spirit, *Yetaita,* who must be kept away.

All these ceremonies serve as a means of welcoming the adolescents into adulthood with no regard to why certain practices ever started or why they still exist. The pubertal ceremony, recognizing the adolescent status of youth, has tremendous significance for the adolescent, his parents, and the members of the community or tribe. It makes the transition from childhood and signals a change in the attitude of the parents and society toward the youth. Through the pubertal ceremony the taboos, prohibitions, and customs of the society are preserved, and the authority of the older members of the society is maintained. Such ceremonies tend to inhibit the adolescent from usurping the privileges and powers of his elders and from aspiring to overthrow the existing order of things.

The Adolescent's Role in American Culture

Adolescence in our culture is a period of transition when the individual faces new and frequently difficult problems. Concerning this Lawrence Frank (1951) has stated:

> . . . the second decade of life—the teen ages—are necessarily difficult and problematic because the child is being transformed into the adult, physically, intellectually, culturally, and socially. In that process the boy and girl must relinquish much of their previously learned patterns of action, speech, belief and feelings, and learn new patterns as they struggle to master their life tasks (66).

The adolescent assumes the roles he must assume by the nature of his biological inheritance, his developing personality, his socioeconomic opportunities, and cultural demands and expectations. Unlike primitive youth, who is the product of a group within a single relatively static culture, the American adolescent moves in a "ring of cultures." These are alike with respect to basic human needs but are different by virtue of varying beliefs, sentiments, and customs. The adolescent in the United States lives in a society committed to the freedom and dignity of the individual, to equal opportunities for all, and to the security and general welfare of the nation as a whole—although his observations of special conditions and events may call this into question.

The adolescent is a member of a variety of groups large and small, formal and informal. His activities and roles in each vary considerably from group to group. As he moves into new and different groups his role is frequently uncertain, and he often feels insecure as he attempts to cope with the expectations and demands of the respective groups. In our democratic society he finds an absence of consistent patterns of behavior and a lack of clearly defined goals and purposes among the different groups. He finds himself going around in circles as he whirls through these "rings upon rings of cultures" in the short-lived orbital space commonly called the "teen age."

The Emergence of Adolescent Culture

The groundwork for the emergence of an adolescent culture was laid with the Industrial Revolution which at first enslaved many children and adolescents but later freed them from the toil involved in making a living and providing for their material needs. As the Industrial Revolution progressed, assembly-line production came into being, and automation became an important feature of the revolution. As a result of these developments children and adolescents were gradually removed from active participation in our economy. The withdrawal of adolescents from agricultural activities followed the mechanization of farming and the movement of farmers to the city—urbanization. This deactivated a large and energetic segment of our population without clearly redefining its status and function. Childhood was separated from youth and youth from adulthood. Middle-class teen-agers as compared to working-class adolescents are therefore faced with contradictory expectations. They are not expected to engage in productive labor, but rather to prepare themselves for their future role in a middle-class society. They are given many priviliges and a large measure of individual financial freedom but without the obligatory ties to significant others.

We go to the shopping centers and see adolescents "huddled together," carving out a culture all of their own. Most of them are from middle-class families and display their affluence by their clothes and money. Moving on to what Schrag (1970) refers to as Mechanic Street, we meet the "forgotten" adolescents: "children of factory workers and truck drivers, of shop foremen and salesclerks, kids who live in row houses above steel mills and in ticky-tack developments at the edge of town" (59).

THE NATURE OF ADOLESCENT CULTURE. Those who perceive adolescence as a youth culture clearly distinct from the prevalent adult culture "postulate a severe and widespread generational conflict arising out of the allegedly clashing values, interests, loyalties, and reference groups.

They usually depict the deviant subculture as characterized by preoccupation with romantic love, glamour, popularity, and sports; rebellion against adult standards; and repudiation of interest in adult roles" (Himelhoch, 1970).

In recent years a number of sociologists have questioned the assumption that a distinct adolescent subculture exists. Himelhoch (1970) used data derived from the questionnaire replies of about 1,000 high school students from public and parochial schools in three communities. The students were asked to rate their degree of liking or disliking for each of a set of goals and activities devised by Palmer[1] and to estimate their friends' ratings of hypothetical attributes of a teen-age boy and a teen-age girl.[2] When the different factors were arranged according to the mean ratings of their constituent items, the following rank order of value clusters appeared:

1. *Very high values:* School Success, Civic Idealism, Active Pleasure, and Restrained Heterosexuality
2. *High values*: Utilitarian Work, Personal-Social Competence, Materialism
3. *Moderately high values:* Familism, Passive Pleasure, Sociability
4. *Low-to-medium value or mild disvalue:* Artistic and Intellectual Experience
5. *Disvalues or very low values:* Negativistic Hedonism, High Professional Position (Himelhoch, 1970: 3–4)

Based upon a careful analysis of the data Himelhock concludes:

1. Adolescents share the same basic culture as their parents, and except for small differences in emphasis, peers and parents have similar perspectives. There is, however, evidence that parents place somewhat more stress on the stern, puritan values than do the children.
2. Based upon their perception of the vital influences on their lives, adolescents are more directed by family, a single friend, school, church, and different adults than by their peer group.
3. Regarding his own research and its limitations, Himelhoch states: "The degree of adherence by youth to puritan, work-oriented, altruistic, and familistic values and, similarly, the absence of serious parent-youth value conflict may be more marked in rural and small-city New England than in most of America" (11).

Observations reveal that there are differences in interests and behavioral patterns, although these may not be as great as is sometimes suggested. Also, differences between adolescents and their parents are more pronounced among minority groups. We are presently witnessing differences in religious attitudes and behavioral expressions between

[1] Mimeographed questionnaire, Department of Sociology, University of New Hampshire, 1960.
[2] "Peer group norms" developed by Jerome Himelhoch.

adolescents and adults. These differences may be partly a result of disparities in the educational and intellectual development between adolescents and their parents.

THE NEEDS OF ADOLESCENTS

Need theories describe the dynamics of behavior involved in the attainment of developmental tasks. According to the basic need theory, behavior patterns develop as a result of an individual's efforts to satisfy his needs. In support of this theory a number of lists of needs have been proposed, notably those of Murray (1938) and Maslow (1943).

Adolescent needs have been studied in many ways. Carroll (1968–69) has described adolescent needs in terms of the conditions and problems of growing up in the United States today. Relevant to this emphasis is an emphasis on the personal self or self-structure, which involves his beliefs, values, ideals, expectations, and demands which he has formulated with respect to his own behavior.

Categories of Needs

Maslow (1954) proposed a useful list of needs derived from experimental studies, observations, and clinical experience. According to his theory, needs have a sequence of priority; when needs of low priority have approached gratification, those at the next higher level become prepotent. The hierarchy of needs theory postulated by Maslow is presented in Figure 2–1. These are in order of priority: (1) physiological needs, (2) safety needs, (3) belongingness and love needs, (4) status or esteem needs, and (5) self-actualization needs. Any attempt to separate the needs into discrete categories meets with difficulty. Although authorities are not in complete agreement over the classification, they recognize that personal-social needs are very important during adolescent years but that basic physiological needs must first be satisfied.

Lucas and Horrocks (1960) constructed a questionnaire to investigate categories of needs that consisted of ninety items. It was used on 725 adolescents, aged twelve through eighteen. The results were scored according to a key prepared for the twelve postulated needs included in that questionnaire. Through factor analysis five identifiable needs emerged as somewhat independent clusters. These were: (1) recognition-acceptance, (2) heterosexual affection and attention, (3) independence-dominance with regard to adults, (4) conformity to adult expectations, and (5) academic achievement.

The recognition-acceptance need appears early, as may be observed in the efforts of preadolescents to gain the attention of those whom they admire among both their peers and adults. Needs for heterosexual affection and attention appear during the adolescent years and have an important bearing on the personal and social adjustment of teen-agers. The independence-dominance need, evident during the adolescent years,

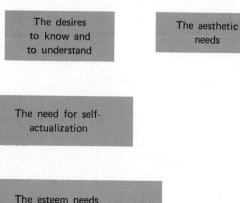

FIGURE 2-1 Maslow's hierarchical need system.

is a source of conflict between the adolescent and parents or other adult authority figures.

In American culture the adolescent boy's need for mastery is more conscious and overt than the girl's. We note this in his play, for example in driving an automobile, and in his work. The girl's efforts at mastery are far more subtle. She may try to gain favor by wearing stylish clothes that give her the desired feminine physique; she may use cosmetics to indicate her social development; or she may respond to social situations so as to win favor from other members of the group. Conflicts frequently appear when the needs relating to acceptance and mastery among peers do not conform to the same needs in the adult culture.

PHYSIOLOGICAL NEEDS. Among the needs of the adolescent Maslow places the physiological first in the hierarchy. Hunger and malnutrition are rampant among children and adolescents in the United States. According to government studies there were in 1970 15,000,000 hard-core hungry in the United States—mostly children (Hollings, 1971). The brain of the child suffering from malnutrition fails to develop completely, thereby affecting his intellectual development; thus, we have the nutritional reasons for some high-school dropouts. Adolescents need additional food to sustain the growth spurt of puberty. The appetite usually takes care of this with increased demands for second helpings, for milk, snacks, and sweets between meals. Rapidly growing children sometimes do not get either enough food or the needed nutrients; they become less active and may be regarded by their parents and teachers as lazy. A child or adolescent who isn't getting enough food but who is motivated to continue a high degree of physical activity will become quite thin.

Sexual development and the development of the sex drive are special characteristics of the adolescent age. One of the developmental tasks of adolescents, set forth in Chapter 1, is developing an appropriate sex role—appropriate to the cultural and social demands and expectations of the society in which the adolescent lives and develops. Although the nature of sex-appropriate behavior of adolescents varies with age and cultural expectations, the physiological bases for the sex drive are the same. Studies of both animals and humans show that the strength of the drive is profoundly influenced by the sex hormones. In this connection a distinction should be made between sexual drive and sexual arousal, both of which are related to physiological behavior during adolescence.

The sexual drive has been closely related to the sex hormones—androgens and estrogens. Sexual arousal, on the other hand, refers to the current level of sexual excitement. Sexual arousal in human beings appears to be mediated through the central and autonomic nervous systems and may involve the pituitary gonadotrophic and gonadal systems. Monet (1961) states: ". . . among the coordinates or sexual functions there are three: local genital surfaces, the brain, the hormones, any of which can fail in its contributions without total destruction of sexual function. . . ." Nonetheless, it is evident that the loss of any one of the three coordinates is an immense handicap to effective sexual functioning.

The adolescent not only has physiological needs, he must also accept his body as he grows physically toward maturity. The small girl with poorly developed breasts may cultivate dreams of becoming the ideal American beauty queen that will have to be modified as she grows through the adolescent years.

NEED FOR EXPRESSION OF CHANGED PHYSICAL SELF. Most adolescents experience bodily changes with mixed feelings. These need not become serious problems, provided they are able to understand them. However, they need opportunities to express their new and complex feelings about their physical changes if they are to develop healthy self-concepts. Carroll states (384): "Just as the healthy adolescent must learn to properly express his genuine feelings, he needs to exercise his growing intellectual abilities and skills." Thus, he needs to be challenged and involved in significant and meaningful problems commensurate with his present level of development.

The adolescents of both sexes also need to learn to coordinate, control, and give expression to their physical development—physical stature, strength, and vigor. They also need to be able to experiment with new roles and behavior patterns that are an inevitable part of growth into adolescence. Frequently it will be necessary for an adolescent to "revise his expectations concerning himself and others, devise and experiment with new roles, self-affirm or disaffirm existing moral and ethical values, learn new methods for coping with the demands of both his internal and external environment, establish and elaborate new social relationships, etc." (Carroll, 383).

NEED FOR SECURITY. Once an individual's physiological welfare is assured, he experiences varying degrees of anxiety concerning threats to his body and his sense of security. Emotionally neglected children seem to be dominated by safety-seeking behavior. Succorance, or security, is the heading under which fall the needs most commonly expressed by preschool children. The safety need is followed in Figure 2-1 by the need for love and belonging. There is evidence from studying animals and children that love deprivation is detrimental to the individual's personal and social development. Antonovsky (1959) noted from studies of mother-child relations that children who were given love showed less evidence of dependency and overt aggressive behavior, but were significantly higher in curiosity and initiative.

The insecurity of adolescence gives rise to an intense need to belong, to be like their peers. At this age they will say "This is my gang," "my crowd," "my girl," "my guy." The need to be accepted can become slavishness to the group and will be discussed in depth in later chapters.

The outsiders, or non-joiners, are frequently in that position not by their own choosing and are in need of special consideration and help. They may display their need for security not only by obvious shyness and withdrawal but also by loudness, showing off, clowning, bragging, and unwarranted criticism of others. These are danger signals that teachers and counselors should direct attention to in their appraisal of the needs of particular individuals.

Based on in-depth studies of six adolescents who defined themselves as a group, Joseph (1969) concluded that there is an underlying dimension of independence-dependence, with the subjects moving from the dependence of childhood to the independence of adulthood. He states: "To the adolescents, the school and parents unjustly force their continued dependence and block their movement toward independence. . . .However, unlike the striving for independence from authority figures, the adolescent is approaching dependence with other teenage friends" (32).

Mary expresses well the ambivalence of self-definition for many adolescents as she seeks security through peer relations. She says: "I don't think that I am myself or what I should be. How can I be different from others? It's hard to be different, if you are going to be part of *the crowd.* Everyone is supposed to be like everybody else, or they will say that you are an *oddball,* and I don't want to be thought of as an oddball. But, maybe I shouldn't care, because I should be myself."

NEED FOR INDEPENDENCE. In order to become an adult the young person must break away from physical and emotional dependence on his parents. With growth into adolescence the typical teen-ager grows impatient with his parents' restrictions and expectations. He begins to think for himself and behave in accordance with his own standards, which are usually quite similar to those of his peers. This becomes an important source of conflict with parents, as will be shown in Chapter 3.

Two outstanding characteristics frequently appear among adolescents that are related to the needs that we have been presenting. First, there is a sense of rebellion against the acceptance of authority. This may arise out of the need for independence and for identity. There is a questioning attitude about the self and others in which the adolescent may appear externally to accept and conform to the wishes and feelings of others, but as a thirteen-year-old boy writes, he may not be conforming internally (Konopka, 1966: 6):

> *And within ourselves, it is our feelings,*
> *Our first notions with which we form ideas*
> *That represent us, and our conscience, . . .*

NEED FOR BELONGING. Loneliness is experienced by many adolescents, together with a wish to be understood by peers as well as those in authority and generally to be accepted, to belong, to be loved. The loneliness is intensified when these needs are thwarted or when conflicts arise. When loneliness is combined with feelings of inadequacy and a loss of personal worth, the adolescent becomes unhappy and sometimes desperate, which may lead to suicide or delinquency. As an eighteen-year-old girl in a delinquent situation writes (Konopka, 6):

> *I've traded love for agony,*
> *My joy has turned to fear.*
> *My friends are now my enemies,*
> *My smiles are now my tears.*

ACHIEVEMENT NEED, OR MOTIVATION. What is generally regarded as achievement motivation as it applies to learning at school possesses the components of the needs for belonging, self-esteem, self-actualization, and the desire to know and understand. The need to know and understand may be task oriented in the sense that it involves learning assignments at school. The importance of reinforcement in the establishment of this need has been demonstrated.

A study reported by Winterbottom (1953) supports the hypothesis that differences in achievement motivation are a result of different experiences during early life. In her study, achievement scores were obtained from stories told by twenty-nine normal boys. The mother's attitude toward independence training was obtained from a questionnaire given the mothers during an interview. The main results of the study show that mothers of achievers make more restrictions during the early stages of a learning process such as learning to read, to perform arithmetic computations, and to acquire skills in other tool subjects. The mother largely withdrew the restrictions after the initial learning, around age eight, and left the child on his own. The picture is that of controlling and supervising the child during the early stages of learning while he internalizes certain desires and interests, and then leaving him alone. In this way increased self-control is established through internalized behavior in which there was earlier consistent, outer control from the parents—especially the mother.

During late childhood and early adolescence academic competition against classmates can under certain circumstances constitute a strong motivating force. However, desire for peer approval may depress the academic achievement motive when such achievement is negatively valued by the peer group. This is more frequently observed among lower-class and certain culturally deprived groups than among middle-class groups, where a higher value is placed on academic achievement.

NEED FOR EGO-ENHANCEMENT. Despite the tendency of many educators to look with suspicion on ego-enhancement motivation, research shows that it is present in most cultures. In Western culture it is a dominant component of achievement motivation during late adolescence and early adulthood. Actually the need for ego-enhancement, prestige, and status through achievement are characteristic of personal and social development and maturation in Western culture. A prime disadvantage of excessive ego-enhancement motivation is that it is short lived—that is, a student whose academic motivation is simply to make a good grade so as to enhance his ego, is likely to have little interest in acquiring additional knowledge and understanding of the particular subject after he passes the course. On the other hand, educators prefer to believe that the desire to know and understand is, or could become, the most potent component of achievement motivation as it applies to learning at school.

NEED TO KNOW AND ACCEPT THE SELF. In addition to the need for accepting the physical self the adolescent needs to find and accept the *cognitive self*. The cognitive self comprises the total of a person's ideas and attitudes about who and what he is. It includes all the experiences that constitute a person's awareness of his existence. When an individual is in the process of "finding himself," he faces many alternatives—at least in theory. He cannot be both a priest and a pirate or a playboy and a professor. Another part of finding the self is the formulation of goals toward which one strives; these may appear as a hierarchy of goals in which some have priority over others.

With more self-acceptance, the child seeks to merit the love, acceptance, and attention he receives by his activities and performance. When he receives praise from his parent or teacher for his behavior or unusual performance, he has reason to be pleased with himself for earning the adoration and praise of others. The need for esteem is closely related to the development of a favorable self-concept and the enhancement of the ego. The self-actualization need is closely related to that of self-esteem. According to Maslow (1954) the need for self-actualization involves man's need to express himself, to realize his potentialities, to increase his competence, to be creative, and to develop satisfying and worthwhile roles in life.

Age and Sex Differences in the Development of Needs

In a consideration of the needs of adolescents several significant questions arise. Two of these that will be considered here are: (1) What differences appear in psychological needs at various age levels during adolescence? (2) What sex differences appear in the development of needs during adolescence?

NEEDS AT VARIOUS AGE LEVELS DURING ADOLESCENCE. Horrocks and Weinberg (1969) tried to determine the psychological needs of adolescents at various age levels. The subjects of their study consisted of 654 boys and girls ranging in age from twelve through twenty. A needs questionnaire, developed by Lucas (1951), was administered to the group. The questionnaire required the adolescent to indicate a desire or lack of desire to play various roles. The normative age-related data obtained showed that the most enduring needs during adolescence for the population studied were:

1. To conform to approved behavior, values, and standards designated by reference individuals or groups seen.
2. To be the special recipient of unqualified and deep expressions of affection.
3. To work hard, endeavor, and to attain worthy goals (Horrocks, 1969: 112).

One of the developmental tasks set forth in Chapter 1 for adolescents was that of a sense of belonging. The importance of peers during this stage of life is recognized by all students of adolescent development. During early adolescence this need appears to be very strong, so that a "slavish" type of conformity characterizes the behavior of young adolescents. Costanzo and Shaw (1966) gathered data bearing on this from subjects aged seven to nine, eleven to thirteen, fifteen to seventeen, and nineteen to twenty-one years. They noted that conformity among these children and adolescents reached a maximum during the early adolescent age range (eleven to thirteen) and decreased thereafter. Landsbaum and Willis (1971) used two age groups in studying this problem. The younger group consisted of sixteen males and sixteen females, aged thirteen and fourteen, all of whom were superior high school students. The older group included a like number of males and females, aged eighteen to twenty-one, who were enrolled in undergraduate psychology and sociology courses. Although only two groups of adolescents were used in the comparison, the results offer further evidence that younger adolescents are more vulnerable to the influence of peers than older adolescents. Younger adolescents feel the need for security among peers to a greater degree than older adolescents.

SEX DIFFERENCES IN NEEDS DURING ADOLESCENCE. There are interesting and significant sex differences as well as similarities in needs during adolescence. Studies of child development show that girls display a greater need for security from early childhood. In general both boys and girls are group centered. As they approach adolescence the need for the support, approval, and proximity of age-mates becomes very important. However, girls as they mature show less interest in group membership than do boys; they are more anxious to maintain a favorable status in the groups they wish to join. They find their closest identification with groups that have values and standards of behavior that provide them with personal prestige. In group relationships they are likely to be more egocentric and use the groups in which they are members for their own personal and social advantages.

In contrast to girls, adolescent boys display interest in groups more for the sake of organization. They are more readily regimented and follow the specific rules of the organization. They seem to have less need for close companions and for peer conformity. There is less need for emotional security but an apparently greater need for achievement or proficiency.

There is a fading of interest in group membership among girls after age fifteen and the girls seem to display more self-sufficiency. However, they are faced with more pressures from society in general to conform to adult standards. After age fifteen or sixteen, girls tend to perceive themselves as playing adult roles, while most boys do not.

ADOLESCENT PROBLEMS
AND CONCERNS

A number of investigators have studied adjustment problems of adolescents at different age levels and from different cultural backgrounds. The results of these studies have furnished useful information to those concerned with the education and guidance of adolescents. Methods most frequently used consist of interviews, written essays, and problem checklists.

A number of problem checklists have been used in studying the problems of adolescents. The *SRA Youth Inventory* was constructed under the auspices of the Purdue University Opinion Poll for Young People with the cooperation of many high schools and over 15,000 teen-agers throughout the country (Science Research Associates). The 298 questions making up the inventory were developed from essays submitted by hundreds of students stating in their own words the problems that bothered them most. The needs and problems of these boys and girls were studied and classified into eight major areas. Norms for boys and girls were then developed, based on a national sample of 2,500 cases. The number of items in each category, the mean, and the standard deviation of the total scores for each area of the inventory are presented in Table 2-1.

TABLE 2-1 Number of Items in Each Area, Mean, and Standard Deviation for the National Sample of 2,500 cases of the SRA Youth Inventory

AREA	NO. OF ITEMS	MEAN	STANDARD DEVIATION
My school	33	7.38	4.49
After high school	37	12.05	7.09
About myself	44	9.42	6.10
Getting along with others	40	10.40	6.32
My home and family	53	5.76	6.59
Boy meets girl	32	6.64	4.98
Health	25	3.94	2.77
Things in general	34	6.36	5.06

Source: SRA Youth Inventory (Lafayette, Ind.: Purdue Research Foundation).

The Mooney Problem Checklist was used by Smith (1961) in assessing problems of rural and urban senior high school Negroes. Smith stated, "The three problems that were of major concern to rural youth were (1) finances, living conditions, and employment; (2) adjustment to school work; and (3) the future: vocational and educational. Among urban students the important problems were (1) adjustment to school work; (2) curriculum and teaching procedures; and (3) personal-psychological relations." Both groups were in agreement that social-psychological relations were among the least problems present. Rural students had on the average 33.15 problems, whereas urban adolescents checked 52.68 problems on the average. The results of this study indicate that cultural conditions and the nature of community life influence adolescent problems.

**Adolescent Problems
as a Function of Grade and Sex**

A study of adolescent problems by the checklist approach has a definite limitation because it fails to provide the respondent with an opportunity to list particular problems and to state the seriousness of the problem checked. Also, it is worthwhile to study age or grade progressions or changes in problems for both boys and girls. Adams (1964) used a questionnaire procedure for studying the problems of boys and girls ranging in age from ten to nineteen from over thirty schools.

The respondents' answers were categorized into fourteen areas and analyzed by age and sex. He noted that with the exception of a slight tendency for students from suburban communities to list more academic or school problems than other students, there was remarkable agreement among students of the same age and sex regardless of school. Perhaps significant differences would have been observed in a study of the nature of the problems listed by boys and girls at different age levels. For boys, the greatest number of problems listed were, in order of number, school, interpersonal relations, and family and finances (tied for third place). For girls the problems listed were school, family, interpersonal; these three areas comprised 64 percent of the problems listed. Both sexes saw their peers as having fewer school problems and more interpersonal problems than they reported for themselves.

RANKING OF PROBLEMS. A later study by Chabassol and Thomas (1969) involved 1,366 students in grades eight through eleven in secondary schools in an urban area in British Columbia. Sex adjustments and mental hygiene receive more attention today than formerly. Perhaps this is a reflection of the fact that these problem areas are given more attention in modern society than formerly. Some topics, such as manners, civic interests, and a philosophy of life have declined or remained low as problems.

Table 2-2, showing the ranking of problems by grades and sex, provides some interesting comparisons and contrasts. Money, study habits, and mental hygiene rank high with males at all grade levels; these three problem areas plus personal attractiveness rank high with girls at all grade levels. Of much less importance to both boys and girls are items relating to safety, recreation, manners and courtesy, daily schedule, and getting along with people. Significant changes may be noted with increased grade. For example, whereas health ranked in fourth place for ninth-grade boys, it ranked twelfth for eleventh-grade boys. Home and family problems showed an interesting rank change for boys, reaching third place at grade eleven. This perhaps is indicative of the boys' struggle for independence from home ties.

RANKING OF INTERESTS. The greater interest of the adolescent girl in people and social events may have had its origin when she was an in-

Table 2-2 Rankings of Problems by Grades and Sexes

ITEM	BOYS BY GRADE				GIRLS BY GRADE			
	8	9	10	11	8	9	10	11
Health	9.5	4	8.5	12	8	5	6.5	8
Sex adjustments	4	7	10	7.5	9	7	6.5	5
Safety	12	12	11.5	10.5	13.5	13.5	11	14
Money	2	1	1	2	1	1	3	2
Mental hygiene	5	3	3	4.5	4	2	1	1
Study habits	1	2	2	1	2	8	4	9
Recreation	15	15	15	15	15	15	15	15
Personal and moral qualities	3	5.5	6	6	5	6	9	4
Home and family relationships	14	8	5	3	6	4	8	7
Manners and courtesy	13	14	14	14	12	12	12	11.5
Personal attractiveness	9.5	5.5	7	9	3	3	2	3
Daily schedule	7.5	10	11.5	10.5	11	13.5	13	13
Civic interest	7.5	9	8.5	7.5	7	11	14	11.5
Getting along with people	11	13	13	13	13.5	10	10	10
Philosophy of life	6	11	4	4.5	10	9	5	6

Source: Chabassol and Thomas, 1969: 18.

fant. Lewis and his colleagues (1965) noted that at the age of twelve weeks girls looked longer at photographs of faces than at schematic line drawings of normal or distorted faces, while boys of the same age failed to discriminate between these stimuli. Girls also vocalized more to the faces than to the forms; boys vocalized equally to each. This greater

Table 2-3 Rankings of Interests by Grades and Sexes

ITEM	BOYS BY GRADE				GIRLS BY GRADE			
	8	9	10	11	8	9	10	11
Health	3	4	4	4	4	3	5	3
Sex adjustments	2	1	3	2	1.5	2	1	2
Safety	12	8.5	9	12	14	12.5	12	13
Money	4	3	2	1	5	6	3	10
Mental hygiene	9.5	10	10	9.5	10	7	7.5	6.5
Study habits	9.5	13	13	11	12	12.5	13	14
Recreation	1	2	1	3	3	8	6	8
Personal and moral qualities	5.5	7	7	6	8	10	9	6.5
Home and family relationships	8	8.5	8	9.5	7	5	7.5	9
Manners and courtesy	14	11.5	12	13	9	11	11	11
Personal attractiveness	7	6	5	8	1.5	1	2	1
Daily schedule	15	15	15	15	15	15	15	15
Civic interest	13	14	14	14	13	14	14	12
Getting along with people	5.5	5	6	5	6	4	4	4
Philosophy of life	11	11.5	11	7	11	9	10	5

Source: Chabassol and Thomas, 1969: 19.

interest of girls in people and social activities has been observed in studies of adolescents.

Table 2-3 displays rankings of interest by grade and sex (Chabossal and Thomas, 1969). There is considerable agreement in the interests at the different grade levels and in the ranks given different areas by boys and girls. This holds especially for the high- and low-interest rankings. Furthermore, a comparison between problem and interest areas shows considerable similarity for money, except for the eleventh-grade girls. Both boys and girls are concerned about health, sexual adjustment, recreation, and getting along with people, although these ranked relatively low among the problem areas.

Problems Involving Money and Family

The results of the studies cited show that money and family rank high among the problems encountered by adolescents. In a poll conducted by Louis and Harris for *Life* magazine (1971) involving a cross-sample of youth, 32 percent reported they had trouble communicating with their parents; 74 percent of these believed it to be the fault of both their

What can I get for my dad and mother who think that youth are going to the dogs?

parents and themselves. Answers to other questions relating to the family are given in Table 2-4. The young people expressed a belief that their upbringing was neither too strict nor too permissive. In response to the question: "Does your family have enough money?" 76 percent replied yes; 59 percent of black youth stated their family did not have enough money.

TABLE 2-4 The Percent of Young People Responding *Yes* or *No* to Questions Regarding Their Relations with Parents

QUESTION	PERCENT	
Has your upbringing been too strict?	10	yes
too permissive?	8	yes
about right?	81	yes
Do you accept and agree with your parents' ideals?	84	yes
Do your parents approve of your ideals and values?	64	yes
Do they approve of the way your generation expresses these ideals?	55	no
Do you have trouble communicating with your parents?	32	yes
	66	no

Source: *Life* magazine, 1971: 22.

A Gallup poll taken between April 23 and May 17, 1969, involving 1,030 youths in 55 colleges showed that the inability to communicate with parents is a major problem (*U.S. News*, 1969). This is indicated by the results presented in Table 2-5, which are consistent with the results presented in Table 2-4. The students also felt that parents were too conservative, indifferent, and materialistic. Only 11 percent had no complaints about their parents.

TABLE 2-5 Student's Gripes About Parents

GRIPE	PERCENT MAKING COMMENT
Too set in their ways	36
They won't listen to us	18
Too conservative	8
Indifferent, apathetic	8
Too materialistic	6
Too strict	6
Their views on morals	4
Racial prejudice	4
They stereotype young people	4
Other responses	6
No gripe about parents	11
No opinion	3

Source: *U.S. News and World Report*, 1969: 35.

Personal and Social Problems

Personal and social problems loom large in the lives of adolescents. During this period boys and girls must adjust to conditions imposed by a society in the process of rapid transition. Frequently they are faced with personal and social problems that are not only new to themselves but are different from those faced by their parents and other adults upon whom they depend for education and guidance.

PERSONAL APPEARANCE. As part of adolescent culture we frequently note special fads in clothing, hair style, and other conditions that affect personal appearance. This frequently brings criticism from parents and other adult figures. In the late sixties and early seventies many schools set forth standards of propriety for students. These have at times bordered on the ludicrous, since rules have a tendency to become more and more useless as attempts are made to clarify them—as may be noted from the following examples:

> A girl's skirt must not be more than three inches above the floor when she is kneeling.
>
> A boy's hair must not extend below the chin level or reach within two inches of his shoulder.
>
> A boy's shirt tail must not hang out, unless the shirt is specially designed to be worn on the outside.

A principal who attempts to enforce such rules may find himself facing a parade of students sent by their teachers who want him to confirm the accuracy of their measurements and to punish the culprits. Furthermore, changing styles soon make the rules obsolete by the time they are clarified and explained to students and parents.

IMPORTANCE OF THINGS. In a panel of high school students discussing the goals of life, one student pointed out that she felt a goal most people seek is happiness. An alert and energetic high school junior replied, "Why should you seek happiness? That doesn't make you any money!" Surveys show that "the making of more money" is the main motivating factor that causes young people to seek an increased amount of education. Visiting students from many Asiatic countries often express amazement at the high standard of living in the United States and at the goals of students who seek happiness and satisfaction through the acquisition of *things*.

The American adolescent today lives and functions in a society where material values are considered of utmost importance, as a result of American ingenuity, mass production, and salesmanship. When adolescents have their own television sets, radios, telephones, and subscriptions to glamour magazines, yet neglect the aesthetic and the sublime, it follows that one of the most urgent tasks confronting the home, church, and schools today is to destroy the twentieth-century myth that the accumulation of wealth and the attainment of widespread luxuries are the most important goals of man. There is need to remember that "man does not live by bread alone." The way materialistic values in American life affect the personal and social lives of adolescents helps provide an understanding of some of our youth's problems. Concerning this Bloustein (1971: 46) states:

> Our youth find themselves in a world dominated as never before by bureaucracy and technology. It is a world in which science and rationality have become gods for men to worship rather than tools for men to use. It is a world in which creative comforts and material goods have been sought, produced and accumulated out of all proportion to their appropriate place in the life of man. Finally, it is a world in which the adult population has suffered a failure of nerve, a failure of confidence in its capacity to succeed according to its own lights.

This has had an important bearing on the development of uncertainties on the part of a large percentage of college youth as well as many adults. To sit back and point out that uncertainties have existed at all stages of man's development is to be blind to the impact of the Industrial Revolution and to problems besetting the more highly industrialized areas of the world.

Fears and Concerns of Adolescents

As children grow into adolescence they tend to discard certain childhood fears. Adolescents generally fear the same things as most adults, such as unpopularity, rejection, and failure. However, some of our most thoughtful adolescents fear adults themselves—the older generation, or "The Establishment." There is also a fear of and antagonism toward the police on the part of many young blacks and long-haired whites, who are sometimes subject to brutality or mistreatment by a small segment of policemen, as was the case of Trogdon from Charlotte, North Carolina, in 1971:

> Trogdon's appearance would type him as an outcast in the eyes of some people. He is seventeen years of age and wears bell-bottom trousers —sometimes with red stripes and blue stars when playing bass guitar with a local rock group. The 50 to 60 dollars a week he earns goes into the family budget. His father is separated from his mother, who works at the public library. There is no indication of a generation gap between Trogdon and his mother. Trogdon is not "hung up" on his long hair and had it cut before the court trial, where he was acquitted. "I let it [his hair] grow out when I got in the group." He had earlier reached an agreement with his mother on this.
> He was picked up by the police while in a crowd listening to the rock group "Orphanage" and was charged with disorderly conduct. He recounts

the mistreatment received at the hands of several policemen before they locked him in a cell. The police were unable to prove any disorderly conduct on the part of Trogdon. The police department's Internal Affairs Section investigated four officers involved in Trogdon's case and declared the misconduct charges unfounded. (Maschal and Walls, 1971).

SPECIAL CONCERNS. At a recent youth organization conference a group of adolescents and adults gathered to discuss the year 2,000. Although most of the participants agreed on the technological implications of the future, the young people were horrified at the scientific rather than humanitarian approach toward solving our present-day problems. They expressed a fear of technological manipulation and control by adults who have no significant commitment to moral consequences and to human life in its wholeness. This attitude has been revealed over and over by adolescent discussion groups when dealing with world problems. It was apparent in their feeling about the Vietnam War, in which the federal government at one time displayed a greater interest in saving face than in saving lives. The statement of Deborah Jean Sweet, a nineteen-year-old girl, to President Nixon when she was one of four to be given a medal for service to her countrymen reveals something of the humanitarian attitude of youth toward world problems in general and the Vietnam War in particular. She accepted the medal, shook hands with the President, and said: "I find it very hard to believe in your sincerity in giving an award for service until you get us out of the war" (*Charlotte Observer,* 1970).

THE NOW GENERATION

Never before have adolescents in the United States been so well informed, assertive, articulate, idealistic, and worldly. Due to unprecedented affluence and the welfare state, there is a sense of economic security that has never been equaled in history. This not only makes them a new generation but a new kind of generation—a *now generation* in which the future is now. They have prolonged youth and an increased life span. Most adolescents do not feel the cold pressures of hunger to motivate and inspire them. Perhaps this is what young people who have involved themselves recently in various kinds of youth movements are striving for—the pressures that inspire and motivate.

Because of scientific and technological advancements the adolescent is armed with more tools to help him choose his life pattern and even a marriage mate than he can normally use. Experiences and adventure of immense importance await him—adventures in space, finding a cure for cancer and other deadly diseases, population control, pollution, and the many problems caused by the post-Industrial Revolution that confront the United States in the 1970s.

The Conflict of Cultures

We are living in an environment characterized by diverse cultures that in many respects are opposed to one another. This may be observed in the case of "our old scarcity-oriented technological culture that still predominates and the somewhat amorphous counterculture that is growing up to challenge it. At times this distinction may seem synonymous with old-versus-young, or radical-versus-conservative, but the overlap is only approximate. There are many young people who are dedicated to the old culture and a few old people attracted to the new. . ." (Slater, 1970: 97).

Each culture has its own internal logic and consistency. The older culture, which is closely associated with the older generation, is identified with far right, authoritarian, puritanical, law-and-order fundamentalism. The newer culture, adhered to by a large percentage of middle-class college students, is identified with the New Left, with its emphasis on equalitarianism, social justice, and social commitment. Expediency has been the major force in unifying these views through a sort of compromise—although the two cannot and will not mix, since no morally based unity is possible. The core of the old culture, according to Slater, is scarcity. "Everything in it rests upon the assumption that the world does not contain the wherewithal to satisfy the needs of its human inhabitants" (103). The new culture is based on the assumption that important human needs are easily satisfied and that the resources for doing so are here and now. The dilemma of these cultures is discussed more fully in Chapter 12. It is sufficient to state here that many college-going adolescents adhere to the new culture; they see no reason why changes and reforms advocated cannot be immediately adopted.

For all their knowledge and understanding the now generation remains skeptical. They are looking to additional knowledge and understanding for answers to their problems, but the rules and guidelines that directed their parents' lives do not operate today. Nor will adolescents automatically accept what were given as moral absolutes to earlier generations. This is happening with youth from Tokyo to Berkeley.

WHAT CHILDREN AND ADOLESCENTS ARE THINKING. Once each decade the President of the United States has convened a White House Conference on Children to obtain from lawyers, parents, educators, physicians, scientists, and others their assessment of the needs of the nation's youth. The 1970 conference was different from its predecessors in that for the first time a national administration gathered and made use of the impressions of the children. Responses to the question What would you tell the President of the United States if you had a chance? were gathered from children from all areas of the United States. Some representative responses of eleven-year-old children are here presented (Shearer, 1970):

Well, I'd tell him that the war must stop in Vietnam.

I'd ask the President to do something about pollution. You should see the back of our building. Everytime the wind blows, trash falls out all over the yard.

I'd tell the President we need more schools. It's hard to learn when there are too many kids in your class.

I'd ask the President to do as much as possible about the crime situation. Once you could leave your doors unlocked. Now friends of ours even have bolts on their door and bars on their windows.

I'd ask the President to do everything about drugs. I heard about a kid who went to a party and somebody offered her some drugs and she said no, so they put it in her food. I'm afraid of drugs and I watch what I eat a lot.

I'd like to see people associate with one another better—communicate, that's it.

I'd tell the President to work harder on conservation. If people could spend two hours in the woods, they'd see how beautiful it is and maybe they'd care more. Life is important, all kinds of life.

In the fall of 1970 children in Amherst, Massachusetts, ranging in age from eight to fourteen, were invited to tell grown-ups (although grown-ups were not present, except for the moderator) what was wrong with their schools. The youngsters demonstrated a sophisticated understanding of classroom problems that surprised those listening over closed-circuit television from another room. Teachers and grades came in for the most criticism. The youngsters could not see any consistency between the teachers' statements and their behavior on such matters as trust, as well as in other matters. All of the children responding expressed strong disapproval of the standard grading system that awards letter grades as an incentive for learning or as an evaluation of achievement. The pupils also sounded off about outdated textbooks and those that talked down to them rather than challenging them to do some thinking (*Newsweek,* 1970).

Many adolescents fail to see any relation between what they are required to learn and their needs and objectives. They can be heard asking: "Why do we have to study ———?" The results of some studies show that adolescents tend to welcome meaningful activities at school; they want to be heard; they want to participate. Student power to most students means "We want to participate."

YOUTH AND THE CHANGED MORALITY. It has been suggested that with the exception of the mainland Chinese, no people have changed so much during the past quarter of a century as Americans. This change in the United States is most apparent in our sexual attitudes and ethics. The change has been so rapid that the older generation is dazed by it, while the older clergymen and many other church leaders very frequently fail to recognize it, much less accept it (Nichols, 1966).

> Wherever you go, you find people speaking of the "new morality," the "new freedom," the "sexual revolution." They all add up to the same thing—a contagious spirit of permissiveness, of anything goes, in all areas of social conduct, in manners, dress and sexual relationships. It applies at every age level. America seems to be engaged in one vast, all-pervading, all-permissive sexological spree.

To the youth of today religion should be concerned with present-day problems. The notion that adolescents are not religious is not borne out by scientific studies. They are less concerned with the church and religion in its institutional form than adults. This is shown in the results of the Louis and Harris poll taken for *Life* magazine (1971). The results, presented in Table 2-6, show that 77 percent of the high school students interviewed responded *yes* to the question, Is religion important to you? Over two-thirds of the youth responded *yes* to the question, Do liberalized attitudes and new forms of worship make church more interesting? Almost one-half of the youth polled stated that they found more spiritual benefit in nature or in fellowship with others than in going to church. To those who think of religion in terms of values related to nature and fellowship with others these results are encouraging; to those who regard religion in terms of absolutes and as an establishment that remains stable throughout the ages the results are discouraging.

TABLE 2-6 Response of Youth to Questions Bearing on Religion

QUESTION	PERCENT RESPONDING YES
Is religion important to you?	
high school students	77
college students	56
Do you attend church regularly?	
high school students	58
college students	43
Do liberalized attitudes and new forms of worship make church more interesting to you?	69
Do you find more spiritual benefit in nature or in fellowship with others than in going to church?	47

Source: *Life* magazine, 1971: 26.

The world today is committed to accelerating change—radical, wrenching change that evades both traditions and old values. Its inheritors have grown up with rapid change, are educationally better prepared to acclimate themselves to it than any group in history; they embrace change as an inherent part of living. With their skeptical yet humanistic outlook, disdain for fanaticism, and scorn for the spurious, adolescents believe that they will infuse the future with a new sense of morality, a transcendent and contemporary ethic that could infinitely enrich the empty society—and have a great deal of fun in the process (*Time* 1967).

Critical Problems—The Future is Now

The so-called generation gap, adolescent unrest, parent-adolescent con-flict and youth rebellion are usually attributed to the rapid changes that are occurring as a result of the applications of technology to all aspects of our lives. The nature, rate, and significance of change is elaborated upon in Chapter 12. Most commentators, analysts, and educators, in spite of differences in their viewpoints, make predictions for the future on the basis of the past and treat the future as an extension of the past. They ignore the irreversibility of changes that have occurred since the beginning of the Industrial Revolution. Margaret Mead (1970: 24) offers primary evidence that the situation is unique: "the generation gap is world-wide. . . . Recent technological changes or the handicaps imposed by its absence, revolution or the suppression of revolutionary activities, the crumbling of faith in ancient creeds or the attraction of new creeds—all these serve only as partial explanations of the particular forms taken by youth revolt in different countries."

Several conditions are offered by Mead to explain the revolt of youth around the world, the first of which is the emergence of a world community. No single, interacting worldwide community has ever existed before. The young generation, especially the articulate young from the middle and upper classes are speaking out against many of the ills they see today. They are like the first generation in a new country; they live and are at home in an era far different from the one their parents ex-perienced as adolescents. Satellites are familiar in their skies; rapid transit is a commonplace. They do not feel that continued pollution of the air, soil, and water is a necessary part of modern civilization. They fail to see why skin color should be a basis for discrimination. They cannot reconcile the mass murder in North Vietnam in 1972 with this country's avowed humanitarian ideals.

There as still many parents who cling to the past and attempt to answer today's problems on the basis of past remedies that have always worked poorly. Some religious leaders answer our major problems by saying "It is God's will," or advising youngsters to figure it out for them-selves. Most parents are, however, too uncertain to rely upon old dogmas; they depend upon hope and faith. Concerning these Mead (1970: 113) points out:

> It is the adults who still believe that there is a safe and socially ap-proved road to a kind of life they have not experienced, who react with greatest anger and bitterness to the discovery that what they had hoped for no longer exists for their children. These are the parents, the trustees, the legislators, the columnists and commentators who denounce most vocally

what is happening in schools and colleges and universities in which they had placed their hopes for their children.

The youth of today recognize that the resources are available to solve our major problems—both natural and human. They know that the know-how is here or can soon be made available, as has been demonstrated by our walks on the moon and planetary probes. Many adolescents are convinced that we must make important changes if we are to survive not only as citizens of a relatively free society but as citizens of one world.

ADOLESCENCE:
THE CRISIS OF IDENTITY

The identity crisis, according to Erikson (1968), occurs when a youth must forge for himself some central perspective, some unity, out of the remnants of his childhood and the hopes of adulthood; he must detect some meaningful relationship between what he sees in himself and what others judge and expect him to be. The early Greeks recognized this problem among adolescents and described it as the period of trying on and taking off different masks until one is found that best fits.

Not until adolescence, according to Erikson, does the individual develop the prerequisites in physical growth, mental maturation, and social responsibility to experience the crisis of identity. The identity crisis is one of the psychosocial aspects of adolescence. Erikson has developed a chart that depicts the different stages in the life cycle. The diagram formalizes the temporal progression of the differentiation of parts; each comes to its peak, meets its crisis, and moves into the next stage.

The Need for Identity

Modern technology has confronted man with problems more complex and far-reaching than he has ever faced before. Some of the needs and problems of this age listed by Erikson include trust in oneself and in others. Then, according to Erikson, "the adolescent looks most fervently for men and ideas to have *faith* in, which also means men and ideas in whose service it would seem worthwhile to prove oneself trustworthy."

The adolescent comes into contact with various personalities and ideas, both covertly and overtly. And, although the identification process is primarily individualistic, the contemporary scene is extremely important. Identification is made difficult by the fact that roles and adjustments vary considerably from one situation to another. However, when the perceived identity is confirmed by reality the individual's identity is more stable and secure. This becomes an important step toward maturity.

Adolescents are highly dependent upon their parents' example for acquiring their sex role as well as other behavior traits. This identification process will be given special attention in Chapter 8. These learned way of behaving are part of the cultural heritage. In our urban-industrial society, the norms that distinguished masculinity and feminity are not as distinct as they were several decades ago. Long hair, ruffled shirts for boys; pants suits, boyish haircuts for girls—are these part of the current youth movement? or does it go deeper and symbolize the lessening division of the sexes? There are some who look upon the disappearance of sex differences with much concern; others look upon this as a passing fancy of the generation (Deutsch, 1968).

UNIQUE SELF-CONCEPT PATTERNS. The adolescent must develop a realistic yet compassionate self-concept in order to lead a stable and useful life. He must learn to accept his own capabilities, then shape his aspirations accordingly. Those unable to see themselves realistically seek various forms of escape from the real world. For example, a young boy may say, "I am not very popular with the gang because I live too far away from them," rather than "because I am too selfish."

Self-acceptance is to a great extent dependent on intellectual abilities. In a comparison by Strang of two eighth-grade classes in the same school, one made up of poor learners, the other of able learners, the former's self-assessment and hopes for the future were way beyond what their abilities would indicate, whereas the latter's aims were almost entirely realizable. Both groups mentioned the varied factors that enter into self-concepts: physical characteristics, clothes, attitudes of age-mates toward them, interests, educational plans, and future vocation. Both mentioned their good and bad traits, but the intelligent group seemed to be more realistic than the other.

The able learners looked upon themselves more as average than superior, as for instance in the following: "I think that I am what might be regarded as a normal person. Perhaps other people may think of me as shy or timid. I just like to watch television. Most of the time I enjoy my schoolwork." Individuality seemed to be the key feature of the group as a whole. Each person seemed to be smart in his own way or to display unique interests. This group frequently ran into difficulty with teachers in an effort to maintain individuality.

Adolescents are to a marked degree dependent upon their peers for self-concepts. The adolescent personality is so pliable that the tastes and values of contemporaries become an unquestioned norm which must be followed for group approval, without which the adolescent cannot accept himself. One who is not considered a part of his peer group has serious doubts about himself; similarly, a person unsure of himself lacks confidence even in his apparent acceptance by others.

The self-accepting adolescent is likely to be more forthright in recognizing himself as one who at times is troubled, sexually excited, anxious about his place in society. Forced to identify largely with peers, adolescents set up their own structure and develop what has been referred to as teen-age culture. The need for such a culture with its peculiar symbols is symptomatic of their search for identity.

CRYSTALLIZATION OF SELF-CONCEPTS. In the establishment of a unified self-concept the adolescent must draw upon multiple identities. The growing independence and physical strength of the adolescent make it especially important that self-concepts be crystallized, that childlike concepts be reinterpreted in the light of the new autonomy, and the hiatus between the ideal and the real self be breached. The adolescent failing to achieve self-acceptance will find it difficult to cope with his environment.

There is perhaps no period of life more difficult than the adolescent period—the transition stage of life. The adolescent is often not only misunderstood by adults, but also by himself. This will be shown in case studies presented throughout subsequent chapters. The brief case study of Tom, with whom the writer has had close contact, illustrates how an adolescent can be an enigma to himself.

> Tom was slightly late in reaching physical maturity, although he was above average mentally and got better than average grades in school. He developed a keen desire for a repeater shotgun. Over his mother's protest, Tom was given the gun for Christmas. During the next several months he seemed to get much pleasure in going hunting with a good friend of his, a young man his own age.
>
> Most of the usual habits and characteristics common to a large percentage of adolescents were to be found in Tom. He was rather careless; he would forget to clean his gun after hunting, despite his father's continuously calling this to his attention. He would wear a good shirt to school and forget about his clothing and enter into some tumbling or play activities, even though his mother had warned him on many occasions not to. He would leave the lights on in the basement, although he had been reminded of this a number of times. At times he would join the family; at other times he would prefer to remain in his room listening to the radio or go to the movies with his friends. Just two years before, he seemed to be very fond of his family, his father in particular, and spent a great deal of time with him, yet Tom no longer wished to go with him to watch a practice ball game; he preferred other activities—watching television and playing with his friends. Tom himself could not understand why he changed in some of his interests and activities as rapidly as he did, and why he always forgot things. Thus, Tom, a normal adolescent boy, was understood neither by his family nor by himself.

SUMMARY

Adolescents today face problems quite different from those faced by previous generations; however the biological changes occurring during adolescence are similar in all cultures. Adolescence, as a period of life, is closely related to the Industrial Revolution. Among primitive tribes puberty ceremonies appropriate to the particular culture usher the individual from childhood into adulthood. Adolescents in highly industrialized societies are not admitted into the larger adult-oriented culture; therefore they tend to form a culture of their own.

The needs of adolescents may be thought of in terms of problems they face in growing up. Maslow proposes the following general list of needs: physiological, safety, love and belonging, esteem, self-actualization, and desire to know and understand. An understanding of the operation of these needs helps us to better deal with adolescents. The need for self-actualization is frequently repressed during the adolescent years.

The adolescent period is one of rapid transition from childhood to adulthood. The rapid changes operating in our society have created difficult problems for adolescents in their preparation for adulthood. There has been a pronounced extension of the adolescent period, and this has been a factor in the development of adolescent cultures and special problems. Among the immediate problems of adolescents are those related to schooling; these vary with different grades and to some extent with gender. Study habits, money, and mental hygiene problems rank high for both boys and girls. A major family problem is the inability to communicate. In general the fears and concerns of adolescents are quite similar to those of adults, especially young adults.

Adolescents have been described by some students of developmental psychology as the "now" generation. This is perhaps truer for middle-class adolescents than for adolescents from the lower classes. We must recognize that there is a great diversity of adolescent cultures. Adolescence is not a single, monolithic entity.

Contemporary adolescents are better informed than adolescents of any previous period. This may be the basis for the generation gap that is discussed in Chapter 3. Actually, this conflict may result in large part from ignorance and lack of understanding of contemporary problems. Upper- and middle-class adolescents see many present-day practices as outworn, materialistic, and inhumane.

REFERENCES

Adams, James F. "Adolescent Personal Problems as a Function of Age and Sex." *Journal of Genetic Psychology* (1964), 104:207–14.

Antonovsky, H. F. "A Contribution to Research in the Area of Mother-Child Relationships." *Child Development* (1959), 20:37–51.

Benedict, Ruth. *Patterns of Culture.* Boston: Houghton Mifflin Company, 1934.

Bloustein, Edward J. "Why We Ought to Join Our Kids." *Look* magazine (January 26, 1971), pp. 46–47.

Carroll, Jerome F. "Understanding Adolescent Needs." *Adolescence* (1968–69), 3:381–94.

Chabassol, David J. and David C. Thomas. "Sex and Age Differences in Problems and Interests of Adolescents." *The Journal of Experimental Education* (1969), 38 (2):16–23.

Charlotte Observer (December 4, 1970), p. 24A. "Honored She Doubts. . . ."

COSTANZO, P. R. and M. E. SHAW. "Conformity as a Function of Age Level." *Child Development* (1966), 37:967–75.

DEUTSCH, PATRICIA and DON DEUTSCH. "Are Sex Differences Disappearing?" *Family Circle* (October 1968), pp. 30–31, 103.

ERIKSON, ERIK H. *Identity: Youth and Crisis*. New York: W. W. Norton & Co., 1968.

FRANK, LAWRENCE K. "Needs and Problems of Adolescents in the Area of Emotional Health." *The High School Journal* (December 1951), 35:66.

HIMELHOCH, JEROME. "Generational Conflict and Youth Culture: Myth or Reality?" Mimeographed copy of paper presented at the annual meeting of the American Sociological Society. Washington, D.C.: August 31–September 3, 1970.

HOLLINGS (Senator). Report of a commission studying hunger in the United States. *The Today Show* (television program), January 7, 1971.

HORROCKS, JOHN E. *The Psychology of Adolescence*. 3rd ed. Boston: Houghton Mifflin Company, 1969.

———— and S. A. WEINBERG. "Psychological Needs and Their Development." In Horrocks (1969).

JOSEPH, T. P. "Adolescents: From the Views of the Members of an Informal Adolescent Group." *Genetic Psychology Monographs* (1969) 79:3–88.

KONOPKA, GISELA. "Group Work with Adolescents." *Mental Health in Virginia* (Summer 1966), pp. 5–7.

LANDSBAUM, JANE B. and RICHARD H. WILLIS. "Conformity in Early and Late Adolescence." *Developmental Psychology* (1971), 4:334–37.

LEWIS, MICHAEL, HELEN CAMPBELL, B. BARTELS, and D. FADEL. "Infant's Responses to Facial Stimuli During the First Year of Life." Paper presented at the American Psychological Association. September 3, 1965, Chicago.

Life magazine (January 8, 1971), pp. 22–27, 30. "A New Youth Poll."

LUCAS, C. M. *An Emergent Category Approach to the Analysis of Adolescent Needs*. Doctoral dissertation. Columbus: Ohio State University, 1951.

———— and JOHN E. HORROCKS. "An Experimental Approach to the Analysis of Adolescent Needs." *Child Development* (1960), 31:479–87.

MASCHAL, RICHARD and D. WAYNE WALLS. "Arrest Still Puzzles Youth." *Charlotte Observer*, (January 25, 1971), pp. 1A–2A.

MASLOW, A. H. "A Theory of Human Motivation." *Psychological Review* (1943), 50:370–96.

————. *Motivation and Personality*. New York: Harper & Row, 1954, pp. 80–122.

MEAD, MARGARET. *From the South Seas*. New York: William Morrow and Co., 1939.

————. *Culture and Commitment: A Study of the Generation Gap*. Garden City, N.Y.: Doubleday & Company, 1970.

MONET, J. "Sex Hormones and Other Variables in Human Eroticism." In *Sex and Internal Secretions,* VIII, W. C. Young, ed. Baltimore: Williams and Wilkins, 1961.

MURRAY, H. A. *Explorations in Personality.* New York: Oxford University Press, Inc., 1938.

Newsweek (September 21, 1970), p. 80. "What the Kids Think."

NICHOLS, WILLIAM I. "Let's Not Panic at the New Morality." *Reader's Digest* (January 26, 1966), pp. 75–78.

SCHRAG, PETER. "Growing Up on Mechanic Street." *Saturday Review,* (March 21, 1970), pp. 59–61, 78–79.

SCHULTZ, HARALD. "Takuma Maidens Come of Age." *National Geographic Magazine* (November 1959), 116:629–49.

Science Research Associates. *SRA Youth Inventory* and *Examiner Manual.* (Published by Science Research Associates, copyrighted by Purdue Research Foundation.)

SHEARER, LLOYD. "The Nation's Kids Speak Out." *Parade* magazine (December, 13, 1970), p. 10.

SLATER, PHILIP E. *The Pursuit of Loneliness: American Culture at the Breaking Point.* Boston: Beacon Press, 1970.

SMITH, PAUL M. JR. "Problems of Rural and Urban Southern Negro Children." *Personnel and Guidance Journal* (1961), 39:599–600.

STATON, THOMAS F. *Dynamics of Adolescent Adjustment.* New York: The Macmillan Company, 1963. Chapter 6.

Time magazine (April 1967). "Here Comes the Now Generation."

U.S. News and World Report (June 2, 1969), p. 35.

WINTERBOTTOM, M. R. "The Relation of Childhood Training in Independence to Achievement Motivation. Ann Arbor: University of Michigan, 1953.

RECOMMENDED READINGS

ERIKSON, ERIK H. *Identity: Youth and Crisis.* New York: Appleton-Century-Crofts, 1968.
The author has given much attention to identity throughout his life. In this writing he has focused on the adolescent years when the ·crisis of identity occurs. Written from a psychoanalytic point of view, the author gives us a good and rather complete account of the problems encountered by adolescents as they grope for identity.

RAMSEY, CHARLES E. *Problems of Youth: A Social Problems Perspective.* Belmont, Calif.: Brooks-Cole Publishing Co., 1967.
The cultural, social, and psychological problems of youth are discussed in the light of our contemporary social order. Sources of parent-youth conflict are identified; conclusions and generalizations are presented.

SHERIF, MUZAFER and CAROLYN W. SHERIF, eds. *The Problems of Youth: Transition to Adulthood in a Changing World.* Chicago: Aldine Publishing Co., 1965.
The authors point out that the problem of transition involves a conflict in values. The authors also present current thinking about the social psychology of adolescent behavior.

SIMONS, J. L. and BARRY WINOGRAD. *It's Happening—A Portrait of the Youth Scene Today.* Santa Barbara, Calif.: Marc-Laird Publications, 1967.
The authors present a sympathetic discussion of the present-day environment and spirit of the younger generation. A glossary of terms used by some of our youth may be of special interest.

3

adolescence: generation and continuity

Several explanations have been offered for the "conflict of generations," or so-called generation gap in Western societies: (1) the different content of experience of adolescents today compared to that of their parents; (2) the lack of clearly defined steps in the adolescent's growth from dependence on parents to increased independence; (3) the differences in the needs, problems, and values of adolescents and their parents; and (4) stresses and strains resulting from social and cultural changes. The brevity of these explanations should not disguise the complexity of the problem. For example, the notion that social and cultural changes have produced stresses and strains may seem redundant, but the underlying factors and conditions that produce these changes have a bearing on generational conflicts. Although anthropological, psychological, psychoanalytical, and sociological explanations have been offered, any explanation of adolescent-adult conflict must be sought in the sociocultural background in which it occurs.

Theoretical Explanations of the Generation Gap

IDENTITY FORMATION. Erik Erikson noted that identity formation, while critical to adolescents, is really a generational issue. His concept of ego identity represents a search for an inner continuity that is consistent with the outer circumstances. Thus, the term "identity crisis," when applied to the adolescent period, takes on a normative meaning.

Erikson's notion of generational conflict emphasized its social nature. This primarily involved the adolescent's relation with his parents and other individuals in his environment. He contended, however, that the achievement of adolescent ego identity had one element in common throughout all cultures: the adolescent must receive meaningful recognition for his achievements from his parents and society. According to Shimberg (1969:335), Erikson recognized two major sources of conflict between adolescents and their parents: "(1) the failure of parents to accord recognition of adolescent achievement; and (2) adolescent revolt against the values and dominance of the parents."

THE RAPIDITY OF CHANGE. If one is to place the blame for the widespread unrest and dramatic actions of many adolescents today, it should be on an overall assumption that is most questionable if not completely false: that skill in child-rearing and the guidance of adolescents comes naturally by simply being a parent and following the procedures used by one's own parents. This assumption has been carried down through the centuries, but it has had its most serious effects within recent decades because of the rapid and dramatic changes that have taken place in our society.

If we study the course of development in our culture we will note that until relatively recently, children and their parents lived pretty much in the same world. Changes that took place were usually rather slow. Farming methods, for example, had not changed much over the generations. But, following World War I, the momentum of change became more rapid with each passing decade. Concerning this Brown (1969:20) states: "Today, however, so rapid is the pace of scientific and technological development and so rapidly are certain of these new developments being embraced by society, the world in which younger people now find themselves differs dramatically from that in which their parents grew up."

The rapid change of the past half century or more has brought with it a proliferation of knowledge and technical skills, as reflected in the various educational programs today. Thus, what we often observe is a knowledge or educational gap between groups. Cultural transmission in a period of rapid change has created generational problems; it has become disintegrated in contemporary societies. Mead (1970:72) states: "In periods of rapid social change, parents are uncertain of what and how to teach their children. Conflicts arise when, ritualistically, they transmit worn-out dogma which has little meaning for them and even less for their children."

Adolescents and the New Revolution

Adolescents are living today in an atmosphere created by three Americas emerging at different periods in our history. Each one has had an impact on the building of our social and economic structure; each one has also created special problems. There is the first America, which was created by the agricultural revolution—the *preindustrial* (agricultural) *America* of slaves, landowners, sharecroppers, and migrant workers.

The second America was created largely by the Industrial Revolution, which led to the creation of wealth and the concentration of our population in large cities. This America is further symbolized by our factories, steel mills, and industrial enterprises. The skilled blue-collar workers that are an outgrowth of this America are gradually forgetting the economic traumas experienced during the depression of the 1930s but are fearful lest their new social and economic position be threatened by those from an inferior social and economic position. Those that make up this second America look upon an improvement of the lot of the poor, particularly the minority and ethnic poor, with anxiety and fear. Modern-day ethnic groups have been difficult to absorb because they were late in being drawn into the benefits of the more stable industrial society.

The third revolution began to develop momentum after World War II, with the massive entrance of GIs into college, with the explosion in scientific knowledge, with the growing acceptance of the primacy of universal education, and with advancing technological developments. In the process, the third America, the *postindustrial,* has absorbed aspects of the other two and become a social-humanistic movement which is related to both technological advancements and developments in the social and behavior sciences. The third revolution is rapidly changing the nature of our basic institutions and the values of American society, although it is encountering strong resistance from the established members of our society who fail to come to terms with the nature and force of the impending changes.

The new America is symbolized by changes and controversies taking place in our political parties and churches, by the increased interest in eliminating poverty, pollution, and disease, by the increased interest in the fine arts and the preservation of our natural resources.

THE CHALLENGE: THE FUTURE BELONGS TO YOUTH. We can see in the different youth movements in high schools and colleges real evidence of a deep concern over the issues that trouble the world. It is fitting that the demands for action against environmental and social conditions resulting from the Industrial Revolution have been vividly called to our attention by the young generation; after all, they will be the real victims of the environmental and social catastrophe now facing us. This is the first generation of adolescents to have Strontium 90 in their bones and DDT in their fat threatening their health in the years ahead. They see two-thirds of the human race hungry or malnourished while the other third is overfed. They witness racial strife, gross racial discrimination, urban decay, rioting, and an increase in crime at a time when knowledge and wealth are rapidly accumulating. Furthermore, it is the youth of today who must solve the social and economic problems now facing us if we are to survive. Many youths of today are now committed to the idea of using scientific knowledge for man's welfare rather than for greater industrial growth with its waste, pollution, and socioeconomic problems.

THE DIVERSE BACKGROUNDS
OF ADOLESCENTS

The diverse backgrounds of the current adolescent generation are reflected by the educational, cultural, and income levels of the parents. They are further revealed in child-rearing patterns, the juvenile crime rate, religious activities, dating patterns, educational aspirations, and occupational choices of adolescents.

Not all adolescents participate in teen-age culture, although all adolescents are affected by the forces and conditions that brought about our present-day youth culture. Teen-age culture, like the prolonged period of adolescence, is essentially the culture of a leisure class. Most children, regardless of social class, participate in teen-age culture during the early teen years; a relatively large percentage do not participate during the late teen years.

The Suburbian Adolescent

A large percentage of American families are post-World War II suburban families. In contrast to families before World War II they are largely isolated and autonomous without grandparents and cousins; they are unable to absorb teen-agers into their culture and tend to use children and adolescents as status symbols. They live in communities without sidewalks and totally depend upon the automobile.

Although the setting of suburbia appears to satisfy childhood needs fairly well, it fails to help adolescents find their place in the broader adult world. It treats youngsters gently and with a degree of compassion until around ten, eleven, or twelve years of age. Then, as the adolescent begins to assert himself in his quest for independence and his interests and ideas begin to diverge from those of his parents, the togetherness pattern of the child-centered home no longer meets his needs. At this time the adolescent usually prefers to be with other teen-agers than with his parents.

The extended family has been reduced to a nuclear one, and the functioning neighborhood has withered to a small circle of friends plus a number of acquaintances. For millions of American children and adolescents, the neighborhood is a row of buildings or apartments where "other people" live. Most of the people making up the neighborhood have a good and relatively stable income. In the perception of youth these adults live in a standardized, seldom varying routine. Consequently, the suburban family does not function as a social unit.

Since the adolescent spends less and less waking time at home with his parents, where does he spend his time? In the main he is with other teen-agers in school, after school, over weekends, and frequently on holidays. But even here his contacts are restricted; his social life is limited largely to persons of his own age and station, his peers. Bronfenbrenner (1971: 45) states:

> . . . Whereas invitations used to be extended to entire families, with all the Smiths visiting all the Joneses, nowadays, every social event has its segregated equivalent for every age group down to the toddlers. While the adults take their drinks upstairs, the children have the "juice time" in the rumpus room downstairs. In short, we are coming to live in a society that is segregated not only by race and class, but also by age.

It doesn't take children very long to learn the lesson the adult world teaches: "Don't bother us! Latch on to your peers!" And this is what children and adolescents do as revealed by their interests and activities. Brofenbrenner studied 766 sixth-grade children, who reported spending during the weekend, an average of two to three hours a day with their parents, while spending during the same period about twice as much time with their peers, either singly or in groups. When asked whom they preferred to spend an afternoon with, many chose their friends over their parents.

Adolescents from Homes of Blue-Collar Workers

Until the middle of the twentieth century blue-collar workers comprised more than half of the working force. The families were usually larger than those of white-collar workers, and therefore their children comprised considerably more than half of the youth population. Their income was considerably below the national average; consequently, they were unable to provide adequate health and educational opportunities for their children.

Recently, however, the living standards of most blue-collar workers have substantially improved. Many of these families have moved to the suburbs; their children go to school with middle-class children, and many of them have adopted middle-class values and aspirations—particularly the desire to go to college. "The average youngster, who would have gotten just past the eighth grade thirty years ago, now finishes high school, while seven million are in college" (Mothner 1971: 50). It is estimated that there will be ten million enrolled in college by 1980.

> Schooling is youth's busywork, and all our postindustrial goodies are their reward for shutting up and lying doggo until there's room to fit them into an economy that hasn't even got enough jobs for people who need them. So more of them earn more degrees and higher degrees, which then become requirements for the jobs they probably could have filled before they started college. Kids whose parents can't afford to keep them on the conveyor fall off and get ground up in the gears. But plenty of

parents can afford it—barely. They keep their kids on it with bribes and threats and proddings. They do all this because they know the rules for staying within reach of the great American cookie jar, and they don't want their offspring ever to go without the plenty they've been trained to consume (Mothner, 1971: (50).

Not all adolescents from blue-collar homes live in the affluent suburbs, and many of those living in suburbia fail to assimilate middle-class values. Many of these children grow up on what Schrag (1970) described as Mechanic Street. These may be thought of as the "forgotten adolescents," except when they get into trouble. They are visible on the street corners with their special hair styles, in knocked-down cars, or at work on some menial task. Their wedding announcements appear in the newspapers with the names of the parents barely mentioned. Concerning these adolescents at school Schrag writes:

> It is possible to leave Mechanic Street through school achievement—to community and state colleges, to technical schools, to better jobs—yet it is hardly universal. Fewer than half actually do. . . . The honors class is filled with the children of professionals, kids whose parents have gone to college. The general course (meaning the dead end) and the vocational track are composed of the sons and daughters of blue-collar workers. The more "opportunity," the more justified the destiny of those who are tagged for failure. The world accepts the legitimacy of their position. And so do they. Their tragedy and the accompanying threat lie precisely in their acceptance of the low esteem in which school, society, and often their parents regard them, and in their inability to learn a language to express what they feel but dare not trust (60).

They sit in classrooms waiting for the bell. Books are usually a means used by teachers for oppression. A ninth-grader once confided to me: "I didn't want to write a paper for my English teacher, but she said I must, if I expect to pass her course. Well, I did. It was about a visit I made to my uncle, who lived in the country. The teacher laughed about some of the things I said in the paper; so, I just quit school." Teachers usually try to conceal their contempt for certain children—those from disadvantaged homes and others who do not succeed in their studies. Most of these children and adolescents are from Mechanic Street.

Adolescents from Disadvantaged Homes

The economically disadvantaged were once referred to as "those on the other side of the tracks." They are not confined to any one locale or ethnic group. Many are concentrated in urban slums. Others are found in less visible rural areas, undesirable or low-cost housing areas, and migrant labor camps. They are frequently concentrated in the inner city and include a large percentage of blacks and Spanish-speaking minorities. They are characterized by a variety of behavioral styles and value orientations. They have been described by Tannenbaum (1967: 46) as follows:

They are derogated for the instability of their family life, for their failure to internalize a strong achievement syndrome, for the physical ways through which they express their aggression, for their lack of certain graces in interpersonal behavior, for their deficiency in schooling and cultural sophistication, and for their apparent tolerance of noise, filth, intoxication, and sexual promiscuity.

These adolescents develop a culture of their own—somewhat distinct from the more sophisticated culture of the suburban adolescent.

Many adolescents from disadvantaged homes drop out from high school, secure a low-level job, establish some sort of home or family relationship, and continue the life style they inherited from their parents and neighborhood. The problems of these adolescents will be given special consideration in later chapters.

The Adult's Image of Adolescents

To a degree possibly never experienced before, many adults see adolescents as discontented and alienated. This image is only partially true; it has been drawn largely from the culture of upper-, upper-middle and middle-middle-class adolescents who are expected to go on to college. Certainly these do not represent all or perhaps even the majority of youth; clearly there are a number of Americas and American adolescent types, all of whom must be taken into consideration in our concept of adolescence. We cannot stereotype adolescents any more than we can stereotype adults, although many adults tend to do so. Pamela Swift (1971) pointed out that the "Red scare of the fifties tended to give way to the head scare of the sixties and seventies." She states:

> Hippies, yippies and "heads"—beaded, bearded, barefoot members of the dropped-out, turned-on generation—are as incomprehensible to the average Middle American as the Communists were—and they arouse the fear and xenophobia of a middle class which feels its values and way of life threatened.

For years the middle class has been disturbed by the successive appearance of psychedelic drugs, radical activism, terrorism, and other forms of youth rebellion. A watershed may have been reached with the arrest of Charles Manson and his followers in the Sharon Tate murder case in 1970, which seemed to confirm all of middle America's fears.

PERSPECTIVES ON
THE PRESENT GENERATION GAP

The problem of continuity and discontinuity between generations is not new, although it has been aggravated by certain characteristics of contemporary family life in industrialized societies. It has been observed that discontinuities are more visible among some groups than others. Note, for example, the discontinuities found among some minority groups that migrate to our cities or to this country. Adults similarly look with suspicion on pronounced behavioral changes on the part of adolescents.

Those adults who are much concerned with the ear-splitting, foot-stomping, hair-tearing unisexual dances of the sixties and early seventies may well examine how the public first greeted dances of old. The waltz, a West European peasant dance in the early eighteenth century, met with scorn for over a century. In 1807 Washington Irving warned parents of the dangers of permitting their daughters to waltz; while seventy years later Wilhelm I, Emperor of Germany, forbade it in Berlin (Shearer, 1970). The polka, originally a Bohemian peasant dance, suffered a somewhat similar fate. Queen Victoria forbade anyone to polka in her presence, while the *New York Herald* termed the new import, when it came to America in 1944, "indecent, immodest, and scandalous." Twentieth-century moral arbiters found the newer Latin dances equally shocking. The New York State Assembly passed a resolution against the tango. The rhumba, the mamba, the cha-cha, each in its turn met with criticism, but eventually achieved social acceptance (Shearer).

Youth Attitudes and Values

Although the development of attitudes and values is discussed in Chapter 7 in connection with personality integration and character development, it should be recognized at this point that one of the basic ingredients of the generation gap is the unwillingness and perhaps inability of many adolescents to accept the concepts, values, and goals of the older generation. In the adolescent's scheme of values, for example, materialism plays a much less important role. Observations and experiences with youths during the early 1970s revealed a decreased interest in formality, expensive clothes, and all status symbols. It is difficult for many middle-class adolescents to reconcile the vast expenditures for the war in Vietnam, with the slums and poor health conditions experienced by thousands in the United States.

The Generation Gap as Viewed by Teen-agers

In the spring of 1969 Herzog and Sudia of the H.E.W.'s Children's Bureau mailed the following questions to a group of 407 high school students randomly selected from students in college preparatory courses in metropolitan areas situated in the four major areas of the United States.

> We hear a lot these days about the generation gap. We'd like to know what your friends think about it, and whether they think about it at all.

If so, what are the main things that adults do or say or fail to understand that bothers teen-agers so much?

What about the other side of the coin? Do your friends think that some of the problems come from the teen-agers? If so, what are the main things young people do or don't do that make things worse?

A wide range of opinion appeared about the existence and nature of a generation gap with about half reporting that it is a real problem. The other half divided rather evenly between those who viewed it as no problem at all and those who said it was a problem for some young people but not for others. Some of the youngsters pointed out that it wasn't a problem for them personally but was for many others.

The majority of the youngsters see the problem as a gap in understanding. Four out of five refer to failures of communication or understanding or both. "Lagging behind the failure to understand and communicate but nevertheless bulking larger than other complaints, is a cluster of protests against the failure of parents to grant the teen-ager full status as a person entitled to respect and trust. Parents, the complaints go, do not respect the teen-ager's opinion, fail to recognize that his problems are important to him, and do not trust him" (Herzog and Sudia, Youth Report, 1970: 54).

Over one-third of the teen-agers reported value clashes between generations. Frequently these are reported in general terms such as: "We don't have the same values." "We have different viewpoints." However, nearly one in ten explicitly stated that he shared the values of his parents. This seems to be true in general for those whose fathers have liberal attitudes toward present-day problems and relatively high humanitarian values.

Contrary to what some would expect, religion did not emerge as an important issue in the generation gap in the Youth Report by Herzog and others (1970). There were a few (about one in thirty) who gave some indication of a real religious commitment, occasionally referring to a "good Christian upbringing" or the value of a belief in God.

CONFLICT OF CULTURES. It is easy to recognize differences between the cultures of various ethnic groups. According to Margaret Mead (1970) the generational differences that we now have are primarily conflicts between pre-World War II and postwar cultures rather than a rebellion of youth against their parents.

EDUCATIONAL DIFFERENTIAL. There are some who would also introduce educational differences between adolescents and their parents as a condition that produces cultural conflicts. According to the Census Bureau, more than half the nation's college students come from homes (primarily blue-collar homes) in which the head of the family did not attend college (Swift, 1971).

Whatever you do at the university, don't get involved in politics, race, pollution, war policies, taxes, or civil rights.

One reason given for the free-wheeling and defiant attitudes of Japanese teen-agers toward their parents is that parents suffer from a mass inferiority complex resulting from an inadequate education. During World War II, high school and college class work was suspended. Fathers of present-day teen-agers received a scant education. The result is that these parents do not know how to deal with their adolescent sons and daughters, who in most cases are better educated, more oriented to American culture, and much more independent (Swift, 1971).

The Generation Gap and Lack of Communication

It was pointed out earlier that many adolescents attribute the wide generation gap to a lack of communication between parent and child. But why is there a greater lack of communication today than ever before? Strom (1965) attempted to answer this question, in part at least, with diagrams which show the experiences shared by adults and children in different types of society. These are reproduced in Figures 3-1 and 3-2. In a simple society in which change is not so rapid, there are more experiences shared by parents and children together than by each

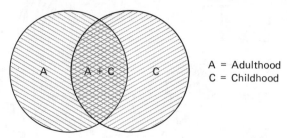

A = Adulthood
C = Childhood

FIGURE 3-1 Life in a simple society—childhood and adulthood. Adapted from R. D. Strom, *Psychology for the Classroom* (Englewood Cliffs, N.J.: Prentice-Hall, Inc., 1969), p. 5.

separately. On the other hand, in a more complex society where change is very rapid because of advanced science and technology, fewer experiences are commonly shared by adults and children. Here, because so much has changed between the time of the parent's generation and the child's generation, few things that the parents have experienced are experienced by the child and vice versa. Many parents say "I know about those things. I was young once. Listen to the voice of experience." But they were young in a different age, with different pressures, different goals, and different values.

In our complex society, adults and children frequently live in two separate worlds with separate schedules and therefore seldom have time to share experiences. But even sharing involves more than doing things together or spending time with one another; its most meaningful dimension is communication. Due to a failure in communication many parents, particularly fathers, admit that they really do not know their children.

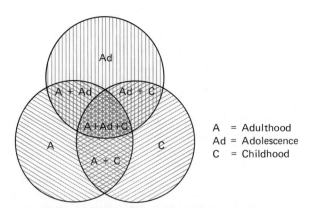

A = Adulthood
Ad = Adolescence
C = Childhood

FIGURE 3-2 Life in a complex society—childhood, adolescence, adulthood. Adapted from R. D. Strom, *Psychology for the Classroom* (Englewood Cliffs, N.J.: Prentice-Hall, Inc., 1969), p. 5.

SOME SELECTED CULTURES

Must there be a conflict between the adolescent and society? Anthropologists have pointed out that there are cultures where this conflict does not appear to exist; however, in such cultures those personality characteristics which we associate with adolescence do not appear. It has been postulated that tensions and frictions develop between the generations to the extent to which social roles, values, and relationships in the new generation deviate from those of the preceding generation. In other words, tension between the generations is not a result of human nature as such, but a consequence of the rate of social change. Since Western society is, above all, a society of change, conflict between our society and the growing child is inherent in the development of personality. The question arises: Must there be a generational conflict in our society? This question will be answered in part by examining parent-adolescent relations found in different cultures within our own society. Light might also be thrown on this question by studying adolescents in certain selected cultures.

One very important culture that has come to the forefront recently is that of China. Intergenerational gaps have appeared with increased industrialization and the widening gap between the culture of the elders and the adolescents. Also, in China more jobs have become available to youth, and traditional dependence of young people upon their elders has largely disappeared in much of China. This family revolution has been accompanied by a generation gap which seems destined to increase as China becomes more industrialized.

Indian society reflects characteristics of Eastern societies which emphasize the quality of interpersonal family relations; little value is placed on the quality of material existence. Shimberg (1969: 339) states: "Indian society has been relatively static for centuries, and as such the traditional values and norms of the society have remained unchanged and unchallenged. Generation gaps have not developed because life styles have remained constant for centuries." The extended family characterizes the Indian household; this alleviates the likelihood of potential adolescent-parent conflict and is consistent with their emphasis upon the quality of interpersonal relationships. A number of interpersonal relationships may exist in the extended family while in the nuclear family there are usually closer and more intense relationships with fewer people. The emotions are more highly concentrated upon a few members of the family, and there is a greater likelihood of explosive intergenerational relationships.

The institution of Asrama furnishes the basis for a smooth transition of authority from generation to generation. The Indian male is supposed to go through four Asramas, or age grades in life. These stages provide a condition for the transfer of authority. Sons owe complete obedience to their fathers, while the fathers are required to finally relinquish their authority. This, then, avoids conflicts between adolescent males and their fathers. According to orthodox Hindu religion, a child is born with three debts: (1) a debt to his ancestors; (2) a debt to the sages, and (3) a debt to the Gods. The developing individual pays these debts in the order named, while respecting his elders at all stages of life.

The description of the nature of the parent-adolescent relations in the Indian family is perhaps most applicable to the more orthodox Hindus and higher-caste families; it is less descriptive of lower-caste families, Muslim communities in India, and families that have been influenced by Western ideals and practices. For thousands of years the extended family has been the main economic unit throughout India. With increased industrialization we can expect changes in the family unit. Already the adolescent in some groups has begun to liberate himself from the strict customs and traditions of the orthodox Hindu religion and the extended family it tends to impose. A higher standard of living would mean increased opportunities of adolescents for a better education and a movement from the extended family toward the nuclear family. Such changes inevitably bring about changes in religious practices among youth—a movement from a more orthodox religious viewpoint toward a modified or reformed religion. This has already occurred among Jews, Christians, and some of the Oriental religions. Sometimes this religious break is itself part of the generation gap that arises.

Some African societies, such as the Massai tribe, handle the problem of parent-adolescent conflict with clearly defined age grades, or initiation ceremonies, or combinations of the two (Ottenberg, 1960). The major importance of the Massai system is that it regulates the behavior of individuals at different age levels. Other African societies such as the Tallensi or Massi, lacking specific age levels or initiation ceremonies, rely on other societal institutions, one of which is the principle of reciprocity. This principle provides for the mutual rights and duties of fathers and their adolescent sons, and acts to prevent conflicts between them (Fortes, 1949: 207). The principle of reciprocity operates in two notable instances to prevent intergenerational conflict: (1) in the use of the son's property by the father; and (2) in the arrangement of a marriage by the father. Parent-adolescent conflicts are reduced by ensuring both father and son that mutual services and favors must balance.

Shimberg describes the means used by the Mossi tribe of Upper Volta just north of Ghana for reducing or controlling parent-adolescent conflict—primarily father-son conflict. A rather drastic means of avoiding parent-adolescent conflict is the removal of the first born male until he reaches puberty because he eventually inherits the wives of his father. These first-borns are only allowed to visit the family compound for important purposes, and even then care is used to avoid any encounters with the father. Besides the Mossi practice of avoidance, their system of solving problems helps to prevent intergenerational conflict. Such decisions involve consultation with the head of the extended family. We note then that parent-adolescent conflict is rooted deeply in the structure and functions of the Mossi culture but is prevented or alleviated within bounds by following certain well-defined rules. The extended family is again the major economic and social force. Shimberg states:

> In order to maintain the solidarity of the family unit, the act of acquiring wives is reserved for the elders of the extended family—the father, and the clan chief or head. All marriages are arranged to enhance the extended family and to ensure that all new family members and new wives will remain loyal to the extended family. The inheritance of wives indicates not only the relatively low position of women in Mossi society but also serves to maintain the continuity and effective operation of the Mossi extended family by retaining effective women workers in the family unit (351–52).

In the Arab world the guidelines for parent-adolescent relationships are set forth in the religious activities and teachings that pervade all aspects of Arab life. According to Muliamed: "Whoever has a son born to him, let him give him a good name, teach him good manners and when he reaches puberty get him married. . . . If he reaches puberty and has not married and falls into sin, it is the father who is responsible. . ." (Patai, 1951; quoted from Shimberg: 352).

One may note that in the peasant culture adolescents are required to show complete respect and obedience to their father, although there is usually a closer emotional tie with the mother than with the father. Concerning the rights and guardianship of adolescents, which are usually fixed by custom or law Shimberg writes:

> . . . The child has the right to food, care, and upbringing. The child has three types of guardianship: (1) guardianship of upbringing (*tarbiya*) which is accomplished by the mother and usually ends when the child is seven or nine years old; (2) guardianship of education (spiritual guardianship) which involves proper training in the values and rules of the society; and (3) guardianship of property, which involves the maintenance of the adolescent's property until he reaches majority status (353).

Wherever education, technology, and the extended family are being challenged, conflicts have arisen between parents and the younger generation over marriage, guardianship, and family rituals.

Village households throughout Turkey contain extended families. The roles of the sexes are clearly defined, with women playing a submissive and secondary role. Older people are held in high esteem and there is no competition between individuals of different age groups for status. Respect for the aged is demonstrated on various occasions. For example, at a feast old men and guests are seated in places of honor and served first. Adolescents address their elders by special titles or kinship terms indicating their age and the respect due them. Elders are seldom addressed by their actual names. According to Shimberg there is little competition between adolescent boys and their parents because of the social concept of status in Turkish life. One simply outranks those of lower age grade and so intergenerational conflicts cannot exist.

SUMMARY

The adolescent is a product of his culture. Since there are a variety of cultures in the United States, adolescents come from diverse backgrounds. However, not all adolescents participate in what we refer to as teen-age culture.

We are living today in three Americas—preindustrial, industrial, and postindustrial. Many adolescents are deeply involved in the postindustrial culture, which places greater emphasis upon human values and less emphasis upon material values.

Significant changes have taken place in the working force, with less than half being made up of blue-collar workers. Schooling is youth's busywork, which causes many adolescents to remain dependent upon their parents. Many adolescents come from economically disadvantaged homes, and are frequently concentrated in slum areas. These make up many of the school dropouts. They do not participate in many aspects of youth culture.

The present-day adolescent spends more of his time away from home and is influenced by forces and conditions outside his home than was the case for adolescents during the first half of this century. As a result of changed conditions enumerated in this and the previous chapter, a youth culture seems to have developed, although some sociologists have questioned the existence of an adolescent culture, since adolescents are reared in an adult culture. The groundwork of an adolescent culture was laid with the Industrial Revolution, which ultimately freed adolescents from agricultural activities and industrial jobs. The adolescent culture soon came into conflict with the ideals of adults, and a generation gap appeared.

The generation gap was stimulated by rapid changes. Adult attitudes and values were questioned. For many adolescents this has been a real problem; for others the problem has been less acute. It is more apparent among boys than girls. A number of theoretical explanations of the generation gap were briefly described: the psychoanalytical explanation, the cultural anthropological, the sociological, and the developmental.

There is a difference between ethnic groups. Margaret Mead has suggested that the generation gap is actually a cultural gap between the older and younger generation. Others hold that the generation gap developed because of lack of communication between generations. One can readily observe major differences between different cultures throughout the world.

REFERENCES

BRONFENBRENNER, URIE. "Parents, Bring Up Your Children." *Look* magazine (January 26, 1971), pp. 45–46.

BROWN, HARRISON. "Why the Generation Gap?" *Saturday Review* (July 19, 1969), pp. 20–22.

ERIKSON, ERIK H. *Identity: Youth and Crisis.* New York: W. W. Norton, & Co., 1968.

FORTES, MEYER. *The Web of Kinship Among the Tallensi.* London: Oxford University Press, 1949.

HERZOG, E. and C. E. SUDIA. "The Generation Gap in the Eyes of Youth." *Children* (March–April 1970), 17:53–58.

————, B. ROSENGARD, and J. HARWOOD. "Teenagers Discuss the Generation Gap." U.S. Department of Health, Education, and Welfare, Office of Child Development, Children's Bureau, Youth Report No. 1., 1970.

MEAD, MARGARET. "Youth Revolt: The Future Is Now." *Saturday Review,* (January 10, 1970), pp. 23–25, 113.

MOTHNER, IRA. "A Few Kind Words for Parents." *Look* magazine (January 26, 1971), p. 50.

OTTENBERG, SIMON. *Cultures and Societies of Africa.* New York: Random House, Inc., 1960.

PATAI, RAPHAEL. *Relationship Patterns Among the Arabs.* New York: Council for Middle Eastern Affairs, Inc., 1951. Pp. 180–85.

SCHRAG, PETER. "Growing Up on Mechanic Street." *Saturday Review* (March 21, 1970), pp. 59–61, 78–79.

SHEARER, LLOYD. "The Nation's Kids Speak Out." *Parade* magazine (December 13, 1970), p. 10.

SHIMBERG, LAWRENCE. "Some Socio-cultural Factors in Adolescent-Parent Conflict: A Cross-cultural Comparison of Selected Cultures." *Adolescence* (Fall 1969), 4 (15):333–56.

STROM, ROBERT D. *Teaching in the Slum School.* Columbus, Ohio: Charles E. Merrill, 1965.

SWIFT, PAMELA. "Keeping Up with Youth." *Parade* magazine (August 8, 1971), p. 16.

TANNENBAUM, A. J. "Social and Psychological Considerations in the Study of the Socially Disadvantaged." *The Educationally Retarded and Disadvantaged.* Sixty-sixth Yearbook of the National Society for the Study of Education, Part 1. Chicago: University of Chicago, 1967.

RECOMMENDED READINGS

BLUMENTHAL, H. E. *Psychological Problems of the Adolescent Immigrant in Israel of Today.* Jerusalem, Israel: Ministry of Labor, Department of Vocational Education, 1958.
Although this was written in 1958, it presents some of the problems faced

by adolescents growing up in a culture which is in conflict with previously established ideals.

FRANK, ANNE. *The Diary of a Young Girl.* New York: Pocket Books, Inc., 1953.
This is a diary of a teen-ager unable to communicate or show her true inner self.

FRIEDBERG, EDGAR Z. *Coming of Age in America: Growth and Acquiescence.* New York: Vintage Books, 1967.
A cross-section of American adolescents was studied to determine the effectiveness of their education and the values they placed on their school and the opportunities and possibilities provided.

————. "Current Patterns of a Generation Conflict." *Journal of Social Issues* (1969), 25 (2):21–38.
The conflicts between the present generation and their parents is different and more far reaching than generational conflicts in the past. Many young people from the middle class are disillusioned with what they see and want to give up many of the values, ideals, and practices of middle-class culture. They (the adolescents) have developed communication patterns that are more or less unique.

HORROCKS, JOHN E. *The Psychology of Adolescence.* 3rd ed. Boston: Houghton Mifflin Company, 1969. Chapter 3.
The teen-ager is described as an activist and a great holder of values. Major topics covered in this chapter are: the teen-ager and society, adolescent tension in American culture, conflict between generations, adult stereotypes of adolescents, the nature of modern American culture, and historical changes.

OFFER, DANIEL. *The Psychological World of the Teenager.* New York: Basic Books, 1969.
The focus of the author is upon the world and problems of the normal teen-ager, especially the conditions which cause conflict with adults and adult view of the world.

SEBALD, HANS. *Adolescence: A Sociological Analysis.* New York: Appleton-Century-Crofts, 1968. Chapter 3.
The topics covered in this chapter are as follows: conflicting norms between generations; Competing authorities: parents vs. experts-parenthood; The last of the amateur; parental reaction I: permissiveness and acquiescence; Parental reaction II: reassertion of traditional authority; The clash of inferiority complexes.

WEINER, IRVING B. "The Generation Gap: Fact and Fancy." *Adolescence* (Summer 1971), 6 (22):156–66.
Although the generation gap is frequently viewed as fancy, the author emphasizes through meaningful examples that it is also *real.*

part two

Adolescent Development and Change

A problem which the student of developmental psychology must concern himself with is the relationship between biological and environmental factors in the emergence of various kinds of behavior. It was pointed out in Chapter 1 that some students view the adolescent primarily in terms of biological factors, others in terms of phychological, social, or psychoanalytical factors. The eclectic approach predisposes one to view the adolescent somewhere between the extremes, or in terms of an interaction approach. If we are to understand the adolescent we must recognize the relation between the physical and physiological and the varied cultural and environmental conditions.

4

physical and physiological development

The physical and physiological changes that occur during the adolescent years have wide repercussions in personal and social behavior and attitudes toward self and others. Hence the student of adolescent psychology needs to understand the course and nature of physical and physiological development so that he can more adequately interpret the behavior of adolescents.

Change goes on constantly in living cells—as was once said, "life is a process of changing." The growing child is constantly faced with new and different forces of two special types. The one is organic, and is in essence the physiological process occurring in all living organisms; energy is being made available through the metabolic processes related to food assimilation and is released through activity. The other force is man's external environment, which continuously stimulates a reaction. Concerning the effect of these forces, Boswell states:

> Each living organism, in relation to internal as well as to external changes and conditions, tends to maintain itself as an integrated whole, as do also social organisms and a wide range of animate things. Each is,

then, not merely something happening, but is a complex, integrated, and unified system of activities. Thus, definite internal changes are taking place within each living being in accordance with its character and mode of life; and all its vital mechanisms, however varied, combine to maintain a uniform dynamic state or "field" within each individual, in the face of fluctuating conditions of internal or external stimulation. (1947: 290)

Thus, it may be noted that the development of the individual is a result of conditions set forth in the germ plasm and environmental stimulation continuously operating on the growing organism.

PHYSICAL GROWTH AND DEVELOPMENT

Near the end of childhood growth becomes slower; this is the period that marks the physical transition between the slow, gradual development of childhood and the accelerated, more irregular growth changes of adolescence. The growth controls of childhood begin to fade, and the adolescent growth factors are not yet ready to function.

Growth in Height and Weight

Tables of averages for growth during childhood and adolescence are likely to be misleading because children of the same age vary enormously in their rate of development. Such tables do furnish useful information about growth trends and about the average height at different age levels. They furnish no useful information about individual patterns of development (Bayley, 1956).

Just prior to the advent of puberty, the rate of growth in height increases. According to Nicolson and Hanley (1953) the average chronological age at which the greatest increment in standing height occurs is 11.5 years for girls and 13.8 years for boys. The height record of 408 girls of known age at the time of menarche showed that the mode of increase was from 2 to 5 inches, with 17 percent of the girls growing

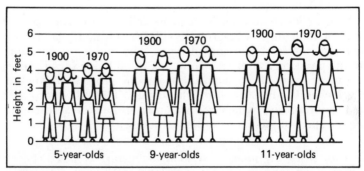

FIGURE 4-1 Growth in average height of children in the United States from 1900 until 1970.

more than four inches after menarche (Fried and Smith, 1962). The average yearly increments for weight show a somewhat different picture. Beginning around the fifth year there is a gradual and progressive gain each year, with girls showing a greater increase than boys. The average thirteen-year-old girl is both taller and heavier than her male contemporary, as shown in Table 4-1 (Martin, 1955). The growth in weight during the early teen years is frequently followed by a falling off in weight on the part of many girls (Bayley, 1956). The ideal slenderness is no doubt responsible for this early stabilization of weight for girls.

Many studies substantiate the conclusions that children today mature physically earlier and are taller at maturity than children a century ago. According to Van Dellen (1971), at the turn of the century fewer than 4 out of 100 men attained a height of six or more feet; today more than 25 out of 100 do. Also, a greatly increased number of women today are reaching the five feet, seven inches mark or higher. This increase in physical development is especially apparent in some recently industrialized nations, where there have been profound changes in diet and living patterns. The results of a recent survey, reported by Japan's Education Ministry, covering 340,000 children and adolescents shows a remarkable change in growth patterns since the early 1960s. The average twelve-year-old Japanese boy in 1972 is 2½ inches taller, 10 pounds heavier, and 1 inch larger around the chest than his counterpart in 1962. Likewise, the average Japanese twelve-year-old girl in 1972 is 2 inches taller, 8 pounds heavier, and 1½ inches larger around the chest than her counterpart ten years earlier (Parade, 1972).

GROWTH RETARDATION. There are many adolescents that fail to reach their physical growth potential set forth by biological inheritance because of adverse conditions during childhood such as a prolonged period of ill-health, malnutrition, insufficient rest, or the lack of sufficient exercise. According to a three-year survey conducted in 1968 by the Public Health Service, one-third of the children up to six years of age in

TABLE 4-1 Average Standing Height and Weight of Boys and Girls During the Teen Years

	MALES		FEMALES	
AGE	Height (inches)	Weight (pounds)	Height (inches)	Weight (pounds)
13	60.7	98.9	61.3	102.2
14	63.6	113.7	62.9	113.6
15	66.6	128.1	63.5	117.2
16	67.9	136.6	63.9	120.8
17	69.0	145.3	64.1	122.0
18	69.3	150.3	64.4	123.0

Source: Martin (1955).

rural slums and urban ghettos have suffered from growth retardation (*Charlotte Observer,* 1971). The study was specifically aimed at low-income families, and its findings do not represent a cross-section of Americans. But it does establish an irrefutable link between poverty, malnutrition, and growth retardation. As pointed out earlier in connection with earlier sexual maturation today as compared to several generations ago, we find significant increases in height and weight among children today as compared to children a century ago.

Wrist-bone X-rays taken of preschool children from poverty areas in five states—Kentucky, Louisiana, Michigan, New York, and Texas—showed that growth retardation among the poor in the United States is quite similar to that of problem areas in Africa, Asia, and Latin Amercia. This has been shown to affect development during subsequent years. There was observed a close relationship between retardation in growth and vitamin deficiencies (*Charlotte Observer,* 1971).

Anatomical Development

The ossification of the bones (skeletal age) proceeds gradually, but is rather advanced at the beginning of adolescence. The bones of the adolescent are both harder and more brittle than those of the child, and grow more brittle with advancing age. The typical girl of twelve is considerably advanced in bone development over the typical boy of the same age. A sex difference also appears on dental age scales.

Both skeletal age and tooth eruption are closely tied to the onset of puberty. Normal skeletal development will not occur in the absence of adequately functioning gonads. In fact, the relation of skeletal age to maturation is so close that an X-ray film of the hand and wrist during preadolescence may be used for predicting the time of occurrence of menarche.

OSSEOUS DEVELOPMENT. Osseous development has been found useful in predicting puberty as well as other aspects of development (Harding, 1952). By the age of thirteen the average girl will have about 30 percent ossification of her wrist bones. In a study by Malina (1970) skeletal maturation was studied longitudinally in American white and Negro children six through thirteen years of age. The data gathered were analyzed in terms of the status and progress of skeletal maturation. "Little, if any consistent difference was observed in the skeletal age and maturity point scores of Negro and white males. Negro females tended to be somewhat advanced in skeletal maturity status over white females from nine through twelve years of age. No consistent race differences were evident in the velocity of skeletal maturity in males" (389).

Miklashevskaya (1969) collected cross-sectional data on some 3,000 girls. These data were compared with previously reported data on boys. In three ethnic groups studied, the head measurements of boys were found to be greater than those of girls at all ages. The growth curves do not cross during the whole period of growth. The process of growth in girls comes to an end by the age of fifteen or sixteen years. "From age fourteen to eighteen years the velocity of growth in girls is minimal while in boys it reaches its peak. Differences between girls' and boys' curves are somewhat dissimilar in cranial and postcranial dimensions, but the growth of the foot resembles growth of the head dimensions in this respect" (261).

Nutrition of Adolescents

The marked physical and emotional growth of adolescents results in strains that frequently precipitate stress and anxiety, as reflected in physiologic, psychologic, and social behavior. The nutrition of the adolescent is affected by these and other growth characteristics during this period. The results may be "(a) an overweight teenager; (b) an underweight teenager; or (c) a teenager whose dietary intake is unbalanced in kinds and amounts of nutrients, but whose caloric intake and weight are commensurate with his level of development" (Peckos and Heald, 1964: 27).

The increased size of the stomach, along with a greater need for food caused by rapid growth, is closely related to the adolescent's cravings for food. When the individual is adding three inches to his height, his calcium need will perhaps be twice as high as during a later period. He will also need about three times the protein required in adult life in order to attain optimum storage of nitrogen in the muscle tissues and achieve a normal metabolism.

Metabolic studies of individuals at different ages demonstrate that the amount of food intake and the specific nutrients retained depend upon the individual's rate of growth and the extent of his physical activity, as well as the composition and relative proportion of the nutrients consumed (Johnston, 1953). It is likely that an unbalanced diet in which certain essential vitamins are lacking may be more harmful to the developing adolescent than an insufficient diet.

TABLE 4-2 Recommended Daily Dietary Allowances (Calories)

	AGE	WEIGHT (pounds)	HEIGHT (inches)	CALORIES
Boys	9–12	72	55	2,400
	12–15	98	61	3,000
	15–18	134	68	3,400
Girls	9–12	72	55	2,200
	12–15	103	62	2,500
	15–18	117	64	2,300

National Academy of Sciences-National Research Council: Recommended Dietary Allowances, Revised, 1963. Washington: National Academy of Sciences-National Research Council, 1964.

Studies of family nutrition involving school groups at different ages indicate that older boys and girls have the poorest food habits and the least satisfactory nutritional status, the diet of girls being less satisfactory than that of boys. A word of caution is necessary about the use of the Recommended Dietary Allowances shown in Table 4-2. As already stated, wide variations among individuals exist in nutritional needs. There is, however, a tendency for many adolescent diets to be low in calcium, vitamin D, and vitamin A. Adolescents should be encouraged to drink milk rather than soft drinks. It has been shown that the addition of milk to the diet of school children improved their mental and physical alertness (Egan, 1969). Milk provides calcium, especially needed during the adolescent years. Clinical examinations and nutrition surveys reported a decade or more ago by Hathaway and Sargent (1962) that 19 percent of our teenagers are underweight and 30 to 35 percent are overweight. However, an accurate diagnosis is difficult to make and should not be based entirely upon height-weight tables, since these do not take into account differences in the relationship between lean body mass, bone, and fat tissue.

Obesity during adolescence. Many adolescent girls, in order to maintain a slender figure, undergo a rigid diet and thus fail to get the desired nutrients for maintaining optimum health. There are others, however, who eat too much, especially carbohydrates and other foods that cause obesity. These girls engage in a minimum of exercise and eat only for pleasure.

Obesity affects both the health and well-being of adolescents as well as their personality. It has a detrimental effect upon a boy's physical activities, which are important to him in his social and personal development. The adverse effects of early exposure to negative sociocultural attitudes toward obesity was shown in a study of Stunkard and Mendelson (1961). They noted that obesity with the onset in childhood or adolescence caused more permanent ill-effects than did the onset of obesity during the adult years. Those obese from childhood felt it to be a serious handicap, while subjects who became obese later did not display such negative feelings. In a later study (1967) the investigators found that of the many behavioral disturbances to which the obese are subjected, two were unique to obesity: overeating and a disturbance of body image characterized by a feeling that the body was grotesque, and that others regarded it with contempt. This syndrome most frequently appeared among those whose obesity began during childhood or early adolescence.

PHYSIOLOGICAL
GROWTH AND DEVELOPMENT

It has been recognized by students of human development since the turn of the century that important changes occur prior to and following puberty. However, the early students of adolescent psychology gave little attention to the physiological changes, due to the lack of scientific knowledge. Although individuals differ in the rate of development, we note that certain developmental patterns exist for different organs and parts of the body. Today is it generally recognized that the young child is not a miniature adult; likewise, the adolescent is neither a child nor an adult in his physiological development and reactions.

Longitudinal studies are the best means for arriving at a valid index of the rate and periodicity of physiological growth during childhood and adolescence. However, since reliable and interpretable data on changes in body chemistry are difficult to obtain, a relatively small number of studies has been conducted in some areas of physiological development. Those that have been made have furnished valuable data, and serve as a basis for understanding and guiding growing boys and girls. For example, a study of the differences in the rate of physiological development of boys and girls can supply a perspective on the earlier changes in social-sexual interests of girls as they pass from childhood into and through adolescence. Behavior problems and disorders and personal maladjustments can also be better understood by studying physiological changes that occur during late childhood and adolescence.

Adolescence—A Period of Physiological Changes

It was pointed out in Chapter 1 that important changes occuring during childhood signal the beginning of adolescence. There are, however, no "normal" physiological changes commensurate with each age level. Today, it is generally recognized that although universal changes occur during late childhood, each child's rate of development is unique. Thus, children and adolescents should not suffer from expectations in physiological changes based upon some statistical norm.

PHYSICAL SYMPTOMS OF EARLY ADOLESCENCE. It was pointed out earlier that there is a pronounced growth in height followed by an increase in the rate of growth in weight just prior to puberty. Some adolescents gain from twenty to thirty pounds during the year. The girls again pass the boys of their age level in weight during a two- or three-year period. Accompanying this increased growth, one finds important changes in body proportions. There is at first a rapid growth of the arms and legs, followed later by a more rapid growth of the trunk of the body. The hands, feet, and nose seem to play an important part in adolescent development. By the time the boy is thirteen to fourteen years of age his hands and feet have achieved a large percentage of their total development at maturity.

One of the earliest indications of the development of the girls during the preadolescent stage is the development of the breasts. The mammary nipple usually does not project above the level of the surrounding skin structures until the third year after birth. The nipple after this stage shows a slight elevation above the surrounding structures. There is no further pronounced change for the average girl until about the tenth year, when the so-called "bud" stage appears. This is soon followed by the development of the "primary" breast, resulting mainly from an increase in the fat surrounding and underlying the papilla (nipple) and adjacent skin area.

The Endocrines and Their Relation to Development

The pituitary gland is the most important organ related to growth. It is a pea-sized gland located at the base of the brain. The ten known hormones secreted into the blood stream by the forward part of the pituitary act mostly in controlling the release of hormones by endocrine glands situated throughout the body. Unlike most other pituitary hormones, the human growth hormone acts on tissues throughout the body. If there is a deficiency of the growth hormone, normal growth will be retarded, and a form of pituitary dwarfism will result. On the other hand, if an excess is produced during the growing period, pituitary gigantism will follow. The other pituitary hormone of special importance in maturation is the gonad-stimulating hormone. A deficiency of this hormone during pre-adolescence would interfere with the normal growth and development of the ovaries or testes; an oversupply would tend to produce precocious sexual development. The importance of properly timed action of the growth and gonad-stimulating hormones has been pointed out by Greulich (1942):

> If the testes or ovaries begin to function at the requisite level too early in life, growth is arrested prematurely and the child ends up abnormally short. If, on the other hand, the adequate production of the ovarian and testicular hormones is unduly delayed, growth, particularly that of the limbs, continues for too long a period and the characteristic bodily portions of the eunuch are attained. It appears, therefore, that normal growth and development are contingent upon the reciprocal and properly timed action of pituitary and gonadal hormones."

A number of studies have been conducted on gonadotrophic hormone secretion in children. In general these studies indicate that the excretion of gonadotrophic hormones in early childhood in both sexes is too slight to be detected by the methods used; these studies indicate that measurable amounts first appear in the urine during adolescence. Data early reported by Greulich and others (1942) on the results of 120 urinary gonadotrophin assays performed on sixty-four boys are useful to our understanding of certain physiological changes. Concerning the significance of gonadotrophin excretion in adolescence, they conclude:

> The results show that with advancing developmental status there is a general tendency for gonadotrophin to increase in amount from the undetectable levels of early childhood to levels more characteristic of the adult.

. . . It seems reasonable to suppose that the primary changes of puberty, namely an increase in size of the testes and the initiation of spermatogenesis are related to the action of the gonadotrophin upon the seminiferous tubules. Secondary sex changes related to the secretion of the steroid sex hormones may be ascribed to the action of the hormone upon the interstitial gland of the testes (62).

Nathanson and others (1941) have reported somewhat similar results. Average curves for boys and girls are presented in Figure 4-2. Note that before the ages of ten or eleven, both boys and girls excrete measurable amounts of male and female hormones. The increase of female sex hormones in the girl leads to the growth of breasts at menarche, and the increase of male hormones in the boy produces significant changes.

Blood Pressure, Heart, and Pulse Rate

The growth of the heart, like that of other organs of the body, follows a course of its own. During the adolescent years its weight nearly doubles, and its transverse diameter increases by almost one-half (Marsh, 1953). During most of the childhood, boys' hearts are a little larger than girls; then from approximately nine to fourteen, girls' are larger. From thirteen on, boys' hearts continue to grow at a rapid pace, girls' very slowly.

The heart rate falls gradually throughout the entire period of growth, the decrease being checked about the time of peak stature growth. A sex difference is also established during early adolescence that persists during early adulthood (Iliff and Lee, 1952). This difference may be a result of the greater size of the male's heart, or it may arise simply from the difference in basal body temperature. The mouth temperature of girls and boys shows a gradual decrease during childhood, although this decrease for girls seems to stop around the age of ten or eleven. The heart rate is fairly closely related to body temperature in healthy persons. Thus, the difference of about 0.7° F. between boys' and girls' temperature at age seventeen may account for the difference of about five beats per minute in their heart rate at this age.

Systolic blood pressure rises steadily throughout childhood, but during adolescence the rise becomes more rapid and adult values are quickly reached (Downing, 1947; Schwenk, et al., 1955). There is also a rise of pulse rate during the preadolescent years, with the maximum for girls reached during the years just prior to menarche. There is a marked change in both blood pressure and pulse rate with physiological maturity. The relation of these changes to sexual development may be seen most easily in girls, since their menstrual period furnishes conclusive evidence of sexual maturity at a particular time, whereas there is no single criterion to give us a specific date for sexual maturity of boys. Shock (1944) presented data on fifty girls tested every six months for a number of years, for both blood pressure and pulse rate. A tabulation of the data on each girl's first menstrual period irrespective of chronological age showed that blood pressure rose sharply during the three years before

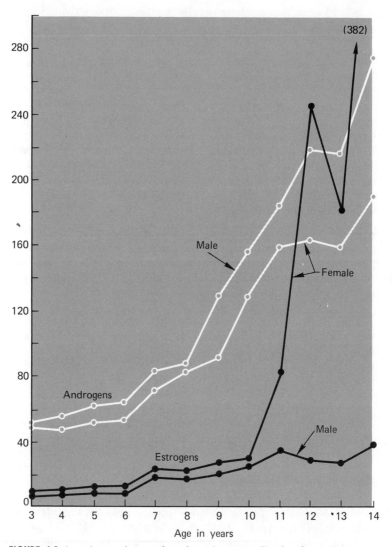

FIGURE 4-2 Age changes in secretion of sex hormones. The female sex hormone, produced by the ovary, is the chief estrogenic hormone. Adapted from Nathanson *et al.* (1941).

puberty and for six months afterwards, then settled to a new level of about 106. It seems then that sexual maturity operates to stabilize the upward trend of blood pressure and to reverse that of pulse rate. After menarche there is a gradual decline in pulse rate.

It is mainly because of the red cell increase that the blood volume increases more in boys than in girls at puberty, so that whereas in childhood there is no sexual difference in the relationship of blood volume to height or weight, after puberty the male value is higher (Sjöstrand, 1953). However, not all the blood volume increase is attributable to an increase in cells; there is also a greater increase in plasma volume in the male than in the female (Morse, *et al.*, 1947; Russell, 1949).

The veins and arteries do not follow the same growth pattern as that of the heart. Prior to adolescence they grow quite rapidly, whereas they show little growth during adolescence, when the heart is growing rapidly. Thus, the preadolescent may be said to have a relatively small heart with large arteries. Changes during adolescence in the relative ratio of the size of the heart to the arteries are reflected in changes in blood pressure (Richey, 1931). During early childhood, blood pressure is nearly the same in both sexes, but between the ages of ten and thirteen blood pressure is higher in girls than in boys; after the age thirteen the pressure of boys exceeds that of girls, the difference increasing with age. This is an example of the general trend toward an earlier incidence of maturity among girls, a trend which has been observed in connection with other developmental characteristics.

Respiratory Changes

The lungs grow steadily during childhood; their rate of growth is much accelerated during adolescence, especially in boys. A common measure of lung growth is vital capacity, which consists of the amount of air that can be exhaled from the lungs after one has drawn a deep breath. Most girls fail to develop their maximum capacity, since they do not usually engage in vigorous activities. Growth data for liters of air exhaled presented by Ferris and Smith (1953) for boys and girls from ages 5½ to 17½ years shows that girls excel boys during the first 9½ or 10 years. Beginning about age 11½, vital capacity of boys exceeds that of girls, and the difference increases during the growing years from 11½ to 17½ years. This increased difference is affected both by the larger lungs of boys as well as the greater amount of activity of boys.

Age Changes in Metabolism

With the beginning of the puberty cycle there is a reversal of unstable physiological processes. This may be observed in the metabolic processes that show marked fluctuations at this time. There is a continuous decrease in basal metabolism throughout the teen years for both boys and girls. This decline presents quite a contrast with the change in blood pressure pointed out earlier; there is little change registered in blood pressure after the menarche, yet there is a continuous decrease in basal metabolism throughout the teen years for both boys and girls. This is shown in Figure 4-3, which is based upon materials from the California study. Over one-half the cases illustrated in the figure showed a pronounced decrease.

Individual curves show a marked increase just before or at puberty,

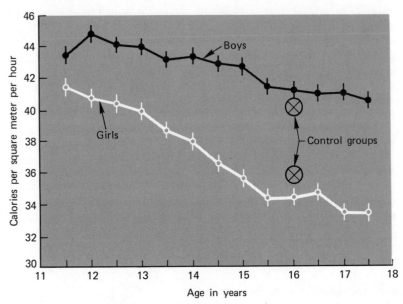

FIGURE 4-3 Age changes in basal metabolism from repeated tests on the same subjects (smoothed data). Adapted from Shock (1944).

followed by a conspicuous decrease. This is shown, in Case C9, for an adolescent girl in Figure 4-4. The adolescent decline is followed by a recovery to an adult level which is then maintained. There are, however,

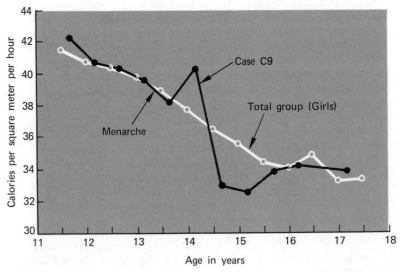

FIGURE 4-4 Average and individual growth curves of basal metabolism for girls. Adapted from Shock (1944).

cases which do not conform to this pattern. The individual slump in metabolic rate exists among both boys and girls, and should be taken into consideration by those concerned with the guidance of adolescents. For example, the adolescent who appears sluggish in his activities may be suffering from a low metabolic rate.

Sexual Development

Based on studies involving thousands of girls, four generations of Harvard boys, early records of the choir of Johann Sebastian Bach, and many other studies, students of child development have concluded that the rate at which boys and girls mature sexually has been increasing steadily (Sullivan, 1971). Careful studies of girls from different areas of the world show that the average age of menarche has dropped by at least two years during the past century although it seems likely that the age of menarche may be leveling off in the more affluent populations. Hints of a strong nutritional effect run through many of the reports of earlier menarche in many populations.

RANGE AND AGE OF SEXUAL DEVELOPMENT. The range and age of puberty, or first menses, for girls may vary as much as ten years. The information in Table 4-3 is based on the Health Examination Survey used to estimate current age at menarche of women in the United States. "Overall, the median age of menarche is 12.80 years for white girls and 12.52 years for black girls" (MacMahon, 1973: 3). There is no clearly defined method for determining puberty among boys. In an early study reported by Ramsey (1943), complete histories were obtained from personal interviews of 291 boys between the ages of ten and twenty. These boys were from the middle or upper socioeconomic strata of a midwestern city. His findings are shown in Table 4-4. Although pubescence

TABLE 4-3 Percentage of Girls in the United States Whose Menstrual Periods had Started, by Race and Age

AGE[a]	ALL RACES[b]	WHITE	BLACK
6–9 years	0.2	0.2	0.2
10 years	1.2	0.8	4.0
11 years	12.8	11.6	21.3
12 years	43.3	41.7	51.2
13 years	73.2	72.9	74.1
14 years	91.7	91.4	93.5
15 years	98.3	98.2	98.7
16–17 years	99.7	99.6	100.0

[a] Age at last birthday.
[b] Includes data from other races which are not shown separately.
Source: MacMahon, 1973:3.

is earlier today than at the time of Ramsey's study, these data show the wide range existing in the timing of certain sexual changes.

The beginning of menstruation does not mean that the girl has reached sexual maturity as measured by fertility. For most girls menstruation begins before the ovaries are capable of producing ripe ova. The ovaries at the time of the first menstruation are relatively small compared to their size at the time of complete physical maturity. Ovulation tends to occur before the uterus is sufficiently mature to support pregnancy (Ford and Beach, 1951). The pubescent period for girls is approximately three years while that of boys is more variable, being from two to four years. Also, girls are more nearly their adult size when they become sexually mature.

FACTORS INFLUENCING SEXUAL RIPENING. Quite frequently we observe that children in some families mature earlier than children in other families. This may be observed in the case of first cousins. However, environmental influences sometimes reinforce hereditary influences and sometimes cancel them out. Thus a girl whose mother matured early, may, because of deficiencies related to illness or poverty, mature late. On the other hand, many children today are brought up in better circumstances than their parents were, and these children are in general maturing earlier than their parents.

TABLE 4-4 Percentage of Each Age Group of Boys Showing Different Aspects of Sexual Development

AGE	EJACULATION	VOICE CHANGE	NOCTURNAL EMISSION	PUBIC HAIR
10	1.8	0.3	0.3	0.3
11	6.9	5.6	3.7	8.4
12	14.1	20.5	5.3	27.1
13	33.6	40.0	17.4	36.1
14	30.9	26.0	12.9	23.8
15	7.8	5.5	13.9	3.3
16	4.9	2.0	16.0	1.0

Source: Ramsey (1943).

In the highly industrialized countries the average age of menarche (first menstruation) has declined steadily for several decades. Burrell and his colleagues (1961) made a study of different races to determine possible genetic influences on the age of menarche. They found that, although significant differences existed between girls from different families, the incidence of menarche was heavily dependent on living standards, including diet and medical care. When living standards are similar there does not seem to be significant scientific evidence that race differences exist. A comparative study of the age of menarche for Negro schoolgirls in Alabama with that of white schoolgirls in Georgia by Henton (1959) revealed no significant difference. However, the results of MacMahon's study (Table 4-3) indicate that between the ages of ten and fifteen, the percentage of black girls whose periods had begun is slightly higher than for the white girls. According to Tanner (1969) nutrition is probably the most important of the many socioeconomic differences between girls in the age of menarche, with protein playing an important role. He notes that the mean age of menarche of well-to-do Iraqi girls is somewhat higher than that for the highest classes of Western Europe, which is around 13.0 years. This is contrary to the formerly widely held notion that girls living in hot climates menstruate earlier than those living in more temperate climates.

There is considerable evidence from scientific studies that the age of puberty has become stabilized among adolescents from homes or areas where a high standard of living has been maintained for several generations. This was noted in an investigation by Poppleton and Brown (1966) in which data about the age of menarche were obtained from a sample of girls in three schools in West Riding, England. Care was taken to ensure the accurate reporting of this event. They conclude: "When the more recent figures were compared with data obtained from other surveys conducted in the last sixteen years, no consistent secular trend was revealed." The age of menarche according to various surveys is shown in Table 4-5.

TABLE 4-5 Age of Menarche According to Various Surveys (1949–1965)

AGE	1949 OXFORD N = 1,338	1950 FRANCE N = 75,000	1952 OSLO N = 11,618	1960 ABER-DEEN N = 1,385	1961 ENG. AND WALES N = 1,812	1965 WEST RIDING 3RD YR. N = 313	1965 WEST RIDING 4TH YR. N = 343
Median	13:6	13:2	13:3	13:2	13:2	13:4	13:14
Semi-interquartile range	9 mos.	12 mos.	9 mos.	incomplete	10 mos.	incomplete	10 mos.
Method	School records	Yes-No	Yes-No	Recall 13–16	Recall at 15	Recall at 13+	Recall at 13+

Source: Poppleton and Brown (1966).

Age of puberty is also markedly influenced by body build. The child with an endomorphic build—broad hips and relatively short legs— is likely to mature earlier than the average, while the child with an ectomorphic build—slender body, broad shoulders, and long legs— usually matures later than average. Like the endomorphic child, the one whose build is muscular and compact—the mesomorph—is slightly earlier than average in reaching maturity (Lea, 1956). Obese children as a group reach puberty earlier than their age-mates whose weight is more nearly average.

SECONDARY SEXUAL CHARACTERISTICS

The secondary sexual characteristics are the physical features which distinguish the male from the female. Unlike the sex organs, they have no direct relationship to reproduction; however, like the sex organs they follow a predictable pattern of development. At the beginning of puberty, when the primary sex characteristics have a growth spurt, the secondary sex characteristics likewise begin to develop.

Changes in Hair

Throughout the growing period there is a gradual darkening of the hair of the head, but at adolescence this becomes more marked. Very likely the darkening is due to an increase in adrenal androgens (in the adrenogenital syndrome the hair tends to darken). There is also a distinct change in the shape of the hairline on the forehead as the individual begins to mature; this has been referred to as a secondary sexual characteristic. The hairline of immature boys and girls follows an uninterrupted bow-like curve, as illustrated in the upper row of Figure 4-5. In mature males, the curved hairline is interrupted by a wedge-shaped re-

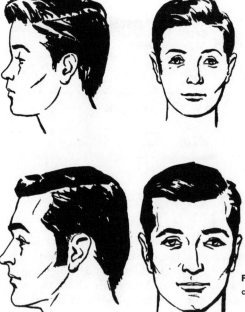

FIGURE 4-5 Adolescent changes in hairline and facial contours.

cess on each side of the forehead. Greulich and others (1942) found this characteristic to be a late rather than an early developmental feature.

FACIAL HAIR. There are no marked sexual differences during childhood in the vellus of the upper lips, cheeks, and chin. Among boys, the downy hairs at the corners of the upper lip become noticeable beginning with puberty. This development extends medially from each corner of the upper lip, and eventually forms a mustache of rather fine hair which is perceptibly larger, coarser, and darker than the vellus hair it replaces. The mustache becomes progressively coarser and more heavily pigmented as the individual passes through adolescence. During the period when the mustache is developing, the vellus over the upper part of the cheeks increases in length and diameter. It persists as long, coarse down until the juvenile mustache is fairly well developed. Somewhat later, a thin growth of long, rather coarse, pigmented hairs appears along the sides and lower parts of the chin and on the upper part of the face just in front of the ears. These, too, gradually become coarser and more heavily developed, eventually forming a beard.

PUBIC HAIR. Pubic hair is a secondary sex characteristic that appears during puberty. However, not until the growth of the genitals is well under way does the terminal hair appear to replace the vellus. It has been customary to associate the amount and extension of terminal hair over the body with the degree of masculinity in terms of sexual potency; however, there is no indication that a close association exists.

AXILLARY HAIR. The axillary hair does not usually appear until the development of the pubic hair is nearly complete. The transition from vellus to terminal hair in the axilla is quite similar to changes in hair in other regions of the body, and the amount of axillary hair appearing is closely associated with the development of other body hair. Among boys, the development of terminal hair on the limbs and trunk begins during the early stages of adolescence, with growth rather rapid at first. Terminal hair on the limbs begins to appear first on the upper part of the forearm, later on the sides of the lower arms, and then on the back of the hands.

After the transition from long down to terminal hair has made considerable progress, a similar process begins on the distal half of the leg. It gradually extends upward toward the knee. The extension of the hair-covered areas from the centers on the trunk and limbs proceeds at different rates of speed in different boys, and the amount of hair developed will vary considerably from individual to individual. By the age of eighteen or nineteen the growth of hair on the arms is fairly heavy for the majority of boys. Also, there is a moderate growth of terminal hair over the legs, thighs, and buttocks as well as a varying amount on the ventral surface of the trunk.

The Skin Glands

Marked changes take place in the structure of the skin and in the activity of the skin glands as the individual matures sexually; the soft, delicate skin of childhood gradually becomes thicker and coarser, and the pores become enlarged, a development closely related to adolescent skin disturbances and blemishes.

There are three different kinds of skin glands, each of which is distinctly separate from the others. They are (1) the *merocrine glands,* which are scattered over most of the skin surfaces of the body, (2) the *apocrine sweat glands,* which are limited primarily to the armpits, mammary, genital, and anal regions, and (3) the *sebaceous glands,* the oil-producing glands of the skin.

MEROCRINE AND APOCRINE SWEAT GLANDS. The merocrine and apocrine sweat glands of the armpits become increasingly active during adolescence, even before the growth of axillary hair. Their secretion is fatty and has a pronounced odor that is usually not detectable in boys prior to puberty but becomes more pronounced during the early adolescent years. Among girls the apocrine sweat glands appear to undergo a cycle of secretory activity during the menstrual cycle.

SEBACEOUS GLANDS. The increased size and activity of the sebaceous glands during puberty is thought to be closely associated with skin disturbances during adolescence. There is a disproportion between the size and activity of these glands and the size of the gland ducts that begins at puberty, so that they frequently become plugged with dried oil and turn black as a result of oxidation of the dried oil upon exposure to air. These plugged gland ducts are generally referred to as blackheads, and are most often found on the nose and chin. The glands continue to function, even though the opening has been blocked, and raised pimples then appear on the surface of the skin. High on the list of problems of teen-agers is acne, which may last years beyond adolescence. Although it seems to be a normal manifestation of growing up, it may have a very harmful emotional influence on the adolescent boy or girl. Based on the results of a study of 1,254 high school students Schachter and others (1971) reported that 69 percent of the boys and 58 percent of the girls had acne vulgaris on the face. The results from questions dealing with the psychological impact revealed significant differences between the group with acne and those without acne. Those with acne did not enjoy social activities as much as those without acne; however, they received more help from their parents with problems of grooming. Important factors that can aggravate an oily skin's tendency to acne are glandular disturbances, nervous tension, overwork, lack of sleep and irregular hours, dietary habits, and constipation (Michaelson, 1973). Although some cases are aggravated by chocolates, nuts, or some other specific food, the most important thing about nutrition is for the individual to eat three nourishing meals each day with food particularly rich in proteins, minerals, and vitamins.

Distribution of Subcutaneous Fat

During childhood there is a pronounced reduction in the amount of fat over the thorax, abdomen, and back. The reduction is less marked in girls, and the fat over the abdomen continues to increase during childhood. After about the tenth year, the fat gradually increases in boys. In later years, the amount of fat over the back, the thorax, and especially the abdomen increases in girls more than in boys.

A study by Reynolds (1950) furnished certain quantitative information about the amount and distribution of subcutaneous fat in various regions of the body. Means and medians for different age levels, measurements based on results obtained from six individual tissue areas reveal differences in growth patterns for the different areas; however, in general, the similarities were striking. A second observation resulting from this study showed consistent sex differences; girls displayed a pattern of greater fat thickness than boys, in all six areas. The steady rise, during the period studied, in mean values for girls, and the drop at adolescence in boys were in harmony with results obtained by other investigators.

Change in Voice

Closely connected with muscular development are the obvious changes of voice in early adolescence. They are much more evident in boys and constitute one of the external signs of the advent of puberty. They are the effect of the rapid growth of the larynx, or the "Adam's apple," and a corresponding lengthening of the vocal cords that stretch across it. The cords approximately double their former length with a consequent drop of an octave in pitch. Girls' voices are not subject to such an outright transformation; at maturity, they are little, if at all, lower than in childhood, although fuller and richer. Boys' voices not only change pitch but also increase in volume, and often become more pleasant in quality. They require two or more years to achieve control in the lower register, and during that time the roughness of their tones are often embarrassing. They are mortified by unexpected squeaks which punctuate bass rumblings. Such whimsical "breakings" cause them to feel they are making themselves ridiculous—an opinion that is often confirmed, unfortunately, by the mirth with which others greet their vocal vagaries.

The voice change, however, is not an accurate index for use in studies of the development of a boy, since there is no satisfactory way of evaluating it objectively. It could be studied if a recording device were used for comparing the depth and other qualities of the voice at varying stages of development. In this connection, it should be pointed out that it is the progressive deepening of the voice, rather than the absolute pitch, that is significant as an indication of progress toward maturity, since the voices of young men at maturity will vary widely in pitch and other qualities.

A difference in rate of physiological maturity may be a source of anxiety to the adolescent. When Bill's pal, Henry, suddenly surpasses him in physical development, develops a bass voice, and begins to shave, Bill may wonder whether he is normal. The difference between his own appearance and that of his friend may become so pronounced that he begins to seek other friends, and may even resort to behavior not socially acceptable in an effort to prove himself.

MOTOR DEVELOPMENT DURING ADOLESCENCE

Our discussion of physical development would be incomplete without some consideration of motor development, which includes the development of strength, motor coordination, physical prowess, and both simple and complex motor skills. Although we frequently think of physical prowess in relation to adolescent boys, it is also important to girls. Both boys and girls get much satisfaction from the performance of both simple and complex motor skills. It will be pointed out later that there are different kinds of motor skills, and the course of their development will vary with the individuals concerned.

Age and Motor Performance

Motor performance reaches its peak during the adolescent years, except for complex performances requiring years of practice and excessive strength. Still, some have described the adolescent period as an "awkward age" because of apparently awkward movements made by many adolescents. However, there is a biological principle that functional capacity must follow physiological or structural growth, and individuals actually reach their peak in motor skills during this period. Two factors seem to account for any awkwardness that may appear among adolescents. The adolescent is growing rapidly; he is expanding his physical activities, doing many things that he has never done before requiring motor coordination. Any period of life when one is called upon to learn many new motor coordinations will involve awkward movements.

As with body shape, body strength and agility are closely related to sexual maturity. Muscular development in the studies that follow is plotted in average chronological age, but it must be kept in mind that the ages also indicate stages of sexual development. It must also be remembered that the lower performance of girls is partly due to their mechanical disadvantage; the arms and legs are proportionally shorter than boys', the trunk larger, pelvis broader, and the femur is attached to the pelvis at an oblique angle.

The California Adolescent Growth Study found some interesting facts about development of strength (Jones and Seashore, 1944). Figure 4-6 compares growth in right-hand strength in two groups of girls representing contrasting extremes in age at menarche. Among these girls, the earlier-maturing group showed a rapid rise in strength before age twelve. The later-maturing group was relatively retarded in strength, but the two groups eventually reached the same level. Significantly, the greatest increase in strength occurred near the time of menarche.

In comparison with the group means for strength of grip, each of the early-maturing boys studied was above the norm in strength at ages thirteen to sixteen, whereas the late-maturing boys tended to fall below the norm at these ages. Results for boys and girls classified as early-, average-, and late-maturing, are presented in Table 4-6. The early- and late-maturing groups represented approximately the 20 percent at each extreme of a normal public school distribution at the different age levels; the average group consisted of those whose maturational level was approximately that of the norm for their age level. Jones (1944: 56-57) states: "It is apparent that the three curves are more or less parallel, with some divergence of the early- and late-maturing groups between the ages of thirteen and fifteen, and with a later convergence which, however, fails to bring them together at the end of the series of measures." A further study of the results of the table shows that the early-maturing girls, although stronger at the age of thirteen, failed to maintain their superiority in subsequent years, and actually dropped below that of the average-maturing group, just as they did in their height and weight. Thus,

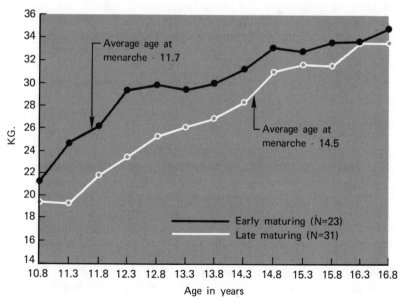

FIGURE 4-6 Manual strength development of girls in two maturity groups. Adapted from Jones (1944).

TABLE 4-6 Mean Scores for Early-, Average-, and Late-Maturing
Boys and Girls* (K.G., Right Grip)

	PERCENT OF BOYS			PERCENT OF GIRLS		
AGE	Early N = 16	Average N = 28	Late N = 16	Early N = 16	Average N = 24	Late N = 16
11.0	27.1	24.0	22.7	21.1	20.9	20.6
11.5	29.3	25.9	25.2	24.4	23.2	21.2
12.0	29.3	26.9	26.0	26.1	25.8	22.5
12.5	31.3	28.4	27.0	29.1	26.8	23.7
13.0	33.3	30.4	28.1	30.3	28.8	25.7
13.5	37.6	32.5	30.0	29.3	30.3	26.8
14.0	44.2	34.3	30.2	29.7	30.7	26.4
14.5	47.1	38.6	33.3	31.0	32.2	28.4
15.0	50.0	43.0	36.3	32.5	33.3	31.4
15.5	52.2	47.6	41.1	33.4	35.2	32.7
16.0	54.3	49.0	43.9	33.4	35.8	32.4
16.5	55.9	50.9	48.4	34.7	36.1	34.4
17.0	57.2	53.5	51.3	34.3	36.5	34.8
17.5	...	55.8	54.3	33.9	37.8	35.3

* The boys are classified on the basis of skeletal maturing, the girls on the basis of age
at menarche.
Source: Jones (1944).

precocious sexual development of girls appears to be associated with an
early arrest in physical and motor development; this is not true for boys.

MacCurdy (1953) found further evidence connecting strength and
sexual maturation in adolescent boys. He stated that strength grows
gradually to age twelve then quite rapidly, reaching a maximum for
most boys around the eighteenth birthday. McCloy (1935) confirmed the
fact that the most rapid increase in strength for boys was between ages
thirteen and sixteen; for girls between twelve and fourteen. Boys increased
only slightly after age seventeen; most girls actually decreased after their
fifteenth birthday.

Jokl and Cluver (1941) studied the development of physical fitness
among a group of children from five to twenty years of age. In endurance,
measured by the 600-yard run, both boys and girls improved from age six
to thirteen. The improvement up to thirteen years was about the same
for both sexes; but afterwards boys continued to improve, whereas girls
actually lost in efficiency, so that from seventeen to twenty the girls'
ability was about that of six- to eight-year-olds. Their decline in efficiency
was reflected not only in their running time, but also in their pulse
rate, respiration, and fatigue. It seems likely that the early decline in
motor ability among girls is a result of their way of life: that is, they
show an increased interest in social activities at a fairly early age, and a
lack of interest in athletics and other forms of muscular activity as they
grow older.

Sex Differences

The smaller size, lesser muscle mass, lower metabolism and energy level of the female, along with the more vigorous overt activity of the male, occurs at such an early age that it seems clearly biologically based. The assumption of a biological basis is supported by evidence that male-hormone treatment of pregnant primates increased the incidence of rough overt play among female offspring and decreased their tendency to withdraw from threats and approaches of others. In humans girls affected by male hormones in utero displayed more of a developmental tendency toward vigorous overt activity than did other girls (Money and Ehrhardt, 1968).

Significant sex differences became greater at each age level on the gross motor performances studied by Espenschade (1947). The greatest gap recorded was in the distance throw, although differences in the broad jump became as great among the older adolescents. Jones and Seashore (1944) and Sardon (1944) found that girls are inferior to boys in many tests of manual celerity, however, Travis (1945) found from a study of dynamic and static equilibrium a small difference in favor of women. It seems rather that girls may excel in one type of motor skill but display inferiority in another type. Thus, sex differences may be in part due to sanctions by adults and peers that encourage girls to practice to develop a particular skill but discourage it for another motor skill.

Although strength and motor coordination increase with age, the bones and joints reach their maximum flexibility at a relatively early age. One study measured the flexibility of twelve areas of the body in 300 girls ranging in age from 5.5 to 18.5 years. The girls showed greatest flexibility of the shoulder, knee, and thigh at age six. Head rotation was most flexible at age nine; the remaining eight areas at age twelve. Although individual differences were observed in the degree of flexibility among girls of the same age group, the figures indicate that it is highest during childhood and early adolescence, so that for education in motor skills, exercises requiring a high degree of flexibility should be started during the pre-school years and continued during the elementary school years to reach the potentially highest level.

Relationship of Strength to Other Traits

Significant relations have been reported by various investigators between dynamic and static strength and certain physical measurements. Dynamic strength is strength in action—in field events or other sports, whereas static strength is sheer strength of pull—in grip or lifting—and is frequently measured by means of dynamometric tests. Some interesting similarities in the operation of these two aspects of motor performances are revealed in the results of a study by Bower and reported by Jones (1949). Correlations were obtained among a group of boys between these aspects of strength and chronological age; skeletal age, based on assessments of X-rays of the hand and knee; height; an evaluation of "good looks"; and intelligence, based on an average mental age obtained from the results of two forms of a group intelligence test. These correlations are presented in Table 4-7. An interesting feature of the results of the table is that whereas chronological age and physical measurements correlate highest with total strength, more closely related to the gross motor scores are popularity and "good looks." This is to be expected, when one realizes the prestige value of motor performances among adolescent boys. The low correlation between motor performances and intelligence is also significant.

TABLE 4-7 Motor Performance Correlations with Other Developmental Traits—Boys

VARIABLE	TOTAL STRENGTH (grip, pull, thrust)	GROSS MOTOR SCORES (track events)
Chronological age	.39 ± .06	.18 ± .07
Skeletal age	.50 ± .055	.36 ± .06
Height	.65 ± .04	.40 ± .06
Popularity	.30 ± .07	.39 ± .06
"Good looks"	.21 ± .07	.38 ± .06
Intelligence	—.17 ± .07	.05 ± .08

Source: Jones (1944).

Physical Fitness

Adolescents and adults alike depend on machines to do their work, carry them from place to place, and entertain them while they relax. The general practice has become, "Don't run if you can walk, don't walk if you can stand, and don't stand if you can sit." Walking several miles to school and to church over muddy or snow-covered roads is a part of the past that no other form of exercise has replaced. Also, much of the time now spent watching television was formerly spent doing different chores that helped keep muscles fit. Even athletics have changed: they have become so highly specialized that the typical adolescent must be a spectator. Less than one percent of the average American youth's time is spent on physical education, and only a fraction of that time is in vigorous activities that produce physical fitness.

The ill effects of such habits appeared in comparisons of American boys and girls with their European counterparts on different physical fitness tests and attracted the attention of our national leaders. A study reported by Ikeda (1961) compared the physical fitness of children aged nine to twelve in Iowa and Tokyo. There were 172 girls and 178 boys from Iowa, 221 girls and 174 boys from Tokyo. The Iowa girls and boys were taller, heavier, and had longer legs than the Tokyo children of the same age, yet the Japanese exceeded the Iowans in all but the sit-up test.

A summary of findings from a checklist of the activities of the groups showed that the Tokyo children pursued various physical activities more than the Iowa children, although the physical education classes in Tokyo were larger with less desirable facilities. The explanation of this, no doubt, lies in the differences in culture and in living standards. The Tokyo children must walk to school and have different customs of entertainment and recreation.

Good Posture Habits

The importance of good posture habits in maintaining the organs of the body in their correct position and in enabling them to function at maximum efficiency has been stressed by physicians in recent years. Charts have been devised, exercises recommended, and clinics held, all in an effort to provide for the development of good posture among children, adolescents, and adults. Although training should begin in early childhood, adolescence is the period when so many bad posture habits are formed. There are several reasons why adolescents are susceptible to incorrect habits. First, much of the energy from food during the adolescent years is used up in providing for growth. Thus the adolescent is inclined to slump from a tired feeling. Second, the adolescent years are active years. Adolescents use a great deal of energy in their social, recreational, and play activities. This, again, brings on a feeling of tiredness and the tendency to slump. Third, the individual may feel self-conscious over his long legs, or general height, leading him to assume an unhealthy posture in an effort to hide his height or gangliness. This is much more prevalent among girls than among boys. If proper posture is not acquired during childhood or adolescence, it will never be acquired.

An appraisal of posture is not a simple matter; individual differences in body build must be taken into consideration. Where teachers are available—usually teachers in physical education and health—measurements and careful evaluations based upon observations may be made. Where such help is not available, other means should be used to get a more accurate appraisal of posture, for example, a simple check to see that the individual stands erect, with the head, trunk, hips, and legs well aligned. Also, all children should be observed for sagging shoulders, correct manner of walking, and lateral curvatures.

SUMMARY

The most obvious changes that take place during childhood and adolescence occur in physical and physiological growth—thus, adolescence is frequently thought of as a period of rapid and pronounced growth. The endocrine glands play an important part in the growth changes. Longitudinal studies show that physical growth is irregular, with a period of decelerated rate of growth during preadolescence followed by a period of rapid growth. The ossification of the bones furnishes us with a good basis for estimating anatomical or skeletal growth. Many children suffer from malnutrition, which retards physical growth and the onset of adolescence or puberty. Improved diets have produced a generation of adolescents that are on the average taller and heavier than their parents.

There are also significant changes that take place in blood pressure, heart and pulse rate, basal metabolism, respiration rate and physiological conditions of sexual maturity. The range of sexual maturity is very great; it is affected by hereditary factors and living conditions. Under-privileged children in the United States and elsewhere in the world are late in sexual development. Obese children and those with an endomorphic build usually reach puberty earlier than their age-mates.

Important secondary sexual characteristics appear with the onset of adolescence. Some of these involve changes in hairline, pubic hair, skin structure, skin glands, voice, and subcutaneous fat. Differences in rate of maturity frequently create embarrassing problems for adolescents.

Motor performance reaches its peak during the adolescent years. Body strength, agility, and coordination are positively related to sexual development. Sex differences in motor performance become more pronounced during the adolescent years. Part of this is a result of differences in size and amount of practice.

Physical fitness is frequently neglected by adolescents from more affluent families. This has been observed in comparisons made between adolescents from different countries of the world, some of which have good physical education programs and some where adolescents are generally more physically active. Good posture is an acquired trait; and some adolescents, because of their body build, weight, or state of health need special help if they are to develop good posture.

REFERENCES

BALDWIN, B. T., L. M. BRESBY, and H. V. GARSIDE. "Atomic Growth of Children: A Study of Some Bones of the Hand, Wrist, and Lower Forearm by Means of Roentgenograms." *University of Iowa Studies in Child Welfare* (1928), 4 (1).

BAYLEY, NANCY. "Individual Patterns of Development." *Child Development* (1956), 27:64–65.

BOSWELL, F. P. "Trial and Error Learning." *Psychological Review* (1947), 54:290.

BURRELL, J. W., M. J. R. HEALY and J. M. TANNER. "Age at Menarche in South Africa Bantu Schoolgirls Living in the Transkip Reserve." *Human Biology* (1961), 33:250–61.

Charlotte Observer (March 24, 1971), p. 1. "Slum Kids Growth Retarded."

DOWNING, M. E. "Blood Pressure of Normal Girls from 3 to 16 Years of Age." *American Journal of Diseases of Children* (1947), 73:293–316.

EGAN, MARY C. "Combatting Malnutrition Through Maternal and Child Health Programs." *Children* (1969), 16(2):17, 71.

ESPENSCHADE, E. "Development of Motor Coordination in Boys and Girls." *Research Quarterly,* American Physical Education Association (1947), 18:30–43.

FERRIS, B. G. and C. W. SMITH. "Maximum Breathing Capacity and Vital Capacity of Female Children and Adolescents." *Pediatrics* (1953), 12:341–53.

FORD, C. S. and F. A. BEACH. *Patterns of Sexual Behavior.* New York: Hoeber, 1951.

FRIED, R. K. and E. E. SMITH. "Postmenarchael Growth Patterns." *Journal of Pediatrics* (1962), 6:562–65.

GREULICH, W. W., R. I. DORFMAN, H. R. CATCHPOLE, C. I. SOLOMON, and C. S. CULOTTA. "Somatic and Endocrine Studies of Puberal and Adolescent Boys." *Monographs of the Society for Research in Child Development* (1942), 7 (3).

HARDING, V. S. V. "A Method of Evaluating Osseous Development from Birth to 14 Years." *Child Development* (1952), 23:247–71.

HATHAWAY, M. L. and D. W. SARGENT. "Overweight in Children." *Journal of the American Dietetic Association* (June 1962).

HENTON, COMRADGE L. "A Comparative Study of the Onset of Menarche Among Negro and White Children." *Journal of Psychology* (1958), 46:65–73.

IKEDA, NAMEKO. "A Comparison of Physical Fitness of Children in Iowa and Tokyo." Ph.D. dissertation. Ames: Iowa State University, 1961.

ILIFF, A. and V. A. LEA. "Pulse Rate, Respiratory Rate, and Body Temperature of Children Between Two Months and Eighteen Years of Age." *Child Development* (1952), 23:237–45.

JOHNSTON, J. A. *Nutritional Studies in Adolescent Girls and Their Relation to Tuberculosis.* Springfield, Ill.: Charles C Thomas, 1953.

JOKL, E. and E. H. CLUVER. "Physical Fitness." *Journal of the American Medical Association* (1941), 116:2383–89.

JONES, H. E. "The Development of Physical Abilities." *Forty-third Yearbook of the National Society for the Study of Education,* Part 1. Chicago: Department of Education, University of Chicago, 1944. Chapter 6.

———. *Motor Performance and Growth.* Berkeley: University of California Press, 1949. Pp. 56–57.

——— and R. H. SEASHORE. "The Development of Fine Motor and Mechanical Abilities." *Forty-third Yearbook of the National Society for the Study of Education,* Part 1. Chicago: Department of Education, University of Chicago, 1944.

LEE, KRALJ-CERECK. "The Influence of Food, Body Build, and Social Origin on the Age of Menarche." *Human Biology* (1956), 28:393–406.

MCCLOY, C. H. "The Influence of Chronological Age on Motor Performance." *Research Quarterly,* American Physical Education Association (1935), 6:61–64.

MACCURDY, H. L. *A Test for Measuring the Physical Capacity of Secondary School Boys.* New York: Harcourt Brace Jovanovich, 1953.

MACMAHON, BRIAN. "Age at Menarche in the United States." *Vital and Health*

Statistics, Series 11, no. 133. Washington, D.C.: U.S. Department of Health, Education, and Welfare, 1973.

MALINA, ROBERT M. "Skeletal Maturation Studied Longitudinally over One Year in American Whites and Negroes Six Through Thirteen Years of Age." *Human Biology* (1970), 42:377–90.

MARSH, M. M. "Growth of the Heart Related to Bodily Growth During Childhood and Adolescence." *Journal of Pediatrics* (1953), 2:382–404.

MARTIN, W. E. *Children's Body Measurements for Planning and Equipping Schools.* Special Publication No. 4. Washington, D.C.: U.S. Department of Health, Education, and Welfare, 1955.

MICHAELSON, MIKE. "Acne Is More Than Skin Deep." *Today's Health* (1973), 51 (2):14.

MIKLASHEVSKAYA, N. N. "Sex Differences in Growth of the Head and Face in Children and Adolescents." *Human Biology* (1969), 41(2):250–62.

MONEY, JOHN and ANKE A. EHRHARDT. "Prenatal Hormone Exposure: Possible Effects on Behavior in Man." In *Endocrinology and Human Behaviors,* R. P. Michael, ed. London: Oxford University Press, 1968. Pp. 32–48.

MORSE, M., SCHULTZ, F. W., and D. E. CASSELS. "Blood Volumes of Normal Children." *American Journal of Physiology* (1947), 151:448–58.

NATHANSON, I. T., L. E. TOWNE, and J. C. AUB. "Normal Excretion of Sex Hormones in Childhood." *Endocrinology* (1941), 28:851–65.

NICOLSON, A. and CHARLES HANLEY. "Indices of Physiological Maturity: Deviations and Interrelationships." *Child Development* (1953), 24:3–38.

Parade magazine (December 24, 1972), p. 5. "Bigger Japanese."

PECKOS, PENELOPE S. and FELIX P. HEALD. "Nutrition of Adolescents." *Children* (1964), 11 (1):27–30.

POPPLETON, PAMELA K. and P. E. BROWN. "The Secular Trend in Puberty: Has Stability Been Achieved?" *British Journal of Educational Psychology* (1966), 36:95–100.

RAMSEY, G. V. "The Sexual Development of Boys." *American Journal of Psychology* (1943), 56:217–23.

REYNOLDS, E. L. "The Distribution of Subcutaneous Fat in Childhood and Adolescence." *Monographs of the Society for Research in Child Development* (1950), 15:1–189.

RICHEY, H. G. "Blood Pressure in Boys and Girls Before and After Puberty." *American Journal of Diseases of Children* (1931), 42:1281–1330.

RICHEY, H. G. "The Relation of Accelerated, Normal and Retarded Puberty to the Height and Weight of School Children." *Monographs of the Society for Research in Child Development* (1937), 2 (8):1–67.

RUSSELL, S. J. M. "Blood Volume Studies in Healthy Children." *Archives of Diseases of Childhood* (1949), 24:88–98.

SARDON, M. A. "El Desarrollo de Algunas Dotes Manuales en el Escolar de Lima." *Boletin del Instituto Psicopedagogico Nacional.* Lima, 1944.

SCHACHTER, RUBIN J., ERNEST S. PANTEL, GEORGE M. GLASSMAN, and IRVING ZWEIBELSON. "Acne Vulgaris and Psychologic Impact on High School Students." *New York State Journal of Medicine* (1971), 71 (24):2886–90.

SCHWENK, A., G. EGGERS-HOHMANN, and F. GENSCH. "Arterieller Blutdruck, Vasomotorismus und Menarchetermin bei Modahen im 2. Leben sjahrzchut." *Arch. Kinderheilk* (1955), 150:235–49.

SHOCK, N. W. "Physiological Changes in Adolescence." *Forty-third Yearbook of the National Society for the Study of Education,* Part I. Chicago: Department of Education, University of Chicago, 1944. Chapter 4. Pp. 59–60.

SHUTTLEWORTH, F. L. "The Physical and Mental Growth of Girls and Boys Age Six to Nineteen in Relation to Age at Maximum Growth." *Monographs of the Society for Research in Child Development* (1939), 4 (3).

SJÖSTRAND, T. "Volume and Distribution of Blood and Their Significance in Regulating the Circulation." *Physiological Review* (1953), 33:202–28.

STUNKARD, A. J. and M. MENDELSON. "Disturbances in Body Image of Some Obese Persons." *Journal of the American Dietetic Association* (1961), 38:328–31.

————. "Obesity and the Body Image, I. Characteristics of Disturbances in the Body Image of Some Obese Persons." *American Journal of Psychiatry* (1967), 123 (10):1296–1300.

SULLIVAN, WALTER. "Boys and Girls Are Now Maturing Earlier." *New York Times* (January 24, 1971), pp. 1, 36.

TANNER, J. M. "Growth and Endocrinology of the Adolescent." In *Endocrine and Genetic Diseases of Childhood,* L. Gardner, ed. London: Saunders, 1969.

TRAVIS, R. C. "An Experimental Analysis of Dynamic and Static Equilibrium." *Journal of Experimental Psychology* (1945), 35:216–34.

VAN DELLEN, T. R. "Is It Better to Be Taller?" *Charlotte Observer* (March 29, 1971), p. 14C.

RECOMMENDED READINGS

GARRISON, KARL C. and ROBERT A. MAGOON. *Educational Psychology: An Integration of Psychology and Educational Practices.* Columbus, Ohio: Charles E. Merrill Publishing Co., 1972. Chapter 2.
    In this chapter the authors present recent findings on basic principles of growth, physical growth, motor development, sensory development, the development of thought, and theories of development.

HORROCKS, JOHN E. *The Psychology of Adolescence.* 3rd ed. Boston: Houghton Mifflin Company, 1969.
    Especially useful are Chapters 17 through 20 which give considerable attention to physical growth, physiological growth, anatomical and structural growth, and physical functioning and efficiency.

JONES, MARY C. "Psychological Correlates of Somatic Development." *Child Development* (1965), 36:899–911.
    This is a longitudinal study in which the rate of physical maturity is related to certain psychological variables. Comparisons are made between boys who are accelerated in physical development and those who are retarded.

Tanner, J. M. "The Course of Children's Growth." *Education and Physical Growth*. London: University of London Press, 1961.
A careful study is presented of the course of children's growth. Charts are presented for individual growth curves, adolescent spurt in height growth for boys and girls, growth curves for different parts and tissues of the body, changes with age in the amount of subcutaneous fat, growth of strength of hand grip, arm pull, and arm thrust, changes in composition of the blood with age, and skeletal age plotted against chronological age.

5

intellectual development

In the previous chapter special consideration was given to physical and physiological development. Another important area of development in which profound changes occur during adolescence is that of intellectual abilities, including cognition and creativity. Intellectual development may best be described as a continuum from the simple to the complex. As the child develops intellectually, he learns to differentiate and to think hierarchically. Elkind (1966) describes the adolescent as well into the hierarchical thinking stage.

The discussion in this chapter will be confined mainly to the adolescent stage of life, although certain background materials are presented for the sake of clarification. Since many problems relating to intellectual development are highly controversial, the materials presented are given in the spirit of what recent scientific studies tend to point out. Some of the major problems to be studied are: concepts of intelligence, mental growth, conceptual development during adolescence, factors or conditions related to mental growth, and the creative adolescent.

INTELLIGENCE:
ITS NATURE AND MEANING

Few terms in educational psychology have been so generally used with functional meaning and yet are so difficult to define operationally as the term intelligence. Certainly it is not an entity that can be readily defined, manipulated, and measured. It is perhaps easier to describe behavior that indicates intellectual functioning than to describe intelligence as such. Yet, for many decades writers have attempted to provide us with notions of the meaning and nature of intelligence.

Concepts of Intelligence

The concepts of the nature of intelligence held by early students of psychology were quite simple. Intelligence was conceived by many as a general mental power or a multiplicity of mental powers that could be measured on a vertical scale by a single score. These scores were either divided by chronological age and the resultant quotient called the intelligence quotient (IQ), or transmuted into mental ages. (A child's mental age, according to the early Binet tests and revisions of his test, was expressed in terms of the average age of children making that test score). Any significant changes in a child or adolescent's IQ from year to year were regarded as exceptions. Thus, the theory of "the constancy of the IQ" was developed and generally accepted. Binet regarded intelligence as directness of thought, capacity to adapt, and autocriticism; others described it as the ability to learn, to solve problems, or to adjust to new or complex situations. One of the most complete definitions of intelligence was that presented by Wechsler (1960:7). He states: "Intelligence is the aggregate, or global, capacity of the individual to act purposefully, to think rationally, and to deal effectively with his environment."

THE CONCEPT OF PRIMARY MENTAL ABILITIES. Thorndike, Terman, Goddard, and others furnished us with useful definitions of intelligence. Beginning in the 1930s the Thurstones, among others, questioned the validity of the concept of general intelligence. They conceived that five or more tests may correlate with one another because of group factors common to the different tasks rather than a "g," or general factor, as posed by Spearman (1927). Consequently, L. L. Thurstone worked out a statistical technique for what has been termed factor analysis. Using this method, he found a set of separate factors to account for the correlations in a battery of tests.

In 1938, Thurstone assembled a battery of fifty-six psychological tests for use in a study designed to determine factor loadings. These tests were administered to 240 college students. From a factorial analysis of the data nine primary abilities were identified. In a later study, 1,154 eighth-grade students were given a similar battery of tests; seven primary abilities were identified from a factorial analysis of the data. The primary mental abilities found among both college and eighth-grade students were as follows:

Space: visualization of geometrical figures in different positions in space.
Perceptual speed: quick observation of details.
Number: quickness in making arithmetical computations of all sorts.
Verbal meanings: grasp of ideas and meanings of words.
Word fluency: speed in manipulating single and isolated words.
Memory: ease in memorizing words, numbers, letters, and other materials.
Induction: ability to extract a rule common to the materials of a problem or test.

Other investigators have given other explanations of the formation of factors. Ferguson (1956) proposed a transfer of training in which abilities emerge through a process of differential transfer. The breadth of transfer determines whether an ability is broad or narrow; verbal comprehension is a relatively broad factor. While recognizing the importance and applicability of transfer, Vernon (1969) explained factors through contiguous educational experiences. The broad verbal-educational factor is frequently found across intellectual functions learned in school, and its nature and function may vary in different cultures because of the nature of the culture and the varying content taught in the schools. Both educational and socioeconomic differences in factor patterns were noted by Filella (1960) in a study of high school students in Colombia, South America. Verbal tests had marginally low loadings among boys enrolled in technical high schools, while the verbal factor was prominent among those enrolled in academic high schools. Also, the differentiation between verbal and nonverbal factors was sharper in the private school group than in the public high school group. The extensive cross-cultural studies of mental factors indicate that the growth of different mental abilities is affected by many factors, including the experiences of a particular individual.

Mental Growth—Intellectual Development

The data now available on mental growth are those obtained from administering intelligence tests to the same individual or group of individuals repeatedly for a number of years. Since each person develops at a unique rate, curves made from studies of individual mental growth vary greatly in shape; a plateau period frequently appears, and it will vary in duration from one individual to another. Such variations may be observed in the individual growth curves for five boys shown in Figure 5-1 (Bayley and Oden, 1955). These curves show further that some children forge ahead and maintain their relatively advanced position

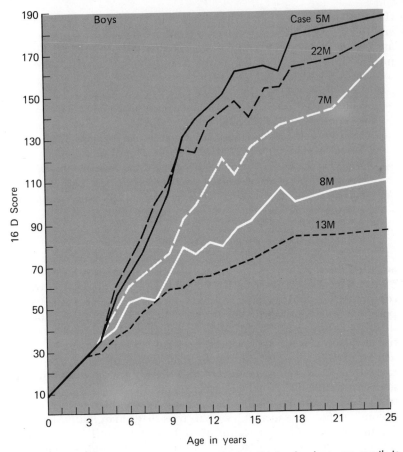

FIGURE 5-1 Individual curves of intelligence (16 D units) for five boys, one month to 25 years. From Bayley and Oden (1955).

after the early years, whereas others grow slowly and tend to fall further and further behind. Compared to the adolescent years, the early years are a period of rapid growth.

MENTAL GROWTH DURING ADOLESCENCE. Long-term predictions of intelligence test scores based on earlier scores are unreliable (Bayley, 1949). However, correlations between scores obtained at different periods become increasingly higher as scores are obtained at ages closer to maturity. In a study by Eagle (1966), tests were administered to 115 eighth-grade boys and 150 eighth-grade girls who had previously taken the test when they were in grades three or four. The correlations obtained between the verbal IQ scores secured earlier and those obtained in the eighth grade was .592 for boys and .777 for girls; the correlations be-

tween the earlier and later nonverbal IQ scores were .494 for boys and
.666 for girls. These results indicate that verbal IQ scores are more stable
from the third to the eighth grade than nonverbal IQ scores and that
the scores for girls were more stable than those for boys. In an earlier
study, the Primary Mental Abilities Test (Intermediate Form) was administered to a sample of eighth-grade pupils and readministered when
they were completing the eleventh grade (Meyer and Bendig, 1961). The
correlations show that academic abilities remain stable during the period;
there is, however, less stability in word fluency and nonacademic ability.

In a relatively early study by Stone and Barker (1937), 175 postmenarcheal and 175 premenarcheal girls of the same chronological age
were compared with respect to Otis Intelligence Test scores, personality,
and socioeconomic status of the parents. The postmenarcheal girls made
a mean score on the intelligence test which was 2.25 points higher than
that made by the premenarcheal girls, but the difference was not
statistically reliable. The Pressey Interest Attitude Test scores and the
Sullivan Test for Developmental Age showed the postmenarcheal girls to
be more mature than the premenarcheal of the same chronological age.
The two groups were from families of about the same socioeconomic
status, and did not show a difference in their general personality traits as
measured by the Bernreuter Personality Inventory. Apparently, then,
pubescence has much more significance as a physiological change affecting
various glandular secretions—especially those relating to sexual characteristics—and the rate of growth in height, weight, and other physical
measurements than it has as a criterion for mental growth. Physical and
emotional changes are much more closely related to the onset of puberty
than are the more specific mental abilities.

FORMATION OF FACTORS. The formation of factors, referred to
earlier, was explained by Ferguson (1956) in terms of transfer of training.
He looked upon the different abilities as prior learned acquisitions and
attributed the correlation among the abilities to positive transfer. Thus,
different abilities emerge through a process of differential transfer.
Since cultural factors influence what the child learns at different ages,
different cultural environments lead to the development of different
ability patterns. The breadth of transfer effect will determine whether
the resulting factor is broad, such as verbal comprehension, or narrow,
like a specialized motor skill. Traditional intelligence tests measure
intellectual skills or abilities that transfer widely to tasks within our
culture.

Whiteman (1964) explained the origin of factors differently by
pointing to a relation between the formation of learning sets and the
development of factors. This was observed in Harlow's experiments with
monkeys (1960), in which the monkeys established a learning set by
differentiating between certain shapes such as triangles and circles. This
enabled them to learn more rapidly when given another problem requiring the differentiation of shapes. Differences in the amount of prior

shape-discrimination experience (or degree to which the animal had profited from such experience) would be reflected in the strength of the learning set when presented with a new problem. These explanations emphasize the role of learning in the formation of factors.

There is much similarity among these explanations in the generality of concepts, extent of transfer effects, and intersituational applicability of learning sets. There is also an explanation offered by Vernon (1969) based upon contiguous educational experiences. Thus, what we designate as the verbal factor may be a result of the intellectual functions involving verbalization taught in our schools. The fact that mental factors seem to become more pronounced during and following adolescence may result from early specialization in learning interests and experiences. Narrower factors are then seen to be associated with the organization of course content in different types of schools or in different curricula.

COGNITIVE DEVELOPMENT
DURING ADOLESCENCE

With advancement from childhood into and through adolescence there is an increased stability of patterns of mental abilities, shown in the results of a study by Meyer, (1960: 800) presented in conjunction with another study. Meyer concluded: "These studies clearly demonstrate (a) increasing stability of test patterns with age and (b) increasing differentiation of the primary abilities with age." This would seem to result from training and practice. The individual with a high score in numerical ability will probably make considerable use of this ability, and thus increase it. On the other hand, if he has a low verbal score, he will probably shun activity that requires use of words, and as a result his verbal ability will not increase at the same rate.

The Development of Memory Ability

The period of childhood has been frequently described as the "golden age of memory" and adulthood as the age of reasoning. Studies of the growth of different mental functions show, however, that memory, reasoning ability, critical thinking, interpretive ability, and other mental functions grow continuously, in an orderly manner. There are a number of reasons why certain misconceptions have developed about the memory ability of children. In the first place, much of that memorized by children is mechanical. On that basis, the child competes favorably with adults. Children have not developed a wide range of associations and understandings; therefore, they are compelled to rely largely upon mechanical memories, and are not distracted by meaningful elements that may appear in the situation. Furthermore, children are more limited in the scope of their mental activity and spend considerable time in going over certain materials. The developmental curve for memory ability is

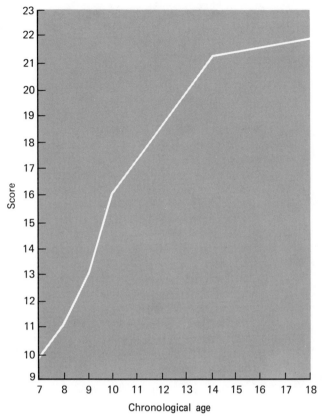

FIGURE 5-2 The relation of age to scores made in memorizing poetry. From Stroud and Maul (1933).

somewhat similar in nature to that of other mental functions; it increases with age and experience.

The problem of the influence of age upon the learning of poetry
and nonsense syllables was studied by Stroud and Maul (1933). The subjects consisted of 172 grade-school children, 26 ninth-grade students, and
23 college freshmen. The average chronological ages ranged from 7.7
years to 18.1 years. The different groups were approximately equal in
average IQ. The growth with age in the ability to memorize poetry is
shown in Figure 5-2. The memory curve for nonsense syllables was found
to be similar to that shown for poetry, and a high correlation existed
between memory ability and mental age.

Vocabulary Growth

Early studies by Terman, Thorndike, and others have shown that
there is a continuous growth of vocabulary with maturation and verbal

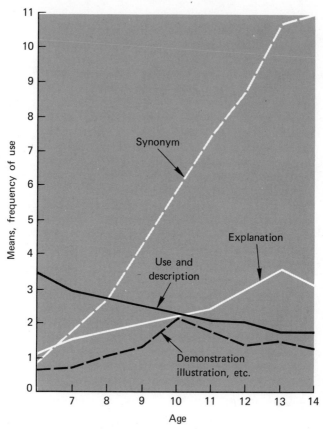

FIGURE 5-3 Mean frequency of use of four qualitative categories by age. From Feifel and Lorge (1950).

experiences. Studies of the qualitative aspects of vocabulary reveal also a change in the character of word definitions. Feifel and Lorge (1950) administered the vocabulary test of Form L of the Stanford Revision of the Binet Tests to 900 children aged six to fourteen, slightly above average in intelligence except at age fourteen. The definitions given were studied for their completeness and qualitative nature. The results are presented in Figure 5-3. It is apparent that children at the six- and seven-year age level define by giving the use and description of the object most often; *orange* would be "something to eat." The explanation type of response is used very little at this age, but appears to grow slowly and continuously in use until the thirteen-year age level. The decline noted at the fourteen-year age level may be partially accounted for by the lower intelligence of this group in comparison with that of the other groups. The synonym type of response, although seldom used by the six- and seven-year-olds, is used quite frequently by children around the ages of nine and ten, and continues to grow in use throughout the following years. The decline in the demonstrational and illustrative types of response during the adolescent years may be attributed to the growth in the size of vocabulary and the ability to symbolize things and events in terms of opposites and similarities.

Piaget—Stages in Concept Formation

Piaget (1952) noted in his studies of the development of quantity concepts that abstract responses to mass, weight, and volume appear in a sequence related to age. Despite the limitations in his method of collecting and evaluating data, he has made valuable contributions to our understanding of the stages of the child's development. His ideas are of widespread interest, due in part to Flavell (1963), who translated and summarized a number of his publications. Piaget has set forth the following chronological order of the development of the mental processes involving cognition:

> *Birth to two years:* the period of sensorimotor adaptation.
> *Two to four years:* the period of preconceptual thought.
> *Four to seven years:* the period of intuitive thought
> *Seven to eleven years:* the period of concrete operations
> *Eleven to fifteen years:* the period of formal operations.

According to Piaget, the eleven-year-old is able to apply operational thinking to concrete situations and problems. The child or adolescent who has reached the formal operational level will systematically attempt relatively complex operations; he will consider different combinations; and he will make use of an array of possibilities, since relations involving more than one variable can be dealt with. Thus, he looks for different combinations to employ in dealing with a problem. The individual at this stage is concerned with the possible, not just the concrete or real. The adolescent is better able to carry on abstract thought. This opens to him the deductive procedures of science, mathematics, and formal reasoning. Since a variety of new intellectual techniques are available at this stage, the individual can, through guided instruction, plan scientific investigations, develop theories and models as guides, and conduct logical thinking in different life areas.

Piaget's studies of intellectual development suggest that there are basic differences between the adolescent and young child in scientific thinking and reasoning. For the adolescent, possibility dominates reality. He states:

> Confronted with a scientific problem, he begins not by observing the empirical results, but by thinking of the possibilities inherent in the situation. He imagines that many things *might* occur, that many interpretations of the data *might* be possible, and that what has actually occured is but one of a number of possible alternatives. Only after performing a

hypothetical analysis of this sort does he proceed to obtain empirical data which serve to confirm or refute his hypothesis. Further, he bases experiments on deductions from the hypothetical; he is not bound solely by the observed (quoted in Ginsburg and Opper, 1969: 203).

Intelligence and Formal Thought

According to Piaget (1972), formal operational thought becomes established around the ages of twelve to fifteen years. This is reflected in the adolescent's ability to reason hypothetically and independently of concrete states of affairs. However, the rate at which children progress through the developmental succession may vary, especially from one culture to another. Significant differences appear in areas of functioning to which they apply formal operations, depending on their intellectual abilities. Individuals with an IQ range between 70 and 89 are retarded in their intellectual development and thus do not begin to fully utilize formal operations until ages fourteen, fifteen, or sixteen. According to Yudin (1966), subjects with superior intelligence show an efficient use of formal and logical operations as early as age twelve. In addition, changes in performance from age twelve to ages fourteen and sixteen are more nearly linear with a considerable increase with increasing age. It is this quality of mind—the ability to continue to profit from experience and to manifest continued growth—that characterizes the individual of superior intelligence. This is further shown in the case of a study of college students with a mean age of eighteen (Kates and Yudin, 1964). These students were found to be capable of attaining concepts at a level beyond that found by Yudin (1966) with superior fourteen- and sixteen-year-old high school students. This would indicate that mental growth in concept attainment continues for college students into late adolescence.

Perhaps the most important implication of Yudin's findings is that an interaction of age, or maturity, and intelligence contributes toward concept attainment and cognitive development. The attainment of logical operations as an integral aspect of mental functioning during adolescence is far from uniform. Intellectually superior adolescents are capable of functioning to a greater extent and perhaps continue to grow in this ability longer than those less intellectually endowed. It should also be pointed out that development, whether accelerated or retarded, brings with it a shift of emphasis from concreteness to abstractness and a new or different way of dealing with facts and relations—operational thought.

The Role of Experience
in Cognitive Development

In contrast to Piaget's belief in a neurophysiological basis for cognitive development, Ausubel and Ausubel (1966) emphasized the importance of experience. They presented three trends to account for the changes that take place during adolescence: (1) increased vocabulary of abstract words; (2) growth of stable, higher order concepts; and (3) increased ability in manipulating relationships with the help of concrete props, so that relationships and interpretations can be performed more readily without props. Elkind's findings (1966) are closely related to these trends; he suggests that adolescents are more successful than children in the facility to shift conceptual orientation in the course of resolving a concept-formation task. The findings of his study further suggest "that the thought of the adolescent is not only more logically elaborate than that of the child, . . . but also that it is more mobile and flexible" (496).

Older children and adolescents are able to gather information by asking questions in a directed, sequential order that leads to a goal or a solution. The idea of enhancing human cognitive development by surrounding a young child with an environment that provides rich and stimulating experiences is a relatively recent one. In a study by Wolman and Baker (1965), a sample of 117 children ages four to twelve drawn from the middle to upper-middle class, was used as subjects. Each child was presented a list of forty-three carefully chosen words to be defined by answering the question: "What is an X?" "What does Z mean?" One important finding was that as age increases, the percent of *use* definitions tends to decrease. This is shown for three age groups:

Four-year-olds	78 percent
Eight-year-olds	63 percent
Twelve-year-olds	25 percent

The investigators conclude, ". . . the transition from the infantile mode of defining words to the more mature form is gradual and slow. It was also found that intelligence and sex play no important role in this development. Factors that do correlate with the mode of defining are (1) age and (2) number of words known" (165).

FACTORS RELATED TO MENTAL GROWTH

The vast amount of research showing the ill effects of adverse conditions, beginning with conception, upon intellectual development has affected notions earlier held about the nature and growth of these abilities. A brief review of the results from some of these studies should give us a better understanding of intellectual development during the adolescent years along with the factors and conditions affecting such development.

Influences of Undernutrition During Infancy

The results of a number of studies reveal that undernutrition during the first year of life is detrimental to the later development of the brain. The greatest growth spurt for the brain occurs during the fetal period. By the end of the first year after birth the brain has reached approximately 70 percent of its adult weight, while by age two its growth is almost complete. In a study by Chase and Martin (1970) of nineteen children who were admitted to Denver General Hospital between 1962 and 1967 at less than one year of age with the primary diagnosis of generalized undernutrition, a positive correlation was found between early undernutrition and later retardation of physical development. An exception was a boy who gained rapidly in the hospital and seemed to catch up in his physical development, although head growth and brain function remain impaired.

Stock and Smythe (1963) in an earlier study recorded the results of an eleven-year follow-up of the head size and intellectual development of a group of children on whom they reported in an earlier study. They took twenty of the most grossly undernourished infants they could find and matched them for age and sex with an adequately nourished control group from a similar socioeconomic level. They noted: "Throughout the period of study, members of the undernourished group had smaller heads, lower heights and weights, and lower intelligence quotients than the controls. The most important physical difference was considered to be the smaller mean head circumference, suggesting that the brain had reached maturity at a suboptimal size" (233).

Cravioto and Robles (1965) studied a group of twenty Guatemalan infants and preschool children who had recuperated from severe protein malnutrition, following some of them for six and a half months. These children scored lower than a control group of children, matched for age and ethnic background, who had never manifested symptoms of severe malnutrition. Infants who had recovered from severe malnutrition before they were six months old continued to show deficits in adaptive, motor, language, and personal-social behavior. The results from this, supported by related studies, suggest that early malnutrition during the time of rapid brain growth and cell division will produce permanent mental deficits.

Sex Differences

Soon after birth cultural forces begin operating to develop and reinforce a differentiation of mental growth based upon sex. The nature and extent of differences in treatment and training based upon sex will vary with different cultures. Boys and girls from the lower classes are made aware of sex-role behavior earlier than children of the middle and upper classes. At the first-grade level the average girl seems to articulate clearly and has a larger vocabulary than the average boy (McCarthy, 1954). One explanation for this among lower-class children is the differences in the play and recreational activities of boys and girls—the girls' play life involves the use of language to a greater degree.

Lynn postulates that "the intellectual development of women is based on an interaction of: (1) biologically rooted potentials which predispose women toward some roles more than others; (2) parent-child relationships, seemingly inherent in the typical family pattern, which predispose toward certain cognitive styles; and (3) both blatant and subtle cultural reinforcement of traditional feminine-role prescriptions" (1972: 241). It might be pointed out that these same forces operate to direct the intellectual development of the male. Differential parent-child interaction seems to be an important factor in the development of specific mental abilities and characteristics.

Influence of Parent-child Interaction

In a study of the environmental processes related to intelligence, Wolf (1964) hypothesized that thirteen process variables could be used to describe the interactions between parents and children insofar as intelligence development is concerned. These were classified as follows: Press for Achievement Motivation, Press for Language Development, and Provisions for General Learning. An interview form was devised and used in interviewing mothers of sixty fifth-grade students in a midwestern community. Each family or home was rated on each of the thirteen process variables. Wolf obtained a multiple correlation of .76 between these ratings and IQs obtained from Henmon-Nelson Test results. This correlation is significantly higher than that found between such environmental variables as social status, parent's occupation, or parent's education—the correlations with these variables being .40.

The results of this and related studies are especially significant in that they show that child-parent interaction is more important in determining the IQ level of the child than social status and other factors usually emphasized in studies of cultural deprivation. Perhaps the term stimulation deprivation should be used in this connection. The results of this study have been borne out by other investigators. Bloom, Davis, and Hess have summarized the research bearing on the various aspects of the home environment which seem to be most significant in affecting the level of measured intelligence of the child. They state:

> . . . In most general terms these may be described as involving provisions for general learning, models and help in language development, and parental stimulation and concern for achievement and learning on the part of the child. For the most part, it is the adults in the home who serve to stimulate the child's intellectual development (1965: 12).

The Social Class Structure

Continued exposure to differential environmental conditions, found in different social classes favors the development of certain abilities and discourages the development of others. Most of the tasks to be learned at school are more closely related to the background of middle-class than of lower-class children. Consequently, middle-class children tend to excel in the tasks. The importance of an enriched and stimulating early environment was pointed out earlier. An inquiry by Hess and Shipman (1965) dealt with the question: How does early cultural deprivation act to shape and depress the development of cognitive abilities? The investigators noted that one of the most striking and obvious differences between the environments provided by the mothers of the research group was in their patterns of language use. They suggest that the most obvious social class variations were in the total amount of verbal output in response to questions and tasks calling for verbal responses.

Somewhat related to class structure are certain cultural differences and practices. Witkin's (1967) review of cross-cultural studies dealing with cognitive development in different cultures gives some evidence for cross-cultural differences in cognitive styles. A study by Berry (1966) delineates this relationship. A comparison was made of the Temne of Sierra Leone and the Eskimos of Baffin Island. The strict child-rearing practices of the Temne and the permissive rearing of the Eskimos were reflected in the marked independence of the Eskimos in relation to their environment and to other Eskimos compared with the dependence of the Temne upon their environment and upon one another.

**Motivation-Achievement Need and
Intellectual Development**

According to studies conducted by McClelland and Atkinson (1963) and supported by more recent studies, the achievement motive develops during the early years, being closely related to parental expectations. This has been shown to be responsible for some of the differences in intelligence test scores and in the variability and direction of IQ changes. Sontag and others (1958) noted that eagerness to learn or "learning to learn" was closely related to an increase in IQ throughout childhood and into adolescence; lack of such interest or a low achievement need was found to be related to a deceleration of the IQ during the elementary school years. The degree to which an adolescent possesses the achievement need or motivation to learn will depend upon a number of factors, including early parent-child relations, a favorable self-concept, a realistic but worthwhile aspiration level, and past learning experiences.

Research by Rosenthal and Jacobson (1968) suggest that teachers' expectations may have an important effect on a student's intellectual development. The intelligence test scores of a group of randomly selected students who were described by their teachers as likely to show intellectual gains were compared with those of a control group; the experimental group of students scored significantly higher on the test. Although this study has been open to certain criticisms, it is reasonable to hypothesize that a teacher's expectations will have an influence on a student's performance. The results of a more recent study by Rothbart, Dalfen, and Barrett (1971), involving high school students, support the notion that teachers' expectations influence student performance. Teachers spend more time attending to the high-expectation students, and these students talked more, perhaps as a consequence of the greater attention they received from their teachers.

School Achievement in Relation to Intelligence

When one considers the nature of intelligence tests and traditional achievement tests, it seems that a significant relationship should exist between achievement and intelligence. Layton and Swanton (1958) obtained correlations between scores on the items of the Differential Aptitude Test and high school rank, presented in Table 5-1, that indicated such a relationship. The correlations varied with a number of factors but usually ranged between .30 and .75.

TABLE 5-1 Correlations of the Items on the Differential
Aptitude Test with High School Rank

Verbal reasoning	.56
Numerical ability	.57
Abstract reasoning	.45
Space relations	.36
Mechanical reasoning	.29
Clerical speed and accuracy	.32

Source: Layton and Swanson (1958).

Evidence from studies has confirmed the hypothesis that a well-made test of verbal and mathematical ability furnishes useful information about a student's academic promise. Such predictions would be more accurate if the program of studies and the standards of grading were more uniform. Figure 5-4 illustrates the kind of relationship found between the verbal scores on the Scholastic Aptitude Test and college freshmen grades under favorable conditions. The chart indicates, as expected, that the higher the student's SAT score, the better the chances of satisfactory or honor work in college. Colleges have succeeded in greatly reducing the failure rate among students enrolled through their selective admissions policies, and this would affect the relationship that might be expected between SAT scores of students actually admitted to college and grades obtained during the freshman year.

FAVORABLE SELF-CONCEPT. In a study by Winterose (1968) a comparison of high-achieving and low-achieving fourth-grade culturally disadvantaged pupils was made. The investigator compared selected factors in the background and personal-social adjustment between the two groups of pupils. The high-achieving group was significantly superior to the low-achieving group in total academic performance and on mental tests. Acceptance of self and others was significantly related to total ad-

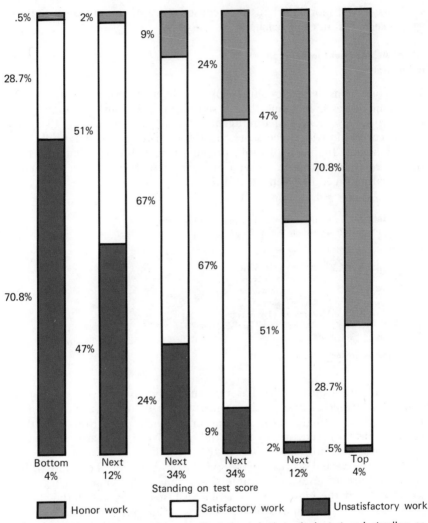

FIGURE 5-4 Relation between standing on scholastic aptitude test and standing on college freshman grades under favorable conditions. From *Educational Testing Service Annual Report* (1963: 41).

justment. Since there is usually little in the disadvantaged culture to encourage children to develop a positive self-concept or an accepting view of others, the classroom teacher should be trained to help them. Caplan (1957) noted that important changes may be brought about in the self-ideals of junior-high boys through counseling, while Perkins and Shannon (1965) reported that ideal-self scores of preadolescent boys are related to academic success.

THE CREATIVE ADOLESCENT

Intelligence has been defined and measured as it applies to classroom learning because the early studies in this field were primarily concerned with students' learning difficulties at school. As Getzels and Jackson state in their description of giftedness:

> If we moved the focus of inquiry from the classroom setting, we might identify qualities defining giftedness for other situations just as the IQ did for the classroom, Indeed, even without shifting our focus of inquiry, if we only modified the conventional criteria of achievement, we might change the qualities defining giftedness even in the classroom. For example, if we recognized that learning involves the production of novelty as well as the memorization of course content, then measures of creativity as well as IQ might become appropriate in defining characteristics of giftedness (1962: 371).

Creativity and Divergent Thinking

Probably the greatest challenge to the existing concepts of intelligence was presented by the emergence of *divergent* or nonconforming facets upon the intellectual scene. Guilford (1950, 1959, 1962) holds that these abilities should be perceived as general in nature, as opposed to specific, and that they can be applied to great varieties of tasks. They can no longer be viewed as the preserve of a few or be limited to aesthetic pursuits. Rather, they must be recognized as existing in many forms and in many different kinds of men. Creativity may be perceived in the plumber, student, professor, engineer, or perhaps the auto mechanic who "listens" to an engine and appears to have a special, mystical *insight* into the solution of a particularly stubborn problem which no mechanic for the last year and a half could solve.

Getzels and Jackson (1962: 39) concluded from student responses that, within four minutes following the presentation of a picture, divergent responses tended to be unrelated to the stimulus whereas convergent responses were stimulus oriented. The convergent thinkers tended to be more inhibited by the stimuli and presented conforming or "expected" responses to the stimuli. Divergent students constructed less inhibited, more creative stories when presented with the same picture. Concerning the growth of creativity Torrance (1962) noted a decline in the sixth and seventh grades and a rather steady rise through the high school years.

**Relationship Between IQ, Creativity
and Academic Achievement**

The relation between intelligence and creativity depends upon the age level of the subjects being tested and the nature of the tests used. When we examine the relevant research conducted during the past decade, the results indicate an increasing differentiation with age. As the child advances through the grades at school, the academic curriculum becomes increasingly structured and differentiated into traditional areas of subject matter. The instructional program, conducted by specialized teachers in special classrooms, furthers the differentiation process already at work. Thus, a comparison of the gifted and talented becomes clearer with this increased differentiation.

A study by Cicirelli (1965) dealt with the relationships between IQ, creativity, and academic achievement. He found an interaction between IQ and creativity as they relate to academic achievement. Beyond a certain level, higher IQ did not usually distinguish students in terms of their academic achievement. However, he noted that within a critical range, both IQ and creativity distinguish students in terms of their academic achievement. In a study of seven- and eight-year-olds, Ward (1968) found a clear distinction between creativity and intelligence; however, Cropley (1966) failed to find one. He suggests that high scores on tests of divergent thinking, characteristic of creative students, will usually be accompanied by high scores on tests of convergent thinking and vice versa.

Teachers have consistently observed some students who are academically superior and other students who are especially talented in one or more of the arts—painting, drama, music. This becomes more obvious as we move from childhood into adolescence. Juniors and rising seniors selected from high schools in North Carolina for the Governor's School, an eight-week residential summer program, were studied by Welsh (1966). There were two major divisions in the school: the Academic Division and the Arts Division. The Academic Division students were selected on the basis of their academic record at school; the Arts Division students were selected on the basis of demonstrated talent in a special area.

The two groups were given the Terman Concept Mastery Test (CMT), (Terman, 1956), D–48 (Black, 1963), a nonverbal test, and the revised Art Scale (RA) of the Welsh Figure Preference Test (Welsh, 1959). The results for the two groups on the three tests are shown in Table 5-2. The Academic Division students averaged higher on both intelligence tests while the Arts Division students average score was higher on the creative measure. Correlations obtained between scores on the three tests showed that the intelligence tests are significantly correlated with each other, but that correlations with the creative measures were insignificant.

Cognitive Functioning and Creativity—
Psychological Differences

In the study by Getzels and Jackson (1962) five alleged tests of creativity were administered to large samples of students ranging from the sixth grade through the end of high school. Four of the five tests correlated

TABLE 5-2 Comparisons of Scores of Two Groups of Gifted Adolescents on Intelligence and Creativity Measures

TESTS		ACADEMIC DIVISION (N = 207)	ARTS DIVISION (N = 161)
CMT	M	67.35	41.55
	SD	26.88	26.89
D–48	M	32.15	27.07
	SD	4.89	7.09
RA	M	29.53	34.22
	SD	15.72	14.12

Source: Welsh (1966).

significantly with IQ for girls; all five of the tests correlated significantly with IQ for boys. However, the results showed that the five tests of creativity did not correlate any higher with each other than with the intelligence tests results, as is indicated by the following results:

	BOYS	GIRLS
Mean correlation between creativity battery and IQ	.26	.27
Mean correlation between tasks on the creativity tests	.28	.32

On the basis of these results there is no basis for considering creativity and intelligence as distinct entities.

The question poised by Wallach and Kogan (1965) was: Is there an aspect of cognitive functioning that can be appropriately labeled "creativity" and is independent of the traditional concept of intelligence? In order to answer this question, standardized intelligence tests and five measures of creativity were administered to 151 children comprising the entire fifth-grade population of a suburban public school system. The tests were given in gamelike situations by two young women who spent two initial weeks with each fifth-grade class gaining rapport with the children. The two experimenters made independent ratings of the children along specifically defined behavioral dimensions during the initial two weeks of observing each class. A rating was made of each child's status on a given dimension in terms of a nine-point scale. These rating dimensions were found to have a high interrater reliability.

From the results obtained, including the case studies, rather distinct pictures emerge concerning the psychological nature of the children in the four cognitive groupings: high creativity–high intelligence; high creativity–low intelligence; low creativity–high intelligence; and low creativity–low intelligence.

HIGH CREATIVITY–HIGH INTELLIGENCE. Girls high in both creativity and intelligence showed the least doubt and hesitation of all the groups, showed the highest level of self-confidence, and displayed the least tendency toward depreciation of oneself and one's work. These girls were sought out by their peers more eagerly than were any other group; and they themselves sought the companionship of others more actively than did any other group. The social relationships of this group were highly reciprocal. Boys and girls "can exercise within themselves both control and freedom, both adultlike and childlike kinds of behavior" (98). This group displays the highest level of achievement; it also may well be brimming over with eagerness about classroom activities and learning, although it may become a disruptive force in the classroom under certain settings.

HIGH CREATIVITY–LOW INTELLIGENCE. The girls of this group seem to be at the greatest disadvantage of all—even more than the group which is low in both creativity and intelligence. They are "the most cautious and hesitant of all the groups, the least confident and least self-assured, and least sought after by their peers and companions, and in addition are quite avoidant themselves of the companionship of others" (92). This group of boys rated highly in relation, or thematic, reasons for grouping things together. It is further described by the investigators as "in angry conflict with themselves and with their school environment, and are beset with feelings of unworthiness and inadequacy" (98).

LOW CREATIVITY–HIGH INTELLIGENCE. As in the case of the high-high group of girls, this group displayed confidence and assurance. An intriguing difference appeared in companionship patterns. The girls were strongly oriented toward achievement and tended not to seek out companions, although they were sought after as companions by others. The boys avoided using thematic or relational bases for grouping. This entire group can best be thought of as committed to school achievement; for them academic failure would be catastrophic, so they continue to strive for academic excellence.

LOW CREATIVITY–LOW INTELLIGENCE. "These girls actually seem to be better off than their high creativity–low intelligence peers. The low–low possesses greater confidence and assurance, is less hesitant and subdued, and is considerably more outgoing toward peers in social relationships than is the high creativity–low intelligence group" (93). The low–low boys seemed to be locked within thematic modes of responding and relatively incapable of inferential-conceptual behavior. "Basically bewildered, these children engage in various defensive maneuvers ranging from useful adaptations such as intensive social activity to regressions such as passivity or psychosomatic symptoms" (98). While the anxiety level was lowest for the high intelligence–low creativity group, it is highest for the low–low group.

In a study of creativity by Nguyen (1970) 110 "High Potential" students were separated into two groups: creatives and noncreatives. A battery of twelve creativity tests, or predictors, was administered to the two groups. The battery consisted of eleven tests for cognitive factors developed or suggested by Guilford, Cattell, and Thurstone, and one test of sensitivity to physiognomic properties based on Wallach and Kogan's work (1965). The idea was to fuse cognitive structure with inner feeling and affective states. The results of the study have been summarized as follows:

1. Creativity is a unified dimension which includes both intellectual and motivational factors linked with personality factors.
2. The creative subjects in this study are distinctly original, thinking, flexible, fluent in ideas, strong in conceptual and abstract learning without losing the sense of perceptual experience. To a lesser extent, they are feeling and more receptive to their culture than the noncreatives.
3. The relationship between creativity and intelligence is high and positive, in contrast to recent findings suggesting a relative independence between creative talent and intelligence (2194-A).

Some Correlates of Creativity
During Adolescence

It appears that various background, motivational, and personality variables interact with situational conditions in producing creative behavior. Encouraging creativity at home and in the classroom is important; but this is not a form of behavior that all teachers are able to turn on and off at will. A number of investigators have completed tests designed to measure creative thinking. Among them are Getzels and Jackson (1962), Torrance (1965), Wallach and Kogan (1965), and Guilford (1967). The Torrance Tests of Creative Thinking (TTCT) provides a measure of creative ability throughout the school period. These tests have furnished us with useful information about the growth of creative ability and the variables and background factors related to it.

SOME BACKGROUND FACTORS. Investigators have repeatedly noted a relationship between creativity among adolescents and the socioeconomic level of the home. Based on results obtained from a biographical inventory, Schaefer and Anastasi (1968) found the familial background of the creative adolescent students was not only academically superior, but the parents tended to provide role models of interest and creative expression in the student's field. College education was more frequent among parents of the creative students, especially mothers. Among creative boys in the arts, both fathers and mothers read more books than those in a control group, and reading was more often listed as the father's favorite leisure-time activity. Also, the fathers had more often won honors or awards in literary or art fields. "The mothers had more often specialized in art or literary subjects in college, had more creative hobbies, more frequently visited art museums or galleries, and were more often listed as the family member who had taught the student most about art" (45).

Based upon biographical information on artistic and literary creativity in adolescent girls, Anastasi and Schaefer (1969) noted: "Typically, the highly creative adolescent girl in this study had manifested an absorbing interest in her field since childhood, and her creative activities had received recognition through exhibitions, publications, prizes, or awards" (271). Thus, her early interest and achievement was continuously reinforced early in life by persons in authority. The creative girls were more likely than the controls to have had a variety of unusual experiences, to daydream about unusual things, to have special and unusual collections, and to have experienced eidetic imagery or had imaginary companions in childhood.

SOME PERSONAL FACTORS. The literature does not furnish us with a complete description of the creative adolescent. The fact is we are most likely to find that personal factors will vary with kinds of creativity, cultural conditions, the nature of the situation or setting, and perhaps sex. There are, however, some significant relationships that have been observed by different investigators. For example, because of their limited experiences many adolescents feel insecure, and this may tend to inhibit creativity during the early adolescent years, as noted by Torrance. On the other hand, adolescents have within recent years been given more freedom by those in authority, and this may account for the increase in creativity that has been observed among many present-day adolescents.

Studies by Torrance and others confirm and expand the relationships between personal factors and creativity during adolescence. Torrance noted that creative persons are more inclined than average to be attracted to unusual vocations, especially those involving risk-taking (1962: 75). He also noted that creative persons seem to have a well-developed sense of humor. Feld (1967) found from a study of creative potential that IQ, age, and personality when combined accounted for approximately 60 percent of the variance in creativity scores; the more outstanding and consistent personality variables between the sexes were acceptance of impulses and fantasy. Both boys and girls seemed to be aware of their own creativity and personality type.

In a study by Dauw (1966) senior boys and girls were administered Torrance's test of creativity. On the basis of scores on the two scales of originality and elaboration, twelve groups of creative thinkers were designated among boys and girls as high and low original thinkers, high and low elaborate thinkers, and students highest and lowest in both abilities. The results from this study show that clear differences appear between high and low creative seniors. Some of the differences noted are summarized by Dauw as follows:

In school and related activities the highly creative students tended to do things over and over until they were satisfied with the results. . . .

High creatives more often appear to set high standards or goals for themselves than they can possibly reach. Yet they do not tend to speak up as much as the low creatives do when someone cuts in line ahead of them.

In playing musical instruments the high creatives more often improvise, bang around, or in any way leave the written score to play the way they wish. While more low creatives tend to have close friends who have almost always been about their own age, the high creatives more often have friends older than they.

Considering grades received in grade and high school, the high creatives tended to receive better marks than low creatives, but the differences do not seem very great in high school. The highly creative students seem to prefer a more competitive or independent work relationship with others, while the whole question seems to make little difference to the low creatives.

The highly creative students—especially the girls—like to attend lectures as often as possible, but there were no important differences between creative levels in attending athletic events, churches, dances, and social parties.

In expressively creative activities, the high creatives more often make up games, build models, compose music, play musical instruments, paint, participate in dramatics, and dabble more in woodworking and tinkering.

Athletically, the low creative students tended to participate more often in most events, especially track, golf, hockey, wrestling, and gymnastics. In only one sport—tennis—did the highly creative boys tend to participate more. . . . (437).

SUMMARY

The early concept of intelligence as fixed and as a unitary trait has given way to the notion that intelligence, as measured by intelligence tests, is quite unstable and consists of a variety of abilities. A number of animal studies have furnished us with valuable information on the neurochemistry of the brain and the effects of early physical states on the growth of the brain.

The most useful data on mental growth has come from longitudinal studies. These have furnished us with individual growth curves for different mental functions. The development of memory ability, vocabulary, and concrete concepts is most rapid during the early years of life. Piaget has set forth in chronological order the development of cognitive mental processes showing that formal operations appear during the adolescent years. He further suggests that for the adolescent *possibility* dominates *reality*.

Among the factors or conditions related to mental growth, undernutrition during infancy stands out as very important. Cultural deprivation frequently present among lower-class children has an adverse effect upon the development of mental abilities. Other variables that influence the growth of intellectual abilities include parent-child interaction, motivation or eagerness to learn, and cultural conditions and practices.

There is a relation between intelligence and school achievement, although motivation plays an important role. High-achieving disadvantaged children are significantly superior to the low-achieving in total school achievement and mental ability. They also have a positive self-concept as well as a positive view of others.

Differences may be observed in any classroom between adolescents who are creative and those less creative. Creativity is further related to the production of novelty, divergent thinking, and a degree of nonconformity.

There is an increasing differentiation of mental abilities with age during the school years, therefore we may note considerable creative ability among some adolescent students. There is an interaction between IQ and creativity as they relate to academic achievement. There is, then, a low but positive relationship between scores on tests for creativity and intelligence test scores. Sex differences have been observed between adolescent boys and girls on the four cognitive groupings: high creativity–high intelligence, high creativity–low intelligence, low creativity–low intelligence, and low creativity–high intelligence.

Creativity appears early in the individual's life and is frequently observed among the parents of creative children and adolescents. High creative subjects set high standards or goals for themselves in the areas of their interest; they are not usually interested in participating in most athletic activities.

REFERENCES

ANASTASI, ANNE and CHARLES E. SCHAEFER. "Biographical Correlates of Artistic and Literary Creativity in Adolescent Girls." *Journal of Applied Psychology* (1969), 53 (4):267–73.

AUSUBEL, D. P. and P. AUSUBEL. "Cognitive Development in Adolescence." *Review of Educational Research* (1966), 36:403–13.

BAYLEY, NANCY. "Consistency and Variability in the Growth of Intelligence from Birth to Eighteen Years." *Journal of Genetic Psychology* (1949), 75: 165–96.

————— and M. H. ODEN. "The Maintenance of Intellectual Ability in Gifted Adults." *Journal of Gerontology* (1955), 10:91–107.

BERRY, J. W. "Temno and Eskimo Perceptual Skills." *Journal of Psychology* (1966), 1:207–29.

BLACK, J. D. *Preliminary Manual to the D-48 Test.* Palo Alto, Calif.: Consulting Psychologists Press, 1963.

BLOOM, BENJAMIN S., ALLISON DAVIS, and ROBERT HESS. *Contemporary Education for Cultural Deviation.* New York: Holt, Rinehart & Winston, 1965. Pp. 12–13.

CAPLAN, S. W. "The Effect of Group Counseling in Junior High School Boys'

Concepts of Themselves in School." *Journal of Counseling Psychology* (1957), 4:124–28.

CHASE, H. PETER and HAROLD P. MARTIN. "Undernutrition and Child Development." *New England Journal of Medicine* (1970), 282:933–39.

CICIRELLI, V. G. "Form of Relationship Between Creativity, IQ, and Academic Achievement." *Journal of Educational Psychology* (1965), 56:303–9.

CRAVIOTO, J. and B. ROBLES. "Evolution of Adaptive and Motor Behavior During Rehabilitation from Kwashiorkor." *American Journal of Orthopsychiatry* (1965), 35:449–64.

CROPLEY, A. J. "Creativity and Intelligence." *British Journal of Educational Psychology* (1966), 36:259.

DAUW, Dean C. "Life Experiences of Original Thinkers and Good Elaborators." *Exceptional Children* (1966), 32:433–40.

EAGLE, N. "The Stability of Lorge-Thorndike IQ Scores Between Grades Three and Four and Grade Eight." *Journal of Educational Research* (1966), 60:164–65.

Educational Testing Service Annual Report 1961–62 (1963). P. 41.

ELKIND, D. "Conceptual Orientation Shifts in Children and Adolescents." *Child Development*, (1966), 37:493–98.

FEIFEL, J. F. and L. LORGE. "Qualitative Differences in the Vocabulary Responses of Children." *Journal of Educational Psychology* (1950), 41:1–18.

FELD, STANLEY. "Creative Potential, IQ, and the Heil-Sheviakov Personality Profiles: An Investigation of the Relationship Between High Creative Potential in Children, and Both IQ and Personality." *Dissertation Abstracts* (1968), 28 (12-A). New York: New York University, 1967.

FERGUSON, G. A. "On Transfer and the Abilities of Man." *Canadian Journal of Psychology* (1956), 10:121–31.

FILELLA, J. F. "Educational and Sex Differences in the Organization of Abilities in Technical and Academic Studies in Colombia, South America." *Genetic Psychology Monographs* (1960), 61:115–63.

FLAVELL, J. H. *The Developmental Psychology of Jean Piaget.* Princeton, N.J.: Van Nostrand, 1963.

GETZELS, J. W. and P. W. JACKSON. "The Highly Creative and Highly Intelligent Adolescent: An Attempt to Differentiate." Paper read at the American Psychological Association Convention, Washington, D.C., September, 1958.

———. *Creativity and Intelligence: Explorations with the Gifted Student.* New York: John Wiley & Sons, Inc., 1962.

GINSBURG, HERBERT and SYLVIA OPPER. *Piaget's Theory of Intellectual Development.* Englewood Cliffs, N.J.: Prentice-Hall, Inc., 1969.

GUILFORD, J. P. "Creativity." *American Psychologist* (1950), 5:444–54.

———. "Three Faces of Intellect." *American Psychologist* (1959), 14:469–79.

———. "Factors that Aid and Hinder Creativity." *Teachers College Record* (1962), 63:380–92.

———. *The Nature of Human Intelligence.* New York: McGraw-Hill Book Company, 1967.

HARLOW, H. F. "Learning Set and Error Factor Theory." In *Psychology: A Study of Science,* Vol. 2., S. Koch, ed. New York: McGraw-Hill Book Company, 1960.

HESS, R. D. and VIRGINIA C. SHIPMAN. "Early Experience and the Socialization of Cognitive Modes in Children." *Child Development* (1965), 36 (4):869–86.

KATES, S. L. and L. W. YUDIN. "Concept Attainment and Memory." *Journal of Educational Psychology* (1964), 55:103–9.

LAYTON, WILBUR L. and EDWARD O. SWANSON. "Relationship of Ninth Grade Differential Aptitude Test Scores to Eleventh Grade Test Scores and High School Rank." *Journal of Educational Psychology* (1958), 49:153–5.

LYNN, DAVID B. "Determinants of Intellectual Growth in Women." *School Review* (1972), 80 (2):241–60.

McCARTHY, DOROTHEA. "Language Development in Children." In *Manual of Child Psychology*, 2nd ed. L. Carmichael, ed. New York: John Wiley & Sons, Inc., 1954.

McCLELLAND, D. C., J. W. ATKINSON, R. A. CLARK, and E. L. LOWELL. "Origins of Achievement Motivation." In *Psychological Studies of Human Development*, 2nd ed., R. G. Kuhlen and G. G. Thompson, eds. New York: Appleton-Century-Crofts, 1963.

MEYER, WILLIAM J. "The Stability of Patterns of Primary Mental Abilities Among Junior High and Senior High School Students." *Educational and Psychological Measurements* (1960), 20:795–800.

MEYER, W. J. and A. W. BENDIG. "A Longitudinal Study of the Primary Mental Abilities Tests." *Journal of Educational Psychology* (1961), 52:50–60.

NGUYEN, G. H. "Reconstruction in Creativity: A Useful Conception of the Creative Person." *Dissertation Abstracts International* (November, 1970), 31 (5):2194-A. University of California, Berkeley, Calif.

PERKINS, C. W. and D. T. SHANNON. "Three Techniques for Obtaining Self-perceptions in Preadolescent Boys." *Journal of Personality and Social Psychology* (1965), 2:443–47.

PIAGET, JEAN. *The Child's Conception of Numbers.* London: Kegan, Paul Trench & Co., 1952. (First published in Switzerland, 1941.)

———. "Intellectual Evolution from Adolescent to Adulthood." *Human Development* (1972), 15 (1):1–12.

ROSENTHAL, R. and L. JACOBSON. *Pygmalion in the Classroom: Teachers' Expectation and Pupils' Intellectual Development.* New York: Holt, Rinehart and Winston, 1968.

ROTHBART, MYRON, SUSAN DALFEN, and ROBERT BARRETT. "Effects of Teacher's Expectancy and Student-Teacher Interaction." *Journal of Educational Psychology* (1971), 62:49–54.

SCHAEFER, CHARLES E. and ANNE ANASTASI. "A Biographical Inventory for Identifying Creativity in Adolescent Boys." *Journal of Applied Psychology* (1968), 52 (1):42–48.

SONTAG, L. W., C. T. BAKER, and V. NELSON. "Mental Growth and Personality Development: A Longitudinal Study." *Monographs of the Society for Research and Child Development* (1958), 23 (2).

SPEARMAN, CARL. *The Abilities of Man: Their Nature and Measurement.* New York: The Macmillan Company, 1927.

STOCK, M. B. and P. M. SMYTHE. "Does Undernutrition During Infancy Inhibit Brain Growth and Subsequent Intellectual Development?" *Archives of Diseases of Childhood* (1963), 38:546.

STONE, C. P. and R. G. BARKER. "Aspects of Personality and Intelligence in Postmenarcheal and Premenarcheal Girls of the Same Chronological Age." *Journal of Comparative Psychology* (1937), 23:439–45.

STROUD, J. B. and P. MAUL. "The Influence of Age upon Learning and Retention of Poetry and Nonsense Syllables." *Journal of Genetic Psychology* (1933), 42:242–50.

TERMAN, L. M. *Genetic Studies of Genius*, Vol. 3. Stanford, Calif.: Stanford University Press, 1930.

———. "Manual" to *The Concept Mastery Test*. New York: Psychological Corporation, 1956.

THURSTONE, L. L. PRIMARY MENTAL ABILITIES. Psychometric Monographs No. 1. Chicago: University of Chicago Press, 1938.

TORRANCE, E. PAUL. *Guiding Creative Talent*. Englewood Cliffs, N.J.: Prentice-Hall, Inc., 1962.

———. *Rewarding Creative Behavior*. Englewood Cliffs, N.J.: Prentice-Hall, Inc., 1965.

VERNON, P. E. *Intelligence and Cultural Environment*. London: Methuen, 1969.

WALLACH, MICHAEL A. and NATHAN KOGAN. *Modes of Thinking in Young Children*. New York: Holt, Rinehart and Winston, Inc., 1965. Chapter 8.

WARD, W. C. "Creativity in Young Children." *Child Development* (1968), 39:737–54.

WECHSLER, D. *The Measurement of Adult Intelligence*. Baltimore: Williams and Wilkins, 1960.

WELSH, G. S. *Preliminary Manual: The Welsh Figure Preference Test*. Palo Alto, Calif.: Consulting Psychologists Press, 1959.

———. "Comparison of D-48, Terman CMT, and Art Scale Scores of Gifted Adolescents." *Journal of Consulting Psychology* (1966), 30:3–88.

WHITEMAN, M. "Intelligence and Learning." *Merrill-Palmer Quarterly* (1964), 10:297–309.

WINTEROSE, HAZEL C. "A Comparison of High Achieving and Low Achieving Fourth Grade Culturally Disadvantaged Pupils." Unpublished thesis. Logan: Utah State University, 1968.

WITKIN, H. A. "A Cognitive-style Approach to Cross-cultural Research." *International Journal of Psychology* (1967), 2:233–50.

WOLF, R. M. "The Identification and Measurement of Environmental Process Variables Related to Intelligence." Unpublished doctoral dissertation. Chicago: University of Chicago, 1964.

WOLMAN, R. N. and E. N. BAKER. "A Developmental Study of Word Definitions." *Journal of Genetic Psychology* (1965), 107:159–66.

YUDIN, LEE W. "Formal Thought of Adolescence as a Function of Intelligence." *Child Development* (1966), 37:697–708.

RECOMMENDED READINGS

CANCRO, ROBERT, ed. *Intelligence: Genetic and Environmental Influences*. New York: Grune and Stratton, 1970.
The book is a product of a conference on intelligence at the University

of Illinois which brought together eminent scholars of intelligence. The three main parts of the book are: theory and measurement, genetic contributions, and environmental contributions.

CARROLL, J. B. *Language and Thought.* Englewood Cliffs, N.J.: Prentice-Hall, Inc., 1964.
Carroll refers to two main categories of language function as follows: (1) as a system of responses by which individuals communicate with each other, and (2) a system of responses that function to facilitate thinking and action. The interrelation of language and thought is stressed.

CLARK, CHARLES M., VELDMAN, DONALD J. and JOSEPH S. THORPE. "Convergent and Divergent Thinking Abilities of Talented Adolescents." *Journal of Educational Psychology* (1965), 56:157–63.
A study of the relationship of convergent and divergent thinking in which the conceptualization of divergent thinking as a dimension of cognitive ability is pointed out.

GALLAGHER, JEANETTE M. "Cognitive Development and Learning in the Adolescent." In *Understanding Adolescence,* 2nd ed., James F. Adams, ed. Boston: Allyn and Bacon, 1973.
Major topics include contrasts in thinking between childhood and adolescence, validity of formal thought, factors in the development of cognition, and conflict in the educational setting.

HORROCKS, JOHN E. *The Psychology of Adolescence.* 3rd ed. Boston: Houghton Mifflin Company, 1969. Chapters 21 and 22.
In Chapter 21, the author presents findings on cognitive development and its nature during adolescence, while Chapter 22 deals with the nature and characteristics of intelligence and mental ability.

McCANDLESS, BOYD R. *Adolescents' Behavior and Development.* Hinsdale, Ill.: The Dryden Press Inc., 1970, Chapter 7.
Intelligence and intellectual growth along with cognitive function are stressed. Their development during adolescence is presented.

PIERS, ELLEN V. "Adolescent Creativity." In *Understanding Adolescence,* 2nd ed., James F. Adams, ed. Boston: Allyn and Bacon, 1973.
The author presents in a clear manner useful and valid materials dealing with the status, nature, and extent of creativity present during the adolescent years.

SEARS, PAULINE. *Intellectual Development.* New York: John Wiley & Sons, Inc., 1971.
A brief historical introduction to the measurement of intelligence; discusses the child's generalized concepts of objects, actions, and relationships in the environment, and shows how language development influences the child's thinking and intellectual development.

6

the self: personal and social development

Physical development during adolescence is profound and rapid, so also are the personal and social changes. These changes take place over a period of years, and therefore the post-adolescent is quite different from the pubescent child. Since there is no clear line of demarcation between adolescents and children, the adolescent at age thirteen or fourteen is more like the child of age eleven or twelve than his older counterpart of age seventeen.

EGO IDENTITY:
SELF-CONCEPT OF ADOLESCENTS

The need to know and accept the self was presented in Chapter 2 as an important adolescent need. One purpose of education should be to help the individual arrive at a more realistic and positive attitude toward the self. An adolescent's concept of self refers to his feelings of self-worth and competency. The *adolescent self* is a continuum, that is rooted in the past; it influences his present and future reactions. Psychoanalysts have emphasized that experiences occurring in early childhood, although buried in the subconscious, are nevertheless very influential. The *self* is an outgrowth of many perceived experiences.

Emergence of the Self-Image

Since adolescents cannot be stereotyped, neither can their self-concepts. Certainly the self-concept of a privileged middle-class adolescent will be very different from that of one who is economically and socially disadvantaged. Also, the self-concepts of adolescents will vary with the educational and cultural backgrounds. Since the United States is actually a culturally pluralistic society, adolescents from diverse backgrounds will have different self-concepts.

The self-image emerges from an interaction of physiological, physical, psychological, and sociological factors in the development of the individual. In a study by Mehita (1968), bright high school students were identified by intelligence test scores; achievers and underachievers were selected on the basis of achievement test scores in the preceding school examination. The two groups—achievers and underachievers—were found to differ significantly on a number of items of a self-concept scale describing positive or negative aspects. Underachievers were characterized by negative self-concepts, and achievers by positive.

A case history presented by Brandt (1957) illustrates the interaction of factors in the development of self-concept.

> . . . Betty Burrows was fourteen years old and in the ninth grade of a junior high school. She was 5 feet 8 inches tall and weighed 137 pounds. She had menstruated at eleven and at fourteen had about completed the growth cycle. Physically she had reached womanhood. Yet her parents treated her as a little girl. According to Betty's report her mother thought she still ought to be playing with dolls. Her father thought it sinful for her to attend movies or dances. In gym classes at school she was encouraged to dance with ninth-grade boys who were several inches shorter than she. Boys and girls whose interests and development were equivalent to hers had long since left junior high school. Her mental capabilities were superior but her school grades were mediocre. She expressed little interest in schoolwork. She was forced to drop art, the only course in which she seemed interested. Deriving no satisfaction from a highly restrictive environment which was completely out of step with her development level, Betty resorted to "nonacceptable" ways of gaining attention and enhancing herself. She seemed to take delight in shocking people. One day she reportedly drank a Coke after taking aspirin because she heard this would make her drunk. Either she actually became drunk or she put on a good enough act to convince people of it. She upset the school nurse another day by volunteering to bring a marijuana plant to class for the project on narcotics.
>
> An early maturer caught in a web of home and school pressures geared only to chronological age, Betty formed pictures of herself and the world about her that were anything but conducive to sound development. The following statements, which she made to a guidance counselor near the end of the year, illustrate some of the worries and concerns that made

up her developing self-organization: "I am taller than you but I don't believe I look any taller. I quit letting them measure me when I got to be 5 feet 8 so I don't know exactly how tall I am and I don't want to. . . . They think I am nuts around here but honestly sometimes I think I will go crazy cooped up with all those little kids all day. Sometimes I run every step of the way home at noon and every step of the way back because I think I will pop if I don't."

Fortunately, the school counselor understood Betty's predicament and began accepting her as the mature young woman she actually was. Adjustments were made in Betty's high school program the next year with the result that she eventually became a popular, successful student. Fear of being peculiar and concern over her growth were alleviated as she received acceptance and understanding from the counselor. In other words, the change in her self-concept brought about an adjustment.

INFLUENCES OF LOW AND HIGH SELF-CONCEPT. There is both empirical and scientific evidence that self-concept has an important bearing on behavior. It seems likely that behavior resulting from a low self-concept is more varied than that resulting from a favorable self-concept. A low self-concept during adolescence leads to self-depreciation, and this in turn leads to withdrawal or aggression.

Studies of individual conformity support the hypothesis that persons with low self-esteem conform more to social pressures than persons with high self-esteem (Crutchfield, 1955; Tuddenham, 1959). In studies of attitude change under group pressure, the usual procedure is to measure opinion before and after exposure to the group experience. This procedure is based upon the assumption that all the individuals studied had the same background of experience and success. League and Jackson (1964) made a preliminary investigation of the prior judgments of a group of college students before group exposure. The low self-esteem subjects made more incorrect judgments on the preliminary test than the high self-esteem subjects. Viewed from the perspective that they have frequently found themselves wrong, it is not surprising that the low self-esteem subjects relied on the judgments of others more heavily than their own in conformity situations.

AGE-RELATED PATTERNS. According to Phillips (1963) there is a progressive and age-related pattern in the development of the self. This is a factor in the accuracy and dimension of self-perception. Older children seem to furnish more accurate information in some types of studies. In the study by Phillips classes of third- and fourth-grade pupils were tested with a modification of Amatora's Children's Personality Scale to secure self-ratings. Teacher ratings and peer ratings were also obtained. The findings indicated that sixth-grade estimates were in closer agreement with those of teachers and peers than third-grade estimates. This study further suggested that older, disadvantaged children with accurate self-perceptions feel that high aspirations are futile. Other studies show that as culturally disadvantaged boys and girls progress through school both their IQ and academic achievement deteriorate.

The self-concept of the culturally disadvantaged child has been shown to deteriorate as he gets older. This is most important, for one's hopes, fears, defenses, and self-esteem are bound up with one's self-concept. It is at the third- and fourth-grade levels that the self-concept appears to take a precipitous drop; it is also at these levels when many culturally disadvantaged children begin to have really serious learning problems at school. Morse (1964) analyzed the responses of more than 600 pupils (in alternate grades from three through eleven) to a self-esteem inventory. The pupils had a high self-regard at the third grade but showed a significant decrease in subsequent grades, so that at the eleventh grade 44 percent of them wished they were someone else. This study suggests that the longer culturally disadvantaged children and adolescents remain in school, the less positive their self-concept.

SEX DIFFERENCES. There are noticeable sex differences in the sources of self-concept and self-esteem. Lynn (1969) suggests that cultural stereotypes determine male sex-role identification. Thus, the first step for the adolescent male is to recognize the cultural stereotype of the masculine role, while the next step is to conform to it. The results of a study by Connell and Johnson (1970) with eighth-grade males and one by Hollender (1972) with undergraduates support the conclusion that the maintenance of high self-esteem in males is contingent upon success in meeting cultural standards of masculine achievement.

The results of the study by Hollender with college students indicate clearly that the maintenance of self-esteem in girls is quite different from that in boys. A girl who indicates in her social position and status a high score on social self-esteem obtains a low score on need for approval, and does not necessarily exert herself to obtain high grades at school. Hollender states: "It may be that both social skills and adolescent self-esteem are dependent on earlier acceptance by parents of the female child for the person she is, an intrinsic valuation, as opposed to the more extrinsic valuation of the male" (1972: 346). This would account for the greater competitive nature of adolescent boys both in and out of school.

THE IDEAL SELF. The ideal self is shown in both aspirations and identifications. The concept in either case has been found useful in studying the development of character and personality. To the Freudians the origin of the ego-ideal is a result of identification with individuals that the child loves, admires, or fears. It is a process of identification through which the child takes on the attributes of such persons. The social psychologists, on the other hand, regard the ideal self as a term for the roles or aspirations that continuously affect the individual's life. A study by Havighurst and others (1946-47) dealt with the development of the ideal self during childhood and adolescence. Boys and girls from eight to eighteen years were asked to write an essay on the person whom they would like most of all to be like when they grew up. This did not have to be a real person, but they were asked to describe the character, appearance, and activities of such a person. The responses of both boys and girls fell mainly into four categories: parents, glamorous adults, attractive and familiar young adults, and composite imaginary characters. Parent substitutes, such as teachers and older adults, were less frequently named. An age sequence was noted, the trend being for the individual to move outward from the family to members of his group or to older peers. This may be noted in the manner of dress, which must now conform to that of peers or older peers.

Interest in Personal Appearance

The self-concept of adolescents is closely related to the physical self; therefore with growth into adolescence both boys and girls become enormously concerned over their appearance. The teen-age girl, especially, spends a great deal of time in front of the mirror experimenting with new hairdos and clothes. Clothes become a symbol for the self; shop windows, fashion shows, and department stores take on new significance. Once uninterested in his personal appearance, except when his parents or friends brought it to his attention, the adolescent boy can now be seen combing his hair, washing his neck, trimming his nails.

Influences on the Self-Concept

As early as 1934, George H. Mead described the self-concept as emerging directly from the behavior of others toward the individual and indirectly from physical and mental attributes of the individual himself. A study by Smith and Lebe (1956) has an important bearing on this problem. Forty-two boys, aged twelve to fifteen were used in studying the relative effects of physiological development and experience on their concepts of heterosexual development and emancipation. Physiological growth status was obtained from ratings of pubic hair development, whereas chronological age provided a measure of the quantity of experiences along with the years of maturity. The following findings and conclusions appeared from comparisons made:

1. Prepubescent and postpubescent boys differed significantly in certain projective aspects of the human figure drawing. "Adequate sex-role identification was assumed from the fact that all subjects drew the male figure first. Postpubescent as compared with prepubescent males appeared to project their stronger feelings of sexual virility or masculinity into the males they drew by their excessive attention to hair. Prepubescent as compared with postpubescent males appeared to express their need for proving masculinity and achieving the body-image by their excessive use of masculine objects such as cigars, pipes, cigarettes, scars, masks, and adam's apples (73).

2. The findings presented in Table 6-1 indicate that measures of

TABLE 6-1 Correlations between Pubescent Maturity Ratings of
Boys and Chronological Age with Self-Concepts of Heterosexual
Development and Emancipation Status

MATURITY MEASURE	SELF-CONCEPT OF HETEROSEXUAL DEVELOPMENT	SELF-CONCEPT OF EMANCIPATION STATUS
Pubic hair maturity ratings	.17	.27
Chronological age	.37	.40

Source: Smith and Lelu (1956).

self-attitudes in the area of heterosexual development are more dependent on chronological age and experience than on sexual maturation.

3. The findings also indicate that adolescent emancipation from
parental ties and concept of independence from parents are more closely
related to age and experience than to physiological maturity.

Mussen and Jones (1957) disclosed that in the group they studied
early-maturing boys are more self-confident than late-maturing boys. They
found that late-maturing boys were likely to have stronger feelings of
inadequacy, feelings of being rejected and dominated, more dependency
needs, and a negative attitude toward parents. Only a few of the early-
maturing boys had these same feelings. Most of the latter appeared
self-confident, independent, and capable of playing adult roles in interpersonal relationships. Perhaps these attitudes resulted to some extent from
the actions of classmates. The early maturer got a more favorable rating
from his classmates than did the late maturer.

A study of three junior-high curriculum organizations by Shannon
(1960) indicates that there is a relationship between the child's class
schedule and his self-concept. The three organizations studied were the
departmental structure, the self-contained classroom design, and the
block-departmental pattern. Shannon found that in the situations he
investigated, the self-contained classroom appears to develop more self-
acceptant attitudes than the others. In this respect the departmental
design appeared to be less successful than the other two.

A direct but unclear relation appears to exist between academic
achievement and self-concept. Shaw and others (1960) indicate that male
achievers feel more positive about themselves than male underachievers.
They point out, however, that female underachievers are ambivalent in
their feelings about themselves. This is perhaps related to the fact that
the female's role is not so clearly defined in terms of academic success
as is the male's.

For many years culturally disadvantaged adolescents have accepted
a given status in society which was important to their own self-image.
Acceptance of this status tends to lower their aspirational level and self-
image. This lowered self-concept not only affects how adolescents learn
but also how they behave. Many Negro boys in their attempt to maintain

their self-image emphasize physical prowess and rebellion, while renouncing artistic, abstract, and intellectual activities. In view of the poor academic concept of many Negro boys, it is not strange that there are usually more Negro girls on the honor rolls than boys (Vontress, 1966: 217).

IDENTIFICATION WITH OTHERS

One frequently hears expressions such as, "She is the exact image of her mother in almost everyway," or "He has his father's good disposition or happy smile." To many people this means that these behavioral characteristics are inherited; however, educators and psychologists tend to ascribe these characteristics to identification, which means they are learned. Some of the consequences of identification with others, especially parents, are: (1) acquisition of sex roles, (2) acquisition of childhood and adult roles, (3) development of a balanced dependent-independent relationship, and (4) acquisition of behavioral standards. The evidence for the first two sets of consequences is greater than for the last two, although studies of identification reveal that parents, teachers, and other adult authority figures are important to the adolescent's personal and social development.

Identity Formation

The term identification originated with Freud, who described it as the process whereby a person molds his own ego after someone he has adopted as a model. Bronfenbrenner (1960) reviewed Freud's use of the term and drew together many references to the concept. According to Bronfenbrenner, Freud distinguished three parental aspects on which the child may pattern himself: overt behavior, motives, and aspirations for the child. Erikson (1956) perceives identity formation as evolving throughout childhood and adolescence through synthesis and resynthesis of the sense of self into a configuration that gradually integrates constitutional factors, special libidinal needs, favored capacities, significant identifications, effective defenses and sublimations, and various roles. This configuration results from simultaneous reflection and observation by which the individual judges himself according to his perception of how others judge him; while he regards their way of judging him according to how he perceives himself in comparison to them and to types that have become relevant to them (Erikson, 1968).

At each step in development, the child must derive a vitalizing sense of reality from the awareness that his way of mastering experience is a successful variant of the way other people around him master experience and recognize this mastery. According to Macintyre (1970), "Erikson's identity concept is focused on the fusion of the elements of identification, capacity, ideals, and opportunity into a viable self-definition. The assembly of all these elements is a formidable task for an adolescent. If this task is not accomplished, he faces the danger of identity confusion—the failure to establish a sense of self-worth. At adolescence, development involves processes of identifying with persons significant to one's life and with ideological forces" (214).

Parents usually think of their children as growing persons who will some day assume the responsibilities of adults, although they frequently fail to realize that their children are actually growing up. The children are reminded of this as parents urge them to do certain things in preparation for adulthood. As a result of the admonitions of parents and other members of the family, children and adolescents gain a sense of continuity—something the foster child fails to sense when he is shifted from home to home or reared without the close family ties experienced by most children.

Over two decades ago Stokes (1950) described the following factors that influence identification:

1. The biological fact of sex and its predisposition of the individual to certain types of behavior.
2. The social pressure placed upon the child to identify with his own sex.
3. The degree of affection given to the child by the person with whom he is supposed to identify.
4. The extent to which the child's needs are supplied by the particular person or model.
5. The degree of acquaintance that the identifier has with the model.
6. The clarity of the role of the person with whom the individual attempts to identify.
7. The attitude of influential people toward this person.
8. The capacity of the child to be like the person with whom he attempts to identify.
9. The temperament of the child in relation to the person with whom he identifies.
10. The existence in the child of strong needs that harmonize or conflict with the patterns furnished by the model.

While identity formation begins long before the adolescent years, the adolescent must achieve a complicated task of synthesis. A study by Maas and Engler (1959) furnished abundant evidence that children who move through a series of families or are reared without close and continuing ties to a responsible adult have increased difficulty in discovering who they are. Macintyre (1970) points out: "Such children tend to develop only shallow roots in relationships with others; they try to please others, but cannot trust them, or they strike out against others before they can be let down. For these children the environment has not been consistent enough to allow them to construct a coherent picture of positive relationships. Their ability to trust others is impaired to the point of hampering the development of their own trustworthiness" (215). The results of this study are borne out by a follow-up study by Meier (1962) of adults who were foster children. It was noted that the removal of children from their own homes has a negative effect on their ability to form an adequate sense of identity, especially in the case of boys. The results of the study by Meier suggest that when a boy spends a major part of his childhood away from his own family, his self-image is likely to be damaged to the degree that it will be difficult for him when he reaches adulthood to maintain a successful marriage or succeed in a job. The young women in Meir's study seem to fare better, their relative success being based on their ability to function as wives and mothers. However, most of them gave no evidence of a feeling of "inner assuredness," which Erickson regards as indicative of an optimal sense of identity. They furthermore demonstrated a lesser sense of satisfaction with their own achievements than would be expected.

Influence of Cross-Age Peers

A review of aspects of adolescent behavior and development reported in the current literature suggests several ways in which younger and older peers influence personal and social development. It is not sufficient for adolescents to learn to work, play, and share with their age group alone, neither is it desirable from the standpoint of satisfying all their basic needs. A study by Lohman (1969) was undertaken to determine and illuminate some of the roles which younger and older peers play in the personal and social development of the individual. The two central problems with which Lohman was concerned included an examination of the individual's psychological orientation toward being older and younger than his peers, and a study of cross-age friendship patterns and activities. An attempt was also made to explore the effects of age, sex, and socioeconomic status on the different areas. Some of the variables examined in the study were self-esteem, sociability and influence status, and utilization of academic ability.

The subjects of the study consisted of 1,313 students from the fourth, sixth, eighth, tenth, and twelfth grades drawn from forty-three classrooms in six different school systems. The classrooms were located in central city, suburban, and rural neighborhoods in the Midwest. The students were from intact families representing a wide variety of socioeconomic levels. The major results of this study may be summarized as follows:

1. Females have more older than younger friends. Males show equal preference, although males rather than females had more younger friends.

2. The degree of intimacy of cross-age friendships is strongly correlated with age, although respondents are most intimate with friends of the same sex.

3. High school youths with older friends report more positive attitudes toward them and toward being helped by them than do those with no older friends; however, elementary school pupils with older friends report less favorable attitudes toward them and being helped by them than do those who have no older friends.

4. Males with younger friends report more positive attitudes toward them and toward helping them than do males without younger friends. In contrast, females with younger friends report less positive attitudes toward younger peers and toward helping them than do females with no younger friends.

5. Being older is valued for its freedom, its opportunities for self-actualization, and the different social roles which may be attained. The younger years are valued for their lack of responsibility, low pressure, fun, and are fantasized as opportunities to start over or remedy mistakes.

Qualities of kindness, mutual help, understanding, and social responsibility are learned through active participation with others—social interaction. This is a matter of social rather than biological transmission. Thus, we conclude with Brofenbrenner (1971: 46): "If children have contact only with their own age-mates, there is no possibility for learning culturally established patterns of cooperation and mutual concern."

THE DEVELOPMENT
OF EMOTIONAL BEHAVIOR

Important changes in emotional behavior take place with increased maturity and wider experiences. Also, the pronounced physiological changes that occur with pubescence have an important bearing on emotional behavior during this period.

Emotions and Behavior

The changed concepts of the nature of the child and adolescent have brought with them different methods and objectives in schools and socializing agencies. There has been a shift from consideration of the intellectual, moral, or social side of the child to that of development of the total personality. An increased understanding of the development and significance of the emotions in the growing personality is of utmost importance to those concerned with guidance. Many people tend to regard the emotions as a stereotyped pattern of expression appearing with certain forms of stimulation. However, the tendency is to recognize that emotional components are in some form and to some degree present in all behavior.

Emotional development must not be considered without reference to physical development. The case of Jo, reported by Zachry in a study of adolescents, illustrates how impossible it is to isolate certain elements as "physical" and others as "emotional." Presented here, the case shows the necessity of considering all the factors that enter into the nature of an individual at any particular stage of life (1940: 69-70).

> Jo's sister was soon to be married and his brother had just started to work, but Jo, twelve years old and the youngest child, was not particularly interesting to any member of the family. He had not been doing well in his school work, especially in arithmetic. One morning at breakfast he ate heartily; he had oatmeal with cream, eggs, bacon, jam, and milk. At the thought of an arithmetic test he was to take that morning, he felt a queer, twitchy feeling of excitement in his stomach. He walked slowly to school, thinking more about the test. His stomach felt strange. He had a vague feeling, hardly a thought, that if he were sick, he would not have to go to school. The arithmetic test came to mind again, and he suddenly found it hard to keep breakfast down.
>
> Shortly after his arrival at school, he was sick. He was sent home with a clear conscience to have a day in bed. The principal telephoned his mother, who immediately became concerned. She put Jo to bed in the guest room and lavished him with attention such as he had not experienced since he was a small boy. His sister showed him her wedding presents; before going out in the evening, his brother had a talk with him, an event that had not occurred for months; and his father spent the evening reading to him.
>
> The upset stomach had a high value: no arithmetic test, and solicitude from all the people from whom he had been wishing attention for some time. The next time Jo was faced with a difficult situation and there was a queer feeling in his stomach, there was no hesitation. He was immediately sick.

DEVELOPMENT OF THE EMOTIONS. According to Bridges (1932) the emotional reactions of the infant are not highly differentiated, but the most common response to emotional stimuli is that of general bodily agitation or excitement. Out of this general excitation develop, during the first several months, the differential responses of distress and delight. Here we note the negative and positive forms of emotional responses that have commonly been recognized and given varied classifications. Anger, disgust, fear, and jealousy emerge at an early age from distress; elation, affection for others, and joy grow out of delight. The different ages for the appearance of different forms of behavior during emotional episodes show that crying, screaming, restlessness, and struggling appear during the first four months of life and may be regarded as general bodily agitation caused by some sort of overstimulation. Following infancy the child passes through a period of growth, coordinating and integrating each new stage with that which has gone before. Emotional development is not great, due to the slow rate of growth of the internal organs of the body controlled by the autonomic nervous system, and thus closely identified with the emotional life.

Most of our fears or angers are acquired ways of responding to various situations. Most of our other emotional patterns are the results of learning and maturation—few of the stimuli that cause fear or anger among adults will frighten an infant. Since emotions are learned, the child or adolescent should be guided in the development of desirable emotional patterns, thus enabling one to avoid the inefficiency, embarrassment, and annoyance that uncontrolled emotions produce.

The word *emotion* was derived from the Latin word *emovere*, "to move out." It is usually defined as a stirred-up state or condition, but should not be regarded as a name for a type of response that is entirely different from nonemotional behavior. Behavior is a continuous, complex process involving simultaneous activity in many parts of the body. Emotion, instinct, and habit do not designate distinctly different types of behavior; they are merely abstractions which are necessary for convenience of study. Emotional behavior is an *emotion* in pure form only within a textbook. The same is true of a conditioned reflex, or a *habit*. However, emotional elements intensify, inhibit, and otherwise modify the behavior in process at any given time and are integral parts of the whole pattern of behavior; they comprise what is sometimes called one's *emotional tone*.

Earlier, James, Lange, Cannon, and others were concerned with the physiological center of emotional responses. Today psychologists recognize that the visceral responses are important components of the emotions. Although the term was recognized by earlier students, Lindsey (1951) clearly defined and described emotional responses by *activation*. Strong emotion represents one end of a continuum of activities, and sleep represents the other, at which time there is a minimum of activation.

INTERNALIZED AND EXTERNALIZED EMOTIONAL RESPONSES. A careful study of early childhood emotions shows that activation is both external and internal; however, important changes in the proportion of internal and external activation appear with growth. One of the most important problems of the dynamics of emotions is determining just this proportion. The galvanic skin response (GSR) is sometimes used as a measure of internalized emotional responses, and observed overt behavior is used for estimating externalized emotional responses. Jones (1950) reports that children who are most overtly excitable are least reactive on the galvanic test. It is thus suggested that the increase of apparent emotional control with age may indicate a shift from externalized to internalized patterns of responses. This results in a large measure from the suppression of overt emotional behavior, since it tends to bring social disapproval and punishment.

In the Adolescent Growth Study at the University of California a series of observations on a group of children was made from age twelve to age eighteen (Jones, 1939). These records included ratings of personal expressiveness and of various social traits. A series of experiments were conducted in which polygraphic records of palm-to-forearm skin-resistance changes, pulse rates, and respiration changes in a mild stress situation of a free association test were secured. A comparison of the overt behavioral characteristics of forty cases, evenly divided at each extreme (high reaction and low reaction) in the average magnitude of GSR, furnished data showing the close relationship of the emotional responses to overt behavior. The first and most striking fact noted was that the high-reactive group showed significantly less overt emotional behavior than the low-reactive group. They were less talkative, less animated, displayed less attention-seeking behavior, and were less assertive in their social behavior. From 85 to 95 percent of the high reactives excelled the average of the low reactives as more calm, more cooperative, more deliberate, more good natured, and more responsible.

Emotional Manifestations During Adolescence

A significant change in the orientation of the individual to his environment occurs at puberty. This change is clearly revealed in the interests that appear at this time. The overt manifestations of emotions become less intense; the reactions of the child to thrills and dangers in the movies become more subdued. Children and preadolescents tend to react violently to thrills and dangers in movies or on television, whereas they are relatively unresponsive to love-making scenes. Four or five years later, with the ripening of the sex impulse, the story will likely be very different.

Fear of animals and other tangible things in the immediate environment appears to decrease as the child develops from age five to age twelve; fear of the dark, of being left alone at night, and the unknown increases. With growth into adolescence, social fears become important, along with anxieties about school achievement and acceptance by peers. In an intensive study of the self-expressed fears and worries of eleven school children aged nine through eighteen, Angelino, Dollins, and Mech (1956) noted a constant increase in fears and worries by girls in activities involving social relations; this increase was less pronounced among boys. In both boys and girls there was an increase in fears after age fifteen, especially in the economic and political areas. The investigators further noted that boys of lower socioeconomic status were more concerned with matters of violence, such as robbery, guns, knives, and whippings; these boys were also more afraid of their parents—especially of being punished. Lower-class girls expressed fears of strangers, drunks, and acts of violence.

Worries are imaginary forms of fear because they are caused by imaginary rather than real stimuli. Worries about school problems are common during the entire adolescent period, and appear to be of greater concern to boys than to girls. Sex and socioeconomic variables have an influence on worries. The girl's greater dependence would naturally lead to a greater concern about social acceptance by peers. The lower-class boy's concern about the lack of money or the economic state of the family is surely more intense than the middle-class boy's concern over whether or not he will be able to use one of the family cars for a date over the weekend.

Anger is a more frequent emotional childhood response than fear; however important changes in the frequency of anger responses and the stimuli or situations that provoke anger appear with age. Impulsive responses appear early and occur in varying degrees of intensity. In older children and preadolescents they appear mostly among those whose parents are inconsistent in their child-training methods, who are emotionally immature, and who fail to give their children either the motive to control their impulsive responses or a good model to follow. The attitudes and behavior patterns of the social group with which the adolescent is identified have a strong influence upon his expression of anger. Among lower-class adolescent boys, toughness and aggression may be rewarded. When boys (and sometimes girls) from such groups learn to suppress their impulsive responses, they may displace their anger by teasing, bullying, torturing animals, rebelling, stealing, lying, or vandalizing.

SOCIAL–SEXUAL DEVELOPMENT

As a full-fledged drive, sex does not mature until puberty. The manner in which a preadolescent reacts to a sex situation or problem will depend largely upon the attitudes toward sex formed during his earlier years. There will be important differences in the social-sexual pattern for different groups and for different members of the same group. For example, boys with several sisters are likely to regard sex somewhat differently from those without sisters. Likewise, girls with several brothers are likely to experience a social-sexual development different from those without brothers. Thus, we may note that social-sex development is influenced by a large number of factors within the home and community.

Social-Sexual Behavior of Preadolescents

A review of research on the social-sexual behavior of preadolescents shows the emergence of new norms in cross-sexual relationships among boys and girls in the ten- to twelve-year age range. The old pattern of avoidance is still present among some groups, but the emerging new pattern has changed the traditional concept of a natural antagonism of boys toward girls during the early teen years. The change is borne out in the results of a 1958 study by Broderick and Fowler (1961) in a Southeastern urban community among fifth to seventh graders, upper-lower to upper-middle in social class status. Table 6-2 shows the percentage of children who chose at least one of four friends across sex lines. Comparing these data with those obtained from preadolescents in

You know, I don't hate girls like Nancy any more.

the twenties and thirties, one finds a remarkable thawing of the antagonisms of boys and girls toward each other.

There has also been an increase in romantic interest among preadolescents. Romance has perhaps always been an element for some preadolescents, although in the past, a twelve-year-old girl was very reluctant to admit that a certain boy was attractive to her and a twelve- or thirteen-year-old boy preferred to pretend that girls were obnoxious to him even

TABLE 6-2 Frequency of Choosing at Least One Friend of the Opposite Sex, by Grade*

	PERCENT			
GRADE	One or more cross-sexual choices	No cross-sexual choices	Total	Total number
5	51.9	48.1	100.0	108
6	41.8	58.2	100.0	79
7	37.7	62.3	100.0	77
Total	44.7	55.3	100.0	264

* Each child had up to four choices. The units in this table are children.
Source: Broderick and Fowler (1961).

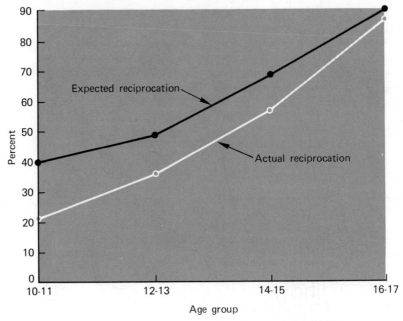

FIGURE 6-1 Expected and actual reciprocation. After Broderick (1963).

if he did have a covert interest in a particular girl. In the study by Broderick and Fowler, the great majority of children in each of the grades studied (fifth, sixth, and seventh) claimed to have a sweetheart. The percentage of children claiming to have a sweetheart did not change appreciably from grade to grade, but Broderick offers evidence, shown in Figure 6-1, from a later study conducted in four Pennsylvania communities that the nature of the relationship changed: the relationship between expected and actual reciprocation became closer with advancement in age (Broderick, 1963).

In both studies, experience with kissing was found to be fairly common, varying to some degree with social class and the area in which the study was conducted. One of the most convincing evidences of growth in preadolescent interest in the opposite sex was the choice of friends for three activities: walking, eating, and attending movies. The preadolescents were asked to rank the desirability of a companion of the same sex, a companion of the opposite sex, or of no companion at all in the three activities. The results are presented in Table 6-3. The majority of sixth and seventh graders felt that when walking or going to the movies a companion of the opposite sex was to be preferred to no companion or a companion of the same sex. Both sexes were more conservative when choosing an eating companion, although almost half the seventh graders preferred an eating companion of the opposite sex.

TABLE 6-3 Preference for Opposite Sex Companion
in Three Situations, by Grade and Sex

| SITUATION | GRADE | PERCENT Prefer opposite sex companion | |
		Boys	Girls
Eating	5th	35.0	30.9
	6th	34.9	31.4
	7th	46.2	47.4
Walking	5th	49.0	50.9
	6th	69.8	51.4
	7th	71.8	68.4
Movie	5th	58.5	45.5
	6th	68.2	51.4
	7th	74.3	65.7

Source: Broderick (1963).

Several factors may explain the lessened antagonism toward the opposite sex on the part of present-day preadolescents. The overlapping
and flexibility now present in sex roles makes it easier for boys and girls
to plan, work, and play together. The increased amount of social events
at school, church, and other community institutions has enabled boys
and girls to gain a better understanding of each other and has resulted
in many common interests.

Also, an increased equality in performance at school and in social
status makes it no longer necessary for the boy to attempt to prove his
superiority, so that there is no need to be hostile toward the opposite sex.
In our middle-class culture, both are working toward similar goals.

Theories of Psychosexual Development

Some theories of psychosexual development emphasize experiential factors but not physiological changes; others stress hormonal changes in the
development of normal sex behavior and exclude social forces and conditions. One source of misunderstanding about the relationship between
physiological and psychological sexual development in humans is the
studies of lower animals that show a close relationship. The mating of
rats, for example, can be eliminated by removal of the sex glands. The
castrated rat will not display an interest in a female in heat, while the
female without ovaries fails to come into heat and does not respond to
the advances of the male. The mating behavior of the castrated rat can
be readily revived by injecting the appropriate hormone and can be
continued as long as the injections are maintained, ceasing again when
they are discontinued. In these animals, learning seems to play a very

minor role in the emergence of mating behavior at maturity. Male rats reared in isolation, with no opportunity for learning, copulate expertly in their first encounter with a female in heat.

The male and female sex hormones are specific in maintaining the genitalia in erotically functioning states, but neither the direction nor the content of erotic inclinations in humans is controlled by them. Insofar as *hormonal* influence is concerned, the sex drive is neither male nor female; rather it is an undifferentiated urge for the warmth and sensation of close bodily contact and genital proximity. The sex hormones are physiologically specific but psychologically rather unspecific.

Development of Social-Sexual Roles

It seems much earier for girls to acquire their social-sexual roles than for boys. This may be accounted for by the fact that girls get a head start on boys during infancy and early childhood, and have the same-sex adult model available during this most important learning period. On the other hand, the boy frequently sees much more of the opposite-sex adult model than of the same-sex adult model. This understandably creates problems and frustrations for the boy. The greater amount of time spent by the daughter in direct face-to-face interactions with her mother, in comparison to that spent by the son with the father, makes the learning of specific behavior attributes of the same-sex parental model much easier for the daughter. Lynn (1959) extended this idea by hypothesizing that the daughter tends to identify with the specific attributes of the mother whereas the son, in the relative absence of a specific paternal model, tends to model his behavior after broad cultural stereotypes of masculinity. Investigations of parent-child similarity support the contention that mother-daughter similarity excedes that of father-son similarity (Sopchak, 1952; Heilbrun, 1962). A further implication of the studies of parental identification is that maladjusted college males are significantly less father identified than well-adjusted college males; maladjusted females were more closely identified with their mothers than were the well adjusted, although the differences for the colleges females were not considered reliable.

Influences Affecting Social-Sexual Development

Although sexual development per se is a physiological phenomenon, we note wide variations in sex-role behavior between different cultures and significant differences within a particular culture. Any appraisal of influences on social sexual development should follow a life-history approach. In a study by Minuchin (1965) a comparison was made of the sex-role concepts of fourth-grade children from homes and schools that stressed socialization and from homes that also stressed the individual development of the child. Differences were found primarily for girls; girls from home backgrounds that stressed individual development showed more open attitudes about sex roles. On the other hand, girls from environments stressing socialization were more committed to their own sex role and to sex-typed play.

In an earlier study by Goodenough (1957) the hypothesis was presented that fathers influence their children's identification more than do mothers because of their differential reinforcements and expectations of sex-typed behavior. According to Goodenough's study, the father seems to display more concern that the children play their appropriate sex role during early childhood as well as during adolescence. The results of this study are supported by Heilbrun and Fromme (1965), who studied the content of sex-role differentiated behavior. Heilbrun noted that fathers are more proficient than mothers in differentiating sex roles. He states: ". . . fathers are more capable of responding expressively than mothers are of acting instrumentally . . ." and that "fathers systematically vary their sex role as they relate to male and female offspring" (796).

A girl usually seems to develop a feminine self-concept early in life, along with her sex-role preference and overt behavior related to her view of her self. In most cases definite sex-role expectations are expressed by her parents and other adults and are continuously reinforced through subsequent interpersonal relationships. Successive age levels may bring new expectations and demands relating to her sex role, and a girl's perception of her sex role at any given age may help to determine the extent of her particular sex-appropriate and sex-inappropriate behavior patterns.

ORDINAL POSITION AND SEX ROLE. There is some evidence that such factors as ordinal position, sex composition of the siblings of the family, and perhaps size of the family will affect the development of sex roles. In larger families, sex roles of siblings are likely to be more clearly defined than in the smaller families. Sutton-Smith and Rosenberg (1965), in their study of the effects of ordinal position on sex-role identification, noted that the development of sex roles is significantly influenced by the presence of siblings of the same sex. Boys with brothers had higher masculinity scores at all the ages studied (six, ten, and college) than did boys with sisters; girls with sisters had higher scores on femininity. The presence of a sibling of the opposite sex did not produce consistent differences in the masculinity-femininity scores for either boys or girls.

Sex-Role Identification and Self-Esteem

White males and females with a mean age of 13.5 years were used as subjects in a study by Connell and Johnson (1970) to test the hypothesis that adolescents with high sex-role identification have more positive feelings of self-esteem than those with low sex-role identification. Groups of high and low sex-role identification were obtained from scores on the Gough Fe Scale. The Cooper Self-Esteem Inventory was used to obtain self-esteem scores. This Inventory provides a measure of general feelings of self-esteem, as well as measures of self-esteem in social interactions with peers, in home life and interactions with parents, and in academic performance.

The findings of this study indicate that high sex-role identified male adolescents have greater feelings of self-esteem than low sex-role male adolescents. This was not true for girls in that low sex-role identified females apparently feel as adequate or worthwhile as high sex-role identified females. This finding can best be understood when we consider the differential value with which the male and female stereotype is usually perceived. The male adult role is viewed in our society as being more powerful and more competent than the female role; it is achievement oriented. The female role is in general conformity oriented with special emphasis given to the security need. Thus, adoption of a male role by the female during the adolescent years may imply the adoption of behavior patterns that have greater reward value. The female adolescent may face a dilemma. On the one hand she is faced with the social stereotype of the female as a passive, dependent, and somewhat inadequate person, while on the other hand she is faced with the achievement, power, and competence associated with the masculine stereotype.

SOCIAL DEVELOPMENT

Social development cannot be considered apart from other aspects of development. Its close relationship with emotional development, physiological changes, intellectual activities, and self-concept may be observed in any adolescent group of boys and girls. Important and significant changes in social behavior occur during the adolescent years, and are usually more pronounced during the early period of adolescence than during the latter years, when a more definite pattern of behavior exists and a more consistent and stable philosophy of life is being realized.

The Importance of Social Interaction

An important developmental task of adolescents is learning to live with their age-mates. They use different methods to obtain approval from and establish good relations with their peers. Adolescent group activities have been found most important to the development of social patterns of behavior. To be successful, they must either have a simple, direct action purpose or have a variety of social experiences in learning to understand each other, both of which will call for social interaction, the only means of learning to understand and get along with others.

Children are directed into their sex roles at a very early age and become conscious of sex differences before they enter school; however, their attitudes toward members of the opposite sex will be closely related to their training and experiences, which serve to identify them

I asked Mother to give me one good reason why
I couldn't go out with Don tonight—she gave me five!

with their sex group. Considerable attention has been given the identification of adolescent boys and girls with their masculine and feminine roles. Lynn (1959) presented the following generalizations on sex identification:

1. With increasing age males become relatively more firmly identified with the masculine role, while females become relatively less firmly identified with the feminine role.
2. A larger proportion of females than males show preference for the role of the opposite sex.
3. A larger proportion of females than males adopt aspects of the role of the opposite sex.
4. Males tend to identify with a cultural stereotype of the masculine role, whereas females tend to identify with aspects of their mothers' roles specifically.

Physical Maturation and Social Behavior

It is a common observation that the twelve- or thirteen-year-old girl advanced in her physical development displays an interest in boys, whereas the girl retarded in her physical development displays little interest in boys. A study reported by Ames (1957), as part of a longitudinal study of forty males and forty females, dealt with the long-term relation between rate of maturation of the forty boys during adolescence and various measures of social participation during adulthood. Physical maturity was determined on the basis of skeletal age. Scores of skeletal age

147

divided by chronological age during the fourteenth to the seventeenth years of life were averaged for each individual to obtain an index of his relative rate of maturation. Ratings of the adolescent social behavior of the subjects were also available. Significant positive correlations were obtained between level of maturation and social ratings, indicating that adolescents advanced in rate of physical maturation were inclined to be advanced in their adult social behavior, whereas those retarded in rate of physical maturation were also likely to be retarded in their social development.

Changes in sex-appropriateness of behavior during adolescence are also related to physical maturation. Girls advanced in their physical maturation attempt to play a feminine role advanced for their age level. This may be observed in their manner of dress, make-up, behavior, and growing interest in boys. Zuk's (1958) analysis of behavior of adolescent boys and girls during the late adolescent years (15 to 17) revealed the following:

1. Sex-appropriate behavior increased significantly in girls from sixteen to seventeen years. Boys showed no comparable increase during this period.

2. Sex-appropriate behavior tended to be more stable in girls from year to year than in boys. For both sexes, however, such behavior was more stable during the sixteenth year than during the fifteenth year.

3. Behavior which was sex-appropriate and more popular with boys tended also to be relatively more popular with girls and vice versa.

4. Sex-appropriate behavior was shown to be related in reasonable directions but in low degree with social, physical, intellective, and temperament factors.

5. The sex-appropriateness of adolescent behavior was shown to vary widely from one area to another. . . . (31–32).

The fifth conclusion has widespread implications: one should be careful in making generalizations from data on adolescent behavior. One can generalize from one group to another, to the extent that sex-appropriate behavior is based upon physiological maturation and to the extent that sex-appropriate behavior is a result of similar cultural forces and conditions. Much of the behavior and growth data on adolescents has been obtained from middle-class cultural groups, making it hazardous to apply such data to lower-class cultural groups. However, as pointed out earlier, there are many educational forces operating to furnish adolescents with what might be termed a universal American (or even Western) culture.

The mass media have been a potent force in informing adolescents from different social classes and subcultures of the manner of dress considered most appropriate for different occasions. Studies show that, in general, there is little difference in the habits of dress and type of clothing worn by adolescent girls in different economic groups. The major difference usually lies in the more expensive clothes and greater number of luxury items worn by those in better economic circumstances; however, girls from all economic levels attempted to conform to the group style of dress and make-up.

Formation of Cliques

According to Smith (1962), cliques are "the first transitional institutions of youth culture." They are made up of informal groups of children or adolescents of the same sex who are usually on or about the same social level. Cliques form within peer groups during adolescence and serve to maintain class socialization differences that are established in the family and are carried on throughout adolescence into adulthood. Adolescents aspiring to advance in social status should become a part of a peer group or clique a class level above. Outstanding athletes and talented and attractive girls have more of an opportunity to be accepted by a clique socially above their own then do other adolescents.

Within cliques conformity to group norms is stressed. The more a member conforms, the more likely he is to be accepted. According to Smith (1962), the selection or rejection of individuals from specific groups is by mutual consent, the emphasis being upon conformity to group norms as a selective factor. A careful study of clique structures reveals a hierarchical ranking implicit in the informal leadership, and a descending rank order determined by the degree of success in fulfillment of the group norms. In attaining leadership, personal factors such as height, weight, intelligence, ability and achievement play a part. Also, facility in speech and depth of voice help to establish a leadership role.

Group norms vary from clique to clique. For example, in one group of boys a beard may be "the thing" and certain behavior patterns may be accepted, while within another group these would be subject to ridicule. The norms of the clique are perpetuated by having older members of the group instill mores of behavior in younger members before the older members move on to another clique that contains older members. The clique among older adolescents evolves toward the framework of the heterosexual crowd as opposed to the more or less monosexuality of the younger clique. Girls' cliques tend to disintegrate more rapidly than boys'. This may be explained by the girls' earlier maturity rate and by competition between girls for dates. Boys whose activities are more athletically oriented tend to remain in cliques longer.

Often the first crowd activities will involve one boys' clique and one girls' clique. Such groups may be observed meeting together in an informal manner at some place, perhaps a favorite spot in a shopping mall after school. More and more frequently this transitional stage is skipped altogether, especially when going steady and dating occurs early.

Formation of Groups and Gangs

Teen-age boys and girls are particularly interested in forming groups, societies, gangs, and clubs. These appear most frequently among heterogeneous groups, such as those found in the large modern high school.

Scientific investigations show that as a rule the members of a gang are likely to be of about the same level of intelligence. They usually come from within a limited geographical area and are very apt to be neighborhood affairs. Individuals are affected by the behavior patterns of the gang, and tend to influence the formation of behavior patterns in others by the activities. The group is generally quite similar in its desires, likes, and dislikes; there is considerable social uniformity in its attitudes and ideals. The results of an experiment by Pratt and Sackett (1967) with monkeys reared under varying conditions of isolation are perhaps applicable to the formation of adolescent groups. The investigators found that these monkeys consequently displayed abnormal behavior of different kinds and tended to prefer social interaction with peers of a similar degree of social abnormality. These animals appear to learn patterns of social cues and prefer "friends" that display similar behavior patterns.

The structure and behavior of a gang are molded in part through its accommodation to the life of its members. The groups in ghettos, in suburbia, along a business street, in the small town, or in an industrial village vary in their interests and activities not only according to the social pattern of their respective localities, but also according to the layout of the buildings, streets, alleys, recreational facilities, and the general topography of their environments. These conditioning factors within which the children and adolescents live and develop furnish a setting within which gang behavior operates. So marked is the influence of such factors as bodies of water, hills, and plant life in determining the location and character of activities, that in some cities delinquent gangs have been classified on this basis.

Reactions to Newcomers

Greater aggression among girls than boys seems to be associated with verbal and indirect forms of aggression such as rejection and exclusion of the newcomer from the group (Feshbach, 1969). The subjects of a study by Feshbach and Sones (1971) of adolescent reactions to newcomers consisted of eighty-seven adolescents—forty-two boys and forty-five girls. The subjects were divided into like-sexed triads, resulting in fifteen girl triads and fourteen boy triads. The first two members of each triad were close friends selected from the eighth grade. The third member, a newcomer of the same sex, was selected from the seventh grade. The students at both age levels were average in ability, white, and from middle-class backgrounds.

Three measures were taken of the interaction between the original group members and the newcomer, each designed to assess an indirect mode of expression of a negative attitude toward the newcomer. The first of these measured latency—the time elapsing before one of the original group members addressed the newcomer. The reactions to the newcomer's suggestions furnished two additional interaction measures.

The elapsed time before speaking to the newcomer was longer for the girls than for the boys. The median time for the girls was seventy-three seconds, in comparison to only twenty-two seconds for the boys. In general, the newcomers directed their remarks toward the original group members earlier than the original group members did to the newcomer. Even here, the girl newcomers waited longer before speaking than did the boy newcomers. In regard to the acceptance or rejection of the newcomers' suggestions, the girls were much more inclined to ignore the newcomer's ideas. Concerning the results, the investigators state:

> The experimental results are consistent with the expectation that female friendship pairs will display more negative, rejecting attitudes toward a same-sex stranger than will pairs of male friends. Girls judged the newcomer less favorably than did boys, were less welcoming, and were more likely than boys to ignore the newcomer's suggestions in arriving at a group decision. . . (385).
>
>   . . . This finding is consistent with those of a prior study of sex differences in response to a newcomer where a much younger age group was employed and where a free play as compared to a social problem-solving situation was used to assess reactions to the newcomer. This continuity over a wide age span suggests a stable sex difference in response to outsiders which has its roots in the early developmental history of the child (386).

Influence of Peer Groups

The peer group does not suddenly take over when the individual reaches puberty or adolescence; neither is it a strictly preadolescent phenomenon. According to Fagot and Patterson (1969), the peer group takes over when the child enters school; and the behavioral patterns begun in home are further consolidated by the peer group. Preadolescent groups are for the most part unisexual in composition, although among some boy groups an outstanding girl (tomboy) interacts successfully with the boys.

With puberty the peer group takes on many of the functions previously provided by the family and is very important in promoting increased independence from the family. The peer group gives the adolescent a useful anchor during the period of rapid transition from childhood to adulthood, from dependence to increased independence, from family control to increased self-control. This transition is gradual in nature and is made easier through identification with peers of a clique, especially the leader. During early adolescence, peers usually identify with members of the same sex. About middle adolescence there is a trend toward heterosexual groups. These become increasingly more important to adolescents, and there is a tendency for late adolescents to establish more stable relations with peers of both sexes (Dunphy, 1963: 45–46).

Peers have an important influence on the social development and behavior of adolescents. It has been pointed out that "the regulation of social behavior termed *conformity*, and its converse, termed *deviation*, are by definition relative to the shared or agreed-upon appraisals of others (social norms)" (Sherif and Sherif, 1965: 6). Thus, peers frequently become the reference groups for adolescents.[1]

SUMMARY

The self-image emerges from an interaction of the physical, physiological, psychological, and sociological factors in development. It is further affected by the attitudes of others and social interactions. Since it is developmental in nature, significant changes take place with age. The ideal self may be observed in the aspirations and identifications of the adolescent. The relation between academic achievement and the self-concept is not uniform from person to person; although the self-concept has an important bearing on behavior. The self-concept is further reflected in the personal appearance of the individual.

Identification begins in infancy and becomes more unified and consistent with development into adolescence. Studies show that normal family relations are important to the development of a sense of identity. Identification with one or both parents has different results for boys and girls.

Important changes in emotional behavior occur during adolescence, although these are related to emotional behavior during childhood. Changes in emotional manifestations take place from early adolescence to late adolescence. Also, emotional manifestations vary with sex and culture.

As a full-fledged drive, the sex drive does not mature until puberty and sometimes after. New norms or standards of social-sexual conduct during the preadolescent and adolescent years have appeared during the past two decades. This is reflected in an increased manifestation of social-sexual interests and behavior. The various theories of psychosexual development recognize the role of the physiological factors, including the sex glands and hormonal conditions. Important differences in social-sexual development appear between boys and girls. Much of this is closely related to cultural differences.

Learning to live with age-mates is an important developmental task acquired in normal social interactions during adolescence. In our culture children are directed into their own age and sex group even during the preadolescent years. Cliques have been described as the first transitional institutions of youth culture. These form within peer groups and serve to maintain class socialization differences. Within cliques, conformity to peer-group norms is stressed, although individuals differ in degree of conformity. Conformity seems to be greater in early rather than late

---

[1] Reference groups refer to those sets of people to which an individual feels he belongs, wants to belong, and to which he relates (Sherif and Sherif, 1965: 6).

adolescence. The structure and behavior of cliques and gangs is affected by the needs, interests, and problems of the members. Sex differences may also be noted, and these are quite important.

REFERENCES

AMES, ROBERT. Physical Maturing Among Boys as Related to Adult Social Behavior." *California Journal of Educational Research* (1957), 8:69–75.

ANGELINO, H., J. DOLLINS, and E. V. MECH. "Trends in the 'Fears and Worries' of School Children as Related to Socioeconomic Status and Anxiety." *Journal of Genetic Psychology* (1956), 89:263–78.

BRANDT, RICHARD M. "Self: Missing Link for Understanding Behavior." *Mental Hygiene* (1957), 41:24–33.

BRIDGES, K. M. B. "Emotional Development in Early Infancy." *Child Development* (1932), 3:324–41.

BRODERICK, CARLFRED, B. "Social-sexual Development in a Suburban Community." Publication data supplied by Broderick, Pennsylvania State University, 1963.

———, and STANLEY E. FOWLER. "New Patterns of Relationships Between the Sexes Among Preadolescents." *Journal of Marriage and Family Living* (1961), 23:27–30.

BRONFENBRENNER, U. "Freudian Theories of Identification and Their Derivatives." *Child Development* (1960), 31:15–40.

———. "Parents, Bring Up Your Children." *Look* magazine, (January 26, 1971), pp. 45–46.

CAMPBELL, E. H. "The Social and Sex Development of Children." *Genetic Psychology Monographs* (1939), 21:461–552.

CONNELL, DAVID M. and JAMES E. JOHNSON. "Relationship Between Sex-role Identification and Self-esteem in Early Adolescence." *Developmental Psychology* (1970), 3:268.

CRUTCHFIELD, A. S. "Conformity and Character." *American Psychologist* (1955), 10:191–98.

DUNPHY, DEXTER C. "The Social Structure of Urban Adolescent Peer Groups." *Sociometry* (1963), 26:230–46.

ERIKSON, E. H. "The Problem of Ego Identity." *Journal of the American Psychoanalytic Association* (1956), 4:56–121.

———. *Identity: Youth and Crisis.* New York: W. W. Norton & Co., 1968.

FAGOT, B. I. and G. R. PATTERSON. "An 'In Vivo' Analysis of Reinforcing Contingencies for Sex-role Behaviors in the Preschool Child." *Developmental Psychology* (1969), 1:563–68.

FESHBACH, NORMA. "Sex Differences in Children's Modes of Aggressive Responses Toward Outsiders." *Merrill Palmer Quarterly* (1969), 15:249–58.

———, and GITTELLE SONES. "Sex Differences in Adolescent Reactions Toward Newcomers." *Developmental Psychology* (1971), 4:381–86.

GOODENOUGH, E. W. "Interest in Persons as an Aspect of Sex Differences in the Early Years." *Genetic Psychology Monographs* (1957), 55:287–323.

HAVIGHURST, ROBERT J., M. Z. ROBINSON, and M. DORR. "The Development of the Ideal Self in Childhood and Adolescence." *Journal of Educational Research* (1946–47), 40:241–57.

HEILBRUN, A. B. "Parental Identification and College Adjustment." *Psychological Reports* (1962), 16:853–54.

———, and D. K. FROMME. "Parental Identification of Late Adolescents and Level of Adjustment: The Importance of Parent-Model Attributes, Ordinal Position and Sex of the Child." *Journal of Genetic Psychology* (1965), 107:49–59.

HOLLENDER, JOHN. "Sex Differences in Sources of Social Self-esteem." *Journal of Consulting and Clinical Psychology* (1972), 38 (3):343–47.

JONES, H. E. "Principles and Methods of the Adolescent Growth Study." *Journal of Consulting Psychology* (1939), 3:172–80.

JONES M. C. and NANCY BAYLEY. "Physical Maturing Among Boys as Related to Behavior." *Journal of Educational Psychology* (1950), 41:129–48.

LEAGUE, BETTY Jo and DOUGLAS N. JACKSON. "Conformity, Veridicality, and Self-esteem." *Journal of Abnormal and Social Psychology* (1964), 68:113–15.

LINDSEY, D. B. "Emotion." In *Handbook of Experimental Psychology*, S. S. Stevens, ed. New York: John Wiley & Sons, Inc., 1951.

LOHMAN, John E. *Age, Sex, Socioeconomic Status and Youths' Relationships with Older and Younger Peers.* Ph.D. dissertation. Ann Arbor: University of Michigan, 1969.

LYNN, DAVID B. "A Note on Sex Differences in the Development of Masculine and Feminine Identification." *Psychological Review* (1959), 66:126–35.

———. *Parental and Sex-role Identification: A Theoretical Framework.* Berkeley, Calif.: McCutchan, 1969.

MAAS, HENRY S. and RICHARD E. ENGLER. *Children in Need of Parents.* New York: Columbia University Press, 1959.

MACINTYRE, J. McEVAN. "Adolescence, Identity, and Foster Family Care." *Children* (November–December 1970), 6:213–17.

MEAD, GEORGE H. *Mind, Self, and Society.* Chicago: University of Chicago Press, 1934.

MEHITA, PERIN H. "The Self-concept of Bright Underachieving Male High School Students." *Indian Educational Review* (1968), 3 (2):81–100.

MEIER, ELIZABETH G. "Former Foster Children as Adult Citizens." Unpublished doctoral dissertation. New York: Columbia University, 1962.

MINUCHIN, P. "Sex-role Concepts and Sex Typing in Childhood as a Function of School and Home Environment." *Child Development* (1965), 36:1033–48.

MORSE, WILLIAM C. "Self-concept in the School Setting." *Childhood Education* (December 1964), 41:195–98.

MUSSEN, P. H. and M. C. JONES. "Self-conceptions, Motivations, and Interpersonal Attitudes of Late and Early Maturing Boys." *Child Development* (1957), 28:243–56.

PHILLIPS, BEEMAN N. "Age Changes in Accuracy of Self-perceptions." *Child Development* (1963), 34:1041–46.

PRATT, C. L. and G. P. SACKETT. "Selection of Social Partners as a Function of Peer Contact During Rearing." *Science* (1967), 155:1135–36.

SHANNON, R. L. "Student Self-acceptance and Curriculum Organization in the Junior High School. *"National Association of Secondary School Principals Bulletin* (1960), 44:35–38.

SHAW, M. C. *et al.* "Self-concepts of Bright Underachieving High School Students as Revealed by an Adjective Check List. *"Personnel and Guidance Journal* (1960), 39:193–96.

SHERIF, MUZAFER and CAROLYN W. SHERIF. *Reference Groups.* New York: Harper & Row, Publishers, 1965.

SMITH, ERNEST A. *American Youth Culture.* Glencoe, Ill.: Free Press of Glencoe, 1962.

SMITH, WALTER D. and DELL LEBE. "Some Changing Aspects of the Self-concept of Pubescent Males." *Journal of Genetic Psychology* (1956), 88:61–75.

SOPCHAK, A. L. "Parental Identification and Tendency Toward Disorders as Measured by the Minnesota Multiphasic Inventory." *Journal of Abnormal and Social Psychology* (1952).

STOKES, S. M. "An Inquiry into the Concept of Identification." *Journal of Genetic Psychology* (1950), 76:163–89.

SUTTON-SMITH, B. and B. C. ROSENBERG. "Age Changes on the Effects of Ordinal Position on Sex-role Identification." *Journal of Genetic Psychology* (1965), 107:61–73.

TUDDENHUM, R. D. "Correlates of Yielding to Distorted Group Norms." *Journal of Personality* (1959), 27:272–84.

VONTRESS, CLEMENT E. "The Negro Personality Reconsidered." *Journal of Negro Education* (Summer 1966), 35:217.

ZACHRY, C. B. and M. LIGHTY. *Emotions and Conduct in Adolescence.* New York: Appleton-Century-Crofts, 1940.

ZUK, G. H. "Sex-appropriate Behavior in Adolescence." *Journal of Genetic Psychology* (1958), 93:31–32.

RECOMMENDED READINGS

BALLER, WARREN R. *The Psychology of Human Growth and Development.* 2nd ed. New York: Holt, Rinehart & Winston, Inc., 1968.
The following topics are covered in Chapter 14: family patterns and personality development, children and fathers, learning from parents, social influences on family living, parent-child conflict, varying family conditions, and sibling relations.

BERNARD, HAROLD. *Adolescent Development.* Scranton, Pa.: Intext Educational Publishers, 1971. Chapters 8 and 10.
Chapter 8 discusses heterosexual adjustments as a phase of socialization. The development and expansion of interests and factors related to interests are discussed in Chapter 10.

HAMACHEK, DON E. *Encounters with the Self.* New York: Holt, Rinehart & Winston, Inc., 1971.
Some of the basic propositions of self-concept theory, along with a dis-

cussion of some of the major contributions to the understanding of the self-concept. Personal anecdotes, case histories, counseling, and therapy excerpts are used throughout the book.

HORROCKS, JOHN E. *The Psychology of Adolescence.* 3rd ed. Boston: Houghton Mifflin Company, 1969.

Special emphasis is given in Chapters 8, 9, and 10 to the adolescent and his family, including parental attitudes, relationships, and perceptions, and environmental factors.

personality integration and character development

Personality development and integration are very important in considering the individual adolescent. And, while personality might be thought of as an individual matter, no individual possesses traits or characteristics that are not to be found in others. It should be pointed out, however, that each age level seems to have its own peculiar characteristics. The very definition of adolescence indicates something general about the personality at this stage of life; but even here no single description characterizes all adolescents. This chapter will present some of the biological and cultural forces that affect the individual during the adolescent years, along with conditions that contribute to personality integration.

Attitudes, ideals, and values are all aspects of personality and hence, the basis of character. During the adolescent years, we note a widening of attitudes, a deepening of ideals, and a strengthening of values. Although personality integration and character development have their beginnings during infancy, it is during the adolescent years that increased maturity, wider social contacts, increased social-sexual development, and influences beyond the home operate to a much greater degree. It was pointed out in the previous chapter that peers come to have an important influence during adolescence; during early adolescence the need to conform to peer expectations is exceedingly great for many adolescents. Other adults, educational experiences, and increased social contacts outside the home have an important influence during adolescence and will be given special attention throughout this chapter.

PERSONALITY DEVELOPMENT

The term *personality* is frequently used in our present-day terminology to refer to man's behavior and characteristics. It has been used widely and loosely by the layman, the personality expert, the orator, and the psychologist. The layman looks upon it in terms of qualifying adjectives such as "good," "pleasing," and "odd," whereas the personality expert considers it somewhat like a pair of gloves or a stylish hat—something that can be bought for five dollars or more and worn effectively with a few hints on how to wear it. Orators—and some psychologists—have clothed the term in a sort of mysticism and abstraction similar to that which surrounds the terms *ego, soul,* and *spirit.* In such a case it does not yield readily to definition or even to adequate description. By personality we mean the total person as a private and social being; it is an integration of the physical, emotional, mental, and social selves. It is the person on the stage playing many roles and being judged by all members of the audience—his total world.

Personality Characteristics or Factors

Although we refer to personality traits, we conceive of these as functioning in an integrated manner. There are, however, significant differences in the manifestations of the characteristics, traits, or factors that comprise the whole personality pattern. Thus, behavior can be described in terms of the functioning of the various traits or factors that make up personality. Trait names describe forms of behavior but fail to furnish information relative to the reasons for such behavior. Many terms have been used that represent personality traits. Furthermore, these traits vary in strength. On the basis of a factor analysis study of personality traits, Cattell (1953) arrived at certain personality dimensions applicable to the age from ten to sixteen. These have been referred to as the primary personality factors. These factors are:

Emotional sensitivity	*versus*	Toughness
Nervous tension		Autonomic relaxation
Neurotic, fearful		Stability of ego strength
Will control		Relaxed casualness
Impatient dominance, cyclothymia		Withdrawal schizothymia
Socialized morale		Dislike of education
Independent dominance, energetic conformity		Quiet eccentricity
Surgency		Desurgency, intelligence

The personality of an individual depends not only upon the manifestation of these traits, but also upon the integration. By integration is meant the general organization of traits into a larger unit of behavior, with some traits becoming subordinate to others in such an organization. There has developed a rather general recognition that personality is concerned with the individual as a unit. Woodworth emphasizes that a study of personality must deal with behavior in its totality (1948: 251–52). Many people lose sight of the integrative nature of personality in their study of the individual; this is especially in evidence in the classification of all individuals with the same educational achievement as similar in personality. The same error is made with regard to criminals, professional groups, people of the same intelligence, and so forth. It is only when two individuals have absolutely identical heredity, identical training, and identical organic conditions that one could expect various personality elements to be integrated into identical personality patterns.

The Growing Nature of Personality

One can expect changes in the personality of an individual during pubescence. There is a continued growth toward mental maturity during adolescence. Physical growth, which was discussed in Chapter 4, is rapid early in this period, but there are some rather abrupt organic changes involved. The thymus gland ceases to function, the sex glands begin to function, and thus a new endocrine balance is established. The child's egocentric nature thus takes on a social form, correlated with the changed endocrine self. The child is now held more responsible for acts committed by the self; society looks upon the personality as a growing social force, and now sees not Smith's child but Mr. Smith's young daughter. The impression the growing individual makes upon others and the attitudes adults take toward him are quite different.

Again, it is interesting to note the personality of an individual as we observe it in different situations. The writer has in mind a fourteen-year-old girl, whom for convenience we shall call Edna. She is very disobedient at home, especially in response to her mother's requests, and the mother thinks of her as "a little smarty." In the presence of her older sister in social situations Edna is quite submissive and timid, but with the boys and girls in the eighth grade at school Edna is quite sociable, and is liked by all. Not only do we notice different behavior patterns when Edna is in three different situations, but even when she is "performing" in any one of these situations we are likely to notice at least a partial exhibition of these other personality characteristics. Thus, personality cannot be considered apart from the situation in which the various traits are exhibited. Some situations will call forth some traits, whereas another situation may call forth a very different pattern of traits. The combination of traits present in a particular situation will depend upon many variables, such as maturity, sex, habit systems, health, present attitude, general social pattern, and so forth.

Development of Self-Discipline

Biological maturity does not automatically bring with it self-discipline. This may be noted from comparisons of adolescents similar in biological maturity but from different backgrounds. However, we may note some interesting trends in the development of self-discipline with increased maturity. At the irrational-conscious level the child is guided by rules or fears created by different situations. He usually conforms to social regulations at home or in public not from a conscious consideration of the rights and welfare of others but from anxiety and fear of the consequences of misbehavior. A young girl may adopt certain aesthetic standards of her mother not because of a conscious desire to emulate her mother, but because of her anxiety of the consequences if she failed to conform.

Various degrees of conformity to rules lead to the internalization of certain ideals, values, and ways of behaving. The highest level of self-discipline involves the altruistic impulse—the consideration of the welfare of others as well as oneself.

Certain developmental trends in self-discipline are supported by experiments. They show that as the child matures, he internalizes moral restraint based upon maturity and experiences. This may be observed in Medinnus's study of the development of moral responsibility (1962). The curves of development show a decline in fear of punishment during late childhood and a growth in social concern. These curves, based upon data gathered from subjects in the lower socioeconomic classes, would probably show an even more distinct transition from the irrational-conscientious to the rational-altruistic stage if the subjects had been chosen from the middle socioeconomic classes.

The Persistence of the Personality Pattern

Children manifest definite differences in personality characteristics not only at the beginning of life but also during growth into adolescence and adulthood. A thirteen-year follow-up study of twenty-eight adolescents who were given the Symonds Picture Story Test and the Rorschach lends support to the theory that certain personality characteristics persist (Symonds and Jensen, 1961). The themes in the stories at both testings showed a marked persistence of certain features, and behavior ratings indicated a high degree of consistency in overt personality. It seems remarkable how we usually reconcile seemingly diverse behaviors into a self-consistent whole. An adolescent may cheat at school, lie to his teacher about skipping a class, go to church on Sunday, and rescue a small boy being beaten up by a bully and still consider himself as basically honest and quite considerate of others. He has transformed these seemingly discrepant behaviors into a unified whole through which there is a basic thread of sound morals. Data from many sources converge in providing evidence for personality stability and continuity (Bronson, 1972). Case studies and introspective observations as well as statistically treated group data indicate that home relationships are most important in the development of personality traits, and that whereas there is some fluctuation of traits, in general there is more persistence than change. Ausubel (1958) states:

> Once organized on a stable basis, distinctive personality structure, like any developmental equilibrium tends to remain intact in the absence of substantial cause for change. The child does not start from scratch in each new situation, but brings with him a precipitate of all past learnings. He attempts to maintain the same orientations, habits, adjustive mechanisms, and modes of striving and interacting with others that he used before. Even if change occurs in the objective properties of a situation (e.g., parent attitudes), habitual apperceptive sets may be strong enough in certain cases to force altered stimulus content into preconceived perceptual molds (perceptual constancy) (99).

The stability of personality factors makes it easier to predict personality development during childhood and adolescence. The fact that the child and adolescent brings his past with him to new and different situations makes it easier for him to adjust to such situations, although past habits may have to be altered because of the changed situation. Thus, new situations frequently present difficult problems of adjustment to the adolescent. The difficulty of adjusting to new situations depends on the individual, since adolescents vary considerably in rigidity of behavior patterns.

PERSONALITY CHARACTERISTICS
OF ADOLESCENTS

The many studies of the characteristics of adolescents reveal first of all that there is no single description that will embrace all adolescents. There are, however, certain personality qualities common to the adolescent period; and any description of adolescents must take into account the period, culture, and setting of the group being studied. The adolescent is usually a member, active or passive, of many groups, large and small, formal and informal, and he plays a different role in each of them.

Emotional Response Patterns

The emotional response patterns of adolescents, like other behavior patterns, are a result of learning. Thus, we would expect the emotional response patterns of adolescents to vary with cultural experiences. This is emphasized in Chapter 9, which deals with adolescents from diverse cultural backgrounds. It has been observed that adolescents from impoverished environments are likely to have a low self-esteem, which serves as a barrier to their educational growth. Upper-class children and adolescents begin earlier to repress and sublimate basic emotions. They are more in-clined to accept long-term goals and values in contrast to the acceptance of immediate goals and values by lower-class adolescents. The fears of lower-class adolescents tend to involve physical conditions to a greater degree than those of middle- and upper-class adolescents. These differentiated reactions are an important aspect of the adolescent's personality.

The findings from the Adolescent Growth Study at the University of California referred to in Chapter 6, indicate that the nature of person-ality is related to the amount of internalized or externalized emotional responses. Those adolescents of the Adolescent Growth Study having the greatest constancy of mood displayed the most intense internal responses to emotionally toned situations. Comparisons of the responses of high and low reactive groups to emotionally toned stimuli on physiological tests for classmate ratings on certain traits are presented in Figure 7-1 (Jones, 1950). The low reactive group displayed more vigorous overt and social responses and tended to be less popular with their classmates than the high reactive group. One might postulate that frank and ready overt ex-pressiveness helps to maintain good personal adjustments, whereas

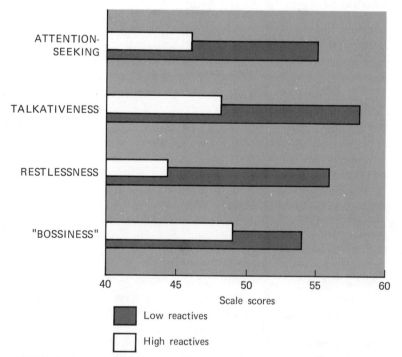

FIGURE 7-1 A comparison of high and low reactives in reputation traits. By permission from *Feelings and Emotions*, E. L. Reymert, ed.; copyright 1950 by McGraw-Hill Book Company.

socialized inhibition of overt responses tends to lead to internal emotional tensions.

**Contrasting Phases of
Adolescent Personality**

Some elements characteristic of adolescent personality tend to make the individual unstable in nature; these elements are here referred to as "contrasting phases." G. Stanley Hall (1904) recognized the importance of emotion in adolescent life. "Youth loves intense states of mind and is passionately fond of excitement." Here we find a valid expression of the contrasting states of vitality and lassitude so characteristic of adolescents. Pleasure and pain are sometimes close together; tears and laughter may closely follow each other; elation and depression; egocentrism and sociability, ascendancy and submissiveness; selfishness and altruism; radicalism and conservatism; heightened ambitions and loss of interest—these contrasts in moods typify this period of life. Individual reactions are more transitory, unpredictable, and unstable; different traits predominate under different conditions; changes are likely to be very marked. However, as the individual has more and more social experiences, his manners of reaction change and his personality characteristics are increasingly modified and made more stable.

Anyone who studies the problems of young people becomes familiar with these common manifestations of behavior: Habit patterns have not fully developed, work in school is not steady, playground activities vary, general attitude toward the school is easily changed. Bronner (1930) makes the following observation:

> Today's enthusiasms may become matters of boredom before long. The desire one day may be to become a missionary, and ere long this has been completely forgotten and the goal of life is to be a dancer. Many an adolescent has said, "I don't know what I want to be. One day I think I want to be one thing and the next day something else, only I want to be someone great." (230).

The newly developed interests and broadened outlook of boys and girls as they reach maturity and come into contact with social reality cause this flightyness. Changes in outlook take place more rapidly than habit systems change, develop, and become integrated into a unified personality.

ADOLESCENT INSTABILITY. Emotional expression, as we have seen, is largely a matter of habit, and from such habits develop behavior patterns characteristic of extroversion or introversion. As attested by giggling, impulsiveness, yelling, loud talking, and other symptoms of instability, extroversion is more universal than introversion. Habits of introversion are likely to be present in individuals who are reaching maturity with poorly developed social and emotional habits. Just how truly such conditions are a result of training is quite evident as we observe many adolescents with varying backgrounds who are socially well-adjusted, wholesome in attitude, courteous in manners, and stable in the exhibition of various habit systems.

Far too many children, as they reach adolescence, are expected to assume the places of adults with only the training that would enable them to follow authority blindly. These individuals have not been given the opportunity for the development of habits of initiative and responsibility so essential in the ordinary pursuits of adult life; they are "too young" to do the things adults are doing and "too old" to act and play as children do. For many individuals this is, therefore, a period of bewilderment. If the individual desires to run and play the "kid-like" games, he is laughed at; if he offers his advice and counsel too freely to the adult group, he is reminded that he is still a child.

ADOLESCENT IDEALISM. Adolescent idealism, as we observe it today in youth demonstrations and youth marches, is not new. This may be noted in the activities of John Adams and Thomas Jefferson in 1776; it was present in the Napoleonic Wars; it appeared in early revolutionary movements in Russia; it was basic to the Nazi movement in Germany; it appeared in the people's movement in China; it has been foremost in the recent civil rights, antiwar, and antipollution movements in the United States. Adolescent idealism was referred to earlier as an important element in the so-called generation gap.

Frequently when adolescents fail to conform to the ideas, practices, and behaviors of the adult world they are considered outcasts. However, many adolescents conform because their ignorance and lack of experience prevent them from recognizing alternatives. Other adolescents conform so as to receive the adult awards derived from conforming. Adolescent conformity and acceptance of the prevailing conditions must be recognized by those in authority if we are to find a realistic and humanitarian solution to the many problems that we face today.

Perhaps adolescents today are best distinguished from most adults by (1) their being better informed on contemporary problems, and (2) their idealistic solutions to those problems. The late Sneator Robert Kennedy was idolized by many adolescents largely because of his idealism. When seeking the Democratic nomination for the presidency in 1968, he quoted George Bernard Shaw:

Some people see things as they are and ask why.
I dream things that never were and ask why not.

INFLUENCES AFFECTING PERSONALITY

Varied influences affect the adolescent's identity formation and personality. These are to a marked degree grounded in his physiological structure and his early childhood experiences, although we should not dismiss the influences of peers.

Physiological Conditions and Personality

A group of structures that exercise great influence over personality development is the system of ductless glands—the endocrine glands. These are especially important in preparing an individual for sexual maturity as well as in promoting other aspects of growth.

Some of the behavioral activities so frequently cited as characteristic of the adolescent period may well have a physiological background. It is well known that the internal environment of individuals is in a state of flux during the early adolescent years. Thus, the unpredictable behavior and variations in mood during this period may often have a physiological basis. Such behavior may range from restlessness, resulting in part from an increased production of sex hormones within the individual, to the opposite state of apathy and listlessness, especially during periods of lowered metabolism. It is at this time that the individual is expected to reconcile his own internal environment with social and cultural demands.

Childhood Experiences

There is evidence from many sources that childhood experiences play an important role in the development of the adolescent's personality. The results of a study by Allen suggest that early experiences are directly related to adult personality adjustment, particularly to ego strength. Allen concludes: "It is the combination of many variables of early experiences, rather than any single factor, that is responsible for the correlations with the ratings of adult personality adjustments; and of these factors, it is the sexual areas of experiences that correlated the strongest with the cultural measure of adult ego strength" (1967: 67).

Students of human development have long stressed the importance of mothering in the development of the child; more recently there has been a growing recognition of the importance of the role of the father in contemporary society. However, the focus has been on the father-son relationship with relatively little thought given to the father-daughter relationship. The importance of the father-son relationship has been documented by many studies and will be given further consideration in connection with adolescent alienation. Psychoanalytic literature abounds with the notion that the girl in her development displays a passively exotic attitude toward her father—the feminine Oedipus complex. The importance of satisfactorily resolving the feminine Oedipus complex has been stressed by Leonard (1966). He points out the need for a girl to "establish a desexualized relationship to her father" so that she may be able "later to accept the feminine role without guilt or anxiety and to give love to a young man in her peer group" (332). Adequate fathering is thought to be essential for the success of this phase of her life. Biller and Weiss (1970) made a rather complete review of the literature bearing on the father-daughter relationship and the personality development of the female. From this they give the following conclusions:

1. It appears that the father influences his daughter's personality development in certain direct ways. He may also influence his daughter's personality development indirectly in terms of his relationship with his wife, who acts as a primary model for his daughter in her sex-role development (86).

2. A healthy father identification for a daughter seems to us to consist of understanding and empathizing with the father rather than acting masculine or wanting to be masculine like him (as might be the case for the boy) (87).

3. It thus appears that certain maladjustive tendencies are fostered by distorted expectations and power assertions by the father or his complete passivity. The effects of paternal inadequacy may leave the child generally limited in social experience (89).

Rate of Maturity

Differences have been observed in the expressive behavior of early- and late-maturers: ratings of early- and late-maturers for "animation" and "eagerness" are presented in Figure 7-2 (Jones and Bayley, 1950). The late-maturers are consistently above the average for the group on both of these traits, as well as on such traits as energy, talkativeness, and laughter. Two factors have been offered to account for the deviate position of the late-maturers. The first is that their childish tendencies persist. Secondly, they feel inferior because of their immaturity. The immature fourteen-year-old boy may be expressing, through his excessive activity, not only his more childlike nature, but may also be using this activity to gain the attention of others and thus compensate for his less favored physical status. It will be noted in Chapter 16 that this is frequently an important factor in juvenile delinquency.

According to Monet (1961) there is a close relationship between the morphological development of the body and social-sexual behavior during adolescence. Late-maturing adolescents tend to display less dating and similar behavior than their age-mates, and conversely, those advanced in sexual maturation show more. It has also been noted that males low in androgen tend to show passive behavior patterns and rank low in dominance hierarchies.

A study of the growth pattern in California of thirty-three boys furnishes worthwhile information about their covert self-concepts. Concerning the influence of late maturity Mussen and Jones conclude:

> Analysis of the data of the present study indicates that this situation may have adverse effects on the personalities of the physically retarded. These boys are more likely to have negative self-conceptions, feelings of inadequacy, strong feelings of being rejected and dominated, prolonged dependency needs, and rebellious attitudes toward parents. In contrast,

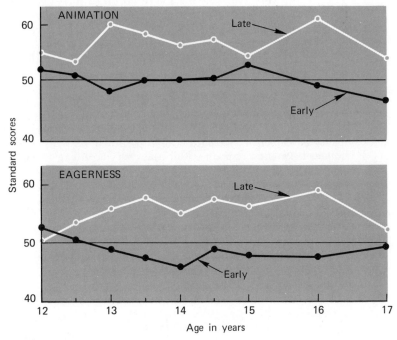

FIGURE 7-2 Mean standard scores for early- and late-maturing groups, in expressive traits. After Jones and Bayley (1950).

the early-maturity boys present a much more favorable psychological picture during adolescence. Relatively few of them felt inadequate, rejected, dominated, or rebellious toward their families. More of them appeared to be self-confident, independent, and capable of playing an adult role in interpersonl relationships (1957: 255).

Reference Groups and Cultural Demands

The continuous stream of interactions between the organism and his physical and social environments tends to shape personality. The individual brings to each adaptive behavior certain properties both of an intrinsic biological nature and those resulting from previous experiences. It is, therefore, obvious that the development of personality depends at all times upon the growing nature of the child and the experiences he encounters. Reference-group theory has been used to explain differences in attitudes and behavior of adolescents. The major reference groups are parents or parent surrogates and others.

CULTURAL DEMANDS OR STANDARDS. Bronson (1972) presented materials from the Berkeley Guidance Study dealing with the continuities and modifications in the behavior of a group of subjects from infancy through adolescence. Data were available on a core group of forty-five males and forty females. Scores descriptive of the emotional *expressiveness-reserve* and *placidity-explosiveness* of the subjects at the four main developmental periods (early childhood through adolescence) were related to concurrent assessments of the subject and his environment. The investigator concludes from an analysis of the data available the following:

> Cultural standards of approved behavior, which differ according to age and sex and which become internalized by the child as a yardstick for self-approval, are seen to play an important role in determining personality development associated with a particular orientation to the environment. Parental responses, which also vary according to age and sex, emerge as an important source of support, modification, or compensation for views that societal reactions lead the child to develop (78).

IMPORTANCE OF PEERS. The importance of peers during the adolescent years has been emphasized in earlier chapters. One of the most important needs of adolescents is to establish secure emotional and social ties with others, beyond the family or home, for the following reasons:

> To have a dependable anchor for a consistent and patterned self-picture, which is essential for personal consistency in experience and behavior, and particularly for a day-to-day continuity of the person's self-identity. Some stability of social ties is a prerequisite condition for the individual to experience himself as the "same person" from day to day, with his characteristic attributes and moorings. There is very considerable evidence that lacking such ties, the individual has great difficulty in establishing a clear self-identity, and that, once developed, the absence of such ties promotes experiences of estrangement and uncertainty, accompanied by erratic and inconsistent behaviors (Sherif and Sherif, 1965: (270).

Reference-group theory has been used to explain differences in the attitudes and behavior of adolescents. Peers become the major reference groups for many adolescents; conformity to peer-group attitudes and behavior may be observed. Hill (1971) investigated the role of peer-group conformity in the cigarette smoking of 186 adolescents attending a rural school. Questionnaire responses and sociometric data showed homogeneity among members on both smoking behavior and attitudes toward smoking. A subsequent experimental manipulation of the responses furnished good evidence that the peer-group conformity motive can be useful in changing the attitudes of adolescents. Subjects who were told that their previous responses differed from those of their peers tended to change their opinion in the direction of the bogus peer norms.

SOURCES OF ADOLESCENT FRUSTRATION

The causes of adolescent frustration and the development of a well-integrated personality are multiple and complex; they lie in part in the biological developments and in part within the culture of our established social and economic order.

Deutsche has emphasized the importance of biological development and the associated psychological component of the increased drive toward independence during adolescence. The immature child accepts the fact that his parents will protect him from dangers and will provide for his physical needs. This has been true for him since birth. The adolescent, however, feels the urge to explore and to use his own drives that have appeared or become intensified as part of his biological structure. He is, furthermore, encouraged in this by institutional forces that furnish opportunities for him to express these urges in a socialized manner.

Such explorations plunge the adolescent into a world outside the domain and protection of the parents. He is on his own, without constant guides and reinforcements from his parents. Josselyn stated:

> By his urge toward independence, the adolescent exposes himself to new and conflicting situations that are beyond the sphere of his adaptive resources, while at the same time he must reject formerly acceptable parental aid in meeting even the usual experience. As a result he is periodically threatened by failure with a resultant loss of confidence in himself (1954: 228).

A factor that complicates growing up and the development of a well-integrated personality for some adolescents is the social mobility of our postindustrial society. This was observed by Sorokin (1927) in the early part of this century. According to his disassociative hypothesis, upward mobility is a disruptive social experience which deprives the adolescent of roots of effective social support—roots especially important during the transition years. This hypothesis has been supported by scientific studies and empirical observations. A disproportionate amount of isolating experiences and social strain is encountered by adolescents when they try to assume a role in a peer group that is higher in status than their home background.

Differences in Physiological Maturity

In the middle period of adolescence early maturing tends to be advantageous to boys, whereas it is a disadvantage to girls (Jones, 1958). The average girl matures earlier than the average boy anyway; for a girl to mature earlier than most puts her at a disadvantageous extreme. She is conspicuously large in comparison to other girls and boys of her age. The case of Louise shows how difficult such a situation can be (Garrison, 1950).

> Louise, a twelve-year-old girl, was much taller than the other girls of her age and grade. Her intelligence quotient of 90 had made it difficult for her to do satisfactory work in school and consequently she was retarded in her school work. Although she was in a grade where most of the children were one year younger, she was still unable to do satisfactory work, es-

pecially in reading. This was accounted for in part by her inferior cultural home background. The poverty of the home did little to overcome an unhappy home situation and tended to make her still more unattractive to the others of her class, since she was usually poorly and untidily dressed.

The teacher recognized her problems and showed a very sympathetic and understanding attitude toward them. Louise recited from her seat entirely and was never called upon to go to the blackboard for fear that this would embarrass her. Furthermore, Louise did not like to march in line with the other members of the class. Although the teacher was rather formal in conducting her class work, she was lenient in allowing Louise to remain in the room and complete certain tasks while the other students were going out of the room in the line. However, the teacher's efforts did not solve Louise's problems. For, in fact, the problem was more than one of self-consciousness. Her self-consciousness developed into a defiant attitude. Louise came to feel that if she did not wish to do certain things then she should be excused from doing them.

At the end of the school year, Louise, now thirteen years of age, was promoted to the seventh grade. The seventh-grade teacher was informed of Louise's problems, and was thus in a position to profit from some of the well-meaning mistakes of the former teacher. The teacher set as her goal the bringing about of a better social adjustment on the part of Louise. Through visits to the home she was able to enlist some cooperation from the parents. Fortunately for Louise, one of the neighbors employed her to remain with their children, as a "sitter." This provided her with some spending money and gave her needed confidence in her ability and worth. At the end of the year considerable improvement was noted in her socialization.

On the other hand, the early-maturing girl is frequently the envy of her slower-maturing age-mates who are anxious to begin dating. Boys find that early maturing places them on a par with girls and ahead of most boys in physical development. This gives the boy an advantage in his social relations with girls. Late-maturing boys, usually unable to compete successfully in athletics and many social activities, frequently turn to individual pursuits such as academic work at school in an effort to satisfy the need to succeed.

Based on data gathered on 731 girls enrolled in the sixth, seventh, eighth, and ninth grades in a suburban community, Faust presents the following generalizations about the relation between developmental maturity and prestige among their classmates:

> . . . When all of the prestige-lending traits of a given grade are considered as a whole, it appears that prestige is more likely to surround those in the sixth grade who are developmentally "in phase" (prepuberal), whereas during the junior high school years being ahead of the group developmentally seems to be an advantage. While prepuberal status may be hazardous for girls in junior high school, it is not considered "immature" nor undesirable in sixth grade. A prepuberal girl in sixth grade is developmentally "in phase" with the great majority of her classmates, while a prepuberal girl in ninth grade is a "developmental isolate." A

girl's level of physical maturity is not only relative to the development of others in the class, but it is seen against a background of developmental differences within the whole school. Being at the prepuberal level of development seems to lend different qualities to the composite picture of an individual in elementary school than it does to one in the junior high school grades (1960: 180).

Conditions and Conflicts at Home

Just as the home is important to the adolescent's socialization, it is also an important source of conflict. The cultural and economic levels of the home are important to the adolescent's socialization and to his personality development. Many adolescents come from underpriviliged homes. That such conditions are not conducive to favorable development and learning is borne out by the large percentage of such children found among the educationally retarded, school dropouts, truants, and delinquents. The anxieties built up in the home or in some community activity become a source of frustration when such anxieties are beyond the scope of likely or possible fulfillment. Often the child from the upper-lower-class group has built up ambitions for his education and for the future which are practically impossible to attain. Likewise a boy or girl from the middle-class group may have only average ability, but because of the expectations of the family and friends he may have developed an anxiety to reach a level equal to that attained by an older and more capable brother or sister.

Another source of frustration among adolescents is that of achieving emotional independence from the home and family ties. This problem is often made difficult by the failure of parents to realize that boys and girls grow up. The results of parental domination may be observed in the case of a thirteen-year-old boy described by Mohr.

> The parents of a boy aged thirteen complained of his lack of responsibility. He was argumentative, would accept nothing readily from his parents. He argued constantly with his younger brother and with his friends. He was impatient unless his friends would do just what he wanted to do. He did rather poorly in his school work, did not concentrate, "fiddled around." He was rather slender and did poorly in athletics. He whined, acted silly when the mother had company, so that she was ashamed of him and sent him from the room; seemed generally unhappy; spent a great deal of time reading; was unpleasant about family outings; did not even like to accept when the father invited him to go to a motion picture with the father and younger brother; always felt abused and identified with the underdog.
>
> The picture as seen from the boy's point of view is interesting. Though thirteen, he had never been allowed to come into town by himself and was accompanied to the office by the mother until she was sure he had learned the way. The boy complained that there was too much arguing with the mother, and when he got irritated with her the father chimed in on her side. His father offered to take him to motion pictures and insisted even when there was no picture which the boy cared to go to. He finally went

because his father would be angry or the father's feelings would be hurt. His mother insisted that he come in to greet her friends when she had visitors, but she watched him all the time to see how he behaved and he knew that she did not want him to stay. When he decided he would like to have a party, the mother first insisted that he have all the children in his room and it took him two days to convince her that would be too many. Then the mother wanted certain children of her own friends invited, but he knew that they would not have a good time because they went to different schools and "the kids do not know them." Finally he got it down to just one girl that mother insisted on, though he knew that the others would not want her and he did not think that she would have a good time (1948: 1590).

The reasons for adolescent dependency are numerous, and are both psychological and social in nature. Striving for independence and emancipation are natural and common aspects of the adolescent period and may be observed in different cultures. Significant shifts occur usually in the direction of alienation from parents, between the early and late high school years. The question of the extent and nature of parental control cannot be answered in a precise manner. The process of achieving emancipation from parental ties is a problem that sometimes extends beyond adolescence. Parents must realize that adolescents are a product of their time, that many conditions and problems today are vastly different from those of a generation ago.

Cultural Demands

The sex code operates differently for the sexes, although the so-called double standard does not apply today in the same manner that it applied several generations ago. The societal code requires that the girl take on a feminine sex role and at the same time places restrictions upon her that sometimes make it difficult for her to do so. This tends to make the inner acceptance of the sex role a frustrating and complex one for the adolescent girl.

Our culture allows boys to express their emotionality to a greater degree than girls, except for the act of crying. Crying on the part of the adolescent boy or man is looked upon as an indication of weakness. The code demands greater conformity from girls, so they must express their emotions in conformance with fairly clearly defined mores. This is observed in the attitude of parents toward their "sassy" eleven-year-old son, whom they regard as "all boy." However, the sassy eleven-year-old girl is regarded as a spoiled child. As a result girls tend to attack the problems of growing up in a more thoughtful and careful manner, and rely to a greater degree upon expediency. Girls seem to grow up by evolution, boys by revolution.

Many teen-agers, particularly those of certain minority groups such as the blacks, live in a different culture. New developments are underway that are designed to improve the educational and cultural opportunities of the different culturally disadvantaged groups. This is presenting many difficult adjustment problems. Segregation, based on a combination of race, culture, and ethnic background, presents a special adjustment problem for those adolescents who do not fit into the culture of the disadvantaged—especially for the more talented adolescents. This was noted in the case of Willie Armsted, a black student at David Starr Jordan High School in the black ghetto of Los Angeles. He states: "It's not so much that I mind being in an all-Negro school. What I care about is not being able to get together with white kids, or just kids with other backgrounds, and discussing ideas" (Time, 1965: 57B).

Armsted is college bound, and perhaps an exception among ghetto kids. For most slum adolescents the American dream of equality and a good life for all is a "hollow dream" not an American fact. The ghetto youngster has been unable to respond to what is being taught. He frequently drops out of school to protect himself from a system with which he is unable to identify.

INFLUENCE OF THE FAMILY PATTERN. Although many studies have been conducted dealing with parent-child identification, most of them used males as subjects (Becker, 1964). Volunteers from three midwestern colleges served as subjects in a study by Doherty (1969) of the influence of parental control on the development of feminine sex role and conscience. The parents of these girls also completed questionnaires. The parent identification was obtained from responses to statements which directed the subjects to select the parent who was best described by statements. The girls indicated the parent (1) whose ideals are more like theirs, (2) whose personality is more like theirs, and (3) who influenced them most. The parent chosen on two out of the three responses was considered the parent with whom the daughter identified.

For girls who chose the mother as model, a significant positive relationship was found between their perception of the mother as controlling and the similarity of their femininity to their father's view of the feminine sex role. This relationship was not significant for father-identified young women. However, father-identified girls were seen as more feminine by their fathers when the girls perceived the fathers as controlling. Mother control was seen as having diverse effects in mother-identified young women. The girls in this study who chose their mother as model did not adopt her standards. There was a significant negative relationship between the perceived control of the mother and the daughter's standards of morality as they were appraised by the mother. Doherty concludes: "In light of the diverse effects of parental control found in this study, we should question whether sex-role standards and developing moral standards can be ascribed to a single identificatory process as has frequently been done in the past" (1969: 5).

Data bearing on the relationships of parental authority patterns and personality adjustments were gathered from 4,310 high school seniors in Washington State (Landis and Stone, 1952). A questionnaire including a check list of 250 problems was used for gathering the data. The problems were grouped into seven areas of adjustment and comparisons were made between the number of problems checked by boys and girls from democratic, intermediate, and authoritarian pattern homes. The problem areas included family, personal, social, boy-girl relations, school, vocational, and morals and religion. In all seven areas, the young people from the authoritarian homes checked the most problems, although the differences were greater in some areas than in others. The two problems that showed the greatest difference were "quarreling in the family," and "getting along with my parents." The desire to leave home was more pressing among both boys and girls from authoritarian homes than from democratic and intermediate homes.

The effects of the home atmosphere on some resulting behavior patterns during adolescence are shown in Table 7-1. The firm, warm, democratic home seems to result in increased self-direction with less tension and increased initiative and independence. The home characterized by indulgence and overprotection fails to promote self-direction and a sense of responsibility, while it tends to delay personal and social maturity. The stern, autocratic home produces either covert or overt

TABLE 7-1 Effects of the Home Atmosphere on Some Resulting Behavior Patterns of Adolescents

HOME ATMOSPHERE	RESULTING BEHAVIOR PATTERNS
Firm, warm democratic	Self-direction Lack of tension Realistic compliance Initiative, independence Friendship with peers Exchange of ideas Social interaction
Indulgent, protective	Delayed maturity Lack of self-direction Lack of responsibility Low self-reliance Social interaction
Pressure for compliance	Slavish conformity, or rebellious, independence Withdrawal, moodiness
Inconsistent discipline	Lack of self-direction Lack of growth in independence Open rebellion Lack of responsibility
Stern, autocratic	Blind obedience, or aggressive independence Conflict over dependence Covert or overt rebellion Lack of responsibility Withdrawal, moodiness

conflict. It furthermore leads to the development of blind obedience to authority or to a more rebellious nature and aggressive independence.

Parental Identification and Adjustment

A study by Payne and Mussen (1965) dealt with parent-child relations and father identification among adolescent boys. Seventy-two juniors and seniors from a public high school in a medium-sized city were used as a sample, and their attitudes, orientations, and preferences were compared with those of their mothers and fathers. The number of father-son and of mother-son agreements (identical answers) on a fifty-item questionnaire selected from three scales of the California Psychological Inventory (tolerance, social participation, and masculinity-femininity) was counted. Each boy's father-identification score was determined by the number of father-son agreements *minus* the number of mother-son agreements. The twenty boys most highly identified with their fathers and the twenty who were least identified with their fathers were selected for further study.

Significant positive correlations were obtained between the father-identification score and two measures of the reward value of the father. The results of this study have been verified by more recent studies. These may be summarized as follows:

1. Boys are more likely to identify with fathers whom they perceive as rewarding, gratifying, understanding, and warm than with fathers who are not perceived in these ways.
2. Boys who feel comfortable in their relationships with their parents adopt more of their fathers' behavior and attitudes than boys who experience less favorable parent-child relationships.
3. Mothers' masculinity scores were significantly correlated with their sons' identification scores; the more masculine the mother, the less strongly the boy tends to identify with his father.
4. Fathers of the highly identified boys did not have significantly higher masculinity scores than the fathers of the less strongly father-identified boys.
5. According to teachers' rating of the boys on nine personality characteristics, boys who were strongly father-identified were significantly more calm and friendly than their less highly identified peers.

Heilbrun and Fromme (1965) attempted to determine female-identification adjustments by breaking down father and mother models into psychological and sex types. They found that there was no relationship between parental identification and level of adjustment among late-adolescent girls from homes where the parents presented atypical sexual models (feminine father and masculine mother). When the parents presented sex-typical models (masculine father and feminine mother), the best adjusted girls identified slightly more with their fathers; the most poorly adjusted girls identified strongly with their mothers. However, one cannot generalize too freely from these results to teen-agers in junior high school, since these late-adolescent girls were actually enrolled in college. Furthermore, there is a possibility that these results which were obtained on a college sample would not be applicable to girls who are not college oriented.

In another study by Longstreth and Rice, the perceptions of parental behavior and identification with parents by three groups of boys differing in school adjustments were compared. The three groups differed as follows: One group was made up of aggressive acting-out boys (*AGG*, N = 61); a second group was made up of nonaggressive, underachieving boys (*UA*, N = 57); and a third group consisted of well-adjusted boys (*WA*, N = 116). These three groups were compared on two psychometric instruments, one determining perceptions of parental behavior on love and control dimensions, and the other determining identification with parents as compared to identification with peers. The major findings of this study are summarized as follows:

> (a) *AGG* boys describe their parents as significantly lower in love than *WA* boys with UA boys between these two groups; (b) *AGG* boys describe themselves significantly less identified with their parents (and thus more identified with peers) than *WA* boys, with nonaggressive *UA* boys again occupying an intermediate position; and (c) description of parents as high in love and control were positively correlated with descriptions of self as high in parental identification (1964: 149).

ATTITUDES, IDEALS, AND VALUES

Attitudes, ideals, and values are not learned through formal instruction, neither do they appear ready-made at different stages of life. Rather, they are absorbed from the social milieu in which the child and adolescent lives, grows, and experiences. We will now give special consideration to the development of attitudes, ideals, and values and to the influences affecting their development.

Attitudes: Their Nature and Development

An attitude is more than a state of mind. It is here used to express a phase of development more complex than factual learning. Attitudes are inclinations, prejudices, or preconceived notions and feelings toward things, persons, situations, and issues. We speak of one's attitude toward racial or religious groups, or toward fundamental social and economic issues such as price controls, reciprocal trade agreements, and public welfare.

Many differences in attitudes are related to the social and financial standing of the family. In the lower socioeconomic groups, parents and children appear to be in closer agreement in their attitude toward church, war, and communism, than they are in the higher socioeconomic groups. One reason may be that children and adolescents in the higher

Our wildlife is being killed off, the air is polluted, our rivers and lakes are filthy, racial tensions are all around us, there is crime on the streets, and politics is corrupt, and still you want to defer part of my allowance until next month.

socioeconomic groups read more widely, travel more, and enjoy broader and richer experiences. Since adolescents come from such diverse environmental backgrounds, one cannot expect to find a universally applicable attitude although certain attitudes are more widely held by adolescents than by older adults. No attempt will be made here to set forth specific attitudinal patterns as characteristic of the adolescent age. It should be pointed out that an individual's attitudes, ideals, and values are expressions of his character and personality.

Pubescence and Changed Attitudes

With the onset of puberty there is an increase in sex hormones that brings about an increased sexual tension. This has been observed in the animal world as well as in the case of man. In our society the maturing individual learns that associations with members of the opposite sex are rewarding in that they both produce and relieve sexual tension. However, in our society these adolescent drives are not ordinarily relieved through direct sexual behavior but through substitute behavior. These substitute forms of behavior, which appear with the onset of puberty, differentiate the responses of more physiologically mature adolescents from those less mature.

The changed attitude appearing at this time is emphasized in a study by Jones and Bayley (1950), a study in which comparisons were made between two groups of boys approximately equal in chronological age but two years apart in skeletal development. The early-maturing boys from twelve to seventeen were all more natural and unaffected than the average. As expected, the early-maturing boys displayed a greater interest in personal grooming and had better personal appearance than the late-maturing boys.

There are also pronounced changes in attitudes and interests among girls with the onset of pubescence. These changes, appearing at an earlier age for girls than for boys, aggravate the socializing problem in the seventh, eighth, and ninth grades. Girls select books of romance; in their social activities they prefer those activities involving both sexes; they tend to shun sports and strive to play the feminine role.

In order to determine the effect of the menarche, Stone and Barker (1939) studied interests and attitudes in 1,000 girls of two large junior high schools in Berkeley, California. These girls were matched with respect to chronological age and social status, but were significantly different in physiological development—one group postmenarcheal, the other premenarcheal. More postmenarcheal than premenarcheal girls of the same chronological age indicated an interest in and favorable attitude toward the opposite sex. The postmenarcheal girls were more interested in adornment and display of the person; they engaged in daydreaming and imaginative activities of such types to a greater degree; they indicated less interest in participation in games and activities requiring vigorous activity. There was, however, no noticeable difference found in the extent to which the two groups rebelled against or came into conflict with family authority. These comparisons indicate a growing interest in adult activities, an increased independence, and an increased interest in the opposite sex, as a result of forces associated with the menarche.

Attitudes Toward Authority

Attitudies toward authority, ranging from conformity to rebelliousness, were evaluated and studied by Tuma and Livson (1960) in three interpersonal situations for a sample of boys and girls at ages fourteen, fifteen, and sixteen. In general, girls proved to conform more than boys, but they consistently tended to increase their degree of conformity from age fourteen to sixteen in the three situations studied, whereas boys showed no clear age trend, except that there was a decided decline in conformity at age sixteen. (See Chapter 6.) That adolescents are not typified by a radical nature is brought forth in a cross-sample of the 26 million Americans between the ages of fifteen and twenty-one by Louis and Harris

(Life, 1971). Based on answers to the question, "What are your politics?" the following results were obtained:

Conservative	20 percent
Middle-of-the-road	39 percent
Liberal	23 percent
Radical	5 percent
Others and not sure	13 percent

In the study by Tuma and Livson a negative relation was found between the conformity of boys and socioeconomic ratings. In contrast, no significant relationships were found between the girls' conformity and socioeconomic indices. In lower-class and lower-middle-class families, parents are more likely to instill in their children the importance of obedience and acceptance of their status—and thus of authority. Upper-middle-class families encourage high aspirations and a nonacceptant attitude toward existing patterns and conditions.

The adolescent is likely to resent authoritative control. The self-conscious attitude so clearly displayed at this stage of life marks him as an individual on the alert, watching for someone to consider him as a child and thus boss him around. He is idealistic in nature and expects the teacher to play fair with him in his activities; he may question many of the procedures of the teacher for this reason. His personal manner of regarding everything as directed toward the self is a factor that should be watched. He is impulsive, oversensitive, and impressionable to mistreatment or unfair dealings.

Persistence of Attitudes

Attitudes, ideals, values, and self-concepts are important motivationally; they are interwoven with conscience. One has no feelings of guilt so long as one acts consistently with these internalized systems (conscience). Scott (1960: 154) noted "that an individual's attitude toward an event, X, tends to be consistent with his values and the way he sees X as relevant to them. Thus there is a tendency for one to act consistently with his attitudes, ideals, and values. This tendency is to a marked degree responsible for the persistent and consistent behavior or reactions toward families of related persons, situations, and objects."

Perceptual research has furnished evidence that attitudinal changes are closely related to personality structure. Katz et al. (1956) advanced the idea that attitudes may serve to protect and enhance the ego of the individual. Resistance to attitude changes may arise from the possibility that a change would deprive the individual of an important defense mechanism. For example, negative attitudes of many people toward the Negro may stem from feelings of inadequacy. An antiblack attitude enables such individuals to automatically feel superior to a large segment of our population.

There is evidence from many studies that attitudes do change as a result of education, wider social experiences, and intense specialized experiences. The influence of intense specialized experiences upon attitudes was especially evident in the case of a large percentage of U.S. soldiers engaged in the Vietnam War. Changed attitudes seemed to appear in connection with killing (the sacredness of life), drugs, the Vietnamese people, and other matters relating to the war and life in Vietnam.

This problem was studied by Lehmann and others (1966) with college students as subjects. A battery of cognitive and affective tests involving critical thinking ability, beliefs, dogmas, and values was administered to 1,051 college freshmen. These were later administered to the same students, when they were seniors. He found a significant decrease in stereotyped beliefs and a significant increase in critical thinking ability.

Ideals and the Adolescent

Ideals and values differ from attitudes in their ever-present imperative nature. It was suggested earlier that the adolescent has an indefinite number of attitudes and that these are often most inconsistent. Ideals are fewer in number; they are broad, guiding principles of behavior. Ideals, like attitudes, are developed from the total environment in which the child and adolescent lives, learns, and grows to maturity. The child's early experiences are frequently quite narrow, and his ideals are limited to his immediate environment involving the self and those with whom he is closely identified. Thus, the ideals of many adolescents, like those of many adults, are very narrow and limited, involving mainly the welfare and pleasure of the ego.

Although materials bearing on the nature of adolescents' ideals will be presented in later chapters, it should be pointed out at this time that the home, school, church, various youth-serving agencies, peers, and cross-age peers are the sources for adolescent's ideals. Movies, television, radio, and reading materials also affect the development of attitudes. Since a great deal of idealism runs throughout these sources, it is little wonder that most adolescents develop an idealistic outlook upon life and the problems confronting society.

DEVELOPING MORALS AND IDEALS. Ideals and morals develop in accordance with the adolescent's background and needs. They are closely related to parental attitudes, ideals, and values. In a study by Hoffman (1971), data were collected from 664 seventh-grade pupils on several moral attributes. Father-identification was found to be positively related to internal moral judgment in middle- and lower-class boys, to rule conformity in middle-class boys and girls, and to moral values in middle-class boys. Although the home background is related to moral development, its influence will vary with the educational level of the home, control patterns of the parents, birth order of the adolescent, age of parents, and sex of the adolescents.

We frequently hear demands for moral instruction in the classroom. There is evidence from many sources that Sunday school and classroom instruction, which have relied largely upon verbal teachings, have been ineffective in meeting the moral demands of modern life. Moral development, like the development of social habits and attitudes, will be most effective when it takes place in connection with situations arising naturally in the classroom or on the playground. The Sunday school can teach appreciation of one another and respect for the rights and feelings of others; but if this is done in a vacuum, and children see no relation between such teachings and the problems they meet on the street, at school, and in the park, the teaching will be so much babbling. Inconsistencies in moral concepts between parents, other adults, and his peers are a source of confusion to the adolescent and cause him concern and uncertainty.

Another essential in moral teachings is the harmonious correlation of all agencies affecting the moral life of boys and girls. The concepts presented in the home, on the playground, in school, and at church are usually too unrelated to have any great functional significance. The program of the church is in so many cases too far divorced from the other interests of the child, and the materials presented are too archaic to have any meaning for him in connection with present-day living. What seems to be needed is a positive approach to morals. Or, as Fleege states, "It would seem that too much emphasis has been placed on impurity and not enough on purity. The virtue has been left in the shadow while the failings have been paraded across the stage" (1944: 286).

In a study of moral judgments, Morris (1958) asked pupils what they would do in fourteen situations such as the following:

> Someone in your class at school has broken the school's rules and the teacher wants to find out who did it. He asks the pupils to own up; but no one does. Then he asks anyone who knows anything about it to come and see him afterward. J. knows who did it. What should he do?

> The pupils' responses were tabulated and the following conclusions were drawn: (1) Marked discrepancies were found between what pupils thought should be done in the problem situations and what they thought would actually be done. These discrepancies increased with age. (2) There was a slow decline with age in judgments based upon self-interest, with the greatest decline on the level of actually expected behavior. (3) There was a decline in moral dependence upon authority and an increase in independence, both subject to considerable fluctuations at the thirteen to fifteen-year age level. These results indicate a change from judgments purely egocentric in nature to those involving the welfare of others.

THEORETICAL CONSIDERATIONS. Most children emerge from a home background in which morality is based upon authority—the authority of the parent or some other adult figure, the church, or some other source. There they have acquired many behavior patterns based upon ideas or rules regarded as sacred and unchangeable. These are usually modified to some degree through interactions with peers and cross-age individuals. A form of mutual respect grows out of the demands involving some reciprocity made by peers. On the other hand, Kohlberg (1970) suggested that the quality of social participation and social responsibilities was associated with accelerated development. Middle-class boys tend to be at higher stages of moral development than lower-class boys, as did popular boys when compared with unpopular ones.

Results obtained from replicating in 1970 a survey conducted in 1963 showed that there have been very significant changes in the moral beliefs of students in maintained grammar schools in England (Wright and Cox, 1971). The subjects consisted of 2,276 seventeen to nineteen-year-old subjects in the 1963 survey and 1,574 in the 1970 survey. The greatest change noted was in sexual behavior, although changes extended to other issues such as racism and gambling. The changes were for the most part away from uncompromising condemnation toward acceptance, permissiveness, or ambivalence. There were clear signs that girls had changed more than boys. These changes, noted in the upper teen years, may also be observed in the lower teen years. This is perhaps related to the generation gap.

Cognitive development theories agree with the psychoanalytic theory that with advanced maturity and social participation there is a genuine development from an early, rigid moral judgment position to a later, more relative or flexible one. This is in harmony with the results of the study by Wright and Cox. They noted further that changes in moral behavior are largely independent of religious commitment. Thus, the influence of peer reference groups during the adolescent years is further substantiated.

Values—Their Meaning and Importance

Any attempt to completely separate attitudes, ideals, and values would be misleading. Values refer to what we regard as important rather than what we know. They are organizing factors within the personality and are especially important in relation to morals and character. They may best be understood from a brief description of the six types of men, presented by Spranger (1928). These six types are: (1) the *theoretical*—the individual who regards theories and knowledge as all-important; (2) the *esthetic*—one who places a high premium on beauty and loveliness; (3) the *economic*—one who cherishes things because of their material or economic value; (4) the *social*—one who places considerable importance upon the social factors; (5) the *political*—the person who has a strong desire for power and control; and (6) the *religious* —the person who finds satisfaction and joy in his relationships with the whole of life's experiences and purposes. These values have been organized into measurable test items, and considerable research has evolved from these and other attempts to measure an individual's values.

The importance of values in character formation has been emphasized by a number of investigators. Leckley (1945) postulated that after values are integrated into the personality they act as barriers to the acceptance of new ones which might be in opposition to them. This is necessary if the personality is to remain consistent and somewhat stable. Four prevailing sets of conditions are set forth by Leckley: (1) new values that are in opposition to those already accepted by the individual may be rejected; (2) new values may be so modified that they are no longer in opposition to the accepted values; (3) new values that are in opposition to old values may be ignored and thus not incorporated into the value system; and (4) old values may be modified in such a way that the new values are incorporated into the total value-system.

The relationship between value patterns of college students and economic status, level of education, and size of home town was shown in a study by Woodruff (1941). Groups of individuals with similar socioeconomic backgrounds engaged in similar educational or vocational pursuits tend to have similar value patterns. This is to be expected, since values, the foundations of attitudes, are a result of learning. Consequently they are subject to change, as may be noted from the results of varied experiences. However, attitudes and values are an individual, not a group matter, as is so frequently thought when considering a group of adolescents. Studies which trace the longitudinal development of a single individual reveal the nature of values and how they are acquired.

Developmental Sequence of Ideals and Values

The fact that adolescents are maturing earlier today, are better informed, and have had broader experiences than those of three or four decades ago most likely accounts for the differences in values. It is noteworthy, however, that ideals and values do go through a developmental sequence in harmony with increased physiological, intellectual, and social maturity and greater independence from parents and other authority figures.

Descriptive catalogs of values of attitudes have been provided by a number of investigators interested in the developmental sequence of attitudes and values. Such a list is likely to represent a particular sample taken in a school setting. There is no one list that would characterize all or even most adolescents. Subsequent chapters will deal with different subcultural groups of adolescents. The ideals and values of each group are products of learning based upon different experiences and needs. Developmental characteristics based upon age have been noted by students of developmental psychology.

In a study by Adelson and O'Neil (1966) of the growth of a sense of community during the adolescent years, a sample of 120 adolescents, thirty each at ages eleven, thirteen, fifteen, and eighteen was used as subjects. The investigators noted that younger adolescents find it difficult to conceive of the community as a unitary whole and hard to imagine the consequences of political action. Rather, they look upon government as a means of furnishing specific and tangible services of a personal nature. With increased age and maturity, adolescents are more apt to conceive of the community as a whole and use philosophical principles in making political judgments.

SUMMARY

Personality and character development begin during infancy; during adolescence, increased maturity and broader experiences have an important bearing on the direction of development. Important emotional and intellectual developments contribute to the internalization of many behavioral patterns. However, at all stages of development there is a consistency and continuity operating. The personality characteristics of the adolescent are characterized as dynamic, somewhat unstable, frequently ambivalent, but in general idealistic.

Although adolescent personality has its roots in biology, the early childhood years are crucial. It is the combination of many variables during childhood that determines the adolescent personality, with the sexual areas of experience correlating strongest with measures of ego strength. Childhood mothering has been stressed, although father-identification is extremely important to both daughters and sons.

During early adolescence, peers become very important, providing an anchor during the rapid transition from childhood to adulthood. Adolescents from certain minority groups and other disadvantaged groups are at a distinct disadvantage in their development of a well-integrated character. Religion affects the lives of many adolescents. Present-day adolescents are not following so closely the religious practices of their parents, although this does not mean that they are less religious.

Attitudes, ideals, and values are learned through interactions of the adolescent with varied forces and conditions in his environment. With pubescence there are changes in attitudes toward the opposite sex, the direction of which is determined largely by earlier experiences. And, although prejudices appear at this stage, they are closely related to social and cultural background. However, adolescents in general do not display extreme radicalism. There is to a marked degree a persistence of personality characteristics and attitudes, although these are subject to change under extremely different conditions.

REFERENCES

ADELSON, JOSEPH and ROBERT P. O'NEIL. "Growth of Political Ideas in Adolescence: The Sense of Community." *Journal of Personality and Social Psychology* (1966), 4:295–306.

ALLEN, MARTIN G. "Childhood Experience and Adult Personality—A Cross-cultural Study Using the Concept of Ego Strength." *Journal of Social Psychology* (1967), 71:53–68.

AUSUBEL, DAVID P. *Theory and Problems of Child Development.* New York: Grune and Stratton, Inc., 1958.

BECKER, W. "Consequences of Different Kinds of Parental Discipline." In *Review of Child Development Research,* H. L. Hoffman and L. W. Hoffman eds. New York: Russell Sage Foundation, 1964.

BILLER, HENRY B. and STEPHEN D. WEISS. "The Father-Daughter Relationship and the Personality Development of the Female." *Journal of Genetic Psychology* (1970), 116:79–93.

BRONNER, A. F. "Emotional Problems of Adolescence." *The Child's Emotions.* Chicago: University of Chicago Press, 1930.

BRONSON, WANDA C. "The Role of Enduring Orientations to the Environment in Personality Development." *Genetic Psychology Monographs* (1972), 86:3–80.

CATTELL, R. B. *et al. Handbook for the Junior Personality Quiz.* Champaign, Ill.: Institute for Personality and Ability Testing, 1953. Pp. 8–10.

DEUTSCHE, H. *The Psychology of Women,* Vol. 1. New York: Grune and Stratton, Inc., 1944.

DOHERTY, ANNE. "The Influence of Parental Control on the Development of Feminine Sex Roles and Conscience." Mimeographed Edition, 1969. Pp. 1–5.

FAUST, MARGARET S. "Developmental Maturity as a Determinant in Prestige of Adolescent Girls." *Child Development* (1960), 31:173–84.

FLEEGE, U. H. *Self-Revelation of Adolescent Boys.* Milwaukee: Bruce Publishing Co., 1944.

GARRISON, KARL C. *The Psychology of Exceptional Children.* Rev. ed. New York: The Ronald Press Co., 1950.

GOUGH, H. G. "Identifying Psychological Femininity" *Educational and Psychological Measurements* (1952), 12:427–39.

GREENBERG, PAUL and A. B. GILLILAND. "The Relationship Between Basal Metabolism and Personality." *Journal of Social Psychology* (1952), 35:3–7.

HALL, G. STANLEY. ADOLESCENCE, Vol. 2. New York: Appleton-Century-Crofts, 1904. Chapter 10.

HEILBRUN, A. B. and D. K. FROMME. "Parental Identification of Late Adolescents and Level of Adjustment: Importance of Parent-Model Attributes, Ordinal Position, and Sex of the Child." *Journal of Genetic Psychology* (1965), 107:49–59.

HILL, DAVID. Peer Group Conformity in Adolescent Smoking and Its Relationship to Affiliation and Autonomy Needs." *Australia Journal of Psychology* (1971), 23 (2):189–99.

JONES, MARY C. "A Study of Socialization Patterns at the High School Level." *Journal of Genetic Psychology* (1958), 93:87–111.

———, and NANCY BAYLEY. "Physical Maturing Among Boys as Related to Behavior." *Journal of Educational Psychology* (1950), 41:129–48.

JOSSELYN, IRENE. "The Ego in Adolescence." *American Journal of Orthopsychiatry* (1954), 24:223–37.

KATZ, D., I. SARNOFF, and C. McCLINTOCK. "Ego Defense and Attitude Change." *Human Relations* (1956), 9:27–45.

KOHLBERG, LAWRENCE. "Moral Development and the Education of Adolescents." In *Adolescents and the American High School*, R. Purnell, ed. New York: Holt, Rinehart & Winston, Inc., 1970. Pp. 144–62.

LANDIS, P. H. and C. L. STONE. "The Relationship of Parental Authority Patterns in Teenage Adjustments." Pullman, Wash.: State College of Washington, Rural Sociology Series on Youth, Bulletin No. 538, 1952.

LECKLEY, P. *Self-Consistency*. New York: The Island Press, 1945.

LEHMANN, I. J., B. K. SINHA, and R. T. HARNETT. "Changes in Attitudes and Values Associated with College Attendance." *Journal of Educational Psychology* (1966), 51:89–98.

LEONARD, M. R. "Fathers and Daughters." *International Journal of Psychoanalysis* (1966), 47:325–33.

Life magazine (January 8, 1971). "A New Youth Poll."

LONGSTRETH, LANGDON E. and RAGAN E. RICE. "Perceptions of Parental Behavior and Identification with Parents by Three Groups of Boys Differing in School Adjustment." *Journal of Educational Psychology* (1964), 55:144–51.

MEDINNUS, GENE R. "Objective Responsibility in Children: A Comparison with the Piaget Data." *Journal of Genetic Psychology* (1962), 101:127–33.

MOHR, G. J. "Psychiatric Problems of Adolescence." *Journal of the American Medical Association* (August 1948), 137, Part 2: 1590.

MONET, J. "Components of Eroticism in Man. I. The Hormones in Relation to Sexual Morphology and Sexual Desire." *Journal of Nervous and Mental Diseases* (1961), 132:239–48.

MORRIS, J. F., ed. "The Development of Adolescent Value Judgments." *Journal of Educational Psychology* (1958), 28:1–14.

MUSSEN, P. H. and M. C. JONES. "Self-conceptions, Motivations and Interpersonal Attitudes of Late and Early Maturing Boys." *Child Development* (1957), 28:243–56.

PAYNE, DONALD E. and PAUL H. MUSSEN. "Parent-child Relations and Father Identification Among Adolescent Boys." *Journal of Abnormal and Social Psychology* (1965), 52:358–62.

SCOTT, W. S. "Personal Values and Group Interaction." In *Decision, Values, and Groups*, Vol. 1, Dorothy Milner, New York: Pergamon, 1960.

SHERIF, MUZAFER and CAROLYN M. SHERIF. *Reference Groups*. New York: Harper & Row, Publishers, 1965.

SOROKIN, P. *Social Mobility*. New York: Harper & Row, Publishers, 1927.

SPRANGER, E. *Lebensformen*. Halle, Germany: Niemeyerm 1928.

STONE, C. P. and R. G. BARKER. "The Attitudes and Interests of Premenarcheal and Postmenarcheal Girls." *Journal of Genetic Psychology* (1939), 54:27–72.

SYMONDS, P. M. and ARTHUR R. JENSEN. *From Adolescence to Adult*. New York: Columbia University Press, 1961.

Time magazine (January 29, 1965), pp. 56–57. "Education."

TUMA, ELIAS and NORMAN LIVSON. "Family Socio-economic Status, and Adolescent Attitudes to Authority." *Child Development* (1960), 31:287–99.

WOODRUFF, A. D. *A Study of Directive Factors in Individual Behavior.* Ph.D. dissertation. Chicago: University of Chicago, 1941.

WOODWORTH, R. S. *Contemporary Schools of Psychology.* New York: The Ronald Press, 1948.

WRIGHT, DEREK and EDWIN COX. "Changes in Moral Beliefs Among Sixth-form Boys and Girls over a Seven-year Period in Relation to Religious Belief, Age, and Sex Differences." *British Journal of Social and Clinical Psychology* (1971), 10 (4):332–41.

RECOMMENDED READINGS

ELMER, ALAN C. ed. *Role Playing, Reward, and Attitude Change.* New York: Van Nostrand Reinhold, 1969.

All but the last of the fifteen papers in this valuable collection are abridgments of journal articles, originally published between 1953 and 1967. The editor has selected and arranged these so as to present a running argument on the effects of experimentally manipulated "role" inductions upon expressed attitudes.

GARDNER, RILEY W. and ALICE MORIARTY. *Personality Development at Pre-adolescence: Explorations of Structure Formation.* Seattle: University of Washington Press, 1968.

The authors report the results of a study of sixty boys and girls between nine and thirteen at the Menninger Foundation in Topeka, Kansas. The team's assessments of the children are based upon a battery of tests. Evidence of individual consistency is impressive among the subjects.

HORROCKS, JOHN E. *The Psychology of Adolescence.* 3rd ed. Boston: Houghton Mifflin Company, 1969.

Interests and activities of adolescents are dealt with in Chapter 23, while Chapter 24 furnishes useful materials, based on research studies, on the attitudes and ideals of adolescents.

LAMPEL, RUSIA. *That Summer with Ora.* New York: Franklin Watts, Inc., 1967.

Written specifically as a diary, this is a clever, realistic account of a sophisticated young American girl who visits friends of her parents in Israel. Her problems of American superiority and snobbishness, lead to an explosive climax.

McCANDLESS, BOYD R. *Adolescents' Behavior and Development.* Hinesdale, Ill.: The Dryden Press Inc., 1970.

Changes in function and sexual socialization are presented in Chapter 4. Chapter 5 deals with the importance and role of physical factors on personality.

ROBERTS, JOAN I., ed. *School Children in the Urban Slum.* New York: The Free Press, 1967. Pp. 425–506.

The topics covered by different authorities in this area are: I want to get out; socialization and social class through time and space; child-rearing practices in low socioeconomic groups; status and the socialized son; some effects of paternal absence on male children; and impact of employment of mothers by social class.

THOMPSON, GEORGE H., ed. *Social Development and Personality.* New York: John Wiley & Sons, Inc., 1971.

Readings dealing with social development of adolescents. The papers show how social actions, preferences, motivations, learnings, and the internalization of social controls appear and shape social development during adolescence.

part three

Cultural and Social Influences

Many young people express an interest in psychology because they are interested in understanding themselves and their own lives. As a psychologist and a sociologist, we have frequently encountered students eager to utilize the insights of these disciplines as a means of greater self-understanding. In this respect, psychology and sociology are quite different from other areas of learning: they deal directly with our personal and social lives. This has been kept in mind in preparing this book and is especially pertinent to Part III.

The five chapters that make up this part examine operation of cultural and social forces and conditions on adolescents. The diversity of adolescent subcultures can best be attributed to the different cultural and social influences in their lives. Adolescents, whether in school or elsewhere, face many uncertainties, difficult problems, and conflicting situations as they grope for a way of life. Unless we as adults interested in human behavior can view adolescents in a humanistic manner rather than as people to be manipulated, the consequences may be very serious.

8

family, peers, and related influences

The personal and social development and personality integration of the adolescent proceed apace with his development as an independent person who is distinct from others. Interwoven with his childhood experiences and intimately related to his basic needs, are close ties with others, especially members of his family and peers. As he matures, he becomes conscious of himself as a separate being; the quest for independence begun during childhood continues into adolescence and is manifested in many different ways. With growth and development there is a widening of social contacts, which have an important bearing on the adolescent's personal and social development.

THE PROBLEM OF GENERATIONS

The problem of generations has received the attention of philosophers and other scholars for centuries. More recently these problems have fallen within the interests and domain of sociologists and social psychologists. Although attractive and interesting, the multiplicity of points of view, resulting from the various backgrounds of scholars, has failed to give us a well-organized schematic approach to the problem. Perhaps the work of Karl Mannheim (1953) is as enlightening as any that we can draw upon; therefore many of the ideas here presented are adapted from this source. According to Mannheim, "the social phenomenon 'generation' represents nothing more than a particular kind of identity of location, embracing related 'age groups' embedded on a historical-social process. While the nature of class location can be explained in terms of economic and social conditions, generation location is determined by the way in which certain patterns of experience and thought tend to be brought into existence by the *natural data* of the transition from one generation to another" (292).

The unity of a generation is not comparable to the unity of organized groups, although there is at times during the adolescent years a unified feeling with peers or others of a similar age and bond. This may be observed in modern youth movements. In this case groups are often cliques formed to further some cause or demonstrate against certain felt wrongs or injustices. Such groups are based upon the consciousness of belonging to one generation, and they frequently abandon a cause once it is embraced by older members of the society.

Fundamental Facts About Generations

We should gain considerable insight through an examination of the characteristics of generations as noted in different societies. There is first of all *a continuous emergence of new participants in the cultural process.* Cultural creation and cultural accumulation are not products of a single individual or group of individuals. Instead, there is a continuous emergence of new age groups, each of which is born into a culture and each of which reacts to that culture and makes certain changes, modifications, additions, and deletions.

A second characteristic listed by Mannheim is that *the participants in the process of culture are continuously disappearing only to be followed by others who are coming into the cultural process.* There are two ways in which past experiences can be incorporated in the present: (1) as consciously recognized models on which patterns of behavior are developed, and (2) as unconsciously implicit or newly discovered patterns are fashioned. This enables youth to graft new truths to the old ones found in earlier cultural movements. Thus, while the older generation is living within a framework of usable past experiences, "youth, on the other hand, where life is new, formative forces are just coming into being, and basic attitudes in the process of development, can take advantage of the moulding power of new situations" (Mannheim, 296).

A third fundamental fact about generations listed by Mannheim is that *members of any one generation can only participate in a temporarily limited section of the historical process.* Members of a generation are similarly located with respect to time and world conditions. They are exposed to the same phase of the collective process. This, however, must not be taken literally, since each individual interprets the world and happenings about him in accordance with his own memory of events, past experiences, and potentials. Each generation is able to start afresh with a new life, to build a new destiny, a new framework of references and expectations based upon a new set of experiences. We must not conclude that each generation has a common bond or unity; each is presented with an angle of vision imposed by a particular time location. Thus, mere contemporaneity becomes sociologically significant only when it also involves participation in universal historical and social circumstances. Also, we must take into consideration the phenomenon of "stratification." Some older generation groups experience certain historical processes together with the young generation, notably in a strictly rural culture; yet we cannot say that they have the same generation location.

We must not assume that because each generation starts life afresh that youth will be liberal or progressive, while the older generation will become conservative over the years because of their experiences. Biological factors and time of birth do not in themselves produce a progressive or conservative point of view. Mannheim states: "Whether youth will be conservative, reactionary, or progressive, depends (if not entirely, at least primarily) on whether or not the existing social structure and the position they occupy in it provide opportunities for the promotion of their own social and intellectual ends. Their 'being young,' the 'freshness' of their contact with the world, manifest themselves in the fact that they are able to re-orient any movement they embrace, to adapt it to the total situation" (297).

A fourth basic fact of generations listed by Mannheim is *the necessity for constant transmission of the cultural heritage*. The traditional ways of life, feelings, prejudices, and attitudes are automatically passed on by the older generation to the younger generation. This may be noted in the case of attitudes toward different racial and religious groups. This is accomplished not so much by conscious teaching but rather by ways of living. And, as pointed out in Chapter 7, such attitudes are absorbed by the younger generation from the social milieu. Ideas and attitudes transmitted by conscious teaching are of more limited importance, while those which serve as the basic inventory for most life activities are unconsciously and unwittingly handed down and transmitted through generations. The adolescent is open to new ideas and influences if placed in a new setting; schools, camps, and other organizations and institutions strongly influence the attitudes, habits, and emotional patterns of children and adolescents.

In the transmission of the cultural heritage, unconscious changes proceed slowly. Ideas appear to precede real social transformation. We have observed this in the integration movement of the blacks into church activities. Middle-class whites early accepted the idea of equality and the acceptance of all individuals into the church, but this acceptance was not unconscious. This was further illustrated by a group of women at a religious meeting. The question was raised, What would our attitude be if a retired black clergyman wished to buy a home and retire in this area? (an area where only people of a certain faith lived.) Although the group had favored an integrated church movement, no one replied to the question raised. Belief in white superiority was firmly entrenched. On problems of this nature there is likely to be a gap between the feelings of the younger generation and those of the older. "This tension appears incapable of solution except for one compensating factor—not only does the teacher educate his pupil, but the pupil educates his teacher too. Generations are in a state of constant interaction" (Mannheim, 301).

A fifth fact about generations listed by Mannheim is *the uninterrupted series*. The fact that one generation moves into another generation in an uninterrupted manner tends to render this interaction smoother. Fortunately this process does not take place at thirty- or forty-year intervals. Although biological differences between generations exist, intermediary groups play an important part in the transitional process. It was pointed out in Chapter 3 that the problems of generations become greater to the degree that the dynamism of society increases. As pointed out by Mannheim: "Static conditions make for attitudes of piety—the younger generation tends to adapt itself to the older, even to the point of making itself appear older. With the strengthening of the social dynamic, however, the older generation becomes increasingly receptive to influences from the younger" (302).

The Generation Gap: Its Nature and Depth

The dynamic nature of our political, economic, social, and industrial society has produced problems for adolescents that are different and far greater than those experienced by the previous generation. The concept of a generation gap was presented in Chapter 3; to deny its existence is to fail to understand the thinking of a large percentage of high school and college youth.

Unsettled though he may be by our role in the Vietnam War, political pay-offs, injustices toward minority groups, a man of fifty looks back at the progress made during his life with a great deal of pride and satisfaction. He, the father of present-day youth, saw a great and crushing depression as a boy; but he saw his government assume greater responsibility for the welfare of its people. He can remember the first jet flights, space shots, television, and polio vaccine. He has witnessed the institution of social security and pensions for the aged, two-car families, paid vacations, and rural electricity.

If world events and national problems overwhelm him, he still nourishes a faith that we will be able to find the right leaders to see us through, just as we have in the past. In any case he is now middle-aged, has survived many hardships or problems, and now lives in a country with the highest average living standard of all times. Thus, it is frequently difficult for him to understand why his 20-year-old son or daughter doesn't appreciate the accomplishments of the past generation and can't be happy with present conditions.

The present middle-class generation is the first in our history, experts generally agree, that is not going to college to prepare for a profession and to earn a living. Due to the prolonged period of education, the middle-class adolescent is able to delay the burdens of adulthood and is free to examine his mind and conscience, to concern himself with the qualities of life and the problems and needs of others less fortunate than himself.

This generation of young middle-class whites is a product of both the good and bad in our society. They take for granted food on the table, a car in the garage, spending money, and freedom to move up or down in our social structure. Accustomed to economic security, religious creeds based upon the brotherhood of man, noble ideals of their country, they are more shocked than their parents were to discover that the government in their own country suppresses historical facts and news, that so-called Christian leaders display racial bigotry, that poverty and disease among the unfortunate are an accepted part of life. Contemporary youth has witnessed police violence, the killing of innocent people by our soldiers in Vietnam, calculated lying by national leaders, and a mindless arms race.

Not only has the present-day youth witnessed these forces and conditions, most stirring of all he has seen the sudden death of his heroes. Such men as John F. Kennedy, Martin Luther King, and Robert Kennedy furnished youth with hope; they provided a vital link between youth and the problems of today. While the silent majority of youth

Dad, what was meant by the New Deal?

may find that their social and economic relations satisfactorily prepare them for the transition into the adult roles of marriage, family, work, and citizenship, a substantial minority finds that school, family, and other institutions inhibit them in the acquisition of the kind of adulthood they strive to achieve. Special materials bearing on the alienation of this section of youth will be presented in Part IV.

Family Authority Patterns

The authority pattern found in the home refers to the power that controls the activities of the family. This power may be exercised in a number of ways, although, since there are only two parents, there can be only three general divisions of parental control. Authority may be in the hands of the mother or the father, or it may be divided in some manner between the two. An investigation by Ingersoll (1946), based on an intensive study of thirty-seven homes, revealed the major types of authority patterns as listed in Table 8-1. A careful study of this table shows that the control may be either democratic or autocratic, although these are not discrete and may be found in varying degrees in either father-controlled or the mother-controlled homes.

TABLE 8-1 Types of Authority Patterns

Mother-controlled—autocratic patterns of authority
Mother-led—democratic pattern of authority
Balanced control:
    Equalitarian—democratic patterns of authority
    Equalitarian—indulgent patterns of authority
    Equalitarian—laissez-faire pattern of authority
    Equalitarian—conflicting pattern of authority
Father-controlled—autocratic patterns of authority
Father-controlled—pseudoautocratic pattern of authority
Father-led—democratic pattern of authority

Source: Ingersoll (1946).

The laissez-faire families are characterized by a father who delegates the major tasks of rearing the children to the mother. The mother, on the other hand, sets up fairly definite standards for child behavior, but neither she nor the father enforces the rules and regulations. The children do as they please and show little respect or consideration for their parents. It seems likely that this type of control is most undesirable, while the democratic home appears to be most desirable as reflected in child and adolescent adjustment. Data bearing on this were presented in Chapter 7.

THE ADOLESCENT VIEWS HIS PARENTS. The adolescent strives for increased independence, primarily because its achievement means he has reached adulthood; he has become grown-up, self-sufficient, and able to chart a world of his own. As he assumes more independence and more authority over his own life, he frequently comes into conflict with his parents. The boundaries of his freedom are frequently not clearly defined, and this leads to parental conflicts.

The adolescent from the autocratic home may become critical and sometimes acutely hostile toward his parents, especially when his prestige with peers or his self-esteem is challenged. Wider contacts with peers and other adults enable him to make comparisons and acquire new understandings. The results frequently cause him to lose confidence in his parents, since he had earlier conceived of them as ideals. Sometimes the child from the lower culture is actually ashamed of his parents. Such was the case of Celia.

> One day while walking home from school a very poorly dressed man stopped his well-worn automobile and called to her. Celia tried to ignore him, but he was insistent. So, she got in the automobile with him and he drove away. The next day some of her friends asked her who the man was with whom she had ridden away on the previous day. She told them that he was an old man who worked for them, doing odd jobs on certain occasions. Actually the man was Celia's father.

The adolescent who is insecure with his peers is more likely to be ashamed of any shortcomings or unfavorable home conditions than the one who is secure. This frequently accounts for the critical attitude of some adolescents toward their parents. Many adolescents take an ambivalent attitude toward their parents, seeing them as affectionate dictators.

TEEN-AGER'S COMPLAINTS. A frequent complaint of teen-agers is that parents are dictatorial. Parents sometimes cut off discussions with "I don't want to hear any more about that," or appeal to children's sympathy by saying, "You are driving me mad," or "You are driving me to my grave." Often, parents blindly make rules and decisions. To stop a romance, they will punish, deny permission for a normal request, or inflict new rules. Further discussion is not permitted; neither is there an appeal from the ruling.

Teen-agers are not by any means unanimous in their complaints. For every complaint or accusation made, there are some who say the opposite. The most common complaint found in the study by Herzog and others (1970) was a failure in understanding and communication. Most youth want to be understood, although understanding does not mean agreeing. Understanding furnishes a basis for further communication and compromise. Many teen-agers stated, "If only my parents would try to understand. They won't even discuss problems with me." Herzog and others noted further certain sins of omission within the family circle: "They are too busy." "They don't take the time." "They're too wrapped up in their own problems." "They don't give enough love."

The sins of omission frequently contribute to such sins of commission as "nosiness," "suspiciousness," and "inconsideration." Some parents inquire into the details of their teen-ager's social life and attempt to keep abreast of all his movements away from home.

A different objection to parental behavior is reported by about one in ten of the correspondents. "This concerns parents who set a poor example for their children, especially those who 'say one thing and do another.' These are described with biting scorn as being 'hypocritical,' 'phony,' 'setting a bad example.' They drink, they smoke, they tell half-truths, they practice 'loose morality,' and at the same time urge their children to practice what the parents preach" (Herzog and others, 1970:8).

THE FAMILY STRUCTURE

The variables included here under family structure have an important bearing on the development and behavior of children and adolescents. These variables include the absent father and broken homes, ordinal position and siblings, rural-urban-suburban living, social class, and self- or peer-orientation of parents. These variables do not operate in isolation from each other. For example, the rural adolescent from a middle-class home may have a horse and be an active member of the 4-H Club, while another rural adolescent from a lower-class home suffers from malnutrition during early childhood and has no spending money except what he can earn or steal. The varieties of family structure are many; the influences are inestimable.

The family as we witness it today in the United States and other Western countries consists of a father, a mother who is married to the father in some manner prescribed by custom or law, and the offspring of this union. This is the *nuclear family*. There are some variations, but they are not of special importance at this point of our discussion. The *extended family* is the most numerous type to be found throughout the world. In this family unit there will be two or more generations involved. Such families are more often patriarchal, although some are matriarchal.

The emergence of the nuclear family resulted from the Industrial Revolution and the modernization of society. The geographic mobility of our population supported the development of the nuclear family rather than the extended family. Aside from the biological functions of the family, there are also educational, economical, psychological, and social functions. The extent to which these functions are carried out depends upon the nature, structure, and goals of each family. There are some who claim that the role of the family has largely been displaced by different secondary conditions and institutions such as schools, clubs, camps, and social and recreational activities and programs.

RELIGIOUS INFLUENCES. There are many tangible and intangible forces and conditions operating in every community that affect the personal and social development of adolescents. Any effort to evaluate the influences of these forces and conditions will be most difficult. However, there seems to be a decided decline in the influence of the home and church accompanied by the assumption of greater responsibility and control on the part of the community; consequently, at some point, the adolescent comes face to face with problems that are not solved on the basis of authority or of sentiment, as are problems arising at home. The importance of the home and community in the development of character was well stated many years ago by John Dewey when he wrote:

> In its deepest and richest sense a community must always remain a matter of face-to-face intercourse. This is why the family and neighborhood, with all their deficiencies, have always been the chief agencies of nurture, the means by which the dispositions are stably formed and ideas acquired which lay hold of the roots of character. The Great Community, in the sense of free and full intercommunication, is conceivable. But it can never possess all the qualities which mark a local community. (1927: 211–12).

Favorable personal and social development will not take place in a vacuum. Neither will these result from too limited experiences. The adolescent must be given an opportunity to make social contacts outside the home and immediate neighborhood, to accept responsibility, and to display a reasonable amount of initiative in order to develop the personal and social self. The churches, schools and different youth agencies have sponsored many programs designed to help adolescents solve their problems. The failure of many of these offers a challenge. Some of these difficulties are given special consideration in later chapters dealing with the alienation of young people and some of the problems faced by them as they grow toward maturity.

Influences of the Home

The different studies of early home influences on the personal and social development and adjustment of children and adolescents have furnished us with considerable evidence that satisfactory adjustments are closely related to the extent basic needs for affection, security, status, and belongingness are met during the early years of life. Families which do many things together, where everyone participates in the varied home activities, produce well-adjusted and happy children. Children reared in such homes tend to catch the spirit of the home and develop good dispositions and favorable outlooks upon life. On the other hand, parents who display habits of selfishness, and who are unable to accept their children as unique personalities may well hinder their personal and social adjustment, and consequently, their outlook and disposition.

A study by Carlson (1958) had for its hypothesis that parental attitudes would, in part, determine aspects of the child's self-concept and social status. Forty-three sixth-graders completed a questionnaire specially designed to furnish descriptions of the self and the ideal self. Their mothers and fathers completed the same questionnaire. The findings confirmed expected interrelationships among children and parents in their self-acceptance, social orientation, and peer status.

Various studies have shown that children in long-term foster-care homes usually experience two or more placements and that the more placements experienced, the more problems they display (Dinnage, 1967). The difficulties which long-term foster-care children experience in establishing an adequate sense of identity and a positive self-image was brought out in Chapter 6. The home environment of such children has not been consistent enough to enable them to construct a coherent picture of positive relationships. They may try to please others, but are unable to trust them, or may strike out against their best friends.

Influence of Ordinal Position

Much research has been directed at determining the effects of ordinal position and sex of siblings on personality development. Oberlander,

Mom just can't understand. She still uses books to raise me by. Her Book says this is the year I start wanting perfume and makeup for Christmas. She couldn't understand when I told her No.

Frauenfelder, and Heath (1969) found that first-borns were more disposed, in their interest choices of a semiprojective instrument, toward intellectual patterns and second-borns seemed to prefer social activities. A subsequent study by Oberlander and Frauenfelder (1970) attempted to relate objectively derived measures of interest to ordinal position and sex of sibling in order to test three hypotheses that were supported by previous investigations: "(a) Later-borns score higher than first-borns in their preference for being active in groups. (b) First-borns have greater preference for working with ideas than do later-borns. (c) First-borns have stronger preferences for directing others than do later-borns" (122).

Kuder Preference Record scores were obtained on a sample of 217 eighteen-year-olds. The data obtained confirmed the above findings and revealed that those with a male sibling showed greater preference for working with ideas than those with a female sibling; and they also preferred to avoid conflict.

According to Nichols (1966), being first-born in a family of three children is more advantageous than being first-born in a family of two. In two-child families, first-born children, either male or female, with younger brothers have been found to be more intelligent than those with sisters (Altus, 1965). Altus further notes that first-borns in college have more verbal ability than later-borns. Studies have shown that there is throughout history a relation between achieving eminence and being first-born. There are a number of possible explanations for this. Historically the first-born male has in many cultures been in an advantageous position in the inheritance of wealth, power, position, and responsibility. The first-born is actually the only child until a second-born appears. Thus, he has the advantage of all of the parents' attention. There is also a likelihood of greater parental expectations from the first-born.

The results of a study by Robertson (1971) support the hypothesis that the relationship between birth order and personality varies with social class. A group of 297 fourteen to fifteen-year-old boys from different social backgrounds was administered Cattell's High School Personality Questionnaire. Data obtained from the questionnaire revealed differences particularly between middle and lower working-class subjects. Boys from lower working-class homes were more anxious and more introverted than their later-born counterparts, whereas in middle working class subjects this position was reversed. A study by Smith (1971) showed that the authority of parents is accepted more completely by first-born than by later-born male adolescents. Thus, any conclusions about the effects of ordinal position must take into consideration a number of variables such as the socioeconomic status of the family, age of the parents, control pattern of the parents, size of the family, and sex composition of the family.

The Broken Home and the Absent Father

The importance of the home for generational continuity has been pointed out. Certainly children and adolescents in the broken home miss some of the family culture that would be learned by living in a healthy home where both parents are present. However, one cannot conclude that all unbroken homes have a desirable emotional climate and are superior to broken homes. As pointed out earlier, there are many patterns of home situations. More than one-tenth of the children in the United States live in households where no father is present (Clausen, 1966; Schlesinger, 1966). The incidence of fatherless families is especially high among the lower class and particularly among lower-class Negro families, approaching 50 per cent in some areas.

The influences of paternal absence on personality development have been discussed and studied by a number of students of education, psychology, and sociology. There is considerable evidence that the death of one of the parents may have quite a harmful effect upon the growing child and thus the adolescent (Bartlett and Horrocks, 1958). Homes broken by divorce may also present difficulties for adolescents. Since there are many variables present in a home situation, it is not possible to assess the ill-effects of the divorce per se on the adolescent's development.

EFFECTS ON BOYS. The results of a study by Hoffman (1971) indicate that the effects of father-absence on boys are similar but somewhat more pronounced than the effects of nonidentification with a father who is present. This suggests that the ill-effects of father-absence are not all attributable to the lack of a parental model. Results of the study suggest further that the effects of father-absence may be partly mediated by the resulting changes in the mother's child-rearing practices.

McCord, McCord, and Thurber (1962) reported that boys' behavior problems were related to father-absence only if the mother was deviant or rejecting. A direct relationship between father-absence and inadequate sex-role functioning has been called into question by Biller (1970). He suggests that other factors in the home situation can greatly influence the extent to which a boy's personality is disrupted by father-absence. For example, the age of onset of father absence was found to be important. The boy's self-concept did not seem to be affected if the father's absence occurred after the age of five; if the absence occurred before the age of five, masculine identification was hampered.

EFFECTS ON GIRLS. Although most of the discussions of the effects of father-absence deal with adolescent boys, Biller's (1970) and Biller and Weiss's reviews (1970) of this problem show that the personal and social development of daughters may also be seriously affected. There is empirical and scientific evidence that the effects of father-absence is different for girls than for boys. Furthermore, this is affected by the makeup of the family. In a study by Hetherington (1973) of adolescent girls without fathers, three groups of first-born daughters of lower or lower-middle-class families, thirteen to seventeen years of age, were used as subjects: twenty-four from families in which the parents lived together; twenty-four from families divorced, and the girls had minimal contact with the father; twenty-four from families in which the father had died. None of the girls had brothers; therefore contacts with males at home were minimal. The results of the study showed that girls whose parents were divorced sought more attention from male adults than did the girls in the other two groups. Girls whose fathers were dead displayed severe anxiety, shyness, and discomfort in the presence of adult males. It seems likely "that for both groups of fatherless girls the lack of opportunity for constructive interaction with a loving, attentive father has resulted in apprehension and inadequate skills in relating to males" (52).

The results of the study by Hetherington support those of an earlier study by Bartlett and Horrocks (1958). They noted that adolescents from homes where one parent is deceased tend to receive less recognition and affection from adults. Thus, they tend to seek attention from the opposite sex in order to compensate for this condition. This frequently presents a problem and a hazard to the adolescent, especially the adolescent girl.

Influence of a Disturbed Mother

The relative importance (and to some degree the roles) of father and mother will vary with culture and with the age of the children. However, since the earliest family records and throughout all cultures, the role of the mother has not changed very much. Blum (1964) states, "It can't, because it is biologically determined. It has been proved countless times, in war, disaster, and tragic experiment, that an infant who does not receive from someone what we traditionally think of as mothering—being held, played with, talked to, loved—will grow mentally or physically sick, and may even die" (38). The importance of motherhood has been further substantiated in animal studies using monkeys as subjects.

A study of social workers' observations of ten- to fifteen-year-old boys by McCord, McCord, and Thurber (1962) showed that the presence of a rejecting or disturbed mother was associated with behavior problems such as sexual anxiety, regression, and delinquency in father-absent boys. Father-absent boys who had seemingly well-adjusted mothers were much less likely to exhibit such behavior problems. The results of a later study by Pedersen (1966) of eleven- to fifteen-year-old boys from military families suggest that psychologically healthy mothers may be able to counteract the effects of father-absence. Both the disturbed and nondisturbed boys in the Pedersen study had experienced long periods of father-absence; however, the mothers of the disturbed boys exhibited significantly more psychopathology than the mothers of the nondisturbed boys.

It appears, therefore, that a mother can help a father-absent son by her positive attitude toward the absent father and other males and by generally expecting and encouraging masculine behavior. This is most important in light of population studies (*Current Population Reports,*

1972) since 1960. These studies show an increasing proportion of young people under eighteen years of age living with their mothers only.

Determinants of Peer Orientation

Although parents and peers may well be regarded as alternative agents of socialization, parents furnish orientations for the child and adolescent's interaction with peers. The fact is that parents themselves usually foster, not necessarily consciously, a peer- or self-orientation. Hollander and Marcia (1970) tested the hypothesis that children who perceive their parents' rearing practices to be peer-oriented tend to be peer-oriented themselves.

The subjects used in the study by Hollander and Marcia were two classes of white, fifth-grade pupils (thirty boys and twenty-two girls) in a middle-class, suburban elementary school. The subjects were individually interviewed to ascertain their own and their parents' attitudes toward their peers. Through the interview the experimenters gathered information about recent activities that the child or adolescent had been allowed or forbidden to do. From these data the investigators determined whether the father or mother was dominant. The most consistent findings were:

1. Children with peer-oriented parents were more peer oriented on the different measures than children with self-oriented parents.
2. Boys were more peer oriented than girls.
3. Children who see their parents as dominant, most of whom were boys, were more peer oriented.
4. Influence over other children in terms of "getting other children to do things," seems to be greater for peer-oriented boys in father-dominant, peer-oriented families.
5. Influence over peers appears to be least in mother-dominant, peer-oriented families.
6. Self-oriented girls are seen as having more influence on their classmates than peer-oriented girls.
7. Conformity in terms of "getting along with what the other children are doing," is greater for children from father-dominant families and least in children who are inclined to choose self over others.
8. Obedience to authority is most marked among parent-oriented children whose parents are not peer-oriented.

INFLUENCE OF PEERS

The transition of adolescents from the nuclear family to the wider adult society takes place in many ways in Western society. The peer group has become one of the most important avenues through which this occurs. It has been suggested by some students of adolescent psychology that adolescents follow parents' wishes in future-oriented situations and

TABLE 8-2 Adolescent Choice Patterns in Hypothetical Situations

HYPOTHETICAL SITUATIONS	ADOLESCENT CHOICE PATTERNS (in percentages)		
	Parent Compliant	Best Friend Compliant	N[a]
Current Situations			
X₁ Club Membership[b]	65.9	34.1	(1508)
X₂ Party vs. Parents[c]	69.7	30.3	(1483)
X₃ Party vs. Best Friends[c]	47.9	52.1	(1491)
Future Situations			
X₄ Character vs. Best Friends[d]	52.6	47.4	(1499)
X₅ Character vs. Parents[d]	54.4	45.6	(1502)
X₆ College vs. Best Friend[e]	78.0	22.0	(1488)
X₇ College vs. Parents[e]	33.9	66.1	(1483)

[a] Nonresponses are excluded.

[b] Joining club against parents' wishes.

[c] In the party vs. parents situation the adolescent is urged by his parents to stay home and by his best friends to go to the party. The party vs. best friends represents a reversal of this situation to ascertain whether the situation or the parent-best friend cross-pressures are operating.

[d] In the character vs. best friends situation and adolescent is urged by his parents to tell the principal who broke the glass and by his best friends not to tell. This situation is reversed in the character vs. parents situation.

[e] In the college vs. best friends situation the adolescent is urged by his parents to enter the college preparatory program and by his best friends to enter the general program. The college vs. parents situation is a reversal of this situation.

Source: Larson, 1972.

peer wishes in immediate situations. In a study by Larson (1972), data were collected on 1,542 students from the seventh, ninth, and twelfth grades of schools in southern Oregon. Parent and peer orientations were measured by fifteen questionnaire items, each of which provided three alternative response categories: parent orientation, best friend or peer orientation, and orientations about the same. Responses were obtained from each of seven situations.

The findings presented in Table 8-2 show that the majority of the adolescents studied chose to accept the wishes of their parents in three situations, and the wishes of their best friends in one (pressure against entering the general program in school). The remaining three situations showed a fairly even split. The major results of this study are:

1. The majority of the adolescents studied are pro-parent in their orientation.

2. A substantial proportion of the adolescents see no reason to differentiate between parent and peer societies.

3. The responses of youth in this study differ very little between future- and current-oriented situations.

4. The club membership and party situations (social) are more conducive

to parent or peer compliance than the character and curriculum situations.

5. Parent-oriented youth tend to make parent-compliant choices, peer-oriented youth tend to make best-friend choices.

6. Most adolescents chose in terms of the *content* of the situation, parental and peer pressure notwithstanding.

Peer Relations During Adolescence

We tend to explain the behavior of children and adolescents on the basis of the family and organized institutions they have been associated with —thus minimizing the importance of their experiences with each other in their day-to-day activities. However, Bronfenbrenner (1969) points out that the increase of the distance between generations in the United States is a result of the fact that adolescents spend more time, compared to past generations, in the company of peers. In England, according to Bronfenbrenner, peer groups are largely autonomous—that is, independent of adult society—and develop their own behavioral norms. In contrast to the United States and England, children and adolescents in Germany spend much time in the family. The U.S.S.R. offers another contrast, the "children's collectives," which are well organized and carefully regulated by the adult society and deliberately try to inculcate adult social norms.

Peer relations during adolescence are extremely important. It is with their peers that adolescents have opportunities to intimately share their problems and experiences, and it is from their peers that they are able to find sympathy and relatively complete understanding. Through doing they learn to cooperate, give, and take, and clarify their sex role. The American teen-age subculture developed as a result of the failure of society to clearly define the roles of adolescents. There is considerable evidence that a boy's peer relationships are much influenced by his display or lack of sex-appropriate behavior and masculinity; this relationship does not appear to exist for girls. Thus, boys are driven to conform to those traits or behavior patterns that are regarded as masculine by their peers.

Peer Acceptance and Conformity

Adolescents' need for peer acceptance is quite generally recognized. It was pointed out in Chapter 2 that conformity to peer expectations or perceived expectations characterizes early adolescence and diminishes in the later adolescent years. Concerning conformity and age, Costanzo and Shaw (1966) state:

> . . . By the postadolescent and early adulthood stages, the individual has learned that there are both situations which call for conformity and those which call for individual action. Thus, he becomes more confident about his own judgments despite the disagreement of a unanimous ma-

jority. However, since the individual in this postadolescent and young adult stage has experienced socialization, and since he has at some earlier time experienced the penalties of nonconformity, he does not attain the degree of individuality of judgment that is evident in the presocialization stage (973).

It should be pointed out, however, that conformity will vary with situations—some situations promote more peer conformity than others. Brittain (1963) studied this problem by presenting a sample of adolescents with hypothetical situations involving conflicting parent-peer expectations. The results revealed that peer- or parent-conforming by the adolescent girl depended largely upon the situation with which she is confronted and upon the alternatives given her.

Conformity also varies with the nature and needs of the individual adolescent. In the study by Landsbaum and Willis (1971), referred to in Chapter 2, it was noted that younger adolescents, "low-competency" subjects, and subjects with "high-competency" partners working in pairs displayed the most conforming behavior. The data also offered experimental evidence to support the view that younger adolescents are more vulnerable to the influence of peers than older adolescents.

By wearing long hair a boy is saying something to his peers, parents, and teachers. The message he is trying to get across depends upon his subgrouping. If most of his friends have long hair, he is likely saying: "I want to be a member of the group." He also may be saying: "I am growing up, so the length of my hair is my own business." What makes the conflict with parents so great is the suddenness of the behavior; if it were gradual, parents might more readily accept it. Parents are also continuously competing with other parents through their children. In the case of some parents their son or daughter is a status symbol, a "front runner." To these parents, long hair or some other deviant appearance or behavior is a symbol of failure, and instead of sitting down with the teen-ager and talking the matter over, they frequently ask themselves: "Where did we fail?"

CONFORMITY TO PEERS AND ADJUSTMENT. Conformity to peer culture or peer-group norms has been associated with good adjustment. In a study by Langer (1954) designed to test this hypothesis, various clinical and social-psychological tests were administered to a sample of 600 school pupils from the fourth to the twelfth grade, one-third of whom were Indian, one-third white Protestant, and one-third Spanish or Mexican. The results revealed that, although conformity to peer group behavioral norms was positively correlated with emotional adjustment, deviance did not necessarily indicate maladjustment. Several factors made it possible for the individual to deviate from the peer-group norms and not suffer an emotionally bad consequence. Deviance brought maladjustments mainly when such deviation separated the individual from the group, automatically cutting off an important source for the satisfaction of certain needs of the individual and producing frustrations and conflicts. The effects of the peer group on adolescent behavior will depend on the attitudes and activities prevailing in the peer group and on the needs of the individual. Where group norms emphasize achievement, most of the members of the peer group perform accordingly; where the prevailing expectations involve delinquency or violations of adult norms, these are just as readily translated into action.

Cultural Forces and Social Class Influences

The social class of a child's family determines not only the neighborhood in which he lives and the group with whom he associates, but also—to a very large extent—the goals, aspirations, and social skills of the child and adolescent. There is evidence from many sources that children and adolescents from low socioeconomic neighborhoods are likely to have feelings of insecurity and hostility to a much greater degree than those from more privileged neighborhoods. Some of these influences are presented in subsequent chapters dealing with adolescent subcultures, school dropouts, alienation, vocational choices, and delinquency. Adolescents from some minority groups often find themselves discriminated against by their classmates, although today's adolescents are not as likely to display deep-seated racial prejudices to the extent that their parents and other adults in their neighborhood show.

Many psychologists and sociologists have given special attention to the effect of parental class and status on adolescent personality development and integration. Class and status are widely used in the field of stratification; they refer to inequalities in the rewards our culture regards as worthy and desirable. Examples of status differentials are income, educational attainment, living standard, influence and power, family and prestige, and the like. Social class influences, although important at all age levels, become more pronounced during the high school years. These influences may be observed in the cliques formed, the social activities pursued, dating patterns, and even in the curriculum pattern.

Social Class and Cultural Differences

The latest statistics on minority groups show that the two largest are blacks and persons of Spanish origin. As of 1971, the black population was about 22.3 million, while the Spanish-speaking population was about 9.2 million. These two groups constitute 31.5 million people, or 16 percent of the total population. Both minority groups, taken as a whole, average considerably less education than the population as a whole, with little more than a grade school education. The national median is a high school education.

When we speak of adolescents, we frequently think of those from middle-class homes. But there is a large segment of our society whose way of life, values, and behavior patterns are the product of a fairly distinct cultural system—the lower class. The segregated organization of our housing, neighborhoods, schools, recreational activities, and religious programs contribute to the development of rather distinct cultural patterns. There is some evidence that this group is becoming increasingly distinct and growing larger. According to Miller, Guertz, and Cutter (1961), the adolescent street-corner gang is usually made up of lower-class boys and is a breeding place for delinquency. One of the most striking and clear-cut findings in their study of the Junior Outlaws (a street-corner gang) was that most acts of aggression performed by the members were directed at each other. This is no doubt a result of interaction—the more frequent and accessible the contact, the greater the likelihood of aggression.

Social class influences the interests and social activities that adolescents pursue. A study reported by Knapp, Brimner, and White (1959) revealed that even esthetic preferences depend on economic station: middle-class adolescents prefer tartans with a complex design and without saturated color or striking contrast, whereas lower-class adolescents and younger children prefer designs of simple massive pattern, saturated color, and strong contrasts.

Since sex differences in interests are not so pronounced among middle-class as among lower-class parents, and since the home is the model of behavior for the child and adolescent, the teen-ager from the middle-class home does not have a masculine or feminine role so strictly delineated as the lower-class teen-ager's. This was indicated in the results of a study by Pierce-Jones (1959). He noted that the adolescent of high status background was less interested in outdoor and mechanical activities and more strongly attracted to literary, esthetic, persuasive, and scientific pursuits than his low-status age-mates.

Differences that appear will depend in a large part upon the factors that produce class groupings. It has been observed, however, that outstanding class differences frequently exist in the social goals, mores, attitudes, and patterns of behavior of children and adolescents from different social classes. Considerably more anxiety appears among middle-class than among lower-class parents in connection with education, thrift, sexual behavior, manners, and respect for law. The lower class is more honest and frank in social situations; the middle class is more tactful.

Goldstein (1955) noted that children from low socioeconomic neighborhoods are likely to have feelings of insecurity and display hostility to a much greater extent than children from more priviliged neighborhoods.

In "tough" neighborhoods boys from fatherless homes may be as masculine (or even more so) than their father-present peers. Over compensation may be a defense against their mother's feminine behavior. Miller (1958) states:

> The genesis of the intense concern over toughness in lower-class culture is probably related to the fact that a significant proportion of lower-class males are reared in a predominantly female household and lack a con-

sistently present male figure with whom to identify and from whom to learn the essential components of a 'male' role. Since women serve as the primary objects of identification during the preadolescent years, the almost obsessive lower-class concern with 'masculinity' probably resembles a type of compulsive reactive formation" (9).

The findings of Carlsmith (1964) with middle-class boys as subjects are quite at variance with the observations of Miller. The data from Carlsmith's study indicated that middle-class boys whose fathers were absent in their early childhood are more likely than boys who had fathers to have a feminine patterning of aptitude test norms. Citing evidence from other studies, Carlsmith reasoned that such a score pattern was a reflection of a feminine global conceptual style.

The differences in class behavior of boys may have resulted from different forces and conditions in the social environment of the two groups of boys. One must take into account variations in the cultural level and child-rearing patterns of the parents. The less refined lower-class parent may have emphasized the need for toughness, for standing up for one's rights.

Differences in educational background and social class, as defined by father's occupation, influence the way parents react to their children's use of television (Martin and Benson, 1970). Based on interviews with the mothers and fathers of 183 white families in 1966, Martin and Benson noted that the attitudes and behavior of mothers toward television viewing by their children were similar across class and educational lines, although working-class mothers tended to make the strictest rules for televiewing; working-class fathers tended to be the most indifferent. Upper-class and professionally educated fathers discussed the content of television programs with their children more frequently than other groups, although the next most frequent group in using television as an educational aid for its children was the working-class mothers with less than a high school education. It seems most likely that children and adolescents are influenced by the amount and nature of the programs viewed by parents.

Religion is one of the cultural forces that affect the lives of children and adolescents. To arrive at sound conclusions about the part the church plays in the lives of young people is not a simple task. The obvious difficulties are aggravated by the fact that it is impossible to isolate the church as a single factor in the experience and background of youth. It is quite possible, of course, to discover the conditions under which the youth of different church groups are living, and also to find out whatever differences may exist in the ways that they react to current problems. However, to presume to measure the extent to which these differences are due to dissimilarities in religious backgrounds and affiliations is not only unscientific but highly dangerous. Differences which, on the surface, may appear to be basically religious in character are, in fact, profoundly affected by such factors as race, nationality, locality of residence, and educational attainment.

In the past, adolescents have adopted the religion of their parents. This is still true for many adolescents today, although they are less dedicated than their parents to the church. This is especially true for adolescents from the lower class who, through education and varied cultural contacts move to a higher cultural level.

As the child grows into adolescence he needs some integrating ideal to supplement or replace his parents as the objects of faith and trust. He needs to have some conception of the universe and his place in it. Religion supplies many adolescents with this world-view. There are many, however, who question the effectiveness of religious beliefs and practices. Based on reviews of a number of studies related to the role of religion in mental health and personal well-being, Sanua (1969) concluded that contemporary religious education does not seem to ensure healthier attitudes.

RURAL-URBAN-SUBURBAN DIFFERENCES. A study by Strauss (1962) showed that parents were concerned about furnishing meaningful work experiences for their sons. Farm parents gave the greatest emphasis to work and were able to find more work experiences for adolescents. Also, farm youth were expected to do certain chores and were paid less for work done. This is usually explained by the closer integration of the family and work activities in the farm family than in the nonfarm family. Young people from farm families seem to retain the virtue of hard work as an important value; furthermore a higher proportion of farm boys found the work enjoyable and regarded this as an aspect of personal and family living. It appears, however, from studies in rural sociology that rural-urban differences have diminished in many ways, although psychological differences still seem to exist. These differences are perhaps greater within either the rural or the urban groups than between them, since many of these differences result from parental influences which may reflect class differences or rural vs. urban attitudes, interests, and values.

The suburban way of life is first of all a segregated one. Housing developments have contributed to social class segregation, since the homes of any one development usually fall within a somewhat limited price range. Children in the lowest class live in the abandoned area of the city that becomes the slum area. Here is civilization at its worst, a breeding place for juvenile crime. In contrast, the different suburban areas are made up of different social class groups. The children of a particular suburban area tend to go to school together and to a church where there is again social class segregation. Within a middle-class suburban community there are strong pressures for conformity. The parents are preoccupied with "keeping up with the Jones," and the adolescents are supposed to achieve and behave in certain prescribed ways.

The rapid development of suburbia has presented special problems involving adolescents and their parents. Some major differences in life-style variables of urban and suburban blue-collar families were studied by Tallman and Morgner (1970). The investigators noted that "Suburban families are more likely than urban families to adopt life-styles resembling the middle class as indicated by measures of local intimacy, social isolation, family organization, church activity, orientations to social mobility, and political perspectives" (334).

INFLUENCE OF COMMUNITY SETTING. The importance of community forces and conditions in the development of children and adolescents is hard to evaluate. With the decline in size and function of the family unit, forces within the community have assumed a more important role. The community operates in a variety of ways in affecting the behavior and development of adolescents. In the first place, it is characterized by somewhat common patterns of behavior which are both taught to and forced upon the adolescents. In the second place, the community furnishes boys and girls guidelines to attitudes, conduct, morals, and frequently religious beliefs and practices. The various agencies and forces of the community often exert pressure on adolescents to accept and conform to the codes and ethical standards presented. A third way in which the community affects adolescents is through its cultural content. The language spoken in the community makes a deep impact at an early age. The likes and dislikes, prejudices, tastes, and appreciations of the adolescents are to a marked degree a result of community influences.

A great deal of hypothesizing has been done about the relation of community size to the personal and social development of the individual. However, it has already been pointed out that social interactions may be found in communities of all sizes. Conservatism is one aspect of the personality system that is often mentioned as varying with community size. Descriptions of city-dwellers generally represent urbanites as less conservative in their behavior than their rural counterparts. In a comparison of the worldmindedness of college students from different backgrounds Garrison (1961) found that students with a rural background were the least world minded, while students from the large urban areas were most.

SUMMARY

A review of the problems of generations reveals certain basic facts: (1) There is a continuous emergence of new participants in the cultural process. (2) The participants are continuously disappearing only to be followed by others who are coming into the cultural process. (3) Members of one generation can only participate in a temporarily limited section of the historical process. (4) A constant transmission of the cultural heritage is necessary. (5) The transmission from generation to generation is uninterrupted.

The present generation of young people is more advanced in its educational and intellectual development than any previous generation. This has aggravated the conflicts with parents. The adolescent's view of his parents is closely related to the control patterns of his family, although the foremost complaint is that parents are dictatorial.

The nuclear family has to a marked degree replaced the extended family in the United States. Case studies as well as studies of children in foster homes indicate that a favorable home atmosphere is important to the child's development of a sense of identity and trust. Even the ordinal position within the family has a bearing on personality development. Although father-absence affects identification, especially for the adolescent boy, there are also indirect ill-effects of father-absence such as may result from a disturbed mother.

The transition from the nuclear family to a peer-oriented society takes place during the adolescent years and is accentuated by the schools and other agencies that bring young people together. A rigid peer conformity characterizes early adolescence. In addition to peers there are cultural forces and conditions within the home and community that influence the adolescent. Among these is the social class status of the home. Important differences in behavior patterns and values exist between different social classes. These are passed on to the children. The religion of the home is also passed on to the adolescent, although this is frequently modified as a result of education and broad experience. Rural, suburban, and urban differences may be noted, although rural-urban differences have diminished within the past two decades.

REFERENCES

ALTUS, W. D. "Birth Order and a Brief (Ten Point) Measure of Aptitude." *American Psychologist* (1965), 19:506.

————. "Birth Order and Scholastic Aptitude." *Journal of Consulting Psychology* (1965), 29:202–5.

BARTLETT, CLAUDE J. and JOHN E. HORROCKS. "A Study of the Need Status of Adolescents from Broken Homes." *Journal of Genetic Psychology* (1958), 93:153–59.

BILLER, HENRY B. "Father Absence and the Personality of the Male Child." *Developmental Psychology* (1970), 2 (2):181–201.

———— and S. D. WEISS. "The Father-Daughter Relationship and Female Personality Development." *Journal of Genetic Psychology*, (1970), 114:79–93.

BLUM, SAM. "What Makes a Good Parent?" *Redbook Magazine* (January, 1964), pp. 38, 98–101.

BRITTAIN, C. V. "Adolescent Choices and Parent-Peer Cross Pressures." *American Sociological Review* (1963), 28:385–91.

BRONFENBRENNER, U. "On the Making of Men: Some Explorations for Research." *Canadian Journal of Behavior Science* (1969), 1:4–24.

————. "Parents, Bring Up Your Children." *Look* magazine (January 26, 1971), pp. 45–46.

CARLSMITH, LYN. "Effect of Early Father-absence on Realistic Attitude." *Harvard Educational Review* (1964), 34:3–21.

CARLSON, BETTY RAE. *Parent-Child Relationships and the Self-Concept of Children.* Ph.D. dissertation. Ann Arbor: University of Michigan, 1958.

CLAUSEN, J. A. "Family structure, Socialization, and Personality." In *Review of Child Development Research,* Vol. 2, Lois M. Hoffman and M. L. Hoffman, eds. New York: Russell Sage Foundation, 1966. Pp. 1–53.

Current Population Reports, Series No. 237, p. 20. "Household and Families by Type: March, 1972."

COSTANZO, PHILIP P. and MARVIN E. SHAW. "Conformity as a Function of Age Level." *Child Development* (1966), 37:967–75.

DEWEY, JOHN. *The Public and Its Problems.* New York: Holt, Rinehart & Winston, Inc., 1927. Pp. 211–12.

DINNAGE, ROSEMARY, PRINGLE, M. and L. KELLNER. *Foster Care: Facts and Fallacies.* New York: Humanities Press, 1967.

GARRISON, KARL C. "Worldminded Attitudes of College Students in a Southern University." *Journal of Social Psychology* (1961), 54:147–53.

GOLDSTEIN, ARNOLD. "Aggression and Hostility in the Elementary School in Low Economic Areas." *Understanding the Child* (1955), 24:20–21.

HERZOG, ELIZABETH, CECILIA SUDIA, BARBARA ROSENGARD, and JANE HARWOOD. "Teenagers Discuss the Generation Gap." Youth Reports No 1. Children's Bureau, U.S. Department of Health, Education and Welfare, 1970.

HETHERINGTON, E. MAVIS. "Girls Without Fathers." *Psychology Today* (February 1973), 6:46–55.

HOLLANDER, EDWIN P. and JAMES E. MARCIA. "Parental Determinants of Peer-orientation and Self-orientation Among Preadolescents." *Developmental Psychology* (1970), 2 (2):292–302.

HOFFMAN, MARTIN L. "Identification and Conscience Development." *Child Development* (1971), 42 (4):1971–82.

INGERSOLL, H. L. "A Study of Transmission of Authority Patterns in the Family." *Genetic Psychology Monographs* (1946), 38:225–302.

KNAPP, ROBERT H., JANET BRIMNER, and MARTIN WHITE. "Educational Level, Class Status and Aesthetic Preference." *Journal of Social Psychology* (1959), 50:277–84.

LANDSBAUM, JANE B. and RICHARD H. WILLIS. "Nonconformity in Early and Late Adolescence." *Developmental Psychology* (1971), 4:334–37.

LANGER, THOMAS S. *Normative Behavior and Emotional Adjustment.* Ph.D. dissertation. New York: Columbia University, 1954.

LARSON, LYLE E. "The Influence of Parents and Peers During Adolescence: The Situation Hypothesis Revisited." *Journal of Marriage and the Family* (1972), 34 (1):67–74.

McCORD, J., W. McCORD, and E. THURBER. "Some Effects of Paternal Absence on Male Children." *Journal of Abnormal and Social Psychology* (1962), 63: 361–69.

MANNHEIM, KARL. "The Problem of Generations." In *Essays on the Sociology of Knowledge*, Paul Kecskemeti, ed. London: Routledge and Kegan Paul, 1953.

MARTIN, CORA A. and LEONARD BENSON. "Parental Perception of the Role of Television in Parent-child Interaction." *Journal of Marriage and the Family* (1970), 32:410–14.

MILLER, WALTER B. "Lower-class Culture as a Generating Milieu of Gang Delinquency." *Journal of Social Issues* (1958), 14:5–19.

———, HILDRED GUERTZ, and HENRY S. CUTTER. "Aggression in a Boys' Street-corner Gang." *Psychiatry* (1961), 24:283–98.

NICHOLS, R. C. "Birth Order and Intelligence." Unpublished study. Quoted by W. D. Altus, "Birth Order and the Omnibus Personality Inventory." *Proceedings of the 74th Annual Convention of the American Psychological Association* (1966). Pp. 279–80.

OBERLANDER, MARK I., KENNETH J. FRAUENFELDER, and H. HEATH. "Ordinal Position, Sex of Sibling, Sex, and Personal Preferences in a Group of Eighteen-year-olds." *Journal of Consulting and Clinical Phychology* (1970), 35:122–25.

PEDERSEN, F. A. "Relationship Between Father-Absence and Emotional Disturbance in Male Military Dependents." *Merrill-Palmer Quarterly* (1966), 12:321–31.

PIERCE-JONES, JOHN. "Vocational Interest Correlates of Socioeconomic Status in Adolescence." *Educational and Psychological Measurement* (1959), 19:65–72.

ROBERTSON, ALEX. "Social Class Differences in the Relationship Between Birth Order and Personality Development." *Social Psychiatry* (1971), 6 (4):172–78.

SANTROCK, JOHN W. "Influence of Onset and Type of Paternal Absence on the First Four Ericksonian Developmental Crises." *Developmental Psychology* (1970), 3:273–74.

SANUA, VICTOR D. "Religion, Mental Health, and Personality: A Review of Empirical Studies." *American Journal of Psychiatry* (1969), 125 (9):1203–13.

SCHLESINGER, B. "The One-parent Family: An Overview." *Family Life Coordinator* (1966), 15:133–37.

SMITH, THOMAS E. "Birth Order, Sibship size and Social Class as Antecedents of Adolescent's Acceptance of Parents' Authority." *Social Forces* (1971), 50:223–32.

STRAUSS, MURRAY. "Work Role and Financial Responsibility in the Socialization of Farm, Fringe, and Town Boys."*Rural Sociology* (1962), 27:257–74.

TALLMAN, IRVING and RAMONA MORGNER. "Differences Among Urban and Suburban Blue-collar Families." *Social Forces* (1970), 48:334–48.

RECOMMENDED READINGS

GLASSER, PAUL H. and LOIS GLASSER, eds. *Families in Crisis.* New York: Harper & Row, Publishers, 1970.

The topics covered by the authors represent three variables: the hardship of the event; family resources, including role structure and previous history with crisis; and the family's definition of the situation.

HORROCKS, JOHN E. *The Psychology of Adolescence*. 3rd ed. Boston: Houghton Mifflin Company, 1969.
Useful and selected materials bearing on cultural and social influences affecting adolescents are presented in Chapters 11–15. The influences of the home, group membership, and friends on personal and social development are emphasized.

JOSEPH, THOMAS P. "Adolescents: From the Views of the Members of an Informal Adolescent Group." *Genetic Psychology Monographs* (1969), 79(1): 3–88.
From the answers to interviews of six adolescents who defined themselves as a group, fourteen hypotheses and one underlying dimension of adolescents were proposed.

McCANDLESS, BOYD R. *Adolescent Behavior and Development*. Hinesdale, Ill.: The Dryden Press Inc., 1970. Chapter 12.
The author presents materials bearing on dimensions of socialization, with special emphasis on cultural influences. Stages and theories of socialization are also given special consideration.

THOMPSON, GEORGE H. ed. *Social Development and Personality*. New York: John Wiley & Sons, Inc., 1971. See references to Chapter 7.

9

alternative cultural influences

Most of the discussion on adolescent culture has related largely to middle-class adolescents. Adolescence has been considered to be a fairly distinct period of life; in some ways it is a product of the Industrial Revolution and has given size to a teen-age subculture in the United States and other Western countries. The subculture has been described by Parsons (1950) as a social reaction of adolescents to their uncertain status in the adult world, it functions to aid "the transition from the security of childhood in the family orientation to that of full adulthood in marriage and occupational status" (614). According to Parsons, the adolescent subculture includes three main aspects: (1) the rebelliousness of youth against adult expectations and demands; (2) the tendency toward peer conformity, along with a tolerance toward certain differences; and (3) a romantic adherence to emotionally significant subjects and situations.

ADOLESCENT SUBCULTURES— YES OR NO?

The controversy concerning the existence of an adolescent subculture, like that of heredity vs. environment, cannot be answered simply.

Adolescents have developed in a home and community culture and share some attitudes and values with other adolescents growing up in a culture with many common variables. Furthermore, some of these attitudes and values are shared with the adults of the community, with whom they have had many quite similar experiences. There are, however, experiences that are unique to their generation that they share primarily with their peers. These behavior patterns and attitudes frequently are discontinuous with the broader community and regional experiences of adults. Parents frequently recognize multiple loyalties on the part of adolescents; some of these relate directly to their peers, others relate more closely to home ties. We may conclude, then, that there is both an adolescent subculture and an adolescent-adult culture; both of these are important to their growth to maturity.

The assumption of a relatively distinct adolescent culture has been challenged as a myth by some investigators. Elkin and Westley (1955) questioned this notion in their article based on the results of an early 1950 study of adolescents in a Montreal suburb. They concluded that teen-agers are relatively well integrated into the customs, norms, and values of adult society. They pointed out that parents expressed few complaints about the socialization problems of their teen-agers and that the continuities of socialization were more striking than the discontinuities. This seems to have some support from the Louis and Harris youth poll of a national sample of the 26 million Americans between the ages of fifteen and twenty-five. The results presented in Table 2-4 of Chapter 2 (p. 54) showed that 84 percent stated that they agreed with and accepted their parents ideals, while only 32 percent stated that they had trouble communicating with their parents. However, 55 percent of the youth interviewed in the Louis and Harris poll stated that their parents did not approve of the way youth *expressed* their ideals, and only 64 percent stated that their parents approved of their ideals.

It seems that most adolescents do not experience serious conflicts with their parents, but a sizeable minority of them does. We believe that the adolescent subculture is an empirical reality and that most adolescents are affected by it.

If we are to appreciate the differences between adult and adolescent orientations to society and social reality, we must examine the importance and meanings peer-group norms have for adolescents. Again, these do not affect all adolescents in the same manner. The insecure adolescent becomes a greater conformist to peer norms than the secure adolescent. However, the social categories in the adolescent status terminology furnish this age group with its own world view, which may be different or even at variance with that held by its parents (Schwartz and Merton, 1967).

Adolescent Subcultures Defined

Although we have discussed adolescent subcultures in the previous chapters, no attempt has been made to define them. Culture is regarded by sociologists as a blueprint for the behavior of a total society. They further regard that the purpose of school and to some extent the family is to pass a culture on to the next generation. As the word implies, subculture refers to the blueprint for behavior of a smaller group within the total society, in the case of adolescents it is the behavior of this segment of the total society. James S. Coleman in his study of high school students, arrived at a good description of the adolescent society. Concerning the adolescent, he stated: "With his fellows, he comes to constitute a small society, one that has most of its important interactions within itself, and maintains only a few threads of connection with the outside adult society" (1962: 3). The function of this subculture is to supply definite status, a feeling of belonging, and acceptance.

ROLE OF LANGUAGE. The role of language in the socialization process has been emphasized by students of child development for several decades. Its importance has recently received the attention of students of adolescent culture (Nelson and Rosenbaum, 1972). It has been suggested that the adolescent is a member of two linguistic communities—one employing the language of adults, the other the language of peers. Schwartz and Merton described youth culture as consisting of "those adolescent norms, standards, and values which are discussed in language particularly intelligible to members of this age group" (1967: 457).

If a special language or vocabulary does play a significant role in the socialization of the child and adolescent, we should note its presence in the subcultures of adolescents. It should furthermore reflect variations due to cultural age-grading. Anyone well acquainted with adolescents will note the special vocabulary, which is somewhat foreign to most adults. This language varies with each generation of teen-agers, and to a degree, with different cultural levels. However, in all cases language serves to distinguish adolescents from adults, and is a very important force in the socialization process.

LIFE STYLE AND IDENTIFICATION. Life style as a means of identification is not a recent development; neither is it confined to the youth of today. It appeared among the "gentlemen" during the Elizabethan period. It was noted among the intellectuals on the college campus throughout the nineteenth century. Today it is a means of identifying a particular subculture. The multiplication of subcultures in our society has brought forth an equally explosive multiplication of life styles. Their importance today has been set forth by Toffler:

> How we choose a life style, and what it means to us, therefore, looms as one of the central issues of the psychology of tomorrow. For the selection of a life style, whether consciously done or not, powerfully shapes the individual's future. It does this by imposing order, a set of principles or criteria on the choices he makes in his daily life (1970: 271).

The life-style selections an adolescent makes are anything but random. The black-jacketed motorcyclist of 1970, with his steel-studded gauntlets and rugged boots, his swagger and authoritarian platitudes, is displaying a consistency. The 1960s and early 1970s saw a proliferation of dress styles through which adolescents could express their social concern. For example, the Vietnam War protester often donned blue jeans and army surplus jackets, while youth involved in the drug culture would wear beads and psychedelic colors.

Adolescent Subsociety

An intense youth subsociety can be found in most highly developed cultures. This appears in our society in adolescent interest in special types of dancing, music, style of dress, and language. Their sharing of experiences, problems, and secrets furnishes them a strong sense of solidarity. The youth houses of some primitive societies institutionalize this better than our schools and youth organizations, which are frequently ridden with adult supervision and regulations.

Paul Goodman has pointed out that the development of a subsociety into a full-blown subculture is not a normal phenomenon, but a reactive one. He states: "It signifies that the adult culture is hostile to adolescent interests, or is not to be trusted; that parents are not people and do not regard their children as people; that the young are excluded from adult activities that might be interesting and, on the other hand, that most adult activities are not worth growing up into as one becomes ready for them. . . ." (1968: 106). Through the development of a teen-age culture, adolescents have created a relatively stable, though temporary, social structure. They recognize that they have common problems and interests, that they belong together and have their own norms of conduct that are not always consistent with those of the adult world.

Our consideration of teen-age subculture is in itself a recognition of this age as a unique period; however, allowance must be made for the fact that not all adolescents are members of teen-age subcultures. It is possible for an adolescent to be socially or physically isolated from peers and not be a member of any discernible peer culture. Also, it is possible for an adolescent to be a member of the teen-age subculture and suffer minimally from adolescent tension, conflicts, and confusions. He may be so completely involved in the teen-age subculture and follow peer standards so fully that he has a feeling of total belonging. He may be completely immune to adult cultural norms and suffer little or no conflict in his loyalties or standards. On the other hand, an adolescent may be a member of a particular group and accept its culture not because of psychological needs but rather because of proximity or coincidental acquaintances and friendships. His participation in the teen-age culture is merely perfunctory and not especially important to his personal needs and development. There are still other adolescents who, because of their minority status, are excluded from the dominant youth culture and may seek to form their own subculture. This is especially true in large cities where there are large minority groups. All told, most adolescents are members of a peer culture, although some are affected by it more than others.

THE DIVERSITY OF ADOLESCENT SUBCULTURES. There is no one uniform, monolithic adolescent subculture. Important differences in adolescent peer culture exist, even within a single city. These are based upon such variables as socioeconomic class, age, race, ethnicity, family history, and place of residence. Concerning the concept of a subculture, Sebald states:

> When the concept of subculture is applied to lower socioeconomic levels, it most often refers to delinquent behavior forms. Some segments of the upper-middle and upper socioeconomic classes of the American population can hardly be said to have an adolescent subculture. In these social strata one would most likely encounter a type of nonadolescent youth who is integrated in his family and community; as a result, he suffers little status uncertainty—often to the point where there is no need for a compensating and security-extending teen-age subculture (1968: 202).

Although variations exist in the attitudes and behavior of adolescents, it is possible to identify some areas that are stylistically distinct from other age groups. Behavioral norms are markedly set by peers, and deviations from these standards are likely to be met with disapproval. There are still some adolescents who are largely unaffected by peer standards; however these are likely to be limited in number, since all adolescents are subjected to long periods of schooling that inevitably bring them into contact with classmates or peers.

NEGRO ADOLESCENT CULTURE

The racial status of Negro adolescents together with their usually lower socioeconomic status marks their adolescent transition and sets their subculture apart from that of other American adolescents. Negro teen-agers are a part of a racial category that suffers today, although hopefully less than yesterday, from discrimination, deprivation, and feelings of inferiority and inadequacy. Thus, discrimination against blacks is an unfortunate American tradition.

However, contemporary Negro youth are part of a process now operating in which many traditions, attitudes, and values are being reassessed. They are faced with the problem overcoming a legacy of alleged racial inferiority. Concerning their condition Sebald states:

> . . . Negro teen-agers find themselves in ambivalent situations. On the one side, a full and clear identification with a Negro culture is difficult, since [the] American Negro population has grown diffuse and diverse and, moreover, is often integrated into the white community to an extent defying a clear characterization as a "Negro community." Furthermore,

identification with Negroes "in general" is usually not ego strengthening or self-enhancing, since it is reminiscent of the subservient and inferior Negro stereotype. On the other side, identification with the full incorporation into the white community is extremely difficult (1968: 266).

The higher Negro birth rate has produced a population markedly younger than the whites; the black median age was 21.1 in 1966 as compared to 29.1 for whites (Kerner, et al., 1968: 238). At the beginning of the major Northern and Western urban migration in 1910, only 11 percent of the American Negro population lived outside the South, while today approximately 50 percent do. Also, there has been a migration from the farms in the South to nearby cities. The black population today is to a large degree urban, and mostly inner-city urban.

The Negro Self-Concept and Self-Esteem

One of the problems confronting many black teen-agers during the first half of this century was their low self-esteem. This was a carry-over from the attitudes of their parents and most whites. That this has not been entirely dispelled has been shown in a study by Williams and Byars (1968). The self-esteem of Negro adolescents was studied in Southern communities where public facilities and schools were being desegregated. Negro self-evaluation was to be measured in a period of increasing social and academic integration. Generally the findings indicated that Negro students were low in self-confidence, defensive in their self-description, and confused about their identity.

A study by Webster and Kroger (1966) compared selected perceptions and feelings of black high school students with and without white friends. Over 300 Negro adolescents were tested with a questionnaire dealing with personal independence, social competence, intellectual self-esteem, self-concept, physical self-esteem, vocational aspirations, expected vocational attainment, social acceptance, ethnic concern, and ethnocentrism.

The Negro adolescents without white friends expressed a preference for associating with Negroes. The investigators concluded from their study that the generally accepted attitudes and behavior of any racial or ethnic group exert a powerful influence upon its members. It would appear that the black adolescent with white friends displayed a higher degree of independence, inner strength, and self-concept than average. In addition the group with higher self-concepts and the Caucasian friends would naturally raise the level of its experiences, human contacts, and vocational goals. Perhaps their lives were thus enriched. Inasmuch as a positive self-concept contributes to optimum educational attainment, this group probably displayed higher academic achievement.

THE BLACK ADOLESCENT IN SCHOOL. Racial integration is not complete mostly because of white attitudes toward integration and housing patterns within our large urban areas that contribute to de facto segregation. With increased integration we can expect drastic changes in the personal and social problems faced by black adolescents at school. While the problems of the past have usually related to inferior schools, the problems of the future will relate more closely to social participation in the total school program. These are already in evidence in many schools where black students are demanding quotas in student government, classroom officers, cheer leaders, and other student activities and organizations.

There are many black adolescents in school who do not fit the lower-class, urban-slum stereotype. There has developed a large middle-class group with the same basic aspirations and interests as other middle-class students. Even lower-class adolescent blacks follow the ordinary pursuits of most teen-agers. One fundamental difference may be noted in the motivations of their protests and demonstrations; the black teen-ager is more likely to be a rebel *with* a cause. Teachers and others concerned with the guidance and training of black adolescents need to recognize the divergent background, abilities, aspirations, needs, and interests of black students.

Profile of the Young Black Militant

The majority of political authorities tend to categorize young black militants who advocate social and economic change through open confrontation as primitive, irresponsible, juvenile criminals, unassimilated in their culture and a menace to society. By attributing the causes of riots to the actions of the "riff-raff" whites are employing the "scapegoat theory" which relieves them of most of the blame. This theory suggests that young black militants are either criminals or emotionally irresponsible outcasts. "Law and order" approaches that use punitive and coercive forms of control are advocated for dealing the "problem."

Results of studies show that the profile of young black militants held by a large percentage of whites is incorrect and based primarily upon prejudices. Tomlinson concludes from his study of riot ideology among urban Negroes that the militants are "the cream of urban Negro youth in particular and urban Negro citizens in general" (1968: 238). The young militants, both male and female, no longer accept the fatalistic viewpoint that their ghetto existence is a result of their own inherent weaknesses over which they have no control. Compared with nonmilitants, the riot supporters have strong beliefs in their ability to control events in their own lives and to shape their destinies. However, they have a new sense of self-efficacy and a better understanding of the forces and conditions that prevent them from realizing their aspirations—discrimination, prejudice, exploitation, and legal injustices.

A unique opportunity for studying the characteristics of students occurred in 1967 during the Detroit riot. Considerable data had been collected during the preceding year on the students' background, future educational and occupational aspirations, and family, plus many personality and attitudinal scales. Also, within five days of the start of the riot and before the sniping had ended, black interviewers questioned students and former students from the riot area about their perceptions of the riot, who started it, who was responsible, whether it was good or bad, and what would happen. These data furnished the basis for studying the profile of those participating in the riot.

The results for personal control give support to the theory that riots arise from *blocked opportunity* to reach their goals in life. The young militants are made up of those who have developed some confidence in their ability to shape their lives if given a chance. They are not defeated fatalists with strong feelings of alienation and powerlessness. On the contrary, riot supporters and nonsupporters alike believed in the Protestant work ethic with its relationship between self-denial and future rewards. The study showed that mothers of young black militants were better educated than mothers of nonmilitants. The most important set of psychological characteristics that distinguish young black militants show that they will no longer accept a second-class status for themselves. Concerning the willingness of black youth to resort to violence Forward and Williams state:

> The combination of a heightened sense of personal effectiveness and the shift from self to system blame may help to explain the willingness of young ghetto militants to resort to violence as a means of forcing a change in the opportunity structure which at present excludes them. On the one hand, the growing tendency to blame the system rather than themselves provides militants with sources of justification for the use of violence (1970: 88).

THE PUERTO RICAN ADOLESCENT

As of 1970, about 9.2 million persons living in the United States identify themselves as being of Spanish origin. A majority of these are native-born American citizens. A breakdown by the Census Bureau shows that 5,073,000 were of Mexican origin, 1,454,000 Puerto Rican, 565,000 Cuban, 556,000 Central and South American, and 1,582,000 of other Spanish origin. Those of Mexican origin reside primarily in the Southwest while the second largest group, the Puerto Ricans, live in New York City and in scores of cities, towns, and villages from Chicago to upstate New York and New England. Except for a tiny minority who have achieved a relative degree of success, there has been little assimilation into the total American culture.

Puerto Ricans are citizens of the United States and as such are legally entitled to migrate to this country.[1] The two general types that migrate are: (1) the urban Puerto Rican who usually moves from the cities of

---

[1] Puerto Rico is a self-governing commonwealth, associated with the United States through a voluntary compact established in 1954.

Puerto Rico to urban centers in the United States, and (2) the rural Puerto Rican who migrates from the cane fields to become a seasonal farm laborer in the East and Midwest. In either case the reason for migrating to the United States is to improve their economic lot.

Puerto Rican Culture

Puerto Rican national culture is primarily a blend of Iberian (Spanish) and United States culture. It is relatively weak in indigenous folk arts and aboriginal culture. Catholicism is the dominant religion, although it is in competition with certain Protestant groups that affect some 15 percent of the population (Cruz and Ricks, 1969: 92–93). Witchcraft seems to serve as a supplement to Western religious forms, and spiritualism appears to be prevalent among all class groups.

The Puerto Rican family is patriarchal and authoritarian, with the adult male commanding obedience and respect from the members of the family; it differs from the European peasant family mainly in the prevalence of consensual or common-law marriage. It is estimated that one-fourth of the marriages are of this type, and that about one-third of the births are out of wedlock.[2] Provisions are made for the child to take the father's name, in line with the patriarchal nature of the society.

There is special concern for the virginity of female children, and their associations with males are closely guarded. Puerto Rican marriages at an early age are frequent and allow the young daughter to escape the male members of her family, who tend to guard her closely. In spite of obstacles, the girl, especially the lower-class girl, is expected to have married by the age of eighteen or nineteen. Marriage at the age of thirteen or fourteen is not uncommon; and consequently many girls move directly from childhood into marriage, early child-bearing, and the responsibilities of a wife, although the husband assumes control and makes most of the decisions.

Problems of Adjustment

The relationship of adolescents with their parents becomes strained in the new environment of New York City. The result of the conflict between the Puerto Rican cultural patterns and the new standards of behavior and values experienced in the United States has serious consequences. Concerning this Cruz and Ricks state:

> Left to their own resources in the new environment, boys are frequently exposed to opportunities for falling into bad company, learning antisocial habits and developing patterns of disrespect and disobedience toward the illiterate and old-time parent. The girl is frequently seen to rebel against the restrictive patterns of staying at home and dating under the stifling conditions of a chaperone. The desire to emulate the behavior of their

---

[2] Some of these children are living with parents married by common law and may not be considered illegitimate in one sense at least.

classmates sometimes results in deception on their part in order to gain their freedom. The settlement house or social center which encourages dancing, for example, may be seen as unwholesome by the parents. Yet, the girls may "steal" time to attend such activities.

Conservative Puerto Rican parents are subject to confusion and shock in the face of such situations. A feeling of inadequacy tends to result in several courses of action: (1) they "give up" their responsibility for the children and often desire that the child be taken over by some institution that will teach discipline and respect, (2) they exercise even tighter discipline and further alienate or increase the emotional disturbance of the child, or (3) they may send the recalcitrant child back to stay with a relative in Puerto Rico until he is mature and learns to face responsibilities.

An additional difficulty in adjustment lies in the fact that the main task of child-training is traditionally relegated to the mother. Outside of demanding respect and obedience, the father has little to do with children or management of the home. Indeed, such tasks are considered to be beneath male dignity. Left to her own resources, the Puerto Rican mother is often confused by the variety of patterns of child-rearing she observes in her new cultural setting. Even though she may be amenable to change, she finds herself at a loss to choose a standard of discipline and behavior for her children (95).

CONFLICTS AT SCHOOL. Major adjustment difficulties also appear at school and in social relations. Gruz and Ricks list three:

1. School is usually a frustrating experience because of the language barrier as well as cultural differences. This is also a stumbling block to employment and participating in the daily life of the larger community.
2. Many darker-skinned Puerto Ricans, unaware of the extent of discrimination in the United States, find that the color of their skin has an adverse effect upon their acceptance by others and their ability to find employment.
3. The Puerto Rican student is frequently faced with teachers who do not understand his background and cultural behavior patterns, and may be reprimanded for conduct at school that is quite normal when viewed in terms of Puerto Rican family customs and traditions.

Concerning the reactions of Puerto Rican children and adolescents to authority Cruz and Ricks state:

. . . When faced with criticism or reprimanded, a primary-grade child may run into a corner to cry rather than have conflict with an authority figure. Older children tend to withdraw in silence. This behavior grows out of a socialization process in which children are taught to respect adults and not talk back; they are also taught not to look at the face of an adult when speaking to him.

However, the Puerto Rican youngster sophisticated in mainland ways may present quite a different attitude. This is especially true of teen-agers who have been conditioned to the lifeways of slum areas in large cities

These youngsters are apt to rebel against the authority of parents, teachers, and even law-enforcement officers. Their behavior is frequently quite different from the docility exhibited by the youngster who has come directly from Puerto Rico (97).

ADOLESCENT IDENTITY. The Puerto Rican adolescent in the process of adjustment goes through many psychological changes as he moves from his home into some larger community in the United States. Perhaps the most difficult phases of his adjustments relate to the process of identification. At home the boy is taught the value of Puerto Rican culture and the extended family. He is expected to act like a man while still in his teens. This cultural background tends to conflict with the culture he is exposed to at school. At school he is treated like an American adolescent and is thus faced with a conflict between his Puerto Rican culture assimilated from home and the American culture at school. The school therefore presents a threat to the Puerto Rican adolescent. When he is called upon to communicate in English, he reveals his inadequacy and difference from others. Thus, he tends to dissociate himself from others in school except for his Puerto Rican peers.

MEXICAN-AMERICAN ADOLESCENTS

Mexican-Americans make up the second largest minority group in the United States. They are located primarily in the rural areas of the Southwest. In general they are characterized as poor and belong to the lower class. They suffer many of the same disadvantages as American Negroes. A common attitude of many young Mexican-Americans is that they are trapped and kept in a state of poverty and inferiority. Mexican-American adolescents in the Southwest are torn between two cultures. They can best be described as belonging primarily to the culture of northern Mexico, with the Spanish language favored over English at home. The young Mexican-American student entering school is torn between his own culture and that of the United States.

Self-Concepts

The attitude prevailing at home that they are destined to remain second-class citizens carries over with many youngsters when they enter school. Thus, they see themselves in a less favorable way than the dominant group of adolescents. The self concept of Mexican-American students seems to be permeated with feelings of inadequacy and low self-esteem. Carter (1968) conducted research in the secondary schools of one of California's rich agricultural valley. The subjects of the study consisted of seventh- and eighth-grade schools and one high school. The school population was approximately 65 percent Mexican-American. During the course of the study, parents, teachers, students, and school administrators were interviewed, in some cases several times. Also, classes were repeatedly observed.

Comparisons were made between the self-ratings of 190 Mexican-Americans and 98 Anglo-American ninth graders on a five-point semantic differential rating scale. Students told how they rated themselves by indicating where they fell on the five-point continuum between two adjectives such as wise-foolish. Little or no difference in self-view was found between the two groups on the self-rating scale, although the Mexican-American students were well aware of the way teachers and others viewed their group. They knew the stereotypes. Many students reported examples of derogatory remarks made by teachers and others. Yet, most of the students seemed to be able to adjust to the prejudices frequently imposed upon them. One must be careful in interpreting the behavior of adolescents from a different culture, as may be noted in the case of this Mexican-American girl.

> . . . The apparent submissiveness of some Mexican-American girls often is judged as reflecting the girl's negative view of herself. However, this behavior may be well established in the girl's home culture as normal and desirable. Educators tend to interpret a minority's behavior from the "Anglo" frame of reference. Actions which may manifest a negative self-view in one society are interpreted equally in children from another ethic group (Carter, 1968: 218).

Educational Achievement

In a study by Mayeske (1967) the Mexican-American students' sense of control of their environment was found to be closely related to their educational achievement. This is in harmony with findings by different students of educational psychology for more broadly representative populations. A United States Department of Agriculture (USDA) report in 1967 indicated that in the five Southwestern states, sixteen- and seventeen-year-olds with Spanish surnames were significantly below the national norm of educational achievement. It seems that children from Mexican-American homes are disadvantaged when they enter school, especially in their language activities.

It was pointed out earlier that the Mexican-American adolescent in the Southwest is torn between two cultures. In many areas of the Southwest, most Mexican-American families could best be described as belonging primarily to the culture of northern Mexico, with Spanish spoken at home. The young Mexican-American student entering school is torn between his own home background culture and that of the dominant American culture. It has been noted that achievement was lowest for those coming from homes where Spanish is spoken, usually lower-class homes. Furthermore, it has been observed that few students from small Mexican-American communities and villages participated in extracurricular activities at consolidated high schools.

Adjustments

Wherever Mexican-Americans are concentrated together, they display increased militancy. The Chicano movement is based on race and ethnic pride and a determination among adolescents to go forward, not backward. The Chicano movement has come forth with great force among youth. They state in protest. "We want our rights." "We want our schools." "We want jobs." Girls tend to play a minor role in the movement, so the task lies largely with the male youth.

SEX ADJUSTMENT. Schmidt and Gallessich (1971) compared the adjustment of first- and sixth-grade Mexican-American and Anglo-American pupils in self-contained and team-teaching classes. The Phillips Anxiety Test was used to measure the anxiety of the pupils. The school adjustment of girls was found to be more variable than that of boys in that they reported more anxiety. They also perceived their teachers more favorably than did the boys. This perhaps resulted from the identification needs of girls at this stage of their development. The investigators state: "Perhaps the greater anxiety of the females is related to the physical, psychological, and social adjustments of puberty which result in concerns typically faced by girls in the sixth grade but not faced by boys until the seventh or eighth grade" (331).

EDUCATIONAL ADJUSTMENT. A review of the literature on the Mexican-American high school student shows that certain characteristics and values of his culture are likely to produce differences in attitudes which place him at a distinct disadvantage and furthermore cause him to come into conflict with the school value system. A study by Ramirez, Taylor, and Petersen (1971) was designed to test the hypothesis that there are differences in attitude and behavior between Anglo-American and Mexican-American adolescents of the same socioeconomic class.

The adolescents studied were 600 junior and senior high school students from two high schools in Sacramento, California. Half of the students were Anglo-American and were not identifiable with any ethnic group. The other half were Mexican-American students. The students were of the lower socioeconomic class. They were administered an attitude scale consisting of sixty-two items that assessed attitudes toward teachers and education. In addition, sixty students were selected from each ethnic group and given a projective test constructed for this study, consisting of ten pictures depicting students, teachers, and parents interacting in settings related in some way to education.

The results of the attitude scale showed that Mexican-Americans had expressed views toward education which were significantly less positive than those expressed by Anglo-Americans. They expressed more agreement with items of the attitude scale which indicated that they were unhappy with the school and desirous of escaping it. "The aggression toward domineering females expressed by Mexican-American males, and the rebelliousness against authority evidenced in the data of the Mexican-American females indicates that Mexican-American adolescents react negatively against control" (146).

The Mexican-American adolescents agreed significantly more than Anglo-Americans with the items stating that parents should put pressure on their children to get as much education as possible. There was further evidence that when parents demonstrated an interest in their children's education, they became motivated to achieve. When parents approved of the school and its practices, the Mexican-American adolescents also approved of it.

The results of this study support those of an earlier study by Kimball (1968) of parent and family influence on the academic achievement of Mexican-American junior high school pupils. The groups studied included 1,457 ninth-grade students—899 Mexican-Americans and 558 Anglo-Americans. Sampling within the schools was from required classes so as to eliminate bias. The variable found to be most closely related to achievement was parental educational aspirations for the child.

THE INDIAN ADOLESCENT

Contrary to a rather widespread belief, American Indians are not a vanishing race. Although many of the younger generation are leaving the environment of the reservations and are becoming deeply involved in the acculturation process, they constitute a distinct Indian subculture. They are in the process of changing their traditional ways, but have not fully accepted the ways of the dominant culture. The fact is, the ways of the dominant culture are somewhat unstable, since it itself is rapidly changing.

Tribal Diversity

It is perhaps more difficult to regard the American Indian culture in the singular than the dominant white Anglo-American, since the many tribes that are scattered throughout the American continent differ markedly in their languages, customs, rituals, manners of living, and so on. The forces of change operate on all Indians, whether they are Navahos, Seminoles, Apaches, Sioux, Cherokees, or Crows. One of the recurrent and typical results is that the Indian teen-ager has become marginal to both his native Indian culture and the white man's. It is quite obvious that the Indian teen-ager is faced with more confusing problems than the white teen-ager.

The tribal diversity of the American Indians makes it necessary to deal with general and abstract adjustment problems of Indian teen-agers rather than with distinct problems experienced by those from different tribal groups. Comparisons were made by Goodey (1972) of scores of Indian high school students on Gordon's Survey of Interpersonal Values from Bureau of Indian Affairs high schools in three tribal areas. Major findings from this study may be summarized as follows:

1. Scores for the Indian sample population were significantly different from non-Indian norms in five of the six categories for both males and females.

2. A comparison of scores of Indian males and females revealed differences in four of six categories. Differences were considerably less, however, than those occurring in norms for non-Indian populations.

3. The differences between schools varied significantly according to the tribes represented in the school population.

4. The study revealed both similarities and marked differences in scores of students from the various tribes represented by the school populations.

Bass and Burger (1967) pointed out a number of years ago that American Indians are the most economically disadvantaged rural group in the United States. In comparison to the general population, their income was found to be only two-ninths of the average, while their rate of unemployment was almost ten times greater. Their school dropout rate was almost double that of the general population, and they had less than half the years of schooling.

The distinctive psychological dispositions of the different Indian tribes are changing, although semblances of them may still be observed. School enrollment has steadily increased over the past decade, so that today, according to reports of the Bureau of Indian affairs, more than 93 percent of all school-aged Indian youth are in school. Young Indians must usually leave their homes if they are to be educated beyond the sixth grade. This brings them into a totally different world that is adult and white dominated and produces continuous conflicts.

The more acculturated youths suffer severe conflicts between their new aspirations and the traditional attitudes and behavior patterns. They are no longer satisfied with the simplicity of their parents' life. New materialistic goals evolve that can be attained in the white-dominated society or the few exceptional reservations that offer advanced economic development. The vocational training of Indian adolescents places them in a difficult position—Where and how will they use their vocational skills? Sebald states:

> The only constructive function of this life experience may be that he retains his identity as a member of the Indian minority group—a rather negative manner of preserving identity. And yet, every aspect of public life to which he is exposed exerts pressure on him to adjust to the dominant culture. A near paradox ensues: the young Indian is forced to retain his identity, while at the same time pressured to live like a white man and adjust to the white culture. The difficulties growing out of this

paradox leave many Indian teen-agers frustrated and inclined to either react in drastic, sometimes delinquent, styles or to turn to substitute gratification (1968: 209).

Characterization of the Indian Adolescent

The characterization frequently presented of the Indian teen-ager is one who is faced with conflicts involving cultural change. This is the marginal type—the teen-ager suspended between two cultures with little allegiance to either. "The two poles, the white and the Indian appear hopelessly equidistant and unattainable to the teen-ager. He knows that the Indian heritage is beyond recall, and he also realizes that the attainment of the white man's style of life is an aim too high and too ambitious to ever materialize for him" (Sebald, 1968: 315).

The *native type* teen-ager has had little contact with whites and their culture. Thus, he represents the aboriginal personality type. His transition to adulthood is guided and directed by tribal rules and regulations in which adult models are involved. The *reaffirmative type* refers to the teen-ager who spent his teen years outside the Indian reservation, usually in boarding schools, and has become closely involved in the white man's cultural and economic system. Finding that the white culture fails to meet his needs, he reverts to Indian culture and attempts to identify closely with it. In many youngsters a degree of doubt appears as they attempt to reaffirm their native heritage.

The *deviant type* is not necessarily delinquent. This also includes those teen-agers who join a specific religious or ultraethnic subgroup that provides an emotional outlet by channeling hostility and frustration into acceptable avenues. This also gives these teen-agers a sense of belonging and an identity which is important to their personality integration. The *acculturated type* of teen-ager, whose parents have become integrated in the white community, grows up almost exclusively according to the norms and values of middle-class white culture. There is a marked absence of most of the traditional traits of the native Indian. This type of teen-ager is assimilated into the white society; he affiliates with the white man's religion; and he participates in the general teen-age subculture in the community of his residence. The adolescent experiences of these Indian teen-agers conform to those of their peers, and they normally have the approval and encouragement of their parents.

Indian Youth Identification

A reluctance of young Indians to enter the white man's world because of strong feelings of Indian identification was shown in a demonstration project designed to explore the possibility of intercultural exchange between the students of an Indian boarding school and white families in the surrounding community (*Children,* 1970). The primary objective of the project, called the Transitional Opportunities Project for Students

(TOPS), was to learn if young Indian students' process of accomodation to the dominant society would be aided by their association with white families. The project was started in August, 1967, by the Lutheran Social Services of South Dakota, with support from the Children's Bureau, and was discontinued in June, 1970, because of lack of participation. A description of the activities shows something of the nature of Indian adolescents, some of the problems they encountered, and the attitudes of the dominant white group.

. . . Each TOPS student was to be invited by a host family for weekends and if possible to live with the family all or part of the summer. This was to give the student an opportunity to live and perhaps to work in an off-reservation community.

From its inception the project encountered many problems. Prejudice and fear among both Indian students and prospective host families hampered arrangements. Many of the students had severe social and emotional problems and so found it difficult to relate to any adult, particularly a white adult. Nearby communities were hostile toward Indians. Some host families were unrealistic in their expectations of the young people. Other obstacles were refusal of parents to grant permission for a young person to participate in the summer program; inability to find suitable host families; the scarcity of available jobs; and reluctance of students to carry through their plans.

Although thirty-two students had expressed interest in living with host families during the summer of 1968, only eight did so. However, largely through the efforts of a student corrdinator, twenty-four students stayed with host families in the summer of 1969. Weekend visits during the school year were the most popular part of the project; thirty-six students participated in the 1968–69 school year.

Summer placements with local families were most successful for girls, for students who showed unusual motivation, and for students who had no acceptable alternative living arrangement, the project found. It also found that families that welcomed the students with warmth, but without pressure or intimacy, were the most successful. (24).

THE JEWISH ADOLESCENT

The stability and integration of the traditional Jewish family has hardly been matched by any other ethnic group in the United States. Jewish family life is interwoven with ethnic practices that give the children and adolescents pronounced psychological benefits. Meaningful rituals and ceremonies mark the traditional religious occasions, family events, and rites of passage from one age level to the next. Since they represent a sizeable number of American adolescents and also since our dominant culture is to a marked degree a Judeo-Christian one, we would find the study of Jewish adolescents a necessary part of American cultures.

Diversity of Jewish Teen-age Subculture

As with other groups of teen-agers, it would be misleading to describe adolescent Jewish subculture as collective or cohesive. There just isn't such conformity among the nearly six million Jews in the United States. A brief description of the diverse subcultures found among Jewish teen-agers and the factors and conditions associated with the diversity will give us a better understanding of Jewish adolescents. Thus, a more realistic picture of Jewish teen-agers can be attained by subdividing the Jewish population in the United States into more unique groups based upon place of residence (New York City, the South, Southwest, West, and Midwest), social class, theological orientation (Reform, Conservative, Orthodox), time of immigration to the United States, country of origin, plus any other variables that might affect the cultural pattern. Significant differences may be observed between Jewish teen-agers based largely upon the educational level of the home and occupation of the father. Thus, today it is harder than ever to generalize meaningfully about American Jews, primarily because "American Jewry is currently groping toward a redefinition of what it means to be a Jew and what the Jewish role in America should be. . . . The rise of anti-Semitism among blacks, bewilderment over the rejection of traditional American Jewish mores by some of their children, and the erosion of support among Christian leaders for the Israeli cause, all have prompted many Jews to feel they have entered a new phase in the perennial problem of coming to grips with their identity" (Newsweek, 1971: 56).

Since World War II there has been a continuous upward mobility of the Jews, so that today half of the Jewish families in America enjoy middle-class status. A major reason for this upward mobility has been their commitment to education. As of 1965, 80 percent of the Jews of college age were enrolled in college in contrast to 40 percent for the total population (Newsweek, 1971: 63). Within weeks after the outbreak of the six-day war in 1967, Jewish groups in America raised more than 170 million dollars in emergency aid for Israel. On the other hand, there is a community of needy, forgotten Jews who need help and have been neglected.

In daily life it may be difficult for a Jew to determine precisely how Jewish he and his family are. Employing one useful model, political scientist Daniel Elazar of Temple University has divided Jews into four degrees of attachment: The first group, which constitutes about 20 percent of the total Jewish population, is truly committed to regular worship and to Jewish communal organizations. Another 40 percent continue a nominal affiliation with organized Jewry, but usually attend religious services only twice a year on the high holy days of Rosh Hashanah and Yom Kippur. A third group—perhaps 30 percent—consists of those who are simply unconcerned about their Jewishness and the remainder according to Elazar are "unhappy and self-hating." (Newsweek, 1971: 63).

Declining Sense of Identity

For more than a century American Jews have struggled with the problem of blending smoothly in American society and at the same time maintaining their sense of identity. Traditionally they have been able to do this to some degree in most societies, although they have frequently met with serious problems. They have debated their problems within the confines of the family, Jewish community, synagogues and fraternal organizations. The one political issue that seems to have united American Jews is their attachment to the state of Israel. This has been a burning issue with them, even on a national scale, for some time and has also given a boost to their self-esteem.

American Jewish youth's disengagement from the Zionist zeal has been manifested in several ways. There has been a falling off of membership in the Intercollegiate Zionist Federation of America from 10,000 during and after World War II to approximately 2,500 members in the early 1960s (Jospe, 1963). Another indication of declining Jewish passion for the Zionist movement is the results of surveys. One survey question submitted to Jewish students was: Assume that you had sufficient funds to visit two foreign countries during your lifetime, and could make your decision now, which countries would you choose? The results were: 69 percent selected France, with Paris as the main attraction, 24 percent selected England, and about 20 percent selected Israel. Zionism as an instrument against injustice has not succeeded in enlisting a collective sense of identity or zeal among Jewish adolescents, especially during the oppressions in Russia in 1970–71.

The sense of identity among Jewish postadolescents has declined further with the increased number of mixed marriages. A number of surveys have traced this upward trend. Rosenthal (1963) noted a significant increase in the late fifties over that of earlier surveys. He further noted that college-educated Jews showed the highest rate of intermarriage. Also, his study estimated that approximately 70 percent of the children of mixed marriages were not brought up as Jews. In a survey made in 1965, 83 percent of U.S. Jews were opposed to mixed marriages. A similar survey made in 1971 showed that the opposition had dropped to 41 percent, with two-thirds of those opposed being over the age of forty-five (*Newsweek*, 1971: 57).

Behavior Patterns of Adolescent Jews

Since most Jewish teen-agers are from the middle-upper socioeconomic class, one would expect them to adopt the sexual patterns of their peers. A significant trend towards stabilization of sexual patterns has been noted among Jewish adults, the Jewish college students have abandoned the traditional sexual behavior code. Premarital continence as a standard has to a large degree been replaced by a petting-with-affection, further modified by the prevalence of premarital intercourse approximating that of non-Jews. There is considerably more deviation in sexual behavior between the religious and nonobservant within the three faiths than between Protestants, Catholics, and Jews. The adolescent American Jew, like his Catholic and Protestant counterparts, is strongly influenced by mass media, socioeconomic status, education, and peers. Thus, abandoning the traditional sexual code is an important part of adolescent culture, but varies considerably with social class as will be pointed out later in this chapter.

Within recent years there has been a new sense of pride among many Jewish youth and a major symptom of this has been their strong support for Soviet Jewry. Ties between Jewish youth in different parts of the world have been intensified. Most young American Jews grow up with gentiles; they play with them, go to school with them, socialize with them, and marry them; they are more accepted today than ever before.

Is THERE A JEWISH STEREOTYPE? Like other minority groups in America, Jews have been stereotyped. Today it is difficult to identify a Jew from his behavioral patterns. The American Jew is said to be groping toward a redefinition of just what it means to be a Jew in the United States. Does his religion give him an identity? "The synagogue has been the first bastion of assimilation in American society," says Temple University's Elazar. Because of this, he contends, most young American Jews grow up with "no experience of what being a Jew means except going to a different church" (*Newsweek*, 1971: 64). No one can predict the course of the young Jew of today. That is he is being assimilated into the larger culture and playing an important economic, political, and social role no one can deny. He is freer in America than ever before to be himself and to make important contributions to society.

THE CHINESE-AMERICAN ADOLESCENT

Prior to the twentieth century, Chinese communities in the United States were characterized by the dominance of the traditional family and neighborhood associations. The wife and children acknowledged the superiority and authority of the male elders. Adolescents readily accepted parental controls in matters of courtship and mate selection. Since 1960, Chinese-American communities have increasingly become involved in the process of urban change and acculturation and assimilation. This has resulted in an increasing divergence from traditional family practices, decentralization of the Chinese community, and a dispersion of families. Family associations are declining in importance, since they no longer meet the needs of contemporary community life. With women gaining a more equal footing in the financial, recreational, and socializing practices of the family, the father's role has been weakened. This is further reflected in his control over the children, especially as they grow into adolescence.

General Pattern of Interracial Dating

A significant and dramatic departure from traditional Chinese-American life appears in the Chinese-Caucasian dating patterns. This further emphasizes Chinese adolescent's new-found independence and freedom from familial dominance and increasing adherence to western dating patterns.

The results of different studies show that Chinese-American females have internalized the dominant dating values of Caucasian teen-agers and have adjusted to American dating and marriage demands better than males (Weiss, 1970). Chinese-American girls desire and expect to be treated like their Caucasian contemporaries. Many Chinese-American boys are unable to meet these expectations. As a result, many girls seek romance, companionship, and adventure with Caucasian boys.

Chinese-American males have experienced many successes in American society as have other Oriental males. They have frequently proved themselves as scholars in our educational system. This upward mobility has enabled some of them to enter into interracial marriages with middle-class Caucasians, although many Chinese-American men have not been as successful as the women in interracial social relations. Chinese-American boys who demonstrate proficiency in Caucasian manners and behavior on a date are quite popular and much in demand both by Chinese-American girls and others as friends, dates, and husbands.

Social Interactions

Historically the American stereotype of Oriental men is negative. They have been characterized as gangsters, drug addicts, and family tyrants. Chinese youth are not characterized by the American ideal of being athletic, romantic, extroverted, and sociable. On the other hand, the Chinese female image is better accepted by the American public. This has been observed in popular songs and movies. Thus, Chinese girls with Caucasian escorts are more favorably received than Chinese men with their Caucasian escorts.

Chinese-American male adolescents seldom participate in school activities involving social interaction such as parties and dancing. They rarely join predominantly Causasian fraternities at college, while Chinese-American females are better represented in women's social organizations. Females state that they are usually at ease in the company of their Caucasian peers; males frequently indicate insecurity and anxiety in interracial situations involving social interactions. The females generally consider themselves more Americanized than the males.

Based on a study of dating practices of American Chinese Weiss concludes:

> Perhaps a major factor affecting the dating attitudes of Chinese-American males and females is not so much in the rate of acculturation but the sphere in which acculturation takes place. Chinese-American women be-

come integrated primarily in the expressive sphere of interpersonal relationships while Chinese-American men appear to be acculturated in the instrumental sphere of work (their dedication towards their studies including part-time work suggests a real commitment to the American dream of social mobility). The strong motivation of Chinese-American men to achieve social status through educational means also suggests that the striving for occupational success takes precedence over and may actually impair their ability to "socialize" with other people (1970: 276).

PERSONAL AND SOCIAL ADJUSTMENTS. The adjustment problems of the Chinese-born adolescents resemble those of many others who migrate to another culture and carry over culturally acquired meanings, values, and role expectations. When the two cultures are vastly different, new role meanings frequently come into conflict with traditional ones, and this may result in personal maladjustment. Furthermore, this may be greater for one sex than the other and present sex-role problems. A study by Fong and Peskin (1969) dealt with the differential adjustment of Chinese male and female college students in America. As students, the sexes face different role strains because the student role has always been reserved for the male.

Results on the California Psychology Inventory with forty-three male and forty-three female Chinese students supported this expectation; females scored lower on "Socialization" and "Good Impression." The naturalized American citizens (twenty males and twenty-one females) were more self-confident, freer from self-doubt and disillusionment, more responsible and dependable, more accepting and tolerant of others, more flexible and adaptive in their intellectual functioning, more in touch with the implicit and underlying values of the American scene (565–66).

Based on results from Rorschach protocols, Weiss concluded:

> Chinese-American females have a less rigid role to maintain than their male counterparts. They are not as responsible for carrying on family "tradition" and are less subjected to parental pressures to conform. They, therefore, find it less challenging to adjust to contemporary American life. Male feelings of inadequacy are not complemented by female "adjustments" to acculturation. It takes but little imagination to project these suggested sex-role discrepancies directly into the dating situation (277).

Parental Conflicts

Perhaps the generation gap between Chinese-American adolescents and their parents is as great or greater than almost any other group. Most Chinese parents disapprove of interracial dating, yet certain aspects of social life in a Chinese-American community seem to encourage Chinese-American females to date non-Chinese men and even discourage dating within the Chinese-American group.

Although the Chinese have become more dispersed than formerly, a sense of community existence still exists. This is maintained in part by an informal information exchange system by friends which unites the community by cutting across age, sex, and generational barriers. Dating stories are readily carried from Chinese family to other Chinese families. Some of these become "juicy gossip," which is readily spread to the detriment of the female in particular. This is in a large measure due to casual or consistent dating. Chinese-American youth, like their Caucasian peers, regard dating as a pleasant end in itself and not necessarily a prelude to marriage. On the other hand, parents have traditionally looked upon dating as a direct prelude to serious marital intentions and, when continued, to a commitment. The grapevine gossip functions best when Chinese-American males date Chinese-American females. Chinese-Chinese dates rarely remain secret affairs, while the Chinese-Caucasian dates are unlikely to become widely known within the Chinese grapevine community.

Interracial dating is not the only source of parental conflict. Chinese-American adolescents are better informed and experienced in the American ways of life than their parents. This, in itself, creates problems between them and their parents in homes where traditionally the father is the authority on all matters. Also, parents have retained emotional ties with their country and certain family rituals and practices. By contrast, their children through the process of acculturation have broken from these ties and adopted the culture of their Caucasian peers; they recognize, sometimes unconsciously, that their world is quite different from that of their parents. Strains develop within the family that are often quite severe. One Chinese girl once remarked to one of the writers concerning problems she was experiencing with her parents: "I suppose I have become too much American for my parents. I am going to make my own decisions."

Perhaps because of the increasing acclimation of dominant American culture by Chinese youth, many members of their older generation are afraid this Oriental group may lose their ethnic uniqueness. This was demonstrated in the fall of 1971 when Chinese parents in San Francisco strongly protested the bussing of their children out of their own neighborhood to suburban white schools.

LOWER-CLASS ADOLESCENTS

The problems of the lower-class adolescent are frequently unique. It was pointed out in Chapter 2 that adolescents on Mechanic Street are often the forgotten adolescents and many of them are dropouts. Mason (1968) has pointed out that the behavior of disadvantaged American Indians, Mexicans, and European ethnics shows a generalized more negative, poorly adjusted behavior pattern among females regardless of ethnic background than among males. This was especially noted for American Indian girls.

**Lower-Class Youth and
Middle-Class Demands**

Adolescents from the lower classes tend to either drop out of school,
enroll in a terminal or vocational course at the secondary-school level,
or adopt middle-class values and make plans to further their education
by going to college.

The adolescent from the lower class who maintains lower-class
values rejects the "eager-beaver" attitude toward school activities, respect
for teachers, and a conformist attitude toward the total school program.
These attitudes are most obvious among lower-class boys, although they
frequently appear among lower-class girls. However, there is a preponderance of delinquents from the lower-class with the boys outnumbering girls by a ratio of five to one or more.

INFLUENCES OF LOWER-CLASS CULTURE. Lower-class youth are highly
influenced by lower-class cultural norms. This frequently sets them in
opposition to and often in conflict with middle-class demands, standards,
and the law. A strong peer loyalty develops, and a simplified social-
structural involvement. These form a bridge that helps the adolescent
during the period of transition. This is very noticeable in the case of
the lower-class Negro who is burdened with a legacy of discrimination
and prejudice. By internalizing these, he has often developed a low
self-esteem. Lower-class family living, the slum environment, preschool
disadvantages, low employment and income, and inferior medical care
are all factors that have complicated his transition from childhood to
adulthood. Following the Supreme Court decision on segregation in the
schools in 1954 and increased automation, jobs for the lower-class adolescents have decreased while jobs and opportunities for the more educated middle class have increased.

This disparity between the middle- and lower-class blacks has given
rise to hostility between the two groups; many middle-class black adolescents have no concern for the plight of the lower-class blacks. One
hopeful sign is that black adolescents are developing a sense of identity
and pride. This should help them overcome their defeatist attitude
which contributes to their unemployment, delinquency, and degeneracy
(*Reader's Digest,* 1967).

Lower Class Urban Youth

The problems involved in living in large cities have been with us
throughout history. They have become more complex and serious with
affluence and poverty present side by side, with the population explosion,
and with automated technology. We find close proximity in crowds
paralleled by loneliness and emotional difficulties (Darley and Latané,
1968). With respect to adolescents there can be little doubt that many
are growing up in a society which has no place for them. Until 1971 they

were even unable to vote in most of the states until they had reached twenty-one years of age. At the same time they furnished the manpower for our war effort, with those from the lower class making up a large percentage of the dead and injured.

VARIABILITY IN BACKGROUND AND EXPERIENCES. There is perhaps more variability in the kinds of environmental experiences of lower-class urban children and adolescents than in most other groups of adolescents. The results of studies by Deutsch (1963) suggest that children and adolescents from upper-class homes have a more common environment due to prolonged schooling, family stability, more exposure to books, magazines, newspapers, and intelligent conversation. The environment of lower-class children and adolescents is less uniform due to inconsistencies in schooling by parents, less exposure to books, magazines, and newspapers, more exposure to superstition, mysticism, and prejudice, and less stability in home life. Thus, we would expect to find greater variability in personality characteristics among lower-class adolescents, although we note a greater differentiation of mental functions or special abilities with increased education and experience.

ATTITUDES OF LOWER-CLASS URBAN ADOLESCENTS. While many adolescents from more affluent lower-class homes succeed in school and develop aspirations to go on to college and move up the occupational ladder, most of them end up in occupations similar to those of their parents but perhaps with a little more schooling. Aspirational level is closely related to home background and peer aspirations.

The adolescent boy's need for autonomy may be observed in the lower-class urban adolescent boy's behavior in asserting his independence and masculinity. The notion of masculinity—toughness, sexual vigor, aggressiveness—is poorly suited to the authoritarian, female-oriented program at school. Thus, they are frequently in trouble with school authorities. This was observed by Jackson and Lahaderne (1966) in their study of teacher-pupil interactions. In a study of four representative classrooms where boys made up from 45 to 59 percent of the class, 70 to 90 percent of the prohibitory teacher-pupil interactions were meted out to boys.

We also note that prejudice against black students in high school tends to be highest among lower-class urban adolescents. This may be in harmony with the idea advanced by Katz, Sarnoff, and McClintock (1956) that attitudes may serve to protect and enhance the ego of the individual. Resistance to attitude change may arise from the possibility that a change would deprive the individual of an important defense mechanism. It seems likely that the lower-class urban white adolescent burdened with feelings of inadequacy is more likely to display prejudice and intolerance toward certain ethnic, religious, or racial groups than an adolescent with a more favorable self-image.

Disadvantaged Rural Youth

When we think of lower-class adolescents we think of the slums, ghettos, and other conditions of urban life. We fail to realize that many rural and small-town youths are also quite disadvantaged. This has been true for a number of decades. In the first place, we have had for the past half century a continuous decline in the percentage of people engaged in farming or even living on farms. Thus, most adolescents must finally find employment in urban areas. Rural youth in general receive less preparation for successful entry into the world of work and have a much smaller range of occupational choices than most other adolescents. Rural schools have for the most part given little occupational information to students. Lindstrom (1965) found that rural schools gave no help to students who were migrating to urban areas to find employment. He concluded that it was a mistake for rural youth to migrate to the cities to find employment. Rather, he suggests that they should attempt to get some vocational training in the type of work in which they hope to find employment.

ASPIRATIONS OF RURAL ADOLESCENTS. An important characteristic that has been observed among a large percentage of rural youth is their low aspiration level, especially white rural adolescents. Haller, Burchinal, and Taves (1963) compared rural and urban adolescents for their vocational aspirations. They found that the college and occupational aspirations of rural youth were lower, that they had more difficulty getting jobs, and that their jobs required less skill and did not furnish as high a wage as those of nonrural youth. Due perhaps to their cultural background rural youth as a general rule do not seem to develop the necessary motivation to achieve success in white-collar jobs. There is some evidence that rural adolescents from the different minority groups have lower educational and occupational aspirations than other rural youth. However, this may result from their place of residence. Drabick (1963) studied the occupational and educational plans of vocational agriculture students in North Carolina. He found that the Negro students did not aspire or expect to enter occupations with as high a prestige value as the white students. Similar results were obtained by Crawford, Peterson, and Wurr (1967) in a comparison of the educational plans of Indian students with those of Caucasians. Likewise Henderson (1966) reported that almost 50 percent of unemployed Mexican-American adults were not looking for work. Thus, one would expect that adolescents from such families would have low occupational aspirations.

SUMMARY

Industrialization, urbanization, technological developments, and the prolonged period of schooling has separated adolescents from many important features of adult society. The subculture furnishes the adolescents definite status and a feeling of belonging and acceptance. Throughout the previous chapters we have emphasized that there is no one adolescent culture. We note differences, even within a single high school, particularly social class differences.

We also find significant differences between adolescent cultures from different ethnic, class, or racial groups. The largest minority group is the blacks. They make up about 11 percent of our total population and are becoming concentrated more and more in the inner city of our large metropolitan areas. This is not a clearly defined ethnic group, since they represent a part of our culture from the time of the early settlements on the Virginia coast. Contemporary black adolescents are part of the process operating in which many traditions, attitudes, and values are being reassessed. Due to the inferior status they have been allocated, they have suffered from a chronically low self-concept. There are indications of change as they become integrated into the larger society.

Another minority group is the Puerto Rican adolescents; they contain a blend of Spanish and United States culture. Although virginity on the part of girls is encouraged, it is estimated that about one-third of all Puerto Rican births are out of wedlock. The relationships of adolescents with their parents are very much strained. Thus, the prognosis for boys is frequently very bad. Another group, akin to the Puerto Ricans is the Mexican-Americans. The self-concept of Mexican-American adolescents is a carry-over from the home of second class citizenship; it is permeated with feelings of inadequacy and low self-esteem. They are acquainted with stereotypes and many have experienced unpleasant relations with teachers and other adults. He, too, is torn between two cultures, and there is considerable intergenerational conflict. Parental educational aspirations for their children furnishes the best basis for achievement prognosis.

There is much tribal diversity in the case of Indian adolescents. There is no one Indian culture and there is no single set of special problems. Most studies indicate that they are in general a disadvantaged rural group. The forces of change may be observed among Indian adolescents, although they are placed in a position of marginality to both their native Indian culture and the American Caucasian culture. The more acculturated adolescents display severe conflicts between their new aspirations and traditional attitudes and behavior patterns. In general they are reluctant to enter the white man's world.

As with other groups of adolescents, it is misleading to think of Jewish teen-agers as a collective, cohesive culture. The emphasis of Jewish parents on education has caused most adolescents to remain in school and go on to college. With the American Jewry groping toward a redefinition of what it means to be a Jew, adolescents are bewildered. There continues a declining sense of identity, and intermarriage with other faiths has increased rapidly. However a new sense of pride and identity arising from happenings in Israel, has inspired some adolescent Jews to identify more closely with Jewry and their parents. There has been a significant and dramatic departure from traditional Chinese-American life by the adolescents in their dating patterns, as well as in values and attitudes. The strong trend toward Western culture has created problems between generations.

REFERENCES

Bass, Willard P. and Henry G. Burger. *American Indian and the Educational Laboratories.* Albuquerque: Southwestern Cooperative Educational Laboratory, 1967.

Carter, T. "Negative Self-concept of Mexican-American Students." *School and Society* (1968), 96:217–19.

Children (November–December 1970), 17 (6):241. "Indian Youth."

Coleman, James S. *The Adolescent Society.* New York: The Free Press, 1962.

Crawford, Dean A., David L. Peterson, and Virgil Wurr. *Minnesota Chippewa Indians: A Handbook for Teachers.* St. Paul, Minn: Upper Midwest Regional Educational Laboratory, 1967.

Cruz, Juan S. and George R. Ricks. "The Puerto Rican Child." In *Children, Psychology and the Schools,* Bryant Feather and Walter S. Olson, eds. Glenville, Ill.: Scott, Foresman and Co., 1969.

Darley, John M. and Latané Bibb. "When Will People Help in a Crisis?" *Psychology Today* (1968), 2 (7):54–57.

Deutsch, M. "The Disadvantaged Child and the Learning Process." In *Education in Depressed Areas,* A. H. Passow, ed. New York: Teachers College, Columbia University, 1963.

Drabick, Lawrence W. *Occupational and Educational Plans of Vocational Agriculture Students in North Carolina: A Comparison with Other Students.* Educational Research Series No. I. Raleigh: Departments of Agricultural Education and Rural Sociology, North Carolina State University, 1963.

Elkin, Frederick and William A. Westley. "The Myth of Adolescent Culture." *American Sociological Review* (1955), 20:680–84.

Fong, Stanley and Harvey Peskin. "Sex-role Strain and Personality Adjustment of Chinese-born Students in America." *Journal of Abnormal Psychology* (1969), 74:563–67.

Forward, John R. and Jay R. Williams. "Internal-External Control and Black Militancy." *The Journal of Social Issues* (1970), 26 (1):75–92.

Gaarder, B. *Education of American Indian Children.* Annual Conference, Southwest Council of Foreign Language Teachers. El Paso, Tex.: The Council, 1967. Pp. 31–39.

Goodey, Darwin. "Joseph: A Study of Personal Values of Indian Adolescents." *Dissertation Abstracts International* (1972), 32 (11):6128-A.

Goodman, Paul. "The Universe of Discourse in Which They Grow Up." In *Adolescence: Contemporary Studies,* Alvin E. Winder and David L. Angus, eds. New York: American Book Co., 1968. Pp. 102–10.

Haller, Archibald O., Lee G. Burchinal, and Marvin J. Taves. *Rural Youth*

Need Help in Choosing Occupations. Circular Bulletin No. 35. East Lansing: Department of Sociology and Anthropology, Michigan State University, 1963.

HENDERSON, RONALD W. *Environmental Stimulation and Intellectual Development of Mexican-American Children: An Exploratory Project.* Cooperative Research Project. Tuscon: University of Arizona, 1966.

JACKSON, P. W. and H. M. LAHADERNE. "Inequities of Teacher-Pupil Contacts." Paper read at the meeting of the American Psychological Association. New York: September, 1966.

JOSPE, ALFRED. "The Sense of Jewish Identity of the Jewish College student." *The Jewish Digest* (May 1963).

KATZ, D., I. SARNOFF, and C. McCLINTOCK. "Ego Defense and Attitude Change." *Human Relations* (1956), 9:27–45.

KERNER, O. *et al. Report of the National Advisory Commission on Civil Rights.* New York: Bantam Books, 1968.

KIMBALL, WILLIAM L. "Parent and Family Influences on Academic Achievement Among Mexican-American Students" *Dissertation Abstracts* (1968), 29: 1965-A.

Life magazine (January 8, 1971), pp. 22–27, 30. "A New York Poll."

LINDSTROM, D. E. "Educational Needs of Rural Youth." *Journal of Cooperative Extension* (Spring 1965), 3:33–41.

MASON, EVELYN P. "Sex Differences in Personality Characteristics of Deprived Adolescents." *Perceptual and Motor Skills* (1968), 27 (1):934.

MAYESKE, GEORGE W. *Educational Achievement Among Mexican-Americans: A Special Report from the Educational Opportunities Survey.* Technical Note No. 22. Washington, D.C.: Office of Education, 1967.

NELSON, EDWARD A. and EDWARD ROSENBAUM. "Language Patterns Within the Youth Subculture: Development of Slang Vocabularies." *Merrill-Palmer Quarterly,* (1972), 18 (3):273–85.

Newsweek (March 1, 1971), pp. 56–64. "The American Jew Today."

PARSONS, TALCOTT. "Psychoanalysis and the Social Structure." *Psychoanalytic Quarterly* (1950), 19:378–79.

RAMIREZ, MANUEL III, CLARK TAYLOR, and BARBARA PETERSEN. "Mexican-American Cultural Membership and Adjustment to School." *Developmental Psychology,* (1971), 4 (2):141–48.

Reader's Digest (January 1967), pp. 70–74. "What the Negro Has and Has Not Gained."

ROSENTHAL, ERICH. "Studies of Jewish Intermarriage in the United States." *American Jewish Yearbook,* (1963), 64:3–53.

SCHMIDT, LINDA and JUNE GALLESSICH. "Adjustment of Anglo-American and Mexican-American pupils in Self-contained and Teen-teaching Classrooms." *Journal of Educational Psychology* (1971), 63:328–32.

SCHWARTZ, G. and D. MERTON. "The Language of Adolescence: An Anthropological Approach to Youth Culture." *American Journal of Sociology* (1967), 72:453–68.

SEBALD, HANS. ADOLESCENCE: *A Sociological Analysis.* New York: Appleton-Century-Crofts, 1968.

TOFFLER, ALVIN. *Future Shock.* New York: Random House, Inc., 1970.

Tomlinson, T. M. "The Development of a Riot Ideology Among Urban Negroes." *The American Behavioral Scientist* (March–April 1968), 11 (4).

Webster, Staten W. and Marie N. Kroger. "A Comparative Study of Selected Perceptions and Feelings of Negro Adolescents With and Without White Friends in Integrated Urban High Schools." *Journal of Negro Education* (Winter 1966), 35:55–61.

Weiss, Melford S. "Selective Acculturation and the Dating Process: The Patterning of Chinese-Caucasian Interracial Dating." *Journal of Marriage and Family Living* (May 1970), 273–78.

Williams, Robert L. and Harry Byars. "Negro Self-esteem in a Transitional Society." *Personnel and Guidance Journal* (1968), 47 (2):120–25.

RECOMMENDED READINGS

Baughman, E. Earl. *Black Americans: A Psychological Analysis.* New York: Academic Press, 1971.
A recent well-organized account of the psychological processes that characterize black Americans. Describes how bigotry, discrimination, and environmental factors have affected the black American's self-image, scholastic performances, attitudes, and general behavioral patterns.

Brody, Eugene B., ed. *Minority Group Adolescents in the United States.* Baltimore: Williams and Wilkins, 1968.
Brody served as editor and contributor to general chapters of this book. The other seven contributors have brought together professional and scientific knowledge as well as their own experiences as members of the minority group about which they write.

Gottlieb, David and A. L. Heimsohn. *America's Other Youth: Growing up Poor.* Englewood Cliffs, N.J.: Prentice-Hall, Inc., 1971.
The subject matter of this book is youth with a focus on the life-style of youngsters living in poverty and from distinct cultures.

Hauser, Stuart T. *Black and White Identity Formation.* New York: John Wiley & Sons, Inc., 1971.
This is a study in the psychosocial development of lower socioeconomic class adolescent boys. Two matched samples of white and black male adolescents are studied throughout their high school careers. The study stresses that divergent patterns of identity formation must be formulated in terms of sociocultural and psychological frameworks.

Roberts, John I, ed. *School Children in the Urban Slum.* New York: The Free Press, 1967. Pp. 371–424.
The topics covered by different authorities are: parent conferences are always tough; West End and Crestwood Heights; rituals in family living; the changing Negro family; up from Puerto Rico; and Chinese culture, social organization, and personality.

10

the schools: education in change and crisis

The institution of the school has evolved in all highly civilized societies as an agency for training children, adolescents, and youth for citizenship. In an industrially developed society such as ours it holds an outstanding and dominant place. Between 60 and 65 million Americans are engaged full-time as students, teachers, or administrators in the educational process. There are thousands of other people engaged as part-time students and teachers, or as trustees of local school systems, state boards of education, or institutions of higher learning. The expenditures for all educational purposes are stupendous and increasing annually. The federal government is being called upon more and more to assure increased educational opportunities for the disadvantaged and to help in financing the schools and colleges.

INTRODUCTION:
THE HIGH SCHOOL POPULATION

The American high school was at one time designed primarily for a privileged group of adolescents, most of whom planned on going to college. The story is quite different today as anyone can observe when visiting a large consolidated high school. The students come from homes of various types; they represent different racial and religious groups; and they have very different goals and aspirations.

Due to the mass media, the wide range of educational agencies, and increased opportunities for broad experience, contemporary adolescents are better informed than any group of youngsters in history. If Booth Tarkington were to write *Seventeen* today, he would perhaps call it *Thirteen*, about the average age of menarche in the American girl. An increasing number of adolescents remain in high school and will enter a technical school or go on to college, thus prolonging their dependent role.

The Case of Pacific Palisades High School

A description of the students at noonday at the Pacific Palisades High School, bordering on Sunset Park, gives us a picture of the groups and activities of upper- and middle-class students. This will be found in certain selected high schools throughout the United States but is not typical of most student bodies described later in this chapter. "Pali," as the students call their school, is a new, seven-million-dollar red brick campus of 2,100 students. The students and the school have been described as follows (*Time*, 1965: 57):

> The natives observe a rigid noonday ritual. The social elite—a breezy clique called the Palisades-Brentwood Singing and Drinking Association—hold court at cafeteria tables reserved by custom for them. Near by, like ladies in waiting, two plain girls snatch at conversational crumbs tossed by a pair of homecoming queens. At another table are the "social rejects" —girls on the fringes of the elite whose boy friends are now tired of them. "They are still allowed to go to parties," explains a guide, "but they aren't in on the really big decisions, like who the elite will back in student elections."
>
> Toward the rear of the hall sit the service club members and the rah-rah crowd, "the squares who really believe in student government." Other tribes are the Saracens, who include a small motorcycling hood element; the clowns, a group of practical jokers who wear Mickey Mouse shirts to signify that all human existence is fradulent; the intellectuals, who lounge on the steps of the administration buiding as the rest of the student body speculates over whether the long-haired girls among them are professional virgins or real swingers; and an amorphous crowd that defies classification by declaring unanimously: "I'm myself."
>
> Parental pressure for grades at Pali is intense; students often retaliate at home by demanding cars, clothes, expensive vacations. "If you aren't aware of the underlying fraud," explains Senior Al Hunsaker, an A student, "then you become a grind. In a way, it's a massive put-on, faking out the community and the family without going through the suffering of a full-fledged revolt." "As long as we don't make waves," a classmate adds, "the administration is happy."

Student Body Characteristics

If we could examine the characteristics of the high school student body in the United States at the beginning of this century, we would find a great deal of homogeneity. The high school at that time was an institution primarily for middle- and upper-class adolescents; most adolescents from blue-collar homes dropped out of school and went to work on the farm or elsewhere upon finishing the sixth, seventh, or eighth grade. Today, however, there is a great cultural diversity in religion, race, and social class, although due to housing patterns and related conditions a great deal of homogeneity exists in some schools. In our cities we find some high schools attended mainly by white or black students despite the Supreme Court ruling in 1954.

> The Supreme Court has found that, even though the tangible provisions of the school are the same, school segregation along racial lines is inherently unequal. The sense of inferiority affects the motivation of the child to learn. The *de facto* segregation brought about by concentration of social classes in cities results in schools with unequal . . . climates which likewise affect the motivation of the child, not necessarily by inculcating a sense of inferiority, but rather by providing a different ethos in which to perceive values (Wilson, 1959: 845).

THE ACADEMICALLY TALENTED. Identification of the academically talented students and establishing his educational needs are important tasks of teachers. Concerning their characteristics, Bish (1961) states:

> . . . Most of these students learn quickly without much drill, organize data efficiently, reason clearly, and show an interest in a wide range of abstract concepts. As a rule they are above average in their use of vocabulary and reading skills.
> Creativity and originality are often distinguishing characteristics. These children are generally persevering. They are capable of a considerable amount of independent study, possess more than the normal amount of stamina, and are usually above average physically (33).

The increased college attendance is reflected in the larger percentage of academically superior high school students who go on to college. The estimates made by Berdie (1954) indicated that about 50 percent of the superior students were going on to college in the early fifties. McDaniel and Forenback's study involved the top 15 percent of Kentucky's 1959 high school seniors who participated in a statewide testing program (1960). The findings indicated that 76 percent of the students from the top 15 percent of the class entered college. Simmons (1963) found from a study of academically superior high school students in Georgia that 88 percent planned to attend college and that approximately the same percentage actually entered college in the fall following their graduation. This study supports the trend for an increasing percentage of academically superior students to attend college. The relationship of background factors related to college attendance indicated some significant differences between superior students who entered college and those who did not enter college. The following factors were significantly related to college attendance:

1. Student Aptitude Test scores
2. Yearly income of the family
3. Extent of student-parent discussion of college plans
4. Occupational level of the father
5. Educational level of the father
6. Educational level of the mother
7. Parental attitude concerning student's college attendance
8. Number of siblings, particular older siblings
9. Size of high school attended
10. Presence of a guidance counselor in the high school
11. Extent of student-faculty discussion of college plans
12. Type of institution preferred for post-high school training
13. Preference regarding the attending of a local junior college
14. Preference for a job rather than college after high school
15. Marital status highly significant for girls

THE NONACADEMIC PUPIL. The traditional academic high school program has not proved appropriate for the increased percentage of boys and girls enrolling in our high schools. Sando (1956) studied problems encountered by high school pupils, especially those who dropped out of school during their sophomore and junior years. The sophomores were asked the following question: "What kind of problems do you have that you would like some help with?" Some answers given were: "I couldn't get along with some of the kids"; "My problem is how to act, how to dress at a banquet, how to act among adults"; "The teachers are too wrapped up in the mass, not the individual." Twenty percent felt history was least valuable—the same things being repeated again and again. Many English teachers have encountered the reaction: "Why should I study this? I ain't going to need it." Complaints frequently made by nonacademic students regarding science are that it is meaningless or lacks relevancy or is too difficult. The biggest and most difficult problem facing the schools is motivating the nonacademic pupils.

The lack of interest and motivation in general in academic achievement looms large in the life of the nonacademic pupil. This also seems to operate in technology programs where there is less emphasis upon what is usually termed academic achievement. In a study by MiDill (1970) an analysis was made of the factors associated with dropouts in a technology program. A comparison was made between those who persisted in the program and those who dropped out in order to determine factors related to dropping out of the program. The study noted that "Interest in technology was the dominating factor in career selection.

Some of the factors influential in program withdrawal were: loss of interest, discouragement with courses, and technology teachers in terms of presentation of material" (1645–A). Since interest in a particular course and discouragement seem so prominent, one can readily see how important the teacher's role is in keeping the nonacademic student in school.

School attendance is only one aspect of the problem. Culturally deprived adolescents at the beginning of the twelfth grade are likely to be several years behind culturally advantaged adolescents in reading comprehension as well as in other areas of academic achievement. Students have been found to do better when they are in school where fellow students come from backgrounds strong in educational motivation and resources (*U.S. News,* 1967). There is a need for the complete restructuring of the social environment of the child and adolescent from the culturally deprived background if he is to compete successfully in our present-day schools.

Efforts are being made to guide educable youth out of the ghetto into trade schools or college. These adolescents usually experience fundamental discontinuities when they leave the ghetto to go to school elsewhere or to enter the world of work. Effective education presupposes good communication—the ability to take the other person's point of view. Taking the ghetto student's point of view should be the first step in any attempt to provide education at the high school or college level for them (Elkind, 1971: 245).

MINORITY-GROUP MEMBERSHIP. Despite efforts over the past two decades to integrate all groups into the high schools, there are still schools in which children of only one particular economic class or racial background are enrolled. Many disadvantaged or otherwise educationally handicapped students are destined to become school dropouts; others will rebel at the school program and remain in school; and others will become covert dropouts—dropouts in their feelings and attitudes toward school while being physically present. According to Ernest Smith, for most slum children, "the American dream is not the American fact. These children cannot respond to what is being taught, and most educators resist changing the curriculum to aid these children" (*Time,* 1965). Although this was written in the middle of the 1960s it is still true to a marked degree, despite innovations of the past decade in many schools.

The Coleman Report (Coleman *et al.,* 1966) showed that pupils from minority groups were more retarded in verbal than nonverbal abilities. The results presented in Table 10–1 also indicate that they fall further behind as they progress from the first to the twelfth grade. Further conclusions and implications of the study are as follows:

1. The differences shown in Table 10-1 should not obscure the fact that some minority pupils perform better than many majority (white American) children and adolescents.

TABLE 10-1 Nationwide Median Test Scores for 1st- and 12th-grade Pupils, Fall 1965

	RACIAL OR ETHNIC GROUP					
TEST	Puerto Ricans	Indian Americans	Mexican Americans	Oriental Americans	Negro	Majority
1st grade:						
Nonverbal	45.8	53.0	50.1	56.6	43.4	54.1
Verbal	44.9	47.8	46.5	51.6	45.4	53.2
12th grade:						
Nonverbal	43.3	47.1	45.0	51.6	40.9	52.0
Verbal	43.1	43.7	43.8	49.6	40.9	52.1
Reading	42.6	44.3	44.2	48.8	42.2	51.9
Mathematics	43.7	45.9	45.5	51.3	41.8	51.8
General information	41.7	44.7	43.3	49.0	40.6	52.2
Average of the 5 tests	43.1	45.1	44.4	50.1	41.1	52.0

Source: Coleman et al. (1966).

2. The schools differ in their relation to the achievement of the different racial and ethnic groups.
3. The achievement of minority pupils depends more on the nature of the schools they attend than does the achievement of the majority pupils.
4. It appears that the average minority pupil's achievement may suffer more in a school of low quality than that of the average majority pupil.
5. The quality of teachers shows a strong relationship to pupil achievement. This seems to be more important to minority-group achievement than to that of the majority.
6. It appears that a pupil's achievement is strongly related to the educational background and aspirations of the parents.

The High School Rebel

The climate of the typical high school is one in which a great many students are not interested in the school program; many of them are in a state of rebellion. We can readily note the climate of change operating as we note the words used to describe the present high school situation: "the words of the involved generation (activist, militant, student coalition, relevant), the words of the electronic generation (computerized, multimedia, video, unisex). Around you science breaks barriers, art forms explode, and new types emerge on the scene, especially the youth scene: antihero heroes, new leftists, rock poets, and leather-jacketed artists" (Reice 1969: 60).

There is some evidence that deviance in behavior results when there is poor articulation between present school activities and future status. The word *relevance* has been freely used with reference to the school program. If the school program fails to link adolescence and adulthood in terms of the most intensely felt needs (future jobs, marriage, child care, citizenship) rebelliousness and alienation are likely to result. Expressive alienation, or the overt acting out of alienation in the presence of authority, occurs when future status is not clearly related to the present educational activities. An outstanding gripe of many rebels is that teachers are not interested in them because they are not planning to go to college. They believe that the teachers merely tolerate them and want them to be quiet.

Probably the most subtle form of adolescent rebellion is under-achievement. It is seldom recognized by either the adolescent, teacher, or parent as rebellion and occurs among bright as well as average or below-average youngsters. Without psychological services to help detect the symptoms of this kind of rebellion, it is likely to be too late for treatment or effective guidance when dropping out of school occurs. Blaine (1966: 30) points out: "What is so commonly termed laziness, lack of will power, or poor attitude is at heart a kind of sullen resentfulness expressed by a stubborn refusal to do anything demanded by authority." He suggests that teachers and parents unintentionally reinforce unconscious feelings of resentment by taking overly punitive attitudes toward students performing unsatisfactorily in their schoolwork. This finally leads such students to rebel against the school program and in a large percentage of cases to withdraw from school.

SCHOOL-RELATED
ATTITUDES AND PROBLEMS

The adolescent encounters many problems at school, some of which he has little control over. In meeting problems of adolescents teachers should first of all recognize individual differences. Each individual is unique, although there are common problems at school encountered by many adolescents. Second, the teacher should not interpret the adolescent's behavioral pattern in terms of her own cultural and educational background. The diversity of cultures found in our high school presents both a challenge and a difficulty to the classroom teacher.

Adolescent Needs and the Schools

The question may be raised: To what extent are our schools meeting the needs of adolescents? An important need of most adolescents is for a sense of belonging and recognition by his peers; he wants to be accepted and respected for his activities at school and elsewhere. Coleman (1963) found from a study of ten midwestern high schools that about 31 percent of the boys wanted to be remembered as "brilliant students," compared to 45 percent who wished to be remembered as "athletic." In the case of girls, 28 percent preferred to be remembered as "brilliant students," with about 72 percent choosing to be remembered as a "leader in athletics," or the "most popular."

The needs of adolescents are clearly related to their achievements at school. Many educational programs fail to meet the needs of the pupils. This is important in student motivation as set forth in the Coleman Report (1966). Too much attention has been given to the manipulation of the external forms of motivation, with too little attention given to the internal. Frequently, among disadvantaged adolescents as well as those at variance with the goals of the schools, teachers are perceived as negative reference figures with attitudes, ideals, and values alien to theirs. In any situation where there are widely different cultural norms and values, the low-status person in particular is likely to feel threatened by the higher-status person.

NEEDS RELATED TO POPULARITY. The problem of the academic-athletic-popularity syndrome in late adolescence was studied by Friesen (1968–69) with 10,019 high school students in grades ten to twelve as subjects in one large Western Canadian city. The results were compared with those of previous research of a similar nature by the investigator involving 2,425 high school students from an Eastern Canadian city and 1,600 rural and urban high school students from eight schools of Central Canada. The results presented in Table 10-2 show that most of the subjects preferred to be remembered as outstanding students, the strongest desire being expressed by mid-western students and the weakest by the western urban students. To be rememberd as an athletic star ranked second by the total group, with popularity running third—15.1 percent of the total.

TABLE 10-2 Percent of Students Choosing To Be Remembered by Three Characteristics

	OUTSTANDING STAR	ATHLETIC STAR	MOST POPULAR	NO RESPONSE	N
Western urban	43.5	26.0	30.5	0.0	10,019
Eastern urban	54.0	25.4	17.3	3.3	2,425
Midwestern urban and rural	60.8	22.6	15.1	1.5	1,600

Source: Frieson (1968–69).

Many high school students find satisfaction in a successful academic role; others find satisfaction through athletics or some other nonacademic role. Concerning this problem Friesen states:

1. The academic area does not receive full support from the adolescent subculture. High marks do not substantially contribute to popularity, or to leading crowd membership. The school's visible honors are awarded mostly to top athletes. Academic honors are reserved only for narrowly defined matriculation students.

2. The athletic area is reserved only for a small group, especially in the large urban school. Half the students have no involvement in any extracurricular activities; they receive no satisfactions from this vital, adolescent "need" zone.

3. Popularity, which occupies a high place in the eyes of the adolescent, is desired by the majority of adolescents. Yet only 25.7 percent claimed to be in the leading crowd. Only 22.6 percent had been elected to any kind of position during their last two years of school. About 28 percent worried most about being accepted and liked by friends. Against this, about 28 percent never went out with friends (49).

NEEDS RELATED TO GROWTH TOWARD MATURITY. The adolescents of today are better informed, better educated, healthier, and more firmly committed to social justice, equality of opportunities, and the improvement of man's physical and social environment than were their predecessors. Many of their needs relate to growth toward maturity, which is dealt with in subsequent chapters on marriage and family living, occupational choice and work, and preparation for citizenship.

The needs of contemporary adolescents are far more complex than those of their forefathers. Rapidly changing conditions have created uncertainties, not only about the future, but even the present. It is most important that the schools and other educational agencies furnish counseling services in almost every area of life- services, most of which were considered unessential a few decades ago. In many cases teachers and counselors will need to refer the adolescent to different sources of help and information. The present generation of adolescents faces problems for which there are no ready-made answers. Teachers and counselors must recognize that they are not infallible, nor do they have all the answers.

RELEVANCY OF SUBJECTS. Many adolescents are disillusioned with their subjects in school. They fail to see how certain subjects are going to help them better understand and participate in solving present-day problems. We have heard many students complain about *relevance* or the lack of it. Just what do they mean by this? Bruner (1970: 68) seems to know what the students have in mind. "The word has two senses. The first is that what is taught should have some bearing on the grievous problems facing the world, the solution of which may affect our survival as a species. This is social relevance. Then there is personal relevance. What is taught should be self-rewarding, or 'real,' or 'exciting,' or 'meaningful.'" The two kinds of relevance are not the same. One may be present without the other. It seems, however, that both should be present in an effective school program.

The primary purpose of subjects is to help students meet more successfully the problems they will encounter as adults. These problems cover all areas of life—vocational, recreational, social, family relations, health, and citizenship. Adolescents who participate in activities at school derive principles of conduct based on their experiences in dealing with the tasks, constraints involved in social activities, and opportunities made available by the nature of the school program. To the question of what is learned at school in addition to academic growth, we can present a hypothetical answer: one of the most important lessons is to accept certain principles of conduct and to act according to them.

INTEREST IN SCHOOL SUBJECTS

Certainly lack of motivation is a prime factor responsible for poor school attendance, achievement, and dropping out of school. Sometimes adolescents are accused of being lazy because they fail to study and prepare assignments given to them by their teachers; actually the real culprit is usually lack of interest.

One of the most complete studies of academic interests is the one completed by Educational Testing Services in 1970. The study was begun in 1966 and involved 15,450 juniors in a nationally representative sample of 187 high schools. Data were gathered by administering the Academic Interest Measures test (AIM). It consists of a list of 192 activities (sixteen in each of twelve academic fields) such as talking about books, collecting and classifying plants, or typing business letters. The directions for marking and scoring the test are to mark each activity 2 to indicate interest, 1 for indifference, and 0 for disinterest. The score for each field is the sum of these numbers; the highest possible score is thirty-two, the lowest is sixteen.

Table 10-3 shows the interest of eleventh-grade students in the twelve academic areas. Boys and girls differed widely in their interests: industrial arts was highest for boys but lowest for girls. The rank-

TABLE 10-3 Rank Order Interests of Eleventh-Grade Pupils in School Subjects Revealed by AIM, 1970

	BOYS' INTERESTS			GIRLS' INTERESTS	
Rank	Field	Mean	Rank	Field	Mean
1	Industrial arts	22.55	1	Home economics	25.35
2	Physical sciences	20.01	2	Secretarial	22.39
3	Business	18.22	3	Foreign languages	20.79
4	Biology	17.39	4	Art	19.76
5	Social studies	17.34	5	English	18.75
6	Mathematics	17.09	6	Business	18.71
7	Secretarial	16.02	7	Social studies	17.03
8	Foreign languages	14.99	8	Music	16.57
9	Art	14.83	9	Biology	15.68
10	English	13.51	10	Mathematics	12.86
11	Music	13.45	11	Physical sciences	11.70
12	Home economics	12.61	12	Industrial arts	10.96

Source: Educational Testing Service (1970).

difference correlations between the interests of boys and girls was —.70. "Boys placed physical sciences, biology, and mathematics near the top, girls near the bottom. Girls like foreign languages to English by two ranks and art to music by two and four ranks respectively. Both gave high rank to subjects with vocational possibilities—industrial arts and business for boys; home economics and secretarial for girls" (ETS, 1970: 2).

Attitudes Toward School

Data from a number of studies indicate that students frequently lose their positive attitude toward their teachers and schoolwork during the elementary-school years. In a study by Flanders, Morrison, and Brode (1968) the Michigan Student Questionnaire (MSQ) was administered to 101 sixth-grade classes in fifteen school districts. Thirty of the 101 classes were selected for additional study. These included the top ten, the bottom ten, and the ten near the average of the 101 classes. The questionnaire was readministered in January and again in May to the thirty classes. Each administration involved more than 800 students.

A test of internality-externality was also administered to the thirty classes. These terms are described by Flanders and others as follows: "by externality is meant the tendency to believe that successes and failures are self-determined and products of one's own behavior. External children . . . would be more likely to associate the good and bad outcomes of classroom learning activities with the teacher, who is a powerful source of influence. Internal children, on the other hand, would see themselves as more closely associated with the good and bad characteristics of learning outcomes" (1968: 336).

The results revealed that the external students had at the time of the initial testing less positive attitudes toward their teachers and schoolwork than did the internal students; there was a greater decline in their positive attitudes. There was no evidence that the attitudes of external sixth-graders were more affected by praise or lack of praise on the part of the teacher than were the attitudes of the internal pupils. However, in classrooms of teachers who gave less praise and encouragement, there was a greater loss of positive attitudes than in classrooms of teachers who made use of more praise and encouragement. Thus, student attitudes toward the teacher and the learning activities at school appear to be related to teacher behavior.

SCHOLASTIC SUCCESS AND ATTITUDE TOWARD SCHOOL. Success and satisfaction in the performance of a task are bound together by logic, if not by fact. Since success would seem to act as a reinforcement to further effort, we would expect it to bring forth satisfaction. However, investigations do not show a close relationship between scholastic success and a favorable attitude toward school (Diedrich, 1966).

The absence of a strong linkage between success and satisfaction has provoked considerable thought among students of educational psychology. Jackson and Lahaderne (1967) examined the accuracy of teachers' judgments of their students' satisfaction with school, and the relationship between scholastic success and attitude toward school. The students comprised the entire sixth grade of the public schools in a predominantly white working-class suburb—eleven classes with a total of 292 students. The students completed questionnaires that assessed attitudes toward their schools and their teachers. Intelligence and achievement test scores and course grades were obtained. In addition, each teacher estimated each of his students' overall satisfaction with school.

Correlations were obtained between attitudes toward school and measures of scholastic achievement. The following conclusions were drawn from the correlations obtained: (1) All the correlation coefficients were small. (2) The correlations were of the same magnitude with teachers' grades as with achievement test scores. (3) There were no significant sex differences in the relationships. The investigators gave several conditions that might have accounted for the lack of relationship and satisfaction. The most important of these is the motivation of the student. This should be recognized by teachers, parents, and others concerned with the education and guidance of adolescents.

IMPORTANCE OF SUCCESS. A good school program will be built upon a pupil's successes rather than his failures. The value of success as a reinforcer may be observed from the results of a study by Steigman and Stevens (1960). Two groups of eighteen children each were matched for ability and given three pretraining problems in discrimination learning. The group for whom successes were contrived made thirty correct choices from thirty-six trials; the failure group experienced only six correct choices. There were also differences in the attitudes and in the approaches of the two groups of children toward the problem. Conditioned to expect failure, the unsuccessful children made little progress.

It has been said that "nothing succeeds like success." Success breeds confidence and enhances one's self-concept. Continuous failure is demoralizing and frequently leads to complete alienation, as will be pointed out in a later chapter. The teacher's definition of success will have a bearing on this problem. The teacher who regards only good grades as the only form of success does a disservice to the student with average or below average academic ability. The teacher who encourages students to set forth realistic goals and commends the student when he has reached them will have a great reinforcing effect.

Some Problems Confronting the Schools

Increased student unrest in various forms, such as student power, underground newspapers, the use of drugs, vandalism, and racism, has brought forth demands for revised courses as well as a general examination of the school program. Surveys and extensive reports on secondary education have called for extensive curriculum reform. The new physics, the new chemistry, the new mathematics, the new social studies, and revised vocational problems followed. There were also changes in teacher preparation and school personnel. There was a marked increase in the number of guidance personnel and a greater concern for disadvantaged students and students with learning difficulties. Concerning the role of the school, Mosher and Sprinthall state:

> In general, then, schools, either city, suburban, or rural, have tended to define their role as the transmitters of academic ideas and skills. Recent efforts at reform have been directed at revitalizing the existing academic curriculum and its teaching. Very little intellectual energy or funding has been directed toward reformulating education—that is, the development of essentially new curricula and new forms of educating adolescents. In most schools and in most eras, the personal side of education has had a lower priority than the academic. The school has always had extensive *rhetoric* about individual growth, but de facto personal or psychological development was largely the result of random (and often inimical) forces in the school (1970: 913–14).

Many students of education have questioned the objectives of education in the post-industrial age and have blamed the multiple problems and failures on educational institutions. The so-called "common school" goal of public education is, as Peter Schrag (1965) and others have pointed out, a convenient myth: equality of educational opportunity, a dream of many idealists, has not yet been achieved. Yet progress is being made despite forces and conditions that would block such opportunities.

Maladjustment at School

Educational problems loom large in the lives of adolescents. Problems relating to failure in school, how to study, pupil-teacher relationships, and the like apparently appear in the lives of many high school boys and girls. A large percentage of preadolescents, adolescents, and post-adolescents disliked elements in the school situation that indicated unfair practices on the part of teachers and snobbish as well as overly aggressive and dominating attitudes and practices on the part of their classmates. *Scholastic Magazine*'s poll of student opinions, taken during the 1971–72 school year, reveals some interesting and startling information of the ways young people see themselves, the schools, and social conditions (*Children Today*, 1973). The polls covered a cross-section of students numbering from 65,000 to 100,000 on each poll, and representing all states, economic levels, and ranges of academic achievement. Some 86 percent felt that very little if any of the course work was up-to-date.

A study reported by Jackson and Getzels (1963) dealt with the differences in psychological functioning and classroom effectiveness of two groups of adolescents—those who are satisfied with their recent school experiences and those who are dissatisfied. Two groups of students enrolled in a midwestern private school identified by means of a student opinion poll instrument as satisfied and dissatisfied were used as subjects in this study.

The results indicated first the dissatisfaction with school appears to be part of a larger picture of psychological discontent rather than a direct reflection of inefficient functioning in the classroom. Each of the test instruments designed to measure psychological health or adjustment was effective in distinguishing satisfied from dissatisfied students. Results on the negative adjective check list presented in Table 10-4 show that although both groups checked negative adjectives when asked to describe their feelings, the dissatisfied students checked negative adjectives more frequently than the satisfied students. Furthermore, interesting sex differences may be noted. It appears that "dissatisfied girls are somewhat less likely than dissatisfied boys to use negative adjectives involving implicit criticism of others. Dissatisfied boys, on the other hand, are less likely than dissatisfied girls to be distinguished from their satisfied counterparts by the use of adjectives *not* involving implicit criticism of others." Boys more often than girls project the cause of their discontent upon the world around them so that teachers and other adults are seen as rejecting and lacking in understanding.

TABLE 10-4 Number of Subjects Choosing Negative Adjectives When Asked To Describe Typical Classroom Feelings

	BOYS		GIRLS	
ADJECTIVES	Dissatisfied (N 27)	Satisfied (N 25)	Dissatisfied (N 20)	Satisfied (N 20)
Inadequate	19	16	17	7**
Ignorant	19	13	15	2**
Dull	25	16*	16	9*
Bored	24	13**	20	13**
Restless	20	15	19	9**
Uncertain	20	21	17	13
Angry	15	4**	13	4**
Unnoticed	19	5**	7	4
Unhelped	18	8*	9	6
Misunderstood	16	5**	5	2
Rejected	12	3**	4	0
Restrained	17	2**	9	3*

* Statistically (Chi Square) significant at the .05 level.
** Statistically (Chi Square) significant at the .01 level.
Source: Jackson and Getzels (1913).

Some of the major sources of maladjustment in school are: (1) lack of intellectual ability to do the work required, (2) failure in socialization, (3) personal maladjustment, (4) lack of parental or adult identification, (5) economic and cultural deprivation, (6) being a member of certain minority group, and (7) unfavorable school conditions.

Correlates of School Attendance

Compulsory education or school attendance is based upon the assumption that school attendance is important. This has been observed especially in connection with vocational preparation and going on to college (see Chapter 11). The influence of school attendance, as a global variable, was studied by Photiadis and Biggar (1962) with a sample of 300 South Dakota men and women as subjects. The amount of formal education was found to be significantly negatively related to church attendance and participation, religious orthodoxy, extrinsic religious belief, concern with status, conservatism, anomia, authoritarianism, withdrawal tendencies, and antisocial tendencies. Other students of adolescent psychology have furnished data supporting these findings. Empirical evidence supports the hypothesis that formal schooling contributes to the development of less orthodox beliefs and a less dogmatic and authoritarian attitude toward religious and social problems.

Attendance in secondary school was observed by Webb (1963) to be related to masculinity-femininity. Boys and girls with good records of school attendance were found to have higher femininity scores than those with poor attendance records. This finding is in general agreement with an earlier study by Cattell and others (1962) in which submissiveness and docility were the personality traits most highly related to school success. These are traits usually regarded as feminine. Since classrooms are to a marked degree dominated by females and encourage or reinforce behavior characterized as feminine, one can readily see why many outgoing boys brought up to play a role different from that encouraged at school are likely to find themselves in trouble with their teachers and other authority figures.

If the school is to help the child in self-actualization, self-acceptance, and realistic self-esteem, those in authority must provide adequate reinforcements rather than the frustrations that frequently accompany the teaching and grading systems. This means that each student is accepted for what he is and does rather than his color, class status, religion, or language. While the writers know many teachers that accept each child for his own personal worth as a human being, we also know personally teachers who speak derogatorily of pupils who fail to fit into their white middle-class cultural prejudices and values.

Coopersmith (1959) noted that parents who use positive noncontingent reinforcement produce children and adolescents with favorable self-concepts or high self-esteem; children and adolescents with high self-esteem are more successful at school and on the playground than those with low self-esteem. While there is little the school can do to damage the self-concept of children who come from homes that furnish them with good models and give them high self-esteem, there is much the school can do to damage or to help children who come from homes less fortunate, homes lacking in good models and in positive noncontingent reinforcement.

PRESSURES AT HOME AND SCHOOL. While pressures at home and school may operate to bring forth increased effort and better grades, it is frequently disastrous to others. One of the outcomes of this growing pressure is the increase of cheating over the past several decades. A general hypothesis in a study by Shelton and Hill (1969) of cheating by high school students is that cheating is done to aversive social consequences. Cheating was operationally defined as the falsification of scores on a word-construction task. The subjects of the study were 111 high school students. The investigators found that achievement anxiety was positively correlated with cheating only when knowledge of reference-group performance was provided. When the students were told of the reference group's superior or inferior performance, cheating was elicited at the high school level. The implications of this for grades and grading are clear; emphasis on grades furnishes students with a strong incentive for cheating.

Although cheating seems to begin at home with parental pressure, it continues with little or no disapproval from peers at school. It is reinforced by the need to be socially accepted, to participate in school activities, and to be popular with classmates. The results of the study by Shelton and Hill would indicate that students who are academically oriented are more likely to cheat to get good grades. Pressure frequently comes from the home, especially middle-class homes where a high premium is placed upon academic learning and going to college. A student who is not academically oriented but needs a passing grade in order to participate in athletics or some other school program may resort to cheating.

The increase in suicides among high school and college students, according to school psychologists, is a result of the difficulties encountered in coping with the twin pressures of their own and social problems (*Charlotte Observer*, 1971: 21A). Suicide is the third most frequent cause of death among adolescents fifteen to nineteen years of age and is outranked only by automobile accidents and cancer. The senior year at high school is frequently the critical period, although suicides among high school and college students appear at all levels. Behavioral scientists recognize the influences of emotional characteristics of the adolescent, frequently accentuated by societal pressures.

COMPULSORY SCHOOL ATTENDANCE. Compulsory school attendance was at one time hailed as a means that would democratize educational opportunities and thus provide equal educational opportunity to all. The Coleman Report (1966) on the equality of educational opportunity brought together a mass of factual data to show that equal educational opportunity in America is more myth than fact. One has only to observe schools in the same general area of a particular state to note wide community differences. Many of these differences result from methods of financing local schools through property taxes, and property evaluations vary widely for different localities.[1] Coleman's studies also showed great racial disparities in opportunities with the blacks at one extreme and the majority whites at the other. He notes: "The average Negro has fewer classmates whose mothers graduated from high school; his classmates more frequently are members of large rather than small families; they are less often enrolled in a college preparatory curriculum; they have taken a smaller number of courses in English, mathematics, foreign language, and science" (1966: 21).

Achievement in school is conditioned by a multiplicity of factors. Compulsory education does not and cannot overcome these differences in opportunity. It sometimes aggravates conditions and presents difficult adjustment problems for many adolescents. This is reflected not only in the increased suicide rate, but also in the increased use of drugs. Clinical psychologists have established a connection between drug usage and compulsory education. Herter Berger, associate professor of clinical medicine at New York Medical College, concluded from a study of 343 addicted adolescents:

> . . . Compulsory education engenders in the individual [drug user] a hatred of society. . . . He attempts to destroy his jail [school]. . . . Finally, he attempts a chemical escape [drugs] from his environment (cited in Mosher and Sprinthall, 1970: 911).

SPECIAL PROBLEMS OF BOYS. While the evidence may be largely empirical, the typical United States school is quite authoritarian and feminine in its orientation. This would seem to account for girls faring better in school than boys as evidenced by grades, dropout rate, and punitive measures used in classrooms (see Chapter 11).

Many of the goals set forth by the schools for adolescents do not seem relevant to the needs of lower-class boys and boys from certain minority groups. Neither do these apply to the high school girl who becomes pregnant. However, some of our city school systems have set up special programs or classes for unwed teen-age mothers. It seems quite likely that the disadvantaged male is in general cheated by most school programs. Datta, Schaefer and Davis's study of the effects of sex and scholastic aptitude show that teachers' ratings operate to the disadvantage of boys. Boys are more frequently scolded, reprimanded, commanded, and disciplined in different ways. The investigators conclude:

> Regardless of ethnic group or scholastic aptitude, boys were more likely to be described as hyperactive, asocial, verbally and physically aggressive, and tense and were less likely to be described as friendly, methodical, persevering, task oriented, and well adjusted than were girls. They were not likely, however, to be described as lower in such traits as enthusiasm, inquisitiveness, leadership, verbal expressiveness, academic ability, nor as higher in conformance (1968: 99).

[1] This is a problem confronting almost all of the states in the country and has come to the attention of the Suprem Court.

Younger adolescents, especially those of lower academic achievement, may resort to minor infractions of rules in order to gain the attention of their teachers and to raise their status with their peers by "daring" acts of courage. By the senior level of high school, though, most students have a fairly concrete idea of their own chances of being "winners" or "losers" in the school system. Often these adolescents, by the time they reach senior high, see the school as blocking any chance they might have to be at least minimally successful. They may resort to vandalism or truancy, while those adolescents who internalize their academic failure may drop out of school.

EDUCATIONAL OUTCOMES

By definition school should provide self-fulfillment and training in skills and cultural values. School experiences should lead to better adjusted and happier adolescents and adults. Each individual should be better off from a psychological, social, and emotional viewpoint as a result of attending school.

Skills training and cultural transmission include the conventional functions of the school. These provide the child with skill in and knowledge of reading, arithmetic, writing, spelling, science, social studies, art, music, literature, health, physical activities, and so on. The teacher has the problem of integrating these functions. All too often the first function is omitted. In fact, our discussion here centers on the latter function, although we are well aware of the importance of the first and have emphasized it throughout our discussions of problems of adolescents.

A democratic society cannot expect the outcome of schooling to be the same for all students; it can have as its goal the provision of equal educational opportunities for all pupils—the typical, the advantaged, the disadvantaged, and the exceptional.

It is well known that intelligence is related to learning ability. This is implied in definitions and descriptions of intelligence presented in Chapter 5. Generally the correlation between intelligence and academic achievement ranges from .40 to .70 or .75. There is little difference between the correlations for boys and those for girls; however, the achievement of disadvantaged adolescents is less well predicted from intelligence test scores than that of average or typical adolescents. The results of a study by Davis (1968) are typical of what is usually found. He studied the role of curiosity in achievement and obtained correlations between scores of eighth-grade Canadian students on the Dominion Group Test of Learning Capacity and their marks on end-of-term examinations. For academic subjects the following correlations from high to low were found: Intelligence with English literature, .67; with English language, .64; with history, .61; with mathematics, .53; with science, .53; and with geography, .41.

Correlates of Academic Achievement

The Coleman Report suggests that home background is by far the most important predictor of academic success in school. Several decades ago *intelligence* was held up as the best basis for predicting academic success, the general viewpoint being that intelligence is inherited and relatively stable from early childhood throughout life. The past couple of decades has brought forth much research on mental and cognitive structures, and the results of this research have changed our notions about cognitive development and factors related to academic success.

SELF-CONCEPT AND ACADEMIC ACHIEVEMENT. The importance of a favorable and realistic self-concept has been emphasized in previous chapters. There is some indication that there is a positive relationship between the adolescent's self-concept and academic achievement. However, Butcher (1968) noted that "There is a pattern of the child's self-concept taking on an increasing negative quality as he progresses through the elementary and secondary schools" (4844–55). This may result from the school's all too frequent emphasis upon failure rather than success. Butcher found further that there is a closer relationship between the measures of self-concept and intelligence test results than with standardized achievement test results.

The purpose of a study by Joyce (1970) was to gain information on personality characteristics which differentiate achieving and underachieving high school students from lower socioeconomic environments. Academic achievement was indicated by discrepancy scores between a student's composite score on an academic progress test and that predicted from his performance on the verbal battery of an intelligence test. Joyce concludes from his comparison that "High achievers were characterized by high concepts of ability, lack of a need for aggression, positive self-concepts, and a tendency to perceive a high press for achievement in their particular school."

SCHOOL ACHIEVEMENT AND HOME LIFE. The few studies of the relation between family life and achievement in high school have indicated a positive relationship between student achievement and happy home life. A study reported by Morrow and Wilson (1961) compared the family relations of bright high-achieving and underachieving high school boys. Several types of information about family relations were obtained from the students through questionnaires. The students' family relations were also evaluated by sixteen self-report Family Relations Scales. High achievers more often than underachievers described their families as sharing recreation, ideas, confidence, and making decisions. They also described their families as approving, trusting, affectionate, encouraging, but not pressuring in achievement and not overly severe in discipline. The overall family morale was considerably higher for the high achievers. The results supported the hypothesis that good family morale fosters academic achievement among bright high school boys by fostering positive attitudes toward teachers and toward school and interest in intellectual activities.

The extent to which the values of secondary-school pupils are a reflection of their social-cultural background was cross-validated through a massive study by Coleman and others (1966). Teachers have been aware of this throughout the years, and it may be observed in their reactions to the behavior of adolescents from different backgrounds. It has also been observed in their educational expectations of adolescents. The study by Coleman and others showed that clear differences existed between children from different backgrounds on such items as: encyclopedia in the home, education of parents, books in the home, interactions of adolescent with parents, and neighborhood.

THE ROLE OF PEERS IN EDUCATIONAL ACHIEVEMENT. There is evidence from many studies that peers have a strong influence on the individual's aspirations and performances during the adolescent years. Porterfield and Schlichtung (1961) found a significant relationship between peer status and reading achievement at every socioeconomic level of the school community. Hudgins, Smith, and Johnson (1962) found significant correlations between peer acceptance and arithmetic ability, while Sears (1963) found a significant correlation between general academic achievement and popularity.

Just as peers are important in connection with delinquent behavior, we find that they are also important in all aspects of behavior at school. Lahov and Robins (1969) have pointed out that "the school environment and school values are plainly not influencing the boys firmly grounded in street culture. The group which does show learning contains a large percentage of boys who do not fit with street culture—who reject it or are rejected by it" (402). These findings have a bearing on the fact that reading failure in the urban ghettos is alarming. The full extent of the cultural background, including peers, on school achievement can readily be seen when we note the academic achievement of students from the ghettos or other adverse home and community conditions.

Television, Radio, and Adolescents

It has been said that children spend more time learning from television than from church and school combined. Johnson writes:

> By the time they enter first grade they will have received more hours of instruction from television networks than they will later receive from college professors while earning a bachelor's degree. Whether they like it or not, the television networks are playing the roles of teacher, preacher, parent, public official, doctor, psychiatrist, family counselor, and friend for tens of millions of Americans each day of their lives" (1970: 14).

Television plays a most important role in the lives of adolescents not only as an educational force but also as a social, recreational, and sometimes therapeutic force. The social aspect may be observed when adolescents get together to listen to specal musical programs; it also provides the music for dancing. There are many lonely adolescents who find comfort and solace in watching television. Some adolescents make the claim that they study best when the radio or television is going.

One of the reason many adolescents are so well informed on national and international problems is that they spend a great deal of time listening to news broadcasts. While many blue-collar adolescents are only interested in the sports section of the daily newspaper, many of them will listen when their favorite politician is about to speak, or when the president is scheduled to make an address. The proverb, "One picture is worth a thousand words," is particularly true when it is accompanied by words and music and is not forced upon the adolescent or tied to a particular and orderly time sequence.

After suffering a decline some years ago following the widespread appeal of television, radio is now occupying a firm place in the lives of adolescents. It has within the past several years devoted itself increasingly to playing the type of music that has an almost universal appeal to adolescents. Several thousand disk jockeys play records over the radio. These are accompanied by running comments. If we add to this the tremendous popularity and adulation displayed by adolescents toward popular music singers, we can readily see why radio is so popular with adolescents.

THE INFORMATION REVOLUTION. Due to the mass media, especially television, and universal education, we have witnessed an information revolution so extensive that some students of adolescent psychology believe it to be the basis for the generation gap. Many high school students are in general much better informed on current happenings and problems than their parents.

Education in the past has often been a form of indoctrination to justify the high crime rate, infant mortality, and social injustice as a way of life in a democratic society. Newsmen were quick to bring to our attention atrocities by American soldiers in the Vietnam War as well as those of the enemy; they enlightened the public concerning the deceit of men in responsible positions. The mass media have struck fear into the hearts of some leaders, and led them to criticize the free press. The intellectual insights of our adolescents should be challenged and encouraged. This will be our one guarantee of a free society (Revel, 1970).

OUR SCHOOLS:
AN ANALYSIS OF THEIR FUNCTIONING

Some of the major criticisms that can be leveled at our schools in their handling of adolescents may be summarized as follows:

1. Most of the school personnel fail to understand the problems and needs of many adolescents largely because their experiences have been so different from those of present-day adolescents.
2. Teachers are not warm and friendly to many adolescents at school, with whom they have little or no empathy.
3. The school curriculum and program are adult-selected and fail to take into account the characteristics, problems, and immediate needs of adolescents.
4. The evaluation program is usually controlled by adults with no student involvement. This tends to put the student against the teacher.
5. Schools try to teach only what is safe and uncontroversial. If it is controversial, care is taken to give the materials a slant in harmony with the attitudes and prejudices of the power structure in the community.
6. The schools are to a marked degree in the "dead hand" of the past, while adolescents are looking ahead to a period their elders scarcely think about.
7. Emphasis is put on the learning of meanings and concepts to be regurgitated; little consideration is given to the acquisition of thinking abilities.

Some Student Reactions

Many attempts by different groups have been made to secure reactions of high school students to the educational program. One of the most representative of these is one that was moderated by David Brinkley (1971). Editors of high school newspapers from eight broad areas of the United States were chosen to appear on a television panel. Some of the major proposals, criticisms, and ideas are presented here:

1. Among the priorities suggested was the need to stress the worth of the individual.
2. Several students pointed out that the schools had been very effective in turning out people to fit into the establishment but had turned off many students.
3. The panel felt that the schools are packaged and channeled toward middle- and upper-class students, occupations, and goals.
4. The schools should face the drug problem and should recognize that it is a symptom of something far more serious in society.
5. There was a feeling that the government has entered into the lives of young people too much.
6. Every time society is faced with a problem, it tries to solve it through legislation. Why not use education?
7. Strong opposition was expressed to wars in general and the Vietnam War in particular. The government should take money out of the defense budget and spend it on education.
8. The problem of when the government should intrude was discussed. A conclusion reached by most of the members of the panel was that when the individual becomes a danger to society the government should intrude.
9. Pollution, urbanization, and overpopulation should be a concern of the schools as well as society at large.

Noncollege Youths

The majority of youth do not go to college, yet little is heard or written about them. Most studies have focused on the segment that go on to college with a number of studies dealing with dropouts and delinquents. There is a large group, perhaps the majority of adolescents today, that finishes high school or a technical school and find employment in their community or city. They marry at a relatively early age, become worthy citizens, and rear a family.

Noncollege youth, compared with college students, have a narrower range of knowledge, understanding, and interests in national and world problems and a stronger work orientation. They tend to hold middle-class values mixed with certain upper lower-class values, to be politically conservative, to be religiously oriented toward rather orthodox beliefs, and to be blue-collar workers (CBS, 1969). Since their attitudes and life style are so much like that of their parents, the generation gap appears to be a myth; therefore much that we have written about the generation gap relates to adolescents from upper middle-class homes and to many students in college.

In April 1969, CBS news and the Daniel Yankelovich research firm undertook a study of the generation gap (Thornburg, 1971: 183). In this study the views of 2,881 noncollege youths, 723 college youths (17 to 23

TABLE 10-5 The Views of College Youth, Noncollege Youth, and Their Parents

QUESTION*	NONCOLLEGE		COLLEGE	
	Youth	Parents	Youth	Parents
Will hard work always pay off?	79	85	56	76
Is belonging to some organized religion important in a person's life?	82	91	42	81
Does competition encourage excellence?	82	91	72	84
Is having an abortion morally wrong?	64	66	36	50
Are premarital sexual relations morally wrong?	57	88	34	74
Should there be less emphasis on money?	54		72	
Should there be more emphasis on law and order?	81		57	
More emphasis on self-expression?	70		84	
More sexual freedom?	22		43	

* Unless otherwise stated answers refer to *yes* or agreement with the statement.

. . . Other results of the survey showed that noncollege adolescents, as compared to college students, are (1) more conservative, (2) more prone to traditional values, (3) more religious, (4) more respectful, (5) more work oriented, (6) more money oriented, (7) more patriotic, (8) more concerned about moral living, (9) more conforming, (10) more accepting of the draft and (Vietnam) war, (11) less activism oriented, (12) less sympathetic with activists, (13) less drug-prone, and (14) less sexually oriented (Thornburg, p. 184).

Source: Thornburg, 1971: 184.

years old), 310 noncollege youths' parents and college youths' parents were sampled. The answers to certain questions used in the survey, presented in Table 10-5, show something of the difference between noncollege adolescents and their parents.

YOUTH IN COLLEGE

Each time a new census compilation is made, we have many surprises. The most revealing clues about what is happening to youth is derived from more specialized census reports. The census report dealing with American youth in 1970 was a surprise to many people, especially that part dealing with their education (*Newsweek*, 1971). From 1940 to 1970 the proportion of all young adults who completed college rose from 6 percent to 16, and the percentage of those who completed high school rose from 38 percent to 75 percent (80). The greatest increase was among black youth, and this promises to show a continued increase. The percentage of blacks who had completed four years of college rose from 1.6 percent in 1940 to 10 percent in 1970.

The College Student Profile

Any attempt to present a portrait of the college student runs into serious difficulty; college students vary considerably, even within a single, small, church-related college. Our portrait of the college student may be colored by the selective concentration of the communication media. The vociferous, atypical, bizarre or unusual members of the college student body are likely to receive the most attention. We have noticed that many lower-class adults unacquainted with the college campus regard them as typical of all college students.

SOME TYPES OF COLLEGE STUDENTS. Although we will not claim to define or describe all college students, we will present several types, insofar as students can be typed. We realize that typing at best is quite inaccurate; however, we believe that some of the following general types will be found on all college campuses.

On most campuses the largest group of students is made up of what Kavanaugh (1970) referred to as the "kept generation." They are closely tied up with the Establishment; they haven't severed the close emotional ties with their families. These students, then, are tied to the status quo because it offers them the security of a future position in life. The hippies make up a second group. They are in many cases alienated from their parents. Their manner of dress and behavioral patterns are ways of telling us that they do not accept many and in some cases most of the ways of the Establishment. Although we do not know the percentage of students who rebel against many of adult ways, the number is likely much larger than what we observe. There are certainly some among the "kept generation" who are alienated from many of the practices of our society, but for various reasons, they conform to the accepted pattern of the community. The campus hippies are distinct from the "unwashed losers" roaming our streets, gathering at shopping centers, and battling against materialism, although accepting money from their families.

Kavanaugh describes the "graveyard generation" as those being choked into inadequacy by standards and requirements that they don't seem to be able to make. They become the "hangers on" or college dropouts. Frequently without hope and in despair, they resort to crime.

THE PROBLEM OF SOCIAL STRATIFICATION. There are some who look to college for social contacts and social status. Several decades ago the senior author asked a peer of his where his son was going to college and what career did he plan to follow. The father, who had become relatively affluent, replied by pointing out the college his son would attend, since it is a prestige institution. His son didn't have any particular career in mind but was hoping to become a member of one of his favorite fraternities, and he listed three that his son was most eager about. Today's social and economic conditions have changed the values of many people, although there are some who regard success in terms of high position in the social hierarchy.

In general adolescent girls are more class conscious than boys, although it seems that this generation of young people takes a broader and sounder attitude on matters relating to human worth than past generations of young people. There was a time when membership in certain fraternities and sororities held as much prestige as being a student at an Ivy League school. Many girls and some boys actually dropped out of college when they failed to be invited to join a fraternity or sorority of their choice. Such things have changed rapidly during the past decade or more. At Davidson College (N.C.) a very strong academically oriented college for men, every boy has an opportunity to become a member of a fraternity if he so chooses. However, many of the boys do not choose membership. Only 363 girls registered for fall rush at the University of Missouri in 1971, although 680 young women registered five years ago. It is reported that twenty years ago at Northwestern, 80 to 90 percent of the girls who enrolled were sorority girls, but in 1970 sorority members represented only 40 percent (Voights, 1971: 9C).

The Reactions of College Students

Although college students do not make up a homogeneous group, there are certain responses to the college environment characteristic of a large percentage of the students. In a study of undergraduate peer relations in a midwestern university, Bauer (1970) found that two-thirds of the seniors felt that social development had been the most valuable part of their college experience. We note here that despite the general notion that the major goal of a college education is intellectual development, the goal of satisfying social development ranks first in the thinking of most college students.

Despite the relative personal freedom of living away from home or commuting to school, college students have a common complaint. College is too much like high school. In the majority of colleges in this country, curriculum requirements force students to take a relatively determined course of study for their first two years. Little emphasis is placed on relating one class to another or in directing students to relate their educational experience to their own personal needs or goals.

The choice of academic fields of interest is a major one for college students. Unless a student has definitely decided on a profession after college graduation, his choice is apt to be haphazard with little or no guidance. One of the current criticisms of many colleges is that a graduate may have difficulty in obtaining employment because he has not been trained to "do" anything except go to school.

New colleges have been founded and in many older institutions curricula are being modified in an attempt to bring a sense of relevance into the classroom. Many students have questioned and some have revolted against the old concept of an academic ivory tower set apart from the rest of society and the world. Much of the campus unrest of the last half of the 1960s revolved around the question of whether administrative policies and classroom emphases recognized and dealt relatively with the social, political, and ecological questions which confront society and the world.

COLLEGE STUDENT SUBCULTURE. Any attempt to describe the subculture of college students is made difficult because of the diversity of cultures. Gottlieb and Hodgins (1963) defined the college students' subculture by categorizing students into four groups: (1) the academic group, consisting of students who really want an education and are willing to study to obtain it; (2) the vocational subgroup, consisting of those students pursuing primarily the same vocational choice (we view the vocational subgroup as those whose concern for an education is almost solely vocational; they have little interest in the theoretical and aesthetic values of education); (3) the nonconformist subgroup, who concentrate on social issues and use the university setting as an avenue for expression; and (4) the "collegiate" or social subgroup, whose main interests are in social and athletic activities and sorority and fraternity functions.

Gottlieb and Hodgkins suggested that the reason so many studies have failed to show significant changes in values of college students as a result of education is that student bodies are treated as monolithic entities, when, in fact, they are composed of a number of subcultures. It was in connection with this that Lewis (1969) attempted to isolate members of the different subcultures and to ascertain the effects of college on each of them. From a sample of 646 undergraduates, he was able to place 401 in one of the four categories, according to their responses to two questions. First, they were asked how important they believed the stimulation of new ideas was to them; those who replied that new ideas were of the highest importance were considered to be involved with them, while those who ranked them as less than third in importance were considered not to be involved with them. The second question related to identification with school. Those who felt close or fairly close to the school were said to identify with it, while those who felt indifferent about their college were said not to identify with it.

REACTIONS TO CLASSROOM SITUATIONS. For a large percentage of college students the classroom situation is a boring experience; and it is tolerated only in order to receive the needed credit. The typical college instructor has had little or no supervised teaching experience; he tends to follow the procedure of his teachers. Thus, much college teaching follows a lecture procedure. The lectures are about as boring as the typical 11:00 o'clock sermon in an institutional church.

The writers have collected notes from students, notes that were left in books, on the floor, and on desks or tables. These notes present in a picturesque manner how students feel about some of their classes or instructors. One student had scribbled on a worksheet, "Now I can see why students riot!" Another student's notes gave some indication of her thoughts while in a lecture. "Dean _____ was up nearly all night nursing her sick cat. No wonder she was so cross this morning. Did you notice?"

A third reaction concerned the instructor of a class in counseling: "Gee! won't it be exciting to be a full-fledged counselor—just like playing 'God'." In this particular class the instructor, like many college instructors, was more interested in expressing his own ego then in helping students learn.

ATTITUDES TOWARD CHEATING. That cheating is widespread has been shown from surveys of high school and college students. Extensive interviews by the authors of high school teachers verify the results of various surveys. Based on an extensive survey of over 5,000 students at 99 colleges Bowers (1964) found that 50 percent of the sample studied had cheated on an examination or turned in papers done wholly or in part by another student. A third study by Hetherington and Feldman (1964) involved a group of 78 college students. The students were exposed to three different examination situations in which cheating was possible. According to the results, 46, or approximately 59 percent of the students, cheated in at least one of the three possible situations. Approximately 64 percent of those who cheated did so in two situations, while 24 percent cheated in all three situations. It should be noted, however, that all three situations involved academic examinations.

Many studies have identified personal characteristics of cheaters; others have indicated college settings where cheating and other deviant behavior most often occurs (Centra, 1970). Cheaters, in comparison to noncheaters, tend to be more vocationally or socially oriented and to be fraternity or sorority members; they also have lower grades and are more frequently from lower socioeconomic backgrounds. Furthermore, colleges with higher cheating rates tend to be large, coeducational, and not very selective of students (1970: 366-67).

Centra posed two questions: What are the characteristics of students with lenient attitudes toward cheating? Do different types of colleges enroll students who are more likely to cheat? A significant question related to this second one is: Is the cheating incidence at these types of colleges related entirely to the kinds of students who enroll, or are there climates at some that discourage cheating? Two samples of students were used to investigate these questions. The first included 1,500 entering freshmen from 37 institutions. The second sample consisted of institutions: 119 four-year colleges and universities involving nine types.

The entering freshmen from the 37 institutions responded to the College Student Questionnaire (CSQ), Part I (Peterson, 1965). Reactions to cheating by the sampling of students revealed that girls were inclined to be slightly more disturbed than boys. About one-third of the students stated that they were concerned but would do nothing about it. Some major conclusions from this study are the following:

1. Males and commuters were slightly more prevalent among those responding that they were not disturbed and would do nothing about it.
2. Students with less academic motivation and fewer artistic and literary interests tend to be more accepting of cheating.
3. Lower-ability students tend to cheat more often and have more lenient attitudes toward cheating; they also tend to come from lower socioeconomic backgrounds.
4. Males have higher reported rates of cheating and more lenient attitudes toward cheating than females.
5. There is evidence that collective peer attitudes may be more important than known personal characteristics in determining cheating.
6. "In all likelihood, both incoming students' dispositions toward cheating, and the climate for cheating resulting from these collective attitudes, determine the amount of cheating that occurs" (Centra, 1970: 372).

SUMMARY

The American high school was formerly designed primarily for the upper- and middle-class students. There is a diversity of students in our high schools with most of the adolescents between ages twelve and seventeen enrolled. In the present-day high school we find talented students, nonacademic students, hard-to-reach students, and students from different ethnic groups. Many of these students come from culturally deprived homes and are at a great disadvantage in learning to read and write. Instead of catching up with other students, most of them get further behind them in academic achievement as they proceed into junior high school. A large percentage of them drop out of school after they have passed the compulsory school age requirement; others become rebellious as they face continuous failure at school.

The schools have become more than transmitters of knowledge and skills. The problem of relevancy has loomed large in the minds of adolescents. Students are concerned that materials and skills should have some bearing on present-day world problems and upon problems of students. One of the important learnings at school today is to accept certain principles of conduct and act accordingly. This does not mean that the school's task is to indoctrinate. Rather, the school of today strives to teach students to think reflectively and find solutions to problems that they have never faced before.

Evidence is overwhelming that the school best serves middle-class students. It is also a means for social mobility, especially for the students from the lower class who accept middle-class values and goals.

The problem of grading is one of the most complex faced by teachers; it is also a far-reaching problem for many high school students. Many innovations are being used by different schools in an attempt to overcome some of the problems created by grading. Grades are frequently a source of frustration to many students. They also encourage cheating and studying to pass examinations rather than acquiring useful knowledge and skills. They sometimes create a breach between teacher and pupil. The value of success at school as a reinforcer is well recognized. Grades that emphasize failure serve as negative rather than positive reinforcers. If the school is to help the adolescent in self-actualization, self-acceptance, and self-esteem based on personal worth, it must make use of positive reinforcers.

There is evidence from many sources that boys experience more difficulties and problems at school than girls. This stems in part from the effeminate nature of the school programs and personnel. Many of the needs of boys run counter to the school program.

Radio, television, newspapers, libraries, and magazines serve as educational devices. Values are acquired from the total school situation and may run counter to those met at home or even at church.

College has become important in the lives of an increasing number of adolescents. Some of the same problems confronting high school students also confront college students. The college student is more mature and independent in reacting to situations. Thus, he is interested in current domestic and world problems and is willing to go on record for his opinions if necessary.

REFERENCES

BAUER, RUDOLPH H. "An Experimental Approach to the Concept of Ego Identity as Related to the Achievement Motive and Other Variables." *Dissertation Abstracts International* (October 1970), 31 (4):1611–12A.

BERDIE, R. *After High School—What?* Minneapolis: University of Minnesota Press, 1954.

BISH, CHARLES E. "The Academically Talented." *Journal of the National Education Association* (1961), 5:33.

BLAINE, GRAHAM B. *Youth and the Hazards of Affluence.* New York: Harper & Row, Publishers, 1966.

BOWERS, W. J. *Student Dishonesty and Its Control in College.* New York: Bureau of Applied Social Research, Columbia University, 1964.

BRINKLEY, DAVID, moderator. "Some Student Reactions. Eight Editors of High School Newspapers from Different Areas of the United States." NBC television program. January 4, 1971.

BRUNER, JEROME. "The Skill of Relevance or the Relevance of Skills." *Saturday Review* (April 18, 1970), pp. 66–68, 78.

BUTCHER, DONALD G. "A Study of the Relationship of Student Self-concept to Academic Achievement in Six High Achieving Elementary Schools." *Dissertation Abstracts* (1968) 28:4844–45.

CATTELL, R. B. *et al. Prediction and Understanding of the Effect of Children's Interest upon School Performance.* U.S. Department of Health, Education, and Welfare. Office of Education, Cooperative Research Project No. 701 (8383). Urbana: University of Illinois, 1962.

CENTRA, JOHN A. "College Freshmen Attitudes Toward Cheating." *Personnel and Guidance Journal* (1970), 18:366–73.

Charlotte Observer (August 8, 1971), p. 21A. "Young People Resort to Suicide."

Children Today (January–February 1973), p. 35. "Students Voice Opinions."

COLEMAN, JAMES S. *The Adolescent Society.* New York: The Free Press, 1961.

————. "The Adolescent Subcultures and Academic Achievement." In *Readings in the Social Psychology of Education*, W. W. Charters and N. L. Gage, eds. Boston: Allyn and Bacon, 1963.

————, *et al. Equality of Educational Opportunity.* Washington, D.C.: U.S. Department of Health, Education, and Welfare, 1966.

Columbia Broadcasting System (1969). "Generation Apart" (television program).

COOPERSMITH, S. "A Method for Determining Types of Self-esteem." *Journal of Educational Psychology* (1959), 59:87–94.

DATTA, L. E., E. SCHAEFER, and M. DAVIS. "Sex and Scholastic Aptitude as Variables in Teachers' Ratings of the Adjustment and Classroom Behavior of Negro and Other Seventh-grade Students." *Journal of Educational Psychology* (1968), 59:94–104.

DAVIS, H. "Role of Specific Curiosity in School Achievement." *Journal of Educational Psychology* (1968), 59:37–43.

DIEDRICH, R. "Teacher Perceptions as Related to Teacher-Student Similarity and Student Satisfaction with School." Unpublished doctoral dissertation. Chicago: University of Chicago, 1966.

ELKIND, DAVID. "From Ghetto School to College Campus." *Journal of Social Psychology* (1971), 9:241–45.

ETS Developments (1970), 18 (1): 1–2. "News of Research and Testing Programs at Educational Testing Service.

———— (October 1970), 18 (1):1–2. "Study Shows Interests in Twelve School Subjects."

FLANDERS, N. A., B. M. MORRISON, and E. L. BRODE. "Changes in Pupil Attitudes During the School Year." *Journal of Educational Psychology* (1968), 59:334–38.

FRIESEN, DAVID. "Academic-Athletic Popularity Syndrome in the Canadian High School Society." *Adolescence* (1968–69), 3:39–52.

GOTTLIEB, D. and B. HODGKINS. "College Student Subculture: Their Structure and Characteristics in Relation to Student Attitude Change." *School Review* (1963), 71:266–89.

HETHERINGTON, E. M. and SOLOMON E. FELDMAN. "College Cheating as a Function of Subject and Situation Variables." *Journal of Educational Psychology* (1964), 55:212–18.

HUDGINS, B. B., L. M. SMITH, and T. J. JOHNSON. "The Child's Perception of His Classmates." *Journal of Genetic Psychology* (1962), 101:401.

JACKSON, PHILIP W. and JACOB W. GETZELS. "Psychological Health and Classroom Functioning: A Study of Dissatisfaction with School Among Adolescents." In *Studies in Adolescence*, Robert E. Grinder, ed. New York: The Macmillan Company, 1963. Pp. 392–400.

JACKSON, PHILIP W. and HENRIETTE M. LAHADERNE. "Scholastic Success and Attitude Toward School in a Population of Sixth Graders." *Journal of Educational Psychology* (1967), 58:15–18.

JOHNSON, NICHOLAS. "What Do We Do About Television?" *Saturday Review* (July 11, 1970), pp. 14–16, 34.

JOYCE, JOHN F. "An Investigation of Some Personality Characteristics of Achieving High School Students from Lower Socioeconomic Environments." *Dissertation Abstracts International* (1970), 31 (4):1623A.

KAVANAUGH, ROBERT E. *The Grim Generation.* San Diego, Calif.: United States International University, 1970.

LAHOV, WILLIAM and CLARENCE ROBINS. "A Note on the Relation of Reading Failure to Peer-group Status in Urban Ghettos." *Teachers College Record* (1969), 70:395–405.

LEWIS, LIONEL S. "The Value of College to Different Subcultures." *School Review* (1969), 77 (1):32–40.

McDANIEL, E. and MARY S. FORENBACK. *Kentucky's Top 15 Percent: A Case Study of the College Attendance Patterns of Superior High School Students.* Special Report, Kentucky Cooperative Counseling and Testing Service. Lexington: University of Kentucky, 1960.

MIDILL, JOHN A. "An Analysis of the Factors Related to Dropouts of Technology Programs." *Dissertation Abstracts International* (October 1970), 31 (4): 1644–45A.

MORROW, WILLIAM R. and ROBERT C. WILSON. "Family Relations of Bright High-achieving and Underachieving High School Boys." *Child Development* (1961), 32:501–10.

MOSHER, RALPH L. and NORMAN A. SPRINTHALL. "Psychological Education in Secondary Schools: A Program to Promote Individual and Human Development." *American Psychologist* (1970), 25 (10):911–24.

Newsweek (February 15, 1971), pp. 80–81. "Census Surprises."

PETERSON, R. E. *Technical Manual: College Student Questionnaires.* Princeton, N.J.: Educational Testing Service, 1965.

PHOTIADIS, J. D. and J. BIGGAR. "Religiosity, Education and Ethnic Distance." *American Journal of Sociology* (1962), 67:666–72.

PORTERFIELD, O. V. and H. J. SCHLICHTUNG. "Peer Status and Reading Achievement." *Journal of Educational Research* (1961), 54:291–97.

REICE, SYLVIA. "Under 21." *McCall's* (October 1969), pp. 6–44.

REVEL, JEAN-FRANCOIS. *Without Marx or Jesus.* Garden City, N.Y.: Doubleday & Company, 1970. Translated by J. F. Bernard.

ROTHNEY, J. W. M. *The High School Student.* New York: The Dryden Press, 1953. Pp. 103–8.

SANDO, RUDOLPH. "Education of the 'Non-Academic' Pupil in Secondary Schools —This They Believe." *California Journal of Secondary Education* (1956), 31:45–49.

SCHRAG, PETER. *Voices in the Classroom.* Boston: Beacon Press. 1965.

SEARS, P. S. *The Effect of Classroom Conditions on the Strength of Achievement Motive and Work Output on Elementary School Children.* U.S. Department of Health, Education, and Welfare, Office of Education. Cooperative Research Project No. 873. Stanford, Calif.: Stanford University, 1963.

SHELTON, JEV and JOHN P. HILL. "Effects on Cheating of Achievement and Knowledge of Peer Performance." *Developmental Psychology* (1969), 1 (5): 449–55.

SIMMONS, NORVILLE G. *College-Going Plans and Actual College Attendance of Academically Superior High School Seniors in Georgia.* Ed.D. dissertation. Athens: University of Georgia, 1963.

STEIGMAN, M. J. and H. W. STEVENS. "The Effect of Pretraining Reinforcement Schedules on Children's Learning." *Child Development* (1960), 31:53–58.

THORNBURG, HERSHEL D. *Contemporary Adolescence: Readings.* Belmont, Calif.: Brooks/Cole Publishing Company, 1971. Pp. 181–85.

Time magazine (January 29, 1965), pp. 56–59. "Education."

U.S. News and World Report (1967), 63 (26):44–45. "Controversial Report on Education."

VOIGHTS, MADELYN. "There May Be More Sororities, but Girls Don't Seem Interested." *Asheville Citizen-Times* (October 24, 1971), p. 9C.

WEBB, A. P. "Sex-Role Preferences and Adjustment in Early Adolescence." *Child Development* (1963), 34:609–18.

RECOMMENDED READINGS

GOODLAD, J. I. ed. *The Changing American School: Sixty-fifth Yearbook of the National Society for the Study of Education.* Chicago: University of Chicago Press, 1966.
Thoughtful surveys and discerning projections of innovations in our schools. Special consideration is given to the changing role of the teacher, curricula changes, expanding instructional resources, grouping pupils for instruction, and philosophical, psychological, and sociological factors underlying the changes.

KING, EDMUND J. *Education and Social Change.* New York: Pergamon Press, 1966.
A comprehensive study which shows how the teaching and learning roles have changed through the years. The author points out the ways in which the population, aims, and general structure are evolving.

McCandless, Boyd R. *Adolescent Behavior and Development.* Hinesdale, Ill.: The Dryden Press Inc., 1970. Chapters 9 and 10.

Chapters 9 and 10 deal with two major institutions designed to provide opportunities for young people: the school and the church. Major emphasis, however, is given to problems at school faced by adolescents with diverse home backgrounds. The importance of relevancy in the motivation of youth is discussed.

Purnell, Richard. *Adolescents and the American High School.* New York: Holt, Rinehart and Winston, Inc., 1970.

Designed for secondary school teachers, guidance counselors, parents, and youth workers. It provides useful, practical behavioral information about adolescents in school.

Silberman, Charles E. *Crisis in the Classroom.* New York: Random House, Inc., 1970.

A report on American public education commissioned by the Carnegie Foundation. A strong indictment against the traditional American school.

Spaulding, Robert I. "Personality and Social Development: Peer and School Influences." *Review of Educational Research* (1964), 34:588–98.

The author reviews the results of research on the influence of peers and the school on personality and social development from 1960 to 1964.

Webster, Statem W. *Discipline in the Classroom: Basic Principles and Problems.* San Francisco: Chandler Publications, Science Research Associates, 1968.

The author emphasizes that persistent acts of pupil misbehavior should not be viewed as isolated incidents. In Part Two cases are presented and analyzed. Suggestions for improving behavior are offered by trained and experienced teachers.

11

the school dropouts

It was pointed out in Chapter 10 that there has been an enormous increase since 1940 in the number of students who remain in high school until graduation and also in the number who go on to college. Among the nation's fourteen- to seventeen-year-olds, 94 percent were enrolled in school in 1969 compared with 90 percent a decade earlier; half of the eighteen- to nineteen-year-olds were in school in 1969 compared to 38 percent in 1960 (*Newsweek,* 1971). However, within the decade of the 60s seven and one-half million adolescents left school before graduation. Unless continued efforts and changes are made in our school programs, the number will increase during the decade of the 70s.

Many of these youngsters, unable to find full-time employment, get into trouble with the law; they have become one of the major problems of this generation. Many dropouts end up terrorizing the nation's cities in roving street gangs looking for excitement because they have nothing else to do. Many agencies have shown concern for this problem. The federal government has proposed different programs for these teen-agers. To many people the job seems simple, "Get tough with them." Slogans are brought forth such as "Uphold Law and Order." Unless jobs are found for these teen-agers, we expect a wave of juvenile crime, according to president of the National Council of Juvenile Court Judge in 1971 (Dygert, 1971).

In this chapter we will deal with the profile of the school dropout, factors associated with dropping out of school, runaways, married and unmarried teen-age girls, problems encountered by dropouts, and stop-outs.

THE POTENTIAL DROPOUT

Although all adolescents are potential dropouts, there are some with certain characteristics or who face particular problems that make them more likely to drop out than others. To the behavioral scientist, the deviant who fails to measure up to expected normal standards is a potential dropout. If he lacks intellectual capacity to do satisfactory work at school, his chances of graduation are very slim and his chances of dropping out of school are great. The lower-class child who deviates widely from the interests and values of most of his classmates at school and the teachers he encounters is certainly a potential dropout.

The Misfit as a Potential Dropout

The beginning stage of many dropouts may be observed in the failure of a boy or girl to have friends at school. In school the future dropout is outside the in-groups, especially those in-groups involved in school activities. He may belong to a group that engages in acts of mischief or illegal activities outside of school. For example Erik Adams, a nineteen-year-old who has twice dropped out of school, gives us some good insight into the potential dropout as one who finds friends only among other misfits. He is a truant both at school and in the neighborhood. He spends much of his time with other school misfits on the streets or in juvenile delinquency.

The potential dropout finds that his friends at school are gradually dropping out and he becomes more lonely at school. If, after dropping out of school, he returns, he is faced with even more problems than he had prior to dropping out. Most teachers will be kind at first, but the returned dropout soon feels that they have not forgotten. He will not find most students particularly friendly to him and may experience antagonism and embarrassment from fellow students. With no one to turn to, he usually leaves school a second time, perhaps for good.

Academic Failure and the Potential Dropout

Clinical psychologists frequently turn to the IQ test as a logical clue to the potential dropout and are sometimes surprised by what they observe. Although many dropouts rank below their graduating peers in IQ, there is a great deal of overlapping in intelligence test scores. Lack of intellectual ability alone may explain some early withdrawals; most cases of dropping out of school result from a combination of factors or conditions.

A more telling factor than IQ is school achievement. Nationwide surveys of school dropouts show that the great majority were in classes one or more years below the grade level they should have reached at the time of their withdrawal. Most of the girls who were served in the Community Services Project of the Chicago Board of Health in 1963 had already repeated one or more grades, and were academically on a level two to four years below normal expectations (Wright, 1966). They were true potential dropouts, and were what might be termed covert dropouts for some time before leaving school.

Fitzsimmons and others (1969) presented a report on the scholastic characteristics associated with both high school dropouts and poorly performing graduates. They conducted an extensive analysis of the academic records of 270 students from elementary school to high school. The results revealed that most poorly performing students could be identified as early as the third grade and that the failure pattern of dropouts began somewhat later. Early English-language problems were found to be critical; early failure in one or two areas frequently spread to other areas; and certain early performance patterns were associated with dropping out later. The investigators concluded that remedial programs in the very early grades should lead to improved school performance. Measures designed to decrease dropout rates should begin in the lower grades if they are to be most effective.

Attitudes and Values

Attitudes and values are closely related to family background and family interactions. In one study, a random sample of two groups of thirty family triads was selected which had been stratified on the basis of the father's occupation (Crawford, 1970). Each triad consisted of an adolescent male high school graduate or dropout of average IQ and his English-speaking natural parents. The homes of the parents were visited and data collected on questionnaires, TAT-like protocols, and tape-recorded family interactions. A careful analysis of the data furnished the basis for the following conclusions:

1. No differences appeared between the boys in achievement motivation.
2. The graduates and their mothers more likely subscribed to achievement-related values than did the dropouts and their mothers.
3. The graduates regarded achieving success at school a highly valued goal while the dropouts placed high values on achieving success in non-school work.
4. The graduates seemed to realize more egalitarian relationships with their parents in family interaction than did the dropouts.
5. The graduates' mothers were better educated and less demanding than the mothers of the dropouts.

There is evidence from many studies that an adolescent's attitudes toward school and teachers are closely related to those of his parents; many parents from the lower classes hold unfavorable attitudes toward school. There are also many studies that show that the extent of the parents' education is frequently reflected in the dropout rate of their offspring. Education which involves graduating from high school and going on to college is an accepted and expected way of life for many adolescents, while dropping out of school either before graduation from high school or at the time of graduation from high school is an expected way of life for others.

Some Early Signals

The tendency to leave school early begins to manifest itself in elementary school and gains momentum by age sixteen. The child who enrolls in the first grade at the age of six but is not educationally, psychologically, or socially ready for school is a prospective dropout from the beginning. It has been observed that many children grow up in an environment that seriously handicaps them in the essential skills in learning to read upon entering school at age six. Preschool educational programs have been established to help the culturally disadvantaged child learn to read and thus prevent continuous school failure throughout the elementary and high school years.

Prevention is obviously the best means of combating school dropouts, and this requires the cooperation of parents and teachers. Being alert to the causes of reading failure, poor grades, repetition of grades, mischief-making, lack of self-confidence, and a poor self-concept furnishes parents and teachers with useful insights. Lack of interest in school, truancy, and persistent tardiness are danger signs that should not be ignored. Evidence was presented in Chapter 10 that pupils frequently lose their positive attitude toward their teachers and school in general with advancing years. This is particularly true for nonacademic students and others who lack the motivation to succeed.

We might say that one doesn't have to actually quit going to school to be a dropout. Covert dropouts can be seen in almost every school and exist in large numbers in some. They can best be defined for what they are not, and in the minds of many people in the community they do not exist, except when they get into trouble. These are the students who do not participate, who do not study, who do not make satisfactory grades at school, who do not plan to continue their education beyond their enrollment period in the public school. They have no plans for the future. Their attitude toward teachers is one of contempt because their teachers are preoccupied only with order and control. Studies by Flanders (1963, 1965) indicate that teacher behavior is a dominant factor in determining the attitudes of these frequently forgotten or overlooked students.

Family Interactions

There is a general agreement among research studies that the *quality of interaction* in the adolescent's family has the greatest bearing on his behavior and achievement at school. A study by Cervantes (1965b) focused on the dimensions of family interaction such as depth of communication and joint leisure activities. Comparisons were made between dropouts and those graduating from high school. In all cases the dropouts ranked significantly lower in family interaction. For example, 81 percent of the dropouts were characterized by infrequent communication within the home, while only 20 percent of the graduates fell into this category.

A lack of parental interest in education can be cited as one of the major contributing factors to the large number of dropouts. Thus, adolescents who drop out receive little encouragement or reinforcement from their parents for any efforts expended at school. By and large it appears that the parents of many dropouts do not themselves have a high school diploma, nor do they have jobs which show them and their children the values of a completed secondary education. As a consequence, their aspirations for their children do not include graduating from high school.

A FAMILY PATTERN. It has been observed that the number of years children attend school tends to be only slightly higher than that established by their parents. Dropouts have significantly lower scholarship and attendance records than do those who remain in school. Scholarship and attendance seem, however, to be more a manifestation of orientation toward the value of education, level of aspiration, degree of participation in school activities, and whether or not the individual finds an adult in the school with whom he can identify than it does a manifestation of intelligence. Therefore, dropouts are associated with economic pressures, peer relationships, participation in school life, and treatment by the teacher—in short, a function of the social class. The importance of social class, which is discussed more fully later in this chapter may be noted in that little difference appears in intelligence ratings of lower-class boys who drop out and those who remain in school. Intelligence is more of a factor in whether girls stay in school or drop out than it is for boys; boys are more likely to stay in or drop out according to their position on the social status scale.

Bertrand (1962) found an inverse relationship between the years of schooling of the parents and the dropout rate of their children. The results of his study are presented in Table 11-1, indicating that the higher the educational level of the parents the greater the likelihood that their children will remain in school.

Subculture of Dropouts

Although there is a lack of agreement as to whether an independent adolescent subculture exists, there is evidence of a dropout subculture.

TABLE 11-1 School Attendance of Adolescents
in Relation to Education of Parents

EDUCATION OF PARENTS	PERCENT IN SCHOOL	PERCENT DROPOUTS
Father		
0–8 grades	55	76
9–12 grades	38	24
College experience	7	0
Mother		
0–8 grades	34	69
9–12 grades	53	31
College experience	13	0

Source: Bertrand (1962).

This was noted by Cervantes (1965a) in a questionnaire study of working-class youth in six metropolitan areas. The response of dropouts and high school graduates to questionnaire items dealing with intergenerational mutual understanding and reactions to parental disapproval of their choice of friends are shown in Table 11-2. Almost three-fourths of the graduates' responses indicate that they are in harmony with parental values; however, 58 percent of the dropouts retain friends in opposition to parents, and only 22.7 percent of the dropouts reject friends. The results of this study do not support the notion of an independent youth culture pervading all groups of teen-agers.

TABLE 11-2 Teen-agers' Reactions to Parental Opposition
to Their Friends*

	DROPOUTS		GRADUATES	
	%	N	%	N
Ignore parents, retain friends	53.3	80	7.3	11
Retain friends secretly	4.7	7	2.0	3
Evaluate objectives as see fit	19.3	29	17.3	26
Gradually reject friends	12.0	18	30.0	45
Reject friends, internalize parental values	10.7	16	43.3	65
Total	100.0	150	100.0	150

* The hypothesis that dropouts more characteristically reject parental authority is sustained at the .001 level of statistical significance.
Source: Sebald, 1968: 442.

The dropout rate is very high among many minority groups where a relatively distinct subculture may be found. Many adolescents come from a culture that fails to prepare them for school. Thus, when they enter school at the age of six they are not ready to learn to read and perform many other activities at school. The dropout rate for adolescents from culturally and/or economically disadvantaged families is much higher than for adolescents from culturally stimulating, more affluent homes. The home environment motivates and prepares boys and girls for academic or nonacademic pursuits from early life.

The Failure Habit

A large percentage of dropouts have been school failures throughout most or all of their school life. It has been pointed out that "the common denominator of crime and delinquency is failure in school." According to Judge James H. Lincoln, "Most chronic delinquents read at three or four grades below their average grade placement. They're the lowest achievers among dropouts. They account for 90 percent of the severe behavior problems in this country" (quoted in Dygert, 1971:23).

The dropout begins and ends as a misfit. He is essentially a friendless boy or girl, except for other misfits with whom he identifies. The future dropout is outside the in-group. Boys who perform poorly in school are likely to select friends who are also poor students. Since failing students are more likely to be misfits at school and misbehave, it becomes difficult to separate the delinquency of a boy's friends and his grades at schools.

FEELINGS OF INADEQUACY. The dropout frequently develops a feeling of inadequacy resulting from constant failure in school. Unless he has been able to succeed in some extracurricular activities at school or in other outside activities, this failure complex becomes very serious. Many reckless teen-age automobile drivers must outdo others on the highway because they haven't been able to succeed in any other activity. Their souped-up automobiles become great compensators that allow them a measure of success.

FACTORS ASSOCIATED WITH DROPOUTS

Many studies have been conducted to ascertain the reasons for students dropping out of school. Some closely associated factors are: (1) low academic aptitude, including failing grades; (2) personal and social maladjustments; (3) home conditions—lack of parental reinforcement; and (4) lower-class attitudes and values.

Low Academic Aptitude

It is clear from many studies that progress in school is clearly related to academic aptitude, which is frequently determined by intelligence tests. In a study reported by Havighurst and others (1962) over a decade ago, it was noted that 40 percent of the dropouts came from the lowest quartile of IQ scores. However, the fact that 6 percent of the dropouts came from the top IQ quartile shows that other factors are extremely important as causes for dropping out of school.

Studies uniformly show a lower IQ of adolescents from slum areas and other disadvantaged home conditions. Solomon and others (1971) obtained intelligence quotients of black inner-city adolescents (Table 11-3). The mean IQ of the boy dropouts is higher than that of the girls. This may best be accounted for by the greater number of dropouts among the boys, thus the IQ was less selective.

TABLE 11-3 Mean Sixth-Grade IQs for High School High Achievers, Low Achievers, and Dropouts

MEAN IQs		MEAN IQs	
High boys	93.9	High girls	102.8
Low boys	93.1	Low girls	92.9
Dropouts (boys)	91.0	Dropouts (girls)	86.6

Source: Solomon, 1971: 482.

GRADES AND FAILURE IN SCHOOL. It was suggested earlier that failing grades hang over many students from the early years into high school. Solomon and others (1971) examined this relationship among black inner-city adolescents. High and low achievers were selected according to overall grade average—the high and low grade point averages for boys were 2.48 and 1.37, for girls 2.59 and 1.47. He noted that future high-achieving boys were significantly higher than future low achievers at the elementary school level on five of the nine school subjects (oral recitation, spelling, social studies, art, and arithmetic); the future low achievers and dropouts were not significantly different. For the girls future high and low achievers were essentially undifferentiated; but six of the school subjects significantly differentiated future low achievers and dropouts.

The results of the study by Solomon and others suggest that dropping out of school is more related to academic success for girls than for boys. It seems likely that factors outside of school are relatively stronger motivational determiners operating for boys remaining in school than for girls.

Gold (1970) found from a study involving a sample of 522 thirteen- to sixteen-year-olds in Flint, Michigan, that sons of semiskilled and unskilled workers were hardest hit by poor grades. The results in Figure 11-1 indicate that two-thirds of them were actually failing, while only one-third of those in the high-status group were making unsatisfactory grades.

The problem of failing grades is of greater significance to the adjustment of boys than girls. This was shown in a study by Douvan and Adelson (1966). In the first place parents, especially the father, put more

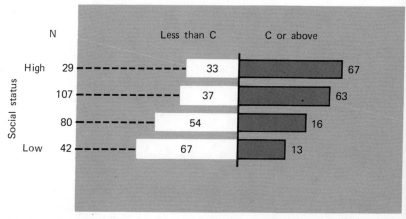

FIGURE 11-1 School grades of thirteen- to sixteen-year-olds by social status. From Martin Gold, *Delinquent Behavior in an American City* (Belmont, Calif.: Cole Publishing Co., 1970), p. 123.

pressure on the son to succeed than they do the daughter. This perhaps results from the parents' concern about a son's future occupational choices, although Women's Liberation may increase pressure for girls to also prepare for a greater range of occupational choices. Good grades mean to the boy an increased opportunity to attend a prestige college, enter a prestige occupation or profession, and fulfill the American dream of material success. The most common academic failure of dropouts is reading, and because of their lack of reading skills, they are unable to succeed in academic subjects.

Maladjustments and Dropouts

There are many students with the ability and parental encouragement to complete high school who withdraw because of emotional or social difficulties. They often strike out with resentment by misbehaving and thus calling attention to themselves. Other maladjusted adolescents meet frustrations at school by withdrawing altogether. They are in many cases emotionally immature; they are not ready to grow up, and "graduation is like the last step in walking the plank." They cannot tolerate the self-sufficiency that school demands. They are not motivated by the remote and often abstract rewards that education has to offer.

ATTITUDES TOWARD TEACHERS AND PEERS. Typically the dropout often feels that the teacher doesn't encourage and support him in his school activities and efforts. He resents the teacher's classroom mannerisms, and doubts his ability to instruct. He feels that the teacher is pedantic, boring, and unfair in meting out punishment and rewards.

In his relationship with fellow students the dropout often sees himself victimized by people who don't understand him and really don't care to. He is usually not a member of any school group. He doesn't feel he belongs. As a result of President Kennedy's 1963 campaign to get dropouts back to school, half of the dropouts in twenty-three states returned to school after having been contacted personally by counselors. The reason dropouts most often gave for returning and staying in school was that someone thought them important enough to contact.

The adolescent who has withdrawn from all school activities and develops a low self-concept is a potential suicide. This was the third most important cause of death in 1966 among those aged fifteen to nineteen; it was the second most frequent cause of death among college students (Gavzer, 1966). They have reached the stage in their lives where they can no longer accept their continued failure in school, in extracurricular activities, and with their peers.

Influence of Cultural and Social Backgrounds

Most dropouts are from the lower social classes. It is frequently said that dropouts leave school in order to get a job and earn money, but this is only part of the story. An examination of the conditions and forces in their cultural and social backgrounds reveals that they are not motivated to take an interest in school and remain there, or to graduate and perhaps go on to college, or enter some vocational area for special technical training. Only a small percentage of lower class boys returning from service in World War II, the Korean War, and the Vietnam War took advantage of the GI Bill which would have enabled them to secure additional education. Lower-class adolescents usually go to work, get married, and establish their independence at an early age.

SOCIOECONOMIC STATUS. Bertrand (1962) found the percentages of dropouts from the lower, middle, and upper classes to be 63 percent, 24 percent, and 13 percent respectively. Hathaway and Monachesi (1963) used a carefully constructed design on more than 15,000 Minnesota high school students in a follow-up study spanning several generations. The findings, presented in Table 11-4, show that more boys drop out of school before graduation than girls and that the day laborer and semiskilled occupational backgrounds accounted for more than half of all dropouts.

A study by Namenwirth (1969) was designed to determine the orientation of dropouts and graduates and the extent to which they changed it so as to fit more readily into middle-class values. The investigators found that many New Haven high school students change their orientations, attitudes, and behavior but that dropouts do so to a far lesser extent than graduates. Three hypothetical explanations for this were considered. The investigators conclude: "adaptation to middle-class values rather than autonomous maturation predispositions at an early age provide the most likely explanation of the survey findings" (23). The high school pupil from the lower class, unable or unwilling to adjust to

TABLE 11-14 Dropout Rate of High School Students
by Socioeconomic Background and Sex

SOCIOECONOMIC CATEGORY*	BOYS PERCENT	GIRLS PERCENT
Day laborer	38	32
Semiskilled	19	18
Farmer	21	11
Clerical	13	12
Professional	5	5

* One of the most important criteria in socioeconomic classification is the occupation of the father.
Source: Hathaway and Monachesi (1963).

middle-class values, will lack interest in the high school program, fail to become an inpart of the school, and will not be able to identify with teachers or other adult figures at school.

The lower-class students confront expected middle-class behaviors and values on many levels and in many different ways, some of which are quite subtle. The practices of teachers and other school personnel indicate an implicit rejection of other behavior and values. In this the teacher displays a lack of care, interest, and sympathy for the problems faced by the potential dropout. Namenwirth states:

> Traditionally, schools have tried to bridge the chasm between middle-class school values and the values of the student minority by acting upon two conflicting educational philosophies: encapsulation and forced induction. By isolating the school and students from the competitive structure of society (and the inequities thus produced and sustained) it is hoped to create an atmosphere which will be conducive to the acceptance of middle-class amenities and values. By forced induction at an early age, the system has tried to create greater conformity *and* equality at the onset which in turn would allow for a greater realism and more competitiveness during the remainder of the school career. Both philosophies have been of little use in ameliorating the problem of school failure, partly because they are often only rhetoric, partly because the true causes of school failure are not of the school's making (1969: 34).

ETHNIC DIFFERENCES. Significant cultural differences between adolescents from several ethnic groups were described in Chapter 9. In some of these minority groups, adolescents are at an extreme disadvantage. The largest minority group, the Negroes, has been at a distinct disadvantage throughout its history in the United States. Racial prejudice and legal restrictions have frequently in the past deprived the black adolescent of opportunities for better schooling and jobs. And, although the legal restrictions have been removed, we find that their home and community environment fails to provide them with the needed background and motivation for remaining in school.

Studies of achievement motivation show that it varies with different ethnic groups; however, it has been passed down through generations in the attitudes, aspirations, and values of the parents. Ethnic differences in motivation were first studied by McClelland (1955) who noted a close relationship between early independence training and achievement motivation. McClelland observed that Protestants and Jews favored earlier independence training than the Irish and Italian Catholics. Data were gathered by Rosen (1967) on the relative emphasis given by different ethnic groups upon achievement training—that is, imposing standards of excellence, setting high goals for the child to achieve, and reinforcement of excellence on tasks well done. A comparison of the mean achievement motivation scores shows the Negroes to be lowest in all social class groups except for the I–II group. The largest difference noted among the ethnic groups is between the French-Canadian and Negro on one hand and the Greek, Jew, and Protestant groups. However, the results indicate that social class remains more important in the development of achievement motivation than ethnicity. This must be taken into consideration in interpreting the results. There are relatively more middle- and upper-class Jews, Greeks, and Protestants than among Italians, French-Canadians, and Negroes. Rosen concludes from his examination of differences in motivation, values, and aspirations of six racial and ethnic groups:

> . . . The data show that the group places different emphasis upon independence and achievement training in the rearing of children. . . . The data also indicate that Jews, Greeks, and Protestants are more likely to possess achievement values and higher educational and vocational aspirations than Italians and French-Canadians. The values and educational aspirations of the Negroes are higher than expected, being comparable to those of Jews, Greeks, and white Protestants, and higher than those of the Italians and French-Catholics. Vocational aspirations of Negroes, however, are the lowest of any group in the sample. Social class and ethnicity interact in influencing motivation, values, and aspirations; neither can predict an individual's score (1967: 346).

Teen-Age Marriage

One factor frequently associated with dropping out of school is early marriage, especially on the part of girls. Early dating practices, quite prevalent in our society today, lead to early marriage. Also, pregnancy is a prime factor leading to early marriage. Recent statistics indicate either a leveling off or a decline in early marriages. Two factors would seem to have an effect: (1) More permissive sex practices have permitted many engaged couples to have sexual relations and in some cases live part-time together without the formality of marriage. (2) More widespread knowledge of birth control means, including the pill, as well as other, recently developed devices, have reduced the likelihood of pregnancy—a frequent cause of early marriage.

Perhaps marriage counseling in schools would help in reducing teen-age marriages and school dropouts. As of 1971, California was the only state in the nation to require counseling for young brides (Parade, 1971).

The Pregnant Schoolgirl

The problem of the pregnant schoolgirl continued to grow through the decade of the sixties; it is still with us in the seventies. From medical, educational, social service, and psychological aspects these girls are faced with extremely complex problems and until recently most of them received little or no help in meeting their problems, just condemnation. In some states pregnancy has been the primary reason for teen-agers leaving school before graduation; in fact, it occurs more than twice as often as all other medical and physical conditions combined (Stine, Rider, and Sweeney, 1964).

The neglect of these girls results in many medical problems such as toxemia, excessive weight gain, anemia, fetopelvia disproportion, and miscarriages. Among the newborn infants there is a preponderance of prematurity, prenatal mortality, deformities, and neurological impairments.

A YMCA medical program was set up in Syracuse and Onondaga, New York, in the fall of 1965 for the overall care of pregnant teen-age girls; it was a comprehensive, interdisciplinary approach (Osofsky et al., 1968–69). The first 125 admissions that were reviewed statistically revealed that only 26 percent of the girls were living with both parents; 21 percent of the girls had been pregnant twice in the past. Over half (56 percent) were sixteen to seventeen; 22 percent were younger than sixteen; and 22 percent were eighteen or over. The girls came largely from the lower socioeconomic families, since the mobile middle-class girl would more likely conceal (or even abort) her pregnancy.

TEEN-AGE MOTHERS. Teen-age mothers have been on the increase. Just now it is difficult to predict the future course, since we do not know for certain what the effects of birth control information, improved birth control methods, and legalized abortion will have on pregnancy prior to marriage (see Chapter 14). One thing is certain, teen-agers need counseling. In the fall of 1970, California became the first state to pass a law requiring any couple with one of the partners under eighteen applying for a marriage license to submit to premarital counseling (Amon, 1971).

The counselors do not attempt to talk the youngsters out of marriage but suggest that they think about it carefully and consider the different alternatives open to them. Most of the young girls who become pregnant during their teens are enrolled in school; they are not delinquent; and they come from all social class groups. Of course they face difficult problems. Society, because of its punitive attitude toward unwed mothers, tends to withhold the care and emotional support that the girl (and sometimes the father) desperately needs at this time. Restrictive practices have at times limited her educational opportunities, although these are hopefully disappearing. The Atlanta public schools are among those that have taken the lead in providing for the educational needs of the unwed teen-age mother. The girls drop out of school long enough to have their babies and recuperate. They are given special help so they can keep up with their classmates. Special classes or schools tend to set the unwed mothers apart from others their age. These are truly normal girls who got caught. They have many options open to them; but their continued education in normal classroom situations seem to best provide for their needs.

Single pregnant teen-agers in school today are more likely to suffer from self-consciousness than from guilt. Their school classmates take a better attitude toward their problems than do parents in general. These girls need understanding and help from their teachers and parents; they need acceptance from their peers; and they need to be able to communicate their ideas, thoughts, and feelings about matters that concern themselves and about problems that confront others and even society at large.

THE DROPOUT IN THE LABOR MARKET

When the dropout leaves high school or college he is likely to meet with frustration, since he is dealing with a labor market in which he has little bargaining power. The high school dropout, when asked about his education, must admit that he is not a high school graduate. That is very frequently a sufficient answer to cause the personnel manager to tell the youngster that he has no job to offer him. If he is fortunate enough to secure a job, he is likely to begin and end at the bottom of the job pile. He will face recurrent periods of frustration as he observes others with more education and the resourcefulness that accompanies it pass him by through promotion.

Need for a Job

Though dropouts give many reasons for quitting school, the major reason is to escape the conditions and pressures at school: failure, boredom with dull courses, friction with teachers, lack of friends, feelings of inadequacy because of experiences in class. There are unquestionably many students who drop out because they need a job to maintain their cars.

The governor's Task Force, which met in Denver in 1971, concluded that providing needed jobs should be the first consideration for returning veterans from the Vietnam War. This was regarded as the major problem. It may also be the major problem for many dropouts. During the late adolescent period many young people from the low socioeconomic strata leave school to secure employment. For these adolescents the absence of money is often a constant problem which continually haunts both the parents and children alike. However, curriculum-makers should be aware that they could partially solve this condition by providing old and young alike with information and skills in money management. Today, it is generally accepted that the problems of low-income families are often compounded because they do not have the skill to realize the maximum benefit from their limited funds. With reference to the "imagined" or desired financial needs of adolescence, it should be recognized that a number of people in this age group aspire to the same materialistic possessions as their affluent acquaintances, such as clothes, cars, spending money, and heterosexual acceptance. If sufficient money is not available to satisfy these learned needs and the drive is sufficiently strong, the individual may leave school and seek employment.

Judge James H. Lincoln of the Detroit Juvenile Court links crime with school dropouts. These dropouts are not rebelling against materialism, as is the case of certain commune groups. Rather, they feel the "pinch" of poverty and the need for materials thing that their more affluent peers have: cars and money in their pockets. This would give them status and enable them to fulfill certain desires and needs. Thus, stealing a car is one of the main crimes of juvenile dropouts. No real success can be achieved in combatting crime among dropouts without an organized effort to furnish young people with a legitimate way to acquire a car and other material things and at the same time give them something to do—namely a job. What seems to be needed is an appropriate work program, the cost of which may be far less than the cost of juvenile crime. Lincoln states:

> But it's the only way. The issue is how to make millions of people succeed who are failing. What other reasonable alternative has been proposed? The nation has to focus on making juveniles feel successful in their day-to-day life. This means a vast shift in national resources, but we'd better take it on. There's no other way (quoted in Dygert, 1971: 23).

DROPOUTS AND EMPLOYMENT. There is a greater need today than ever before to keep potential dropouts in school and to get the out-of-school, out-of-work youth back onto an educational track that will prepare them for a job.

One reason for this is that the country is becoming more and more urbanized, with white-collar workers outnumbering blue-collar workers for the first time in 1956; the gap has widened ever since. The cities have become "paper cultures" where the written word is a vital medium of production and transaction.

Each year increased automation makes obsolete many unskilled and semiskilled jobs. The result is a situation where there is already not enough low-skill work to go around for those who must rely on it, while high-level openings go unfilled for want of enough people with advanced education or with the skill and training necessary for the job. Early dropping out of school only aggravates a difficult task.

UNEMPLOYED AMONG THE DROPOUTS. Dropping out of school is likely to be a dead-end road. This may be observed among high school dropouts

I wondered about Harry's secret industry. He's making a list of outstanding men who didn't finish high school.

who seek a job. Most dropouts think that they will soon find employment and through experience move a rung or more up the ladder only to find that their lack of education and experience are serious obstacles when applying for a job—despite the fact that a smaller percentage of students is dropping out of our schools than ever before, perhaps 25 percent today as against more than 50 percent thirty years ago.

The results of a study by the Michigan Institute for Social Research of more than 2,000 young men over a four-year period from the time they were tenth graders do not bear out all the consequences of dropping out usually presented (Thomas, 1972). The investigators suggest that the greatest harm from dropping out was the stigma of failure that was acquired. The dropping out made it more difficult to obtain employment; however, the weekly income of those employed compared favorably with that of employed high school graduates. The investigators suggest that perhaps schools should give a ten-year diploma and offer additional vocational training or work-study programs.

Problems of Employment

Problems of employment loom large for the high school dropout who has not had special vocational training. Some of the major difficulties faced by the dropout when seeking a job are:

1. Employers feel that adolescents are too immature to be dependable workers.

2. State and federal child labor laws limit the eligible jobs.

3. Adolescents lack experience.

4. Employment in certain occupations is forbidden to people under eighteen years of age.

5. Lack of education or training.

6. Because of his lack of training and his recent hiring the dropout is most likely to be among the first fired in the case of any recession.

RUNAWAY TEEN-AGERS

The supposedly free and easy life of the hippies with the promise of love and excitement has been a powerful lure to thousands of adolescents unhappy at home and school. Running away from home is as traditional as Tom Sawyer; yet the story of the runaway today is quite different from that of yesterday. Far from finding the anticipated fun and excitement, most runaways are disillusioned by the end of the first or second day when faced with a shortage of money, or the loneliness and fear. Some return when their friends in another city tire of their uninvited, long-staying, free-loading "guests." Some return when they find that the "world away from home" is not so beautiful after all.

> Stephen and Paul, high school students bored with their small town, decided to hitchhike to the West Coast and "make the big scene." Their trip got off to a bad start when what they called a "redneck cracker" picked them up and purposefully dropped them off on a dead-end dirt road five miles off the main highway. Just getting halfway through Texas took a week, and Stephen was down to the spare change in his pockets. Disillusioned, he sent a collect telegram to his parents who wired him money to fly home. Paul, who wasn't going to ask his parents for a "damn thing," stuck the trip out and reached California. Once there, he soon became "turned off" after he had experienced a "bummer" on bad acid given to him by one of his new friends and after some of the "groovy chicks" at the pad he was staying passed syphilis on to him. Paul then decided to get a job pumping gas for a month until he saved enough money to return home. His only comment on his three-month adventure was "It's something everybody ought to do ONCE."

The case of Deborah, described by Surface (1970), was less fortunate, but is typical of the fate that may befall the runaway girl.

> One Saturday in July, 1968, thirteen-year-old Deborah Neill, a rather frail girl with long reddish-brown hair, decided to run away from her home in Vickery, Ohio. She hitchhiked with another teen-ager to New York City's Greenwich Village. After spending most of her money, she ended up sleeping in Washington Square. However, Deborah was so disillusioned that she telephoned an uncle in Vickery and promised to return home in a day or two.

While wandering around the East Village, a notorious hangout for teen-age runaways, Deborah was approached by two young men. They took her to the fifth floor of a tenement house, stripped her, and raped her. While attempting to escape further attack by fleeing through a bathroom window, the girl fell down an air shaft to her death.

The "National Missing Youth Locator," a bimonthly published in Hayward, California runs photos and descriptions of some of the 1,500 daily runaways for a relatively small fee, the money usually paid by anxious parents. Far from finding the anticipated glamorous life, most runaways are soon disillusioned. It has been estimated that for every determined runaway who remains away a year or more, at least ten either talk to the police, contact a friend, or in some cases their parents within a few days following their running away from home.

Like the case just cited, the runaways soon realize that you "don't get love and protection for nothing." Boys, in particular, must help by providing money, groceries, and goods by begging, stealing, or any other method that seems to work. Girls are usually more readily accepted by occupants of communal apartments. Frequently they are forced into shoplifting, drug addiction, and prostitution. The personable older leaders, who set themselves up as protectors and as providers, are misfits and usually untrustworthy.

Reasons for Running Away

The question frequently asked by parents is, "Why did he (or she) run away from home? We provided him (or her) with . . . " Apart from a few incorrigibles, most are confused over interactions at home and are unable to communicate with either parent. Thus, we hear about their problems with parents over hair styles, use of the car, dating, choice of friends, social values, and frequently grades at school (among middle-class parents). Running away from home may be to adolescents any one of a number of things, ranging from an actual need to get away from an intolerable situation to a victory yell at being able to have their own way about dating hours or about hair-dos.

Whatever the reasons, attentive parents can usually detect them if they are not too wrapped up in their own affairs and are willing to listen to their adolescent son or daughter. It has been emphasized in previous chapters that adolescents have problems, and they need to be heard. Parents who are willing to simply listen with a sympathetic ear will do much in solving the problems of their adolescent son or daughter and thus prevent their running away from home. When an adolescent runs away from home, he is either running away from something he regards as very unpleasant or to something that he needs and wants very much, or both. It has been observed that parents and runaways, when reunited, hopefully recognize that both were at fault and that the ordeal could have been avoided if communication had not broken down.

THE COLLEGE DROPOUT

Today approximately half of our young people enter college, and there has been a proliferation of colleges, especially community colleges. The outlays for higher education, public and private, have been increasing at approximately two and a half times the rate of the gross national product. The goal has been that every college-age boy and girl should have access to a college education. Yet access alone does not automatically lead to a successful education. The importance of aspiration or motivation should not be overlooked in any consideration of why adolescents drop out of school or fail to go on to college.

According to Harvard psychiatrist, Dr. Armand M. Nicholi, almost half of all college dropouts are bright students who suffer from self-doubt and depression. This is based upon a study of the relation between high intelligence and psychiatric disorders in 1,454 Harvard dropouts between 1955 and 1960. Forty-three percent left for psychiatric reasons, and the psychiatric dropouts as a group were above average in intelligence (Parade, 1970).

Stopouts

The number of students who plan to go to college but expect to stay out of school for a period of three months to a year or more has increased during the past two decades. This number is found mainly among males partially because females tend to marry earlier. Also, the problem of choosing and preparing for a vocational career looms larger in the lives of boys than girls.

Each fall as millions of young people enter college, many college-oriented high school graduates decide not to go to college—6 percent in 1970 (*Time,* 1970). This disenchantment with college education affects many students already enrolled in college. This trend is sometimes discomforting to colleges, although many colleges accept it and make provisions for it.

Wisconsin's Beloit College is thoughtfully offering its delayed freshmen a bit more: counseling on everything from personal problems to finding a job. From the University of Kansas to Yale University, high school graduates find it easy to get leaves of absence for up to two years; at Harvard last year, one out of every eighteen students was on leave. Stanford's sympathetic advisers often work out projects in which students receive academic credit for analyzing the nonacademic jobs they take (*Time,* 1970: 79).

Not every stopout returns to college; the longer a student waits before returning, the lower his chances of ultimately graduating. Those dropping out for psychiatric reasons return to college sooner than others but have a higher incidence of quitting a second time. Students upon returning are more mature, have more definite goals, and are better able to relate college experiences to their problems and to the outside world. As some have suggested, "School may be a preparation for life; life is also a preparation for school."

NEED TO FIND ONESELF. Many failures in college can be attributed to immaturity. In some cases the child has never been away from home and on his own before; he hasn't had the need or opportunity to make his own decisions. Suddenly he finds himself away from his parents and other adults to whom he looked for the solution of his problems and to make decisions for him. The security of his home is gone and he has gained more independence. The more intelligent adolescent begins to think of his future, and raises many questions such as: Why am I going to college? Why should I be taking certain courses? What do I want to do when I have graduated from college? Just what is my future anyway? While some of these questions may be male oriented, there are significant questions in the mind of most girls as they enter college.

The senior author encountered the case of Nell, a high school senior, who had been accepted at every college to which she had applied. Nell suddenly confronted her parents with the idea that she wanted to drop out of school after graduating, skip college, and get married. The parents were much surprised and couldn't at first believe that she was serious. The father, a successful person in the business world, was adamant and unwilling to listen at first to Nell's ideas or plans. He could not easily conceive of the oldest of his two children (both daughters) not going to college. The mother was less insistent about Nell going to college. As an answer to the father's arguments and questions, Nell responded: "I am tired of school." "I want to get married." "I want to be myself."

This is a common theme and thought of many bright girls and also boys from middle-class homes—where education means so much to the parents. It is indeed a real blow to parents to suddenly learn that many of their middle-class values that they cherished so much are not important to their teen-age daughter or son.

Nell seemed to have made up her mind about schooling. It had not been a sudden decision on her part, but it came as a shock to her parents. There are many Nells. Some find themselves and return to school. Others find themselves and happiness in worthwhile pursuits. Others get into trouble in their efforts to find out what life is all about. In any case communication between adolescents and parents or other responsible adults should not be broken. The approach to success in such a situation must be based on respect and understanding of the individual rather than authoritarianism. If possible, parents should try to keep contact with adolescents who feel the way Nell feels. Sound decision-making is one of the keys to maturity, and adolescents need the opportunity and independence to experiment with this ability as it affects their own lives. Youth have the ideals and questions but not all the solutions, and if parents can realize the difficult lesson that they don't have all the answers either, there is a chance for dialogue and rapport. Many adolescents who do not follow the plans their parents set forth for them are not so much rebelling as taking a break from their school-oriented, programmed lives. Often they are not seeking to march to a different drummer as much as asking for a period of peace to see if they can hear any music at all.

The Covert Dropout or Involuntary Stay-In

Access to a college education alone does not automatically lead to successful education. It simply means the exposure of an individual to whatever education institute he is able to attend. We have observed at first hand many cases of boys and girls who commuted some distance to college, and whose major goal was simply to accumulate college credits and finally a diploma. Most of these cases displayed no interest in the musical programs, art displays, lectures, or even the sports programs. Their sole interest was to attend classes and study so as to receive the needed credits to graduate after a period of time. Such students may end up with a college diploma, but with minimum of a college education. Thus, the notion that one goes to college to secure an education is only true for some students.

THE COVERT DROPOUT. Almost every college instructor has observed the student who displays little or no interest in the materials or skills being taught. His thoughts are usually quite foreign to those of the instructor and to most of the students. He is unable to see any relevance of the materials being taught to his problems and goals. However, he stays in college because of certain conditions and pressures. These pressures take different forms (*U.S. News,* 1971: 62):

1. Parents' attitudes, which reflect their own aspirations rather than a thoughtful assessment of the needs of their adolescent son or daughter.
2. Pressure from peers—"they stay in college, so why shouldn't I also remain?"
3. The knowledge that *now* is the time in one's life to go to college, if one expects to go to college.
4. Lack of a suitable alternative—"what would I do if I dropped out of school? What about my peers?"
5. The social stigma attached to dropping out of school.
6. The inability to get a decent job without a college education.
7. The need to remain in college for the sake of one's future. The girl may wonder about her marital future if she drops out of college and must find friends among noncollege youth.

These students have not been turned off by college. They are able to make passing grades, even though they don't have any special interest in most of the courses they are studying. These students remain in school and may be thought of as "involuntary students." The longer they remain in the academic atmosphere, the more they are likely to become dependent upon it; it is actually the only life they know as a young adult. The sum of these conditions and circumstances leaves many students unprepared to make sound career choices—a serious problem for most adolescents, since there are few opportunities for actual work experience.

THE DRIFTERS. Although it is difficult to measure motivation, there appear to be many college students without a vocational or career choice, who are willing, and apparently prefer, to remain in college as the easiest and safest way of life. They are capable of successful college work and put forth enough effort to pass most of their courses. These students sometimes drift from one college to another. In a larger university they may drift from one school or college to another, where regulations permit. Certainly not all transfer students are drifters, for there are frequently good personal reasons why a student desires to transfer to another college. "In a study of the graduating class of 1967 in one major state-college system, 30 percent has attended three colleges and 17 percent had attended four or more. . . . Since fewer than a third of the students who enter this system graduate, these figures represent a conservative estimate of the actual amount of drifting" (*U.S. News,* 1971: 63).

Many of these students display little interest in any particular educational objective—either to prepare for a career or to learn to think. Their major concern is with the immediate enjoyment of life and will try to perpetuate it as long as possible. This same phenomenon may be observed among young workers.

Factors Related to Withdrawal

The causes of withdrawal from college are perhaps even more complex than those for withdrawing from high school. In either case the apparent cause is frequently not the real one, and most often there is more than one cause. One of the complexities results from mass tabulation of data which fails to differentiate between students who withdraw because of academic difficulty and those who are in good academic standing when they withdraw.

VOLUNTARY VS. INVOLUNTARY WITHDRAWALS. Problems related to college withdrawal are quite different from those found among high school dropouts. This was observed in a study by Rossman and Kirk (1970) involving students who enrolled as freshmen in the College of Letters and Science at the University of California, Berkeley. These were classified as (a) persisters (b) voluntary withdrawals, and (c) failures based upon their first-year cumulative grade-point average and whether or not they returned to the college the following fall. Data were collected during the registration week from a questionnaire, Omnibus Personality Inventory (OPI), and the School and College Ability Tests (SCAT). Significant differences in academic ability as measured by SCAT scores were found between the failures and the voluntary withdrawals on all items except on the SCAT Quantitative section for women. However, the higher academic ability of the female voluntary withdrawals is supported by data from the Omnibus Personality Inventory. The investigators state: "The differences suggest that the female voluntary withdrawals are more reflective, more esthetic, have a greater need for independence; are more other-directed, less concerned with practical matters, and more intellectually oriented" (60).

The psychological effects of failure are perhaps the worst consequence of withdrawal from college. Thus, special counseling is needed at different stages in the college student's educational career.

NEED FOR BROADER EXPERIENCES. Young people definitely need to experience situations in which they are held accountable for their actions. Youth from affluent homes have many privileges and luxuries, from hi-fi stereos to the latest sport cars. Going to college may simply serve as a means to prolong adolescence. One may regard such youths as a deprived class—deprived of the need and opportunity to experience adult responsibility. Many of these become bored and frustrated by their experiences; some rebel by dropping out of school; some remain in school and give vent to their feelings in various ways, while others attempt to adjust to college conditions.

The *Report* of the Carnegie Commission on Higher Education in 1970, based on the assumption that problems of higher education are problems of society as a whole, urges the expansion of educational opportunities outside of college. Young people should have the option after high school graduation of deferring further education for a period of time in order to get service or work experience and to learn more about their own needs and aspirations. There is plenty of work to be done in improving the countryside, making our parks more beautiful, caring for the sick, aged, and young children, and campaigning against pollution, illiteracy, political graft, racism, and unhealthy social conditions. Some efforts have been made to provide needed services or work through such agencies as VISTA, the Peace Corps, the Teacher Corps, or Youth for Service (a new version of the Civilian Conservation Corps).

SUMMARY

The potential dropout in high school is usually a misfit. His friends have dropped out in many cases. He has been labeled a school failure throughout most of his school years. More boys drop out than girls. This stems in part from the greater stress and number of problems boys encounter at school. There is a positive relationship between the parents' years of schooling and the children's staying in school.

An independent subculture may appear among dropouts that is

different from the stay-ins. The dropout rate is high among most minority groups. Most dropouts have developed feelings of inadequacy and compensate for such feelings by getting into trouble with teachers and school officials. There is also a lack of goals among potential dropouts; they see little value in what they are doing at school.

Certain scientific findings bear on dropping out of school: (1) low academic aptitude, including failing grades; (2) personal and social maladjustment; (3) home conditions, especially lack of parental reinforcement; (4) lower-class attitudes and values that are usually at variance with those found at school.

Many dropouts feel that a job and money will solve their problems. They find that full-time jobs are to a marked degree closed to them. Money earned comes largely from part-time employment at menial tasks. The federal government has made different gestures toward solving the problem; however there is usually a great deal of unemployment among dropouts.

The runaway adolescent is most likely to come from a home where communication with parents is bad. These children are faced with problems and believe that running away will solve them. Most of the runaways are soon disillusioned but find nothing to return to, while a few find something that fits their need better than their homes did. The answer to why adolescents run away is not a simple one. Failure in communication stands out prominently as an important home factor.

Prominent today among the college dropouts are the stopouts. Some of these, like Joel, are eager to find themselves. Others stop out for different reasons. Stopouts are in need of counsel. The covert dropout appears both in high school and college. He usually lacks goals and sees little relevance in what is being taught. The major causes for dropping out of college are somewhat similar to those for dropping out of high school. Again, lack of goals and motivation are prominent.

REFERENCES

AMON, RHODA. "Teen-age Mothers Want to Love and Be Loved." *Newsday,* 1971. From *The Charlotte Observer* (August 31, 1971).

BERTRAND, ALVIN L. "School Attendance and Attainment: Functions and Dysfunctions of School and Family Social Systems." *Social Forces* (1962), 40: 228–33.

CERVANTES, LUCIUS F. "American Youth Culture: Independent or Dependent?" Paper read at the Annual Convention of the American Sociological Association, Chicago, 1965.

———. "Family Background, Primary Relations, and the High-school Dropout." *Journal of Marriage and Family* (1965), 27:218–23.

CRAWFORD, DOUGLAS D. "Family Interaction Achievement—Values and Motivation as Related to School Dropouts." *Dissertation Abstracts International* (November 1970), 31 (5):2173-A.

DOUVAN, E. and J. ADELSON. *The Adolescent Experience.* New York: John Wiley & Sons, Inc., 1966.

DYGERT, JAMES H. "We Must Give Jobs to School Dropouts." *Parade* magazine (August 29, 1971), p. 23.

FITZSIMMONS, STEPHEN J., JULIA CHEEVA, EMILY LEONARD, and DIANE MACUNO-VICH. "School Failures, Now and Tomorrow." *Developmental Psychology* (1969), 1 (2):134–46.

GAVZER, BERNARD. "5,000 Adolescent Suicides: Assault on Accepted Values." *Charlotte Observer* (November 6, 1966), p. 5.

GOLD, MARTIN, *Delinquent Behavior in an American City.* Belmont, Calif.: Brooks/Cole Publishing Company, 1970.

HATHAWAY, STARKE R. and ELIO D. MONACHESI. *Adolescent Personality and Behavior.* Minneapolis: University of Minnesota Press, 1963.

HAVIGHURST, R. J., *et al. Growing Up in River City.* New York: John Wiley & Sons, Inc., 1962.

MCCLELLAND, D. C. "Some Social Consequences of Achievement Motivation." In *Nebraska Symposium on Motion,* M. R. Jones, ed. Lincoln: University of Nebraska Press, 1955.

NAMENWIRTH, J. ZVI. "Failing in New Haven: An Analysis of High School Graduates and Dropouts." *Social Forces* (1969), 48:23–36.

Newsweek (February 15, 1971), pp. 89–90. "Census Surprises."

Parade magazine (December 13, 1970), p. 12. "Keeping Up with Youth."

——— (December 13, 1970), p. 13. "Missing Kids."

——— (February 14, 1971), p. 24. "Marriage, Teen-style."

OSOFSKY, HOWARD J., B. B. DIFLORIO, ROBERT HAGAN, and PEGGY W. WOOD. "A Program for Pregnant School Girls: A Progress Report." *Adolescence* (1968–69), 3:89–108.

ROSEN, BERNARD C. "Race, Ethnicity, and the Achievement Syndrome." In *School Children in the Urban Slum,* Joan I. Roberts, ed. New York: The Free Press, 1967. Pp. 327–46.

ROSSMAN, JACK E. and BARBARA A. KIRK. "Factors Related to Withdrawal Among University Students." *Journal of Consulting Psychology* (1970), 17 (1): 56–62.

SEBALD, HANS. *Adolescence: A Sociological Analysis.* New York: Appleton-Century-Crofts, 1968.

SOLOMON, DANIEL, DANIEL R. SCHEINFELD, JAY G. HIRSCH, and JOHN C. JACKSON. "Early Grade Performance of Inner City Negro High School High Achievers, Low Achievers, and Dropouts." *Developmental Psychology* (1971), 4:482.

STINE, C. C., R. V. RIDER, and E. SWEENEY. "School Leaving Due to Pregnancy in an Urban Adolescent Population." *American Journal of Public Health* (1964), 54:1–6.

SURFACE, BILL. "The Case of the Runaway Teen-ager." *Reader's Digest* (May 1970), pp. 143–45. Condensed from *Christian Herald* (May 1970).

THOMAS, JO. "Dropout Concept Wrong." *Charlotte Observer* (February 27, 1972), p. 16A.

Time magazine (September 27, 1971), p. 79. "As College Starts, There Go the
   Stopouts."
U.S. News and World Report (March 22, 1971), pp. 62–63. "Dropouts, Drifters,
   the 'Lock Step'—A Critical Report on Colleges."
WRIGHT, MATTIE K. "Comprehensive Services for Adolescent Unwed Mothers."
   Children (September–October 1966), 13 (5):171–76.

RECOMMENDED READINGS

CERVANTES, LUCIUS F. *The Dropout: Causes and Cures.* Ann Arbor: University
   of Michigan Press, 1965.
   Presents data indicating the dropout rate and some factors closely related to it in a population over a four-year period. Prevention of dropouts
   by emphasizing the school program is suggested.
COMBS, J. and W. COOLEY. "Dropouts: In High School and after High School."
   American Educational Research Journal (1968), 5:343–64.
   An elaborate and revealing analysis of the 440,000 students participating
   in Project Talent. Reasons for leaving school are discussed both for
   males and females.
HATHAWAY, S. R., P. C. REYNOLDS, and E. D. MONACHESI. "Follow-up of the
   Later Careers and Lives of 1,000 Boys Who Dropped Out of High School."
   Journal of Consulting and Clinical Psychology (1969), 33:370–80.
————. "Follow-up of 812 Girls 10 Years after High School Dropout." *Journal
   of Consulting and Clinical Psychology* (1969), 33:383–90.
   The results of these studies indicate that the prospects for the dropout
   returning to school or succeeding outside of school are quite dim.
HAVIGHURST, ROBERT J., PAUL H. BOWMAN, GORDON P. LIDDLE, CHARLES V.
   MATTHEWS, and JAMES V. PIERCE. *Growing Up in River City.* New York:
   John Wiley & Sons, Inc., 1962. Pp. 57–64.
   A special study of 432 students with complete educational career records.
   Of this number 35 percent dropped out of school. Comparisons are made
   between the dropouts and a control group.
SCHREIBER, D., ed. *Profile of the School Dropout.* New York: Vintage Books,
   1968.
   Many dropouts are near illiterates, and their chances of steady employ-
   ment are very poor. This study questions the value of remaining in school.
SEVALD, HANS. *Adolescence: a Sociological Analysis.* New York: Appleton-Cen-
   tury-Crofts, 1968. Chapter 10.
   The chapter discusses educational trends in the United States, the extent
   of the dropout problem, and prevention.
TANNENBAUM, A. J. "Dropout or Diploma: A Socioeducational Analysis of Early
   Withdrawal." In *Education of the Disadvantaged,* A. H. Passow *et al.,* eds.
   New York: Holt, Rinehart & Winston, Inc., 1967.
   A careful analysis of the causes of dropping out with special attention
   given to the social, economic, and psychological backgrounds of dropouts.

12

adolescents and work in a changing world

Traditional definitions for the idea of work have been changing with the technological and social advances taking place in this country. In many instances, there is no guarantee today that a given career specialty will last throughout a young person's lifetime. Adolescents are now faced with both more career specialties to choose from and the fact that increased automation may phase out the very job they want.

THE DIVISION OF LABOR IN SOCIETY

Two relatively distinct divisions of labor have appeared that affect the educational aspirations and vocational goals of adolescents from different classes. The earliest colleges were created to prepare men for certain professions or for the "gentleman's" life. The first girls' colleges were created to prepare girls to be ladies and to teach them the arts or at least how to enjoy the arts. Education for them was not career oriented.

The early Latin grammar school was established in the East to prepare students for college. At a later time, academies, institutes, and high schools were established for the growing middle class. These schools trained students not for vocations or menial jobs but for white-collar employment. Education has been a means of upward social and economic mobility for increasing numbers of young people. Secondary education during most of the nineteenth century was primarily for the growing middle class. Private schools were established for the privileged, and they were taught the traditional academic curricula.

A Historical Perspective on Work

In nonindustrialized, primitive societies there are no adolescents. The young children are either pampered or ignored until they are accepted into their society as adults after an often painful and dangerous ceremony which occurs almost always at the time of puberty. In Europe, into the seventeenth century, work began at an early age for children, often as early as five or six. The young were considered small adults. By the time a person reached what is now known as adolescence, he had been a member of the working force for a number of years. In that period of shorter life spans and little education, teen-agers were in the "prime" of life. Ivan the Terrible was seventeen when he had himself crowned czar of Russia and began to make his name; and Joan of Arc was the same age when she led the French troops which overtook the British force in Orléans. Youth derived a sense of identity from its own position in the larger society. The feudal identity included: (1) the class to which one was born, (2) the European universalistic religion of Roman/Catholicism in which each person was a child of God, and (3) work, which was an integral part of one's status.

The seventeenth century brought the beginnings of the Industrial Revolution and increasing urbanization. The younger members of society were forced into periods of training through apprenticeships. No longer were they able to participate in work with adult status; a separate period of learning or training began to emerge. The young could no longer serve and follow the work arrangements of their elders. Even though many children of eight or ten worked in the sweat shops of the urban industries, their place of work and their place of living were now separated from each other. As the Industrial Revolution progressed, machines changed the nature of work. Fewer workers were needed as machines became increasingly sophisticated and took over much of the manual labor. Furthermore, new and different skills were needed to operate the machines. The Industrial Revolution, which brought urbanization, separation of work and living environments, and the necessity for a training period, also initiated the stage known as adolescence.

THE EMERGENCE OF THE PERIOD OF ADOLESCENCE. Whether one is discussing England in the seventeenth century, the United States in the 1850s, or the newly emerging nations in the last half of the twentieth century, the era of industrial development is concomitant with the emergence of adolescence. The child labor laws and minimum required schooling (usually to the age of sixteen) signaled the fact that there was in society a section of people who could not be classified as children and could not be considered adults. They were forced to grow up with no practical knowledge of actual work; it was left to separate institutions to prepare them to enter the work force.

Urban migration greatly changed the position of formerly rural youth. They were no longer closely integrated members of a family work situation. The migrants who streamed into the United States in the early 1960s faced much the same abrupt change in living patterns. Neither group could participate as active members in their parents' worlds, as they attempted to adjust to the new city conditions. Education became a key to participation in society, and assimilated peers became the examples to guide them.

THE TECHNOLOGICAL-CYBERNETIC REVOLUTION. The trends begun in the early seventeenth century have become accentuated. The multi-specificity of labor has produced an apparently ever-increasing complex division of labor. As Durkheim (1947) predicted, occupations have become a source of meaning and identity for people. The work pattern has become almost completely separate from the home. In the early 1900s four Americans in five were self-employed, but by the 1970s, only one American in five was self-employed. Work has resulted in individuals being trapped in specialized roles apart from a community or family continuity that could give them meaning. To the adolescent, the father's influence as a working, intrinsic member of society and as a stable transmitter of adult work patterns has become fragmented. Work is no longer linked to some intrinsic value but has become an externally imposed, impersonal, competitive and universalistic standard of society. Economics, rather than family or cultural ties, influences a family's geographic location. The adolescent is forced to rely upon a fragmented nuclear family that has cut ties with the past and left grandparents behind in the search for the good life through job promotions. The practical and pleasurable values are the only ones that count. One works in order to live better. Rather than all members of a culture or society working together, it is "everybody for himself," with a potential multitude of choices and an intense degree of individualism. For the youth seeking identity there are no ultimate answers, only a variety of roles in, as Sorokin (1941) termed it, a "sensate culture."

The primary cultural transmission parents give to their children is their own feeling of anomie. They are no longer able to train children to participate in society. There has been a pronounced reliance on schools to teach the young what they need to know to participate in an ever more complicated society. In our technological-cybernetic world, education is mandatory for societal participation; and adolescence is often prolonged into the mid-twenties so that a young person may gain enough training to participate in specialistic work and play his role in adult-oriented social situations.

The emphasis on high school education was profoundly affected in the later 1950s as the schools strained to produce the scientists needed to allow the United States to catch up with the Russian Sputnik space effort. However, by the late 1960s and early 1970s, many adolescents were rejecting this highly fragmented perspective of life and dropping out of high schools and colleges in order to seek other alternatives to the prevailing society.

Vocational Aspirations of Adolescents

Aspirations for finishing high school, attending college, specializing in some trade, preparing for a profession, going to work, or dropping out of school relate to one's self-concept and his total background of experience. Obviously the importance of an education and the prestige hierarchy of occupations are not the same for all adolescents. Not everyone wants to be a professional or go to college. For the lower-class boy ownership of a small business and a modest home with a family may represent his life ambition. In discussing this with a high school junior who had worked the previous summer on a dairy, we found that his greatest ambition was to some day own a small herd of cattle and a small farm or become a manager for a larger dairy. Since the manager of the dairy where he had worked did not have a college education, the high school junior saw no particular relationship between an education and fulfilling his aspiration.

IDENTIFICATION WITH THE FAMILY. One factor influencing vocational aspirations involves family relations. A study by Crites (1962) dealt with the relationship of parental identification to the vocational interests of the adolescent son. A son's identification with both parents significantly affects the patterning of his interests, although close identification with the father is the most important. This is in harmony with the findings of Cohen (1965), who noted that fathers are more concerned with the son's vocational aspirations and life, whereas mothers give more consideration to his status in society.

Data on the vocational preferences of junior high school students and their parents' occupational levels were gathered and studied by Krippner (1963). He found from his study that ". . . At all occupational strata (except the highest), the fathers apparently suggested careers that would boost their sons slightly above their own job level."

IMPORTANCE OF THE SELF-CONCEPT. We should not overlook the importance of the self-concept of an adolescent in his vocational aspirations. This was noted in a study by Korman (1967) in which he found support for the hypothesis that high self-esteem led students to aspire to occupations they perceived as requiring their higher abilities to a greater degree than did students with low self-esteem. Thus, it appears that high scholastic achievement in high school tends to escalate the adolescent's level of occupational aspiration and attainment to the extent that it is accompanied by high self-esteem.

One of the major difficulties confronting the high school student in choosing a vocation is the lack of available jobs in many occupational fields that offer prestige and status (Parade, 1974, p. 26). Technology and its associated effects have presented difficult problems. Even many college students do not find lucrative jobs awaiting them, although they have the specialized training. Certainly one of the problems facing many adolescents upon completing their education is finding suitable and worthwhile employment.

The complexity of modern vocations calls for guidance in choosing a career. A trained person who cannot make use of his training is in an unfortunate position. Likewise, a person forced into a job for which he is poorly prepared or ill-adapted finds little or no job satisfaction.

Teen-Agers at Work

Teen-agers make up a relatively large percentage of the present-day working force. During 1971, approximately one in every eleven workers was in the sixteen- to nineteen-year-old age group, making a total of about 7.5 million workers, or almost half of all the sixteen- to nineteen-year-olds in the nation (Perella, 1972). Even more impressive than this is the number of teen-agers who work at some time during the year. This was, according to Perella, about 10 million in 1971, or two-thirds of all the sixteen- to nineteen-year-olds. Furthermore, these do not include a large number of fourteen- and fifteen-year-olds who work at part-time, irregular, or seasonal jobs.

The kinds of jobs which teen-agers are able to get depend in part upon the nature of the community; however, within a particular community they will depend in part upon such factors as age, sex, social class, and school status. There are some jobs closed by law to younger teen-agers but open to eighteen- and nineteen-year-olds. Adolescents in the fourteen- and fifteen-year-old bracket frequently work at such irregular or part-time jobs as baby-sitting, mowing lawns, cleaning, or at seasonal jobs involving harvesting fruits and vegetables. High school students are more likely than nonstudents to be working in different service occupations, in which part-time and temporary jobs are available. Also, teen-agers are being called upon for many voluntary service activities.

Part-time employment of adolescents may be said to have three important functions. First, it furnishes many with needed money that would not be available otherwise. To others it supplements the small allowance provided by parents who have to live on a rather limited budget. Second, gainful employment has educational value in that it trains the individual for holding down a job by actually participating in the world of work. Third, gainful employment helps to satisfy certain psychological needs. This may be observed in a study reported by Scales and Hutson (1955) with 150 Negro boys of the Hill District in Pittsburgh grades. In grade placement the boys ranged from seventh to twelfth grades. Two-thirds were from broken homes. The developmental tasks that gainful employment helped to accomplish, as identified by responses of the boys, are shown in Table 12-1. The four most important satisfactions the boys obtained from gainful employment were in order of frequency as follows: (1) feeling of independence, (2) feeling of growing up, (3) improved relations with family and parents, and (4) status with peers.

CAREERS AND VOCATIONAL NEEDS

As an adolescent reaches the period when he must be responsible for his own living—spending money, an automobile, clothes and food, and a home of his own—he gives more thought to finding a job or preparing for a vocation. He soon observes and is told that getting a job depends upon preparation. He then begins to think about the kind of work that will best satisfy his present and future needs. The importance of a job or career becomes very important at this stage of his life.

TABLE 12–1 Developmental Tasks That Gainful Employment Helped to Accomplish

DEVELOPMENTAL TASK	PERCENT
Establishing economic independence	68.0
Achieving emotional independence of parents and other adults	48.0
Acceptance of the proper sex role	20.0
New relations with peers	20.0
Accepting, desiring, and achieving socially responsible behavior	3.3
Selecting and preparing for an occupation	0.7
No developmental task identified	7.3

Source: Scales and Hutson (1955).

The Concept of Career

The concept of career is associated with a period of apprenticeship or professional training. Blue-collar jobs, other than those which require a good deal of skill and apprenticeship, are not generally considered to be careers. A career implies some degree of esoteric knowledge and specialization, and some degree of responsibility for the distribution of information, goods, or services. Only within a highly differentiated division of labor in a complex, modern society can the term career apply to large numbers of people. The diversification and increase in potential career opportunities, until very recently, has offered a growing variety of employment choices for young people in our society. There are over 30,000 job categories and subcategories in American society; and in our technological society requiring increased specialization career choices are likely to become more and more difficult.

An important development since World War II is the broadened vocational opportunities available for girls. This has more recently been supported by federal legislation prohibiting job discrimination based upon sex. Thus, we find women presently employed at tasks formerly denied them. Fifteen girls from Cedar Crest College in Allentown, Pennsylvania, worked out at a local garage for one month in a scholastic course called "The Care and Feeding of the Automobile" (Parade, 1972: 71). High schools are being urged to offer vocational guidance and courses for girls oriented toward careers formerly reserved for males.

Education and Upward Mobility

Upward mobility has almost always been an aspiration of most parents for their children. The percentage of young adults with college degrees almost tripled between 1940 and 1970, while the proportion with one or more years of college education increased about 2.4 percent. U.S. Census figures demonstrate this in the median number of school years for adults: 1940—8.6 years; 1950—9.3 years; 1960—10.5 years; 1970—12.1 years (New Republic, 1972). This increased consumption of education is in part reflected in the massive rural to urban migrations since the 1940s. The manual laborers had sufficient skill to work in rural settings. However, the children of these migrants have had to cope with a highly competitive, industrially technical setting in their first jobs, all of which demands increased technical training.

In the past, generally, upward mobility has been supported by both parents and their children alike. In many instances, where the aspirations of upward mobility exist without avenues for achieving this goal, the result has been the experience of marginality. In such cases aspirations remain unfulfilled, and individuals must settle for fewer gains. The myth of upward mobility still remains, especially among disadvantaged young people and many older Americans, as the road to happiness and fulfillment. This myth is recently being questioned by many contemporary young people who have grown up with relative affluence in a world beset by change and instability.

ATTITUDES AND VALUES. The interdisciplinary theory of vocational choice proposed by Ginzberg and others (1951) was an outgrowth of various investigators who were interested in vocational choices. According to this theory, vocational choice involves the following significant variables: (1) reality, (2) education, (3) emotions, and (4) individual values. In reaching a vocational decision an individual may be confronted with a conflict between these variables, e.g., the emotional variable and the reality or educational variable.

Attitudes and values become important determiners for a large percentage of adolescents from the lower social class, since they view work as a means of making money and thus providing them with material comforts. Many adolescents view work as a choice between working with people and working with things. In general girls have displayed a greater desire for working with people. A job for some adolescents may be a means of making money so he can quickly complete his education. In such a case the economic value of a job is very high.

Ability and Vocational Choice

There is ample evidence that the hierarchy of occupations is closely tied to intelligence test scores and academic aptitude. Those being trained for professional pursuits or whose fathers were members of a profession rank highest, with clerical and business groups following, and the semiskilled and unskilled ranking lowest. The intelligence test score remains the best single criterion for judging an individual's ability to succeed in a given occupation—there being an optimal range for most occupations. This means further, of course, that there are other factors important to vocational success.

THE FIRST JOB. The first job for many teen-agers is only temporary; it is a means to satisfy certain immediate wants, or an educational experience on the way to a better position. The level of the first job of the young worker in more permanent employment will depend primarily upon his educational level and social status. However, success on the job and promotion to a better or more productive job will depend to a marked degree upon the individual's willingness to work, dependability, and ability to get along with others, including his boss.

NEED FOR VOCATIONAL TRAINING. Interviews with youths verify that, if a student once drops out of school, he is unlikely to return. The decline of the need for unskilled and semiskilled workers presents a real problem for such youngsters. The vocational needs of adolescents may be summarized as follows: (1) a better understanding of their own aptitudes and limitations, (2) occupational information—including occupational opportunities and job requirements, (3) vocational training, both in school and through work experiences, and (4) the opportunity to use their abilities once developed—i.e., the right to a job.

The vocational needs of a large percentage of adolescents are being met through vocational training in our high schools and technical schools. It seems likely that society is creating a large number of college-educated youth who are unprepared for the jobs available. Between 1965 and 1970 the number of college students grew from 4.6 million to 7.4 million. During this period, the number of youths enrolled full time in technical or training courses above the high school level grew from 150,000 to approximately 2 million (*Gastonia Gazette*, 1971). Although vocational training has not received the publicity of college training, the U.S. Office of Education estimates that half of all jobs opening up in the 1970s will require training beyond high school but less than four years of college.

It is conceivable that, as college degrees come to offer less job security or preparation, many of the more academically inclined young people may look toward technical or vocational education as an avenue for growth and making a living. In the past, middle-class families have frowned upon technical education, even when their son or daughter's aptitude was more in harmony with a technical school's curriculum.

Paraprofessionals

The term *paraprofessional* has come to describe activity which can be utilized as gainful employment for ordinary citizens without formal educational training. One of the better-known among these types of positions, especially for younger people, is that of the teacher's aide. Sometimes misused as disciplinarians or used to perform menial tasks, teaching paraprofessionals are involved in such activities as teaching dancing steps, grading exams, working with flashcards, and reading lessons—activities sometimes indistinguishable from those of the assigned teacher. Another example of this is the current use of medical corps veterans as doctor's assistants. These paraprofessionals will be increasingly employed as aides and assistants in schools and hospitals, which so frequently are almost hopelessly undermanned and unmanageable. The use of local citizens in this capacity will reintroduce some degree of community participation and community control in the schools and other public institutions.

The student who participates in a vocational training program differs radically from the student who drops out of high school or college. The dropout is hampered by a feeling of failure and a lack of direction, while the student pursuing a vocational education program has a sense of immediate accomplishment and purpose. He knows what type of work he is being prepared for, and his course of study is intense.

Jobs for Dropouts

Some of the problems faced by the dropout were discussed in the previous chapter. In the decade ahead, millions of young people will be entering a job market which will be shrinking because of automation. In the recent past it apparently took a war, sky-rocketing defense expenditures, a "red scare," or some other questionable set of events to provide the needed jobs. That the middle and late 1970s are perilous and crucial years no one can easily deny. The major problems involved in adolescents aged sixteen and seventeen securing a job include these factors (Sharkey, 1970):

1. Employers frequently feel that youth of this age are too immature and are thus reluctant to hire them.
2. State and federal laws frequently limit the amount and kinds of work these young people can do.
3. About half of the states require work certificates for minors.

4. Employment in certain hazardous jobs are forbidden by law to individuals under eighteen. (The United States bars them from seventeen categories considered to be dangerous.)

5. Lack of experience looms large as a factor.

However, a four-year study has led University of Michigan social scientists to a conclusion contrary to the basic assumptions of American education (*Charlotte Observer*, 1971). There was very little evidence that dropping out of school made things either better or worse. The earlier socialization had already had its major effects upon such variables as self-esteem and self-concept. An interesting secondary finding was that the high school diploma now seemed to make little or no difference in earning potential as compared to dropping out of school before graduation. Clearly, the high school diploma still has some importance, but simply completing high school without further training does not guarantee greater earning potential than dropping out without a diploma. Such studies raise serious questions about the "purposiveness" of many high school curricula (Leonard, 1968).

The number of unemployed young people is greatest in the technologically developed nations. One hopeful avenue, among others, is the increase in vocational training oriented toward contemporary job opportunities, rather than diminishing technical and vocational jobs. There is serious question about really meeting these needs rapidly, without a far larger amount of funds for vocational training than even the recent increase. There is still also the question of any technological society that operates on a free basis offering something approaching full employment, especially for its younger citizens. Many who are critical of our educational and occupational structures have pointed out that one of the functions of education in our society, not only higher education but also secondary, is to keep young people out of the job market because there simply are not enough jobs in our society. The problems are by no means solved, even with the rapid increase in vocational and technical training.

VOCATIONAL GUIDANCE

It has already been pointed out that today's job world has become highly specialized and extremely complex and covers a wide range of occupations. This makes the adolescent's task of selecting the kind of work that he desires to pursue much more difficult than it was when our economy was primarily agricultural. Also, the different jobs require varying amounts and kinds of training. This places a burden upon the schools to try to provide the training that is needed for different kinds of work. There is also the problem of helping students better understand their abilities and characteristics and of providing them with information and experiences about the world of work that will help them make sounder vocational decisions. Thus, the problem of vocational guidance has become extremely important in a modern school program designed for the needs of today's youth.

Need for Vocational Guidance

Choices that have vocational implications must be made during the adolescent years; failure to make a decision during this time is actually a decision by default. Most boys and girls do not have a clear-cut vocational plan and need help in making educational and vocational choices. The vocational-guidance counselor is usually able to help the individual better assess his own aptitudes, characteristics, and needs. In addition, he will be able to furnish information about job requirements, employment opportunities, working conditions, and other matters relating to different jobs or careers.

Although vocational guidance has been assigned to the high school period there is considerable evidence that it takes place over a period of years. Ginzberg and colleagues (1951) identified three periods in the process of occupational choice. The first period is one of fantasy choices and coincides with the early elementary school years. During the adolescent years tentative choices, frequently unrealistic, are made. At this time choices are based largely upon interests with little consideration of the requirements of the occupation. As the individual grows emotionally and mentally he begins to recognize his own assets and limitations and frequently revises his choice more in harmony with his newly recognized abilities as they relate to the requirements of the occupation. Super and Overstreet (1962) conclude from follow-up studies conducted with ninth-grade pupils that it is frequently premature to require ninth-graders to make specific vocational choices. Education at this stage should be concerned with helping pupils make preliminary choices of a broad nature that will "keep as many doors open as possible for as long a time as possible."

Table 12-2 shows the difference between job desire and realities. These data are based upon a study by Kuvlesky and Bealer (1967) in which they completed 1,001 interviews with high school sophomores and interviewed them again ten years later to determine the difference in their job aspirations and their attainment. The results of this study clearly show the need for vocational guidance.

At one time it was generally felt that girls needed very little vocational guidance. The social revolution that has changed the status of women has made it imperative that increased consideration be given to the vocational needs of adolescent girls. Many girls graduate from high school without a vocational skill or vocational plans. Certainly graduating from high school no longer assures any girl that she will be able to secure a satisfying job, although most of them will ultimately be on the labor market.

Table 12-2 Aspirations and Attainments: A Longitudinal Study of Rural Youth

OCCUPATIONAL TYPE	ASPIRATION 1947		ATTAINMENT 1957	
	Number	Percent	Number	Percent
Professional	294	29	147	15
Glamor	81	8	0	0
Managerial	51	5	40	4
White-collar	72	7	181	18
Skilled worker	196	20	163	16
Unskilled worker	93	9	350	35
Farmer	214	22	72	7
Unemployed	—	—	48	5
Total	1,001	100	1,001	100

Source: Kuvlesky and Bealer (1967).

OCCUPATIONAL CHOICES AND OPPORTUNITIES. Occupational choices have been so affected by social factors that they are frequently out of harmony with occupational demands. This becomes evident from a study of choices commonly made by high school boys and girls. The influence of parents on the choice of occupations, discussed earlier, shows that they often have unrealistic expectations of their adolescents. This has created special problems for many adolescents, especially those of average or below average academic aptitude from middle-class homes. While we have observed a continuous increase in college enrollment, there has been enlarged demands for service employees. Consumer and labor statistics show that we are in a full-fledged service economy in the United States. According to Reavy, more than 50 percent, perhaps 60 percent, of the work force, excluding government, is busy supplying services (1973: 220).

Based on the President's *Manpower Report* (1969), prospects for youth are brighter in the professional fields than they are in the ranks of wage earners:

Equally important during the coming decade will be the increased demand for professional and technical workers, in the social as well as natural and engineering sciences. The past two decades have witnessed a heavy concentration of the engineering and natural sciences. The next decade must provide for a sharp rise in physicians, dentists, and other highly qualified health workers. It must also provide for a great increase in scientists and engineers who are both able and willing to serve in the difficult task of rebuilding the cities, developing transportation for the people within them, rescuing the environment from enveloping pollutions that destroy the quality and may, in time, destroy the viability of urban life. The next decade must also provide for the upgrading through training and higher pay of personnel to serve in state and local governments, which currently suffer from severe shortages of workers to serve the public need.

The manpower future is promising for those who have or will achieve the education and training essential for professional and technical jobs. It is promising also for those who achieve the skills necessary for work in clerical jobs and in such burgeoning areas of service as practical nursing. In blue-collar jobs, only those who are able to develop the required skills will find good job opportunities. In the semiskilled trades which have in the past provided great numbers of jobs for people with limited education, a high school education or prior skill training (or both) is likely to be increasingly necessary as the supply of persons with such preparation becomes larger. And all workers, regardless of the level of education, are likely to need continuing education to prepare for the constant changes in jobs that are characteristic of our society (68).

Task of the Counselor

The vocational choice of the adolescent and the task of the counselor has not always been clear. To many counselors and most secondary school teachers, social mobility is a virtue that should be given encouragement. The American dream that if a child works hard he will be able to climb from an underprivileged place on our cultural ladder to a privileged place has infiltrated their thinking. Often boys and girls with the ability and aspirations to move up the socioeconomic ladder become fraustrated because they are stymied in their efforts and blocked by circumstances beyond their control. There are also many boys and girls with good ability, who, with drive and willingness to postpone certain immediate needs and satisfactions, could move into an occupation requiring aptitude or ability and training, but lack the aspirations to make the sacrifices and efforts necessary for such training. Such was the case of James.

> James' father was dead. His mother taught the first grade in a mill village. Since she assisted with the recreational program she was given a comfortable home in which to live without having to pay rent. James was the older of two children. He had access to the family car and learned to play his roles as a boy and a member of the community. His mother was ambitious for him to go on to college after finishing high school. However, none of James' close friends were planning to continue further schooling. James was a better than average student in high school. His ambition, however, was to finish high school, secure a job as a clerk in a store in a nearby town or city, and purchase a sport-model automobile. With some sacrifice and drive on the part of James he could have gone on to college and received additional training for a higher occupational level. Lack of aspirations for additional education prevented James from seeking further training.

The task of the counselor is not that of deciding what James and others should do. Rather it is to help adolescents make sounder decisions in their efforts to solve their problems. Specifically his task may be summarized as follows:

1. To help the adolescent decide to which occupational level he should aspire.

2. To assist teachers in their efforts to help students make sound decisions and arrive at realistic vocational choices.
3. To have a realistic knowledge of the job market and trends and know what is a saleable skill.
4. To help the adolescent discover his own identity and talents and have these fit the job rather than vice versa.

Crises in Vocational Guidance

Many crises now current in the career structure of American society may quickly make obsolete much of the data that has been collected on vocational aspirations, opportunities, and needs of youth emerging into the occupational marketplace. The college degree as a symbol of elitism and upward mobility is increasingly less relevant to the dizzying uncertainties of our work structure. As of 1973, for instance, the recent frantic scramble for admission to college, one of the great traumas for high school seniors, has abated. This trend is not attributable alone to the nation's economic difficulties as the United States moves further into the 1970s. Increasing numbers of high school graduates at that time were deciding not to go to college at all by voluntarily postponing decisions on higher education. Placement services at such prestigious universities as Harvard and Columbia were suggesting to many of their graduating students that they seek alternative forms of employment, learn trades, go to technical school, and explore alternative lifestyles.

Many males postpone a vocational decision either by enlisting or by being drafted into military service. However this is only a stop-gap measure except for those who decide on the armed forces as career. Despite training programs and military experience, veterans are having difficulty in obtaining jobs after they are discharged. They are little more prepared to enter the working force with a salable skill than the high school or college graduate.

Employment Issues, Uncertainty, and Marginality

Any society with an overtrained young elite without sufficient work opportunities is prone to a high degree of instability (see Chapter 18). In technical areas, the young teach the old, and those in such fortunate positions frequently receive preferential treatment with their more recent exposure to newer technological ideas. This is a particular problem in a society which has attempted to create educational elitism as the privilege of many of its young, as has increasingly been the case in the United States in recent years. Thus, working-class youth and educated youth as well have to take positions not equal to their training. Middle-class youth especially, growing up in today's society, do not have the assurance that educational training will provide them with career stability and secure incomes.

Hopper (1965) identifies three areas of employment displacement that are coming about as a result of cybernation. First is the *displacement of numbers*—i.e., fewer people are needed with cybernation. Job displacement is no longer confined to the unskilled and blue-collar workers. It has crept upward and invaded such seemingly invulnerable areas as the highly specialized Ph.D in many fields. Thus, vocational guidance and training must take into account the uncertain employment picture. Sufficient alternatives to traditional trades and professions are simply not emerging rapidly enough to provide full employment for young people throughout the 1970s.

A second area which Hopper discusses is *obsolence*. Individuals may need to be retrained for two or three different jobs or careers in a lifetime. The problem also is compounded by older people in technical fields who have to relearn frequently from younger persons. A third type identified by Hopper is *displacement "through the unwitting undermining of the basic cultural values which make sense of the human drama"* (321).

SUMMARY

Work situations and the meaning of work are changing rapidly for adolescents. The Industrial Revolution and the technological-cybernetic revolution caused extended periods of education for young people and have also divorced work situations from the homes and daily life. There is an increasing reliance upon the educational institution, rather than parental example, to train and guide young people in their choice of vocation and career.

The vocational aspirations of adolescence are related to their own self-concept and also to their total background of experience. Education, prestige occupations, ability, and opportunity are not the same for all adolescents. Vocational aspirations are related to a number of factors and conditions. One of the strongest influences is the adolescent's relationship with his family, especially with his father. Fathers tend to suggest careers for their sons that will boost them above their parents' level. An adolescent's concept of self is another important variable. Those who have high scholastic achievement in high school tend to aspire to a higher level of occupational attainment than those whose high school record is poor. Of course, the availability of jobs is a deciding factor.

Many teen-agers are employed, some full-time, most part-time, in conjunction with high school education. The kinds of jobs which teen-agers are able to get depend upon the nature of the community and such variables as age, sex, and social class. Even part-time work supplies important functions for adolescents. The developmental tasks that gainful employment helps accomplish are a feeling of independence, a feeling of maturity, improved relations with family and parents, and status with peers.

The diversification and increase in potential career opportunities offer a growing variety of employment choices for young people in our society. However, there are so very many highly specialized jobs that adolescents need occupational and vocational guidance. This applies also to girls, who are increasingly entering careers formerly reserved for males. Upward mobility jobs have been supported by parents and their children alike for at least the past three generations in this country. For many adolescents aspirations and opportunities to fulfill them do not always coincide. The attitudes and values that young people have towards work is an important variable. The social position and the educational level of an adolescent's father bears a direct relationship to the first job that an adolescent has.

It is estimated that half of all jobs opening up in the 1970s will require training beyond high school but less than four years of college. As college degrees come to offer less job security, many young people may begin to look for technical or vocational education as an avenue for growth and work. Vocational guidance is needed by adolescents as today's job world becomes more and more specialized and complex. One thing that must be considered is the difference between a young person's desire for a job, the realities of the job market, and the chance of his attaining his aspiration. The counselor has several important functions. Among these are to help the adolescent decide which occupational level he should try to attain, gain a realistic knowledge of the job market in order to have a salable skill, and discover his own identity and talents and in order to fit these to a job. Intelligence and aptitude tests are very useful in this effort; interest inventories have been widely used in recent years.

The high school diploma is no longer a ticket to success on today's job market. The qualitative choice for us today is whether we can offer our youth positive choices of values and careers. The teacher is an important influence in the adolescent's educational and vocational expectations and aspirations.

REFERENCES

Charlotte Observer (November 7, 1971), p. 5c. "High School Diploma Not Vital."

COHEN, E. G. "Parental Factors in Educational Mobility." *Social Education* (1965), 38:407–25.

CRITES, J. O. "Parental Identification in Relation to Vocational Interest Development." *Journal of Educational Psychology* (1962), 53:262–70.

DURKHEIM, EMILE. *Division of Labor in Society.* New York: The Free Press, 1947.

Gastonia Gazette (February 24, 1971), p. 2A.

GINZBERG, E., S. W. GINSBERG, S. AXELRAD, and J. L. HERMA. *Occupational Choice and Approach to a General Theory.* New York: Columbia University Press, 1951.

HOPPER, REX. "Cybernation, Marginality, and Revolution." In *The New Sociology,* I. L. Horowitz, ed. New York: Oxford University Press, 1965.

KORMAN, A. K. "Self-esteem as a Moderator of the Relationship Between Self-perceived Abilities and Vocational Choice." *Journal of Applied Psychology* (1967), 51:65–67.

KRIPPNER, STANLEY. "Junior High School Students' Vocational Preferences and Their Parental Occupational Levels." *Personnel and Guidance Journal* (1963), 41:590–95.

KUVLESKY, WILLIAM P. and ROBERT C. BEALER. "The Relevance of Adolescents' Occupational Aspirations for Subsequent Job Attainments." *Rural Sociology* (1967), 32:290–301.

LEONARD, GEORGE B. *Education and Ecstasy.* New York: Delacorte Press, 1968.

Manpower Report of the President. Washington: U.S. Department of Labor, 1969.

New Republic (October 28, 1972), p. 4. "U.S. Census Figures on Adult Median Education."

Parade magazine (December 13, 1970), p. 12. "Keeping Up with Youth."

Parade magazine (March 31, 1974), p. 26. "Keeping Up with Youth."

PERELLA, VERA C. "Working Teenagers." *Children Today* (May–June 1972), 1 (3):14–17.

REAVY, EDWARD P. "Business Communications Needs." *Vital Speech of the Day* (1973), 39 (7):219–62.

SCALES, ELDRIDGE E. and PERCIVAL M. HUTSON. "How Gainful Employment Affects the Accomplishment of Developmental Tasks of Adolescent Boys." *School Review* (1955), 63:31–37.

SHARKEY, SAMUEL. "Jobs for Dropouts Are Disappearing Fast." *Charlotte Observer* (December 6, 1970), p. 3-B.

SOROKIN, PITIRIM. *The Crisis of Our Age: The Social and Cultural Outlook.* New York: E. P. Dutton & Co., Inc., 1941.

SUPER, DONALD E. and P. L. OVERSTREET, in collaboration with C. N. MORRIS, W. DUBLIN, and M. B. HEYDE. *The Vocational Maturity of Ninth-Grade Boys.* Career Pattern Study Monograph Two. New York: Bureau of Publications, Teachers College, Columbia University, 1962.

RECOMMENDED READINGS

BERNARD, HAROLD W. *Adolescent Development.* Scranton, Pa.: Intext Educational Publishers, 1971. Chapter 16.
The author deals with occupations and opportunities as they relate to occupational choices of adolescents. The lack of orientation of many high schools to the vocational needs of adolescents is emphasized. Special attention is given to vocational trends and their implications for vocational choices.

HORROCKS, JOHN E. *The Psychology of Adolescence.* 3rd ed. Boston: Houghton Mifflin Company, 1969. Chapter 25.
Special consideration is given to the adolescent's need to make a vocational choice and to the vocational aspirations of adolescents. Data are presented on factors that influence vocational choice and vocational development. Present and future perspectives of employment opportunities are presented.

National Association of Secondary School Principals Bulletin (1969), 53. "Idea
Forum: IV."
The entire issue deals with problems of occupations and vocational
education. Four very significant topics are (1) the potential for vocational
education, (2) occupational preparation in the secondary school, (3) economic analysis of youth employment, and (4) some characteristics of high-
ability dropouts.

SHERTZER, BRUCE and SHELLEY C. STONE, eds. *Introduction to Guidance: Selected
Readings.* Boston: Houghton Mifflin Company, 1970. Pp. 303–76.
These readings consist of ten articles bearing on vocational counseling and
career development.

TERKEL, STUDS. *Working.* New York: Pantheon Press, 1974.
This book, based on many interviews, corroborates the assumption than
most people are not happy with their jobs.

VANN, G. "Occupational Education for Everyone." *National Association of
Secondary School Principals Bulletin* (1968), 52:112–22.
The author advocates vocational programs especially designed to help
the horde of dropouts find a place in the work force. He points out that
many of these adolescents lack realistic work goals. Schools, he states,
should give occupational orientation and guidance to students and cooperate with business and industry in providing work-experience programs.

part four

Contemporary Issues and Problems

Part 4 centers on the problems of the alienated segment of our population that has failed to find a place for itself in the mainstream of our society. This notion is supported in the statistics from our courts, dropouts from school, runaways, teen-age suicides, public welfare case loads, youth on drugs, unmarried pregnant teen-agers, and the many chronic or sporadically underemployed or unemployed.

According to Brown there are five social pressures that make for alienation in the youth of today. They are: (1) the trend toward urbanization, (2) the drive to succeed, (3) the concept of "fit," (4) the egalitarian thrust, and (5) the absence of "caring."[1]

The revolutionary change from rural to urban living has deprived adolescents of the opportunity and necessity for close personal relationships with adult models. They have been pressed into their own age groups, while the period of adolescence has been continuously extended. They are unable to establish their independence through work opportunities, since they must remain in school and under adult domination. They are told that continued education is the one way to enhance their chances of success—and succeed they must.

The problems of adolescents are not a result of their own actions. We have studied many postadolescents in college, and our observations, borne out by scientific studies, reveal that adolescent problems are very complex. They have their roots in the social and cultural order, and they cannot be dismissed as the "sins" of lack of discipline or immaturity.

[1] William Neal Brown, "Alienated Youth," *Mental Hygiene* (1968) 52:330–36.

13

societal change and adolescent uncertainties

Adolescence is an especially turbulent period of life in societies that seemingly make the adolescent a "marginal man," societies that continuously postpone adult status for their children and the responsibilities that go with it. In addition to the adjustment problems created by the coming of age, there is also the array of problems created by a rapidly changing society in which many past behavior patterns are inappropriate.

The problems of adolescent adjustment are multiple and complex such as postindustrial society, the elimination of the extended family, the rate of societal change, affluency and poverty, the failure of the homes and schools to keep up with and meet the challenges of the new era, the declining role of the church, materialism, the exposure of adult hypocrisy, legal and political injustices, nuclear war, and the Vietnam War. Concerning this condition Allport offers a pointed comment:

> No longer can youth contemplate its future under the protection of the great social stabilizers of the past. No longer can one counsel within the

328   Contemporary Issues and Problems

framework of the Victorian decorum, theological certainties, or the Pax
Britannia. . . . The comfortable stabilities of culture, caste, the gold
standard, and military supremacy are no longer ours (1965: 18).

CREATING A TECHNOLOGICAL STATE

If there is one constant in the process of development, that constant
is the ubiquitousness of *change*. In traditional societies, the rate of
change is slow and visible only over long periods of time. The seasons
change, but life is cyclical and spring returns annually. Every society, of
course, is subject to calamities—natural disasters, disease, invasion by
another society—but, apart from these, the values and life styles of the
young follow very much the pattern of their elders. Time moves slowly,
and the horizon is the next village. In some primitive societies, the
horizon may not even extend to the next village, as with the Stone Age
society that was discovered in 1971 in the Philippines.

Societies undergoing industrial and technological development cannot escape rapid change. Shifts in values, clashes between traditional
definitions and newer definitions, changes in life styles, roles, and statuses
are everywhere present as the society reorients itself to meet the impact
of industry and technology.

Change, Uncertainty, and Instability

The United States has gone through this process more thoroughly than
any other contemporary society. The United States has been a visibly
changing society ever since the first highly dispersed and highly diversified Europeans settled on the East Coast. However, until the present
century, village, town, county, and state ties were able to provide a sense
of order and continuity. Even the Civil War of the 1860s could not
destroy this sense of continuity, but rather, as wars generally do, resulted
in reinforcing local and regional traditions and mythologies. However,
the recently accelerated rates of industrial and technological change in
this century have destroyed tradition and created discontinuities. Increasingly, time has become more compressed and the horizon has receded
from Richmond or New York City to the Moon and Mars.

The three tables compiled from data in Fabun's *The Children of
Change* (1968) illustrate this increased rate of social change and its attendant consequences in social discontinuity. Fabun attempts to order
the experiences of four recently discrete age groups in American society
around differential technological statistics, imprints, and inputs when
they were children, adolescents, and young adults. Fabun concentrates
upon leadership elites and middle-class Americans and others who shared
and participated in the national style of that era, and the effects of the
communications media of their time. Those in more isolated communities
may have received a tardy awareness of the statistics and inputs, but the
descriptions are valuable in defining the nearest thing to a national

Weltanschauung, or world view, for many Americans born during that period.

Group I consists of those Americans still living who were born around 1896. In the 1970s, this would be the equivalent of the tribal elders in a traditional society, the European American equivalent of Black Elk, the famous Oglala Sioux who saw the entire span of white encroachment upon plains Indian society. European tribal elders born at the turn of the century are still living in the 1970s and have some degree of influence in Congress, news media, publishing, and corporations. Theirs was a world of certainty and security, compared with the experiences and influences on Groups II, III, and IV. Authority was still thoroughly generational, although the traditional bases of authority were beginning to weaken. The cluster of Americans born around 1896 had no telephones, radios, or television sets. They had no automobiles. Their films carried traditional values forward. As Fabun cites, *Quo Vadis* (1913) and *Birth of a Nation* (1914) reaffirmed a stable past and a degree of continuity. That generation also provides us with a romanticized, inaccessible past when "things were much simpler" and an opportunity to understand what is genuinely worthwhile in the past; it is enabling us to refocus our own contemporary presence in accelerated change, much as figures similar to Black Elk are doing currently for young Indians.

Group II is composed of individuals now in their late 50s and represents the Establishment. This was the generation of Manifest Destiny, and it grew up believing in the doctrine of economic progress. Utopia was always "just around the corner," and its achievement was simply a matter of increased American technological expertise. Truth had already been weakened, however; it was not something already established by divine sanction. Instead, substitutes for divine sanction were now interwoven with nationalistic patriotism. Human nature, especially if it was American human nature, and nationalistic pride had all the answers. Americans could do anything. However, this was disturbed by the experiences of the Depression, World War II, and the Cold War.

Group III experienced the acceleration of change; however, they were caught between the older values of nationalistic or religious certainty and the newer values of economic and technological change for its own sake, change that was good in itself. Technological determinism came to be embraced as a normative order. Progress for progress' sake became a tentative norm.

Group IV, those born between 1945 and 1951, represent the generational revolt in the 1960s, which has continued through the early part of the 1970s. This is the television generation which has experienced the *real* impact of depersonalized life, extreme mobility, the semblance of a runaway technology, and the fear that such runaway technology, if extended on a global scale, will lead to universal bewilderment and the potential annihilation of mankind.

TABLE 13-1 What Kind of a World Was It?

	WHEN GROUP I WAS BORN (ca. 1896)	WHEN GROUP II WAS TEN (ca. 1924)	WHEN GROUP III WAS FOUR (ca. 1941)	WHEN GROUP IV WAS FIVE (ca. 1953)
U.S. population	66,970,000	114,113,000	133,402,000	159,636,000
Gross National Product	$13,600,000,000	$87,600,000,000	$125,800,000,000	$365,400,000,000
Price Index (1929 = 100)	46	99	91	170
Motor vehicles	—	7,612,940	34,849,134	56,221,089
Telephones/1,000 pop.	5.7	139.7	175	312.7
Families owning radio sets	—	1,250,000	29,300,000	44,800,000
Families owning television sets	—	—	—	20,400,000
Productivity/man hour (1929 = 100)	49.5	91.7	134.6	190.9
Power input (horsepower)	65,045,000	459,000,000	2,759,018,000	5,726,886,000

Source: Fabun, The Children of Change (Beverly Hills, Calif.: Glencoe Press, 1968), pp. 18–20.

TABLE 13-2 Imprints: What Their *Parents* Were Talking About When They Were Ages 1–7

GROUP I (b. ca. 1896)	GROUP II (b. ca. 1914)	GROUP III (b. 1935–42)	GROUP IV (b. 1945–51)
God's in his heaven; all's right with the world. Truth has already been established. It is simply a matter of transmitting it to the young. Man, through his rationality, can solve *all* problems. Authority was vested in the elders. Of concern to *parents* was the Spanish-American war, the South African (Boer) War, the Filipino War, the Boxer Rebellion in China, the Cuban Revolution, and the assassination of President McKinley. Stirring times.	Their parents were filled with the wave of nationalism and pride that followed America's participation in World War I. Parents' concerns: Mexican Revolution with Pancho Villa, Gen. Pershing in pursuit; Amundsen reached North Pole. Scott reached South Pole. First transcontinental airplane flight. S.S. *Titanic* sank. Chinese Revolution under Sun Yat-Sen overthrew Manchu dynasty. Income tax authorized. Panama Canal opened. World War I. The I.W.W. Prohibition law passed. Russian Revolution began. Influenza epidemic killed 20 million people, including 548,000 Americans. They talked much about the war, America's role in it, and their own parts. They did this while playing "500" and Mah-Jongg while the kids (Group II) "slept" on the day-beds and drank it all in.	Parents still caught up in the Depression (in 1935). Largely preoccupied with jobs, money, material acquisition. Some things were better, due to war contracts around the world, in Morocco, Ethiopia, Spain, China, and Europe, creating demand for American goods. Parents had romanticized American role in World War I, though isolationism persisted. But involvement increased. Parents talked about the loss of Amelia Earhart; sinking of U.S. gunboat *Panay* by Japanese; nationalization of Mexico's oil industry; world's first surviving quintuplets; killing of John Dillinger; New York World's Fair. Parental emphasis still on thrift and saving. Tin and aluminum foil, grease, and paper were saved. Although the "enemy" had no aircraft capable of flying either the Pacific or Atlantic, children were instructed in air-raid procedures, and coastal cities were blacked out.	Parents and grandparents had survived two world wars and the Depression. Parents enjoyed new affluence, brought about by application of rapidly advancing industrial technology. Family problem was still money, but in different context: not whether there was any, but how best to spend it. Contemporary events that parents talked about in presence of children were signing of Korean War armistice, death of Stalin, Mt. Everest climbed; Russia's H-bomb ten years ahead of time, the McCarthy hearings, the fall of Dien Bien Phu (although its relevance to future of Group IV children in the U.S. was not then apparent). Sputnik I was launched in 1957. Although few saw its significance then, Sputnik was to profoundly influence the American educational system, by turning its emphasis from the humanities to science and technology. By time Group IV entered college, this had become an important point.

Source: Fabun, 1968: 18–21.

TABLE 13-3 Inputs: Experiences of Each Group During Their Growing Years

GROUP I (b. ca. 1896)	GROUP II (b. ca. 1914)	GROUP III (b. 1935–42)	GROUP IV (b. 1945–51)
See items under *Imprints* for Group II. Group I was especially influenced by the first transcontinental airplane flight and, mostly, by participation in World War I and the fervor of American nationalism. *Over There.* The stars in their galaxy were Sara Bernhardt, Florenz Ziegfield and Rudolph Valentino. The big pictures were *Ben Hur* (1907, 16 scenes), *Quo Vadis* (1913) and *Birth of a Nation* (1914). The first time they heard sound with a motion picture was in *Don Juan* (1926). The cartoons they read in their newspapers were "Little Nemo," "Old Doc Yak," and "Col. Heeza Liar." Popular cartoons with more polished techniques were "The Katzenjammer Kids," "Krazy Kat," and "Mutt and Jeff."	Group II's inputs included the automobile (increasing mobility, privacy, and sexual freedom), radio (breaking down provincial restraints on information); most of all the Depression and some kind of participation in World War II. Concerns were strongly economic. The *Sat. Even. Post* furnished input for nonintellectuals. "Tugboat Annie," "Tutt & Mr. Tutt," Chief Engineer Glencannon, *S.S. Inchcliffe Castle,* etc. reinforced American mythology. Mom's Apple Pie. Cigar-smoking monkeys. Everything fiercely patriotic. Heroes: Wylie Post, Will Rogers, Amelia Earhart, Schoolboy Roe, Lou Gehrig. Fourth of July parades, flags waving, picnics in the park. *The Grapes of Wrath* (1940) with unforeseen implications at the time, James Stewart, *The Philadelphia Story.* Ginger Rogers, *Kitty Foyle,* and *Rebecca.* F. D. R. and Wendell Wilkie's "One World" in 1940. An old-timey sort of world suddenly shattered at Pearl Harbor, and Group II discovered an Asia different from that in *The Mikado.* The experience was traumatic.	Radio and Saturday afternoon matinees constituted most of the educational input for this group. Roy Rogers, Gene Autry, Hopalong Cassidy, and the Cisco Kid were film heroes. The cowboy image, as created by Hollywood script writers, was very strong, e.g., Gary Cooper, *High Noon.* Television did not significantly influence this group. The Korean War and prospects of military service did. The Bomb, and then the Bigger Bomb, the ICBM's, the Cold War, the McCarthy hearings were all realities for teen-age minds. Comic books formed the fantasies for many youngsters; the "good guy," "bad guy," mythology of the parents was reinforced. There was little questioning of the values of American society, either in the schools or out of them. The mass movement of the more affluent out of the cities and into the suburbs created little enclaves of people of the same race, age group, and economic and educational background. For the next twenty years, this is the group to watch. Isolation and alienation had begun, and it	The TV generation. TV was the baby-sitter, mother, father, and teacher. Differed in becoming the first mass medium, audio-visually, to "tell it like it is," relatively unedited. Sometimes fantasized in movies and commercials. But sometimes highly *real* and *now.* What was taught in school appeared to some so irrelevant that some quit. Entire experience of Group III has been the Age of the Bomb, television, Vietnam, space exploration, nuclear energy, jet transport, computerized technology, urban and suburban change, public awareness of poverty and racism; most of all, a world order dominated through institutions by Group II leaders in the form of a military-industrial complex of political and economic forces in which they have no voice. When they try to change "The System," they find themselves confronted by the Establishment. Some keep trying. Some drop out. Some don't care. Group IV knows it will inherit the System. The question it asks is whether it wants to. Group IV fed on the transistorized, street

Group II never re-
covered. The "Cold
War" was part of
the result. Someplace
in there, a Bomb
went off. It was
Group II's bomb.
It is mainly against
Group II, now in
their fifties, that
Group IV have been
directing their hos-
tility and vice versa
in the 1960s and
1970s.

mostly affected
Group III.

radio, on informa-
tion-songs of protest,
nonfiltered words
and images—not the
type likely to be
found in the class-
room.

The graphic descriptions of the three tables, arranged in terms of differential contact with a culture, illustrate the extensiveness of the difficulty in reconstructing a given set of values and norms appropriate to contemporary societal problems. A *fourth* table deals with experiences of youth emerging into the adolescent subculture in the early 1970s.

Acceleration of Change

The "triple revolution" of cybernation, weaponry, and human rights was coined as a term to describe our human dilemma some years ago. Now, we see that this triple revolution is compounded by the problems of population control and pollution.

Anyway, it's good to know that over there is civilization with all its problems.

TABLE 13-4 Experiences of Group V: Tentative Observations on the Emerging Adolescents of the Early Seventies, Born *ca.* 1958–60.

THE WORLD WHEN THEY WERE BORN

1960		1970
80,684,000	U.S. population	204,351,000
$503 billion	G.N.P.	$932.2 billion*
198	Price Index	(1929 = 1000)
73,869,000	Motor vehicles	104,702,000*
408	Telephones/1000	563*
50,000,000	Families: Radios	62,500,000
45,500,000	Families: TV Sets	619,000,000 black and white
11,008,000,000	Man hour productivity	24,000,000 color
	power input (HP)	18,781,000*

IMPRINTS FROM THEIR PARENTS, AT AGES 1–7	INPUTS FOR GROUP V, ca. AGE 14, (EARLY 1970s)

Parents had grown up with change defined as progress. A New Frontier President asked "not what your country can do for you, but what you can do for your country." First Roman Catholic President, showing how the U.S. has changed since the 1920s. His opponent, Richard Nixon, defeated by the presidential TV debates in 1960, later was defeated as candidate for governor of California and publicly retired from political life, blaming the press.

By the early 1960s, public uncertainties broke through earlier masks of optimism. Cuban missile showdown. Civil Rights Movement began. Parents chose sides. Young parents in this cohort began to question problems of defining "the good life" in consumption terms. Some of them were young enough to be involved in the activist movements of the 60s. 1963: Assassination of President Kennedy. Demise of youthful, charismatic image of presidential leadership. 1964: Presidential choice was between a liberal "wheeler and dealer" (as perceived) and an extreme conservative who, Democrats accused, would involve the U.S. increasingly in Vietnam if he were elected. Confusion mounted, and children could watch it all on TV.

Inputs for this cohort include the credit card; manned lunar landings; violent dissent and repression of some of their older brothers and sisters, environmental and population crises, and a general sense of societal uncertainty. On TV or in family discussions, they knew of black youth confronting older whites; white youth confronting older whites and police on issues of war and peace, education, and technology. They saw their older brothers chastized for long locks (while parents were critical or letting their hair grow). This generation knew about marijuana and some had tried it before age fourteen. 1968: Robert Kennedy and Martin Luther King assassinated. They learned about My Lai, public confusion on Vietnam, distinctiveness of then-current youth dress terms like "hippie" and "pig," and were exposed to activism, Zap comics, and ideas from varieties of religious movements and gurus. They heard some speak of the state of the world in apocalyptic terms especially about the environment and developed economics. Would the young "turn off" to consumption? First peacetime freeze on prices and wages in U.S. history in 1971. Parents were as confused as they. Not especially happy with an uncertain world of overbombardment from media and other influences of potential identity-choices, they weren't quite sure what it would mean to reach their teens. With increased societal confusion would come greater susceptibility for these emergent young people to sporadic youth.

* 1969 statistic

"Future shock," as Toffler (1970) defines it, is the distress resulting from an overload of both physical and psychological stimuli (290). He notes in his discussion of future shock what has been noted generally in other studies: the rate of change in a person's life is closely related to his state of health (293). Being forced to adapt to a high rate of change is correlated with a high rate of illness. Toffler discusses four forms of maladaptation by the victims of future shock.

1. *Denial.* This involves blocking out new information and refusing to accept the evidence. The denier, when finally forced to adapt, probably will face a massive life-crisis.

2. *Specialism.* The strategy here is to keep pace with change in one area and block out the rest. Stay within one's own sphere and forget the changes in others, for it is too complex to deal with the whole spectrum of unrelated changes. The danger here is that one may find that change elsewhere has transformed one's own specialism.

3. *Obsessive reversion.* In this instance, one returns to previous, now mal-adaptive patterns. One attempts to reinstate the past unrealistically.

4. *Super-simplification.* In the extreme of this, one grasps at each new idea or guru in an attempt to resocialize around the perceived simplicity of that idea, sometimes embarrassing more modest gurus in the process. In super-simplification, the quest is for a unitary solution to one's abrupt contact with change. One dances from activism to withdrawal to re-ligion to one guru, another guru, and so on (1970: 319–21).

Toffler traces the pathology of society to the "uncontrollable, non-selective nature of our lunge into the future" (325). However, in his strategy for the future, Toffler finds himself, as with Slater, highly tenta-tive. It is much easier to describe a problem than to offer alternatives, apart from charismatic or traditional involvement in the authority of an intense religious or social movement (which may happen, as indicated later in this chapter, if chaos increases in our contemporary world). The experience of transience or of the breakdown of a unified culture itself is a culture-bound phenomenon. Inevitably, many of the suggestions for preparing for the future involve a degree of exhortation and preaching, in terms of the author's own personal interests or suggestions. There are some areas in which Toffler is especially helpful, however, and some of these might be suggested here as they apply to youth of technological societies.

NEED FOR ADAPTATION. Toffler suggests, for instance, that within the system of learning, young and old must now be taught how to *adapt.* Once "transience" is recognized as a source of alienation, we can create situations which allow more people to accept the absence of deep friend-ships or to accelerate friendship-formation (367). Toffler suggests also that we need to provide "advance information about what lies ahead" in order to help individuals to adapt better (371). If societies anticipate change and incorporate the expectation of it their child-rearing, they have a much better chance of adapting with their culture relatively intact. Mead states "The greater the expectation of change, the less disruptive introduced configurations are likely to be" (1970: 56). The degree to which man has responded irrationally in the past to situations of transience leads some to think that humanistic, utopian projections for the future may only be tenuous possibilities at best.

In any event, in terms of the critiques of contemporary, technological, and determined societies offered by Toffler, Slater does succeed in isolating some important problems. There are those who, in fact, suggest that "development" is an improper concept to describe the growth of a tecnological society. Paul and Anna Ehrlich (1970), for instance, have used the term "overdevelopment" to describe the United States, Canada, Western Europe, the Soviet Union, Japan, Australia, New Zealand, and some other smaller nations which have already undergone a high degree of technological development. The Ehrlichs contend that such nations should undergo a process of "de-development."

The British historian, Arnold Toynbee, discusses the following present concerns of the middle 1970s through the early 1980s.

> Can anything be predicted now with any confidence? Two things, at least, do seem probable: Within the next 10 years the population explosion is going to continue, especially in the "developing" countries, and, during these same 10 years, the price of our technological advance is going to rise so steeply that it may become manifestly prohibitive. The price has to be paid in terms of loss of health and happiness. . . . Technology does produce wealth and power beyond our grandparents' dreams, but we, their grandchildren, are now asking ourselves whether the price, in nonmaterial terms, is going to be higher than we can afford. . . . Air, earth, and water, including the deep sea, are already being polluted to a degree at which we are being poisoned. At the same time, the nature of the mechanized work, which is poisoning us physically, is making us unhappy, discontented, rebellious and violent. . . .
>
> Every generation, and every individual, inherits the burden of Karma, the consequences of earlier action. We have it in our power either to mitigate our inherited Karma or to aggravate it, but we cannot jump clear of it, and we ignore it at our peril. We cannot transform this polluted and distracted world into Amida's "pure land", but this unattainable ideal can inspire us to exert ourselves to leave our impure world less impure than we have found it when we have taken over the burden of Karma from our predecessors. This is a modest objective, but, if the rising generation achieves it, it will have done a great service to itself and its descendents (1971: 3-M).

DILEMMA CREATED BY TECHNOLOGY. Slater (1970) describes three human desires as being deeply and uniquely frustrated by American culture. These are as follows:

1. the desire for *community*, frustrated by *competition;*
2. the desire for *engagement*, frustrated by *uninvolvement;*
3. the desire for *dependence*, frustrated by *independence.*

He discusses all of these in terms of the "Toilet Assumption" of American society. He describes the toilet assumption as

> a notion/that unwanted matter, unwanted difficulties, unwanted complexities and obstacles should disappear and be removed from our immediate field of vision (15).

Trash thrown from a car window is not associated with trash in the street; replacing old buildings with new, expensive ones alleviates poverty in the slums; throwing the aged and psychotic into institutional holes decreases their visibility: out of sight, out of mind. Everything unpleasant, Slater contends, including a riot, a generational conflict, a sewage problem, or any other problem which we have decided to ignore, and which we cannot deal with makes us react with an unusual degree of violence and anger until we "wish it away" again. Slater, for instance, applies this assumption to the depersonalized nature of killing in modern warfare. Phrases used in the war in Vietnam such as "wasting a village" reflect the toilet assumptions of modern technological warfare as well as our domestic assumptions on ghettoes and sewage. These mechanisms, Slater contends, are very much "core" American phenomena, although they are spreading to other societies. They can be seen in suburban life styles and architecture, the immaculately "unreal" self-service discount store, the automobile, and other expressions which substitute for personal involvement.

The dilemmas of dealing with technology are not limited to any one country. Slater states that

> the Soviet Union and other planned economies are as enslaved as we. . . . Technology makes core policy in every industrialized nation, and the humans adjust as best they can (46).

However, Slater contends that the American heritage of individualism compounds the problem.

> . . . Individualism finds its roots in the attempt to deny the reality and importance of human interdependence. One of the major goals of technology in America is to "free" us from the necessity of relating to, submitting to, depending upon, or controlling other people. Unfortunately, the more we have succeeded in doing this, the more we have felt disconnected, bored, lonely, unprotected, unnecessary, and unsafe (26).

Individualism and individuality are, of course, two quite different things, much as uniformity and community are two quite different phenomena, as will be noted again later in this chapter.

THE UNCERTAINTIES OF TECHNOLOGY-BASED FUTURISM. The concept of "transience," resulting from our continuous contact with technological change, differentiates the situation of contemporary man from the past, Toffler contends (42). Certainly, transience has been experienced by man many times in the past. As noted earlier, transience is found in traditional societies that face natural calamities, invasion, or innovation. Societies have been uprooted in the past. However, for the survivors of calamity or invasion, transience is replaced with order over time. It may be an order unwillfully imposed, as in the case of black slaves coming to the United States from diverse cultures to be "reordered" according to the needs of eighteenth-century white American settlers; it may, on the other hand, involve a rewarding basis, even among slaves, such as the case of the Ottoman Turks and the Romans "winning over" their Greek slaves by providing alternative rewards and status privileges in their armies and in civil positions in return for accepting their culture.

The difference, Toffler argues, between today and much of the past is the contemporary acceptance of a technologically based futurism and its accompanying uncertainty. The invention of the wheel and the printing press and other comparable "breakthroughs" in the past may have greatly influenced societal developments and changes, but they did not dramatically reinforce or introduce *transience as a way of life*. Margaret Mead (1970) contends that the present generation of adolescents is totally new and is growing up in a world that its parents never knew. Technology has so completely changed the behavior and thought patterns of adolescents that they cannot experience what their parents experienced and vice versa. She continues, "In the past there were always some elders who knew more than any children in terms of their experience of having grown up within a cultural system. Today there are none" (78).

This leaves adolescents with no guide or sense of continuity with the past. The experiences of the 1920s, 30s, 40s are ancient and not applicable. They have no relevance to today's youth. "The more things change, the more they stay the same" no longer applies to adolescents who find the past a failure and face the future with equal dismay. With no patterns to fall back on, the young face change qua change.

A fictional report of the Department of Population and Environment to the President of the United States, January 1, 2000, is of interest. The prognosis, alarmist or not, is worthy of citation (Ehrlichs, 1970: 245):

> This is the first report of the Department in which the prognosis for the United States is mildly positive. In spite of this, a cautionary note must be added. In the national press there has been some comment to the effect that the environmental and public health disasters of the 1970s and 1980s were the result of "bad luck" or "Acts of God." As you know, Mr. President, if we had any luck it was good—for with bad luck the famines, disease, and competition for resources could have precipitated a thermonuclear war. It is only because most of the physical apparatus and records of our culture survived intact that recovery to the present point has been possible. We now can say with certainty that a major thermonuclear war in the 1970s or 1980s would have ended civilization permanently.
>
> The Department urges you to remind our citizens that all of the trends leading to disaster were clear twenty years before the end came, and that

we and the rest of mankind did nothing substantive to avert it. As a single example, the vulnerability of the world population to epidemic disease, due to large population size (overcrowding), hunger and environmental deterioration was repeatedly pointed out by scientists. No substantial action was taken to correct the situation by a nation addicted to economic growth and ignorant of the limits of technology.

The cost of inaction, apathy, and unwarranted optimism has been the payment of nearly four billion human lives over a fifteen-year period— and we are still paying. We cannot permit a repetition of such a disaster. Mr. President, it is imperative that this generation and those to follow be kept mindful of mankind's recent history.

> Respectfully submitted,
> (Signed)
> L. PAGE KENNEDY
> Secretary

Certainly the Ehrlichs and others have their counterparts in the technological optimists—e.g., Richard H. Meier of the University of California, Berkeley, who, in his publications on technological solutions, at least up to 1971, was confident that he and other physical and social scientists "have the technological answers." In a lengthy conversation with the junior author (1971), he stated with great confidence and optimism that technology can and *will* solve all the problems posed by technological development, including diminishing natural recources and population pressures, because *theoretically* it is possible. However, the concept of "cultural lag" may also apply, in some form, to technology, with the accelerated rate of resource-depletion and overcrowding, as well as with the tensions of uncertainty and transience it has created. If technological crises occur on acute societal scales, the timelag between the crises and the solutions may be too great to prevent catastrophies. Cultural lag was a term once used to describe the difficulties of values and institutions in keeping up with technological change.

Man usually responds to change only when the situation approaches crisis proportions. Order and the status quo are man's normal orientation. Other societies have responded only when the potential destructiveness of change has led to acute crises. They collapsed because of cultural lag, and they could not make the sudden necessary imaginative leap soon enough. Are we different, in allowing technology to plot much of its own course and development in the same indiscriminate way?

The prognosis of the Ehrlichs and others like them cannot be ignored, since the Ehrlichs are eminent scientists and not laymen in their fields. However, the layman's fear of the future must be taken seriously, what with the evidence of societal disintegration offered by Slater, Toffler, and others, as they view the current upheavals and tensions among many adults as well as adolescents.

TECHNOLOGICAL DETERMINISM
AND ORDER

Earlier Forecasts of Technological
Determinism

In 1941 Pitirim Sorokin foresaw the crisis of meaning engendered by technological change. In *The Crisis of Our Age,* he correctly predicted that technology would accelerate what he termed as the already existing "sensate culture" with its high degree of individualism to a point of near normlessness over perhaps a thirty-year period, from 1941 to 1971. He stated that this culture would break up with violence and chaos. Among other signs of disillusionment with technological determinism and the sensate culture, there would be the turning away from technological careers by the brighter young leaders who would concentrate on studies in the humanities, philosophy, and art. He predicted that the disenchantment with the older culture would lead to the emergence of a new "ideational" or "Faith" culture.

ACCEPTANCE—THE END OF IDEOLOGY? Daniel Bell in *The End of Ideology* (1962) pointed to a world in which we would have to learn to live with change as a constant and without deep-rooted causes or ideologies in the future. In *The Uncommitted* (1965) Kenneth Keniston dealt with the same issues as they related to youth. He foresaw the possibility of noncommitment as a way of life for many young people who are growing up in an increasingly technological society. Both viewed technological determinism as mitigating against idealism and vision. But can we develop a nation of uncommitted adolescents? It is well known that many causes come to naught when there is no commitment. Adolescence are characterized by their *idealism.* Perhaps the greatest difficulty faced by adolescents lies in the uncertainties of the time and the lack of commitment to a cause. Can we develop a society committed to human values rather than material values? This presents a challenge to education and different religious forces. It seems that many youth groups in our colleges are reexamining our universal values; they are restudying the purpose of life; and they are quite willing to throw aside many traditions and established beliefs in order to arrive at what seems to them a better answer to present-day problems.

There were some in the 1950s and 1960s who foresaw the acceleration of change and the spread of technological determinism. They predicted there would be an increase in anxiety and tension and attempts to reorient society toward a more intrinsic basis of order. David Riesman, in *Abundance for What?* (1953), forecast that the young American suburbanite of that period would, within fifteen years or so, become increasingly alienated from a consuming and increasingly depersonalized society.

The Chaos of Our Times

The evidence of the 1960s and early 1970s has forced a reexamination of Bell's *End of Ideology* premises and those of others who treated the constancy of "change" and "cultural drift" as necessary and primary determinants of contemporary life. The same year Keniston's *The Uncommitted* was published, the Civil Rights Movement erupted and, until it became a predominantly black liberation movement, directed the idealism and loyalties of thousands of middle- and upper-class youth. The student rebellion that followed in the middle and late 1960s was essentially a rebellion against technological determinism. The initial goals of those who initiated the student rebellion were stated as follows:

> We seek the establishment of the democracy of individual participation, governed by two central mains: that the individual share in those social decisions in determining the quality and direction of his life; that society be organized to encourage independence in men and provide the media for their common participation (SDS, n.d.).

Following bombings and fires at several colleges and universities, student leaders came to realize that change, though inevitable must come about otherwise. Larry DiNardo, captain of the Notre Dame football team in the fall of 1970, stated:

> There's a general consensus that change is necessary but that violent change is silly, it's childish. . . . change has to take place and it even has to take place rapidly, but not at the cost of burning buildings, destroying people, getting people killed . . . (*Charlotte Observer*, 1970: 23A).

THE EFFECTS OF
RAPID CHANGE ON YOUTH

The uncertainties of living in a changing society are especially felt by youth. Adolescence is a period when they must establish their own identities as individuals and as members of society. In a stable, traditional culture, youth may be able to choose their future vocations, and there is little or no question of how they are going to live. Adolescents in developed, technologically determined societies are presented with additional decisions of life style and meaning with a conflicting variety of adult patterns to guide them.

The Interruption of the Socialization Process

Socialization is essentially an ordering process. The intrusion of rapid change disrupts this process and heightens confusion over the question of identity formation. Instead of the range of choice being well defined and limited, it becomes increasingly open. The concept of reference groups may be helpful here. Reference groups are those groups from which the individual derives a sense of his own identity. As pointed out in Chapter 6, the child early identifies with the members of his family. Thus, the family normally functions as a primary reference group. There are also class and occupational reference groups which are not necessarily continually visible or physically present. Reference groups in this broader abstract sense are generally either of two types: membership or anticipatory membership groups. A reference group may also be (and, in a society with low status mobility rates, generally is) a *membership group*— i.e., the son taking over his father's occupation.

In societies with a high degree of status mobility, the term reference group has been extended to include anticipatory membership groups. The classic instance of this is the young person from a lower-class background who, together with his parents, anticipates a college degree and elevation to the middle class. Thus the socialization process involves anticipatory socialization toward preparing for a middle-class status as both a reference group and an anticipatory membership group.

THE MARGINAL MAN. The concept of reference groups has been utilized, together with the concept of *marginality*, to explain some types of alienation and rebellion. The marginal man is the individual who is caught among potential reference groups, none of which he can aspire to for membership. A classic history of this process in American society was the widespread movement of blacks in the 1940s from the rural South, where jobs were diminishing, to the urban areas of the North, which promised better employment and possibly even middle-class status for their children. The promise of the city as a reference group and the actual realities of black urban existence turned out to be two quite different things. Faced with the comparative anonymity of the city and no possibility of retreat, the American black has become the classic marginal man; and throughout history, marginal men have been the major source of revolt and revolution.

Adolescence is a period of *potential* and, to some extent, *actual* marginality between childhood and anticipatory membership in the reference groups in the adult world. The security and orderliness of the socialization process is the prime determinant of the extent to which the potential marginality of the adolescent years is actualized. The multiple varieties of exposures provided for today's adolescents, especially when combined with the limitations of order as transition imposed upon the highly mobile nucleated family and the intense American encouragement of early independence, may combine to create too many potential reference groups without allowing any one of them to be assimilated thoroughly enough over a given period of time to assist with identity formation. Toffler's concern with the overload of choices and decision-making in *Future Shock* may be highly appropriate to increasing numbers of adolescents in the 1970s.

Adolescents' Changes in Values

The senior author once heard a high school girl arguing with her father about the slowness of winding down the Vietnam War. The father's argument involved the economic problems that would be generated, while her argument for getting out of the war quickly involved the saving of life. Finally the girl, exasperated, said to her father, "Dad, don't try to communicate with me about this, you can't speak my language." As suggested in earlier chapters, in spite of overlapping, basic distinctions do exist between the youth and adult cultures, especially in values. The needs, values, and outlooks of adolescence impose a unique humanistic world view and style of life not shared by most adults. The long hair controversy of the sixties and early seventies may not be entirely over, and its results are certainly not clear. Many authorities—educators, psychologists, physicians, sociologists—have suggested that long hair in young men is a symbol of their disillusion. Some have identified this with a growth in independence. For many it is no doubt a matter of the influence of peer culture or life style. Stuart Wilson, a clinical psychologist, stated:

> The people who get up tight to an incredible degree about long hair or other outstanding variations from the norm are the people who value changelessness, who find it difficult to cope with change in their lives or anybody else's life. They want the "good old days" to go on as always. They don't know it, but that's been done away with in this country. There are people here who value change, who live by the credo of change. That's where the real war is—between the belief that we should have change and that we shouldn't (Newton, 1970: 30).

CHANGED VIEW OF THE VALUE OF EDUCATION. There has been a change in high school students' views of the value of education. According to Leidy and Starry (1967), in 1953 most high school students considered the acquisition of social skills the most important aim in education; but in 1961, the academic area was selected as much more important than others. However, by 1966, discipline and responsibility ranked first, followed closely by academic skill. Asked what they liked best about school, many students preferred the intellectual aspects. Other things liked about school were: friends formed at school, mature ideas and information from the teacher, learning new things, discussing the news of the day or week, peer group activities. Adolescents are concerned about contemporary problems and are in general relatively well informed. This has had an important bearing on their acceptance or rejection of status quo conditions.

The Potential Radicalism Inherent in Youth

Karl Mannheim, the German phenomenologist, defined history in terms of the stability in the relationship between the concept of generation and the concept of time. A society by definition has a cosmos within which the past is mythologized and ordered, and which also gives meaning to the future in the present. The continuity between past and future is transmitted through generation and time in the ever-precarious present tense. In periods of relative stability, generation and time function to provide us with a sense of security through continuity. Mannheim defines the time span of a generation in the terms of the degree to which a society is capable of transmitting its culture reasonably intact from the elders to the young. The degree of rapidity of societal change is, for Mannheim, the primary determinant in defining the time span of a generation. Thus, in a highly stable society, a single generation might span 100 or 200 years or more if this society has been relatively undisturbed. In such societies, terms like adolescence and the younger generation have little or no meaning. Those contacts which are most important are those between older and younger members of the society. The question of whether a new generation may be emerging depends upon whether or not a given age group's contact with the culture *at a given age* involves experiences similar to the content of culture which their elders had experienced *at the same age* (1952: 276–322).

In discussing the potential radicalism of youth, Mannheim distinguishes between two kinds of fresh contact with existing culture. The first is a shift in social relations for adults, such as individuals migrating from one territory to another or changing status. The second is that of vital or generational factors. Mannheim states that

> The latter is potentially much more radical, since with the advent of the new participant in the process of culture, the change of attitude takes place in a different individual whose attitude toward the heritage handed down by his predecessors is a novel one (294).

Davis indicates how, during periods of rapid societal change, this potential is much more likely to be actualized:

> The time interval (between parent and child) . . . becomes historically significant. . . . Not only are parent and child, at any given moment, in different stages of development, but the content which the parent acquired at the stage where the child now is, was a different content from that which the child is now acquiring (1940: 523).

Thus, generation location always makes possible the facilitation of a fresh evaluation and selection of values and norms and other cultural possessions, and the discarding of others. The actualization of this potential, Mannheim states, takes place

> only where a concrete bond is created between members of a generation by their being exposed to the social and intellectual symptoms of a process of dynamic de-stabilization (303).

The Generational Style

Rapid societal change, in undermining the stability of the transmission of a given culture, at the same time opens alternative possibilities. Generational *units* may emerge from the experience of a generational actuality—i.e., the realization of youth in a given age group that among themselves they have more in common in their contact and experience with the culture as a reference group than their parents' contact with and experience of the culture when they were the same age. These generational units or, as Mannheim describes them, "specific groups of youth working up the material of their coming experiences in different specific ways" (304) may converge to produce their own *generational entelechy* or *Zeitgeist*—an emergent, common cultural or subcultural ethos and life style.

Mannheim is using the concept of generation in its basic meaning as *social* equivalent of the *biological* process of *procreation*. To Mannheim the generation signifies the young Negro male of the 1920s who worked with his father on the same tenant farm and anticipated the same experiences in his own adult life; the young, white Appalachian of the 1950s who goes to work at sixteen in the coal mines just as his father did; the 1930s New England craftsman who learns and carries on his father's trade; the young inheritor of the cotton plantation in the antebellum South; and the attorney's son in the small midwestern town who goes to law school and returns home to practice law in his hometown. To the extent that they are not affected by mainstream changes within American society, these individuals represent, to a degree, single generations. On the other hand, the young Negro who breaks out of the dominant white culture's definition of him, becomes a "black man," wears an African hairstyle, adopts some traditional African clothing, takes an African or Muslim name, reconstructs some forms of language with different meanings, takes pride in soul food and soul music, and rediscovers his African heritage that has been removed from his life, is, in Mannheim's terms, part of the attempt at creating a generation. Urban middle-class young people who decide that country music, organic farming, communal living, sitars, and certain gurus are to be endemic to them also represent generation, as defined by Mannheim.

Looking back at the history of the United States as possibly somewhat phototypical of some of the more random elements of societal change produced with industrialization and later technological revolution, one can see clearly the relationship between the frequency and emergence of new generational styles with the rate of societal and cultural change. One finds, for instance, on a comparative level, a far greater degree of longevity of social generations among the European settlers of the U.S. in the eighteenth and nineteenth century than in our present century. Especially in the more settled areas of eastern U.S., societal crises of those times tended to result in an affirmation of generational unity. Many of those who might otherwise have fostered intergenerational unrest had the Western frontier as their safety valve, or other alternatives. Roger Williams founded Rhode Island; most of the followers of Joseph Smith moved to Utah; the Irish rioted in New York City over the inequities of the draft laws during the Civil War, but that was a class and cultural phenomenon supported by young and old Irish alike. It is predominantly in the present century that we find discussions of "generation" involving attempts at social procreation, which Mannheim discusses. For instance, in American society, we speak of the "generation of the 1920s" and associate with this flapper girls, bathtub gin, songs of the period, and a general buoyancy and liberality. This does not mean that everyone in that generation experienced the same things, but that, in our assessment of the 1920s, a given set of experiences defined a "style." It is sufficient, for Mannheim, in terms of the mythology of the generation, to have a minority which can speak for and define the experiences of a generation, even though all in that age group may not be experiencing the same processes at the same time. This is comparable to an early conclusion by Brinton (1938) that 5 percent or less of a given population can define and articulate for others the appropriateness of a given response to the general sense of unrest and anxiety. Charismatic leaders are the crucial variable in articulating the conditions of unrest and the need for solution. Many of the leaders of the youth movements of the 1960s and early 1970s have been rock stars and innovators.

We recognize the biological meaning of generations as the traditional thirty-year span in child-adult terms. However, in our rapidly changing society, the concept of generations of consciousness in the Mannheim sense is not altogether unfamiliar to us. The mass media continually attempt to define generation in terms of a common set of experiences but increasingly in terms of an ethos which may or may not be common to youth as a "generational expression." In more recent times, possibly as an attempt to restore a sense of generational continuity, the press and mass media tend to define generation precisely in Mannheimian terms, but have found it increasingly difficult to do so.

Fabun, for instance, found it much easier to categorize earlier generations than those born after 1945. One still tends to speak of the generation of the 20s, described earlier; the Depression generation of the 30s; the "silent" generation of the 50s. However, we arrive at the 1960s with such an accelerated change that the concept of generation becomes increasingly difficult to define. The Civil Rights Movement was a "generation in the making"; however, this was quickly followed by a succession of black and white upheavals, black separation, unrest, and violence. A life style for young blacks began to emerge as a generational phenomenon: however, among those white youth attempting to create a generational *Zeitgeist,* the experience went from youthful activism to the withdrawal culture of the hippies to the generation of religious movement, such as interest in easten religions and the Jesus revolution.

Mannheim is also helpful in interpreting this contemporary situation, for he relates very closely the frequency and emergence of new generational styles to the rate of social and cultural change. He postulates, in fact, that "too greatly accelerated a tempo might lead to mutual destruction of the embryo entelechies" (310). With an acceleration in the rate of social and cultural change, closely graded age groups following upon each other may respond to their respective situations differently enough to prevent achieving sufficient continuity to create a real formulation of a distinctive generational style. Different experiences of contact with the existing social structure and culture may become increasingly compressed into more compact age groups, so that any one generational style can not emerge and flower. This seems to have been the case in the 1960s and early 1970s. It is indeed a most volatile and dangerous situation where neither adults nor peers can function as reference groups, as transmitters of the culture in relation to time. It does appear that in American and Western European societies we have witnessed something of Mannheim's implicit assumption that

> a generational system can become even more differentiated than a class system. Just as a class system can evolve with multiple levels from upper-upper to lower-lower, *so repeated historical crises within a short interval of time* can multiply the political generations which exit at any given time (26).

The United States in the 1960s and 1970s illustrates this well. In just over one decade we have seen six political generations in which youth, primarily older and postadolescents, participated and through which they set examples for their younger peers as well as for adults. In a family of several children, a teen-ager in the early 1970s may not share the same generational concepts even with his older brothers or sisters who may have been influenced by sit-ins, drug-inspired be-ins, political activism and peace marches, the ethnic search for identity, the ecology movement, or the back-to-Jesus movement.

The Restoration of Order

Rex Hopper (1965), building upon the theoretical presupposition that social movements arise out of the experience of marginality, contends that, with the acceleration of technological determinism, increasing segments of American society will experience the phenomenon of marginality, and the equivalent of Toffler's future shock. Since the United States has been, in the past, a composite of subcultures, with a very loose form of tradition, most semblances of societal unity have involved charismatic rather than traditional leadership. In the clash of cultures and values that accompanies marginality, man does not behave rationally. Young people who throw bags of urine at police in extreme situations are not behaving rationally; by the same token, neither are the police who rioted against young people in the 1968 Chicago Democratic Convention, and in the indiscriminate shootings at Kent State University and Jackson State University.

Order *will* be restored in the midst of chaos in one form or another, but it seems at the present time that order will not be restored before a clash of competing, embryonic, and frequently abortive "generational cultures." Those in power may try to force a return to the good old days, but if they succeed, it will have to be through totalitarian means, and the results will be only temporary. An individual can drop out and recreate a past for himself, but a society that has gone through a technological revolution cannot.

NEED FOR GENERATIONAL ORDER AND CONTINUITY. As teachers of adolescents, we need to be aware that the issue of values *is* of foremost importance and that we need to define for ourselves what is meaningful if we are to influence pupils. Perhaps, as Toffler and Slater indicate, simply illustrating the problem may be enough. It has been said that "If men define a situation as real, it is real in its consequences." This applies as much to the restoration of values as to the current processes of destruction and "futurist inaccessibility." Simply knowing about the potential for future destruction may bring about corrective processes and values.

Reich's *The Greening of America,* published in the early 1970s, was one of a number of attempts to give direction to yearnings for new values. However, there is no guarantee of any specific direction that youth will take for any extended period of time unless and until the elders of societies such as the United States are willing to dismantle the old culture without calamity, as Slater so clearly indicates (126). The paradox, in the early 1970s, is that the older generation is still concerned with technological innovation, renunciation of traditional ties, and short-term goals. On the other hand, the youth who want to create a new culture are *preoccupied* with tradition, community, relationships, and religious experiences.

There is no doubt that generational order and continuity will have to be restored if technological societies are to survive. The manner in which this takes place may be humane and healthy, or it may be bizarre, violent, and vicious. As indicated, youth, in periods of uncertainty, are the most susceptible and, potentially, the most radical element in society.

SUMMARY

Adolescence is a turbulent period of life when a person becomes marginal in the sense that he is neither a child nor an adult. In industrialized countries there is a continuing postponement of adult status. The United States is a model of visibly changing, technological society. The acceleration of change in our society is now so rapid that change is our only real constant factor. The triple revolution of cybernetics, human rights, and environmental imperatives is a special concern to the adolescent in today's world. The dilemmas created by the increased technology of society are keenly experienced by adolescents.

The effect of allowing technological change in and for itself to order our lives results in a concept of transcience. This has happened before to other societies in times of calamity or innovation. The difference between today and much of the past is the contemporary acceptance of a technologically based futurism and its accompanying uncertainties. Transcience to the adolescent has become a way of life. In the past the experience of the elders has alway surpassed that of children. However, to today's adolescents the relevance of parents' or grandparents' lives is not applicable. One thing which may help the youth of today adjust to the instability and lack of direction of the future may be the ability for adolescents to learn to adjust to change as a constant—i.e., how to adapt to a sense of transciency. When faced with a crisis or problem, adolescents are not as quick as the older generation to fall back upon "outmoded" or traditional solutions. Well-educated and mass media indoctrinated, the adolescents of today, however, do not readily or necessarily accept either technological determination or their own depersonalized, technologically determined lives.

The intrusion of rapid change has disrupted the ordering in process that usually takes place with traditional youth. The adolescent faces heightened confusion over the question of identity formation in our society with its high degree of status mobility. An adolescent may be a part of an anticipatory membership group and his own peers' membership group. With today's highly mobile nuclear family and the intense American encouragement of early independence, the teen-ager may end up with too many potential reference groups without allowing enough time or circumstance for any particular one to assist in forming his own ideas. There has been a definite change in the high school student's view of the value of education.

One finds on a comparative and social level today far greater longevity or social generations among European settlers in the U.S. in the eighteenth and nineteenth century than with adolescents. The frequency and emergency of new generation styles among adolescents is closely correlated to the rate of social and cultural change. Change is happening at such a rapid rate that it is almost impossible to achieve sufficient continuity to create a real formulation of a distinctive generation style even among brothers and sisters that may have only several years apart in age. Order in the sense of a continuous stability will be restored in the midst of chaos in some form or another. At the present time especially among adolescents and those in their twenties, order will not be restored prior to a clash of competing and frequently abortive generation cultures.

Today's adolescents are concerned with the intrinsically past values over traditional community religious or quasireligious experiences. Many young people are searching for and finding their own system of values in different expression. Many are waiting and many are just lost. There is a communality of generational style that has in common the "search" which is taking many directions, and there is no doubt that general order and continuity will have to be restored if technological societies such as the United States are to survive. The manner in which this takes place may be humane, bizarre, or violent. However, youth, being in a period of marginality and uncertainty, is the most susceptible and potentially the most radical element in society.

REFERENCES

ALLPORT, G. W. "Psychological Models for Guidance." In *Guidance Examination.* R. L. Mosher, R. D. Carle, and C. D. Kehas, eds. New York: Harcourt, Brace and World, 1965.

BELL, DANIEL. *The End of Ideology.* New York: The Free Press, 1962.

BRINTON, CRANE. *The Anatomy of Revolution.* New York: W. W. Norton & Co., Inc., 1938.

Charlotte Observer (December 1, 1970), p. 23A. "Notre Dame: A New Look in Life Style."

EHRLICH, PAUL R. and ANNA H. EHRLICH. *Population, Resources, Environment.* San Francisco: W. W. Freeman and Co., 1970.

FABUN, DON. *The Children of Change.* Beverly Hills: Glencoe Press, 1968. Pp. 18–21.

HOPPER, REX. "Cybernation, Marginality, and Revolution." In *The New Sociology,* Irving L. Horowitz, ed. New York: Oxford University Press, 1965.

KENISTON, KENNETH. *The Uncommitted.* New York: Harcourt, Brace and World, 1965.

LEIDY, THOMAS R. and ALLAN R. STARRY. "Youth Culture." *Journal of the National Education Association* (October 1967), 56 (7):9–12.

MANNHEIM, KARL. "The Problem of Generations." In *Essays in the Sociology of Knowledge,* Paul Kecskemeti, ed. London: Routledge and Kegan Paul, 1952. Pp. 276–322.

MEAD, MARGARET. *Culture and Commitment.* Garden City, N.Y.: Natural History Press, 1970.

NEWTON, JOSEPH. "The Great Hair Hassle: A Victory for Youth." *Today's Health* (March 1970), 48 (3):30–33.

REICH, CHARLES. *The Greening of America.* New York: Random House, Inc., 1970.

RIESMAN, DAVID. *Abundance for What?* Garden City, N.Y.: Doubleday & Company, Inc., 1953.

SLATER, PHILIP. *The Pursuit of Loneliness.* Boston: Beacon Press, 1970.

SOROKIN, PITIRIM. *The Crisis of Our Age.* New York: E. P. Dutton & Co., Inc. 1941.

Students for a Democratic Society (SDS). "Port Huron Statement." Chicago: n.d.

TOFFLER, ALVIN. *Future Shock.* New York: Random House, Inc., 1970.

TOYNBEE, ARNOLD. "Mothers of the World Will Be Next to Revolt." *Miami Herald* (January 17, 1971), p. 3-m.

RECOMMENDED READINGS

Flacks, R. "The Liberated Generation: An Exploration of the Roots of Student Protest." *Journal of Social Issues* (1967), 23:52–75.
The author regards most activism as stemming from the brighter and advantaged youth. Most of the article deals with social-psychological roots of student protest. It thus furnishes some basis for an understanding of our present social-psychological climate.

Mead, Margaret. *Culture and Commitment.* Garden City, N.Y.: Natural History Press, 1970.
Mead defines society in terms of those who transmit the culture. She contends that youth are primary and somewhat autonomous in transmitting culture and providing continuity with the past.

Slater, Philip. *The Pursuit of Loneliness.* Boston: Beacon Press, 1970.
A highly readable interpretation of fragmentation and loss of community in contemporary American society, resulting from both societal changes and from many variables in our societal ethos which mitigate against the realization of "community."

See additional references at the end of Chapters 17 and 18.

14

adolescents and sex: issues and problems related to sexuality

Observations of adolescents at school or elsewhere will lead anyone to realize that the sex drive plays an important role in almost every aspect of their lives. Sex-role identification, biological forces and conditions, social norms, cultural and moral background, and immediate needs form an interrelated complex that is responsible for the adolescent's behavior. In this chapter we attempt to furnish some insights into the adolescent's involvement in heterosexual experiences—dating, sexual behavior, and marriage. Some of the outcomes and conflicts will be examined in light of traditional values and recent changes in our concept of the role of sex.

TRADITIONAL SEX CODES

Codes and behavioral norms involving sexual expression provide a model that has an important bearing on the pattern of sexual activities of members of a given society. The endocrine glands are very important in preparing an individual for sexual maturity; they may be said to usher in the period of adolescence. Sebald has pointed out that "ado-

FIGURE 14-1 Study carefully. This is a sample of youth in the early 1970s. (Courtesy of Electronic Companies Advertising Program.)

lescents may *overtly behave* as if there were no specific cultural pronouncements regarding sex and yet covertly react on the emotional level to their deviance from the cultural blueprint" (1968: 393).

We cannot understand contemporary adolescent sex, dating, and marriage patterns without some understanding of Western tradition. Concerning this background Rosenberg and Bensman state (1968: 61):

> . . . Jerusalem, Athens, Rome, and their several sequelae constitute, or symbolize, that tradition. From it, that is to say, from the Hellenic and Judeo-Christian past, Western man derives not only certain prescriptions and prohibitions, but a whole framework of ideas, concepts, and theories that are his heavy cultural burden. Diffusion and dilution notwithstanding, the sexual analyst and those he discusses share that burden. To be sure, neither need recognize or acknowledge the connection that binds them together in an inescapable matrix.
>
> We have come to our present sexual pass through devious and tangled paths, still strewn with innumerable laws, parables, images, aftereffects, and reflections.

Judeo-Christian Tradition

The cultural heritage of our society is rooted in the Judeo-Christian tradition, which for single people dictates ascetic standards; it forbids premarital coitus—the only approved sexual activity consists of marital coitus. Concerning this tradition Sebald states:

> Although these dogmas are gradually giving way to more secular and sensate-oriented views, hardly any young American can avoid exposure to orthodox views on sex that equate premarital sexual activities with sin and evil. Some teen-agers more than others come under the influence of such religious and moralistic evaluation in the course of their association with parents, relatives, church, and school. Inconsistent with this general negative pronouncement is the tacit agreement on a double standard that has been part of informal religious tradition as well as folklore. In effect, it calls for strong condemnation of female sexual transgression, but only mild condemnation, if not tolerance or even encouragement, of male sexual adventure (1968: 393).

The contradiction between the ideas and beliefs about love and sex has been handed down through the literature. We note, for example, that the seventeenth-century bawdy period was followed by the Industrial Revolution, Calvinism, and Protestantism in general, and the rise of the mercantile and middle class that put an end to blatant sexual adventures. Rosenberg and Bensman point out in this regard that "the Victorian double standard was, in its own time, mainly an upper-middle-class phenomenon, rarely affecting higher and lower social strata. Similarly, the revolt against it seems to have liberated segments of the middle class at least from the idea of sexual repression. For some time now, as Theodore Dreiser noted over and over in his early novels, the relatively stable blue-collar working class has best exemplified puritanical prudery and sexual hypocrisy" (1968: 95).

The word "sex" existed in the vocabulary of the nineteenth century and earlier, but it was confined to secret places or uncultured groups; it was not used in polite conversation. The apparent contemporary obsession with sex was not unknown to other civilizations. As pointed out by Rosenberg and Bensman with *eros* and *agape,* Plato spiritualized sex. "Erotic joy" was celebrated among the Greeks and Romans in poems, while the Middle East has always been an area of high intense sexuality. The exaltation of eroticism tends to be academic with the proponents of increased sexual freedom who contrast it favorably with the hypocritical Victorian ideas and practices.

Sources of Sex Information

Realizing the dilemma of many adolescents regarding sex information, educators have shown much concern about the inadequate and incorrect information about human sexuality. Many schools have incorporated materials into the curriculum to give youth accurate and more complete information designed to reduce their naiveté. In doing this, the schools hope to supplement rather than supplant the authority of the home and church.

Thornburg's studies (1970a, 1970b) of the sources of sex information show that many adolescents are poorly informed and have negative, unwholesome attitudes about human sexuality. Their peers, rather than the home, school, or church dispense the greatest amount of sex information. A comparative analysis of sex information sources is presented in Table 14-1. The data presented show that peers furnished the greatest amount of sex information, although much information is obtained through literature. The mother is the primary source of sex information in the home, with the father playing a relatively minor role. He noted that almost all information about petting, intercourse, and homosexuality came from age-mates. An examination of school programs in sex education shows that the schools provide much information about venereal disease, menstruation, pregnancy, origin of babies, and the reproductive system. However, surveys show that there is a great deal of misinformation among young people regarding the whole realm of sex and point to the need for improvement in sex education programs.

TABLE 14-1 A Comparative Analysis of Sex Information Sources

SOURCE	ARIZONA (N = 191)	OKLAHOMA (N = 190)	TOTAL	PERCENT
Mother	382	406	788	19.3
Father	23	20	43	1.8
Peers	688	829	1,517	37.9
Literature	461	360	821	20.6
School	377	213	590	14.8
Minister	20	13	33	.8
Physician	12	9	21	.5
Street talk experience	62	107	169	4.3
Unanswered	76	133	209	—

Source: Thomburg (1970).

THE SEXUAL REVOLUTION

Accompanying the rapid and tumultuous changes that have taken place during the past half century have been important changes in sexual-social relations. And, although we cannot state the exact time, we are well aware that we have parted from the Victorian period, and many of the restraints of past generations have disappeared. Among these that will be discussed here are: (1) Female Emancipation; (2) The New Morality.

Female Emancipation

Beginning especially with the Feminist Movement of the 1920s and 30s, a number of significant social and economic changes regarding the activities of women have become noticeable. First, we have seen women entering colleges and universities in increasing numbers. They have more than held their own in the academic competition with men. They now are found in all professions. This movement has been worldwide. In Russia approximately 85 percent of all physicians are women. In the United States laws have been passed providing fair treatment for them in employment. They are now found in the different branches of the armed services.

ABORTIONS ON DEMAND. The clamor for abortion is widespread throughout Western culture, in spite of the opposition of the Roman Catholic Church. It is estimated that there were 500,000 abortions in France in 1971. The young people in France have demanded an end to the strict laws against abortion, but the fact that France is strongly Roman Catholic and the Church has not relented makes it unlikely that abortions will be legalized there any time soon.

The New York abortion law—the most liberal in the nation at the time of its adoption in 1970—permits abortions to be performed at any time up to the twenty-fourth week of pregnancy as a matter of discretion between the pregnant woman and her doctor. Legalization of abortion in New York brought about a significant reduction in maternal deaths; it also produced a noted decline in the illegitimacy rate during 1971. All the shelters that care for unmarried pregnant girls reported a sharp decrease in the number of applicants for admission (Tuthill, 1971). According to a report of the Center for Disease Control for twenty-seven states and the District of Columbia there were more than 586,000 legal abortions in 1972 (*Charlotte Observer,* May 11, 1974). About one-third of these were performed on women under twenty years of age. In ten states, according to the report, abortions outnumbered live births for women less than fifteen years of age.

The Supreme Court ruled on January 22, 1973, that states may not outlaw abortions during the first six months of pregnancy, although during the second three months a state may regulate abortion procedure, short of a ban. This decision was met with an outcry by certain church groups opposed to usual birth control procedures and abortions.

THE SINGLES. As part of the sexual revolution, an increasing number of girls choose to remain single. One of the most popular courses offered at the University of Southern California in 1970 was entitled "The Challenge of Being Single." The enrollment in the course the first time it was offered consisted of sixty-eight students—eighteen men and fifty women in the thirty to forty age-group. Generally speaking, society is unkind to singles. It continues to ask the question, "Why isn't a nice person like you married?" (Parade, 1971: 7).

According to the 1970 Census, there are in this country approximately 93 million married individuals and 36 million single individuals over the age of eighteen. This indicates that the problems of the unmarried cannot be passed over. Some of the advantages of staying single are: (1) freedom to grow, to make one's own decisions; and (2) opportunity to travel, to accept a new job or promotion, and to broaden one's life. There are now apartments, social groups, and social programs for singles. The man or woman who is divorced need not suffer a life of loneliness. Nor, do single people feel today that they must lead sexless lives. Society has become more permissive and understanding regarding personal and sexual relationships which do not include marriage, and we are noting a great increase in number and variety of such relationships between individuals who prefer the state of singleness.

The increased emancipation of women is reflected in their attitudes toward sex and sexual behavior. The greatest change in sexual attitudes has appeared among college girls (*McCall's*, 1968). It has also appeared in the attitude of the armed forces. The Air Force tried in vain to discharge an unwed pregnant twenty-six-year-old nurse because of her pregnancy. The nurse, however, was able to get a court injunction against the discharge until the case could be brought before the Court of Appeals (*Charlotte Observer*, 1970). Parental control and community attitudes no longer control the lives of single women as they once did. The growth of vast metropolitan areas with highly mobile populations has pretty well destroyed small-town scrutiny.

The New Morality

Young people now in high school, college, and the armed services are living in a new milieu of sex and sexual relations—the New Morality. In a paper presented at the 1965 annual meeting of the American Orthopsychiatric Association, Farnsworth (1968: 8) presented three points of view regarding sexual behavior: (1) the traditional morality, (2) the New Morality, and (3) amorality. The following principles govern the traditional and the New Morality. In the traditional morality:

1. Renunciation or control of instinctual gratification permits a reasonable degree of civilization (Freud).
2. Restraint tends to aid in developing a capacity for thoughtfulness concerning the welfare of others, particularly in a parental sense. Restraint also is thought to aid in the sublimation of sexual energies.
3. Marriage becomes one of life's most cherished institutions when sexual restraint is practiced.
4. The total moral fiber of a society is strengthened if sexual standards are maintained and weakened when sexual standards are ignored.
5. Young people need help in controlling their strong impulses during their formative years.

In the New Morality:

1. Fidelity and consideration of others occupy a very high place.
2. Physical sex is supposed to occur only after the establishment of friendship and love.

3. Exploitation of the sexual partner is very much opposed.

4. A high ethical component is apparent in the thinking of those who adhere to this general view even though it may not be in accordance with views traditionally held, nor with the views of many religious groups.

THE NEW MORALITY AS A SOURCE OF CONFLICT WITH PARENTS. Although many aspects of the New Morality are not new to present-day parents, they were formerly kept out of sight and hidden under a cloak of secrecy. A significant aspect of the sexual behavior and attitudes of contemporary adolescents is frankness. No longer are adolescents ashamed of holding hands or even kissing under certain circumstances in the presence of their parents. The idea of the unchaperoned date is another example. The grandparents of today's adolescents (and in many cases even the parents) would never have been permitted to go out on a date alone. Dating was conducted almost exclusively under adult supervision in the home or in group situations such as church socials. With the widespread use of the automobile, it has become increasingly prevalent for an adolescent couple to spend an entire evening completely unchaperoned. This, of course, gives the adolescents freedom to move about as they please and control their own sexual behavior, a trend which has lead to many conflicts with parents.

THE NEW MORALITY AS A SOURCE OF CONFLICT WITHIN THE SELF. In the New Morality sex experience has become linked with love rather than marriage. Many young people are confused by this break from old moral standards. Furthermore, the convincing arguments of the New Morality make it doubly difficult for the young people to make decisions about their own sexual feelings. The scope of this confusion and vagueness about sexual values and codes is reflected in the disagreements among guidance counselors. This was strikingly illustrated at the 1964 Conference of the National Association of Women Deans and Counselors; the "Work Conference on Current Sex Mores" failed to reach a consensus on sexual mores and codes of behavior.

Leaders of church groups are also unable to agree about premarital sex, dating, marriage, and divorce. It is only natural that adolescents should be very confused. In this light it is becoming more difficult to defend the old morality. In the past, it was protected by three fears: fear of venereal disease, pregnancy, and Hell fire. None of these fears has very much meaning today. Venereal disease can be easily cured, and young people are well aware of it. The young are not afraid of pregnancy because they think they know all about contraception; but pregnancies do occur frequently. The reasons are complicated, some having to do with unconscious motivations of both men and women, some with the failure of contraceptive methods. Because now, practically 100 percent guaranteed methods such as the pill and the IUD are at the disposal of girls, young men assume that pregnancy and contraception are exclusively the girl's responsibility.[1]

WE CAN'T TURN BACK. The New Morality has brought forth much confusion. It is always easier to follow a "beaten path," but the ways of living today are vastly different from those at the turn of this century. Unlike reports on marriage and crime, data on the sexual behavior of adolescents today cannot easily be compared to those of a half century ago. One thing is certain: adolescents of today are biologically similar to those of centuries past, but they are living in a cultural and social setting that has never existed before. The problem of guiding boys and girls so that they will be happy and effective family members in a society that is vastly different from that of the past is a superhuman task. But, we do know that we aren't going back to a Victorian or post-Victorian morality.

Today's adolescents are better informed than any previous group of adolescents. They reach sexual maturity earlier today than ever before. They have more scientific information and technological innovations to help them solve their problems than any previous group. Needless to say, they have more complex problems to solve than did their parents, despite their parents' protests about their adolescent years. One might say that many adolescents are experimenting. They are not guided or held back by some authoritarian religious dogmas. Frequently they are groping for a standard as a guide. They realize that in some respects "the future is now," and the decisions they make today will be important for the rest of their lives as well as the lives of others. They are caught up with the "One World" concept, and an increased concern for humanitarian values.

HETEROSEXUAL INTERESTS AND ACTIVITIES

As a child's interest in his peers grows, his interest in activities involving his parents declines. The early adolescent years are marked by unisex friendships and by like-sexed chums and play groups. A natural extension of this is the movement toward boy-girl pairing, as pointed out earlier in connection with social-sexual development during adolescence.

Heterosexuality

An early study by Harris and Tseng (1957) revealed important changes in attitudes toward members of the opposite sex as the individual grows from childhood into adolescence. Using a sentence-completion method of

[1] The condom, the male protective device, is considered old fashioned by many adolescents. The discarding of the condom is unfortunate, for this directly contributes to the skyrocketing rate of venereal disease among youth. By considering it solely a birth control device, today's adolescent does not realize that the condom was specifically used to protect those engaged in coitus from receiving or transmitting venereal infection.

studying children's and adolescents' attitudes toward peers, they were able to compute "negative," "positive," and "neutral" attitudes.

By combining percentages of boys and girls in each grade who gave responses of a particular classification, the investigators were able to draw curves expressing certain trends in attitudes. Boys' attitudes toward their peers are shown in Figure 14-2. The favorable and neutral responses are shown in this figure. The attitudes of girls toward other girls and boys are shown in Figure 14-3. The curves for boys' attitudes show that approximately two-thirds of the boys gave positive responses to other boys at all ages. Boys at the lower grades are more positive to boys than to girls. Taking into account the proportion of neutral attitudes, boys in the middle grades are more favorable than unfavorable in their attitudes toward girls. The decline around age 15 or 16 perhaps indicates a growing interest in particular girls with a slightly declining interest in girls in general. There was, however, throughout late childhood and the teen years a fair proportion of boys who gave a negative completion response to the general stimulus, "Most girls ———."

A noticeable trend in girls' attitudes was the increase in negative responses to other girls following the ninth grade. This is probably an indication of the competitiveness of girls for boys' attention during the adolescent years. The investigators state, "Perhaps girls personalize their feelings more toward their own sex in adolescence, while boys shift more toward neutrality, and do not move into negative feelings." A wide range of reaction patterns relative to the opposite sex exists in adolescents, and it is very difficult to generalize concerning the reactions of the group as a whole. However, since the sexual urge is present in every individual and probably begins to function influentially, if indirectly, quite early in life, it is evident that the differences between the reactions of various adolescents result from the direction that this urge has been given, rather than its mere existence. The presence of this urge may be observed in the responses of two ninth-grade girls to the statement, "List what you would like to have *now* more than anything else:"

"I would like to have more than anything—one certain BOY!"

"I would like a real nice boy friend."

Heterosexuality itself can be properly established only by social contacts with members of the opposite sex, and in these contacts two environmental conditions are essential: first, members of the opposite sex must be of sufficient numbers, of appropriate age, and of attractive personal qualities; second, an intelligently encouraging attitude is necessary on the part of parents and others concerned with the individual's guidance and welfare. If these essentials are absent, the child may emerge from adolescence with warped and shameful attitudes toward sex matters that may encumber him permanently.

Dating During Adolescence

Dating takes place at an earlier age today than before. This is particularly true of middle-class families and frequently has their blessings. The fact

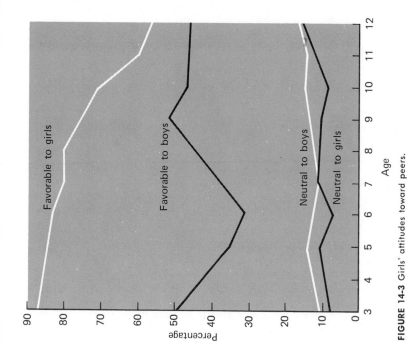

FIGURE 14-3 Girls' attitudes toward peers.

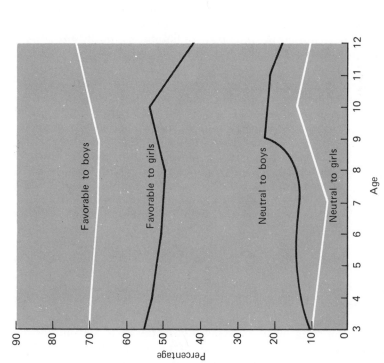

FIGURE 14-2 Boys' attitudes toward peers. After Harris and Tseng (1957).

that boys and girls mature physically earlier today than they did a century ago will certainly have an influence on the etiology of their sexual interests. It should be pointed out, however, that on matters relating to dating, dancing, hair style, clothing, and club activities junior-high school students tend to follow closely the opinion, advice, and behavior pattern of their peers.

Dating practices among sixth-, seventh-, and eighth-graders have undergone important changes during the past two decades. The great amount of shyness, timidity, and antipathy toward members of the opposite sex has given way to dating and going steady on the part of a large percentage of preadolescents. Frequently such dating, especially prevalent among middle-class suburban families, is encouraged or fostered by mothers anxious for their daughters to be popular and not to be left out of social events. The extent of dating by high school students will depend upon the customs, living conditions, social backgrounds, and special interests of the particular age-group concerned. Seniors date more than freshmen, and report chaperonage less frequently. This no doubt reflects their greater social and physical maturity and the increased willingness of their parents to allow them, as they grow older, to associate freely with members of the opposite sex.

The importance of social class may be observed in the dating activities of adolescents as well as in other aspects of their activities. The intra- and interclass dating patterns closely parallel the clique patterns. This is maintained and supported by parents through housing development patterns, church or religious affiliation, club membership, recreational pursuits, and the neighborhood schools.

FALLING IN LOVE. Most young people have two main goals: first, finding a suitable life occupation, and second, getting married and establishing a family. These do not necessarily come in this particular order, for we note that falling in love appears in the lives of most teen-agers at one time or another. This is another milestone in the lives of adolescents, and is preliminary to a major decision relative to a mate and family. It is not always easy for young people actually to know when they are in love. Being in love is very intangible, and may not affect all individuals in the same manner. The element of physical attraction is much stronger in some than in others. Also, some individuals have learned to play their sex role much better than others. Love for modern adolescents represents respect and comradeship to a higher degree than perhaps at any other period. The aspect of love involving partnership grows and develops through the enjoyment of common experiences. Similar tastes, ideals, aspirations, and outlooks are most important in the development of wholesome comradeship.

In the United States, in contrast to much of Europe, dating in not perceived as courting behavior, especially in the early and middle years of adolescence. Adolescents look upon dating as a convenient and satisfying social relationship rather than a preliminary stage in mate selection and marriage. High school students who date can be expected, by the time they graduate, to have passed through two or more dating episodes without any serious consideration of marriage.

Because of modern dating practices, many high school youngsters believe they are in love. There is mutual attraction; they can hardly wait to see each other daily at school; they talk at length over the telephone in the evenings. There are no tests available for measuring the genuineness of love, but thousands of high school students display many symptoms of being very much in love.

Being "pinned" and then engaged is typical of a high school romance, and every year many adolescents marry by the time they are eighteen and have completed their high school work. In many cases they, with the cooperation of both sets of parents, work out a very good arrangement for their marriage in which they remain in school, go to college, or find employment.

SOCIAL DATING AND ACADEMIC ORIENTATION. A major objection parents have to excessive dating is that it will interfere with school grades. A study reported by Grinder (1966) was concerned with this problem. The subjects of his study consisted of 393 boys and 346 girls from the tenth, eleventh, and twelfth grades. A scale was prepared listing reasons for dating: sexual gratification, independence assertion, status seeking, and participation eagerness. Problems were presented and the students chose the ones that best fit their particular case. The investigator also secured by means of a questionnaire personal information about each of the subjects.

No significant differences were found in grades of those who dated frequently and those who seldom dated. However, major reasons for dating were related to grades; those students primarily interested in sexual gratification or in asserting their independence had a grade-average lower than others. Grinder concludes further:

> Boys who are nonparticipants in extracurricular activities seem especially interested in participating in dating and in using the dating system for seeking status. Sex differences also emerge in respect to peer relations. Having friends per se is an important correlate of boys' motivation for all the resources of dating, whereas having close intimate friends appears to be the more critical variable for girls (33).

Premarital Sexual Freedom

One hears much about the sexual freedom of the present generation of adolescents. While there is evidence for increased sexual behavior, one should be careful in making comparisons with previous generations. However, it was pointed out earlier that we have experienced a sexual revolution and this, like other rapid changes, has accentuated the generation gap. The results of the Kinsey studies (1948, 1953), while a shock to

But Mom, **Love** *and* **Sex** *are real today. They are* **now** *things.*

many people, were somewhat of an awakening to the fact that a revolution was at hand.

Packard's (1968) nationwide study of sex on college campuses reveals the nature of the sexual revolution among postadolescents. This study shows that postadolescents, like their younger adolescent counterparts, display more frankness about sexual problems. There is also evidence that the double standard has not entirely disappeared, although college girls are not as passive as their mothers were several decades ago. Questionnaire replies were obtained from juniors and seniors from colleges and universities in the four major geographical areas of the United States. Five times as many males as females were willing to condone premarital coitus as reasonable under ideal circumstances. Quite pronounced regional differences were obtained from students who felt that coitus is reasonable "only if married" when the participants are under eighteen. Only 46 percent of the college girls "specified that marriage was the only reasonable basis for coitus if the participants were over twenty-one" (116). These responses are especially interesting in light of the fact that these are college girls, well past eighteen. No doubt the younger group would respond quite differently.

SOCIAL CLASS INFLUENCES. The sociological literature frequently suggests that adolescents from higher socioeconomic status homes are more conservative in their sexual behavior than persons from lower status backgrounds. Reiss (1967) has pointed out, however, that the expected inverse relationship between permissiveness and social class is frequently masked by other factors. He hypothesized that "among conservative people, those of higher status would be less permissive than those of lower status, while among liberal individuals, the relations would be in the opposite direction" (750).

Welsh (1970) noted among college freshmen that the higher the social status, the more likely a student is to have a standard similar to that of his parents, although the association for men was not statistically significant. However, he found considerable misperception of parental attitudes; therefore any associations noted between students' sexual behavior and that of their parents may be based upon their misperceptions of parental permissiveness rather than their actual permissiveness.

PATTERNS OF PERMISSIVENESS. It has been pointed out that sexual behavior patterns are diverse and result from a variety of conditions and forces including the personality of the individual concerned. Reiss (1967) has brought together many factors from his quite inclusive study of this problem; he notes that although seemingly diverse they actually fall into definite patterns, or clusters of relationships. He has described these patterns in seven basic propositions:

1. The *less* sexually permissive a group is, traditionally, the *greater* the likelihood that new forces will cause its members to become more permissive. Traditionally high-permissive groups, such as Negro men, were the least likely to have their sexual standards changed by social forces like church attendance, love affairs, and romantic love. Traditionally low-permissive groups, such as white middle-class women, showed the greatest sensitivity to these social forces. Also, the lower social classes are reported to have a tradition of greater sexual permissiveness, so the findings that their permissiveness is less sensitive to certain social forces fits this proposition.

2. The more liberal the group, the more likely that social forces will help maintain a high degree of sexual permissiveness. For example, female students from upper-class liberal families and urban students have by and large accepted more permissiveness than those from more conservative settings. In fact, liberalism in general seems to be yet another cause of the increased permissiveness.

3. According to their ties to social institutions, especially marriage and the family, people will differ in their attitudes toward permissiveness. Thus, we note sex differences in dating and courting practices. Romantic love leads more women than men to become permissive. Reiss noted this in particular among women who were faithful churchgoers.

4. The higher the overall level of permissiveness in a group, the greater the extent of equalitarianism within abstinence and double-standard subgroups. Thus, permissiveness is not only a measure of what a person will tolerate for himself and his sex, but what he is willing to allow the opposite sex. Equalitarianism within the double standard means that intercourse is acceptable for women only when in love, but anytime for men.

5. The potential for permissiveness derived from parents' values is a key determinant as to how rapidly, how much, and in what direction

an individual's premarital sexual standards and behavior change; 63 to 68 percent of the students studied by Reiss felt that their sexual standards were close to those of their parents; a still larger number felt their standards were even closer to those of peers (77 percent) and to those of close peers (89 percent).

6. An adolescent tends to see permissiveness as a continuous scale with his parents' standards at the low point, his peers at the high point, and himself at some point between that of his parents and peers but closer to his peers. Those who consider their standards closer to their parents than to peers are less permissive than the others. The most permissive within a particular group reported the greatest difference between their standards and the standards of their parents.

7. Greater responsibility for other members of the family and lesser participation in courtship are both associated with low permissiveness. The only child, according to Reiss, has the most permissive attitudes. As the number of children and their ages increased, the parents' permissiveness decreased; however, the more daughters a white father has, the more strongly he feels about his standards; the more sons he has the less strongly he feels about his standards. White mothers showed the reverse tendency but not as strongly.

Cultural Influences on Sexual Attitudes and Behavior

Since learning plays a very important role in determining sexual attitudes and response patterns within a culture, we would expect that sexual behavior during adolescence would vary markedly from one culture to another. We note important differences between cultures not only in the amount and type of sexual behavior during the adolescent years, but also in the consistency of a society's sexual standards as development proceeds. It has been observed that illegitimacy rates are not evenly distributed among the teen-age population, being higher among groups in the lower socioeconomic class.

A Gallup poll, based on personal interviews with 1,114 college students on fifty-five campuses, shows that almost three out of every four students believe it is not important to marry a virgin of either sex (Parade, 1970). It was observed that students who attend church-affiliated colleges place more emphasis upon marrying a virgin than do students from private or state-supported institutions. Students who consider religion a relevant part of their life find virginity more important than students who do not.

There was also a relation between a student's political and social philosophy and his attitude toward virginity. Those students who regard themselves as liberal were more permissive in their attitude toward virginity than students who regarded themselves as conservative, although the differences here were not large, 79 percent as opposed to 58 percent. As students progress from the freshmen year to the senior year, their attitudes toward virginity become more tolerant.

The sexual behavior patterns of a number of unmarried adolescents in Minnesota was studied during a period of fifteen months (Martinson, 1968). Researchers spent a month in each of four communities—two rural, one suburban, and one inner-city—observing and interviewing adolescents around the general theme: What is it like to grow up in a Minnesota community? The study was made primarily with middle-class adolescents; dating histories of 500 high school students were studied.

In Minnesota middle-class homes beginning in the sixth or seventh grade or sometimes earlier, young people get together in groups and, often with the assistance or at least the consent of parents, plan parties in their homes. Eating, drinking (usually soft or nonalcoholic drinks), listening to music, and "chit-chat" or talking takes place at parties. At the same time they are reminded by suggestions from the mass media, older youth, adults, that there is more in relating to the opposite sex than just laughing, talking, and listening to music and perhaps dancing. So they frequently turn to suggestive games, turn out the lights, and "make out." "Making out" among the young adolescents usually refers to kissing, necking, and perhaps some degree of petting and fondling.

Frequently the parents plan to go out, perhaps to the movies or some other educational, recreational, or social pursuit. In such cases, adolescents not only make out in the kitchen, family, and living rooms, but also in the bedrooms. Drinking was found to be prevalent among Minnesota high school youth. This seemed to help in speeding up the progression of petting from one stage to another, culminating in sexual intercourse.

DATING PATTERNS. Besides group parties, which continue on into senior high school, Martinson (1968) found that some Minnesota middle-class adolescents began paired dating in junior high school, with parental approval or support. Parents may encourage early dating, especially when the daughter's and son's classmates and peers are dating. One Minnesota girl stated:

> In the selection of my friends my mother did let me make my own decisions. One time though, she was quite perturbed when, in sixth grade, I turned down my first date offer because I felt I was too young to accept.

Paired dating develops into going steadily or even steady. Going steady means more than going steadily with only one particular person; it also includes the exchange of expressions of love, promises to be faithful, and some rituals or symbols such as an exchange of rings, wearing matching clothing, or making use of some other identifying pairing. Most Minnesota adolescents studied go steadily or steady rather than "play the field." If a boy or girl are going steadily, they need not "make out," but if they are going steady, it is usually understood among their peers that they will be with each other a great deal and will "make out" whenever the occasion arises.

Nudity or seminudity was found to be not at all uncommon among Minnesota high school daters. One teen-ager stated: "He had seen me without clothes and neither of us felt especially guilty." One adolescent expressed the feelings of many adolescents who were going steady:

> . . . We progressed rapidly from one stage to the next. . . . We were alone quite a lot of the time, either at his home or mine, and our involvement became quite serious. Many times we would be in bed with no clothes on. We got so completely caught up in this sexual exploration, however, that all other aspects of our relationships suffered.

However, Martinson did not find that Minnesota young people indulged fully in sexual intercourse. This seldom occurs unless the two are in love or think that they are in love and do not know how to cope with their feelings. Love makes sexual intercourse right. This adolescent morality has been labeled "Permissiveness with affection." When they feel strong affection for another person, they become sexually permissive. Petting to sexual climax is frequently used by couples who do not desire to engage in intercourse, which they have been taught to avoid by their parents. This does not leave them with a feeling of guilt, although Reiss (1967) found from rather large and widespread samplings that guilt feelings do not generally inhibit sexual behavior.

Double dating, going steadily, and other related heterosexual practices vary with social and cultural conditions. As of 1972 going steadily had declined in favor of the group activities (Parade, 1972). Groups gather in places where they can listen to music, or else go for a hike. Group activity, they pointed out, takes the awkwardness out of being alone with someone you don't know very well and gives you the opportunity to become better acquainted with more young people. In such a case there are no wallflowers—you don't have to have a partner to participate. Dr. John Milner of the University of Southern California's School of Social Work contends there is more sincerity in teen relationships than formerly, and that boys treat girls as they used to treat each other. He states: "They believe in love and warmth and caring for one another; I suspect they'll make great parents themselves one day" (Parade, 1972: 26). That we are witnessing a great social revolution seems obvious. It is difficult to predict future dating patterns or heterosexual relations, but the honesty, idealism, and sincerity of present-day youth should contribute to constructive and wholesome sexual relationships.

TEEN-AGE MARRIAGES

Recent statistics indicate either a leveling off or decline in rates of youthful marriage. There has also been an increase in varying degrees of mate relations in which mature adolescents in college or elsewhere make a home together. In some adolescent cultures communes are formed; however these represent a very small percentage of adolescents. Several reasons may be offered to account for early marriages:

1. Marriage seems to satisfy one's basic needs in general better than the single state.
2. Marriage is the least undesirable of two or more alternatives—note for example the pregnant teen-ager.
3. Girls who see marriage as their main goal in life intrinsically prefer it to being single.
4. Mating is part of man's biological nature. It is through marriage that adolescents ultimately fulfill certain developmental tasks in our culture.
5. For adolescents, marriage is one and perhaps the fastest way to achieve an adult role and status.
6. Early marriage among those with certain strong religious convictions relieves them of the guilt feelings that arise from premarital sex.

Factors Influencing Dating and Marriage

Although we refer to the social mobility that is possible in our democratic society, actual studies of dating and marriage practices show that teen-agers tend to date and marry from the same economic class. There is further evidence that persons occupying adjacent social classes or are on the borderline of their own social class are more likely to form a stable marriage.

Through a variety of associations adolescents are able to learn the special characteristics of those whom they date. Adolescents of each sex have their ideas about what makes for a good marriage partner, although this will vary to some degree from age to age and from one person to another. In general maturity seems to bring forth a sounder basis for selecting a marriage partner. Karp and others (1970) studied a group of engaged female undergraduates at Wellesley College. The girls completed questionnaires consisting of fifty-four adjectival phrases taken from the Leary Interpersonal Check List. The results of the study supported two hypotheses that were earlier set forth: (1) homogeneous traits matched, so that a mate will be chosen who resembles the self; and (2) where the actual self differs from the ideal self, a mate will be seen as resembling the ideal self rather than the actual.

Pregnant Brides

In 1970 it was estimated that 200,000 American girls under eighteen would give birth; nearly two-thirds of the girls would be married by the time of delivery. Of the 200,000, 60 percent were white, 40 percent non-whites (*JNEA,* 1970). It is difficult to establish the percentage of teen-age brides who are pregnant at the time of marriage. In England, according to the Family Planning Association, the answer is 35 percent. In the United States, according to Dr. Paul Popenoe of the American Institute of Family Relations, it is somewhere around 40 percent. Were it not for contraceptive devices it would be much larger. Liberalized abortion laws will likely reduce this further.

The school-age pregnant girl, whether married or single, faces three life crises: the rapid transition from adolescence to adulthood, the acceptance of her role as a wife and mother, and the physical and emotional upheaval accompanying pregnancy. These are girls with problems— medical, social, and educational. The Committee on Maternal Nutrition pointed out that

> The occurrence of pregnancy during adolescence presents both physical and psychological risks. Girls are at increased risk if pregnancy occurs before their own growth has been completed. The majority of girls attain physical maturity by seventeen years of age, and pregnancy after this age has not been found to present special biological hazards. Thus, the course and outcome of pregnancy of girls seventeen to twenty years of age resemble those of mature young women (twenty to twenty-four years of age), whereas there is a sharp increase in infant mortality for each year of age under 17 (1970: 9).

Difficulties of Early Marriages

Teen-agers frequently marry with little or no preparation for marriage, family living, making a living, family budgeting, and child-rearing. The college students in the study reported by Beggs and Copeland (1971) were asked their opinion about financial support from their parents. The answers were couched in the following conditional responses:

Yes, parents should help financially	8.0%
Yes, but only if the parents can afford it	11.0%
Yes, but only if the couple asks for help	13.7%
Yes, but only if both conditions above are met	27.6%
No, parents should not help financially	30.5%
No opinion	9.2%

It is of interest to note from this survey that college males were more willing to accept financial help than were females. Nearly twice as many females answered that parents should not contribute financial help than did males. A large percentage of early marriage partners soon find themselves facing rather serious financial problems. In most cases the husband is poorly prepared for family living; they haven't developed a useful and accurate conception of the roles of husbands and wives. They have had little or no financial experience and may soon find themselves in serious financial trouble. Glick and Norton (1971) noted that the males with an incomplete high school or college education had high probabilities of early divorce and early remarriage.

THE PROBLEM OF CHILDREN. Just a few decades ago most brides could be expected to give birth to a child within about a year after their marriage. The births of a second, third, and fourth child burdened the family financially and caused a great deal of tension, since it has been found that money is the chief factor responsible for most marital difficulties.

With more widespread birth control information and methods available, the problem of unwanted children can be controlled. A 1974 Gallup Poll survey showed a decline in the percentage of people in the United States favoring large families, with the decline being greater for young adults and persons with college or high school backgrounds. The median response on the ideal number of children in a family is 2.0, slightly below the replacement level.

In Berkeley, California, ecology-minded youths have proclaimed that they will stay childless to help save mankind. A large number of affluent, urban young marrieds are also taking the pledge, openly declaiming that they prefer an unfettered, mobile, pleasure-seeking life to the responsibilities of parenthood. According to Dr. Nathan Ackerman, a distinguished psychiatrist and an expert on family problems, a favorite slogan these days among many urban middle-class couples is: "Make love, but don't make babies" (*Newsweek*, 1970b).

Teen-age Divorce

Glick and Norton (1971) have furnished us with information on the probabilities of marriage and divorce based upon the Survey of Economic Opportunity, which the U.S. Bureau of the Census conducted in the spring of 1967 for the Office of Economic Opportunity. The data are limited to persons fourteen to sixty-nine years of age—persons in the principal ages for marriage and divorce. The results presented in Figure 14-4 show that the probability of divorce is greater among those who marry early, have little education, and little money. The age of men at the time of marriage having the lowest rate of divorce was the 25 to 29 age group.

California, after relaxing its stringent divorce laws, instituted legal obstacles to teen-age marriage. Formerly, any prospective bride under the age of sixteen needed both parental and court permission to marry. Under a new law, court permission will be required until the age of eighteen. To secure court permission, one must undertake some form of counseling on the social, economic, and personal responsibilities of marriage (Parade, 1971a). According to the Bureau of Vital Statistics, 39.2 percent of all California divorces in 1966 involved couples who had married in their teens. Also, teen-age brides have children earlier and more frequently than those marrying later in life, so more young lives are disturbed by divorce. About 31 percent of all teen-age marriages ending in divorce in 1966 involved three or more children.

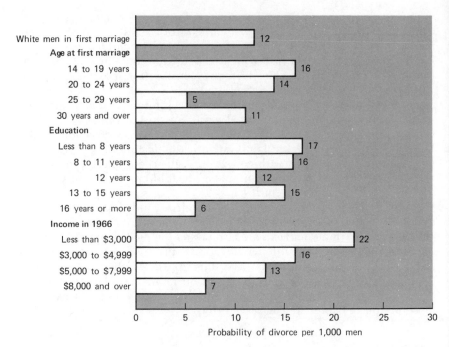

White men in first marriage — 12

Age at first marriage
14 to 19 years — 16
20 to 24 years — 14
25 to 29 years — 5
30 years and over — 11

Education
Less than 8 years — 17
8 to 11 years — 16
12 years — 12
13 to 15 years — 15
16 years or more — 6

Income in 1966
Less than $3,000 — 22
$3,000 to $4,999 — 16
$5,000 to $7,999 — 13
$8,000 and over — 7

0   5   10   15   20   25   30
Probability of divorce per 1,000 men

FIGURE 14-4 Average annual probability of divorce per 1,000 white men in their first marriage less than five years by selected characteristics: 1960–1966. After Glick and Norton (1971: 307).

ADOLESCENT UNWED MOTHERS

More than two million adolescents get into serious trouble each year because they do not know or fail for some reason to face the facts: sexual intercourse may cause babies. "Nationwide, illegitimate births have now topped 300,000 a year. . . . A shocking 243,900 of these are from mothers between the ages of fifteen and twenty-four" (*Reader's Digest,* 1970: 153).

In 1964, a Chicago Board of Health report indicated that 2,833 girls aged seventeen and under had given birth out of wedlock; this number rose to 3,144 in 1965—an increase of 11 percent. "Over 75 percent of these girls resided in areas of the city characterized by the lowest per capita incomes, the highest rates of illegitimacy, and the lowest levels of educational attainment; 83 percent in 1964 and 85 percent in 1965 were Negroes" (Wright, 1966: 171). These figures do not give the total picture because of the hidden pregnancies in the middle class and other groups that never come to the attention of the health or social welfare agencies.

Atlanta reported approximately 1,500 school age pregnant girls eighteen and under in the Atlanta community. Delivery at Grady Hospital is 750 a year, ranging in ages from eleven to sixteen (Cash, 1970). The number of pregnant girls in New York secondary schools reached 2,487 in 1969, twice as many as the year before (*Newsweek,* 1970a: 56). Health officials, concerned about the school's policy of keeping unmarried pregnant girls in class as long as possible (with the natural consequence that some might give birth in school), wrote a booklet as a practical precaution and sent it to all elementary and secondary school principals. The instructions cover everything that school officials might be able to do in an emergency from stillbirths to breech births. Although teachers and school officials are not enthusiastic about the prospect of delivering a baby, these emergency instructions could be invaluable.

Pregnancy in Adolescence

The dangers of pregnancy before the girl has reached her full development was pointed out earlier. Weight reduction in pregnant adolescent girls is dangerous and should certainly not be undertaken except under the supervision of a physician. Girls who smoke during pregnancy are more likely to have underweight infants than nonsmokers. Other items that have been set forth on pregnancy in adolescence are as follows:

1. An increasing number of infants are being born to girls seventeen years of age and younger.

2. Disproportionately more low-birth-weight infants are born to mothers under fifteen years of age.

3. The mortality rate for infants of mothers under fifteen years of age is 58.7 per thousand live births, compared with the U.S. average of 25.1 for all infants.

4. Among pregnant girls under seventeen years of age the incidence of iron-deficiency anemia, toxemia, premature births, and deaths of infants within twenty-eight days after delivery is higher than among older pregnant women (*Children,* 1970b: 239).

In a study by Wagner and Slernboski (1968), Rorschach responses of pregnant unwed women were compared with those of pregnant married women. Significant differences appeared on light shading variables of the test indicating a fearful, compliant, and anxious attitude on the part of the pregnant unwed adolescent. The investigators conclude from the comparisons that the psychological trauma induced by out-of-wedlock motherhood may not be as severe as is popularly believed and that illegitimate pregnancy does not appear from the test results to be as emotionally injurious as is frequently envisioned.

UNMARRIED FATHERS. The idea of considering the plight of the unmarried father is of recent origin; it is perhaps related to the sexual revolution and the New Morality in which love and sex seem to have been brought together to a greater degree than before. The pregnant girl today is in a large percentage of cases "the good girl" who is in love but needs sex education and birth control information. The boy is frequently willing to marry the girl, but parents are in many cases unwilling to cooperate. The fact that such a large percentage of teen-age brides are pregnant at the time of their marriage is evidence of the New Morality and the attitudes of the boys toward their "steady."

The Prevention of Unwed
Adolescent Pregnancy

There are several facets to the problem of preventing unwed teen-age pregnancy, but the most necessary step would be to institute a thorough course in sex deucation in all high schools. The various religious groups could play a role if they would take a constructive and compassionate attitude rather than moralizing and haranguing about loose teen-age morals. Adolescents are not antireligious, but they are obviously not interested in the traditional authoritarian church programs.

In the Sorenson report of adolescent sexuality in contemporary America (1973), most adolescents describe the church's attitude toward sex as being negative, although some theologians and churchmen have publicly declared sex to be a humane and liberating force. According to the report, some 49 percent of all adolescents believe churches teach that the enjoyment of sex is sinful, and 37 percent agree that this is one of the reasons young people have stopped going to church.

NEED FOR COMMUNICATION. According to Dempsey (1969), follow-up studies of programs serving adolescents during their first out-of-wedlock pregnancy have found an alarming high recurrence rate. One study that followed girls for eighteen months after delivery of a first out-of-wedlock child found a recurrence rate of nineteen out-of-wedlock deliveries for each 100 girls; another study covered a five-year period and found a recurrence rate of ninety-five out-of-wedlock deliveries for each 100 girls. The question at once appears, Why the enormous difference? Part of the explanation must lie in the inability for one reason or another of the girls to communicate with responsible adults.

Many girls from lower socioeconomic backgrounds have been raised in families in which communication with the parents is largely nonverbal, and in which there is little steady contact with a father figure. The failure of adolescent girls to identify with men in their home life is a serious disadvantage in their relationships with male classmates at school.

THE USE OF BIRTH CONTROL. The increased permissiveness in the New Morality has produced serious problems for many adolescents and their parents. Parents who are willing to face the situation realistically have increasingly turned to programs for preventing adolescence pregnancy. The Adolescent Family Life Service (Gordis, et al.) is open to any adolescent girl living in Baltimore regardless of race or socioeconomic status. "The program provides a broad spectrum of health services by an interdisciplinary team comprising pediatricians, gynecologists, public-health nurses, social workers, psychiatrists, clinical psychologists, dentists, and other personnel" (1970: 1078). During the first two years of the program, 100 girls were placed on oral contraceptives. The program has been helpful despite the fact that many of the girls did not continue using "the pill"; no harmful side effects were found from using the contraceptives.

A gynecologist from the University of North Carolina suggests that pharmacists openly display contraceptives and birth control information. Dr. Takey Crist raised a serious question in an address delivered at a symposium on health education sponsored by the University of North Carolina's School of Pharmacy (1970). If in fact the easy availability of contraceptives to unmarried people encouraged greater sexual activity, it would be no more harmful than the unwanted pregnancies and unwanted children.

ABORTION. Closely related to birth control as a means of preventing pregnancy is abortion, although this occurs after pregnancy. Legalization of abortion during the first six months of pregnancy in accordance with certain guidelines should have a significant effect on the birth rate, especially among the unwed teen-agers and adults. This may not significantly affect some groups who are strongly opposed to abortion on moral and religious grounds. Although problems related to abortion are controversial, it seems likely that opportunities for abortion when needed or desired will increase among the ignorant and poor in the decades ahead.

HOMOSEXUALITY

Homosexuality, sometimes referred to as homoerotism, refers to a personality whose sexual interests are inclined toward members of the same rather than the opposite sex. Although differences in physical make-up and balance between male and female hormones exist between adolescents of the same sex, there are also certain environmental factors that contribute to homosexuality.

In Western civilization environmental pressures sometimes operate to make adolescents deviate sexually. However, due to hormone differences not all adolescents of the same sex would be affected to the same degree by such pressures. Some boys may be made very effeminate in their behavior by mothers who persist in treating them as they would their daughters. The overprotected girl shielded in a strict girls' school has only the opportunity to associate with girls and to satisfy her sexual needs through these associations. Such social and psychological experiences have been thought of as related to the development of homosexuality.

Although we tend to think of homosexuality only among adults, such behavior also appears among the young. The militancy of the Gay Liberation Movement is an indication of the increased permissiveness in sexual matters. ". . . In major cities across the country, thousands of young homosexuals, their arms locked affectionately around one another and their fists defiantly clenched in the air, parade proudly through the streets chanting: 'Two, four, six, eight, Gay is just as good as straight' " (*Newsweek*, 1971: 45). Although this group is militant and vociferous, it doesn't likely exceed 100,000 of the estimated 4 million homosexual men and women.

The traditional view is that homosexuality is purely social and psychological. Recent improvements in biochemical assay methods have shed some information on the physiology of homosexuality. Margolese (1970), a Los Angeles endocrinologist, attacked the problem of homosexuality in a different manner, concentrating on the male hormone. The subjects of his study consisted of ten heterosexuals and ten active homosexuals in "good health," and four heterosexuals not in "good health." Urine collected over a twenty-four hour period was analyzed for seventeen ketosteroids, androsterone, and etiocholenolone. A statistical analysis of values obtained from the ten heterosexuals and ten homosexuals revealed a clear discrimination between the two groups. The results for an additional group of six healthy subjects, whose classification was withheld prior to the urine analysis, furnished a discrimination score which accurately predicted the four homosexuals and the two heterosexual males.

The andosterone etiocholenolone ratio and the discrimination scores of the four heterosexuals who did not fulfill the criteria of good health were in ranges similar to those of homosexuals. One of these subjects had diabetes mellitus; the other three had severe depression. Thus, the change in ratio and discrimination scores may occur in cases of individuals other than homosexuals. This suggests that the reversed ratio does not in itself furnish a safe basis for predicting homosexuality. Margolese concludes further:

> . . . the present data, could lead to the hypothesis that the metabolic condition which results in a relatively high andosterone value is the cause of sexual preference for females by either sex, whereas a relatively low andosterone value is associated with sexual preference for males by either sex (154).

SEX EDUCATION

Although sex education in schools is not new, it remains one of the controversial issues in the curriculum. Many parents and professionals have strong reservations about what should be included in a comprehensive sexual educational program. That adolescents are ignorant of the biological facts of sex and reproduction has been shown from different studies, however, they have shown an interest in more information about themselves—their needs, biology, and basic drives. "The

American Medical Association has endorsed proper sex education programs and has urged physicians to help in the development of such programs" (Goodheart, 1970: 28).

Needs and Purposes

In 1969 the West German government came out strongly in favor of sex education. They recognized the need for meeting the problem. Consequently the Bonn government

> made available to the public a revolutionary *Sexual Atlas* that will be used to instruct fourteen- and fifteen-year-olds in optional school programs.
> The forty-eight page book begins with a detailed explanation of the human reproduction process, then goes on to shatter sexual myths. It states that sex is not fearful, that "self-enjoyment" by both sexes is not sinful but rather "a normal development process," that venereal disease is most difficult to contract from toilet seats and showers.
> A lengthy section deals with birth control methods, concluding that the pill is the safest. The book also discusses abortion (*Parade*, 1969: 8).

No doubt many problems of teenagers relate to either lack of information regarding sex or incorrect information. This is indicated in part by the frequency of teenage pregnancy and the increase in venereal infection among adolescents. Some of the special problems which the schools must become more concerned with are:

1. how and when to furnish adolescents with the needed information about problems related to sex;
2. just what information is most needed;
3. how to provide for the needs of the pregnant high school girl and the unwed teenage mother;
4. what provisions should be made for teenagers who marry;
5. how to best deal with information and problems related to venereal disease at school;
6. how to deal with parents of pregnant or unwed school girls;
7. what kind of materials should be provided in an educational program for the pregnant teenagers.

NEED FOR BIRTH CONTROL INFORMATION. A sad feature of teen-age pregnant girls is their ignorance about the causes of pregnancy and birth control methods. This is especially true among adolescents from the lower social class, where there is little communication and understanding between parents and adolescents. The consequence of this in increased pregnancies was referred to earlier. Increased birth control information for adolescents has helped reduce the rate of second pregnancies in San Francisco (*Newsweek*, 1970a). According to the findings of a follow-up study of 158 girls who gave birth out-of-wedlock at the age of seventeen or younger, more girls in the noninterviewed groups had a second child than girls in the interviewed groups. "Most of the girls told the interviewers they had not wanted their first pregnancy and had lacked knowledge about reproduction processes when they had begun having sex relations. Only two of the forty-eight girls who were fifteen years of age or under and thirteen of the 110 girls who were sixteen or seventeen said they had 'known enough' about sex at the time" (*Children,* 1971: 159).

INFORMATION ABOUT VENEREAL DISEASE. There has been a sizable increase in the amount of venereal disease during the past two decades, especially in adolescents. The Public Health Service's Center for Disease Control in Atlanta estimated in 1970 that about 1,300 new cases of infectious venereal disease—gonorrhea, primary syphilis, and secondary syphilis—occur each day in the fifteen- to, nineteen-year-old group, and about 1,900 new cases occur in the twenty- to twenty-four-year-old group. These data indicate a sharp upward trend during the 1960s which seems likely to continue through most of the 1970s (*Children,* 1970a). One of the major reasons for the increase in venereal disease among children and adolescents is ignorance, which points to the need for sex education. "In California, children as young as ten are being infected with venereal disease. In 1970 there were 700 reported cases among children aged ten to fourteen and probably five times that amount of unreported cases (*Parade,* 1971d).

In the case of gonorrhea, the rates among teen-agers and young adults showed a sharp increase so that "from 1965 to 1968 there was an increase from 401 to 611 reported cases per 100,000 persons in the fifteen to nineteen age group (240). Public health officials believe that reports are available for only one out of four treated cases of venereal disease.

The incidence of syphilis is on the increase, following a period in which it was thought that modern drugs had almost eliminated this disease.[2] Adolescents are as uninformed about venereal diseases as they are about effective contraception. This is especially true of girls who do not manifest the symptoms as obviously as men.

SUMMARY

To understand contemporary attitudes toward love, sex, dating, and marriage we must understand Judeo-Christian traditions and the

---

[2] Through federal, state, and county health programs children are checked and inoculated against infectious diseases such as smallpox, diptheria, pertussis (whooping cough), and now both kinds of measles. School children are also tested for tuberculosis. The rapid increase in venereal infection, even among eleven- and twelve-year-olds may make it imperative that society give some consideration to the control of syphilis and gonorrhea. Some have suggested that junior high school adolescents should be tested regularly and that an easily administered diagnostic test should be developed.

double standard of sexual behavior for men and women. The wide gap in standards between male and female is being closed as a result of many conditions, including the Woman's Liberation Movement. Peers remain the main source of sexual information, with the parents providing for less than one fourth of it. Attitudes toward abortion, singles, and petting have changed. The New Morality, which is more permissive than the old morality, has provided another source of generational conflict.

Family and social class, as bearers of tradition, have an important influence upon the morality of adolescents, although the family has lost much of its influence as a result of the increased influence of peers. In general the more liberal the group the greater the permissiveness. Thus, sexual permissiveness is an aspect of the increased liberalism in general. The importance of virginity has faded in favor of sex accompanied by affection. The increase of pregnancy among teen-agers, in spite of greater knowledge of birth control methods, is evidence of the operation of the New Morality. With the decline of religious influences and the increased knowledge of birth control, we find a pronounced change in attitudes toward premarital sex and a surging rate of venereal disease among adolescents.

There has been a leveling off of youthful marriages with an increase in sexual relations and various living arrangements. Marriages motivated by pregnancy are on the decline in many areas due to better and more widespread birth control information and more liberal abortion laws.

In the past, the rate of divorce has been very high for teenage marriages, but may become lower in the near future as a result of significant changes that are beginning to operate in connection with marriage and a family.

There is a tremendous need for additional information on and medical help with venereal diseases. Teenagers must also be educated in the areas of family relations, child rearing, and operating a home.

REFERENCES

BEGGS, DANIEL C. and HENRY A. COPELAND. "Large Majority of Students Plan Church Wedding." *Charlotte Observer,* March 19, 1971, p. 5A.

CASH, SARAH. "Teen-age Parents Get Community Services." *Atlanta Journal and Constitution* (February 8, 1970), p. 10G.

Charlotte Observer (November 29, 1970), p. 17A. "Airforce's First Unwed Mother Still Waiting."

———— (April 18, 1974), p. 1F. "Appeal of a Large Family Lowest in 38 Years."

———— (May 11, 1974), p. 8A. "586,000 Abortions Reported."

Children (November–December 1970a), 17 (6):240. "Child Health."

———— (November–December 1970b), 17 (6):239. "Nutrition."

———— (July–August 1971), 18 (4):159. "Unmarried Mothers."

Committee on Maternal Nutrition. Food and Nutrition Board, National Research Council. *Maternal Nutrition and the Course of Pregnancy: Sum-*

mary. Washington, D.C.: U.S. Department of Health, Education, and Welfare, 1970.

DEMPSEY, JOHN J. "Proposed Standard Measure of Recurrence of Out-of-wedlock Births to Adolescents." *Public Health Reports* (October 1969).

FARNSWORTH, DANA L. "Sexual Morality and the Dilemma of the Colleges." In *Adolescence: Contemporary Studies,* Alvin E. Winder and David L. Angus, eds. New York: American Book Co., 1968.

GLICK, PAUL C. and ARTHUR J. NORTON. "Frequency Duration and Probability of Marriage and Divorce." *Journal of Marriage and Family Living* (May 1971), p. 307.

GOODHEART, BARBARA. "Sex in the Schools: Education or Titillation." *Today's Health* (February 1970), pp. 28–30, 70–71.

GORDIS, LEON, RUTH FINKELSTEIN, JACQUELINE FASSETT, and BETTY WRIGHT. "Evaluation of a Program for Preventing Adolescent Pregnancy." *New England Journal of Medicine* (May 7, 1970), p. 1078.

GRINDER, ROBERT E. "Relations of Social Dating Attractions to Academic Orientation and Peer Relations." *Journal of Educational Psychology* (1966), 57: 27–34.

HARRIS, DALE B. and SING CHU TSENG. "Children's Attitudes Toward Peers and Parents as Revealed by Sentence Completions." *Child Development* (1957), 28:401–11.

Journal of the National Education Association (October 1970), pp. 26–29, 89. "Pregnant Teen-Agers."

KARP, ELLEN S., JULIE H. JACKSON, and DAVID LESTER. "Ideal-self Fulfillment in Mate Selection: A Corollary to the Contemporary Need Theory of Mate Selection." *Journal of Marriage and Family Living* (1970), 32:269–72.

KINSEY, ALFRED C. *Sexual Behavior in the Human Male.* Philadelphia: W. B. Saunders, 1948.

———. *Sexual Behavior in the Human Female.* Philadelphia: W. B. Saunders, 1953.

MARGOLESE, M. S. "Homosexuality: A New Endocrine Correlate." *Hormones and Behavior* (1970), 1:151–55.

MARTINSON, FLOYD M. "Sexual Knowledge, Values, and Behavior Patterns of Adolescents." *Child Welfare* (1968), 47:405–10, 426.

McCall's (August 1968), pp. 58–59, 114–18, 122. "Sex on the Campus."

MEHRABIAN, ALBERT. "Communication without Words." *Readings in Psychology.* Del Mar, Calif.: CRM Books, 1969.

Newsweek (February 9, 1970a), p. 56. "Until the Doctor Comes."

——— (June 15, 1970b), p. 111. "Make Love, Not Babies."

——— (August 23, 1971), p. 45. "The Militant Homosexual."

PACKARD, VANCE. "Sex on Campus." *McCall's* (August 1968), pp. 58–59, 113–18, 122.

Parade magazine (July 20, 1969), p. 8.

——— (July 5, 1970), p. 7. "Differences."

——— (February 14, 1971a), p. 24. "Marriage, Teen Style."

——— (May 8, 1971b). "How Come a Nice Girl Like You Isn't Married?"

———— (November 14, 1971c), p. 26. "Reagan's VD Vote."

———— (May 21, 1972), p. 26. "Going Steady."

Reader's Digest (December 1970), pp. 153–56. "What Kids Still Don't Know About Sex."

REISS, IRA L. *The Social Context of Premarital Sexual Permissiveness.* New York: Holt, Rinehart & Winston, Inc., 1967.

ROSENBERG, BERNARD and JOSEPH BENSMAN. "Sexual Patterns in Three Ethnic Subcultures of an American Underclass." *Annals of the American Academy of Political and Social Sciences* (1968), 378:61–75.

SEBALD, HANS. *Adolescence: A Sociological Analysis.* New York: Appleton-Century-Crofts, 1968.

SORENSON, ROBERT C. and DAVID HENDIN. "Few Teens Agree with Parents' Views on Sex." *Charlotte Observer* (February 19, 1973), p. 1D.

THORNBURG, H. D. "Age and First Source of Sex Information as Reported by 88 Women." *Journal of School Health* (1970), 40:156–68.

————. "The Adolescent and Sex." In *Contemporary Adolescent Readings,* H. D. Thornburg, ed. Belmont, Calif.: Brooks/Cole Publishing Co., 1971.

TUTHILL, SUE. "More Abortions, Fewer Pregnancy-related Deaths." *Today's Health* (November 1971), p. 7.

WAGNER, R. E. and JEAN SLERNBOSKI. "Psychological Reactions of Pregnant Unwed Women as Measured by the Rorschach." *Journal of Clinical Psychology* (1968), 24:467–69.

WALSH, ROBERT H. "Intergenerational Transmission of Sexual Standards." A paper presented at the American Sociological Association Annual Meeting, August 31-September 3, 1970, Washington, D.C.

WRIGHT, MATTIE K. "Comprehensive Services for Adolescent Unwed Mothers." *Children* (September-October 1966), pp. 170–75.

RECOMMENDED READINGS

BRISKIN, JACQUELINE. *California Generation.* Philadelphia: J. B. Lippincott Co., 1971.
A novel based on a group of high school students which follows them from their graduation in 1960 through 1968. Characters were created to play different roles. Education was pictured as a mockery, religion as mostly forgotten, and parents as mainly drab.

DESCHIN, CELIA S. *The Teenager and VD: A Social Symptom of Our Time.* New York: Richards Rosen Press, 1969.
The nature of venereal diseases and the problems involving the rising incidence among adolescents is discussed against a background of a changing social climate and sexual behavior patterns.

OSOFSKY, HOWARD J. *The Pregnant Teenager: A Medical, Educational, and Social Analysis.* Springfield, Ill.: Charles C Thomas, 1968.
The author discusses the social and psychological effects of out-of-wedlock pregnancies. He mentions the lack of adequate medical care and the all too frequent inferior medical care received.

PACKARD, VANCE. *The Sexual Wilderness.* New York: David McKay Co., Inc., 1968.
Surveys numerous studies of the effect of premarital intercourse on marital happiness. Caution is suggested in interpreting and generalizing from data on sexual relations.

REISS, IRA L. *The Social Context of Premarital Sexual Permissiveness.* New York: Holt, Rinehart & Winston, Inc., 1967.
Reiss's primary interest was in attitudes of college students. He collected data on 268 students in an Iowa college on sexual attitudes and behavior.

SAGARIN, E., ed. "Sex and the Contemporary American Scene." *Annals of the American Academy of Political and Social Science* (1968), 376.
This entire issue consists of fourteen articles on human sexuality from several perspectives. Articles dealing with the sexual behavior of different groups and types of people are presented along with special sexual problems in our society. Major issues discussed are (1) sex within our society; (2) the double standard; (3) role of the family, school, and church in human sexuality; and (4) attitudes toward sex.

SIMON, W. "Sex." *Psychology Today* (1969), 3:23–27.
The writer traces a shift in concerns about sex since 1900. He notes that this has been more discernible since World War II. He feels, however, that few new patterns of sexual practices are likely to occur among contemporary adolescents, especially girls. He sees most sexual behavior as leading toward marriage and family.

TOFFLER, ALVIN. "The Fractured Family." *Future Shock.* New York: Random House, Inc., 1970. Chapter 11.
The following topics make up the materials of this chaper: the mystique of motherhood; the streamlined family; bioparents and proparents; communes and homosexual daddies; the odds against love; temporary marriage; marriage trajectors; the demands of freedom.

15

adolescent
drug use

The widespread use of drugs by adolescents and adults is alarming. Perhaps the major concern results from our inability to adopt a consistent viewpoint on drugs, since some drugs are part of our culture while others are largely new to us. Certainly, drug abuse is not confined to the present generation of adolescents; however, the widespread use among adolescents today is recognized by both parents and teachers.

This chapter will focus on the use of both illegal drugs and also alcohol and nicotine, which are legally and socially sanctioned in American society. Nowlis (1969) made a study of drugs and the extent of their use for the National Association of Student Personnel Administrators; he pointed out that a considerable part of the average family's budget is spent on drugs, alcohol, and beverages that might be classified as drugs. American faith in the curative power of chemical compounds is vividly portrayed in the advertising of the mass media. There is a drug for every ailment, and even the shy or insecure can gain instant confidence and popularity by availing themselves of the advantages of innocuous substances such as toothpaste or deodorant. It is estimated that the average household has about thirty drugs in its medicine cabinet.

Drugs range from those mild, daily consumed ones to those which are medically necessary, and to those which are addictive and destructive.

A complete definition of drugs would include any substance which, because of its chemical nature, affects the structure or function of a living organism. This includes coffee and other caffeine-containing drinks, vitamins and other food supplements, all alcoholic beverages, as well as legal and illegal drugs.

DEFINITIONS AND CATEGORIES
OF DRUGS

Many reports tend to consider as drugs only those substances that are experimented with by youth and make exceptions of alcohol, nicotine, and caffeine. However, these last three, while they are culturally sanctioned, have the pharmacological properties of drugs and will be discussed. The term "drugs" will therefore have a broader meaning and will include substances that produce a definable physical and psychological reaction. These will be grouped as: stimulants, depressants, narcotics, hallucinogens, and chemical solvents.[1]

There is a wide range in the use and abuse of drugs. A heroin addict has to have his fix even though an overdose can kill him. Another person has to have his morning coffee and cigarette, and too many cigarettes can cause lung cancer and heart attacks. Sniffing gasoline is a cheap, easily available "kick," but few persons try it.

Because of the illegality of drugs and the very strong social and parental sanctions against their use, adolescents rely on their peers for knowledge about and accessibility to drugs. This can lead to very grave dangers to the drug user. The first danger is the ready availability of many different types of drugs the properties of which the teen-ager is totally ignorant, other than the fact they are "groovy highs." The other danger is that, because of the drug's illegality, the teen-ager cannot be sure of the dosage or the purity of a compound. For instance a tablet of LSD may be enough for one, two, or even four persons and may contain an additive such as amphetamine of strychnine (rat poison). Milder hallucinogens may be cut with an opiate that could lead a user unwittingly into addiction.

Stimulants

Stimulant drugs are chemically classified as members of the amphetamine family. Amphetamine was first prepared in 1887 and synthesized in the form of benzedrine in 1927. Its use received a big boost during World War II when battle troops and scientists working on war-related projects used them often to relieve exhaustion. Both American and German pilots packed stimulants in their survival kits.

---

[1] In the discussion of the history and pharmacological property of drugs, we have relied heavily upon the studies of Geller and Boas (1969) and Taylor (1966).

After the war two new amphetamines were developed. They were dextroamphetamine (dexedrines or "dex" or "pep pills") and meth-amphetamine (methedrine or "speed"). Stimulants act directly on the central nervous system and their effects include alertness, an increased heart rate, a rise in blood pressure, and dialated pupils. The milder dosages are used too by students cramming for exams or truck drivers on overnight runs to stay awake, by housewives to "pep" up, and are in-cluded in many diet drug preparations. Coffee, tea, and chocolate are included in this group, and if taken in sufficient quantity over a period of time are at least habit forming.

With excessive or prolonged usage the body develops a tolerance, which means the steady user requires increasing dosages. Heavy users, or "speed freaks," use methedrine crystals which are dissolved and taken by injection or sniffed in the nostrils. Large dosage or frequent use re-sults in insomnia, loss of weight, paranoia, and sometimes hallucinations. The aftereffects include extreme exhaustion and depression. Some use depressants to minimize the effects of "coming down."

Depressants

The first sleep-producing barbiturate was synthesized in 1903. In clinical use they reduce mental stress, induce sleep, and control convulsions; they are used in psychiatry as a diagnostic and therapeutic aid. Depressants slow down nerve action, heart beat, breathing, and muscle coordination. There are many barbiturate derivatives; the best known and strongest is phenobarbital. Two of the many intermediate lasting ones are seco-barbital (seconal) and amobarbital (amytal). Other drugs such as bromides chloral hydrate ("knockout drops"), and some tranquilizers such as meprobamate produce effects similar to those of barbiturates. These pills are often called "goof balls" or "red devils," "yellow jackets," and other names which denote the color of the capsules.

Barbiturates are both physically and emotionally addicting, and abrupt withdrawal from excessive use can result in convulsions, coma, and death. Many of the depressants have a cumulative effect with re-peated doses, and traces of barbiturates can be detected in the blood stream as many as eight to twelve days after a hypnotic dosage. Over-doses can cause death especially if the pills and alcohol are consumed simultaneously.

Alcohol is perhaps more widely used than all other depressants combined. Its effects on the body are very similar to barbiturates. Re-peated excessive dosages of alcohol definitely result in psychological addic-tion, and can possibly produce physical addiction. Chronic alcoholism is more common and more costly to society than narcotic addiction.

Like alcohol, nicotine is an addictive depressant whose use is wide-spread and legalized with only age restrictions as to its purchase. Tobacco, thought to have aphrodisiac properties, which it does not, was extremely popular in England in the late 1500s and early 1600s. The

English, having found neither gold as the Spaniards had nor the abundant fur trade of the French, found their fortune in the New World in Indian tobacco in Virginia. In the late 1870s James Buchanan Duke began and continued to monopolize the making of tobacco into cigarettes with the use of light-cured tobacco, rolling machines, and aggressive advertising.

Nicotine, found in small amounts in tobacco leaves, is one of the most poisonous alkaloids found in the plant world, and causes physical addiction. The smokers of tobacco inhale minute amounts of tar which show definite results of being cancer inducing. Since the 1950s cigarettes have been known to be so physically detrimental that now U.S. law requires each package and advertisement of them to state: "Warning: The Surgeon General Has Determined That Cigarette Smoking Is Dangerous To Your Health."

Narcotics

Narcotics are by far the most addicting and dangerous drugs in these five groups. They are depressants and were introduced as pain killers. Opium comes from the opium poppy; morphine was derived from opium in 1812. The hypodermic syringe and needle were developed shortly before the Civil War, and many veterans of the conflict became medical addicts. Heroin, first produced in 1898, was first thought to be a "cure" for the opium habit.

Until the passage of the Harrison Narcotics Act in 1914, opium-derived narcotics were freely available and could be purchased without prescription from drug and even grocery stores. It is estimated that there were approximately 100,000 narcotic addicts when the Harrison Act was passed. Most of these were "respectable citizens" who were unwittingly addicted to such widely used preparations as laudanum or paregoric,

Over two dozen products have been derived from opium. The most widely known of these are heroin ("smack," "horse," or "H") and codeine, which is still used in some over-the-counter cough syrups. Cocaine ("snow," "coke"), a stimulant, is usually mixed with a narcotic to produce a "speed ball."

The effects of narcotics are an ecstatic rush often likened to a sexual orgasm and followed by a euphoric stupor. Increasing tolerance to these drugs leads to larger dosage requirement and definite physical dependence whether the narcotics are injected (either mainlined into a blood vessel or skin popped) or inhaled ("snorted"), or mixed with another substance such as marijuana and smoked.

Withdrawal from the opiates is a severe process involving violent vomiting, muscle cramps and spasms, diarrhea, and insomnia. Having successfully withstood the withdrawal period is no sure sign of being cured. Present total cure rates are very low. As O'Donnell and Ball report, 75 percent of the *voluntary* patients in a Lexington, Ky., federal hospital leave before the recommended minimum period of four and one half months and 50 percent leave within the first 30 days (1966: 204). Methadone, a drug with milder withdrawal symptoms than heroin has been used to replace it in some drug treatment programs. This has met both success and controversy for, while methadone allows the heroin addict to be a functioning member of society, methadone is itself addicting and also has appeared on the black market.

Hallucinogens

Hallucinogens are neither depressants nor stimulants, and although they may be psychologically addictive, there is no evidence that they are physically addicting. This group of drugs primarily alters one's perception of reality by changing one's concept of time, space, and basic sense perception. They can be divided into two groups: those extracted from plants and those chemically produced.

The most commonly known and widely used hallucinogen, or illegal drug of any kind, is marijuana. Its use has dramatically increased among youth in the past several years. "Grass" is derived from the leaves of the Indian hemp plant and is usually smoked in a pipe or rolled in a cigarette called a "reefer" or "joint." Hashish, or "hash," the more potent derivative of this same plant, is the sticky resin of the flowering female plant. Peyote comes from the aboveground buttonlike growth of the peyote cactus. It has a long history as a powerful hallucinogen used in Indian religious ceremonies of Mexico and the Southwest. From this plant mescaline ("mesc") was synthesized in the 1920s. Psilocybin is derived from a mushroom found in Mexico.

The best known, widely publicized, and most potent man-made hallucinogen is lysergic acid diethylamide (LSD, or "acid"). It was first synthesized from one of the ergot alkaloids that had come from the spoiled rye fungus. For centuries spoiled rye had caused a disease called St. Anthony's Fire until better milling procedures rejected the ergot. It had also been used by European midwives in minute portions to aid in the last stage of delivery. In the 1920s and 1930s scientists isolated some of the active ingredients and LSD was synthesized in a Swiss laboratory in 1943.

LSD is a mind-altering substance which has direct action upon the functioning of the brain without a loss of consciousness. In controlled clinical use it has met with success in the treatment of chronic alcoholics and acute schizophrenics. Illicit, unguided use has produced "trips" into nirvana and into schizophrenia. One of the least understood aspects of this drug is its ability to cause "flashbacks" where the individual seems to be under the influence of LSD months after he has "tripped."

There are also several man-made chemicals that approximate the intensity or effect of LSD. Most of them are known by the initials of their chemical compound—i.e., DMT, DET, and STP.

Chemical Solvents

This last class of drugs is used primarily by younger adolescents or those who want to get high when illegal drugs are either unknown or unavailable. These are often called "garbage highs" and include a wide range of substances such as paint thinner, airplane glue, gasoline, or chloroform. Morning glory seeds, certain mushrooms, and cough syrup may be consumed for their intoxicating effects, while excessive doses of diet pills, caffeine tablets, or sleeping preparations may be used to take one "up" or "down." These chemical solvents are primarily used for a spree, but an overdose of any of them can be extremely dangerous.

ADOLESCENT DRINKING AND DRUG BEHAVIOR PATTERNS

Two important trends may be observed in drug use and abuse. Perhaps the most frightening trend is "that in well-to-do suburban communities and inner-city ghettos alike the age of the youthful drug experimenters has been steadily dropping; there have even been cases of heroin addiction among elementary school children" (*Newsweek*, 1973: 67). The second trend is one that should alarm many parents. "From nearly every quarter of the nation, school authorities and teen-agers themselves report that the latest fad in juvenile drug abuse is one that has a familiar ring to the older generation: the drug of choice these days, they say, is alcohol" (*Ibid.*, p. 68).

According to Federn (1971) drug "misuse" by adolescents should be distinguished from drug addiction. He notes that adolescents are particularly vulnerable to drugs, which accounts for their widespread use. However, there is no single concept that describes a young person and his drinking and drug-taking patterns. The behavior ranges from total abstinence to heroin addiction. It is difficult to draw a line between the somewhat arbitrary distinctions between experimentation and regular and heavy use of alcohol and drugs. The older adolescent who has several beers every night and more on weekends would be considered a regular drinker, whereas a young teen-ager following this same pattern would be labeled a heavy problem drinker. The age of the user of alcohol and drugs is a definite consideration, especially when alcohol and drugs are used by junior high school children. Also the substance used is a factor: beer vs. whiskey, marijuana and hashish vs. LSD, or any of these vs. the opiates such as heroin. For instance a weekend smoker of marijuana is a regular user, whereas the same frequency in taking LSD points to heavy use of that substance.

Feeling of Resentment

The social surroundings in which an adolescent uses these substances is extremely important. Technically, minors who smoke cigarettes or drink alcoholic beverages and all persons who use illegal drugs are breaking the law and are therefore criminals. However, there is a wide range of reaction to such legal infractions. The moral sentiments of an adolescent's community or group of peers define what is considered "bad" behavior and what is really criminal. In addition to peers and teachers, the manner in which an adolescent's parents, neighbors, and friends react to certain behavior determines whether he will conceive his own actions to be rebellious or normal. A youth from a strongly fundamentalist Protestant background who drinks alcoholic beverages with some regularity is equally as deviant from his own social background as is the suburban, middle-class adolescent who smokes marijuana instead of drinking martinis like his parents.

Often cigarette smoking, alcohol consumption, and drug use by adolescents are related to their feelings of rebellion, needs for compensation, or desires to escape social and academic pressures. These are all part of a feeling of *resentment,* defined by Scheler (1961) as a nonspecific, socially oriented form of resentment. As an adolescent told the junior writer, "I don't know exactly why, because nobody ever did anything to me, but I just feel like I've been screwed. And a lot of my friends have too."

The lower-class student sees little relevance in the more esoteric subjects such as geometry and Elizabethan poetry. Adulthood will arrive for him by the end of his teen years. He does not anticipate continued education beyond high school. Chances are that the lower-class student will be placed on a "vocational track" rather than an academic one. In many high schools this is a type of second-class citizenship. If this adolescent begins to drink or smoke, is he rebelling against his prolonged childhood by emulating adult behavior? rebelling against a school system which is irrelevant to his needs? compensating for lack of academic success? or just temporarily escaping from a somewhat unpleasant living pattern?

Very similar types of questions or feelings are voiced by many middle- and upper-class youths. While academic failure is not as great a problem for them, many are pressured to excel in order to gain admittance to the best schools or win a good scholarship. Some of these adolescents question whether later professional success is worth postponing adulthood and "real life" until they are in their mid-twenties. Many adolescents rebel against, compensate for, and escape from their feelings of pressure and resentment by drinking, smoking, and using the milder hallucinogens with some regularity.

Reasons for Using Drugs

All adolescents experience some feelings of marginality and resentment, but not all turn to drugs. Those who do are influenced by three significant factors: (1) their peers, (2) their school experience, and (3) the extent of alienation from their parents.

THE HOME SITUATION. The adolescent's home situation, especially alienation from parents, appears to be the most important factor leading to the use of drugs. The results of a study of high school students by

Herzog, Sudia, and Harwood (1970) show that 70 percent of their correspondents listed an "impulse to escape" as a reason for using drugs. This need was primarily attributed to family-linked problems such as stressful home environment, parental indifference, the generation gap, and pressure to achieve. Adolescent drinking patterns are also closely correlated to their degree of alienation from their parents.

Smart and Fejer (1972) studied the relationship between parental drug use among 8,865 students from the sixth to the thirteenth grade. A positive correlation was obtained between parental use of psychoactive drugs, alcohol, and tobacco and the use of these drugs by the students. The relationship was closest when both parents used psychoactive drugs. These findings suggest that adolescents model their drug use after their parents. Weiner (1971) suggests that the alienated, promiscuous, drug-habituated adolescent needs to be recognized as a psychologically disturbed youngster in need of clinical attention.

The Occasional or Experimental User

The occasional consumption of alcohol or tobacco is in part an imitation of adult customs and usually reflects the patterns of an adolescent's home. Alcohol is often readily available to the teen-ager from his parents' own liquor supply. An adolescent's use of alcohol aids in resolving his dilemma of "Am I a child or an adult?" By indulging in socially sanctioned behavior, such as the consumption of alcohol or smoking cigarettes, and adolescent can partially bridge the gap between childhood and adulthood.

While the occasional user of alcoholic beverages is emulating adult behavior patterns, the experimental user of marijuana is usually following the example of his peers. In both cases there is a curiosity to discover what happens when one is under the influence of such substances. For some the desire to experiment begins in the preteens. As Hager, Wener, and Stuart point out in a study they did on teen-age drug use, 5 percent of the thirteen-year-olds they sampled reported experience with marijuana. They note, "Apparently those desiring to ascertain where drug use begins must consider research at earlier ages" (1971: 296).

There appears to be a definite correlation between an adolescent's social class and whether he will experiment primarily with alcohol or illegal drugs. As Sebald indicates:

> Psychedelic drugs tend to be of greater interest to middle-class teen-agers who are relatively more curious and desirous to experiment than lower-class adolescents who might prefer such escapist drugs as alcohol and opiates, which provide them with instant amnesia concerning the surrounding squalor and poverty (1968: 483).

Occasional or experimental use of alcohol or marijuana is consistently reported to be influenced by peer example and group pressure. Being socially accepted by one's friends is extremely important to an adolescent, and this may mean that he will have a beer or a few "tokes" on a "joint" rather than be considered a drag. Whether an adolescent will move from experimentation to regular use of either alcohol or drugs depends in large part on his association with nonabstemious friends, how he personally views his own actions, and whether or not he found taking the substance to be enjoyable.

The Peer-Oriented Regular User

There is evidence that athletic achievement and heavy involvement in school activities are accompanied by low marijuana use. The results of observation and investigation suggest an association between drinking patterns and the following school conditions:

1. Academic success—"A" and "B" students are less likely to drink than those with lower grades.
2. Interest in school—Those enjoying school are less likely to drink than their opposites who do not enjoy school.
3. Participation in extracurricular or school-related activities—The less participation, the more likelihood of drinking.

Parents and school are also related to adolescent cigarette use. While there is no significant difference in how smokers and nonsmokers feel they live up to their peers' and their own expectations of themselves, both male and female cigarette smokers are more likely to feel they do not meet the expectations of their parents or school.

Herzog *et al.* reveal that students who abstain from drugs tend to feel psychological and social security and strength, often crediting their abstinence to "a sense of identity," "a good family life," and "good friends who are not on drugs". However, in this study, 40 percent of their correspondents cite peers as the influencing factor in drug use. This group mentioned as reasons for drug use: "(1) status or image—a desire to 'look big,' 'be cool,' 'show one isn't chicken'; (2) conformity—a need to follow the crowd and be accepted; (3) curiosity—a desire to 'see what it is about' " (209).

A number of studies have indicated that there is a definite association between adolescent drinking behavior and the amount of time spent with nonabstemious peers. Cigarette smoking was once considered to be primarily influenced by parental example. However, recent studies, such as that by Levitt and Edwards (1970), indicate that the smoking of one's best friend and closest group of friends are an equally strong influence. Reasons for both the use of alcohol and tobacco are similar to those stated above for drug use.

The Addiction-Prone Heavy User

According to Elizabeth Coleman's report (1974), there are 450,000 adolescent alcoholics, the number having tripled in the past decade. Alcoholics Anonymous, once a haven for older adults, now appeals to many young people; in 1974 there were 25 or more AA young groups. However, this does not represent all adolescents and postadolescents that are addiction prone; many younger adolescents are protected from being counted by their parents. Older adolescents who are addiction-prone may become "invisible" persons, unless their actions require police or medical attention.

No one, except for the infant who suffers withdrawal after his birth from an addicted mother, is a "born" addict. There are several specific personality traits exhibited by both the potential chronic alcoholic and the drug addict. These include a sense of personal inadequacy, despair, and intense dependency needs. Since the insecure adolescent is often afraid to display signs of weakness, these inner feelings are often masked. Social relations are a threat to those who are anxious about their own self-image, and some insecure adolescents do not participate in typical peer relationships. For those remaining in school such withdrawal is difficult. To cover up their anxieties, many of these adolescents develop a veneer of toughness. In the case of alcoholism, the characteristic of compulsive independence occurs often. This is apt to take the form of aggressive, overly masculine behavior. Those regularly using drugs, but not yet addicted to narcotics, try to impress their peers with their emotional and psychological strength in being able to handle any type of "trip."

Despite the similarity in the need for escape and the pattern by which an adolescent becomes a heavy user of either drugs or alcohol, there are distinct differences between the chronic alcoholic, the opiate addict, and those who use hallucinogens and the wide variety of other drugs. To a large extent these differences depend on the psychological and physical dangers inherent in the heavy use of any or all of these substances. Some of these differences will be discussed in the next sections.

Effects of Alcohol

Geller and Boas (1969) estimate that there are seventy million persons in the United States who consume alcoholic beverages. Of this number, they estimate that approximately five million are alcoholics. While heavy, escapist drinking patterns often begin by late adolescence, chronic alcoholism is almost exclusively an adult phenomenon because it takes several years of heavy drinking to become sufficiently addicted to experience intense withdrawal symptoms. Many heavy-drinking adolescents may become chronic alcoholics, but they often escape the notice of parents or school officials unless they get into trouble by displaying other more overt signs of social pathology.

Recent findings presented at the International Conference on Alcohol and Addiction in Dublin indicate that alcohol—not marijuana—is more often the stimulant first used by persons who later become heroin addicts (*Parade,* 1972: 14). This conclusion is based on a study of the cross-use of alcohol and drugs used by addicts by Drs. Harriet L. Barr, Donald J. Ottenberg, and Alvin Rosen of the Eagleville Hospital and Rehabilitation Center in Eagleville, Pa. The group studied consisted of 129 male patients diagnosed as alcoholics and 61 considered to be drug addicts. The investigators noted that in a large percentage of cases of drug addiction, the first drug used was alcohol. On the average the alcohol abuse preceded the illegal drug usage by about a year and a half.

The ill-effects of alcohol on school performance, out-of-school activities including recreation and work, and social and sexual behavior have been noted in many studies. Bacon and Jones (1968) state that by and large the students with the highest grades show a higher proportion of abstainers than those with lower grades. However they also note that there is no supportive evidence to show that high school students who do drink are any more socially maladjusted than those who do not. Their results indicate that there is no relationship between the fact of an adolescent's drinking and the likelihood that he will participate in athletics, student organizations, and so on. This would of course be relevant only to the occasional or very moderate regular user of alcoholic beverages.

A specific consideration of teen-age drinking is the part alcohol appears to play in the statistics for young drivers' automobile accident and fatality rates. A Minnesota study (*Traffic Safety*, 1970) reveals that while only 24 percent of that state's drivers were in the sixteen to twenty-four-year-old age group, that group accounted for a disproportionately high 43 percent of drinking drivers killed in 1969. Hames (1971) elaborates:

> But, undoubtedly, normal youthful tendencies for taking dares, showing off, and general exuberance were also involved as much as alcohol. The problem, of course, is that these tendencies seem to be dangerously intensified in the young driver when he drinks. It is a fact, also, that alcohol intensifies those mechanical errors which the beginning driver might normally make, due to inexperience with the task (485).

Effects of Narcotics and Amphetamines

Unlike alcohol, narcotics weaken aggression in the user, and the process of becoming an addict can be very rapid. Opiate users are able to take up to five or six times greater dosages than a typical lethal dose within weeks after their initial experience with opiates. Trice (1966) notes that most regular users of opiates become dependent on them, with regular morphine users having about a 70 percent addiction rate and heroin users almost 100 percent. Medical addicts account for very few of the total number of adolescents using narcotics; however, an increasing number of young persons are becoming "hooked" inadvertently or accidentally through their involvement in the youth drug culture. Many believe erroneously that they will not suffer addiction if they sniff or skin pop narcotics. Heroin is no longer confined to inner-city, poverty-stricken, minority youth. Peer pressures to "try a new high" have brought the opiates to middle- and upper-class adolescents. Secondary to addiction, the prevalent physical disorders encountered by the narcotic addict are hepatitis and related diseases resulting from unsanitary injection equipment, and sexual impotency.

The primary problem facing narcotic addicts is the supply and price of heroin. Ognibene states that in England where the government controls the supply of heroin, the pharmacy cost is $0.04 per grain compared to the United States street price of from $30 to $90 per grain. While taking the profit out of the heroin trade would not lower its use, he notes that the illegality of heroin contributes to its high price and states:

> There are more than a half million Americans who use heroin. Most are addicts who support their habit by committing crimes such as burglary, prostitution, and robbery. A $40 or $50 a day heroin habit would require $150–$200 in stolen property to sustain the addict for a single day. It is estimated that half of all property crimes in New York City are committed by narcotics addicts. The cost to the nation in property losses is several billion dollars a year. The human costs are incalculable (1972: 20).

Amphetamines give the user a sense of well being, as can alcohol and narcotics; however, they also impart a sense of power and confidence. If there is to be one specific category of drugs to be singled out as anti-social or violence producing this would be the one. Amphetamines in fairly large dosages are often used by adolescents to stay awake while studying for exams or to extend and intensify weekends as periods of escape. To the overly insecure adolescent, the lift in spirits and sense of confidence felt when under the influence of this drug can lead him to a psychological dependence upon it. Because there can be extreme depression as the amphetamines wear off, a user may turn to a repeat dosage to stay up or may use barbituates to ease the coming down. Repeated or excessive dosages may result with a user experiencing an altered sense of reality and paranoia which can be physically violent and aggressive.

Influence of LSD and Other Strong Hallucinogens

The potency of LSD and the behavioral effects it causes have been widely reported in the mass media. The three most important factors concerning its use are the user's personality, his emotional state when taking the drug, and the physical setting in which the "trip" takes place. Because LSD alters consciousness, an individual under its influence may not be able to differentiate between hallucinations and reality and is not able to control that difference. The neurotic adolescent who regularly frequents the "drug scene" may use this drug and have severe psychotic reactions, while a stable individual might experience a state of spiritual consciousness close to that which oriental Zen mystics achieve after years of discipline. A primary danger in LSD use is the streetmarket quality of the drug. The chances for a bad trip are almost doubled when LSD is mixed with other substances. Stanley Krippner (1969) reports that he and his colleagues discovered black market LSD containing methedrine, heroin, atropine, and strychnine, as well as some which contained no LSD.

Almost all adolescents who use heroin, amphetamines, or the stronger hallucinogenic drugs have had some fairly regular experience in the drug scene before taking these substances. Youth, turned off by educational programs which equate marijuana with heroin, may not believe facts given by drug experts. This is also true of the younger adolescent wishing to have the apparent freedom of older peers who no longer live at home or attend high school. They are apt to say, "They lied to us about grass, they are lying to us about speed." However, most older adolescents differentiate between marijuana and the other more potent drugs. A study was completed by Beggs and Copeland (1970) after interviewing over 1,000 students in forty-seven colleges. The results are presented in Tables 15-1 and 15-2. A clear majority of college students polled favored the legalization of marijuana while at the same time less than one student in 20 endorsed the legalization of heroin. No significant correlations were obtained on the basis of sex, except that college males favored legalizing marijuana slightly more than did females.

MARIJUANA AS A FOCUS OF CONCERN

Until the early 1960s drugs were not used by an appreciable number of white adolescents. Marijuana was primarily smoked by a very

TABLE 15-1 Differentiations among College Students on the Legalization of Marijuana and Other, More Potent Drugs (in percents)

LEGALIZE	MARIJUANA	HEROIN/OPIATES	LSD/SPEED SYNTHETIC DRUGS
Yes	56.6	4.6	8.6
No	36.5	93.2	88.6
No opinion	6.9	2.2	3.1

TABLE 15-2 Comparative Responses among College Students on Penalties for Selling Marijuana and Other, More Potent Drugs (in percents)

PENALTIES FOR SELLING SHOULD BE:	MARIJUANA	OTHER ILLEGAL DRUGS
More harsh	32.0	68.4
More lenient	61.6	24.9
No opinion	6.4	6.7

Source: Beggs and Copeland, 1970: 13A.

limited number of people: young blacks in urban ghettos, jazz musicians, and older "beatniks" in the New York City and San Francisco areas. Heroin, which in the mid-1950s ran rampant through large city ghetto areas, was a cause for concern but remained out of sight and out of consciousness for the vast majority of adolescents.

Recent Changes in Drug Usage

As late as 1968 Kenneth Keniston noted:

> A recent Gallup poll arrives at the estimate of five to six percent of college youth who have "ever tried" any hallucinogenic drug. Thus while student drug use constitutes an important phenomenon it probably touches directly less than one in ten of the young Americans who attend institutions of higher education (2).

The sudden increase in drug use may be seen in Table 15-3.

TABLE 15-3 The Percentage of Students Using Drugs in 1967 and 1970

	COLLEGE STUDENTS SPRING 1967*	COLLEGE STUDENTS DECEMBER 1970*	HIGH SCHOOL STUDENTS FEBRUARY 1970**
Use marijuana	5%	42%	46%
Use LSD	1%	14%	10%
Use heroin	not asked	not asked	3%

* Gallup polls reported in *Newsweek* (January 25, 1971).
** Survey of a Michigan and a Connecticut high school reported in *Newsweek* (February 16, 1970).

It should be noted in Table 15-3 that the use of these drugs has increased, but since the drugs mentioned are illegal, the precentages are probably low and do not reflect many experimental users. Today we must reverse the Keniston estimate and state that probably over nine young persons in ten have either tried hallucinogenic drugs or have had direct contact with peers who do use them. Scarlet (1972), quoting the National Institute of Mental Health, estimates that between 15 and 20 million people have used marijuana at some time and goes on to state, "In teen-age and young adult groups use is very extensive—in some groups as high as 90 percent have used marijuana at some time" (1972: 6).

The data presented in the tables reflect a promarijuana outlook on the part of young persons. These data also indicate that the prodrug generation of adolescents lacks discrimination in the use of drugs: 3 percent of the seniors in a suburban high school admit having used heroin, and 4.6 percent of college students surveyed approved its legalization.

Some Effects of Marijuana Use

The increased use of marijuana has led to many studies concerning its effects. In fiscal year 1972, the National Institute of Mental Health spent a total of $4,695,000 for grants and contracts in marijuana research. Scarlet summarizes the NIMH 1972 report:

> While heavier marijuana use is clearly associated with the use of other drugs as well—those who use it regularly are far more likely than non-users to have experimented with other illicit drugs—there is no evidence that the drug itself "causes" such use. More frequently users are likely to find drug use appealing or to spend time with others who do so or in settings where other drugs are readily available. . . .
>   . . . Marijuana use does not appear to have a causal role in the commission of crime. . . .
>   . . . It appears that acute toxic physical reactions to marijuana are rare. . . .
>   . . . The amount of evidence bearing on the question of birth defects is modest. . . .
>   . . . In most reports it is simply impossible to distinguish between illness resulting primarily from toxic effects of cannabis and an aggravation of a previously existing serious mental disturbance (1972: 6).

Science (December 13, 1968) published findings of a controlled, clinical experiment by Weil in the Department of Psychiatry and Pharmacology at Boston School of Medicine. This study compared the effects of first experiences with marijuana among nonusers with the effects upon regular users. The psychophysical functions of the "naive" (nonuser) subjects suffered from a small but significant effect when tested in such activities as matching symbols or responding to flashing letters. The habitual smokers not only suffered no such impairment in their performance but actually did better on the test after they had smoked marijuana. Project director Weil offered the explanation that regular users learned to "adapt to and overcome their performance deficits." The study indicates that marijuana does not affect the lower brain centers, which control functions such as reflex action and coordination, as much as it affects the higher brain centers which control thinking and perception. All subjects tended to go off on irrelevant tangents and had trouble maintaining a logical train of thought. Six months after these tests, a follow-up study was made of the "naive" subjects. Only two of them had tried marijuana on their own after the experiment, and both had tried it only once.

The present controversy concerning marijuana is often centered around social rather than medical concerns, although there have been no long-term studies of regular users comparable to studies of cigarette smoking—e.g. only in the 1960's with studies tracing many years of cigarette smoking, did adverse, long-term, medical effects begin to be noticed. Some marijuana smokers maintain that since the housewife has her pep pills and tranquilizers and men have their whiskey and cigarettes, why can't they have their "grass"? The opposing argument to this is that our society already has a sufficient number of vices and escape mechanisms and does not need any more. There is also the question posed by many psychologists and sociologists of what will happen to our nation if a large percentage of adolescents followed the advice of LSD guru Timothy Leary: "Turn On, Tune In, and Drop Out" and thus possibly deprive our society of their energies and talents.

Perhaps the most serious danger of marijuana is that those who use marijuana do so in settings or under circumstances in which other illegal drugs are also available. Thus, it is quite likely that increasing involvement with marijuana leads necessarily to heroin use, delinquency, and deep involvement in the drug subculture.

FACTORS WHICH INHIBIT OR ENCOURAGE ADOLESCENT DRINKING AND DRUG USE

There are several factors which may inhibit or encourage an adolescent's experimentation with illegal drugs and alcohol and his progress from being an experimenter to a regular user of these substances. Many adolescents experience anxiety about their own personal inadequacies and identity, but most do not become heavy drinkers or drug users in their attempts to escape feelings of loneliness and anomie. Social controls, peer influence, and parental example are all important considerations in the discussion of adolescent drinking and drug use. Although the progression from experimenting with a beer or a "joint" to alcoholism or narcotic addiction may be extremely rapid in the case of a very seriously disturbed, escapist-oriented adolescent, even he is influenced and perhaps as much encouraged by the following three factors.

Social Controls

Three important social controls which tend to inhibit drug and alcohol use by young persons are (1) the need for secrecy, (2) access to a supply of alcohol or drugs, and (3) the influence of conventional morality. Secrecy is necessary since the purchase and consumption of alcoholic beverages by underage adolescents and the possession of marijuana and other similar drugs is illegal. Totally apart from the possibility of legal reprimand, the teen-ager must consider the likelihood of repudiation and perhaps punishment from his parents, school officials, and nonindulging peers. Herzog, Sudia, and Harwood (1970) indicate that the degree to which an adolescent respects or fears the opinions of others will greatly influence his decision to try drugs or not.

Two other factors related to the need for secrecy apply especially to adolescents and often inhibit their progressing beyond an experimental stage with marijuana or a very moderate regular use of alcohol.

To become fairly regular in partaking of either liquor or other drugs, a person needs to have a supply, however small, on hand, and this may be discovered by a nonuser. Also, if one is under the influence of alcohol or drugs, he must be able to control the high so that people will not be able to tell. In the first instance, a thorough bedroom cleanup or a school locker inspection might yield evidence of possession or consumption of either drugs or alcohol.

The availability and ease of access to drugs is another influential factor. Drugs appear to be readily accessible for those who want them. As one high school principal said, "I've had kids tell me that if I'll give them five dollars they'll get anything I want, right here in school" (Herzog, et al.). Even in the light of such statements, marijuana can not be procured as easily or as openly as a pack of chewing gum. An experimental user will in most cases be turned on by his friends free of charge. If he is to continue smoking, he will need to reciprocate their generosity and also buy his own supply in a more economical amount than by the single cigarette or "joint." This is a stopping point for many adolescents. Many, besides having limited finances, must often justify expenditures to their parents. At this point the secrecy factor—where to hide the stuff— also comes into consideration. There is also the fear that the seller may be under the observation of an official and both the seller and the buyer could be apprehended. As long as an adolescent is under the influence and control of his family and school, the need for secrecy and the accessibility of drugs will be factors which will influence his use or nonuse of drugs.

The third factor is the adolescent's view of conventional morality. There is a moral imperative in our society, which is emphasized strongly in schools, that one is to behave rationally and be reasonably responsive for his actions and welfare. The stereotype of a marijuana user or an alcoholic as a hedonistic, debauched addict is a direct threat to or violation of these sentiments.

Peer Influence

When an adolescent is aware that his peers are using marijuana or alcohol and also sees that they do not conform to the conventional characterizations of users, he may begin to question society's moral pronouncements on drug use. The adolescent acquires a more "liberated" moral standard on drug and alcohol use "at least to the point that he will not reject activities out of hand simply because they are conventionally condemned" (Becker, 1966: 73). Drug use by high school students is no more limited to student activists and radicals than the use of alcohol is limited to dropouts and academic failures.

A large percentage of adolescents are exposed to and experiment with illegal drugs in peer group situations. A beginner must learn how to use, perceive the effects, and enjoy the sensations of the substance. The adolescent finds himself in a shared learning experience with his friends.

Obviously there is very little technique involved in taking amphetamines or in drinking alcohol as long as, in the case of the latter, one does not overindulge to the point of nausea. With marijuana, however, experimental users must be coached in the technique of sustained inhalation or the drug will produce no effects and they will discontinue using it. Those who turn to injecting heroin or amphetamines must learn the method of preparation and injection. Only those who have had experience with these substances can teach and explain the steps necessary for the successful use of these drugs.

Second, there must be an interpretation of the effects of the substances used. As Becker notes in relation to marijuana: "It is not enough, that the effects be present; alone, they do not automatically provide the experience of being high. The user must be able to point them out to himself and consciously connect them with having smoked marijuana. . ." (1966: 49). Upon perceiving the effects of alcohol or illegal drugs, the novice must learn to enjoy the resulting sensations which are not necessarily or automatically pleasant. This is another stage during which the novice requires the tutelage of more experienced users. Becker elaborates, for instance, that marijuana is a "socially acquired" taste that is "not different in kind than the acquired taste for oysters or dry martinis" (53).

Peer influence is especially important to the addiction-prone adolescent as he progresses from regular to heavy use of drugs or alcohol. This type of young person needs at least a few friends who accept his behavior and will become his "drinking buddies" or fellow "potheads." In his clique, he can find a group-approved release from his own anxieties and also can openly use his means of escape without feeling guilty. The importance of a reinforcing group is explained by Trice (1966) and applies to those who use drugs. The relation between personality readiness and the characteristics of the drinking group forms the basis for learning to turn to alcohol. There is an attraction between personality qualities and typical drinking-group qualities. If repeatedly reinforced, drinking and drug-taking become the predominant way of dealing with the exaggerated emotional needs that furnish the readiness. Alternative ways of adjusting to tension decline and gradually disappear. Thus, peers are important during the early stage of the habit-forming process.

Parental Influence

In many respects drinking and drug-taking are patterned after the parents' example. Alcohol, tobacco, and mood-altering drugs are all widely advertised in the United States. Joel Fort (1970), a former consultant on narcotics to the World Health Organization, bluntly states: "Children are raised on propaganda for drugs, including alcohol and nicotine. They see their parents drinking every time they socialize and come to the conclusion that a meaningful relationship is impossible without the aid of some chemical."

A number of studies have indicated that the children of chronic drinkers are more likely themselves to become alcoholics. In large part, this is because the drinking parent does not present a stable image on which the adolescent can base his own identity. In this situation, the adolescent lacks the security necessary for his own well-being. Anxious and insecure, the child from a home with chronic heavy drinkers can easily fall into his parents' pattern of escape.

There are three ethnic-religious groups in the United States which display patterns of regular drinking but exceptionally low rates of alcoholism. They are the Italian-Americans, the Jewish-Americans (especially the Orthodox), and the Cantonese Chinese-Americans. In all three of these groups, drinking begins in early childhood and is part of family meals and ceremonial festivities. There is a permissive attitude toward drinking, but drunkenness is not allowed. Trice (1966) explains the low rate of alcoholism as follows:

> The norms of the group regulate how to drink, and deviation is effectively controlled. Unlike the pattern in American society generally, the drinker is surrounded by clear negative sanctions. He is not rejected and isolated but is brought under the social controls of the group (23).

However, the majority of adolescents in the United States experience alcohol in peer-group situations with no clearly defined parental or cultural controls. Parental example in drug use is also ambiguous. Adults in the early 1950s took tranquilizers, amphetamines, and barbituates. Geller and Boas (1969) state that over twelve thousand patents for these drugs were filed between the early 1950s and 1967. It might even be said that the adolescent drug use of today is not so different from that of the parents except it is more adventurous. An example of this is a high school student who told his mother that he smoked grass and liked it because school pressures were great and he felt like relaxing every once in a while. His mother immediately denounced marijuana, and he asked her what she did when she got rushed or tense. The mother answered by giving him a bottle of widely advertised tranquilizers with the following advice: "Take these whenever you need them. They always work for me."

The key to parental influence on adolescent drinking and drug-taking patterns is *how the parents use these substances themselves*. This is noted in a survey made by two high school students of their 1,400 classmates in a suburb of New York City (Wyden, 1970). Forty-four percent of the students who had seen their mother drunk were drug users, while only 28 percent of the students who had never seen their mother drunk used drugs. *Twice as many* of their classmates who used drugs had fathers who regularly used either stimulants or tranquilizers as opposed to those whose fathers seldom did. These two high school students concluded that, "Parents can no longer be considered spectators of the drug problem; they are a major part of it."

Parents who use alcohol or drugs as an avenue of escape or a means of coping with reality set an example for their children. To the anxious adolescent, chemical escape is as easy an answer as it is for his parents. After all, "if mother uses it, can it be so bad?"

DRUG EDUCATION

In an attempt to discourage drug use, schools, civic groups, and the mass media have been promoting programs on drug awareness. These efforts appear futile in the light of statistics that show rising drug use, especially of marijuana.

Establishment Efforts

John Finlator, past deputy director of the Bureau of Narcotics and Dangerous Drugs, pointed out that the drug problem has created a unique situation (1970). He explained that the young know more than their parents about drugs and their effects. They rely on "street and marketplace" information rather than on adult lectures. Finlator noted discouragingly that "I have never seen a good film on drug abuse." The study by Herzog, Sudia, and Harwood revealed that only one high school student in eight reported that an educational effort had deterred him or his friends from using drugs (Herzog et al, 1970: 212).

The futility of trying to communicate with adolescents about the use of drugs was strongly brought home to David Lewis (1970), an assistant professor of medicine at Harvard. He appeared with a panel of experts on a drug education program at a Boston high school. He reported that a few days after he participated in this program two students came up to him and said, "If drugs were worth calling off classes for a day, they were worth trying."

There are several reasons for the failure of these programs. The fact that they are adult sponsored is certainly a major one. Another may be that the programs often deal with all the illegal drugs but not delineate how different drugs work on the body and the mind. Adolescents do need specific, reliable information about each type of illegal drug. However a film or program which presents heroin addiction as the inevitable outcome of a single marijuana cigarette will not be believed by this generation of street wise adolescents. Programs which present the straight facts rather than alarmist rhetoric are far more likely to receive attention.

Clinics and Nonestablishment Organizations

Adolescents who use or are susceptible to using drugs are influenced far more by their peers and their leaders, be they musicians or counterculture political activists, than they are by adults. This is perhaps why some nonestablishment groups, clinics, and newspapers are able to influence youth and keep them from "graduating" to the more harmful opiates. Because most of these drugs, other than alcohol and tobacco, are lumped together as illegal, there is a very real fear among young people that any frank discussion may cause adult authorities not only to refuse to help them, but also to inform parents and school and police officials. The nonestablishment influences know what they are talking about when they give information about drugs and they will help a person by accepting his real problem instead of lecturing or threatening him. There are no statistics to gauge the effectiveness of such programs because many of these groups are outside the mainstream of society.

In most large cities there are now established clinics manned by professional volunteers which will help those on "bad trips." Unlike the emergency ward of a municipal hospital, a young person need not fear that his parents or local police will be notified. The following excerpt published in the *Berkeley Tribe* reveals wide variety of poisonous substances on the street market which medical facilities must be ready to cope with:

> *Each week, the Free Clinic posts a list of bad dope, which consists of drugs which have sent people to the Free Clinic in any kind of fucked up condition. The following varieties should be kept clear of:*
> Caps filled with cream colored powder—sold as mescaline—it's pure strychnine with some speed.
> Pink and purple double domes, line down one side, white speckles and tastes sweet—it's pure strychnine with speed.
> Orange tabs with black dots.
> Yellow flats.
> Clear caps with white powder—dealer has short brown hair, scrawny beard—sold for $1.50 a hit and it's pure shit.
> White tabs—sold as acid, mescaline—it's nothing.
> Yellow tab called yellow sunshine—sold as acid—has lots of speed and strychnine—dealer's a woman with shoulder-length brown hair.
> Yellow-orange cap sold as psylocybin—causes pain and respiratory problems.
> Gelatin caps with white powder—sold as mescaline—is nothing.

Both the life style and songs of many popular musical groups emphasize hallucinogenic drugs. However, some of these cultural leaders are attempting to reach adolescents and discourage their using the "hard" drugs. An example of this is a radio spot announcement by a nonprofit foundation for drug education and rehabilitation called "Do It Now." This particular message is directed towards young drug users and is from a leading rock musician:

> This is Frank Zappa from the Mothers of Invention. I would like to suggest that you do not use speed, and here's why: It is going to mess up your heart, mess up your lives, your kidneys, rot out your mind. In general, this drug will make you just like your mother and father.

Because of the possibility of recrimination, most adolescent drug users do not trust either their parents, teachers, or guidance counselors. Parents are not only ill-informed about drug usage but also react with hysteria and guilt. School officials, while they may be more knowledgeable about drugs, are usually unforgiving and threaten expulsion. Schools would be far more successful in drug education efforts if they could follow the example of the nonestablishment groups and combine information and rehabilitation programs free of any threat of punishment. If students knew that a teacher or counselor would not report interest in or experimentation with drugs, they would feel much freer to discuss these things with adults. Drug education programs which gain both the trust of adolescents and the acceptance of school officials will be a challenge and need throughout the decade of the 1970s.

SUMMARY

The first step in the discussion of adolescent drinking and drug use is to define different chemical substances, their properties, and their use, especially as they relate to youth. This includes alcohol, nicotine and caffeine which, while they are culturally sanctioned "vices" with only an age limit on the purchase of the first two, have the pharmacological properties of a drug. The first group discussed is stimulants—the amphetamines. These include benzedrine, dexedrine, and methedrine. Coffee, tea, and chocolate are included in this group. All these substances act directly on the central nervous system. The second category of drugs is the depressants, which include a wide variety of derivatives such as phenobarbital, seconal, and amytal, or drugs such as bromides, chloral hydrate, and tranquilizers. Alcohol is another depressant whose effects on the body are similar to those of the barbituates. Nicotine, which is an addictive depressant present in tobacco, is one of the most poisonous alkaloids found in the plant world. All these depressants slow down nerve action, heart beat, breathing, and muscle coordination.

The narcotics include heroin, opium, codeine, and cocaine. Narcotics are the drugs to which one can become most rapidly addicted and from which withdrawal is both severe and not necessarily permanent. The hallucinogens are neither depressants nor stimulants, and although they may be psychologically addictive, there is no evidence that they are physically addictive. Their primary effect is to alter perception. The most commonly known one is marijuana. Hashish is a more potent derivative of the same plant. Peyote and mescaline are extracted from a cactus. The best-known and widely publicized as well as most potent hallucinogen in the man-made chemical category is lysergic acid diethylamide, or LSD. This and other compounds often known by the initials of their chemical names are mind-altering substances which have a direct action upon the function of the brain without a loss of consciousness. The last category of drugs is a wide variety of chemical solvents such as airplane glue, paint thinner and the like, which are used primarily by younger adolescents when illegal drugs or alcohol are either unavailable or unknown.

In discussing adolescent drinking and drug behavior patterns, one must consider the frequency of use, the age of the adolescent, and the actual substance used. The social surroundings and community standards in which these substances are taken are extremely important.

Adolescents who resort to illegal drugs or alcohol are influenced strongly by three factors: peer influence, school experience, and extent of alienation from parents, with the latter appearing to be the most important. The experimental user of alcohol or tobacco is in part imitating adult customs and usually reflects the patterns of the adolescent's home while it helps him resolve the dilemma of his status as an adult. An experimental user of marijuana emulates his peers. Whether he progresses beyond the stages of experimentation is definitely influenced by his association with abstemious or indulging peers. Only a very small percentage of all adolescents are addiction-prone, heavy users of illegal drugs, or alcohol. Many of this group drop out of their homes and schools, and those who do remain often develop an overt veneer of toughness to cover up their dependence and anxiety.

Marijuana is a focus of special concern since its use has increased dramatically among adolescents. It and other hallucinogens appear to be of special interest to middle- and upper-class youths. Its most serious danger to adolescents appears to be that those who use marijuana do so in settings or under circumstances in which other illegal and more dangerous drugs are readily available.

Three important social controls tend to inhibit an adolescent from progressing from an experimenter to a regular or heavy user of chemical substances: secrecy, availability, and training. It is important for the addiction-prone adolescent to find a group-approved release from his own anxieties and tensions so that indulgence gradually becomes the predominant way of coping with emotional needs.

In many respects adolescent drug use and drinking patterns are very closely correlated with parental example. The key to parental influence is why or how the parents of adolescents use alcohol or drugs themselves. Usually teen-agers are not so different from their parents, only more adventuresome.

The Establishment efforts to promote education have not met with much success. Although there is no exact way to measure the effects of "free" clinics and nonestablishment efforts in drug rehabilitation and education, this type of group seems to have more success in keeping adolescents from graduating to the dangerous substances. Perhaps schools would be more successful in drug education attempts if they were to emulate the nonestablishment efforts and link programs of information with those of rehabilitation, without the fear or threat of official punishment.

REFERENCES

BACON, MARGARET and MARY BRUSH JONES. *Teenage Drinking.* New York: Thomas Y. Crowell Company, 1968.

BECKER, HOWARD S. *Outsiders.* New York: The Free Press, 1966. Pp. 46–58.

BEGGS, DANIEL C. and HENRY A. COPELAND. "Campus Opinion." *Charlotte Observer* (December 4, 1970).

Berkeley Tribe (October 22–28, 1971), p. 7.

COLEMAN, ELIZABETH. "ABC Report." May 13, 1974. (Television program.)

FEDERN, ERNST. " 'Drogenmissbrach' hei Jugendlichen aus einer Sozial-pädagogischen Sicht." *Praxis der Kinderpsychologie und Kinderpsychiatrie* (1971), 20 (60) ; 219–25.

FINLATOR, JOHN. Speech reported in the *Charlotte Observer* (April 16, 1970), p. 17A.

FORT, JOEL. Reported in the *Charlotte Observer* (November 1, 1970), p. H1.

GELLER, ALLEN and MAZWELL BOAS. *The Drug Beat.* New York: McGraw-Hill Book Company, 1969.

HAGER, DAVID L., ARTHUR M. WENER, and CYRUS S. STEWART. "Patterns of Adolescent Drug Use in Middle America." *Journal of Counseling Psychology* (1971), 18 (4).

HAMES, LEE N. "Can Students Be Taught to Mix Alcohol and Gasoline—Safely?" *The Journal of School Health* (November 1971).

HERZOG, ELIZABETH, CECILIA SUDIA, and JANE HARWOOD. "Drug Use Among the Young: As Teenagers See It." *Children* (November-December 1970), 17 (6).

KENISTON, KENNETH. "Heads and Seekers, Drugs on Campus, Countercultures and American Society. Reprint from *American Scholar* (1968), 41:481–87.

KRIPPNER, STANLEY. Afterword in A. Geller and N. Boas, *The Drug Beat.* New York: McGraw-Hill Book Company, 1969.

LEVITT, EUGENE E. and JUDITH A. EDWARDS. "A Multivariate Study of Correlative Factors in Youthful Cigarette Smoking." *Developmental Psychology* (1970), 8:5–11.

LEWIS, DAVID. Reported in *Newsweek* (February 16, 1970), p. 67. "The Drug Scene: High Schools Are Higher Now."

Newsweek (March 5, 1973), p. 68. "The Latest Teen Drug: Alcohol."

O'DONNELL, JOHN A. and JOHN C. BALL, eds. *Narcotic Addiction.* New York: Harper & Row, Publishers, 1966.

OGNIBENE, PETER J. "Treating Heroin Addition." *The New Republic* (December 23 and 30, 1972), pp. 20–23.

Parade magazine (July 26, 1972), p. 14. "Alcohol, Not Marijuana."

SCARLET, MARJORY. "Harmful Pot Effects Judged Minimal." *APA Monitor* (April 1972), p. 6.

SCHELER, MAX. *Ressentiment.* New York: The Free Press, 1961.

SEBALD, HANS. *Adolescence.* New York: Appleton-Century-Crofts, 1968.

SMART, REGINAL G. and DIANNE FEJER. "Drug Use Among Adolescents and Their Parents: Closing the Generation Gap in Mood Modification." *Journal of Abnormal Psychology* (1972), 79 (2):153–60.

TAYLOR, NORMAN. *Narcotics: Nature's Dangerous Gifts.* New York: Dell Publishing Co., 1966.

Traffic Safety (June 1970). "Youths Rank High Among Drinking Drivers."

TRICE, HARRISON M. *Alcoholism in America.* New York: McGraw-Hill Book Company, 1966.

WEINER, IRVING B. "The Generation Gap: Fact and Fancy." *Adolescence,* (Summer 1971), 6 (22):156–66.

WYDEN, BARBARA. "Report of an Anonymous Study." *New York Times News Service* (November 1, 1970), p. 32.

RECOMMENDED READINGS

CAREY, JAMES J. *The College Drug Scene.* Englewood Cliffs, N.J.: Prentice-Hall, Inc., 1968.
Centers around the use of hallucinogens primarily by youth from middle- and upper middle-class homes. Presents a portrait of the recreational and heavy drug users.

ELGIN, KATHLEEN and JOHN F. OSTERRITTER. *The Ups and Downs of Drugs.* New York: Alfred A. Knopf, Inc., 1972.
Explains all kinds of drugs and presents facts about their uses, dangers, and risks.

FALKANEN, ARTHUR W. "Drug Use and the Adolescent." In *Understanding Adolescence,* 2nd ed., James F. Adams, ed. Boston: Allyn and Bacon, Inc., 1973. Chapter 15.
The author presents an overview of the following major topics: effects and descriptions of different drugs, theories of drug use, drug abuse and drug abuse treatment.

GELLER, ALLEN and MAXWELL BOAS. *The Drug Beat.* New York: McGraw-Hill Book Company, 1969.
Deals with the history, distribution patterns, uses, and abuses of marijuana, LSD, and amphetamines. Discusses why adolescents use these drugs, how they procure them, and the effects of the drugs.

JOHNSON, BRUCE D. *Marihuana Users and Drug Subcultures.* New York: John Wiley & Sons, Inc., 1973.
Presents well-analyzed data on drug use in the United States; deals with many of the controversies about drug use and abuse.

TAYLOR, NORMAN. *Narcotics: Nature's Dangerous Gifts.* New York: Dell Publishing Co., 1966.
The history of the use of plants by which man escapes reality. Covers the narcotics and the hallucinogens as well as coffee, tobacco, and alcohol.

TRICE, HARRISON M. *Alcoholism in America.* New York: McGraw-Hill Book Company, 1966.
A concise overview of alcoholism in the United States, along with reasons for indulgence. Gives a comparison between alcohol and opiate addiction.

16

juvenile delinquency

The purposeful disobeying of laws by youth is neither a recent nor exclusively American problem. While considerable delinquent behavior never comes to the attention of the legal authorities, court action is often taken in cases where juveniles have committed no criminal acts. Thus, it is difficult to estimate the actual extent of juvenile delinquency. Any estimate will further depend upon the definition used. This chapter is especially concerned with the extent, causes, and trends in juvenile delinquency. Attention is also given to the portrait of the juvenile delinquent and the means for preventing and dealing with delinquency.

DEFINITION AND EXPLANATION

It is virtually impossible to present a definition of juvenile delinquency that is applicable to all areas of the United States. Standards and mores vary with different groups of people as does the level of tolerance for misconduct. Juvenile delinquency cannot be equated with adult crime. It includes additional behavior such as running away from home, ungovernable behavior at home or at school, and in some cases truancy from school. Since it is more subjectively determined than adult crime, evaluation is frequently difficult.

From a social point of view delinquency means any form of behavior detrimental to the well-being of society. Such a definition, however, does not provide for any practical limits. Actually, juvenile delinquency is a legal term. In most states a juvenile delinquent is an individual under eighteen years of age who is adjudged guilty of violating the law. Thus, it can readily be seen that the great majority of problem adolescents would not be officially designated as juvenile delinquents. In a broad sense of the word, our schools and other social agencies are concerned with all problem behavior, including that frequently classified as delinquent.

Quasidelinquents

If delinquency is defined in terms of wrongdoings alone, acts of mischief, or breaking the law, then almost every adolescent is a delinquent. In American culture many activities by youth are regarded as part of their way of life. This may be noted in connection with high school parades without a permit, bonfires, and escapades that are regarded as harmless although not in keeping with the letter of the law. The quasidelinquent was early defined by Kvaraceus (1958) as "a rather well-integrated youngster who makes a mistake or who misses his target only to do injury to others." Left to himself he will usually work out his problem and develop in a normal manner. The high school youngster celebrating a football victory who accidentally injures some bystander or the Halloween prankster who defaces his neighbor's shrubbery is by no means a true delinquent, although he may have commited acts that may be classed as delinquent. If these and others who commit acts of mischief are classified as delinquents the number of children and adolescents classed as such will be doubled several times. Help is needed in distinguishing pseudo- or quasidelinquents from true delinquents. An attempt will be made later in this chapter to better describe the nature and characteristics of those classified as true delinquents.

The Extent of Juvenile Delinquency

One factor that determines the extent of delinquency is the enforcement of the law. If traffic violations were not enforced, there would then be no violators apprehended and thus no traffic delinquents. Some of the increase in juvenile delinquency may result from changes in definition, laws, or enforcement of laws. Stealing apples from the fruit vendor today to likely to bring the adolescent to a court, whereas stealing apples from the farm orchard a half century ago was not likely to.

Whether an adolescent comes to the attention of the court today is influenced markedly by community and parental attitudes toward the adolescent's behavior. Many delinquents from middle- and upper-class homes never come to the attention of the public. According to FBI data reported by the American Institute for Research in the Behavioral Sciences (1968), the increase in crime since 1960 can be attributed in the main to juveniles. From 1960 through 1970, according to the FBI, police arrests for all criminal acts except traffic violations rose 31 percent. Arrests of those under eighteen years of age more than doubled, an amount over four times as great as the population increase in the ten to eighteen age group. Adult arrests for violent crime during this period increased 67 percent; juvenile arrests increased 167 percent. Again, it should be pointed out that FBI figures represent only formal police contacts; they do not include hidden delinquency and thus underrate the true amount of juvenile delinquency.

Many cases of juvenile delinquency involve vandalism by gangs, and gang vandalism can be interpreted as a phase of social life.

In a town with a population of approximately 10,000, several high school girls set up a club. The only admittance requirement for membership was the shoplifting of a minimum of $50.00 worth of merchandise from local stores. One aspiring club member was apprehended and she told what was going on. Since all the girls involved were from middle-class homes with "respectable" parents, none of the stores officially prosecuted these girls. They were all given the choice of working off or paying off their thefts. In this instance all their parents reimbursed the stores and the whole affair was "hushed up" as much as possible.

SEX DIFFERENCES. Sex differences in the extent and nature of delinquent acts are clearly discernible, with boys committing more delinquent acts. Gold (1970) points out that girls, in particular, are less delinquent than boys in terms of seriousness of offenses. This is in harmony with findings from different studies bearing on juvenile crime. Girls are generally less delinquent than boys partly because adults in general more strongly disapprove of and more actively discourage delinquent behavior in girls than in boys. This may be noted in the reaction of parents to misconduct on the part of small boys and girls. The father boastfully states with regard to misbehavior of his preschool son, "Well, he is all boy." Thus, delinquent behavior among boys is frequently seen as masculine during the preschool and early school years.

The reasons most frequently given by school authorities and police for the general increase in rate of crime by children and adolescents against their peers are the breakdown of family discipline, racial animosities, and changing school patterns that place underprivileged children in closer contact with the more affluent (*New York Times News Service,* 1971). Within the past decade there has been a notable increase in aggressive crime by girls both toward their male and female peers. Such crime usually takes the form of knife fights, throwing objects, or just kicking and biting.

According to government reports, juvenile delinquency among girls aged ten to seventeen rose twice as fast as that among boys during the period 1969 to 1970 (*Charlotte Observer,* 1972: 1A). Of the 1,052,000 juvenile court cases in 1970, based on a national sample, 799,500 involved boys and 252,500 girls. The rise in girls' rate of delinquency has generally been attributed to their changing attitudes toward society and society's changing attitude toward them. Adolescent girls today display more aggressive and independent behavior than ever before, and this is reflected in increased running away from home, drug use, shoplifting, and robbery.

Social Deviancy

Early investigators attributed delinquency to underprivileged and lower-class environments. More recently investigators have studied delinquency from different points of view and have observed new patterns arising from changing conditions.

Two new factors in delinquency and social deviance have produced considerable confusion and misunderstanding. The first of these is that deviancy has multiple causes. Too often the causes of deviancy have been oversimplified, with a single factor brought forth to explain a particular kind of behavior, although it is frequently true that a single factor is of paramount importance. Second, neither delinquency nor other forms of social deviancy make up an entity. There is certainly much difference between a gang of boys that preys upon individuals from other parts of a city, the girl who is sexually promiscuous as a form of rebellion against parental attitudes, and the boy who explodes in a rage when the teacher chides him for classroom misbehavior.

JUVENILE STATUS OFFENDERS. Many juveniles are accused of socially deviant acts that would not be considered crimes if they were committed by adults. Lerman described these as: "The offenses that delinquents are charged with do not involve a clear victim, as is the case in classical crimes of theft, robbery, burglary, and assault. Rather, they involve young people who are themselves liable to be victimized for having childhood troubles or growing up differently. Three major categories appear to be of primary concern: behavior at home, behavior at school, and sexual experimentation" (1971: 39).

Behavior at home involves such acts as running away, incorrigibility, and ungovernability. Behavior at school includes truancy, disturbances in the classroom, and other troubles involving teachers, principals, or other school personnel.

Juvenile status offenders represent quite a sizable proportion of the total number of delinquents. Lerman estimates that this type of charge covers about one out of every five boys' and over one half of all girls' delinquency petitions. He points out that certain young people in our society are more likely to have these types of troubles: girls, poor youth, rural migrants to the city, underachievers and the less sophisticated. Historically, a community's more disadvantaged children and adolescents are more likely to have their troubles defined as "delinquent."

PORTRAIT OF A JUVENILE DELINQUENT. One Saturday Harry's father received a telephone call from the town's policeman telling him that he was holding a boy for stealing an automobile in company with two other boys. Harry's father didn't believe at first that this could possibly be his son. Harry was spending the night with James. What Harry's father didn't realize at first was that James was supposed to be spending the night with Harry. Actually the two boys had joined their friend Kevin, who lived with his divorced mother who didn't keep close watch over him. The trio had spent Friday night together riding around in automobiles they had found unlocked and that they could get started by special wiring. This had been their pasttime on previous Friday nights, but this time they had not been as fortunate as on previous occasions. This time they had used a car, the second one for the night, that was "hot"—the policemen of the town and county had been on the lookout for the car (Garrison, 1961).

This incident of the joyriding by Harry and his friends in 1961 is not unique. It has become one of the most frequent offenses committed by adolescents. According to a report by Mosquwda (1971), about 72 percent of all the auto theft in the United States every year is done by joyriders—typically fun-seeking teen-age boys.

Present-day sociological theories attempt to analyze delinquency in the wider context of deviance, conformity, and control (Phillipson, 1974). There has been a shift from single-factor explanations to an all-embracing perspective, with special attention to the total setting. This theory is supported by results from a three-year study by sociologists at Temple University (*Charlotte Observer*, May 7, 1970). The investigators noted that fear of danger and violence on the way to school, as well as at school, led to truancy and subsequently to delinquency in boys. Increased attention is being given today to the patrolling of school areas. Lower-class families, frequently with little income and little understanding of the needs and problems of their children, lack the resources and authority patterns to maintain adequate social control over their adolescents.

PERSONAL FACTORS ASSOCIATED WITH DELINQUENCY

Attempts have been made to ascribe special characteristics to delinquents. In a relatively early study of the psychiatric aspects of juvenile delinquency, Donet (1951) concluded that delinquency is a biosocial phenomenon, the common psychological denominator of which is a feeling of insecurity. Case studies of delinquents reveal that these boys and girls have the same basic needs and, in general, face the same problems as nondelinquents.

In our study of delinquency, we are especially interested in (1) the behavioral aspects and their etiology as a result of learning and maturation, and (2) in analyzing the causative factors in the social processes in the delinquent's cultural and environmental backgrounds.

Theoretical Considerations

Many theories have been offered as an explanation of juvenile delinquency. We will not attempt a review of these here, since most of them are implied under the topics covered in the subsequent discussions of conditions and factors associated with delinquency. While we reject the criminal type, or the notion that "criminals are born not made," we recognize the importance of personal and social factors that are closely associated with delinquent behavior.

An early theory was based largely upon the value system as it operates in Western culture. This is a theory of differential opportunity or access, and may be especially relevant to delinquency. It is important where one stands *in relation to the goals or ideals* which he seeks, and the likelihood of being able to attain such goals or ideals. In the United States we extoll the value of success and define it primarily in economic and materialistic terms. However in this country, there is little attention given to how a person may achieve success by legitimate means. Opportunities to achieve the "good life" as portrayed in television commercials —the single-family dwelling with a yard and at least one car in the garage—are not equally accessible to all. High levels of educational and professional training are the necessary and legitimate means to success, but this avenue is often not open to the poor and to racial and ethnic minorities who are educated in overcrowded, poorly programmed inner-city schools.

Intelligence and Crime

The fact that many delinquents are failures in school and score low on intelligence tests has caused some students of child and adolescent behavior to relate juvenile delinquency to low intelligence. Early studies of delinquency by the Gluecks (1950) revealed differences in the components of intelligence of delinquents and nondelinquents in the verbal and performance aspects of the Wechsler-Bellevue Scale. The delinquents were inferior to a control group of nondelinquents in verbal intelligence, while the two groups resembled each other closely in performance intelligence. The delinquents do better in those tasks in which the approach to meaning is direct in nature rather than through symbols. They are, in general, inferior in vocabulary and information. This is a source of difficulty for them in much of the learning emphasized in the traditional school program. Thus, the nature of the test used affects the intelligence quotient obtained. Since the delinquent is frequently retarded in his schoolwork, he is seriously handicapped on tests involving language activities and reading materials. In spite of the fact that the various investigators have used different techniques for evaluating the intelligence of delinquents and have in many cases tested subjects in which different criteria have been used for classifying them as delinquents, their data agree in certain respects as follows:

1. There are more mental defectives among the delinquents tested than among unselected groups of children.
2. The average intelligence test scores of children brought before the courts is less than the average for unselected school children of the same age level.
3. The average educational retardation among the children regarded as delinquent is greater than that for public school children in general.
4. There are delinquents with high levels of intelligence as well as delinquents with low intelligence levels.
5. In line with item 4, we note that the distribution of IQs among juvenile-court cases tends to follow the normal probability curve.

ERROR IN SAMPLING. It is quite unlikely that we ever have a truly representative group that can be labeled "juvenile delinquents." Results from different studies are not in complete agreement regarding the average IQ of delinquents. The discrepancies found between the results from these studies may be explained on the basis of differences in sampling. If one bases his conclusion on children already committed to institutions, it is probably true that intelligence superiority among delinquents is rather rare. (Of course, it must be remembered that this group is not the entire body of delinquents in any state; the entire delinquent group, if *all* delinquents are considered, comes very close to being the entire population.) Among institutional cases the percent of intelligence quotients in excess of 100 is small as compared with the percent less than 100; however, for every intelligence quotient below 70 in the penal institution there can be found dozens or more of comparably low-ability persons not in such an institution—and, from the standpoint of behavior activities, no more deserving of being there than the general average of the population. It is probably true, and in most cases proper, that many juvenile-court judges try to salvage from the human wreckage that is brought to their courts as many as possible who appear promising or capable of recognizing the nature and consequences of antisocial behavior—those who can profit from mistakes and thus give promise of making more adequate adjustments under some sort of supervision outside institutions. But these individuals are in most cases not mentally retarded and are therefore not counted among the institutional cases. Hence, counting methods decrease the average mental ability found in our institutions.

Educational Retardation

There is evidence from many sources that educational retardation, leading to dissatisfaction with school and truancy from school, is often the beginning stage of delinquency. A study by Eckenrode (1949–50) of the scholastic achievement of 345 boys committed to an institution for juvenile delinquency revealed a median retardation in reading of five years. In arithmetic, the retardation was even higher, slightly more than six years. More than 90 percent of the group indicated a distinct dislike for school. The results of a study by Critchley (1968) confirmed those of earlier studies showing that 60 percent of 477 delinquent children and adolescents were two or more years retarded in reading. Also, left-handedness, crossed laterality, and faulty pronunciation were found frequently with the retarded readers, suggesting that many are dyslexic.

A survey of the court records for the causes of incarceration of girls aged eleven to sixteen in a Tennessee state institution for correction showed that over 60 percent had been judged delinquent because of school-related problems such as truancy or insubordination. Based on the Gates Reading Survey Test, 90 percent of the 110 girls were functioning two to seven years below grade level. Based upon further evaluations, 68 percent of the girls were found to have a specific behavior disorder which was believed to be related to a learning disability (Rice, 1970). It seems likely that much of the disruptive behavior that brings adolescents before the courts and ultimately to special training or rehabilitation institutions results from failure, frustration, and anxiety experienced as a result of learning problems at school.

MINIMAL BRAIN DYSFUNCTION AND JUVENILE DELINQUENCY. Various studies have reported up to 70 percent of juvenile delinquents with abnormal electroencephalograms (EEGs) as compared with 15 to 27 percent abnormal EEGs in the total population (Tarnopal, 1970). In a study reported by Tarnopal, 102 nonwhite male youths aged sixteen to twenty-three were examined and tested. Almost all of these had dropped out of school and had engaged in varying degrees of delinquency. Untreated medical and dental problems were found in a substantial number of the group. The cumulative evidence of test deficiencies noted on a variety of tests given "tends to support the hypothesis that a significant degree of minimal brain dysfunction exists in the minority group, delinquent, school dropout population" (206). The results from this study may partially explain why special programs to educate this population have in general not attained the results expected. A successful program of educational improvement for the minority poor would likely require early diagnostic testing followed by prescriptive teaching starting in the preschool years.

Attitudes and Values

The fact that delinquents are frequently well socialized within their own group makes the problem of rehabilitation most difficult. Their attitudes are frequently at variance with those of the established order. Delinquents as a group do not conform to the established rules but may be very loyal to their peer group.

A composite study of delinquents and nondelinquents conducted by Allen and Sandhu (1967–68) sheds some light on the attitudes of these two groups. More of the delinquents were out of school and either unemployed or employed full time than nondelinquents. The data on employment implies that they are from lower income homes and have a stronger need for employment in order to have a car and other things which their more affluent peers have. The delinquent boys regard themselves as finished with education and displayed little interest in schooling.

Religious categorization of Protestant, Catholic, Jewish, and nonparticipant did not significantly relate with delinquency, nor did frequency of church attendance (daily, weekly, yearly, never) have any consistent relation to delinquency. In strength of religious feelings, however, the delinquents as a group were significantly weaker than their nondelinquent counterparts. "This evidence suggests that it is the quality of their religious feelings which reflect their socialization rather than the frequency of church attendance or the type of religious preference" (264).

Delinquents in general have an unfavorable attitude toward school and teachers. Furthermore their values distinguish them to a degree from nondelinquents. Data collected by Thompson and Gardner (1969) from several contrasting samples of adolescent boys and girls with an inventory designed to measure their perceptions of what actions typically lead to successful living support the hypothesis that behavioral values in the American adolescent culture are consistently and hierarchically ordered. Delinquent boys and girls assign relatively greater weight to behaviors associated with the need strivings of dominance, aggression, and exhibition; nondelinquents give greater emphasis to nurturant, deferent, and affiliation behavior, as well as to the achievement-related behavior subsumed under endurance and order.

POTENTIAL PROBLEM BOYS. Certain symptoms can indicate likely delinquent behavior among adolescents. In a study by Kulik and others (1971), delinquent slang is specifically set forth as related to delinquent conduct. The adolescent whose language interferes with his social relationships within the wider community is at a disadvantage in the socialization process. An item pool of sixty-two slang words gleaned from various sources was administered to 996 boys of high school age (mean age 16.18 years) of which 605 were enrolled in school and 391 were in institutions for delinquents.

A careful analysis of the data comparing delinquents and nondelinquents led to the following conclusion:

> . . . a good knowledge of slang relative to one's knowledge of conventional usage was most indicative of antisocial behavior by several criteria. Among delinquents, this pattern of unequal development of verbal abilities is found in a greatly magnified form. Institutionalized delinquents as a group, have retarded standard vocabularies, but far outstrip the average boy in their knowledge of street slang (439).

A six-year in-depth study to uncover the important unconscious inner dynamics of the delinquent boy in our culture was conducted by Slavson (1965). Seven seriously delinquent fifteen- and sixteen-year-old boys were studied by use of a "para-analytical method" and an "intro-version technique." The investigators concluded that the boy's sense of identity has been so injured by experiences of rejection that by the time he reaches fifteen or sixteen years of age he can feel "alive" only when acting out hatred, anger, and rage toward others.

POTENTIAL PROBLEM GIRLS. Although there is no unique symptom of trouble for the adolescent girl, one of the first signs of possible delinquency is failure in school (Havighurst, *et al.*, 1962: 64). Frequently the trouble begins with failure in learning to read upon entering school. This is closely related to disadvantaged home and community conditions during the early years. In one sense, we might say that school failure and dropping out of school usually have their beginning in a culturally disadvantaged situation existing before the child enters school. Maladjustments of either the aggressive or withdrawal type become apparent by the age of twelve or thirteen. The combination of a maladjustment and reading failure is a dangerous one, indicating future trouble. In general, boys are likely to display aggressive maladjustment and girls are more likely to display withdrawal tendencies, as noted by Mueller (1966):

> The junior high level represents the period of highest frustration, and for many reasons. Teachers begin to grade more realistically, and reading deficiencies become very significant. Children from many elementary schools come together, and the pressure to assert one's individuality and self-reliance is magnified. The group is larger, more anonymous, more heterogeneous. Economic differences are not only greater among the more diverse groups but also take on more meaning. Self-consciousness becomes acute, and competition is overwhelming. In the larger groups, a little farther from home, one's own identity and individuality count for more, and the failure to achieve pleasant and satisfying social interaction becomes a devastating experience (353–54).

Although delinquency is not as prevalent among adolescent girls as it is among boys, the problems of the adolescent girl are very complex. They involve the self-concept. The central importance of a negative self-concept is well stated by Konopka: "The girls themselves are full of inner helplessness or hostility and frequently unable to express this in any constructive form" (1964: 5). For various personal and social reasons girls do drop out of school; however, this is not viewed with the same alarm as is the case for boys; they commit acts in violation of the sexual teachings at home and church; and they act against the restraints of parents in different and frequently subtle ways.

SOCIAL CLASS CULTURE
AND DELINQUENCY

Cultural anthropologists have been interested in cultural factors which contribute to the low incidence of stress and violence among adolescents in some relatively simple cultures as opposed to the greater incidence in Western countries such as the United States and Japan. This was noted in Tokyo, where the alienation of adolescents has resulted in a rising crime rate, increased extremist terrorism, and a growing obsession with money and materialism (*Parade*, 1973).

The Teen-age Gang and Delinquency

Juvenile delinquency as it exists today may be a means for teen-agers to expend energy and assert themselves. Yablonsky (1962) identified three types of teen-age gangs: the social gang organized for comradeship rather than delinquent behavior; the delinquent gang, primarily organized to conduct illegal acts; and the violent gang, primarily organized for aggressive violence.

These types of gangs have operated in the assimilation of ethnic and minority groups of adolescents, especially boys. In the case of Italian-American teen-agers, the first gangs were largely of the comradeship type and satisfied their need for belonging. However, these frequently took on new functions in harmony with changes in their emotional and social needs. Negro teen-age gangs also developed to satisfy their need for belonging and identity. Caught in a conflict resulting from prejudices, urban Negro gang behavior has been characterized by violence and inward-directed hostility (Cloward and Ohlin, 1961).

The major difference between white American and black American gangs seems to lie in the psychological make-up of the individual members. A larger percentage of white gang members are emotionally disturbed, and this factor motivates them to become members of gangs. The acute disorganization of the Negro slum and the frustrations experienced because of social and economic discrimination are factors that have produced the high rate of juvenile delinquency among Negro adolescents. Much white delinquency involves vandalism—crime committed for "kicks."

From a study of children in the inner city of Toronto, a city of about 500,000 people, Levine concludes: "In general, a disproportionate number of children in the poverty group manifest so-called antisocial behavior. Aggression, impulsivity, stealing, truancy, etc., are seen more frequently here. Children from the immigrant group often present classic psychoneuroses (conversion reactions, phobias, dissociative state, etc.) that are seldom seen so well delineated in North American children nowadays, or with overt parent-child conflict (cultural language barriers). These are the disadvantaged children in our city today. What will they become as adolescents and adults?" (1970: 235–36).

Lower-Class Culture and Delinquency

The lower-class way of life, in common with that of other cultural groups, is characterized by a set of focal concerns. As discussed by Miller over a decade ago, lower-class concerns are different in many respects from those of the middle class. Table 16-1 presents a highly schematic and simplified list of six of the major concerns as presented by Miller (1958). A close look at these concerns reveals that many of them are also present among middle-class adolescents. However, middle-class adolescents have been able to satisfy their needs in a more acceptable manner through constructive channels. Perhaps middle-class norms and values are largely the norms and values of the lower class, but not readily attainable by legitimate or law-abiding behavior.

Much of the delinquency of lower-class teen-agers is due to their attempt to adhere to behavior patterns, standards, and values of their subculture. Among lower-class adolescents, focal concerns are centered around trouble, toughness, endurance, physical prowess, "outsmarting the other guy," fate and luck, desire for autonomy with dependency needs, excitement, escape from boredom and monotony, and the like. Attitudes, values, concerns, and ideals are contagious, and necessarily so, for in order that the youth be accepted into his segment of society, he must adopt the behavior patterns of that society. Thus, the youth born into this lower-class society must make these concerns his own, and with a choice of alternative forms of behavior his decision is frequently on the side of norm-violating behavior.

FOCAL CONCERNS OF LOWER-CLASS ADOLESCENT STREET CORNER GANGS. According to Miller the one-sex peer group is prevalent in the lower-class community. Membership in a stable peer unit is vital to the lower-class adolescent, especially because certain needs are not satisfied by the family and community. Perhaps the strongest impact of the conditions of lower-class living can be observed in the anti-intellectualism of many

TABLE 16-1 Focal Concerns of Lower-Class Culture

AREA	PERCEIVED ALTERNATIVES (State, Quality, Condition)	
1. Trouble:	law-abiding behavior	law-violating behavior
2. Toughness:	physical prowess, skill; "masculinity," fearlessness, bravery, daring	effeminacy; timidity, cowardice, caution
3. Smartness:	ability to outsmart, dupe, "con"; gaining money by "wits"; shrewdness, adroitness in repartee	gullibility, "con-ability"; gaining money by hard work; slowness, dull-wittedness, verbal maladroitness
4. Excitement:	thrill; risk, danger; change; activity	boredom; "deadness," safeness, sameness, passivity
5. Fate:	favored by fortune, being "lucky"	ill-omened, being "unlucky"
6. Autonomy:	freedom from external constraint; freedom from subordinate authority; independence	presence of external constraint; presence of strong authority; dependency, being "cared for"

Source: Miller, 1958: 7.

adolescents and of their parents. This disadvantage is most noticeable in linguistic behavior, especially in the abstract dimension of verbal functioning. This deficiency increases with age and is cumulative in nature, thereby demonstrating the effects of continued cultural deprivation.

The street corner gang member lacks the language breadth that enables him to think clearly and make abstract discriminations. He acquires the concrete language of his gang which is of little value to him elsewhere. Sebald points out:

> The main reasons for the verbal destitution of the lower-class youngsters lie in the deficient models for syntax and vocabulary, the lack of reading at home, and, above all, the lack of *variety* in stimuli. . . . If a child is substantially deprived of the variety of stimuli that he is capable of learning, he invariably falls behind in learning, and the more fortunate peers from the middle and upper social classes will surpass him in intellectual and academic success (1968: 333–34).

Since juvenile status offenders are predominately disadvantaged urban youths, they do not have the safeguard of respectable parents to bail them out of trouble. Also, courts are less likely to return a youth to the custody of economically disadvantaged and often separated parents, than they are to middle- or upper-class parents. This often means detention and incarceration and also encourages criminal delinquency among these youths. They are often sent to reform schools where they are indoctrinated into real criminality by older peers. Often juvenile status offenders are incarcerated for being "incorrigible" for longer periods of time than those who have committed actual crimes against persons or property. Lerman states:

> From the child's point of view, he learns that occurrences that may be part of his daily life—squabbles at home, truancy, and sexual precocity— are just a delinquent as thieving, robbing, and assaulting. It must appear that nearly anyone he or she hangs around with is not only a "bad" kid but a delinquent one as well (1971: 39).

Delinquency and Youth Culture:
Upper and Middle Classes

Juvenile delinquency has all too often been thought of as part of lower-class culture, while delinquency among upper-class adolescents may not be officially reported or prosecuted and therefore is seldom seen in studies or reflected in statistics. Some work has been done by Vaz (1969) with boys from private and public schools of Canada as subjects. Some questions about delinquency among upper- and middle-class adolescents are: Are there subcultural characteristics of upper- and middle-class delinquents? What is the nature of peer orientation of upper- and middle-class boys? What are the attitudes of private and public school upper- and middle-class boys toward selected youth cultural activities? What are some of the changes in attitudes and behavioral patterns among upper- and middle-class boys and girls?

YOUTH CULTURE AND THE UPPER- AND MIDDLE-CLASS ADOLESCENT. Youth culture is not endemic to a society but develops under special favorable conditions. Institutional changes in the social and economic spheres of Canada and the United States has made possible the emergence of a relatively prestigious youth culture. This may be observed in the manner of dress, life styles, traveling, and schools attended by many adolescents from upper- and middle-class homes. The adolescent is being given a prominence never accorded him before, although he retains his youth culture and establishes barriers between it and the more general adult culture.

As part of a larger study Vaz used a questionnaire to gather data from boys aged thirteen to over nineteen in five public schools and one upper-class boys' private school located in five Canadian communities. Table 16-2 compares the delinquent behavior of upper-class and middle-

TABLE 16-2 Self-Reported Delinquent Behavior of Public School Upper- and Middle-Class Boys

TYPE OF OFFENSE	UPPER CLASS	MIDDLE CLASS	UPPER CLASS	MIDDLE CLASS
	Percent Admitting Offense		Percent Admitting Offense More Than Once	
Taken little things of value (between $2 and $50) which did not belong to you	15.5	15.2	4.8	2.3
Remained out all night without parents' permission	27.3	25.9	11.1	8.4
Gambled for money at cards, dice, or some other game	68.8	65.4	35.8	38.8
Taken a car without owner's knowledge	13.9	11.3	3.1	3.0
Taken little things that did not belong to you	71.5	64.7	19.8	15.4
Skipped school without a legitimate excuse	41.0	41.6	12.2	14.5
Driven beyond the speed limit	57.1	48.8	42.1	38.6
Taken money of any amount from someone or place which did not belong to you	36.8	29.2	10.4	4.7
Placed on school probation or expelled from school	7.3	4.7	1.0	1.1
Been feeling "high" from drinking beer, wine, or liquor	38.9	40.4	17.8	29.4
Driven a car without a driver's license	63.2	61.5	28.9	27.8

Source: Reprinted by the special permission of the *Journal of Criminal Law, Criminology, and Police Science*, Vol. 60, No. 1. Copyright © 1969 by Northwest University School of Law.

class boys from private and public schools. Of the seventeen delinquency items, fourteen are reported by proportionately more upper-class private school boys; two items, car theft and driving a car without a license, are reported by upper-class public school boys; and one item, drunkenness, is reported more by middle-class boys. Serious theft and remaining out all night without parents' permission are disproportionately reported by upper-class private school boys. The responses of public school boys from the upper- and middle-class are very similar on almost every item.

Petty theft is reported by over 70 percent and 64 percent of upper- and middle-class boys respectively. It is likely that this type of theft is practiced by practically all boys at one time or another, irrespective of social class. Stealing for fun appears among all social groups; it is an indication of courage and masculinity—integral components of the male role. The data on theft are likely a reflection of the early years; with increased maturity and sophistication, petty theft, vandalism, fist-fighting, and stealing money decrease markedly; gambling, taking a drink, driving beyond the speed limit, and driving without a license assume increased importance. These acts may be termed "sociable delinquency" since they tend to emerge from predominately social events. The data suggests further that breaking and entering, being placed on school probation, automobile theft, and purchasing liquor are relatively unpopular delinquencies among upper- and middle-class boys.

MOBILITY AND MIDDLE-CLASS DELINQUENCY. Students of juvenile delinquency have pointed out that delinquency has been on the increase during the past several decades among middle-class adolescents. A number of explanations have been offered to account for this phenomenon (Bohlke, 1961). First, it may be a result of the increase in percentage of our population who may be regarded as middle class in terms of their earnings and education but remain lower class in attitudes, behavior, and interests. There is a cultural lag in many homes; thus, many so-called middle-class adolescents have assimilated the attitudes, behavior, and values of lower-class culture.

Second, there has been a weakening of self-control and the deferred gratification pattern characteristic of middle-class culture. Many affluent middle-class families indulge their children to such a degree that they fail to develop frustration tolerance and self-control on the part of their children and adolescents.

Third, many adolescent boys are unable to meet their fathers' expectations that the boy equal or surpass the father in his achievements. Fourth, there has been a diffusion of lower-class values and behavior patterns to middle-class youth, aided particularly by public education and mass media. Fifth, lower-class behavior patterns have become fused in part with teen-age culture. It has left its imprint in their music, dance, sexual codes, and attitudes toward authority.

SOCIAL INFLUENCES AFFECTING DELINQUENCY

In 1947 Sutherland developed his generic theory to explain delinquent and general criminal behavior. Its major emphasis is on the processes of learning, and it explains juvenile delinquency on the basis of social interaction and social learning rather than in terms of personality disorganization and social pathology. Sutherland's theory of juvenile delinquency involves the nature of associations and experiences at home, with peers, at school, and in the neighborhood. If the adolescent's exposure to intimate groups favors delinquent behavior, we can expect him to internalize these indirect teachings. Although we recognize the importance of learning, we also recognize individual differences. These may be noted among brothers and sisters within a given family or members of a gang. A study of the influences of home, peers, school, and community should, however, furnish us with additional insight into the causes of juvenile delinquency.

Home Conditions

One cannot well ignore the influence of the home in any consideration of delinquent behavior. A study of case histories of delinquents reveals again and again a picture of rejection, neglect, parent-child conflict, poverty, abuse and ill-treatment, psychotic parents, and social stress. Mizuship and others (1971) noted from their studies that family relationships were related to emotional disturbances and delinquent acculturations, and that the common factor in most delinquents was "lack of rejection of interpersonal ties with socialized persons."

PARENTAL ATTITUDES. An important source of frustration for many adolescents is the unwillingness of parents to "let go." A thwarting of the quest for independence is closely related to the early development of many juvenile crimes. It has been observed that at ten or eleven years of age around 70 percent of girls and 60 percent of boys find greatest pleasure in the home and prefer to spend most of their leisure time there. With the onset of puberty, the wider range of interests, and broadened social activities, adolescents begin to find more pleasures outside the home. Parents should not deplore this fact, and instead of thwarting adolescent desires, should aid the growing boy or girl in his or her emancipation from the dependency of childhood. It has been observed that parents of delinquents resort more frequently to punishment and to a lesser extent to reasoning than do parents of nondelinquents. It has further been noted that mothers of delinquents are inclined to be lax and eratic in their discipline. Both mothers and fathers of nondelinquents tend to display firm but kindly measures of discipline. Sometimes the delinquent behavior of the adolescent is reinforced by parents who consciously or unconsciously sanction it. Such was the case of Jack reported by Baittle:

> An example is Jack, who was a popular member of the group. He was constantly involved in serious fighting with other boys and was expelled from school many times. His father frequently boasted of getting into trouble when he was Jack's age, and refused to recognize the seriousness of his son's fighting. He felt Jack would straighten out as he himself had. Moreover, the father felt that Jack could not possibly compete with his own delinquencies in adolescence, and therefore blinded himself to what the boy was doing. The mother, although verbalizing wishes to impose controls on Jack, could not because of her conscious fear of hurting him. Unconsciously, she wished the boy to get into trouble and be punished, and he acted this out (1961: 108).

A study of subgroups of delinquents by Bassett, Crowder, and Cohen (1968) sheds further light on this problem. They assessed the disciplinary practices of parents in relation to reported degree of involvement in *FA* (Fantastic Aggressive) and *A* (Aggressive) behavior. A thirty-five-item questionnaire was completed by 101 boys aged twelve to nineteen, confined for the first time in the Wisconsin School for Boys. The purpose of the questionnaire was to determine how often, by whom, and in what manner they were disciplined before incarceration.

The results of the study showed that the specific family member who was the main disciplinarian had no significant relation to their involvement in aggression; the nature of the punishment did make a difference. "Boys reporting that they were usually punished by being 'beaten' rather than being disciplined in other ways showed significantly higher scores on the *FA* scale than did other boys. Boys punished typically by someone living outside the home showed significantly higher scores on the *A* scale than those punished by family members in the home" (1968: 29).

CHARACTER AND PERSONALITY ADJUSTMENT OF PARENTS. A factor closely related to parental attitudes is the character of the parents. It has been pointed out that the child is imitative; especially does he imitate those whom he considers authorities. He comes to feel that their acts are an endorsement of such types of behavior. Imitation and suggestion in connection with drinking, immorality, or lawlessness aid in the establishment of delinquent tendencies in adolescent boys and girls. In an early study by Lumpkin (1931) the delinquent girls' parental backgrounds were found to be very unfavorable. Social defective tendencies such as crime, alcoholism, and sexual irregularity appeared 443 times in 189 families.

The Iowa Training School for Boys at Eldora has a capacity of 300 and receives boys between the ages of twelve and eighteen committed by a juvenile court (O'Neill, 1969). Their offenses range from truancy and incorrigibility to murder. The personnel in charge inaugurated a special program in an effort to get whole families to work with them in their boys' behalf. Their efforts were based on the belief that a "delinquent" child or adolescent may be symptomatic of a troubled family—a problem of alienation. Concerning the results of their efforts O'Neil concludes:

> . . . Our experiences convinced us that family dysfunction can lead one or more of its members to adopt delinquent behavior. This seems especially true when the dysfunction is characterized by (1) low parental self-esteem; (2) communication failure between the parents; (3) communication failure between the parents and the children; (4) vague definition and inadequate performance of parental roles in division of labor within the family and in the provision of guidance, nurture, and support; and (5) relationship failures between the family and community authorities, such as school personnel, police, and social agencies" (202).

Family Relations and Delinquency

Bandura and Walters (1959) did a study on juvenile delinquents focusing specifically on family rather than cultural pathology. They restricted their sample to white adolescents who suffered no overt economic hardship and whose parents were living together. Their study revealed that there was little difference between delinquents and nondelinquents in mother-son relationships. However, there was a crucial difference in the father-son relationships. The delinquent youths exhibited much less identification with their fathers and had failed to internalize a set of moral values in part because of the failure of the father to provide a good role model.

It appears that delinquency may be related to a female-dominated home situation. This may be noted in particular among the blacks in large cities, where a large percentage of adolescents grow up in fatherless homes. Clinical studies and investigations of delinquents suggest that father-child relationships, especially father-son, are of considerable etiological importance to both social and psychological difficulties (Nash, 1965). It seems likely that delinquency rates will be higher among adolescent boys and perhaps girls who have lost their father than among those who have lost their mother. This hypothesis seems to run counter to the general notion of the all-importance of the mother to the child's social development. As suggested in earlier chapters, the father is most important to the healthy development of adolescents.

A comparison of the family characteristics of a group of delinquent and nondelinquent boys in Sweden has been given by Johnson (1967). The family can best be described as economically marginal and contains symptoms of pathology, such as alcoholism, irregular marriages, and illegitimacy. The father is frequently absent and is sometimes replaced by a stepfather.

Separation from the mother usually means from the father also. Only 25 percent of the delinquents (compared with 83 percent of a control group) had a continuous relationship with a father figure. Although data are not available on the dynamics of father-son interactions, there were evidences of the presence of underlying factors such as:

1. Punishment in the delinquent families was commonly severe and often brutal.
2. The attitudes of the parents were authoritarian.
3. The mother frequently dominated the home.
4. Delinquents had an unfavorable image of the father.
5. There was a communicative failure between parents and adolescents.

CHILD-REARING PRACTICES. Significant differences exist, even within a particular class or ethnic culture, in child-rearing practices, although lower-class parents are inclined to be quite autocratic in their relations with their children while middle class parents are more democratic. In a study reported by Sollenberger (1968) Chinese-American child-rearing practices were studied as they related to juvenile delinquency. This study is of special interest since it involves a minority group with an alien culture. Adolescents from this group suffer many of the same discriminations as do other subordinate groups whose appearance is different from that of the white majority. These Chinese-American adolescents are of low socioeconomic level and there is a cultural conflict between them and their Chinese-born parents. From interview responses, observations of familial relations, and discussions with neighbors and others in the area, Sollenberger concluded that to produce a low delinquency rate, in spite of environmental variables that ordinarily favor delinquent behavior, the following factors and conditions operate:

1. Through an abundance of nurturance and protection during early childhood, a reservior of security and trust is built up, so that after the age of six, when the rigid demands for conformity are expected, they will be accepted with a minimum of hostility.
2. From an early age, physical aggression is not only not encouraged but it is not tolerated.
3. The child comes from a close-knit, integrated family. He is reared in an atmosphere of mutual respect. Certain filial duties are expected of him, and, on the other hand, the parents accept responsibility for his behavior.
4. Within the family, and within the community, the child is continuously in contact with good models of behavior after whom he patterns his own behavior (1968: 22).

The School and Delinquency

The schools, once thought of as havens of learning where students were prepared for life's activities, have in many cases become sources of discord and violence. One of the by-products of social change and the educational, cultural, and social revolution now operating in our schools is the increase in juvenile crime at school. King in a report by the *New York Times News Service* points out, "Crime by children, some of it serious and committed by youngsters not yet in their teens, is becoming a problem of growing concern to parents and the police across the country" (*Charlotte Observer*, 1971: 23A).

CRIMES AT SCHOOL. Crimes by juveniles in school are not new, but authorities generally agree that the problem has grown increasingly worse during the past decade. For the most part, the crimes are petty and involve money and property—"shakedowns," bicycle thefts, and pilfering from lockers. There are also crimes against persons, including assault, rape, robbery, and, in a few cases, murder. Bicycle theft is the most common. Most major cities have a stolen bike room where youngsters can look over those that have been recovered to see if theirs is among them. Instances of extortion, backed up by threats and actual violence, are increasing. This is usually the work of a small group that may have several peers from whom they secure money. The most frightening aspects of this problem are (1) the enormous increase in frequency of juvenile crimes, and (2) the increased seriousness of crime, especially crime against schoolmates.

EFFECTS OF FAILURE. More and more the problem of individual variation is receiving attention in an endeavor to interpret better the cause-and-effect relations in the development of behavior. The importance of this is brought forth in a study by Wattenberg (1954) of factors associated with repeating among preadolescent delinquents. The records of 90 "repeaters" were compared with those of 235 boys showing only one police contact. Repeating was found to be closely associated with poor school work, low intellectual ability, membership in unruly gangs, and reputation for trouble. One of the most interesting in the context of data offered from other studies dealing with dropouts is the result of a study by Palmore and Hammond (1964) that failure at school, along with sex and age, are the factors most closely associated with official delinquency among youngsters supported by Aid to Dependent Children funds. The delinquent boy in particular presents a phychologi-cal deficit. His behavior may be attributed to a series of inadequacies or failures.

A considerable amount of racial turmoil, crime, and violence in and around schools is perpetuated by young people who have dropped out of school, usually as a result of failure or lack of adjustment to the school program. Most of these nonstudents are unemployed. They return to school sometimes with a grudge against teachers or certain students or they just want to give expression to their feelings. In one sixteen-day period in the fall of 1972, fourteen New York City school teachers were robbed or assaulted. Nearly 1,000 assaults on students and teachers were reported during 1972 in Miami (*Newsweek*, 1973). Nonstudents return to school with firearms at dances and athletic events. The problem has been further aggravated by the drug problem among both students and nonstudents.

CONTRIBUTION TO DELINQUENCY. Although the schools are playing an increasingly important role in the training of future citizens, they are in many cases contributing to juvenile delinquency. Some of the major problems faced by adolescents have been listed in earlier chapters as school problems. It has been pointed out that many adolescents are almost doomed to failure because of an inadequate program, while another large group finds itself at odds with the teachers and school administration because it is not interested in, and in many cases actually dislikes, the program in which it is required to participate at school. We note that the first step of many juvenile delinquents is truancy from school.

NEIGHBORHOOD CONDITIONS

The undesirable effects of the ghetto, slums, and other environmental conditions in our cities where poverty and ignorance play important roles have been emphasized throughout previous discussions. In our cities the detrimental effects of bad home conditions are usually supplemented by undesirable neighborhood influences and a lack of good educational and recreational opportunities. In the first place, congested home conditions are closely related to congested neighborhood conditions. It has been found from various studies that crime is relatively higher in populous areas. In an early study by Maller (1936) of juvenile delinquency in New York City, it was observed that delinquency is largely concentrated in certain underprivileged areas. High delinquency areas are characterized by (1) low rents, (2) low educational level of the adults, (3) excessive retardation of pupils in school, (4) poor recreational facilities, (5) overcrowded conditions, (6) high adult crime rate, and (7) lack of organized activities for adolescents. These conditions are similar in nature to the results obtained from surveys in other cities. These studies indicate that delinquent areas fall into the following general types: (1) deteriorating residential areas in which business establishments are being organized, (2) manufacturing areas, and (3) districts characterized by an unstable population.

VIOLENT CRIMES BY CITY GANGS. There was an upsurge of violent crimes by city youth in the 1960s. The public image is that of adolescent gangs, or "wolf packs," prowling the darkened streets and alleys bent upon doing evil, especially tormenting others—a delight in violence for its own sake. Conclusions presented here about gang violence are based upon findings of an extensive study of youth gangs in "Mid-city," a central-city slum district of 100,000 persons (Miller, 1966).

Information was gathered on some 150 street gangs, numbering about 4,500 males and females, aged twelve to twenty, in the middle and late 1950s. Twenty-one of these gangs were selected for more detailed study; selection was based primarily on their being the toughest in the city. Seven of these gangs, numbering 205 members (four white male gangs, one black male gang, one white female gang, and one black female gang) were subjected to intensive field observation. Detailed qualitative information on the daily behavior of gang members in sixty "behavioral areas" was collected and studied. The bulk of the findings presented is quantitative in nature. They show that most violent crimes were directed at persons, few at property; however, compared to other forms, violent crime was far from dominant. Only a small minority of gang members were active in violent crimes. While race had little to do with the frequency of involvement in violent crimes, social status figured prominently. A clear and regular relationship was found between age and offense-frequency. The yearly rate of court charges rose quite steadily between the ages of twelve and eighteen, reaching a peak of about nine charges per 100 boys per year. These findings do not support an image of violent crimes during adolescence as erratically impulsive, uncontrolled, and unpredictable.

Further insight into gang violence may be obtained by asking the question: "What categories of persons were targets of gang assault, and what kinds of physical objects were the targets of damage?" Findings based on field-recorded data show that of seventy-seven targets of assault whose identity was known, 73 percent were persons of the same age and sex category as the gang members, and 71 percent of the same race. An initial observation of the data lends substance to the "ganging up" notion: one-half of all targets were peers of the same age, sex, and race categories. Miller concludes:

> . . . Most scholars agree that these ends are predominantly ideological rather than material, and revolve on the concepts of prestige and honor. Gang members fight to secure and defend their honor as males; to secure and defend the reputation of their local area and the honor of their women; to show that an affront to their pride and dignity demands retaliation (1958:111–12).

Television and Aggression

There are some who would blame television violence for most adolescent crime; however, the findings of a study of television and aggression by Feshbach and Singer (1970) do not bear out this contention.

Through the cooperation of a number of private schools and boys' homes, the investigators were able to control the televiewing of several groups of boys. Some groups watched such programs as *The FBI, Gunsmoke, The Untouchables;* other groups watched milder programs such as *American Bandstand, Bachelor Father, Lassie,* and *My Favorite Martian.* Records were obtained of changes in aggressive attitudes and values as well as the number of aggressive acts in which the boys engaged during a period of time. The comparisons of the two groups yielded the following:

1. The group that watched the milder nonviolent programs engaged in more than twice as many fist fights than the group that watched the more violent programs.
2. The nonviolent group had over twice as many arguments as the group watching the more violent programs.
3. Both groups cursed and swore a great deal with the group watching the violent program displaying this behavior 12.6 times as much as the nonviolent group.
4. Criticizing or insulting others showed a marked contrast, with the violent group displaying this behavior more than twice as often as the nonviolent boys.
5. The greatest difference between the two groups was in the manifestation of jealousy; the group that watched the milder programs showed 254 instances; the group that watched the violent programs showed only 87 instances, or about one-third the amount of the other group.

The authors point out that the violence of a western or a *Tom and Jerry* cartoon is recognized by the viewer as fictitious. However, the violence on the evening news is realistic. Violence may and perhaps does sometimes result from what children hear and see going on in the world: social injustices, racial discrimination, poverty amidst plenty, and the abuses and horrors of the recent Vietnam War.

SUMMARY

Although a considerable amount of juvenile delinquency never comes to the attention of the courts, it has been and continues to be a major problem. It is the main source for the increase in crime as registered by the FBI. Girls commit far less crime than boys, especially serious crime. The breakdown of family discipline, racial animosities, changing school patterns, and the general increase in crime are reasons usually given for the increase in juvenile crime.

The portrait of the juvenile criminal is not always that of the underprivileged boy or girl, although a large percentage of crime comes from the slums and other undesirable living and educational conditions. The crime rate is higher among those of low intelligence, the dropouts, and truants. Educational retardation and a history of school failure is closely linked with juvenile delinquency.

Many delinquents today are coming out of the middle class. This may be accounted for by (1) the increased size of the middle class, (2) the failure of many homes to assimilate middle-class attitudes, behavior patterns, and values (3) lack of self-discipline, (4) adolescent's inability to satisfy the expectations of their parents, especially those of the father, and (5) the fusion of much lower-class culture in the behavior patterns of teen-age culture.

The causes of juvenile delinquency should not be oversimplified. Sexual promiscuity alone does not cause delinquency, nor do psycho-neurotic tendencies or inferior intelligence. It is not inherited, nor do environmental influences reveal the entire story. The roots of delinquency are usually in the home. Delinquents are often retarded or failures in school and are not accepted by their peers. The needs of the delinquents are not different from those of nondelinquents, but are frequently thwarted at school, especially the need for self-esteem which comes from success.

REFERENCES

ALLEN, DONALD E. and HOYIT S. SANDHU. "A Comparative Study of Delinquents and Nondelinquents: Family Affects, Religion, and Personal Income." *Social Forces* (1967–68), 46:263–69.

AMERICAN INSTITUTE FOR RESEARCH IN THE BEHAVIORAL SCIENCES. *Behavioral Sciences Newsletter for Research Planning* (October 4, 1968), 5 (19):5.

Asheville Citizen (October 18, 1971), p. 4. "Name of the Game Isn't Football."

BAITTLE, BRAHM. "Psychiatric Aspects of the Development of a Street Corner Group: An Exploratory Study." *American Journal of Orthopsychiatry* (1961), 31: 703–12.

BANDURA, ALBERT and RICHARD H. WALTERS. *Adolescent Aggression.* New York: The Ronald Press, 1959.

BASSETT, H. T., J. E. CROWDER, and M. F. COHEN. "The Audio-visual Viewing Habits of Selected Subgroups of Delinquents." *Journal of Genetic Psychology* (1968), 112:37–41.

BOHLKE, ROBERT H. "Social Mobility, Stratification Inconsistency, and Middle-class Delinquency." *Social Problems* (1961), 8:351–63.

Charlotte Observer (April 12, 1972) p. 1A. "Young Girls' Crime Rate Sky-rockets."

CLOWARD, RICHARD A. and LLOYD E. OHLIN. *Delinquency and Opportunity.* New York: The Free Press, 1961.

CRITCHLEY, E. M. "Reading Retardation, Dyslexia and Delinquency." *British Journal of Psychiatry* (1968), 114 (517):1537–47.

DONET, L. *Psychiatric Aspects of Juvenile Delinquency.* World Health Organization Monograph Series No 2. Geneva: World Health Organization, 1951.

ECKENRODE, C. J. "Their Achievement in Delinquency." *Journal of Educational Research* (1949–50), 43:554–58.

FESHBACH, SEYMOUR and ROBERT D. SINGER. *Television and Aggression.* San Francisco: Jossey-Bass, Inc., 1970.

GARRISON, KARL C. Unpublished account given by Harry's father to the author. 1961.

GLUECK, SHELDON and ELEANOR GLUECK. *Unraveling Juvenile Delinquency.* New York: Commonwealth Fund, 1950.

————. *Delinquents and Nondelinquents in Perspective.* Cambridge, Mass.: Harvard University Press, 1968.

GOLD, MARTIN. *Delinquent Behavior in an American City.* Belmont, Calif.: Brooks/Cole Publishing Co., 1970.

HAVIGHURST, R. J. *et al. Growing Up in River City.* New York: John Wiley & Sons, Inc., 1962.

JOHNSON, G. "Delinquent Boys, Their Parents and Grandparents." *Acta Psychiatry (Scandinavian Supplement)* (1967), 43:195.

KING, WAYNE. "Crime by Kids No Longer 'Kid Stuff'." *Charlotte Observer,* (October 10, 1971), p. 23A.

KONOPKA, GISELA. "Delinquent Girls: A Research Report." Unpublished manuscript. Minneapolis: University of Minnesota.

KULIK, JAMES A., THEODORE R. SARBIN, and KENNETH B. STEIN. "Language. Socialization, and Delinquency." *Developmental Psychology* (1971), 4: 434–39.

KVARACEUS, WILLIAM C. *Juvenile Delinquency.* What Research Says to the Teacher Series, No. 15. Washington, D.C.: Department of Classroom Teachers, National Education Association, 1958.

LERMAN, PAUL. "Child Convicts." *Transaction* (August 1971), 8:35–44, 72.

LEVINE, SAUL V. "The Inner City—Setting, Subgroups, Psychotherapy and Service." *American Journal of Orthopsychiatry* (1970), 40:235–36.

LUMPKIN, K. D. "Factors in the Commitment of Correctional School Girls in Wisconsin." *American Journal of Sociology* (1931), 37:222–30.

MALLER, J. B. "Juvenile Delinquency in New York City." *Journal of Psychology* (1936), 39: 314–28.

MILLER, WALTER B. "Lower-class Culture as a Generating Milieu of Gang Delinquency." *Journal of Social Issues* (1958), 14 (3):5–19.

————. "Violent Crime in City Gangs." *Annals of the American Academy of Political and Social Sciences* (1966), 365:96–112.

MIZUSHIP, K., K. MIYAZAKI, and Y. YASHIA. "Diagnostic Scale for Delinquency Proneness." *Report of the National Research Institute of Police Science* (1971), 12 (1):70–76.

MOSQUWDA, JOHN. "Most Juvenile Joyriders Live in Poverty." *Charlotte Observer* (Auguset 12, 1971), p. 11E.

MUELLER, KATE H. "Program for Deviant Girls." In *Social Deviancy Among Youth. The Sixty-Fifth Yearbook of the National Society for the Study of Education,* Part 1, W. W. Wattenberg, ed. Chicago: University of Chicago, 1966.

NASH J. "The Father in Contemporary Culture and Current Psychological Literature." *Child Development* (1965), 36:261–97.

Newsweek (January 15, 1973), pp. 66–67. "The New Three R's."

New York Times News Service (October 4, 1971) . "Rising Rates of Crime by Children Against Children Alarming."

O'NEIL, CARL E. "A Correctional School Aims at Rehabilitation by Working with Families of Delinquent Boys." *Children* (1969), 16 (5):198–202.

PALMORE, E. B. and P. E. HAMMOND. "Interacting Factors in Juvenile Delinquency." *American Sociological Review* (1964), 29:848–54.

Parade magazine (July 8, 1973), p. 17. "Aimless and Alienated."

PHILLIPSON, MICHAEL. *Understanding Crime and Delinquency: A Sociological Introduction*. Chicago: Aldine Publishing Co., 1974.

RICE, RUTH D. "Educo-therapy: A New Approach to Delinquent Behavior." *Journal of Learning Disabilities* (1970), 3 (1) :16–23.

SEBALD, HANS. *Adolescence: A Sociological Analysis*. New York: Appleton-Century-Crofts, 1968.

SLAVSON, S. R. *Reclaiming the Delinquent*. New York: The Free Press, 1965.

SOLLENBERGER, RICHARD T. "Chinese-American Child-rearing Practices and Juvenile Delinquency." *The Journal of Social Psychology* (1968), 74:13–23.

SUTHERLAND, EDWIN H. *Principles of Criminology*. 4th ed. Philadelphia: J. B. Lippincott Co., 1947.

TARNOPAL, LESTER. "Delinquency and Minimal Brain Dysfunction." *Journal of Learning Disabilities* (1970), 3 (4):200–207.

THOMPSON, GEORGE G. and ERIC F. GARDNER. "Adolescents' Perception of Happy-Successful Living." *The Journal of Genetic Psychology* (1969), 115:107–20.

VAZ, EDMUND W. "Delinquency and the Youth Culture: Upper and Middle-class Boys." *Journal of Criminal Law, Criminology, and Police Science* (1969), 60 (1):33–46.

WATTENBERG, WILLIAM W. "Factors Associated with Repeating Among Pre-adolescent Delinquents." *Journal of Genetic Psychology* (1954), 84:189–95.

YABLONSKY, LEWIS. *The Violent Gang*. New York: The Macmillian Company, 1962.

RECOMMENDED READINGS

COWIE, JOHN and ELLIOT SLATER. *Delinquency in Girls*. New York: Humanities Press, 1968.
Unsatisfactory home life emerged as the main cause of delinquency of adolescent girls committed by juvenile courts to an approved residential school in London. Three-fourths of the girls were adjudged delinquent because of sexual conduct and most of the others because of shoplifting.

GLUECK, SHELDON and ELEANOR GLUECK. *Toward a Typology of Juvenile Delinquent Offenders*. New York: Grune & Stratton, 1970.
The authors consider the literature on types of delinquents. The purpose of a typology is to differentiate *qualitatively* different kinds of delinquents.

GOLD, M. *Delinquent Behavior in an American City*. Belmont, Calif.: Brooks/Cole Publishing Co., 1970.
Gold conducted a large-scale study of juvenile delinquency in Flint, Michigan. The book focuses on the character and frequency of delinquency in different parts of the city. Case studies add meaning to the materials presented.

HANEY, BILL and MARTIN GOLD. "The Juvenile Delinquent Nobody Knows." *Psychology Today* (1973), 7 (4):48–56.

The stereotype of the lower-class, minority gang member as a delinquent is challenged by studies showing that many delinquents are found among middle-class white youth and that getting caught is what makes further delinquent acts probable.

HIRSCHI, TRAVIS. *Causes of Delinquency.* Berkeley and Los Angeles: University of California Press, 1969.

The investigator attempts to test the hypothesis or theory that delinquent behavior results when an individual's bond to society is weak or broken. Data were gathered from 4,077 students, a stratified probability sample representative of 17,500 students entering eleven junior and senior high schools. Only the boys' questionnaires were used in the study.

MARTIN, J. M., J. P. FITZPATRICK, and R. E. GOULD. *Analyzing Delinquent Behavior: A New Approach.* Washington, D.C.: U.S. Government Printing Office, 1968.

It is the authors' contention that the sources of crime are to be found in the social and political inequalities in our society. This is an attempt to replace the theory that delinquency is a product of individual pathology and failure.

SELLIN, THORSTEIN and MARVIN E. WOLFGANG, eds. *Delinquency: Selected Studies.* New York: John Wiley & Sons, Inc., 1969.

The first chapter describes an "index of delinquency" developed by the editors. A special system of classification was developed, based on data from police records. Six studies made by graduate students with the cooperation of the Police Department of Philadelphia are presented in which the index is used.

VAZ, E. W., ed. *Middle-Class Juvenile Delinquency.* New York: Harper & Row, Publishers, 1967.

This is a compilation of nineteen articles by leading students in the field and deals with (1) the adolescent subculture, (2) the relationship between socioeconomic status and juvenile delinquency, and (3) patterns of middle-class delinquency.

part five

The Future is Now

Youth movements and issues of the immediate future are presented in Part Five. It has been pointed out that, "Population, technology (human knowledge and skills), and resources from the environment are three factors of extraordinary importance to humankind."[1] Although we have discussed many problems faced by adolescents growing up in a rapidly changing society, it is worthwhile for us to consider the problems suggested by North. These forces and conditions are moving so rapidly toward us that many of the more intelligent adolescents find it imperative to act now rather than wait for the next generation to face the issues. Although government pollution programs may involve much planning, several years must elapse before the effects can be seen, and this creates a great deal of anxiety and frustration. In many cases youth have taken the initiative in social and ecological needs such as day-care centers, tutoring, and recycling.

Scientific advances and technological changes are taking place more rapidly than the ability of social institutions to keep pace with them. Thus, we see conflict and maladjustments arising in almost every area of life. A new world view and much social innovation are needed if we are to move into the future without violence and widespread destruction. The adolescent says, "Why wait? The future is now."

[1] Robert C. North, "Alternate Futures: Some Variables and Parameters," *American Journal of Orthopsychiatry* (1970), 40:252.

youth
movements

INTRODUCTION

In our discussion of youth movements we are not especially concerned with stable, adult-sponsored youth organizations but with the student-oriented movements. Many nonstudents are involved in youth movements; however, the primary youth movements are found in high schools, colleges, and universities. A preliminary statement defining and qualifying the makeup of youth movements may be offered as follows:

> Youth movements are made up of young people who are impressed by the values of some social unit or individuals, around whom they have ordered their basis for meaning, and who see the gap between these values and their own self-fulfillment and that of the society around them. In a pluralistic society, these sources of their ordering values may be varied. These youth will tend to be children of the affluent, many of them being aware of unhappy childhood experiences. In any event, characteristically they have more to gain than the average youth within the framework of the society they reject, in terms of the material rewards the society has to offer. They reject affluence as a dominant goal; they see the

437

present social structure as dehumanizing and oppressive, and they frequently if not always identify with the oppressed poor and with a generalized "humanity." Their alienation from society is primarily social rather than political (Garrison, 1968: 27–28).

Youth Movements within Traditional Societies

Students in traditional or "backward" societies are placed in a position of conflict or strain. They are the bearers of new forms of knowledge which often conflict with the standards of their society and its culture. They often are the elite, and generational authority is reversed because the young teach their elders, particularly in scientific areas. Feuer discusses at some length the interplay between "intellectual elitism" and the extent of "backwardness" of traditional societies as determining factors of the likelihood of the emergence of youth movements during periods of uneven, rapid social change and development. He states:

> The more backward a people is with respect to its culture and intellect, the greater is the likelihood that it will have a student movement of an elitist and revolutionary character (1969: 22).

The tendency among students in backward societies is to seek (sometimes to an extreme) the most advanced technology and philosophical ideas found in "developed" societies. This phenomenon tends to heighten the sense of tension with one's own culture and institutions in traditional societies. This situation is compounded by the tendency among students to form their own "generation" based upon their own common experience of contact with one another and with a similar body of knowledge. On an intellectual level, Feuer describes this as "the law of the universality of ideas, or the law of universal intellectual fashions" —i.e.,

> what is most important to bear in mind is that the culture of the student movement . . . is the one genuine international culture. Students at any given time throughout the world tend to read the same books (23).

This is not totally generalizable, of course, especially to those societies which work towards controlled or repressive intellectualism. However, it has been discovered that even in totalitarian societies, many secondary and university students find their way into the international flow of ideas of their times.

Because of widespread instant mass communications, the music of today's youth has also enhanced the internationality of youth cultures and movements, and has reached far more young people than books and ideas qua books and ideas. A number of totalitarian societies seek to suppress the music from the youth culture of the west. Since it threatens the internal unity of such societies, music is often denounced as a product of decadent imperialism; but still, many of the young clandestinely listen to recordings and radio broadcasts.

Youth Movements in Postindustrial Societies

Adolescents in postindustrial societies also feel the strain between their common culture and the "universalism" of technology. For many, no longer do "intrinsic" cultural values seem to control technological development; rather, technological development tends to determine the directions of cultural values. This has taken a number of different expressions in those societies which are most "developed" technologically, the United States being a prototype. Materials related to the youth movements of the United States during the 1960s and early 1970s will be presented in relation to other youth movements and to general commonalities found among youth movements, in periods of societal dislocation. Much of the material traces some of the "progressions" through recent American history.

Some Characteristics of
Modern Youth Movements

Modern youth movements, as with the student segments from which they tend to arise, are not "bread and butter" oriented; rather, they are almost always composed of middle- and upper-class youth. Unless the political establishment arbitrarily dictates who shall be a "student," this generalization tends to be true in both capitalist and socialist societies. Black students who led the initial sit-ins, white freedom riders of 1961, white students in Mississippi in the summer of 1964, and others who were involved in various forms of youth protests in the 1960s and early 1970s have been sons and daughters of the middle and upper classes.

Affirmation of a generation's own counterauthority is an essential ingredient in youth movements, especially as experienced and reaffirmed in mass rallies and demonstrations by speakers and singers, and simply the contagious power of a group acting in concert on an issue of "rightness" vs. "wrongness." The assertion of authority and independence is usually articulated publicly through a written manifesto. From young Martin Luther to the students of the Kiev Union in Russia to the Free Speech Movement at Sproul Hall in Berkeley to the Port Huron Statement of Students for a Democratic Society, the manifesto challenges the established system and its authority, and asserts generational independence and adulthood.

Youth in youth movements traditionally speak of a new life style and of creating a new "humanity" for the future. From earlier youth movements to the present, there is a sense of having created an intrinsic alternative style of life and meaning. It is not the past qua the past that social movements reject. It is the recent past as it is continued into the present, together with the conditions of the present itself being perceived as oppressive. In all social movements, there is a version of history which includes both an Ultimate Past and an Ultimate Future, each in spiritual and aesthetic harmony.

Alienation and American Youth Movements in the 1960s and 1970s

The concept of alienation is central to understanding contemporary youth movements. The experience of alienation and the experience of various, diverse attempts to deal with it run throughout these movements and especially in their music, sometimes bitterly, sometimes poignantly, sometimes as a prelude to attempts at momentarily experiencing hope and celebration; alienation, a sense of estrangement, loneliness, and struggle are all themes expressed among those youth involved in expressing generational emergence.

Alienation figures prominently in the ideological statements and manifestos of contemporary youth movements—a concept of alienation bearing many similarities to the use of the concept by the young Karl Marx in the 1840s. Marx commented that

> the *devaluation* of the human world increases in direct relation with the *increase in value* of the world of things. Labour does not only create goods; it also produces itself and the worker as a commodity, and indeed in the same proportion as it produces goods (121).

A society which places extrinsic rather than intrinsic value upon man's work and his social relationships makes him an object—a "thing" —for sale in the marketplace. Alienation in contemporary society results, Fromm (1965) contends, because man finds himself treated as a means, a thing to be manipulated, in both economic and social life, and thus treats other men as things to be manipulated. Modern man's relationship to his fellow man is "one between two abstractions, two living machines, who use each other." Many present-day youth, predominantly those of the middle and upper classes, are questioning and rejecting technological determinism as a basis for their society's definition of community of values. Many feel that they are merely "numbers" living in the open market.

Alienation and the Rate of Technological Change

The rate of technological change seems to be the primary precipitating factor in the emergence of youth movements in the United States, together with a new sense of frustrated intellectual elitism on the part of the leaders of the student movements. An increasing need has been felt among youth for self-affirming values, while the pragmatic, technological needs of the nation have seemed to take precedence. There is a turning away from technological determinism toward issues of community and values, especially by youth elites. These youths have been overexposed to the "sensate" culture through the predominantly middle-class and upper-class life-styles of their parents; through commercialism's continual advertising bombardment "the good life" has proven otherwise and brought frustration and loss of identity and meaning.

Fromm's analysis is certainly of significance, especially to adolescents and postadolescents growing up increasingly with frequent experiences of uncertainty from mass media and other sources, even among those from comparatively stable families and communities. Fromm defines the experience of "marginal man," as one who perceives his situation to be structurally defined by a system which "doesn't care"—i.e., a society in which he has neither exchange nor intrinsic value. It is also especially true that adolescents in today's society have very early experiences of the concept of "being only a number." Increasingly, their educational choices are determined by "numbers." When they secure their first job, they have their first experience with a social security number which will follow them in reports and files for the rest of their lives, as a basic means of identification. Whether the technological bureaucracies of modern societies can retain their functional stability is a question raised in an earlier chapter, but, at the present time, it still goes on, with its attendant computerization and depersonalization.

Alienation and Social Class

Many upwardly mobile youth do not experience the same quality of alienation which numbers of middle- and upper-class youth have experienced with the technological revolution. However, as student activists in the 1960s learned, in their frustration with supporting upward mobility for the disadvantaged, achievers, once having achieved in the technological society, may themselves then be led to revolt. Helping the "oppressed" to become "middle class" while themselves attempting to break out of middle-class habits is tremendously paradoxical.

The Black Movement as a
Prototype of Alienation

Scott's discussion of alienation (1965) is especially appropriate concerning the rise of black youth militancy in the middle 1960s. It is appropriate as well to generate propositions concerning other youth movements which tend to rise rapidly through these levels to challenge society on the level of *values*.

ALIENATION FROM PUBLIC FACILITIES. Increased alienation from public *facilities* of blacks in the 1950s led to a few major, dramatic legal breakthroughs in the 1954 Supreme Court decision on school desegregation and access to open seating in public transportation in the South, and finally, after pressures from the early sit-ins, access to formerly white-only restaurants. Initially, there was widespread support for blacks among many non-Southern (and some Southern) whites, in their attempt to eliminate those obvious, legally based forms of discrimination such as segregation on public transportation. It was only a matter of a short time before blacks and whites alike began to realize that sitting together on a bus in Alabama did not solve the real problems which blacks faced. Both blacks and whites came to realize that their mutual problems were not just Southern, but nationwide—it was the problem of an entire society.

Black and white self-definitions came to be radically changed, and, on an incremental level, public facilities for blacks failed to produce the anticipated invitation to middle-class (or even lower-class) white society. Especially was this felt by younger blacks, whose stake in American society was almost entirely in the future. They began to question whether structural facilities, even as redefined and opened up legally, could change the basic problem of being black in the United States.

ALIENATION FROM ROLES AND NORMS: EXPECTATIONS AND ACHIEVEMENTS. Thus, numbers of younger blacks, together with white youth who had participated in the sit-ins in the early 1960s, began to redefine whether the role of Negro would permit access to change in facilities rapidly enough to fulfill rising expectations. The acceleration of expectations among oppressed groups, following initial institutional, legalistic breakthroughs, is a phenomenon perhaps universal in prerevolutionary periods. Coresponding, actual achievements in material and status conditions are comparatively slow. Existing institutions, by opening a few general, legalistic barriers, at the same time generally tend to open floodgates of unfulfilled aspirations among oppressed groups. When the floodgates of unfulfilled aspirations open, institutions respond to the symptoms more than to the causes and attempt to gradualize the process of achievement. The expectations of the oppressed groups, however, continue to rise. Thus, as expectations rise, the gulf between expectations and achievements grows. At various times, there may be revolutionary attempts to close the gap and repression may occur, leading to further redefinitions of expectations and achievements and of identity issues.

ALIENATION FROM VALUES. As young blacks became especially sensitive to the actual problems of achievement in entering American society, as defined by whites, they experienced a progression from the failure of facilities to offer achievement expectations to the failure of roles, norms, and values, as provided by white American society, as a framework for self-identification and sources for group identity. The role of "Negro," and, finally, the whole perspective of white America's society on the concept of "Negro" as a means of entering the society, came to be questioned and, progressively, redefined.

THE FORMATION OF A NEW IDENTITY. Thus, the cycle of alienation as described by Scott (1965) was completed on all four levels, from facilities to roles, norms, and values, to the point of redefining the situation on the basis of *alternative values,* and societal reinterpretation. The level of values is the primary level of identity issues, and thus it is on this level that conflict becomes most intense. There are conflict theorists who claim that conflict is healthy. In any event, conflict is a *natural,* normal process for formerly oppressed groups in their engagement with the process of *identity formation* (Coser, 1956). It is obvious that conflict with white values and conflict between expectations and achievements was a major determinant in the emerging black identity of the 1960s, as blacks clashed with white society on all levels.

The new identity among younger blacks especially in values was that of being proud to be *black* and to define oneself as such ("black is beautiful," "black power," and so on), and rejecting white society's term, "Negro." "Black" redefined norms, roles, and facilities. Norms for the newly defined role of black included for some the adoption of African dress and hair styles, learning Swahili, identification with African culture, soul food, soul music as a new form of their musical heritage's contribution, some attempt as unearthing and teaching black history, and, in some instances, adopting Muslim or African names.

New religious expressions and movements were created both in Christian, Muslim, and other contexts and reinterpreted for their own cultural needs from those names given to them by white society. Facilities came to be redefined, and, at some points, black militants were talking about taking over states or cities, and establishing a black republic within the American republic. It is significant that, as with other youth movements in modern times, those younger blacks who initiated the attempt at a black revolution originated from predominantly middle-class homes.

For blacks, as with European immigrants to the United States, there had to be some transitional basis for entering American society and preserving their own identity. However, white society had made this extremely difficult by giving blacks European names, European culture, the stigma of African inferiority, European language and religion, European dress styles, and so on, together with having annihilated memories of their older cultures from Africa. Even the Mexican-American Chicano brings a language, religion, dress style, customs, food, and musical tradition, rather than having to "create a cultural heritage" from *anomie,* as was the case with black Americans through much of their history. In the 1960s, the attempt to construct a culture was made, independent of and in conflict with the predominantly white-defined interpretation which had dominated their existence since early slavery times.

In many instances, the process led to estrangement between older and younger blacks, especially in the mutual misinterpretations of the purpose of riots. Younger blacks have played more of a leadership role for older blacks in the Civil Rights Movement than white youth have been allowed to play in crises related to the larger white society, such as foreign policy in Vietnam and policy on environmental issues. Those white youth attracted to youth movements from their own alienation found themselves empathetic with their black counterparts and, more recently, with American Indian youth in their attempt to recover their cultural heritage. Many of the terms used by the white youth movement were used earlier among black youth: "dig it," "cool," and other terms associated with "looseness" and also with hallucinogens, as well as such political phrases as "Right On!" and "Power to the People!"

The Search for Identity
Among White Youth

The phenomenon of the search among white middle- and upper-class youth for identity and an intrinsic basis for community can also be analyzed in terms of the hierarchy of alienation discussed earlier. Facilities—i.e., mass high school and university education—have been,governed more by technological considerations than by issues of community. SATs, GREs, and other such tests come to be seen not in isolation but within the context of a whole society centered around numbers, as discussed elsewhere. Here, the problem of values and meaning for an intrinsic basis for identity, where blocked at the level of facilities (e.g., problems with the educational process as not providing these values), can lead youth to question the ability of student roles for redefining facilities in a way that will enable these facilities to be channeled in such directions. Failure at the level of roles may lead to questioning the norms which define role behavior, and, finally, failure at the level of the accessibility of values creates those conditions for alternative redefinitions of social systems. To an extent, this has happened over the past decade or more among numbers of adolescents and has focused the problems within the context of those institutions which service youth—i.e., especially educational institutions. In the late 1960s and early 1970s, among minorities of young people, "free schools" emerged, especially in those urban areas with large university populations. These schools are not "free" financially, but free from the compulsoriness of predefined public teachers and predefined public curricula. At the same time, some traditional educational institutions have begun, in some areas, to respond to this basic issue of bringing together, once again, the rational knowledge available to today's developed societies and intrinsic values related to the use of that knowledge, oriented toward community. In the meantime, numbers, of middle- and upper-class youth have redefined themselves at the level of values, norms, roles, and facilities taking many different directions, as generations have, in a sense, tended to tumble over each other with a multiplicity of choices, in attempts to deal with these issues of community and identity.

It is important, in discussing the phenomenon of alienation in understanding youth movements, that alienation may also take the form of *intergenerational solidarity* and that reaffirmation, in conflict, may take intergenerational forms, as in an external attack upon common values between generations (a "holy war," e.g., which may involve the unity of a society into a single generation, without regard for age or sex). One must bear in mind the distinction between adult-controlled or otherwise adult-youth "united" efforts in institutionalized youth organizations and generationally created, value-oriented movements for societal change, together with new, generational expressions of values and experiences *created among youth* as a distinct expression of their location as youth. The latter results from the inability of society's elders to transmit the culture and a sense of compelling identity with that culture, in the face of rapid societal changes and uncertainties. Yet, in their own reformulation of the culture, youth in youth movements do reconstruct "the past" as well as the future. In a later section of this chapter, social change without generational revolt is discussed as differing from the phenomenon of youth movement attempts at societal change and reconstruction.

**Alienation and Parental Identity Issues
in Youth Movements**

The alienation of significant numbers of youth in our times in the developed societies, as with other periods of youth restlessness and youth movements during periods of rapid societal change in the past, has been linked with a generational revolt against parents, especially their fathers, for many of these youth. The *Mothers of Invention* expressed this theme in the 1960s in, among other songs, *Bow Tie Daddy* (1968) within the context of the culture of drugs. The song tells "bow tie daddy" (the bow tie itself symbolic of irrelevance) simply to go about his business ("drinking" and "stinking" and "getting old") because, in essence youth is charting its own path, including the substitution of hallucinogens and other avenues of new experiences for the old ways. The song, sung in the style of the 1920s, tells parents (notably fathers) essentially to "get lost" and to go on living with their delusions that "everything's under control." The Beatles displayed a compatible theme (noting the mother's concern while "father snores") in *She's Leaving Home* (1967).

Such songs of intergenerational rejection have appeared frequently in the music of the present and recent past in moods of alternating despair, liberation, loneliness, the wish for intergenerational identity, anger, cynicism, indifference, transience, and the fear of having to stand alone as a generation. Such songs are directed toward the lack of an intrinsic parent-child relationship and the lack of ability to relate intergenerationally, with some sense of continuity, to a sense of "validation" of parental authority in the socialization process. Among charismatic *leaders* of modern nineteenth- and twentieth-century youth movements, this lack of validation of parental authority and intrinsic family worth and ties appears as central to their own socialization and identity-formation problems and their current involvement in youth movements, especially as these problems connected with their relationships with their fathers and, frequently, associated, by contrast with an identification with the "nurturant" qualities of their mothers and siblings.

A charismatic student activist organizer in the middle 1960s, in an interview with the junior writer in the course of research, stated of his own childhood:

> My uncle was the mayor of a Southern city. My father was a Vice-President of an Eastern bank. I had a rough childhood. Lots of fights with my father. At nineteen, I decided to become a revolutionary. I realized society had s——— on me, so I decided it had s——— on a lot of other people. I saw what it meant when people could control and buy other people's lives. I came to hate that (Garrison, 1968: 97).

The movement among young blacks in the United States in the 1960s and early 1970s may be seen as, in part, a rejection of the authority of their fathers. The "Uncle Tom" role that their fathers had played in cowed and submissive behavior before white society was for them an intolerable basis for their own identity. This resentment is carried to "Tomism" among black administrators and professors in black colleges, who are perceived as having allowed themselves to live on handouts from white society.

The inability of fathers, in their own values, work, and life styles, to provide a clear basis for identity formation is a highly significant variable in the lives of many youth who join youth movements (as with many older supporters of youth movements, who attach themselves deeply to them). The experience of hostility and rejection on the part of fathers (including perceptions of the father as being "overly materialistic" and "empty of other values") appear to be more important than the father's generally middle- or upper-class status or political convictions, in the assessment by youth in youth movements of childhood influences, as these youth reflect upon them.

Black students, for instance, who have not experienced hostility and rejection from their fathers, are more likely to accept the fact of their fathers having played "Uncle Tom" roles, and are much more likely to place singular blame upon the society itself for forcing that role upon their fathers, rather than blaming both society and their fathers. In this instance, there is a sense of identification with parents' oppression by society, and feelings of some degree of intergenerational solidarity.

YOUTH MOVEMENTS AND SOCIAL CHANGE

There are many who recognize the high ideals in youth movements. Despite the discrepancy between the profession and expression of worthy ideals and despite the disillusionment of many adolescents of today, they are seen to have higher ideals and be more willing to assert them, despite pressure from the Establishment, than adolescents of the past.

As has been indicated elsewhere, youth are especially prone to fads, peer subcultures, and social movements. However, the phenomenon of youth movements as a form of generational expression and conflict on a large scale is new to the United States. By contrast, student movements have been a significant influence in many other societies. Mao Tse-Tung, as a young man, participated in every stage of the Chinese student movement in the early part of this century, as did Lenin in the Russian student movement.

The Importance of "The Event"

Every movement for social change is preceded by growing tensions and a sense of dissatisfaction by certain groups in society. The crystallization of unrest and frustration into a movement for social change, however, is dependent upon a symbolic event which unifies these feelings in a common, responsive set of experiences. Princip's assassination of Archduke Ferdinand was not the cause of World War I; it simply functioned as the incident—the event—which precipitated the war.

The year 1968 was a pivotal one for youth movements in the United States. The assassinations of the Reverend Martin Luther King and Senator Robert Kennedy, both symbolic of youthful idealism and aspirations, left a shattering void for many black and white young people. The Democratic convention in Chicago in the late summer of that year was a chaotic, bloody scene, as police and students fought in the streets, and the convention nominated a candidate who had appeared in no primaries. Society appeared to be coming apart at the seams.

The late 1960s and early 1970s also saw the emergence of the "hippie" culture and of the drug culture, both of which contributed widely to the involvement of numbers of students in eastern religious movements and mysticism. The underground church thrived for a time, although, in the early 1970s, it tended to become overshadowed by the Jesus Movement, which itself proliferated into submovements. The Jesus Movement has its own gospel and rock groups with such names as *The Young Apostles* and its own demonstrations ("Jesus Happenings").

The Importance of Music in
Social Change Among Youth

Much of the experience of youth in our era of instant communication finds its central expression in music. Music in some respects defines the spirit of an era (as do books and films, to an extent, as well). Music itself became a vehicle for defining and unifying emotional experience, and the performers who created and sang the music became charismatic leaders who defined the loyalties associated with their music. The songs of a movement reveal much about its purposes and character.

As for the Civil Rights Movement, *We Shall Overcome* was sung in gatherings all over the United States by "black and white together" in the generating years of the freedom movement. As the movement gained momentum with initial successes, the songs more frequently extolled direct action and confident resistance.

Bob Dylan sang out "The Times They Are a 'Changin'," and indeed they were. Many other folk singers offered various interpretations of the events and the confusion of those times. The music of the past decade or more expresses, in various directions, anger, especially anger with middle-class life styles, loneliness, and hope. Among the most influential stylesetters by far were the Beatles, whose originality and creativity are undisputed. From their beginning as an obscure rock group with English, working-class origins, the Beatles created a unique style and suddenly skyrocketed into a position of unique, international popularity. Some of their earlier music and the raving, fanatical response to it was reminiscent of the sexual hyperidentification of earlier generations. Young people in the 1930s had screamed at verbal inflections by Bing Crosby and at Frank Sinatra's "flatness" in *Shoo, Shoo Baby*. Other young people had screamed in the 1950s when Elvis Presley combined vocal raspings and pelvic movements in such songs as *You Ain't Nothin' But a Hound Dog*. The Beatles moved from semblances of this to distinctive styles of interpretation of experiences for youth in the 1960s, and their influence continued into the 1970s after they had dissolved as a unit.

George Harrison, a member of the Beatles, wrote *Piggies* to describe standardized, middle-class life styles in developed societies, as a means of interpreting and rejecting them. He writes of the little piggies (people) "crawling in the dirt" while "life is getting worse." Then he refers in the second verse to the bigger piggies "in their starched white shirts." The third and fourth verses of the song deal with the life styles and attitudes of the piggies. However, Harrison also wrote for the same album *While My Guitar Gently Weeps* and *Long, Long, Long;* in these songs there is nostalgia for a world which proclaims "community" and solidarity and hope. In a genuinely virtuoso album *Abbey Road* (1969), the group sang songs of hope and escapist fantasy.

Idealism in Youth Movements

The idealism of youth movements may be noted in their literature, music, and actual martyrdoms. There is inherently the potential for violence and terrorism and amorality. Since youth are the most susceptive segment of society, the "purest" forms of moral idealism and "righteousness" are combined with irrational violence, terrorism, and self-destructiveness. Out of the increasing gulf between expectations and achievements arose the terrorist Weathermen and the Black Panthers. Society frequently becomes reactionary when threatened with destruction. The established political authorities "tighten up" society and impede the very goals to which the youth movement is dedicated. The "law and order emphasis" of some Republicans, especially in the 1968 presidential campaign, capitalized upon the unpredictability and demoralizing effects of the deaths of Kennedy and King and the chaos of the Democratic convention. That experience left many young idealists who were not in sympathy with terrorism in a position of being "labeled" and identified with the latter, and thus, they became discouraged and disillusioned.

Youth movements, in some modern societies, have contributed quite basically to social revolution as in Russia, Germany in the 1930s, and China in the 1940s. The Chinese Communist revolution began with members of the Chinese student movement of the early part of this century. Youth involvement was crucial in all three of these social revolutions. However, once successful, as with other revolutions, the possibilities for new forms of dissent were quickly dashed. One of the first aims of a revolution is to consolidate and to prevent the possibility of other alternatives to emerge. Youth must then be disciplined and instilled with the ideology of the revolution in order to create and sustain continuity. Hitler's youth revolution was skillfully led by well-placed, charismatic adults who could continue to inspire and channel the idealism, fidelity, and loyalty of youth toward National Socialism. Other revolutionary leaders who began their involvement in successful revolutionary movements as students have been acutely aware of the dangers of later revolt by a new generation of youth.

SUMMARY

In this chapter we are not concerned with stable, adult-sponsored youth organizations but instead with movements which have been primarily student oriented. These movements, while including many nonstudents, generally take place within the context of common youth gatherings and experiences and are often centered or based at colleges, universities, or high schools.

In traditional, or "backward," societies there is a tendency among students who represent the future elite of their nations to seek the most advanced technology and philosophical ideas found in "developed" societies. This tends to heighten the tension with their own culture and institutions. Adolescents in postindustrial societies also feel tension when the apparent universalism of technology seems to control cultural values.

There are some characteristics which 19th and 20th century youth movements have in common even though these movements occurred in different countries, at different times, and for different causes. Usually articulated publicly by a written manifesto, these movements stress the assertion of youth's authority and independence from the present adult establishment. Modern youth movements condemn the recent past and present state of their societies while they project a romanticized version of the Ultimate Past and a nebulously defined, but harmonious, Ultimate Future.

Alienation, loneliness, and marginality figure prominently in the ideological statements and manifestoes of contemporary youth movements. Many youth, predominantly those of the middle and upper classes, are questioning and rejecting technological determinism as a basis for their society's definition of community or values. Many feel that they are merely "numbers" living in an open market.

The black movement of the 1960s offers a prototype of alienation. Blacks, especially many young blacks, have redefined themselves against American white society. Legal breakthroughs, beginning with the 1954 Supreme Court school desegregation decision, opened facilities to blacks. However access to structural facilities neither produced the anticipated invitation to participate in white society nor changed the basic problem of being black in the United States. Blacks began to question the values of white American society and entered a stage of identity formation in which they could reinterpret their own cultural needs and form a positive identity based on black pride.

While many white youths perceive their activities in terms of carrying out their own parents' unfulfilled humanitarianism, others rebel against the emptiness of their childhood. Only a small minority of adolescents actually become active members of radical organizations; these groups set the style for the wider attack upon middle-class values. Although most adolescents do not directly participate in youth movements, the fact that a movement evolves indicates the extensive frustration, alienation, and dissatisfaction with present conditions.

Every movement for social change is preceded by growing tensions and a sense of restlessness and frustration with the position of certain groups and norms in society. The late 1960s and early 1970s was a period of political disillusionment for many elite youth. The drug-oriented subculture contributed to the involvement of many adolescents in eastern religions, special religious movements, and mysticism. Music was often the message for teen-agers and reflected their social concerns, feelings, commitments, and loneliness.

REFERENCES

Coser, Lewis A. *The Functions of Social Conflict.* New York: The Free Press, 1956.

Feuer, Lewis A. *The Conflict of Generations.* New York: Basic Books, Inc., 1969.

Fromm, Erich. *The Sane Society.* New York: Holt, Rinehart, & Winston, Inc., 1965.

Garrison, Karl C. Jr. *The Tyranny of Freedom.* Unpublished doctoral dissertation. Durham, N.C.: Duke University, 1968.

Marx, Karl. *Early Writings.* Translated and edited by T. B. Bottomore. London: C. A. Watts & Co., 1963. P. 121.

Piggies. Copyright: Northern Songs, Ltd., 1968.

Scott, Marvin B. "The Special Sources of Alienation." *The New Sociology,*

Irving L. Horowitz, ed. New York: Oxford University Press, Inc., 1965. Pp. 239–52.

RECOMMENDED READINGS

ERIKSON, ERIK H. *Identity: Youth and Crisis.* New York: W. W. Norton & Co., 1968.
Erikson, as in his other analyses of issues related to youth and societal changes, skillfully brings together insights from social, historical, clinical, and developmental perspectives on issues of identity for youth in rapidly changing societies and cultures, especially centering upon the experiences of contemporary youth in the acute sociohistorical change.

FEUER, LEWIS A. *The Conflict of Generations.* New York: Basic Books, Inc., 1969.
A meticulous, detailed, historical analysis of youth movements viewed in terms of issues of generational conflict, one of the central theses being that intergenerational conflict is more likely to impede the goals of the younger generation than is intergenerational solidarity working together toward these goals.

FLACKS, RICHARD. *Youth and Social Change.* Chicago: Markham, 1971.
The author makes clear that American youth are not a monolithic category, and that he is dealing with a selective group of young people—those who are white and in college. The author has a strong commitment to social and political change and upholds the college youth who advocate change and pursue an alternative style of life.

LIFTON, ROBERT J. "Individual Patterns in Historical Change: Imagery of Japanese Youth." *Journal of Social Issues* (October 1964), 20 (4).
Studies student movements, especially in Japan, and indicates some of the commonalities among archaic and futurist youth movements.

SCOTT, MARVIN B. "The Social Sources of Alienation." *The New Sociology,* Irving L. Horowitz, ed. New York: Oxford University Press, Inc., 1965.
Scott's analysis of the hierarchy of alienation is helpful to any analysis of young people and others faced with blockage of goals and means.

STREIKER, LOWELL D. *The Jesus Trip.* New York: Abingdon Press, 1971.
A brief but insightful analysis of some aspects of the Jesus Movement of the early 1970s.

18

theoretical issues for the immediate future

The wisdom of the people's gone.
How can the young go straight?
—W. B. Yeats

Through our schools, television, and other media, we have developed the best-educated adolescents of all times. These young people have been equipped with the means (and hopefully with the ability) to sense dislocations, fraud, and hyprocrisy in today's society. All too frequently, however, adults refuse to recognize as legitimate youth's concerns about present-day problems and conditions. As Senator George McGovern (1970) stated in an address given to the Society of Pediatric Psychology in 1969:

> We have raised our children to value the individual, but then asked them to be absorbed into giant bureaucracies that serve themselves before they serve the individual. We have boasted about the great achievements of our society, about our ability to get to the moon, about our money and our goods and our economic system, and young idealists wonder why 15 million Americans go hungry. We teach our young people that American

history is a glowing example of humanistic concern, of the victory of the underdog, and yet we are frequently identified abroad with repressive military dictatorships that use our money and our guns and sometimes our men to suppress indigenous unrest that does not happen to support the status quo (158).

It is certain that in no previous decade in the history of the United States have so many young people experienced such a succession of internal changes, upheavals, and prolonged uncertainties and drift as has been the case in the past decade or so. Hopefully, out of the technological and cultural chaos of our times, youthful idealism may find itself channeled toward viable forms of societal construction and the reaffirmation of individuals as persons.

ADOLESCENCE
AS A CONTINUING PHENOMENON

Adolescence, as a social and cultural phenomenon and as a psychological state of transition and identity formation, is likely to remain in all developed societies, especially the democracies which permit and encourage the expression of individual choice. This period of life will extend beyond the teen-age years into the early and middle twenties, especially for the growing numbers of young people faced with increased vocational specialization. The experience of adolescence for the masses began with the postponement of adult work, as formal schooling was extended through the high school years. For a significant number of young people, undergraduate college and post-high school professional training are today equivalent to a high school diploma for the previous generation. Beginning in the mid-1940s with the influx of World War II veterans with GI educational grants, and spurred in the mid-1950s by Korean War veterans, many persons attended college who never would have had the financial ability to do so. Thus began the rapid expansionist phase of higher education in the United States.

Adolescence and Postponed Adulthood

The period of adolescence has extended to the point that some theorists differentiate between the early and mid-teens, and the late teens and mid-twenties. The extension of this period of education and training, transition and identity formation is being experienced not by small elites, but by millions of young people in the developed nations and increasing numbers of young people in the less developed countries.

The trend toward both undergraduate and advanced professional training for growing numbers has been obvious. However, we cannot say with any surety it is irreversible. Certainly technological societies will continue to require a great deal of specialized training for many professionals in the future; however, the revolution in automation and cybernation could eliminate many mid-level technical jobs. At the present time there are in many fields, especially in the physical sciences, too many trained and overtrained professionals for existing employment opportunities. Possibly a trend will develop toward alternatives, more shortened forms of education, and new types of employment which will not force as high a percentage of young people to seek long years of continuous training.

While the United States is no longer in a period of rapidly expand-ing economic growth, most adolescents in this country are relatively affluent when compared with their counterparts in the rest of the world. There is the possibility that an increasing number of young persons will postpone permanent entry into the adult working world for a couple of years. This group would work at temporary jobs only long enough to accumulate the capital to be able to travel, experiment in communal living, or learn a craft. Growing job shortages, however, may force many other adolescents to accept temporary work whether it fits in with their desires or not.

**Adolescence Today
and the Decline of Youth Movements**

With increased social change, young people are faced with a growing number of conflicting reference groups and too many alternatives in their process of identity formation and decision-making. Unless there is some way to humanize technology and restore intrinsic values as the basis of our culture, an increasing number of young people may react to this country's social structure with undirected, nonspecific resentment (Scheler, 1961).

Delinquent behavior is, on a broad level, closely associated with rapid social change and the inadequacies of the existing society to transmit social control mechanisms and cultural values. Unless and until we begin to find more stable bases for the family and community, we can expect to see more delinquent behavior. This does not mean that all delinquent behavior is violent or actively rebellious or socially unaccept-able. As Merton (1957) clearly indicates, responses to feelings of margin-ality and powerlessness may also involve withdrawal or ritualism, both of which are found in many societies which have been forced into oppressive or repressive conditions. Withdrawal means dropping out of society, and ritualism involves appearing to go along with society and conform to its standards and rules while harboring strong feelings of resentment. These responses are on the increase among a large percentage of adolescents and may well keynote the decade of the 1970s; in fact we can speak of the 1950s as the decade of apathy, the 1960s as the decade of activism, and the 1970s as the decade of alienation.

Many of the feelings of frustration and powerlessness are directly attributable to the failure of youth movements in the 1960s to make any significant gains in changing either the country's cultural values or the politics. The Civil Rights Movement, which gained widespread support in the early sixties, was a radical movement in its vision of social change; however, it was ideologically conservative and called upon the United States to live up to the founding fathers' ideal of "liberty and justice for all." Yet, despite the legal breakthroughs and the successful demonstrations, the social conditions of black persons in this country have not significantly changed for the better. Although there have been great strides made in desegregation, they have not measurably helped the majority of blacks for whom poverty, rejection, and prejudice are part of the American way of life.

The failure of idealism in the 1960s has resulted in an almost contagious feeling of powerlessness and disillusionment with the rationality of social and political structures. The established political and social structures have responded to youth movement protests in this country with a certain amount of hysteria. The shootings at Kent State, Jackson State, and Southern University, the police brutality at the 1968 Democratic convention, and the mass, indiscriminate arrests in Washington, D.C. during the 1970 peace demonstration are not signs of a democratic society rationally using its control mechanisms. This is repression through power and terror—supposedly an anathema to a free society. The adolescents of this decade may learn only frustration; and the chances are great that there may not be major nationwide student movements in the 1970s.

Continued Forms of Generational Expression by Youth

Generational expressions in response to potential anomie or resentment may be expected to continue for some time. All are related to the uncertainties about the future. Growing numbers of young people are concerned more with learning how to live, rather than how to consume, as reflected by anxious articles in the financial section of the *New York Times*. Over the long run, some present youth trends may become quantitatively important, if the present generation continues to remain skeptical of the blessings of mass production and consumption. Wallich comments:

> What about the unemployment that reduced consumer wants might create? That will depend, in the first place, on whether a lessened desire to consume is accompanied by a lessened urge to produce. Suppose the young idealists remain activists and want to keep working. We shall then have surpluses to dispose of. These will show up, as now, in a high saving rate, in a heavy cash flow into banks and other investment media, in falling interest rates. There will still be lots of use for all these resources. If people are tired of cars and gadgets, they may still want their cities and countryside beautified, their environment returned closer to its pristine state. If ever there should be nothing left to do in this country, most of the world will still need help to meet elementary wants (1971: 75).

ISSUES OF INTERGENERATIONAL
STABILITY AND VALUES

**Intergenerational Instability,
Change, and Crisis**

Generational instability is indicated not only in widely varying responses to youth movements but in the inability of polls to predict accurately for any length of time. For instance, a Gallup poll on religion conducted in the spring of 1970 (*Oregonian,* 1970) was concerned with whether or not college students considered organized religion to be a relevant part of their lives. The results were not unpredictable, following past trends, as Table 18-1 indicates.

TABLE 18-1 Response of College Students to the Question:
Is Organized Religion a Relevant Part of Your Life? (in percents)

	YES	NO
National	42	58
East	38	62
Midwest	39	61
South	50	50
West	41	59
Men	37	63
Women	50	50
Freshmen	46	54
Sophomores	44	56
Juniors	37	63
Seniors	38	62
Public	39	61
Private	38	62
Denominational	69	31
"Liberals"	37	63
"Conservatives"	58	42

Some of the usual distinctions were self-evident, as in the comparative higher degree of interest in organized religion in the South, although students in the South were moving closer to students in other parts of the United States, by comparison with the past. The other statistics are also predictable from past studies: greater interest by women than men, greater interest by freshmen than seniors, greater interest in denominational and other private schools than in state institutions, greater interest among conservatives than among liberals. The only surprise was a slightly higher degree of interest in the western part of the United States than in the East or Midwest, since the West has been both the most mobile and the least religious part of the nation in the past. However, the pollsters did not discuss this surprising statistic, nor did they deal with the more esoteric or enthusiastic forms of noninstitutionalized religious expression already developing on a noticeable scale at that time, especially in the West. The theoretical issues of the latter are especially important and involve those who feel themselves to be highly marginal to society and its institutions. It is such small, emergent, marginal minorities whose ideas and styles find their way into the larger population in a more structured and less intense form. For instance, resentment toward the war in Vietnam was somewhat limited to small groups of students and intellectuals in 1962, but by 1964 it had led to growing disaffection all over the country. In 1968 the war led to the unprecedented declaration by a president of the United States that he would not seek reelection; by 1970 a majority of the citizens of the United States wanted to withdraw from the Indochina War as soon as possible. This is despite the fact that war, as a phenomenon, is something a nation usually considers to be moral, holy, and patriotic. The general consensus of amorality concerning the war in Vietnam first penetrated small segments, later led to large demonstrations, and finally to widespread disaffection.

The West was and is the most mobile and marginal section of the country and therefore the area most prone to volatile new movements and life styles. At the time of the Gallup poll, for instance, a significant number of students or quasistudents were increasingly oriented toward mysticism and oriental religions and different kinds of Christian and semi-Christian religion. By 1971 new versions of religious and quasi-religious movements, interpretations, and styles became more prevalent in the larger population. The interest in religion allows young people to share common beliefs and experiences with each other. Whether the Jesus groups and others will have more stability, longevity, or success depends upon factors beyond the level of our discussion here, but these phenomena provide a source of identity formation and values for numbers of youth seeking links with the past and a vision of the future.

Youth May Attempt to Reassert Stability Through Religion

Most attempts by youth to restructure society during periods of rapid change are attempts to reassert stability. The contemporary interest in religion may, for many young people, represent a degree of generational stability and continuity. Although many of these adolescents are not interested in established theology, many do identify with their parents. These religious groups may have more success than the political activists of the 1960s because they appeal to the deeper sources of Western tradition and provide a totalistic view of the past and future.

The Communal Movement and the Nuclear Family

Upper-middle-class and upper-class young people frequently (although not always) are the trend-setters for other adolescents and postadolescents, with older youth generally initiating change and younger adolescents responding. The communal movement appeared to be significant during the late 1960s and early 1970s, initiated by thousands of predominantly middle-, upper-middle-, and upper-class young people, joined later by young people from working-class backgrounds. The movement met with varying degrees of success in attempting to restructure lifestyles within communal settings, as alternatives to the privatism of the nuclear family. In the late 1960s and early 1970s, hundreds of youth communes appeared, particularly in California and Oregon, paralleling similar trends in some other developed nations. Smith and Sternfield conclude that

> Common to most seems to be a belief system of mysticism and nonviolence derived primarily from the use of psychedelic drugs, with LSD and marijuana maintaining premier positions (1970: 527).

There is insufficient data to indicate how generalizable this is, as increasing numbers of communes deemphasize drugs. As with the nineteenth-century commune movement in the United States, the most successful in communal responses to such basic questions as economics, sexual practices, and family ties tend to sustain strongly religious ties. Continuity and stability become major problems for many of these communes oriented primarily toward drugs and mysticism. The successful commune, by definition, becomes something of a "total society" which involves intensely shared religious belief system.

The nuclear family may have trend setters who create new family styles on a more cooperative level, and these, over time, may be absorbed into American society. The nuclear family itself may find new meaning in traditional kinship patterns or involvements with other families, such as with relationships fostered by techniques of humanistic psychology. The nuclear family will probably continue to be a fairly normative phenomenon for some period of time. It has undergone a degree of specialization of function in providing personality development and security, characteristics which have always been basic to the family, and which now are seen in terms of this specialization.

NEED FOR INTERGENERATIONAL UNITY. Far more attention has been paid to intergenerational conflict and rebellion than to intergenerational unity and resocialization. Yet, as noted elsewhere, a degree of intergenerational unity is basic to constructive societal change. Intergenerational revolt rather consistently does *not* lead to idealistic goals, but rather to repression. In order for successful societal changes to take place, it seems that, almost inevitably, intergenerational unity is required. The *Komsomol* in the Soviet Union, the Red Guards in China, and the Hitler Jugend in Nazi Germany were created to build intergenerational solidarity. To a democratic society, such youth groups are anathema. Creating and forging a healthy choice in democratic societies between totalitarian involvement of youth and the rampart individualism stressed in American society is not easy. Most totalitarian movements are an attempt to return to primitivism and to eliminate adolescence as a transition period of identity formation. On the other hand, the American emphasis upon individual choice has led, with the increasing rapidity of change, to generational rebellion and revolt. Possibly, in the resolution of this conflict, the period of transition known as adolescence can be structured for service—i.e., service to a potential adult identity and service in careers which can enable democratic societies to deal with some of their problems and concerns. Such activities as Scouting have always involved mostly preadolescents and have less and less holding power through early adolescent years; as it is currently structured it is appropriate to more stable, small communities than to the megalopolises. More meaningful perhaps would be attempts to deal with the adolescent years as a period in which society utilizes the desires of youth for idealism, fidelity, and loyalty, as Erikson (1968) so clearly indicates. The motivations heightened during those years could promote an idealism that involves personal choice and, at the same time, promotes national and world community. The initial enthusiastic response of older adolescents to the Peace Corps and the Vista program in the 1960s demonstrates that many youth want meaningful work.

A New Generation of Adolescents

Margaret Mead in *Culture and Commitment* discusses culture in three separate groups in terms of the transmission of knowledge and values. The first is the *past,* or *postfigurative,* group in which children learned primarily from their elders. It depended on the actual presence of three generations and, by the example of the elders, answered the questions:

> Who am I? What is the nature of my life as a member of my culture? How do I speak and move, eat and sleep, make love, make a living, become a parent, meet my death? (1970: 5).

The *present,* or *configurative,* generation begins with the absence of grandparents. Perhaps the tribal elders were wiped out in war, or as in this country, young adults moved away from their parents or were caught up in new technological developments in which their parents had no part. Both adults and youth had to learn from their own peers that there are choices to be made: The Past or the Present. The highly mobile nuclear family seeks and sets its own standards and goals in the configuration society, and youth are further separated from the past by being age grouped through institutionalized education. As Mead points out, the elders can say to youth:

> "You know I have been young and *you* have never been old." But today's young people can reply, "You have never been young in the world I am young in, and you never can be" (49).

The world has changed so rapidly in the past twenty or thirty years that future teachers using this book can see that they have grown up in a world their parents never knew: the threat of nuclear destruction, moonwalks, instant global satellite communication, and the use of computers. The teen-ager with his pocket transistor radio is frequently more a native in this new world of today than his parents. According to Mead, we are now in the beginning of an entirely new stage of cultural transmission: the *prefigurative* age in which the youth teach and guide the elders. She continues:

> If we are to build a prefigurative culture in which the past is instrumental rather than coercive, we must change the location of the future. Here again we can take a cue from the young who seem to want instant Utopias. They say: The Future Is Now (75).

These stages can be seen in juxtaposition with Reich's definition of three stages of consciousness as presented in *The Greening of America* (1970). His treatise is based on definitions of "reality," all of which are still present in this country. Consciousness I believes in individualism where success (primarily economic) is determined by hard work and moral character. Consciousness II, which he traces to the liberal reform-ism of the early twentieth century and the later New Deal, envisions a meritocratic world which does not question change per se. For Conscious-ness II the corporate state becomes an interlocked model, and both the state and the individual are judged by their ability to keep pace with new technological breakthroughs. The essence of the corporate state is that it perpetuates itself and becomes something of a technological equivalent of Consciousness I, but without the all-important and neces-sary personal relationships that characterize Consciousness I. Self-dis-ciplined work is important in Consciousness II, although the main value of work is perceived as "functional" rather than "intrinsic." Consumption patterns are separated from the "fullness" of production as the safety valve area where hedonism becomes a reward for tolerating the dullness of work.

Reich contends that Consciousness III is emerging among many of the children of Consciousness II parents. Today's young people are beginning to define man in human terms rather than as a functionary of the technological state. In a sense the beginning of the liberation of Consciousness III combines transcendence and personal affirmation that is reminiscent of the Reformation and the Renaissance.

This "now person," Rogers (1969), Maslow (1967), and other humanistic psychologists contend, is far different from the "Adjusted Man" of the general psychology schools of the 1950s and early 1960s. Maslow described these "Now People" as "self-actualized persons," in-dividuals comparatively free of guilt, shame, and anxiety who accept human nature with its shortcomings in themselves and in others.

Whether one agrees or not with the more optimistic of these statements, it is obvious that the adolescent of the 1970s is a generational modification of his parents or of adolescents of earlier decades. He has been exposed to many, often competing, sets of values and in forming his own identity has the freedom and the attendant uncertainty of choosing his own absolutes. In being among the best-educated youth in history, he has had his horizon expanded beyond his community and nation. The immediacy of mass media, especially television, brought both the moonwalk and the Vietnam War into the living room and carried the adolescent into an interlocking world community. Technological change is so rapid that youth increasingly questions man's ability to answer the question "How?" and increasingly may ask the more difficult question "Why?"

EDUCATION IN A CHANGING SOCIETY

Many have argued that adolescence is now unreasonably extended. Too many young people are forced to enter fields of specialization because of family desires and the American dream of achieving middle-class status. One of the central controversies of our time in education is very much related to the issue of irrelevance and obsolescence. Does education take place simply to teach people technical training, or should those involved in the educational process, as teachers and students, attempt to make educational experiences a means of affirming personal values? The separation of technical education from value orientations is critical to the problems of adjustment and identity for adolescents, especially postadolescents. The continued push on the part of families for competitive success and prolonged educational training has less meaning in a world whose values are increasingly determined by technology rather than personal issues.

ISSUES IN A PLURALISTIC HERITAGE. Our educational institutions can, to an extent, regain their position if they accept the pluralistic heritage of American society as something quite different from the depersonalized, universalistic attempts at tolerance. Tolerance is a great improvement over intolerance, but as a value, it lends itself to blandness and uniformity. In some respects, *pluralism* implies the opposite of tolerance. As Hall indicates (1971):

> Pluralism implies the opposite of toleration. The pluralist does not merely put up with the ideals of others; he assumes from the outset that truth in moral and personal ideals is not black and white, but many blacks and whites and many grays as well; he assumes that there is not simply one good life, but many. Looking at life in this way, he therefore encourages, promotes, and favors differences between men. College education is not the only way to human fulfillment. If someone realized that and drops out because he doesn't belong, because he has other talents to de-

velop or even to find, the pluralist would not only allow his action but would support his ideals or his search for them. Married life is not the only way to human maturity; nor is celibacy. Black is at least as beautiful as white; there is no reason why either should be preferred. And insisting that the poor adopt middle-class mores and ideals with all our proprieties and anxieties, is doing them no favor.

Perry considered pluralism to be a value in affirming persons: "When one sees the inward value of other lives, one acknowledges their right to exist, or even exults in their existence" (1954: 223). Pluralism implies the right of individuals to choose their own culture, while it encourages other cultures to flourish; however, a tolerance (without pluralism) destroys whatever may be unique about a given culture. A recent attempt to resist school busing by the tightly knit Chinese minority in San Francisco indicates the conflict between pluralism and tolerance. Fearing the absorption of their young into the dominant society, the Chinese-Americans in San Francisco sought to retain community controls and cohesion. The Chinese share with many other minority cultures in American society the desire to retain their cultural integrity within a "melting pot" society. This is also true of the Indians and Mexican-Americans, and especially and increasingly with the blacks as well. Our educational institutions must learn to accept the richness from different cultures, rather than attempting to impose a uniformity. These institutions need to utilize philosophers, humanistic psychologists, social scientists, theologians, and others involved in issues of self-development to enable our young to achieve personal, social, and cultural integration and affirmation. Only then can we begin to deal with public education's negative influence on the problems of the emergence of the self and identity formation in today's youth. There is considerable evidence that many schools and colleges are trying out innovations that offer great promise, although there are many that are resisting change and are becoming ineffective.

Educational Revolution

The rapid changes in education as well as in other phases of life in the United States can best be thought of as a revolution. Revel points out that "There are five revolutions that must take place either simultaneously or not at all: a political revolution; a social revolution; a technological and scientific revolution; a revolution in culture, values, and standards; and a revolution in international and interracial relations" (1971: 2). All these are now in process in the United States, but are not following the usual revolutionary guidelines. There is first of all a questioning of values and goals, with movement toward changing them. This revolution resembles many past revolutions in that it is a revolt of the young and includes many intellectuals as well as members of the upper class. This revolution embodies a new approach to moral problems, the rejection of white supremacy, the feministic attack on male domination, the rejection by the young of completely materialistic values, the general adoption of noncoercive methods in education, the embodiment of a diversified culture, the rejection of American imperialism, the rejection of authoritarian culture, and the realization that an unpolluted environment is more important than commercial profit.

Change in Composition of Student Body

Segregated schools—black-white, public-private, rural-urban, and even male-female—have been part of the American heritage. The act of the Supreme Court in 1954 which declared unconstitutional legal segregation based upon race marked the beginning of the educational revolution. Today we find a student body made up of all elements of our society. The high schools are no longer white, middle-class institutions dominated by teachers from the white middle-class group who extoll middle-class values. The values, expectations, and behavior patterns of whites are encouraged by the total school environment and are conveyed primarily by the social relations of the schooling process—student-teacher and student-student interactions. Bowles states:

> Whether established relations among students are competitive or co-operative, whether relations between students and teachers are democratic or authoritarian, and whether relations between students and their work are creative or alienated, are better indicators of what is taught in schools than texts or formal curricula (1971: 478).

Concerns in Contemporary Education

Contemporary education is concerned with problems of day-to-day reality. In its efforts more consideration will be given to happenings reported on TV. The newscaster shapes reality regardless of whether or not he plans to do so. This was pointed out by Small, a news director of CBS news in Washington, as follows:

> The news media make news. . . . That is an uncomfortable fact to reckon with in the 20th century. As the conduit of what is happening, the news media is not only imperfect but frequently shapes or reshapes happenings. (1970: 284).

The schools of tomorrow will give increased attention to special TV programs, especially those on educational channels. Adolescents will be better informed on contemporary economic, political, and social problems. This should help in breaking down many barriers resulting from prejudices, misinformation, and inadequate information. Consider, for example, the effects of news reports on racial discrimination, pollution, legal and social injustices, poverty, and war. The generation gap, resulting in part from differences in education, will continue as a result of improved education and the use of the television media.

Students must be taught to separate facts from half-truths and propaganda. The notion that "one person's opinion is as good as another's" must be seriously challenged and shown to be false, especially on problems where information is available. To say that the man in the street's opinion on heart disease is as good as that of a heart specialist is obviously false. However, teachers cannot rightly define for all students matters such as the quality of life. Each individual must be free to develop his own philosophy of life; but he should be given guidelines to help him evaluate his concepts about the nature and purpose of life.

WORK EXPERIENCE. A program in school that makes use of work experience is not new. A dozen such programs operating over a decade ago are described by Burchill (1962). Work experience may be the central agent around which the attitudes and interests of students are organized. Such a program is started in the junior high school and develops from simple work to experiences involving increased responsibility and time and, eventually, to full-time employment as the student develops the skills, attitudes, and understanding required of the job. The work experiences are so interrelated with the school program that credit toward graduation is given for them.

Work-experience programs seem better fitted for boys than girls, because the careers of workers usually have more of a masculine quality; however, there are possibilities for work experiences for girls in many activities including nursing assistants, teaching assistants, child care, in business offices, or even industry. These programs can be coordinated with the activities and programs of other community agencies. A recognition that education grows out of all life experiences is basic to these programs.

At Warren Wilson College in Swannonoa, N.C., the entire student body of approximately 400 works fifteen hours each week at plumbing, painting, farming, cooking, and other tasks. There is no sex discrimination—girls feed the pigs, ride tractors, and help with painting jobs. If a student doesn't like his work assignment, he applies for a change. In addition, a summer work program enables students to gain credit toward their tuition. Part of the philosophy of Warren Wilson College involves the fundamental educational value of work. This is a good illustration of the more recent concept of the relevancy of education to everyday living.

SEX EDUCATION. It was pointed out in Chapter 13 that the schools must be concerned with sex education. Important changes have taken place in the attitudes of the schools toward sexual behavior and teen-age pregnancy. In one consolidated rural school in North Carolina, there were as of February, 1972, seventeen pregnant high school seniors. An interview with two high school teachers in the school appears to lead to the following conclusions:

1. Teachers display a sympathetic and rational attitude toward the girls and their problems.

2. Students at the school do not stigmatize these girls, but display a sympathetic and helpful attitude.
3. The girls expect to return to school and graduate after the birth of the child.
4. Several of the girls expect to marry the father of their baby; two of the girls are not interested in such a marriage, although the boys are willing.

The problem of sex education in schools is a controversial one. Certainly steps should be taken to meet the problems of teen-age pregnancy, venereal disease, and child care. It is predicted that the population in the United States will climb to 300 million by the year 2000 and to more than 400 million by 2042; and the present administration has set up the Office of Population Education to inform children, adolescents, and adults through television about national population growth and its adverse effects (Palmer, 1972).

CHANGED MORAL ATTITUDES. In general the schools have been slow to change many deep-seated attitudes largely because they are dependent upon the support of the local community. This frequently means that the schools must teach and follow the mores and prejudices of the community. This has been noted relative to problems of integration in the South, or problems related to pollution in areas dependent upon certain industries.

In Houston, Texas, a sixteen-year-old high school honor student was barred from all extracurricular activities, including turning the pages for the school choir piano player, because she had been married and divorced (Criss, 1972). Officials of the high school felt that married or formerly married students should be excluded from extracurricular activities because they might discuss sex with other students. The girl's parents took the case against the regulation to the American Civil Liberties Union (ACLU), and won a ruling from a court. The court ruled that the regulation violated the girl's constitutional rights. Now she not only turns the pages for the piano player but sings in the choir.

INSTRUCTIONAL MEDIA. The primary purpose of *instructional media* is to place the learner closer to reality—to make learning more meaningful. New instructional media include electrochemical devices which are transmitters between the student and what he is supposed to learn. Audio-visual aids are being used effectively in many schools, although the three most important visual aids usually available to the teacher are the chalkboard, overhead projector, and bulletin board. These aids are followed by globes, maps, charts, handouts, films, slides, still pictures, opaque projector, television easel, and models (Garrison and Magoon, 1972: 323). No one visual aid can serve all purposes, although educational TV programs and other visual aid materials will be used increasingly in the schools of the future.

In addition to the sound motion picture, educational TV classes, and audio laboratories, auto-instruction has been introduced to individualize instruction. Auto-instructional devices are varied and numerous. They include multiple-choice apparatus, self-administering and scoring exercises, teaching machines, programmed books, language laboratories, and computer programmed learning experiences for individuals and groups. Although these are useful for certain types of learning, we can never get away from the importance of pupil-teacher interaction. These devices are not substitutes for well-trained teachers and counselors.

EDUCATION FOR SURVIVAL. Four major survival problems may be listed: war and the use of atomic weapons, uncontrolled population, the depletion of our natural resources, and the pollution of the biosphere on which human life depends. Other problems of a humanistic nature can be set forth such as lack of education and worthy goals, the artificiality of modern civilization, and man's own contradictions regarding himself and others.

Our established institutions are self-perpetuating; they create their own meanings and goals, and are more or less resistant to change. Schools are usually one of these instruments and frequently serve to perpetuate ignorance, superstition, and prejudice. Although this is not intentional, it is inherent in their traditional order. An education that is *relevant* must relate knowledge to social and technological changes so that the student can become an integral part and force in historical change. This calls for an education that directs him into the mainstream of human events rather than isolating and shielding him from the reality of our times.

THE WORLD IN THE 1980s

The Presumptuousness of Predictions

Twenty-five years ago only a small minority foresaw the traumas of the 1960s and early 1970s, the dysfunctions of increased technology, and the rapidity of the erosion of a stable world. More frequently than not, predictions involve accepting the technological way of life; in fact many look forward to it. Doctrines of inevitable progress and of human enlightenment were prevalent. We are all culturally bound in our predictions of the future. For instance, in asserting that adolescence will continue indefinitely, we are assuming some continuation of the present and ignoring other possibilities. A deliberate "value-consciousness" on an intrinsic level may emerge to counter the continuance of technological domination. Ecological destruction or nuclear war on a large scale could easily alter the situation, so that generations would join together in the rebuilding process. A shift in societies to totalitarian states could easily create a potential equivalent to the Hitler Jugend or the Red Guards.

However, in attempting to make any predictions, there do seem to be two most likely possibilities; by 1980, if not before, we should be able to discern quite definite trends as to which of these possibilities is more likely to take place. One is the possibility for reasonably widespread, catastrophic destruction resulting from the side effects of technology, overpopulation, ecological disasters, disease, new insect strains, or wars. A second possibility is that of an increasing world of pluralism and an international respect for the vast problems facing us and some affirmation of man's survival needs.

TECHNOLOGICAL AND OTHER DESTRUCTIVE POSSIBILITIES. We are all intrigued with the lemmings who, periodically, as they overpopulate, become increasingly uneasy, restless, normless, and unconcerned about predators and strange situations. Finally, as if compelled simply by movement itself, they leave their home territory, migrate through forests and villages, and plunge into the sea, hundreds of thousands swimming out into the sea until they all drown. Those few who have remained behind and never reach the sea begin the cycle again.

In his experiments with overcrowded, but well-fed mice, Calhoun (1971) found that, over a short number of generations, stress led to withdrawal, normlessness, and, finally, to the infantilism of following any strange, moving object approaching them. While remaining physically healthy, they no longer can learn. They do not reproduce, they are voiceless, and they will crowd around and follow the feet of any human being who comes near. Calhoun comments: "Perhaps the story of the Pied Piper is not so mysterious after all" (31). Man's behavior in situations of extreme stress has led to similar behavior; some prisoners in Nazi concentration camps in World War II emulated the guards and snatched bits of their clothing as a means of securing a basis for personal identity. *The Fireside Theatre* (1969), a "serious comedy" group, caricatured this phenomenon in the depiction of a contemporary individual stricken with Bubonic plague running from thousands of persons who seek to touch him so that they also might die en masse. The descriptions in Toffler's (1970) *Future Shock* also hint at this kind of possibility. Paul and Anna Ehrlich (1970) tell of widespread ecological destruction; and others warn of the still live possibility of accidental or deliberate nuclear destruction.

A WORLD OF PLURALISM WITH AFFIRMATION. In a view of the future more hopeful than the preceding, Revel contends that we are already in a revolution of consciousness in the developed societies, and that the revolution has begun, is centered around development in the United States. He states, ". . . The exchange of one political civilization for another, which that program implies, seems to me to be going on right now in the United States. And, as in all the great revolutions of the past, this exchange can become worldwide only if it spreads, by a sort of political osmosis, from the prototype-nation to all the others" (1971: 15).

Although Revel's predictions may be dampened by Watergate and related events, these are reactionary products of the changes in process, and revolution may be accelerated by the exposure of such political intrigue. Certainly we can see signs of revolution in our changed relations with China and Russia; increased attention to pollution; consideration of birth control on a planetary scale; the use and control of natural resources; and greater moral freedom, to ensure individual happiness through increased plurality of choices.

The Religious Element in
Current Changes in Values Among Youth

Revel states that revolutionary action is most creative and diversified when it occurs within the context of a constitutional, liberal democracy, so that change is wrought within the framework of existing laws. The revolution must be worldwide, Revel states, with a form of government. The important thing is that it has already begun and it is being led within the United States, even if Americans are not fully aware of the process. He cites the recent emergence of the religious movement, and this can be confirmed by the controversies within the different religious groups, the adoption of Buddhist practices, a return to the Indian cult of natural foods; and to a changed perception of the nature and meaning of Christianity. The principle that the best religion for the individual is the one that he finds for himself is being more widely accepted (Revel, 1971: 21).

Revel is, however, deeply concerned about the possibility that the religious undergirdings and sanctions as expressed in certain movements among youth in the United States might lead to an enormous number of dropouts. He contends that the real disaster from this would be a sudden drift toward a right-wing form of totalitarian government.

Bearing in mind that Revel is a democratic socialist and tends to see revolution politically as well as in terms of consciousness, he quite naturally cites evidence to support his own form of democratic socialism. On the other hand, many aspects of his analysis are apolitical, such as his description of the growing consciousness of a need for new values, especially among many young people. He points out that the central problem of our times is a conciliation between revolution and democracy. Thus, it is "essential for humanity that there should exist a society capable of making a revolution without sacrificing democracy" (31). Although the United States seems the most likely to achieve a revolution within the framework of democracy, significant problems have arisen because of increased presidential power.

SUMMARY

While the extension of adolescence for specialized training is a part of the process of modernization at any level, current and future trends may not be so massive in that direction, as the work force alters and many conceivably find themselves overtrained for society's needs. With increasingly rapid societal changes, more anomie will be expressed by young people. Searches for new life style that are less consumption oriented on individual and small group levels probably will continue among youth in relatively noninstitutionalized forms.

The communal movement is a recent phenomenon with young people. Others have reexamined the nuclear family and searched for ways to make it more viable. The stability of any new response to societal change depends, in part, upon creating an intergenerational basis for it. Yet some contend, as does Mead, that times are such that the young today no longer can create a bridge with the past. Reich and others describe what they perceive as fundamentally new patterns of emerging consciousness, although many of these are reminiscent of earlier periods of widespread change.

The schools will be forced to deal increasingly with issues of values rather than simple utilitarianism. A reemphasis upon values and meaning will be necessary to achieve a reintegration between meaning and technical training. The values of pluralism allow individuals, within their own cultures, to develop self-affirming structures for meaning. Revel and others attempt to indicate, by various approaches, that this process has begun. It is essential that our political, religious, economic, educational, and kinship institutions create structures which will enable today's young people to find a meaning for their future.

REFERENCES

BOWLES, SAMUEL. "Cuban Education and the Revolutionary Ideology." *Harvard Educational Review* (1971), 41:472–500.

BURCHILL, G. *Work-Study Programs for Alienated Youth.* Chicago: Science Research Associates, 1962.

CALHOUN, JOHN B. "The Lemmings' Periodic Journeys Are Not Unique." *Ekistics* (April 1971), 185:315–17.

CRISS, NICHOLAS C. "Now Teen Divorce Can Sing." *Charlotte Observer* (February 6, 1972), p. 15E.

EHRLICH, PAUL R. and ANNA H. EHRLICH. *Population, Resources, Environment.* San Francisco: W. H. Freeman & Co., 1970.

ERIKSON, ERIK H. *Identity: Youth and Crisis.* New York: W. W. Norton & Co., 1968.

The Fireside Theater. New York: Columbia Records, Inc., 1970.

GARRISON, KARL C. and ROBERT A. MAGOON. *Educational Psychology.* Columbus, Ohio: Charles E. Merrill, 1972.

HALL, ROBERT T. *Pluralism and the American Ideal.* Unpublished manuscript. 1971.

MASLOW, ABRAHAM. *Self-actualized People.* Harvard University. Mimeographed, 1967.

MCGOVERN, GEORGE. "The Child and the American Future." *The American Psychologist* (1970), 25 (2):157–60.

MEAD, MARGARET. *Culture and Commitment.* Garden City, N.Y.: Doubleday & Company, 1970.

MERTON, ROBERT K. *Social Theory and Social Structure.* New York: The Free Press, 1957.

Oregonian (May 30, 1970), p. 3m. "Gallup Poll."

PALMER, CRAIG A. "New Population Education Office 'as Significant' as the Pill." *Charlote Observer* (February 6, 1972), p. 11A.

PERRY, RALPH BARTON. *The Thought and Character of William James.* Cambridge, Mass.: Harvard University Press, 1954.

REICH, CHARLES. *The Greening of America.* New York: Random House, Inc., 1970.

REVEL, JEAN-FRANCOIS. *Without Marx or Jesus.* Translated by J. F. Bernard. Garden City, N.Y.: Doubleday & Company, 1970.

ROGERS, CARL. *Freedom to Learn.* New York: Charles E. Merrill Books, Inc., 1969.

SCHELER, MAX. *Ressentiment.* New York: The Free Press, 1961.

SMALL, WILLIAM. "To Kill a Messenger: Television News and the Real World." *New Republic* (July 10, 1971), 165:29–30.

SMITH, DAVID E. and JAMES STERNFIELD. "The Hippie Commune Movement: Effects on Child Birth and Development." *American Journal of Orthopsychiatry* (1970), 40 (3):527.

TOFFLER, ALVIN. *Future Shock.* New York: Random House, Inc., 1970.

WALLICH, HENRY C. "Consuming Youth." *Newsweek* (April 5, 1971), p. 75.

RECOMMENDED READINGS

MEAD, MARGARET. *Culture and Commitment.* Garden City, N.Y.: Doubleday & Company, 1970.
A discussion of present and future configurations as noted in this chapter is presented in lucid form.

REVEL, JEAN-FRANCOIS. *Without Marx or Jesus.* Garden City, N.Y.: Doubleday & Company, 1970.
Revel thinks that the United States has the potential for world humanitarian leadership, especially among its youth.

SCHELER, MAX. *Ressentiment.* New York: The Free Press, 1961.
This is a very sensitive and thorough study of *ressentiment*, as was discussed in this chapter.

TOFFLER, ALVIN. *Future Shock.* New York: Random House, Inc., 1970.
This is a thought-provoking book which presents a number of alternatives to the future of the United States and of mankind.

bibliography

ALEXANDER, THERON. *Children and Adolescents: A Biocultural Approach to Psychology and Development.* New York: Atherton Press, 1969.
The author traces the process of growth through middle childhood and adolescence. Case studies are presented showing the importance of early motivation and cognitive processes and the need for self-direction.

BERNARD, HAROLD W., ed. *Readings in Adolescent Development.* Scranton, Pa.: International Textbook Co., 1969.
This is an interdisciplinary study as reflected in the articles dealing with philosophy, sociology, education, economics, technology, and general commentary.

BERNARD, HAROLD W. *Adolescent Development.* Scranton, Pa.: Intext Educational Publishers, 1971.
Adolescence is treated as a psychological, social, and cultural phenomenon, and as a product of technology and automation, population growth, prolonged dependence, and rapid change. The institutional factors in adolescent development and the transition from adolescence to adulthood are discussed.

CANTWELL, ZITA M. and PERGROUHI N. SVAJIAN, eds. *Adolescence: Studies in Development.* Itasca, Ill.: F. E. Peacock Publishers, Inc., 1974
The studies included in this book present adolescence as a unique period in the total life-span. Emphasis is given to the vitality of the adolescent, his

functioning in his environments, and the role of past experiences in his
varied adjustments.

COLE, LUELLA and IRMA NELSON HALL. *Psychology of Adolescence.* 7th ed.
New York: Holt, Rinehart & Winston, Inc., 1969.
A presentation of different points of view of adolescents, based upon
significant research since the publication of the sixth edition. New materials on drugs, sexual freedom, special movements, youth rebellion, and
other recent developments are included.

CONGER, JOHN J. *Adolescence and Youth: Psychological Development in a
Changing World.* New York: Harper & Row, Publishers, 1973.
A comprehensive, contemporary view of adolescent development which
deals with the effects of changes in social institutions and of divisions and
conflicts in society at large.

COTTLE, THOMAS J. *Times Children: Impressions of Youth.* Boston: Little,
Brown and Co., 1971.
A series of essays, mostly about people between ten and twenty years of
age. The author presents a sensitive and deep insight into the wishes, fears,
and motivations during the adolescent period.

EVANS, ELLIS D. *Adolescents: Readings in Behavior and Development.* Hinsdale,
Ill.: The Dryden Press, 1970.
This is a collection of original essays and research papers dealing with
adolescence.

GOETHALS, GEORGE W. and DENNIS S. KLOS. *Experiencing Youth: First-Person
Accounts.* Boston: Little, Brown and Co., 1970.
Twenty-six cases, written by an undergraduate at Harvard about some
aspect of adolescence. The case studies are grouped in three categories:
autonomy, identity, and sexual intimacy.

GOLD, MARTIN and ELIZABETH M. DOUVAN. *Readings in Adolescent Psychology.*
Boston: Allyn and Bacon, Inc., 1969.
This is an important book of readings by well-known authors. The collection includes a review of relevant literature preceding each chapter
grouping.

GRINDER, ROBERT E. *Studies in Adolescence: A Book of Readings in Adolescent
Development.* 2nd ed. New York: The Macmillan Company, 1969.
This second edition compiles critical, current, and provocative selections,
chosen from the empirical literature. The book is made up primarily of
papers focusing on relations between socialization experiences and the
major characteristics of adolescence.

HILL, JOHN P. and JEV SHELTON. *Readings in Adolescent Development and Behavior.* Englewood Cliffs, N.J.: Prentice-Hall, Inc., 1971.
The readings focus on the physical, cognitive, and sexual changes that
mark the onset of adolescence. The reactions of adolescents to their environment and developmental changes, and of adults to adolescents are
given consideration.

HORROCKS, JOHN E. *The Psychology of Adolescence.* 3rd ed. Boston: Houghton
Mifflin Company, 1969.
The author presents a comprehensive view of adolescence based upon
new research and theory. In this review a more explicit theoretical orientation underlies his discussions.

HURLOCK, ELIZABETH B. *Adolescent Development.* 4th ed. New York: McGraw-
Hill Book Company, 1973.

The text covers the traditional areas of development with special emphasis on the transitional nature of the adolescent period. Two new chapters on the adolescent as noncomformist and adolescent status symbols are included.

KOVAR, LILLIAN COHEN. *Faces of the Adolescent Girl.* Englewood Cliffs, N.J.: Prentice-Hall, Inc., 1968.
The author describes behavior patterns of five types of adolescent girls—the peer-oriented, the adult-oriented, the delinquent, the anarchic bohemian, and the autonomous—and the different paths they follow in their development toward womanhood.

McCANDLESS, BOYD R. *Adolescents: Behavior and Development.* Hinsdale, Ill.: The Dryden Press, 1970.
A comprehensive treatment of the behavioral features that characterize adolescents. The conceptual framework of the book involves a blend of the drive theory and the psychology of change and the self-concept.

MEDINNUS, GENE R. and RONALD C. JOHNSON. *Child and Adolescent Psychology: Behavior and Development.* New York: John Wiley & Sons, Inc., 1969.
The authors examine the major aspects of adolescent behavior and development and present findings bearing on childhood. The parent-child relationship and peer groups are given special attention.

MUUSS, ROLF E. *Adolescent Behavior and Society: A Book of Readings.* New York: Random House, Inc., 1971.
This is an interdisciplinary collection involving primarily social and educational issues such as student activism, the youth drug culture, Negro youth, and sex education.

OFFER, DANIEL. *The Psychological World of the Teenager: A Study of Normal Adolescent Boys.* New York: Basic Books, Inc., 1969.
A very intensive study of normal adolescent boys is presented here. The writer sought to answer such questions as: What are teen-agers really like? What are their major psychological problems? What are their goals? What role does sexuality play in their lives?

STONE, JOSEPH L. and JOSEPH CHURCH. *Childhood and Adolescence: A Psychology of the Growing Person.* 2nd ed. New York: Random House, Inc., 1969.
The authors are concerned with all aspects of childhood and adolescence and bring the total picture of growth during this period into focus.

THORNBURG, HERSHEL D., ed., *Contemporary Adolescence: Readings.* New York: Appleton-Century-Crofts, 1971.
The articles were selected to furnish an understanding of the problems of adolescents. Of the fifty-three articles selected, all except five have been written since 1965. The introductions to each chapter are useful.

USDIN, GENE L., ed. *Adolescence: Care and Counseling.* Philadelphia: J. B. Lippincott Co., 1967.
The papers present the normal physical, and physiological changes of adolescence and adolescent relationships with adults as well as the effects of social change on adolescents and their subculture.

WEINER, IRVING B. *Psychological Disturbance in Adolescence.* New York: John Wiley & Sons, Inc., 1970.
Clinical and research data on abnormal behavior are integrated. There are guidelines for assessing and treating the psychological disturbances that account for the majority of problems in adolescent patients: schizophrenia, depression and suicide, school phobia, academic underachievement, and delinquent behavior.

index of authors

index of subjects

Menarche, 71, 82, 83, 178 (see also Sexual maturation)
Menstruation (see Menarche)
Mental ability (see Intelligence)
Mental growth (see Intellectual development)
Merocrine sweat glands, 86–87
Metabolism, 79–81
Mexican-American adolescents, 227–30
  adjustments, 229–30
  self-concepts, 227
Middle class, 7, 21, 56, 208–9, 289–90, 299, 319, 457–58, 463
  and delinquency, 420, 422
Minority group membership, 221–39, 251
Mobility, 312–14, 422
Moral attitudes, 465
Moral development, 180–81
Morality, 40, 357–59, 399
Mothers, 145, 210
  disturbed, 203–4
  see also Parents
Motivation:
  lack of, 250
  see also Adolescent needs; Needs; Sexual drive
Motor development, 88–92
Motor performance, 88–91
Muscular development, 87–88

Narcotics, 386
  effects of, 393–94
Needs, 23–30, 253–56
  for adaptation, 335–36
  to find oneself, 299
  for a job, 293
  vocational, 313
  see also Adolescent needs
Negro adolescent culture, 221–24
  profile of, 223
  self-concept, 222
New morality, 357–59
Nicotine, 385
Noncollege youths, 268–69
Nuclear family, 457–58
Nutrition, 73, 86

Obesity, 74
Occupation:
  choices, 317
  opportunities, 319
  see also Vocation
Ordinal position, 200
Osseous development, 72

Parental attitudes:
  and delinquency, 422–24
  and frustrations, 422–23
Parental identification, 175, 176
  and alienation, 445–46
Parent-child interactions, 111, 175
Parents, 42, 134, 171–73, 204–5, 261, 284, 297, 367
  and delinquency, 423–25
Peer acceptance, 206
Peer orientation, 204
Peer relations, 206

Peers, 44, 151, 266
  importance of, 168
  influences of, 204–9
  see also Gangs
Personal appearance, 37, 131
Personality, 44, 161–68
  and physiological conditions, 165
  stability of, 160
Personality development, 158–61
Petting, 355
Physical development, 70–73 (see also Physiological development)
Physical fitness, 90, 92–93
Physical maturation, 147–48
Physical self, 25
Physiological development, 74–84
Physiological needs, 24–25
Pituitary hormones, 76
Popularity, 254–55
Post-adolescents, 441, 453 (see also Youth)
Posture habits, 93
Preadolescents, 140–43
Pregnancy, 356, 357; see also Adolescent pregnancy
Premarital sex (see Sexual behavior)
Puberty, 18, 70, 81–84, 151
Puberty ceremonies, 19
Pubic hair, 85
Puerto Rican adolescents, 224–27
  adjustment problems, 225–27
  culture, 225
Pulse rate, 77–78

Quasi-delinquents, 409

Radicalism, 343–44
Radio, 180, 266–67
Rejection, 405
Religion, 41, 210, 457–58
Religious influences, 199, 374, 416
Respiratory changes, 79
Revolution, 51–53 (see also Social change; Technological revolution)
Roles (see Female role; Male role; Sex role)
Runaway teenagers, 296–98
Rural, 211, 242

School achievement:
  and home life, 265–66
  and intelligence, 113
Schools:
  attendance, 261–64
  crimes at, 427
  and delinquency, 426–28
  effects of failure, 427
  maladjustments, 259–60
  problems confronting, 258–59
  special problems of boys, 263–64
Secondary school (see High school)
Secondary sexual characteristics, 84–88
Self, 28
Self-acceptance, 44
Self-concept, 113–14, 127–33, 179, 261, 265
  importance of, 309
  patterns, 44–45
Self-discipline, 160

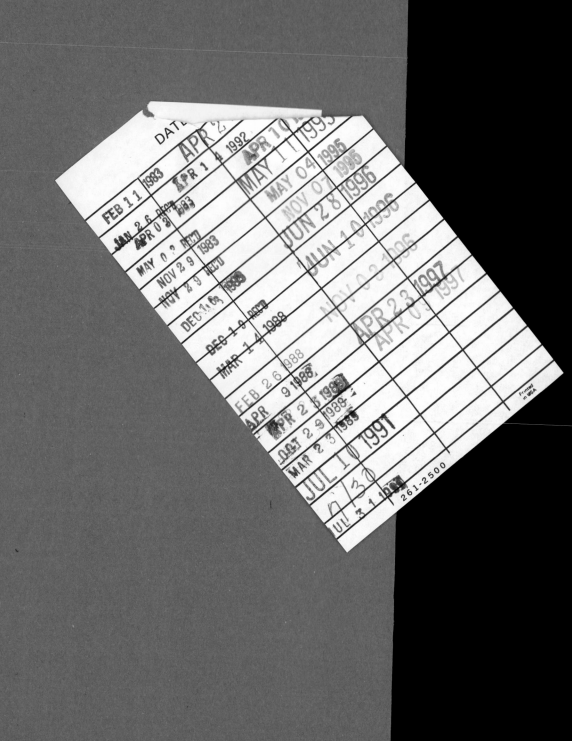